P9-DTZ-603

04119087

Canadian	International	Prime Ministers	
	1899 • Canadian volunteers fight in the Boer War	**1896–1911** • Wilfrid Laurier (liberal)	**1900**
	1903 • Alaska boundary dispute		
1905 • Alberta and Saskatchewan become provinces			**1905**
			1910
		1911–1920 • Robert Borden (conservative)	
	1914 • First World War begins		
1914 • War Measures Act	**1918** • First World War ends		**1915**
	• Spanish flu pandemic		
	1919 • Paris Peace Conference		
1917 • Halifax explosion	• Treaty of Versailles		
• Conscription crisis	• League of Nations established		
• Khaki election	**1922** • Chanak Crisis		**1920**
1919 • Winnipeg General Strike	• Mussolini comes to power in Italy	**1920–1921** • Arthur Meighen (conservative)	
	1923 • Halibut Treaty	**1921–1926** • William Lyon Mackenzie King (liberal)	
1926 • King-Byng Crisis			
• Imperial Conference leads to Balfour Report	**1928** • Joseph Stalin gains control of the Soviet Union		**1925**
1927 • Old-age pensions introduced	**1929** • Stock market crash	**1926 (3 months)** • Arthur Meighen (conservative)	
	• Depression begins	**1926–1930** • William Lyon Mackenzie King (liberal)	
1931 • Statute of Westminster	**1933** • Adolph Hitler comes to power in Germany	**1930–1935** • R.B. Bennett (conservative)	**1930**
1932 • Co-operative Commonwealth Federation (CCF) founded	• Franklin Roosevelt introduces economic "new deal" in the U.S.		
• Federal relief camps established			
1935 • On-to-Ottawa Trek	**1936** • Spanish Civil war begins		**1935**
1936 • CBC created	**1938** • *Kristallnacht* in Germany	**1935–1948** • William Lyon Mackenzie King (liberal)	
1937 • Rowell-Sirois Report	**1939** • Second World War begins		
1939 • British Commonwealth Air Training Plan begins	**1941** • Japan bombs Pearl Harbor		
1940 • National Resources Mobilization Act	**1944** • D-Day		**1940**
	• UN sets up World Bank and International Monetary Fund		
1942 • Canadians vote in favour of conscription	**1945** • U.S. drops atomic bombs on Hiroshima and Nagasaki, Japan		
	• Second World War ends		**1945**
	• United Nations created		
	1948 • Universal Declaration of Human Rights		
	1949 • NATO formed		
1949 • Newfoundland joins Canada	• Geneva Convention	**1948–1957** • Louis St. Laurent (liberal)	**1950**
1951 • Massey Report	**1950** • Korean War begins		
	1953 • Korean War ends		

OKANAGAN COLLEGE-LIBRARY

COUNTERPOINTS EXPLORING CANADIAN ISSUES

second edition

Michael Cranny

Garvin Moles

PEARSON

PEARSON

www.pearsoncanada.ca

Copyright © 2010 Pearson Canada Inc., Toronto, Ontario

All rights reserved. This publication is protected by copyright and permission should be obtained from the publisher prior to any prohibited reproduction, storage in a retrieval system, or transmission in any form or by any means, electronic, mechanical, photocopying, recording, or likewise.

Portions of this publication may be reproduced under licence from Access Copyright, or with the express written permission of Pearson Canada Inc., or as permitted by law. Permission to reproduce material from this resource is restricted to the purchasing school.

The information and activities presented in this work have been carefully edited and reviewed. However, the publisher shall not be liable for any damages resulting, in whole or in part, from the reader's use of this material.

Brand names and logos that appear in photographs provide students with a sense of real-world application and are in no way intended to endorse specific products.

Permission to reprint copyright material is gratefully acknowledged. Every effort was made to trace ownership of copyright material, secure permission, and accurately acknowledge its use. For information regarding permissions, please contact the Permissions Department through www.pearsoncanada.ca. Feedback on this publication can be sent to editorialfeedback@pearsoned.com.

Pearson Canada Inc.
26 Prince Andrew Place
Don Mills, ON M3C 2T8
Customer Service: 1-800-361-6128

ISBN 13: 978-0-13-510613-6

Publisher: Susan Cox
Research and Communications Manager: Patti Henderson
Managing Editor: Gaynor Fitzpatrick
Coordinating Editor: Martha Malic
Developmental Editors: Tricia Carmichael, Sheila Fletcher, Christel Kleitsch, Caroline Kloss, Martha Malic
Production Editors: Allana Barron, Christine Higdon, Marie Kocher, Lisa Santilli
Copy Editor: Kathleen ffolliott
Proofreader: Ann Echlin
Fact Check: Christine Higdon, Tracy Westell
Index: Audrey Dorsch
Permissions Researcher: Marnie Lamb
Photo Researcher: Sheila Hall
Production Coordinator: Zane Kaneps
Cover & Interior Design: Alex Li
Interior Design & Composition: Word & Image Design Studio
Maps & Illustrations: Deborah Crowle
Illustrations: Stephen MacEachern
Cover Photograph/Illustration: © Brian Milne/First Light
Manufacturing Coordinator: Karen Alley
Vice-President, Publishing: Mark Cobham

11 10 9 8   CC   16 15 14 13 12
Printed and bound in the U.S.A.

ACKNOWLEDGEMENTS

Contributing Writers

Jenise Boland
Mike Denos
Rob Lewis
Holly Mair
Tom Morton
Janet Ruest
Glen Thielmann
Paula Waatainen

Course Advisors/Reviewers

Pearson thanks the Course Advisors and Reviewers, who helped to shape *Counterpoints*: *Exploring Canadian Issues*, Second Edition, through discussions and reviews of prototype materials and manuscript.

Werner Kopp	David Thompson Secondary School, Rocky Mountain SD
Rob Lewis	Prince George Secondary School, Prince George SD
Tom Morton	University of British Columbia, Faculty of Education
Glen Thielmann	D.P. Todd Secondary School, Prince George SD
Paula Waatainen	Rockridge Secondary School, West Vancouver SD

Reviewers

Wayne Axford	Burnaby Central Secondary School, Burnaby SD
Jenise Boland	West Point Grey Academy
Sean Chambers	Guildford Park Secondary School, Surrey SD
Dean Cunningham	Clayton Heights Secondary School, Surrey SD
Mike Edgar	Clarence Fulton School, Vernon SD
Holly Mair	Saanich School District
Barry Morhart	Similkameen Secondary School, Okanagan Similkameen SD
Janet Ruest	Chemainus Secondary School, Cowichan Valley SD
Jonathan Vervaet	North Surrey Secondary School, Surrey SD
Keith Regular	Elkford Secondary School, Southeast Kootenay SD
Jennifer Puharich	Enver Creek Secondary School, Surrey SD
Barry Walker	Mark R. Isfeld Secondary School, Comox Valley SD

Pearson would also like to thank the teachers who provided valuable comments and suggestions in surveys, discussions, feedback on the revised page design, etc. throughout the revision process. Your feedback and constructive recommendations have been most valuable in helping us to develop this resource.

CONTENTS

CONTENTS

UNIT 4: Human Geography: The Future in Balance 354

What does it mean when someone tells you that "you can't judge a book by its cover"? They are asking you to think critically about something and to not take it at face value.

Thinking Critically

Critical thinkers are open-minded. They ask questions and communicate with others to form an opinion. They gather relevant information and use criteria, which are the standards used while making a judgement, to guide their responses. Being a critical thinker can help you create an opinion or decide on an option based on sound reasoning.

In *Counterpoints*, you will study the history, politics, economy, and geography of Canada. How might critical thinking apply to your study?

- It can be used to solve a puzzle or problem, or debate an issue.
- It can be a good way to remember the facts of a topic when you learn them in order to make a decision or solve a problem.
- Critical thinking has many uses outside of the classroom. It is learning for life.
- Employers value critical thinking.
- Thinking deeply about issues is part of being a good citizen of Canada and the world.

In History, Geography, Politics, and Economics

Most geographers, historians, and other social scientists agree that there are certain "big ideas" that need to be grasped to understand social studies. One way to understand these big ideas is to ask critical thinking questions. Here are some examples.

Questions to ask while studying history:

- How did things get to be as we see them today?
- What groups of people am I a part of? What are their origins? In what ways am I Canadian?
- How did people in the past see different ethnic groups and women? How has this changed over time?
- How should we judge the actions of others in the past?
- Are things getting better or are they getting worse?
- Which stories about the past should I believe? On what grounds?
- Which stories shall we tell? What about the past is significant enough to pass on to future generations?
- What can we do to make the world a better place?

Questions to ask when studying geography:

- What is life like in a foreign country?
- In what ways is Canada different from and similar to a less-developed country?
- Why are some people rich and some poor?
- What can be done to make a fairer world?
- What is my impact on the planet?
- How can I help our planet?

Questions to ask when studying politics and economics:

- What is the best form of government?
- Who is responsible for the economy?
- What should be the government's role?
- How are the environment and the economy intertwined?
- How can Canada best keep its independence in an interdependent world?

Using the Critical Thinking Icon

In *Counterpoints*, a Critical Thinking icon appears at the beginning of each chapter. Several parts of the icon are highlighted to show you which critical-thinking elements are the focus of the chapter. These elements are meant to guide you in your examination of the people, places, and events that you will study in the text.

On pages x–xi, you will see examples of how each element of the icon can be applied to a specific issue—in this case, food.

A Note on Perspective

Sometimes it can be difficult to understand a different perspective from your own. It can be even harder when that perspective is based on the different belief system of another country or another time.

Recognizing that another person's perspectives may be different from your own is the starting point for mutual understanding and meaningful communication. We also need to recognize that another perspective may make sense when we understand the basis for that perspective. For example, farmers in developing countries who need help with planting and harvesting their crops, and someone to take care of them in old age, may want more children than an urban Canadian.

Another important part of understanding perspective is to recognize that in any given culture and in any given time people held a variety of values and beliefs. Over time, you may find that your perspectives on issues or events may change as you study further or learn more about the perspectives of others. Recognizing perspectives not only can help us to understand others, it may be an essential basis for getting along in a culturally diverse country such as Canada. Social studies should give us practice moving beyond our own perspectives and taking seriously the perspectives of others.

Significance

- How did the potato change the history of the world?

- How important are farmers?

Judgements

- Should the sale of bottled water be banned?

- Which is more important: land for farming or land for housing?

Cause and Consequence

- How has technology influenced where our foods come from?

- What might be the cause of local farms failing to compete on price?

Significance

Judgements

Cause and Consequence

24 HR DRIVE-THRU

BREAKFAST

Patterns and Change

- How has the diet of Canadians changed in the last 20 years?
- What factors influence our change in eating habits?

Evidence

- What do we know about the food we eat?
- How does advertising affect our choices about food purchases?

Perspectives

- How do the ways people eat and the kinds of food they eat reflect their perspective?
- How might parents see mealtime differently from teenagers?

Patterns and Change

Evidence

Perspectives

Canada in Transition: A Nation Emerges

During the first half of the 20th century, many events, trends, and themes shaped Canada and its diverse population. International recognition, domestic changes, acts of intolerance, and economic hardships forced many Canadians to ask hard questions about who they were and what they valued. The tragedy and triumph of two world wars saw Canada come of age as an independent nation, but still a proud and valued member of the British Commonwealth.

CHAPTER 1

In the early 1900s, Canada was seen at home and abroad as a British colony. Several groups, including women, immigrants, and Aboriginal peoples, were struggling for equality.

CHAPTER 2

The First World War provided new opportunities for women and Aboriginal peoples, who had previously been discouraged from participating in military conflicts.

NORTH AMERICA

PACIFIC OCEAN

ATLANTIC OCEAN

CHAPTER 3

Canadians celebrated the end of the First World War by adopting new music and fashions. During the "Roaring Twenties," women fought for social and legal equality, labour unrest gave rise to the formation of unions, and Canada strengthened its status as an autonomous nation.

SOUTH AMERICA

CHAPTER 4

The Great Depression was a decade of hardship and despair that highlighted weaknesses in the Canadian and global economy. As people struggled to survive, tensions divided the country, notably between immigrants and non-immigrants, men and women, and Western and Central Canada.

©P

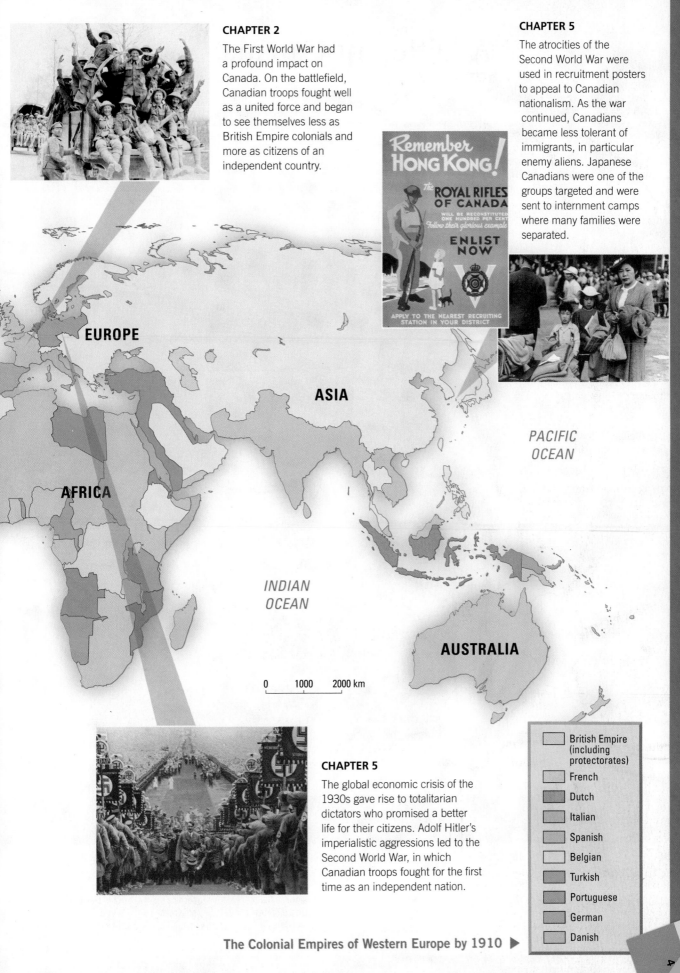

CHAPTER 2

The First World War had a profound impact on Canada. On the battlefield, Canadian troops fought well as a united force and began to see themselves less as British Empire colonials and more as citizens of an independent country.

CHAPTER 5

The atrocities of the Second World War were used in recruitment posters to appeal to Canadian nationalism. As the war continued, Canadians became less tolerant of immigrants, in particular enemy aliens. Japanese Canadians were one of the groups targeted and were sent to internment camps where many families were separated.

Remember **HONG KONG!**

The **ROYAL RIFLES OF CANADA**
WILL BE RECONSTITUTED
ONE HUNDRED PER CENT
Follow their glorious example

ENLIST NOW

APPLY TO THE NEAREST RECRUITING
STATION IN YOUR DISTRICT

EUROPE

ASIA

PACIFIC OCEAN

AFRICA

INDIAN OCEAN

AUSTRALIA

0   1000   2000 km

CHAPTER 5

The global economic crisis of the 1930s gave rise to totalitarian dictators who promised a better life for their citizens. Adolf Hitler's imperialistic aggressions led to the Second World War, in which Canadian troops fought for the first time as an independent nation.

British Empire (including protectorates)

French

Dutch

Italian

Spanish

Belgian

Turkish

Portuguese

German

Danish

The Colonial Empires of Western Europe by 1910 ▶

1

A Different Canada

Society & Identity

- How did women influence Canadian society in the early 1900s?

- Why were the attitudes of English- and French-speaking Canadians different regarding Britain?

- What attitudes did many Canadians have toward minorities?

- What steps did the government take to control immigration to Canada?

- What challenges did Aboriginal peoples face in the early 1900s?

Economy & Human Geography

- How did technology impact Canada's economy during this period?

- What impact did industrial development have on the natural environment?

Autonomy & World Presence

- What was Canada's relationship to Britain at the turn of the century?

TIMELINE

1896

Wilfrid Laurier becomes prime minister of Canada

Klondike gold rush begins

1899

Canadian volunteers fight in the Boer War in South Africa

1903

Alaska boundary dispute settled between the United States and Canada

1905

Alberta and Saskatchewan become provinces

1906

B.C. First Nations leaders take their land claim to King Edward VII of England

CHAPTER FOCUS QUESTION

What defined Canada in the early 1900s, and what attitudes and expectations did Canadians have for the century ahead?

Significance
Patterns and Change
Judgements
CRITICAL INQUIRY
Evidence
Cause and Consequence
Perspectives

On a cool October evening in 1904, a tall, dignified man stood in front of a crowd in Toronto's Massey Hall. He was Wilfrid Laurier, Canada's prime minister. Laurier stepped to the podium that night and presented a bold vision of Canada for the new century:

> *Let me tell you, my fellow countrymen, that the twentieth century shall be the century of Canada and of Canadian development. For the next seventy-five years, nay for the next one hundred years, Canada shall be the star towards which all men who love progress and freedom shall come.*
>
> *–Wilfrid Laurier,* Toronto Globe, *October 15, 1904*

What was Canada like at the beginning of the 20th century when Laurier made his bold prediction? Manitoba, Ontario, and Québec were much smaller than they are today. Newfoundland was still a self-governing colony, and the territory of Nunavut had not yet been created. The census of 1911 reveals that Canada's population was only 7.2 million, less than a quarter of what it was by the end of the century.

People's attitudes about good manners and behaviour in general, the role of women, national identity, minorities, and Aboriginal peoples were also different then. In this regard, Canada fit the claim that "the past is like a foreign country; they do things differently there." In our study of history, it is important to try to see the world through the eyes of Canadians at that time if we want to understand why they took the actions that they did.

KEY TERMS

prohibition
suffragist
imperialists
nationalists
autonomy
head tax
Indian Act
reserves
residential schools
assimilation

1907	1908	1909	1911	1912	1914
Vancouver race riot occurs	*Anne of Green Gables* is published	First airplane flight in Canada	Laurier era ends Robert Borden elected prime minister	RMS *Titanic* sinks off coast of Newfoundland	Passengers on the *Komagata Maru* are refused landing in Vancouver First World War begins

![Canadian flag graphic]

Prime Minister
Wilfrid Laurier

- born 1841, Saint-Lin, Canada East (Québec)
- lawyer
- first elected to Commons in 1874
- prime minister 1896–1911; longest unbroken tenure as prime minister; first prime minister of French ancestry

Domestic Record

- helped resolve the Manitoba Schools Question in 1896 by allowing some Catholic and French instruction in public schools
- supported the construction of a second transcontinental railway in 1903
- oversaw Alberta and Saskatchewan joining Confederation in 1905
- created the Royal Canadian Navy with the Naval Service Act in 1910
- opposed conscription during the First World War (1914–1918)

International Record

- participated in colonial conferences of 1897 and 1902, rejecting England's proposals to unify the British Empire
- sent a force of Canadian volunteers to fight in the Boer War (1899–1902)
- fought for Canada's claim during the Alaska boundary dispute, 1903

● How did women influence Canadian society in the early 1900s?

Society and Manners

By the early 20th century, most Canadians lived on farms or in small villages, yet morals and manners of the day were set by a minority of middle- and upper-class Anglophones. These people were greatly influenced by the attitudes of **Victorian** England. This period—named after Queen Victoria, who was the British monarch from 1837 to 1901—was known for its appearance of moral strictness. Families were expected to attend church regularly; they supported Britain and the monarchy; and they believed in honour, virtue, and duty. It was an age in which right and wrong, good and evil, seemed clear; they were not seen as issues that needed discussion or debate.

There was little tolerance for those who did not obey the law, and the application of the law could be quite harsh. At the time, the death penalty was the sentence for murder. Most convictions, however, were for crimes against people's property. Drunkenness was a close second.

Women of the Era

In the early 1900s, the Woman's Christian Temperance Union, founded in the 1870s, was still actively campaigning for **prohibition**. These women saw alcohol as the cause of many of society's problems. They also supported women's right to vote. With the vote, women believed they could influence the government to address social problems of the day, such as child labour, pollution, and poverty. Nellie McClung was a well-known **suffragist** who, together with other women, campaigned for women's rights (see Chapter 3).

Since moral codes of behaviour were strict and well-defined, the courtship of young, middle-class ladies was a formal affair under the watchful eyes of their families and community. Once married, women had few rights over property or children, and divorce was rare. Women were not considered persons under the law—unless they committed a crime. Even a woman's salary was legally the property of her husband. Women who worked outside the home, usually before marriage, were employed mainly as servants or factory workers. Some women were teachers and nurses; a few even became doctors.

FIGURE 1–1
Woman's Christian Temperance Union convention in Calgary, 1911

Thinking Critically
What class of women do you think this photograph represents? Why would these women be concerned about society's problems?

Arts and Leisure

As Canada started to become more urbanized, its literature and art became more sentimental, expressing a preference for rural life, simple values, and happy endings. In 1908, Lucy Maud Montgomery published the much-loved novel *Anne of Green Gables*, a rural romance set in Prince Edward Island. Stephen Leacock gently mocked small-town Ontario life in his humorous *Sunshine Sketches of a Little Town* (1912). Ernest Thompson Seton wrote moving stories about animals. Pauline Johnson, daughter of a Mohawk chief and his English wife, read poems about her Mohawk heritage to packed halls. Ontario painter Homer Watson gained international recognition with his farm scenes. In Québec, Ozias Leduc painted religious works and landscapes filled with a sense of spirituality. In British Columbia, Emily Carr explored the landscapes and peoples of the West Coast through painting and writing.

For leisure, Canadians enjoyed outdoor activities, such as running, cycling, and rowing. In the summer, trips to the beach were popular despite confining "bathing costumes." In the winter, tobogganing was a must.

Still a British Nation

At the beginning of the 20th century, some of Britain's colonies, including Canada, had their own governments but still depended on Britain to resolve disputes with other countries. The British government often made decisions that did not have Canada's best interests in mind.

The Alaska Boundary Dispute

The dispute was over the exact border of the Alaskan "panhandle," a strip of land running down the Pacific Coast between British Columbia and Alaska. Of particular concern was the question of ownership of a fjord called the Lynn Canal. This waterway provided access to the Yukon, where gold had been discovered in 1896. In a speech, Prime Minister Laurier reflected on the relations between Canada and the United States:

> I have often regretted... that we are living beside a great neighbour who, I believe I can say without being deemed unfriendly to them, are very grasping in their national actions and who are determined on every occasion to get the best in any agreement....
>
> –*Wilfrid Laurier, October 23, 1903*

In 1903, the matter was finally settled. The British, weary from fighting the Boer War in South Africa and unwilling to become involved in another international conflict, determined that the Lynn Canal was part of Alaska, not B.C. Many Canadians were angered by this decision, believing Britain had sold out Canada's interests to keep peace with the U.S.

KEY TERMS

Victorian of or pertaining to the reign of Queen Victoria; also someone who shares the values of that period

prohibition the ban of alcohol

suffragist a person who advocates that women should have the right to vote

● What was Canada's relationship to Britain at the turn of the century?

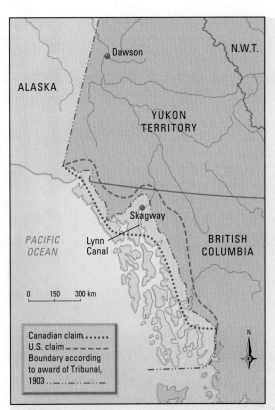

FIGURE 1–2 The Alaska boundary dispute

Using Evidence From the map, explain how the Canadian claim would have allowed easier access to Dawson.

French-Canadian Nationalists

While unhappy with Britain's decision regarding the Alaska boundary, most English-speaking Canadians were proud to be British subjects, and they shared Britain's dreams of expanding the British Empire. These **imperialists** had eagerly supported Britain in the Boer War in 1899.

French-speaking Canadians, however, did not share this enthusiasm for the British Empire. They were the descendants of people who had settled New France more than 200 years earlier, and they saw themselves as **Canadiens** rather than British subjects. French Canadians tended to be **nationalists**, believing that Canada should have **autonomy** and be totally independent from Britain. For example, nationalist leader Henri Bourassa resigned from Laurier's Cabinet when Laurier agreed to send volunteers to fight with the British in South Africa during the Boer War. Bourassa's stand against Canada's involvement in Britain's wars became an even bigger issue during the First World War.

Language rights was another issue that divided French-speaking and English-speaking Canadians. After a bitter dispute, French Canadians first lost the right to French-language instruction in Catholic schools in Manitoba, then in Saskatchewan and Alberta. Henri Bourassa voiced the concerns of many French Canadians when he suggested that Canadiens might not have any reason to stay in Canada if their rights as a minority were not protected, as the people of Québec had believed they would be at the time of Confederation.

KEY TERMS

imperialists people who support imperialism, the policy of one nation acquiring, controlling, or dominating another

Canadiens French descendants of the original settlers of New France

nationalists people who have a strong attachment to their culture or nation

autonomy the power to govern oneself and make one's own decisions

homesteaders newcomers who claimed and settled land

ethnocentric the belief that one's own culture is superior, and that other cultures should be judged by its values

head tax the fee that Chinese immigrants were required to pay after 1885 in order to enter Canada

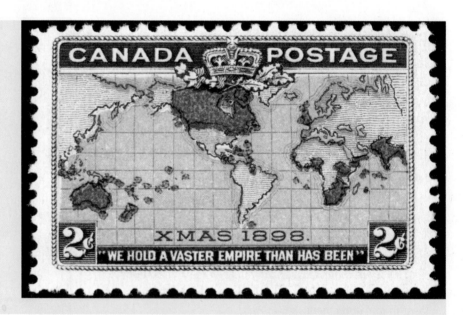

FIGURE 1–3 This postage stamp shows the extent of the British Empire in 1898.

Using Evidence The British Empire was the biggest of the European empires that controlled much of the land and people of the world. What does the expression "the sun never sets on the British Empire" mean?

PRACTICE QUESTIONS

1. **Perspectives** Imagine you could go back to the Canada of 1914. What attitudes would you find most difficult to deal with? Why? What specific social values do you hold that would conflict with those commonly held in 1914?

2. Describe the situation of women in Canada in the years before the First World War.

3. Explain why some Canadians did not share enthusiasm for Canada's ties to Britain. Do you think their objections were justified? Explain.

Canada's Changing Population

After becoming prime minister in 1896, Laurier realized that for Canada to prosper, it needed more people, especially in the West. His government launched an advertising campaign to attract immigrants to Canada. It circulated posters in the United States and northern and eastern Europe promoting the Prairies as the "Last Best West" to distinguish it from the American West, where land was becoming limited and more expensive. These efforts resulted in a significant increase in immigration.

Entry into Canada was easy if you were reasonably healthy and had funds to establish yourself. The federal government offered immigrants willing to farm the Prairies 65 hectares of land for only $10. These **homesteaders**, as they were called, had three years to build a house and begin cultivating the land. The loneliness and harsh conditions of life on the Prairies prompted some to move to urban centres.

Not Everyone Is Welcomed

Some Canadians did not welcome changes to Canada's ethnic composition. Many French-speaking Canadians were concerned that the new immigrants would outnumber the Francophone population. Most Canadians were **ethnocentric**, believing their own race or group was superior, and therefore they disliked "outsiders." As a result, many newcomers to Canada experienced discrimination.

Eastern Europeans, particularly the Ukrainians and Polish people who settled the Prairies, were targets of ethnic prejudice. Their language and customs were unfamiliar to Canadians, who often ridiculed these people.

Many Chinese, Japanese, and South Asian immigrants settled in British Columbia. They, too, suffered from discrimination and racism. R.B. Bennett, a future prime minister, reflected popular prejudice when he declared in 1907, "British Columbia must remain a white man's country." As long as Asian immigrants did work that other Canadians considered too unpleasant—such as hauling coal, packing fish, and washing dishes—their cheap labour was generally accepted. But when Canadian workers began to fear that Asian immigrants would compete against them for other jobs, they joined in denouncing them.

The federal government tried to limit immigration from Asia in 1885 by introducing the Chinese Immigration Act. Under this Act, every Chinese immigrant to Canada had to pay a **head tax** of $50 upon arrival. In 1907, an angry mob of 9000 people smashed windows and destroyed signs on stores owned by Chinese and Japanese immigrants in Vancouver. This race riot resulted in severe restrictions on Japanese immigration. A year later, there was a virtual ban on East Indian immigration.

- What attitudes did many Canadians have toward minorities?
- What steps did the government take to control immigration to Canada?

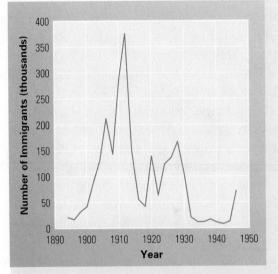

FIGURE 1–4 Immigrants to Canada, 1894–1946

FIGURE 1–5 Today many Canadian communities are multicultural, as shown on this street in Vancouver.

Thinking Critically How does Canada benefit from its ethnic diversity? In what ways is the immigrant experience different today?

©P

Is today's government responsible for injustices of the past?

In the early 1980s, Prime Minister Pierre Trudeau refused to apologize for past injustices committed by Canadian governments. He claimed that we cannot rewrite history; we can only try to be just in our time. Those calling for apologies say it is not about rewriting history. They feel acknowledging that the government and its institutions took wrong turns in the past shows that we are on the right road today.

Since 1988, federal and provincial governments have recognized and tried to compensate for past wrongs by issuing official apologies. In 1988, the Conservative government apologized to Japanese Canadians for their internment during the Second World War (see Chapter 5) and again in 1990 to Italian Canadians for similar reasons. Perhaps the most significant event to date has been Prime Minister Stephen Harper's 2008 formal apology to Canada's Aboriginal peoples, acknowledging that "...the treatment of children in Indian residential schools is a sad chapter in our history" (see Chapter 8). Supporters of this approach hope that such apologies offer closure to a hurtful past. Opponents say that no matter how sincere an apology, it cannot undo what has been done.

The following Canadian immigration case studies examine two apologies and corresponding responses.

The Chinese

As you read earlier, the federal government tried to discourage Chinese people from coming to Canada by imposing a head tax in 1885. The tax was increased from $50 to $100 in 1900, and to $500 in 1903. On July 1, 1923, the federal government introduced the Chinese Exclusion Act—an Act that tried to halt Chinese immigration altogether. Chinese Canadians refer to this day as Humiliation Day. The Act was in place for more than 20 years; it was repealed in 1947.

In 1984, the Chinese Canadian National Council (CCNC) began a campaign for an apology from the federal government. They also asked for a repayment of $23 million, the amount collected from 81 000 Chinese immigrants who were forced to pay the tax.

In 1993, the Canadian government rejected the redress claim stating that it was more important to erase inequality in the future than to compensate people for past mistakes. Dr. Alan Li, the then-president of the CCNC, disagreed. He stated:

> *Returning the money is only basic justice. It is a strong statement of principle that a government cannot, and should not, and must not, benefit from racism.*
>
> *–Alan Li, Speech, 1994*

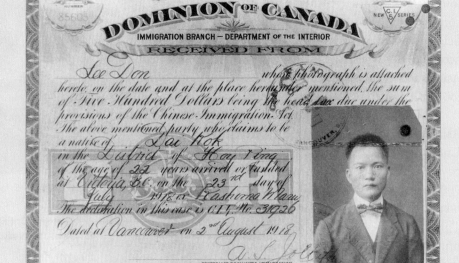

FIGURE 1–6 Immigration certificate for Lee Don, 1918

Gathering Information How old was Lee Don when he was admitted to Canada? How much was the head tax he had to pay? Where do you think he might have obtained the money to pay the tax?

In 1995, the CCNC approached the United Nations Human Rights Commission to ask for their help with this issue. In 2006, the Canadian government agreed to address the claim and offered a parliamentary apology for the head tax and exclusion of Chinese immigrants from 1923 to 1947. The federal government promised financial redress of $20 000 to each of the surviving head tax payers or their spouses.

> *For over six decades, these malicious measures, aimed solely at the Chinese were implemented with deliberation by the Canadian state. This was a grave injustice, and one we are morally obligated to acknowledge.*
> *–Prime Minister Stephen Harper, June 22, 2006*

For Sid Chow Tan, national chairperson of the CCNC and president of the Head Tax Families Society of Canada, the apologies must not distract us from present-day problems. He stated:

> *The historical injustices of the Chinese Head Tax are being replicated today through Canada's exploitative guest-worker programs and restrictive immigration policies. The descendants of these policies will be demanding apologies in future decades. We should deal with this present reality and not just dwell on the past, especially if a history that we are supposed to have learnt from is repeating itself.*
> *–Sid Chow Tan*

The *Komagata Maru*

In 1908, the federal government passed the Continuous Passage Act, a law requiring all immigrants to come to Canada by a non-stop route. This effectively made immigration from countries such as India impossible, since there were not any steamship companies that offered direct routes to Canada. This law was challenged in 1914, when the passengers on the *Komagata Maru*, a steamer chartered to carry Sikh immigrants from Hong Kong to Vancouver, were refused entry to Canada.

FIGURE 1–7 The *Komagata Maru* was docked for two months in Vancouver while the Canadian government decided the fate of its 340 passengers.

In May 2008, the British Columbia legislature extended an apology for the *Komagata Maru* incident. A few months later, at a Sikh festival in B.C., Prime Minister Harper also offered an apology for the incident. Sikh organizations have rejected the prime minister's apology, comparing it to the formal apology to Chinese Canadians in 2006. The Sikh community requested a formal apology in the House of Commons, which would grant this issue the respect and dignity they feel it deserves. The Conservative government has since said there will be no further apology.

Analyzing the Issue

1. Compare the responses of Prime Minister Trudeau to those of Prime Minister Harper. What might explain the differences in their opinions?

2. Official apologies for past wrongs have accelerated since 1988. Why do you think that has happened? Would you support treating all claims for redress for past wrongs equally? Why or why not?

3. Organize a debate on the topic: Should we try to right the wrongs of past generations?

KEY TERMS

Indian Act an Act created to regulate the lives of the First Nations of Canada

reserves land set aside by the government for the use of First Nations

residential schools government-authorized schools, run by the churches, in which Aboriginal children lived apart from their families and were educated in Canadian culture

assimilation adoption of the customs and language of another cultural group so that the original culture disappears

WEB LINK ●

The last residential school closed in 1996. Find out more about Canada's residential schools on the Pearson Web site.

FIGURE 1–8 An Aboriginal man plowing land on a reserve

Thinking Critically Aboriginal peoples traditionally survived by hunting, trapping, and fishing. How would farming change their traditional lifestyle?

Cultural Extinction?

As thousands of immigrants settled into the western provinces, Aboriginal peoples found themselves more and more displaced. Their lives were regulated by the **Indian Act** passed in 1876. By the 1880s, most Aboriginal peoples of the Prairies were living on **reserves**. The main purpose of reserves was to free up land for settlers and immigrants from Europe, and to avoid the violent clashes that had taken place between Aboriginal peoples and settlers in the United States.

On the reserves, Aboriginal people were encouraged to take up farming instead of traditional hunting. But their attempts to adapt to farming were hindered by several factors: the soil on the reserves was often unsuitable for crops. They traded their land for equipment and livestock, but were given hand tools and animals ill-suited for plowing. Even when Aboriginal farmers managed to harvest crops, efforts to sell them were often hindered by government agents who would deny them the passes they needed to leave the reserve and market their crops. As a result, many Aboriginal people experienced hunger.

Loss of land was not the only problem Aboriginal peoples faced. The Canadian government established **residential schools** in an attempt to force Aboriginal children to set aside their identity and traditions and become part of the dominant culture. Children were taken from their communities by Indian agents, police, or priests and sent to schools hundreds of kilometres away. The overcrowded dormitories, unsanitary conditions, and lack of medical care caused tuberculosis and other diseases to spread quickly. Many students were physically and sexually abused. They were punished for speaking their language, forbidden to practise their culture, and denied contact with their families.

Residential schools, reserves, and enforced farming were all part of the federal government's policy of **assimilation**, which was intended to make Aboriginal peoples abandon their traditions and adopt a European way of life. This policy had been in place since 1871, and by the early 1900s the populations of Aboriginal peoples were declining. By 1913, an article in *Maclean's* magazine claimed that "the white man of Canada... is slowly, steadily and surely absorbing his red brother." Aboriginal peoples did not agree. Their struggle to establish land claims and reclaim their culture was just beginning.

PRACTICE QUESTIONS

1. Despite their poor treatment in Canada, immigrants kept coming. Explain the factors that attracted immigrants to Canada.

2. Why were many English- and French-Canadian people upset by the changes to Canada's ethnic composition?

3. Describe the steps taken in British Columbia to restrict Asian immigration.

4. Describe the policies of the federal government that were designed to assimilate Canada's Aboriginal peoples.

Millions of immigrants came to Canada in the 20th century. They were lured by the promise of freedom, land, and a better quality of life. As new people came to Canada, the original inhabitants of the country were forced off their land. First Nations peoples in British Columbia reacted by asserting their rights to Aboriginal land and self-government. Squamish Chief Joe Capilano, a respected and talented speaker, played a major role in championing this cause.

On August 14, 1906, delegates led by Chief Capilano met with King Edward VII at Buckingham Palace. They brought with them a petition expressing their dissatisfaction with the Canadian government and their claim to land. Although they could not present the petition directly to the king because of protocol, they discussed these issues with him during the audience.

The delegates were enthusiastically received when they returned to Canada. Chief Capilano toured B.C., speaking to First Nations peoples throughout the province. He told his audiences that the king supported them in their dispute with the Canadian government. The effectiveness of his speeches was clear in *The Victoria Daily Colonist* headline on May 8, 1907. It claimed, "Cowichan Indians in Restless Mood: Alleged That Tribal Discontent Is Aroused Through Oratory of Joe Capilano."

But Canadian authorities disputed the royal promise of King Edward because there was no written record supporting the chief's claim. This highlighted one of the key differences between European and Aboriginal cultures: Europeans relied on written records while Aboriginals trusted verbal promises.

The more active Capilano became in the cause, the more the Canadian government threatened him with prosecution and labelled him a troublemaker. Until his death in 1910, Capilano continued his struggle for Aboriginal rights. It was not until the latter half of the 20th century that the Supreme Court of Canada began to recognize Aboriginal rights.

1. Describe what the delegates might have hoped to achieve in going directly to King Edward VII.

2. **Patterns and Change** List the differences between the activism of First Nations in the early 20th century and that of First Nations today. How would you relate the early struggles to those of today?

3. During his journey to speak with the king, Chief Capilano wore a blanket crafted to give spiritual protection. In 2009, the Squamish Nation celebrated the historic return of the blanket to Salish traditional territory at the Squamish Lil'wat Cultural Centre. Where should an important artifact like Capilano's blanket be kept?

FIGURE 1–9 Chief Joe Capilano

Thinking Critically Why might this photograph have been taken? Do you think this image shows the "real" Joe Capilano? Why or why not?

What If...

Imagine that the king had convinced the Canadian government to acknowledge the grievances presented in the petition. How might this have changed the attitude of Canadians and the government toward Canada's Aboriginal peoples?

Building Your Skills

Analyzing Evidence: Primary and Secondary Sources

Throughout this textbook, you will be presented with many points of view concerning issues in history, government, and geography. You are not expected to agree with these points of view, but to use them to come to your own conclusions. The following guidelines will help you in analyzing historical information.

Dealing with Evidence

There are two main categories of evidence: primary and secondary. Primary sources are created at the time of an event. Eyewitness accounts are the most obvious primary sources. These are often found in diaries, government documents, photographs, newspaper articles, and political cartoons. Secondary sources are created after the event, often describing or analyzing it. The perspective of time may provide a more balanced analysis in these sources.

Understanding Bias

When you interpret evidence, you cannot help but see it through personal biases. Similarly, primary and secondary sources carry the authors' personal views. Having a bias is not necessarily wrong. It is important, however, to be aware of biases when you analyze evidence. These might include political, racial, religious, ethnic, gender, or economic biases.

Reliability and Credibility

When you read a document, it is important to determine how reliable it is as a source of information. Ask yourself questions such as:

- Who is the author? Was he or she close to the event?
- Why might the author have recorded the event?
- What were the author's information sources?
- What are the author's biases or points of view?
- What was the purpose of the document, and who was the intended audience?

Photographs should also be examined closely when they are used as a historical piece of information. The reader should ask: Who took the photograph? How was the photograph to be used? Sources of information must also be credible, that is, they must be accurate and record the truth. One way to determine the accuracy of a source is to see whether the information is supported by other sources. The following sources offer information about immigrants to Canada in the years before the First World War.

Source 1

Rank	Nationality	Number of People	% of Total Immigration
1	U.K.	150 542	37.4
2	U.S.	139 009	34.5
3	Russian	18 623	4.6
4	Ukrainian	17 420	4.3
5	Italian	16 601	4.1
6	Polish	9945	2.5
7	Chinese	7445	1.9
8	Jewish	7387	1.8
9	German	4938	1.2
10	Bulgarian	4616	1.1
	Other	25 903	6.4
Total		**402 429**	**99.8**

–Canada Year Book, *1914*

FIGURE 1–10 Immigrants to Canada in 1913

Source 2

A historian describes the attraction Canada had for farmers from Eastern Europe:

> *In the mountain trenches of Galicia... the furrows of the strip farms ran to the very edges of houses. No wonder that... pamphlets (promoting Canada) were so successful. Across the oceans lay a promised land where 160 acres [65 hectares] of fertile soil could be had for the asking. Thus was initiated a great emigration of Poles and Ukrainians from Austria-Hungary.*
>
> –*Pierre Berton,* The Promised Land

©P

Source 3

FIGURE 1–11 Galicians at an immigration shed in Québec City

Source 4

Conditions in the slums as described by J.S. Woodsworth, a minister and social activist, in a letter to a Winnipeg newspaper in 1913:

> Let me tell you of one little foreign girl. She lives in a room.... Her father has no work.... The place is incredibly filthy. The little girl has been ill for months—all that time living on the bed in which three or four persons must sleep and which also serves the purpose of table and chairs. For weeks this little girl has had an itch which has spread to the children of the surrounding rooms. She has torn the flesh on her arms and legs into great sores which have become poisoned.
>
> –*J.S. Woodsworth*

Applying the Skill

1. Classify each of the sources as primary or secondary. Explain your choices.

2. How reliable might the statistics in Source 1 be? What are some possible reasons for inaccuracies in population statistics?

3. Make a list of information about immigrants that can be found by examining Source 3. What questions would you ask to determine how reliable this photograph is as a historical source? Given the advances in digital technology, are photographs today more or less reliable than those taken 100 years ago? Explain.

4. How reliable is Source 4? What does it tell us about Winnipeg in 1913?

5. Use all four sources to create a picture of Canadian immigration at this time. List some additional sources that might help you to get a more complete picture of the subject.

KEY TERM

urbanization the process by which an area changes from rural to urban

Urbanization

While thousands of immigrants were settling farms on the Prairies, thousands more were moving to towns and cities. Some immigrant groups, particularly Jewish people, who were not allowed to own land in Europe, chose urban life, which was more familiar to them. For others, living in large communities without having to do back-breaking farm work was appealing. Canada's economy was in transition and the rise in manufacturing meant more job opportunities in urban centres. The population of Canada's western cities exploded in the early 1900s. For example, Winnipeg expanded from 42 340 people in 1901 to 136 035 people in 1911. It optimistically called itself the "Chicago of the North."

The growing cities were filled with contrasts between the wealthy and the poor. The rich lived in luxury. They usually had servants; their houses were lit by electricity, warmed by central hot water heating, and had running water. Across town, the working class lived in shacks and overcrowded tenements. Low wages forced women and children to take jobs and work long hours to support their families. Restrictions on child labour were few and seldom enforced. Lack of clean water and proper sewers, together with pollution from neighbouring industries, caused widespread health problems. Pneumonia, diphtheria, tuberculosis, and typhoid were common in poorer districts. Still, people flocked to the cities, attracted by jobs as well as by cultural and social opportunities unavailable in rural Canada.

FIGURE 1–12 Left: Wealthy home in Toronto, circa 1910; right: One-room home in Winnipeg, 1912

Using Evidence Find evidence in these photographs of the contrasts between rich and poor as described in the text. Which photograph do you think most people would associate with the time period? Why?

Evidence

Innovations
Farther and Faster

While not exactly an information highway by today's standards, the pace of change in communications in Canada in the years before the First World War seemed amazing. Radio messages could be sent over oceans, telephones connected people in cities, and Canadians were experimenting with new and faster ways to travel from place to place.

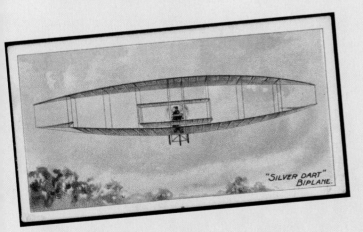

The telephone Invented in the 1870s, the telephone was increasingly popular in the early 1900s. People had to share lines and go through an operator to make a call.

The Father of Radio Québec-born inventor Reginald Fessenden has been called Canada's greatest forgotten inventor. He made the first broadcast of music and voice in 1906. Fessenden was later called the Father of Radio.

Wireless communication Italian-born Guglielmo Marconi invented the wireless telegraph, receiving the first wireless radio message sent across the ocean in 1901, at Signal Hill in Newfoundland.

"SILVER DART" BIPLANE.

Air travel The Wright Brothers made the first airplane flight in the United States in 1903. In Canada, Alexander Graham Bell and Douglas McCurdy developed the Silver Dart, a gasoline-powered biplane.

The bicycle craze Bicycles were the new craze at the turn of the century, when one in 12 people owned a bicycle. Bicycles liberated women from restrictive clothing and from chaperones, even though they were often criticized for riding.

● How did technology impact Canada's economy during this period?

An Economy Transformed

From its earliest days as a young British colony, Canada was known for its abundance of natural resources. The export of timber, wheat, and minerals was an important part of Canada's economy. Canada's export industries also benefited from cheap shipping costs across the Atlantic Ocean. As well, the opening of the Panama Canal in 1914 created a shorter shipping route for Canadian products from the West Coast en route to Europe. Mining also contributed to the economic boom in the early 1900s. Prospectors and investors flocked to the Yukon and British Columbia after gold was discovered near the Klondike River in 1896.

The Manufacturing Industry

In the late 1800s, electric power was becoming more widely available with wood- and coal-burning steam engines. In the early 1900s, **hydroelectric power** stations were built to provide power to Canada's factories. The arrival of electricity in factories was an enormous boost to Canada's industrial growth. With electric power, bigger and better machines could be used to produce many more goods. This **industrialization** created more jobs in manufacturing. Much of the small manufacturing sector was tied to processing resources or providing tools and equipment for farms and homes. Few people could foresee that the rising popularity of automobiles would change the economy of southern Ontario and the way in which Canadians lived and worked.

With jobs came an increase in the demand for consumer goods. Canada Dry, Shredded Wheat, Palmolive soap, Heinz ketchup, and other brands became familiar to Canadian shoppers, along with the first five-cent chocolate bar. In 1913, more than 300 000 telephones were in use in Canada, and more and more automobiles were appearing on Canadian streets. By 1914, wireless radios were used on board many ships, following their much-publicized role in the rescue of passengers on the ill-fated RMS *Titanic* in 1912.

FIGURE 1–13 The 1908 McLaughlin-Buick sold for $1400, which was beyond the reach of most Canadians.

Thinking Critically What recent developments in transportation and communication are comparable to the impact of the automobile in the first decades of the 20th century? Explain.

Corporate Giants

Corporations grew larger during this period of industrial expansion. Huge companies, such as Maple Leaf Milling, Massey-Harris, and Imperial Oil controlled much of industry. With little competition, employers could set high prices for the goods they produced and pay low wages to their workers. Some workers began to form **trade unions** to press for better pay, reduced hours of work, and better safety conditions. When employers refused to give in to union demands, some unions went on strike. Most employers opposed union demands. As a result, strikes could get violent and, in some cases, the police and military were called in to break up the protests. For example, in 1913, coal miners in Nanaimo were involved in a bitter strike that lasted more than two years. The miners were striking over unsafe working conditions and low pay, while the Western Fuel Company, to keep wages low, was trying to stop the workers from forming a union. Eventually, the Canadian government sent in troops to bring the situation under control. They arrested 39 people.

Financial speculation caused by the boom of the previous two decades saw many businesses expand quickly, but by 1910, a series of bank failures led to a collapse in the stock market. By 1914, Canada was in a **recession** after almost two decades of rapid growth. Industries cut back on production, and many workers became unemployed. On the Prairies, most farmers were planting a new, higher-yielding wheat, but the boom was over—the international demand for wheat was down.

KEY TERMS

hydroelectric power electricity produced from the energy of falling water

industrialization change in production systems to large-scale mechanized factories

trade union a group of workers who unite to achieve common goals in discussions with owners and management of businesses and industries

recession a decline in the economy, resulting in lower levels of employment and production

FIGURE 1–14 Workers at the Robert Simpson Company mail-order office, 1909. Mail-order companies became a popular and practical way for many Canadians to shop, comparable to online shopping today (inset).

Thinking Critically Why do you think mail-order companies were so popular in the early 1900s? Compare online shopping today with catalogue shopping of the past.

Resources and the Environment

From the early days of exploration, Canada was seen as a land of plenty with an endless supply of natural resources, such as fur, water, timber, and minerals. For most Canadians in the early 1900s, protecting the environment was not the issue it is today. In 1914, however, residents of British Columbia saw how human interference could seriously damage an important natural resource. Workers for the Grand Trunk Railway were blasting a new railway line in the Fraser Canyon when an explosion caused a rockslide at Hell's Gate Canyon. This rockslide had disastrous effects on the spawning beds of the sockeye salmon. The fallen rocks were massive and partially blocked the river. This blockage increased the river's current, which prevented many salmon from swimming upstream to spawn. The rocks remained in place for about 30 years before a fish ladder was constructed to allow the spawning fish to swim up the rapids. But catches of Fraser River salmon would never again equal the pre-war numbers of 20 to 30 million fish.

The rockslide posed a particular hardship for the Stó:lō First Nation whose culture and livelihood were founded on fishing in the Fraser River. They worked for days to save the fish, carrying them one at a time over the fallen rocks. As stocks improved, commercial fishers were given a monopoly on fishing to help compensate for their financial losses. The Stó:lō, however, were never given back the allocations they had before the Hell's Gate rockslide.

FIGURE 1–15 In 1945, the Hell's Gate fish ladder was built to slow down the water flow in the Fraser Canyon, thus enabling the salmon to reach their spawning grounds upriver.

Incidents like this rockslide demonstrated that our actions could have lasting, negative effects on the environment. Since the first national park was established in Banff in 1885, the federal and provincial governments had been setting aside land to ensure some of Canada's natural landscape was protected. By 1914, British Columbia had three national parks: Mount Revelstoke, Yoho, and Glacier. The B.C. government had already designated Strathcona and Mount Robson as provincial parks. Today, there are nearly 1000 provincial parks and protected areas in British Columbia.

©P

The Athabasca Oil Sands

Canada's landscape still holds a wealth of resources, but today people are more aware of the impact that exploiting these resources has on the environment. One current example is the Athabasca oil sands in northeastern Alberta. The oil sands hold the world's largest reserve of crude bitumen, a sticky, tar-like form of petroleum. About 1.3 million barrels of oil are produced from the oil sands each day. One method used to extract the oil is open-pit mining, in which the oil sand is dug out of the ground and then mixed with hot water to separate the oil from the sand.

Extracting the oil has an environmental impact. Open-pit mining scars the land. Separating the oil from the sand requires large amounts of water, which is diverted from the Athabasca River. The water needs to be heated, and burning natural gas produces greenhouse gases. The Alberta government has programs in place to try to offset environmental effects. However, debate continues over how to best use this resource while minimizing the negative impact on the environment.

FIGURE 1–16 Mining projects in the Athabasca oil sands are expanding.

Thinking Critically Why would a government allow resource development if the production causes environmental damage?

War and Change

When Laurier predicted the 20th century would be the century of Canadian development, he could not have predicted that Canada would play a role in a devastating war involving many countries throughout the world. He also could not have predicted the events and issues that have shaped Canada's identity during the past century. In the following chapters, you will learn about these events. You can be the judge as to whether the 20th century really became "Canada's century."

PRACTICE QUESTIONS

1. Describe the contrasts between rich and poor in cities during this period.

2. What technological changes were taking place in Canada prior to the First World War?

3. Explain why employers and unions had stormy relations in these years.

4. Imagine you are a reporter sent to cover the Hell's Gate Canyon rockslide. Send a telegram to your newspaper describing the tragedy. Include a headline.

CHAPTER FOCUS QUESTION **What defined Canada in the early 1900s, and what attitudes and expectations did Canadians have for the century ahead?**

In the two decades before the First World War, Canada experienced remarkable changes. Wilfrid Laurier skilfully guided Canada through 15 years of prosperity, as well as political and social upheaval. Immigration transformed Canada into a truly transcontinental nation with growing cities and industries. Agriculture and manufacturing prospered. New technologies changed social and cultural habits. However, not all Canadians were part of the new positive outlook. Aboriginal peoples, immigrants, women, and workers struggled for their rights. By 1914, Canada was beginning to resemble the country we live in today.

1. **Perspectives**

   a) People living in Canada in the two decades before the First World War had many different perspectives. Use the organizer to summarize how people in each of the groups might have viewed their place in Canada. Include one or more reasons why they would have had that perspective.

   b) Many factors affect a person's perspective. The boxed list includes those that generally have a significant influence on one's perspective. Add any factors not included that you feel are relevant to your situation. Rank the factors in the chart according to the importance they have in determining your perspective (one being the greatest influence).

   c) What effect do you think your background has on the way you view Canada today?

   d) Your perspective will determine how you view the past as well as the future. Do you have a mostly positive or negative view of Canada's future? Give reasons for your choice.

Groups	Perspective of Canada Before the War	Evidence
Aboriginal peoples		
English Canadians		
French Canadians		
European immigrants		
Asian immigrants		
Women		
Industrialists		
Workers		

Factors Determining One's Perspective	Ranking
Age	
Gender	
Ethnicity	
Religious or philosophical beliefs	
Education	
Family income/parents' occupations	
Place of residence	
Places you have visited	

Vocabulary Focus

2. Review the Key Terms listed on page 5. Form small groups. Each member of the group selects five terms from the list and writes each term and its definition on an index card. Collect and shuffle all the cards. Each player selects one of the cards, reads the definition, and asks another member of the group to identify the term. Alternatively, each player reads the term and asks for the definition. Continue this process until all the cards have been used.

Knowledge and Understanding

3. From what you know of Canadian history before 1913 and from what you have learned in this chapter, how was the French-Canadian view of Canada different from the English-Canadian view? What issues were viewed differently by these two groups?

4. Use information in this chapter to discuss the interactions between the Canadian government and immigrants such as Chinese people.

5. Public hearings on the testimony of Canada's Aboriginal peoples about their treatment in residential schools are underway. What should be the goal of the Truth and Reconciliation Commission? Would you recommend the same process for other groups? Why or why not?

6. Historians look for turning points in history, marking the change from one era to another. Many see the First World War as the end of an era and the beginning of the modern age. What recent event would you choose as a turning point in Canadian or world history? Explain your choice.

Critical Thinking

7. Using the groups from the organizer, list both the positive and the negative impacts of the various changes that were taking place in Canada at the start of the 20th century. Write a paragraph stating which group gained the most and which group lost the most as a result of these changes.

8. Choose three new technologies from today that you think will have as great an impact as did those described in this chapter. Support your choices with at least two reasons.

9. Examine the following quotation from Olga Pawluk, who was 18 years old when her family moved to Canada from Ukraine. What does this document say about some immigrants' perception of Canada at that time? How accurate was Olga in her description of Canada? Upon what was she basing her opinion?

I didn't want to go to Canada... I didn't know where Canada was really, so I looked at the map. There were hardly any cities there. It looked so wild and isolated somehow and I felt that it would be very difficult to live there.... I felt I was going to a very wild place.

–Quoted in Living Histories Series, *2000*

Document Analysis

10. Read through the statistics and information about Canada in the table below. Select the four changes that you think were most significant to Canada's emerging autonomy and explain your choices.

	1914	2009
Population	8 million	33.7 million
National Anthem	God Save the King	O Canada
Nationality	British	Canadian
Flag	Union Jack	Maple Leaf
Governor General	Duke of Connaught (British)	Rt. Hon. Michaëlle Jean (Canadian)
Foreign Affairs	British Foreign Office	Canadian Dept. of Foreign Affairs
Final Court of Appeal	Judicial Committee of the Privy Council	Supreme Court of Canada
House of Commons	221 MPs (all male) 133 Conservative 86 Liberal	308 MPs (69 women) 77 Liberal Party of Canada 49 Bloc Québécois 37 New Democratic Party
Senate	87 Senators (all male)	105 Senators (35 women)
Eligible Voters	1 820 742	23 677 639
Prime Minister	Robert Borden, Conservative	Stephen Harper, Conservative

FIGURE 1–17 Canada's population and government in 1914 and 2009

2

Canada and the First World War

GUIDING QUESTIONS

Society & Identity

- What challenges did Aboriginal soldiers face during the war and upon their return home?

- What effect did the War Measures Act have on the legal rights of Canadians?

- How did Canada's contribution on the battlefield affect Canadian identity?

- What effect did the war have on the role of women?

- What impact did conscription have on Canadian unity?

Autonomy & World Presence

- How did Canada get involved in the First World War?

- What was the war's impact on the home front?

- How did the nature of warfare and technology contribute to a war of attrition?

- What were conditions like for men in the trenches?

- Describe Canada's military role in the First World War.

- What factors contributed to Canada's emerging autonomy?

TIMELINE

1914

Archduke Franz Ferdinand assassinated in Sarajevo

Germany invades Belgium and France

Britain declares war on Germany; Canada automatically at war

War Measures Act passed in Canada

1915

Canadian troops exposed to poisonous gas at the Battle of Ypres

1916

Canadians suffer heavy losses in the Battle of the Somme

Women in Manitoba, Saskatchewan, and Alberta gain the right to vote in provincial elections

CHAPTER FOCUS QUESTION

What effect did Canada's participation in the First World War have on Canadian society and its status as a nation?

When the First World War began in 1914, few believed it would last very long. Many young people in Canada and elsewhere saw the war as an exciting chance for travel, adventure, and glory. Most were afraid that the conflict would be over before they could get into the action. Many people signed up with noble, romantic ideas, such as the honour of fighting for the British Empire to which Canada belonged:

> *These young men were the cream of Canada's youth and chivalry, all volunteers, all willing to face the great adventure for King and country, for freedom and civilization. No conscripts were they, but freemen, glad and willing to demonstrate Canada's loyalty and to make some return to England for the civil and religious liberty we had enjoyed under the protection of her flag....*
>
> –Manliness and Militarism: Educating Young Boys in Ontario for War, *2001*

"The Great War," however, was a far different reality than this romantic vision. It was modern, industrialized warfare on a vast scale. The "war to end all wars" claimed the lives of more than 8 million soldiers, cost almost $350 billion, and changed the map of Europe. What could cause such a devastating international conflict? Why was the war so long and terrible, and what were the long-term effects of the war on our nation? To answer these questions, we must understand the historical forces at work in Canada and around the world at the time—in particular, nationalism, imperialism, colonialism, and militarism.

KEY TERMS

imperialism
militarism
Triple Alliance
Triple Entente
nationalism
War Measures Act
enemy aliens
internment camps
no man's land
Western Front
war of attrition
Battle of Ypres
Battle of the Somme
Battle of Vimy Ridge
Passchendaele
convoy
Victory Bonds
honour rationing
propaganda
conscription
khaki election
Hundred Days Campaign
Paris Peace Conference
Treaty of Versailles
War Guilt Clause

1917
Canadian troops battle at Passchendaele
Canadian troops capture Vimy Ridge
Women in British Columbia and Ontario gain the right to vote in provincial elections
Wartime Elections Act gives federal vote to women related to servicemen
Borden re-elected as head of Union Government
Conscription introduced in Canada
Halifax devastated by an explosion
Income tax introduced as a temporary measure

1918
Enlistment begins
Armistice declared on Europe's Western Front
Women win the right to vote in federal elections

KEY TERMS

imperialism the policy of one nation acquiring, controlling, or dominating another country or region

militarism a nation's policy of enlisting, training, equipping, and maintaining armed forces ready for war

Slavic relating to peoples in eastern, southeastern, and central Europe, including Russians, Serbians, Croatians, Poles, Czechs, etc.

Causes of the First World War

What caused the First World War? There is no simple answer. At the beginning of the 20th century, several factors pushed the world to the brink of war. Industrialization drove the Great Powers—Britain, France, Germany, Italy, Austria-Hungary, and Russia—to expand their territories. As they sought more land, resources, and influence, they also tried to protect their territory by building up their military resources and creating alliances. Meanwhile, the nations colonized by the Great Powers struggled to keep their independence. These power struggles created tension around the world, and one event, as you will read about later, triggered the First World War.

Imperialism and the Age of Empires

Why were the Great Powers so prepared to engage in war? Since the 15th century, several European nations had been aggressively expanding their territory (see Unit opener map). Powerful countries practised **imperialism** by establishing colonies all over the world to create empires. They exploited the land and resources of the weaker nations they controlled. Massive industrialization in the 19th century fuelled the Great Powers' desire to expand their domains, giving them access to more raw materials and creating new markets for their manufactured goods. Africa—with its wealth of gold, diamonds, ivory, agricultural land, and other resources—became the last frontier for colonizers in the late 1800s. European empires aggressively pursued their interests in Africa, often competing for the same territory.

At the beginning of the 20th century, Germany was struggling to establish itself as an imperial power. Its colonies in Africa were not as economically or strategically advantageous as the areas controlled by Britain. Germany's leaders wanted their country to have its own "place in the sun" and to extend its sphere of influence. Germany's aggressive pursuit of this goal brought it into conflict with other imperial powers, in particular Britain and France.

Increasing Militarism

Imperialism brought crisis after crisis, fostering distrust and tension among the Great Powers. As they expanded their empires, the Great Powers developed their military resources to protect their interests and intimidate each other. They glamorized their armed forces, and the size of their armies and navies became essential to national prestige. They embraced **militarism** and saw war as an acceptable way to resolve conflicts and achieve their goals. Militarism was a constant threat to peace in the years leading up to the First World War.

ON THE SWOOP!

FIGURE 2–1 Germany as an eagle in this 1890 cartoon

Interpreting Political Cartoons What is the message of this cartoon?

By the beginning of the 20th century, Britain had established the largest navy in the world to protect its vast empire. Germany's desire to be a major power in Europe drove it to build up its military resources to match Britain's naval strength. In response, Britain dramatically increased the size of its navy and built the HMS *Dreadnought*, the largest and fastest battleship in the world. Germany in turn built more ships, including dreadnoughts of its own. It also increased the size of its army and its reserve of weapons. This buildup of military resources forced France—who had long-standing grudges with Germany—to arm itself in a desperate attempt to maintain the balance of power. This arms race increased international tensions, and by 1914 Europe had become an armed camp.

FIGURE 2–2 Ships such as the British warship HMS *Dreadnought* were heavily armoured to protect them from enemy fire.

The Role of the Balkans

As the Great Powers struggled to expand their colonies around the world, they also fought over limited resources in Europe. Of particular interest were the Balkans, a cultural and geographic region on the Adriatic Sea in southeastern Europe. Three different empires—Russia, Austria-Hungary, and the Ottomans—wanted to control this area.

- Russia's approach was to promote Pan-Slavism, the idea of uniting the **Slavic** peoples of the Balkans. Russia hoped that supporting these nations would allow it access to the region's warm-water ports. This was extremely important to Russia as most of its ports were frozen in winter, limiting its ability to import and export goods.

- Austria-Hungary saw Pan-Slavism as a threat to its power. Several of the nations under its control were Slavic and located in the Balkans, including Slovenia and Croatia. Austria-Hungary feared that it would lose its grip on its territory if these peoples united.

- For more than 100 years, the Ottoman Empire had controlled the Balkans and southeastern Europe, as well as areas of northern Africa and the Middle East. But this empire was crumbling by the beginning of the 20th century. It had already lost its hold of the Balkans and feared losing even more territory.

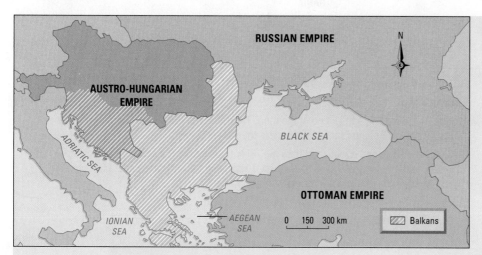

FIGURE 2–3 Imperial struggles in the Balkans

KEY TERMS

alliance a union or agreement among groups working toward a common goal

Triple Alliance the alliance of Germany, Austria-Hungary, and Italy prior to the First World War

Triple Entente the alliance of France, Britain, and Russia prior to the First World War

nationalism devotion to and support of one's culture and nation, sometimes resulting in the promotion of independence

Black Hand a terrorist group of Bosnian Serbs that was determined to free Bosnia from Austria-Hungary

The False Security of Alliances

These intense rivalries in Europe resulted in a rush to make or join **alliances**. By the early 1900s, all the Great Powers in Europe were in alliances with other countries, promising to support one another if they were attacked.

- The **Triple Alliance** was made up of Germany, Austria-Hungary, and Italy. However, when the war broke out in 1914, Italy did not follow the Triple Alliance into battle. Instead it joined the war in 1915 on the side of the Triple Entente.

- The **Triple Entente** (also known as the Allies) consisted of France, Britain, and Russia.

These countries hoped that forming alliances would reduce the threat of war, but it proved to have the opposite effect. Alliances made it easier for a country to be drawn into war. Because members pledged to protect one another, if any one of them was involved in a conflict, its allies would automatically have to fight as well. As you will see, one dramatic event was all it took to drag the whole of Europe into war.

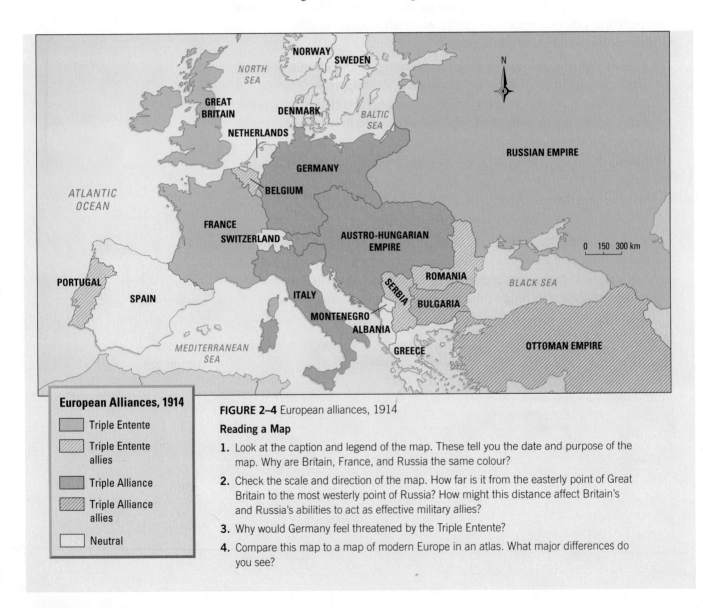

European Alliances, 1914

- Triple Entente
- Triple Entente allies
- Triple Alliance
- Triple Alliance allies
- Neutral

FIGURE 2–4 European alliances, 1914

Reading a Map

1. Look at the caption and legend of the map. These tell you the date and purpose of the map. Why are Britain, France, and Russia the same colour?

2. Check the scale and direction of the map. How far is it from the easterly point of Great Britain to the most westerly point of Russia? How might this distance affect Britain's and Russia's abilities to act as effective military allies?

3. Why would Germany feel threatened by the Triple Entente?

4. Compare this map to a map of modern Europe in an atlas. What major differences do you see?

©P

The Threat of Nationalism

As the Great Powers sought to expand their empires, they paid little attention to the interests of the nations they colonized. They practised their own type of **nationalism**, showing great pride in and patriotism for their mother country. But another type of nationalism—an intense loyalty toward and desire to preserve one's own cultural identity, language, and traditions— simmered in the colonized countries.

The Balkans were a hotbed of nationalism. Some of the countries in the area were newly created while others regained independence as the Ottoman Empire disintegrated. The Austro-Hungarian Empire also controlled several Slavic nations that wanted independence and rebelled against Austrian rule. Bosnia, in particular, was highly contested as Serbia wanted to include this territory within its borders. Some Bosnian Serbs formed the **Black Hand**, a group willing to fight for their nationalistic goals. They wanted to unite the Slavic peoples to form "Greater Serbia." To Austro-Hungarian imperialists, Serbian nationalism was a deadly idea that had to be crushed at all costs.

A Chain Reaction

● How did Canada get involved in the First World War?

In 1914, to demonstrate its imperial rule, the Austro-Hungarian Empire sent its crown prince, Archduke Franz Ferdinand, to Bosnia's capital of Sarajevo. His visit gave the Black Hand an opportunity to strike back at the Empire, whom they viewed as an invader. As their procession made its way through the city, a Black Hand member, Gavrilo Princip, shot and killed Archduke Ferdinand and his wife.

FIGURE 2–5 Archduke Franz Ferdinand and Duchess Sophie, moments before they were assassinated on June 28, 1914

This assassination triggered a chain reaction that started the First World War. Austria-Hungary blamed Serbia for the assassination. As part of the agreement of the Triple Alliance, Kaiser Wilhelm II of Germany offered Austria-Hungary a "blank cheque," promising to support them even if they went to war. When Serbia refused to submit to an ultimatum from Austria-Hungary, the Empire declared war. This caused Russia to mobilize its troops to defend Serbia as part of its promotion of Pan-Slavism. Germany responded with its own mobilization. This prompted Britain to put its navy on alert and France to mobilize its army. When Germany violated the neutrality of Belgium in order to attack France, Britain declared war on Germany to protect its ally. Canada, as part of the British Empire, automatically went to war, too. Gradually, the conflict drew in more and more countries around the world.

TIMELINE

Timeline to War, 1914

June 28   Franz Ferdinand and his wife Sophie are assassinated in Sarajevo, Bosnia.

July 6   Germany promises Austria-Hungary a "blank cheque" to support any military action in Serbia.

July 23   Austria-Hungary delivers an ultimatum to Serbia, threatening severe consequences:
- Serbia must dismiss all anti-Austrian teachers, government workers, and army officers.
- Austrian officials will be allowed to enter Serbia to investigate the assassination.
- Serbia must cooperate with the Austrian investigation.

July 26   Russia begins to mobilize its armed forces in anticipation of war.

July 28   Austria-Hungary rejects Serbia's partial acceptance of its demands and declares war.

July 31
- Russia announces its general mobilization.
- Austria-Hungary and Germany demand that Russia stop mobilizing; Russia ignores this command.
- France agrees to respect Belgium's neutrality, but Germany refuses.

August 1   Germany declares war on Russia.

August 3   Germany declares war on France.

August 4
- Germany invades Belgium and Luxembourg to attack France.
- Britain declares war on Germany.
- Canada is automatically at war as part of the British Empire.

PRACTICE QUESTIONS

1. Build a flow diagram that links the following in sequence, noting any events that occurred simultaneously: assassination of Franz Ferdinand and his wife, invasion of Belgium, creation of the Triple Alliance, Britain declares war on Germany, and Russia mobilizes troops.

2. **Significance** List the causes and contributing factors that resulted in the outbreak of war and then select the three you think are most important. Justify your choices.

3. Imagine you are the prime minister of Canada. Compose a letter to the prime minister of Britain explaining why you do, or do not, support an alliance between Britain, Russia, and France.

4. Write a well-reasoned argument for the following proposition: "The First World War was unnecessary and could have been prevented."

©P

Political cartoons are a useful source of information about historical or current issues. They simplify an issue by portraying political personalities or events in an exaggerated way and using symbols to represent ideas. In this way, they are a very effective means of convincing a reader to see an issue in a specific way. But the perspective about the issue presented in a political cartoon is often extreme and harshly critical. They represent political figures as caricatures, exaggerating their physical and personality traits for comic effect. Political cartoons often use stereotypes to emphasize their message. They also employ analogy to compare people or events to other things that the audience will relate to and understand. While these devices help convey perspectives on historical events or current issues, you need to be aware of the biases and prejudices that may taint political cartoons when you interpret them.

Steps to Interpreting Political Cartoons

1. Read the text and look closely at the drawing.
2. Identify the central issue or event in the cartoon.
3. Identify the devices used by the cartoonist (caricature, analogy, words, symbols, stereotypes, sizing, etc.).
4. Identify the biases of the cartoonist by examining the devices used.
5. Interpret the cartoon.

FIGURE 2–6 The Chain of Friendship. This British cartoon appeared in some Canadian newspapers at the outbreak of war. It highlights some of the main causes of the First World War by representing the European countries in 1914 as different characters.

Applying the Skill

1. Identify the countries represented by the child and the adult who is picking on him. Why is one country shown as a child?

2. The cartoon uses caricatures of speech and clothing to identify European countries. Identify Germany, Britain, France, and Russia. Explain your choice in each case.

3. Use the cartoon to make a list of the countries on either side of the conflict. Compare your list to the map in Figure 2–4.

4. What is the meaning of the title of the cartoon? Could it be interpreted as an ironic or sarcastic title? Explain.

5. Evaluate the cartoon. How effectively does it deliver its message? Explain.

● What challenges did Aboriginal soldiers face during the war?

Canada's Response to the War

Although Canada had become a political union in 1867, Britain still controlled the foreign policy of all its dominions. This meant that when Britain declared war on Germany, Canada was automatically at war, along with the rest of the British Empire.

Mobilizing the Forces

In 1914, most English-speaking Canadians were of British origin, and they supported the war out of a strong patriotic feeling for Britain and the Empire. One Toronto newspaper captured the excitement of the time:

> *Cheer after cheer from the crowds of people who had waited long and anxiously for the announcement of Great Britain's position in the present conflict in Europe greeted the news that the Mother Country had declared war against Germany. Groups of men sang "Rule Britannia," others joined in singing "God Save the King"; some showed their sense of the seriousness of the situation by singing "Onward Christian Soldiers"....*
> –Toronto Mail and Empire, *August 5, 1914*

Wilfrid Laurier, the leader of the Liberals and a French Canadian, joined English Canadians in pledging support for Britain and the Empire. Laurier stated, "It is our duty to let Great Britain know and to let the friends and foes of Great Britain know that there is in Canada but one mind and one heart and that all Canadians are behind the Mother Country."

Prime Minister Borden initially offered Britain 25 000 troops, but more than 30 000 volunteers from across Canada signed up within a month. Many felt the patriotic urge to defend their "mother country." A lot of people volunteered because they believed that the war would be over by Christmas. Others signed up because they were unemployed and the war meant a chance to escape financial hardships at home.

Not all Canadians who wanted to volunteer were welcome. Women were considered too frail and too emotional to partake in battle, so they were encouraged to stay at home and support the soldiers. Women who did join the services worked as nurses and ambulance drivers behind the front lines. Initially, the Canadian forces did not accept Aboriginal peoples and were reluctant to take African and Japanese Canadians. Volunteers from these groups managed to overcome such racist attitudes to join, but few were promoted. Such discrimination did not prevent these recruits from serving their country well (see Case Study, page 48). Tom Longboat, an Onondaga from the Six Nations Reserve in Ontario, was a well-known athlete and Boston Marathon runner. During the war, he became a courier, carrying messages between the trenches in France, a position reserved for the fastest runners in the army.

FIGURE 2–7 At the start of the First World War, crowds gathered to cheer the soldiers on their way.

Thinking Critically What do you think the public attitude was after a few years of war? What might public reaction be to Canada's involvement in a war today?

Rank	Daily Rate
Major-General	$20.00
Colonel	$6.00
Major	$4.00
Captain	$3.00
Lieutenant	$2.00
Sergeant	$1.35
Corporal	$1.05
Private	$1.00

FIGURE 2–8 Canadian Army rates of pay, 1917

A National Identity Emerges

Canada had to prepare for war. When Canada joined the war, its army swelled from 3000 to more than 30 000 soldiers. The enormous task of training and supplying the troops with clothing and munitions went to Sam Hughes, the Minister of Militia. Camp Valcartier in Québec was built in only four weeks to house and train Canada's soldiers. After basic training that lasted only four months, 32 000 enthusiastic, but ill-prepared, Canadian and Newfoundland troops set sail for England.

Before the war, Canada was a patchwork of regions. Few transportation and communication connections existed, and travel across the country was difficult. Regions had little contact with one another; people lived their lives close to home. Wartime training changed that. Young men from all over the country came together to train, first at Valcartier, then at bases in England. As they gathered and worked together, they began to develop a national sense of Canadian identity. In the words of one Canadian soldier:

> We were in Witley Camp [in England] and right alongside us was a battalion from French Canada. We didn't speak much French and they didn't speak much English, but they were the finest sports you ever saw.... You met people from Nova Scotia, or from Prince Edward Island, clean through to British Columbia.
>
> –Ben Wagner

The army formed by these volunteers was known as the Canadian Expeditionary Force (CEF). When the CEF arrived in England, British commanders assumed that, as a colonial army, the CEF would be integrated into the larger, more experienced British units. For much of the war, however, the CEF maintained its independence and fought as a separate unit, which contributed greatly to a growing sense of national identity and autonomy.

● What factors contributed to Canada's emerging autonomy?

WEB LINK ● ⋯⋯⋯⋯⋯⋯⋯
Find out more about wartime training on the Pearson Web site.

FIGURE 2–9 Colourful recruiting posters with urgent messages for volunteers appeared across Canada.

Identifying Viewpoints Compare these two posters. What methods does each one use to appeal to different language groups? What image of war does each one present?

- What was the war's impact on the home front?

Canada's Minister of Militia

Sam Hughes was also in charge of Canada's armament industry. He created the Shell Committee to oversee the manufacture of artillery shells. Canada provided a large portion of Britain's shells. Hughes, however, was a poor administrator and the Ministry of Militia soon became bogged down in inefficiency and war profiteering. While he insisted on using Canadian manufacturers, troops were often supplied with equipment that was inappropriate or of poor quality. By mid-1915, contracts worth about $170 million had been signed with wealthy businessmen, but only $5.5 million in shells had actually been made. Some of the shells were of such poor quality that they exploded before being fired, killing the gun crews. In one case, soldiers were equipped with boots that fell apart in the rain due to soles made of pressed cardboard. Troops came to hate the Canadian-made Ross rifle because it jammed, so they picked up British-made Lee-Enfield rifles from dead soldiers when possible. Hughes was dismissed from his post in 1916, but not before being knighted by King George V.

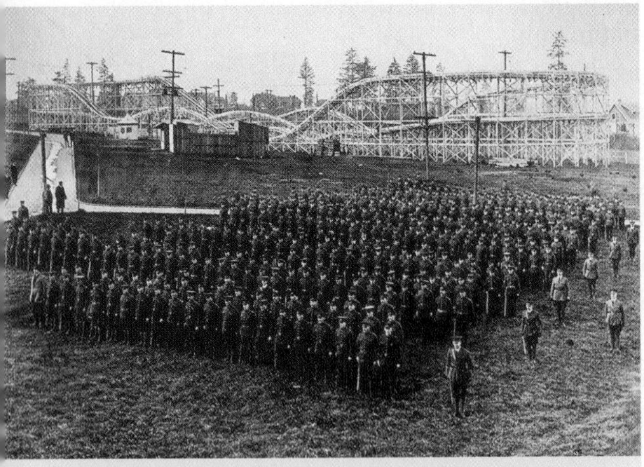

FIGURE 2–10 The 29th Battalion (Vancouver), CEF, in training in Hastings Park, Vancouver, late 1914

Using Evidence How are these men preparing for war?

The War Measures Act

- What effect did the War Measures Act have on the legal rights of Canadians?

To meet the demands of war, Prime Minister Borden introduced the **War Measures Act** in 1914. The Act gave the government the authority to do everything necessary "for the security, defence, peace, order, and welfare of Canada." For the first time, the federal government could intervene directly in the economy to control transportation, manufacturing, trade, and agricultural production. The government also had the power to limit the freedom of Canadians. It could censor mail. It suspended ***habeas corpus***, which meant that police could detain people without laying charges. Anyone suspected of being an **"enemy alien"** or a threat to the government could be imprisoned, or **deported**, or both. Recent immigrants from Germany and the Austro-Hungarian Empire were treated particularly harshly under this Act. Approximately 100 000 of them had to carry special identity cards and report regularly to registration officers. More than 8500 people were held in isolation in **internment camps**. These policies fostered nationalism and prejudice in Canada, and led to attacks on German-owned clubs and businesses.

PRACTICE QUESTIONS

1. Examine the quotation on page 32. What does this document say about the attitude of people in Canada toward Britain at this time? How does the quotation on page 33 demonstrate a growing feeling of Canadian identity among Canadian troops?
2. What prevented women and other groups from participating in the war?
3. Why did the government feel the need to control the economy, transportation, and trade after war was declared? Was this a genuine need? Explain.
4. List the civil liberties suspended by the War Measures Act.
5. Explain why there was such enthusiasm for the war when it began.

©P

The War on Land

Germany's **Schlieffen Plan**, developed years before the First World War began, was a bold strategy for a two-front war. Germany believed it could fend off Russia in the east while it defeated France in the west with a lightning-speed massive attack. The timetable left little room for error. German armies needed to drive through Belgium and swing south to capture Paris within a few weeks. Once this was accomplished, Germany could turn its attention to Russia. The Schlieffen Plan made two critical assumptions:

- It would take Russia time to mobilize its huge army. But Russia's forces were already on the move when Germany declared war.

- Britain would remain neutral. The plan relied on the fact that in the past, Britain had not become involved in disputes between countries in Europe. But, as part of the Triple Entente, Britain had promised to defend France if it was attacked. Also, all the Great Powers had promised not to attack Belgium, so Britain felt compelled to enter the war when Germany did just that.

The Reality of the Schlieffen Plan

The Schlieffen Plan almost worked. By August 1914, German troops were only 50 kilometres from Paris. But German leaders had made some changes that weakened the original plan. They pulled troops from the west to reinforce their defences in the east. The soldiers were exhausted by the pace of their attack through Belgium and into France. The Allies were able to rally and stop Germany's advance at the Battle of the Marne in September 1914, making a quick German victory impossible. Instead, the German army dug a defensive line of trenches along the river Somme and into Belgium. To counter this, British and French troops dug their own system of trenches to face them. Eventually a vast network of trenches stretched from the English Channel to the Swiss border. Between the trenches of the two enemies lay **no man's land**, a terrible wasteland of corpses, barbed wire, and mud. By Christmas 1914, armies protected by trenches that ran through northern France and Belgium on the **Western Front** were locked in a stalemate. With millions of soldiers on each side, neither Britain and France nor the Germans were able to advance, and no one was prepared to retreat.

KEY TERMS

profiteering making a profit by raising prices on needed goods or producing poor quality materials

War Measures Act an Act that gives the federal government emergency powers during wartime, including the right to detain people without laying charges

habeas corpus the right of a detained person to be brought before a judge or other official to decide whether the detention is lawful

enemy alien a national living in a country that is at war with his/her homeland

deport to send a person back to his/her country of origin

internment camp a government-run camp where people who are considered a threat are detained

Schlieffen Plan Germany's plan to stage a two-front war with Russia in the east and France in the west

no man's land the area between the trenches of two opposing forces

Western Front the area of fighting in western Europe during the First World War, characterized by trench warfare and inconclusive battles with heavy casualties on both sides

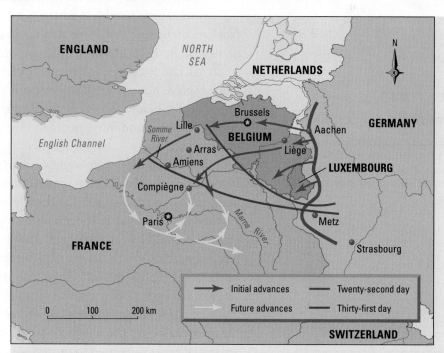

FIGURE 2–11 The Schlieffen Plan

Life in the Trenches

No soldier could ever have been prepared for the horrible conditions of trench warfare. Trenches were cold and damp in the winter and often flooded in the heavy rains of northern France and Belgium. Muddy trenches became stinking cesspools, overrun by rats. Men spent weeks in the trenches without washing, which allowed disease to spread. Soldiers' clothes were infested with lice, and many men developed trench foot, a painful condition that caused their feet to swell and turn black. Many of the wounded were left to die in no man's land because rescue attempts were too dangerous. Mental exhaustion also took its toll. Men were in constant fear for their lives, either from deadly sniper fire or from exploding shells. One soldier reported:

> The air is full of shells... the small ones whistling and shrieking and the heaviest falling silently, followed by a terrific explosion which perforates even the padded eardrums, so that a thin trickle of blood down the neck bears witness that the man is stricken stone-deaf. The solid ground rocks like an express [train] at full speed, and the only comparison possible is to a volcano in eruption with incessant shudder of earthworks and pelting hail of rocks.
>
> –*Quoted in* Toronto Globe, *April 15, 1916*

FIGURE 2–12 Many Canadian soldiers lost their lives in the trenches and suffered psychological disorders and nervous breakdowns.

Gathering Information What can you tell about life in the trenches from this photograph? How might these conditions have contributed to psychological problems?

- What were conditions like for men in the trenches?

- How did the nature of warfare and technology contribute to a war of attrition?

KEY TERMS

artillery large guns used to fire shells

war of attrition a military strategy based on exhausting the enemy's manpower and resources before yours are exhausted, usually involving great losses on both sides

New Technology and the War

New technologies developed at the beginning of the 20th century changed the way wars were fought. In earlier wars, foot soldiers, supported by cavalry (soldiers on horses), tried to outmanoeuvre the enemy to take control of the battlefield. By 1914, however, new weapons were so powerful and deadly that it was suicidal to charge across open ground. Machine guns fired at unprecedented speed; massive **artillery** attacks killed thousands. Airplanes, invented only a decade before the war began, flew over the battlefields to pinpoint the enemy's location and movements and were later equipped with machine guns and bombs.

Although soldiers were using modern weapons on the battlefield, many of their commanders failed to understand how the new technologies demanded new tactics. Over the next three years, generals stubbornly engaged in a **war of attrition**, each side repeatedly attacking the other until one was completely exhausted and unable to continue. To attack the enemy, soldiers were ordered "over the top," meaning they had to leave the relative safety of the trenches to face the horror of no man's land. Hundreds of thousands of soldiers on all sides were slaughtered as they were mowed down by machine guns. These weapons kept either side from advancing, which was the main reason for the stalemate on the Western Front. Later in the war, armoured tanks were used to protect soldiers as they advanced across the battlefield. Tanks could break through the protective wall of barbed wire in front of trenches. By 1918, the trench system was itself obsolete.

©P

Major Canadian Battles

The first division of the Canadian Expeditionary Force (CEF) arrived in France in February 1915. These forces soon became involved in combat along the Western Front, including decisive battles in France and Belgium at Ypres, the Somme, Vimy Ridge, and Passchendaele.

● Describe Canada's military role in the First World War.

● How did Canada's contribution on the battlefield affect Canadian identity?

The Second Battle of Ypres

Some of the bloodiest battles of the early war were fought in and around the Belgian town of Ypres. On April 22, 1915, French and Canadian troops were blinded, burned, or killed when the Germans used chlorine gas, a tactic that had been outlawed by international agreement since 1907. As the clouds of gas drifted low across the battlefield, soldiers tried to escape from the deadly fumes. Many suffocated or choked to death. One soldier described the scene as follows:

> [We noticed] a strange new smell.... A queer brownish-yellow haze was blowing in from the north. Our eyes smarted. Breathing became unpleasant and throats raw.... Some fell and choked, and writhed and frothed on the ground.... It was the gas.
>
> –Canada and the Battle of Vimy Ridge, 1992

Despite the Germans' use of poison gas, the battle continued for a month, but neither side gained much advantage. More than 6000 Canadians were killed, wounded, or captured holding their ground until reinforcements arrived.

One of the doctors serving with the Canada Corps was Lieutenant Colonel John McCrae, who wrote the famous poem "In Flanders Fields" to commemorate Canadians serving at the Second Battle of Ypres. It is said that he wrote the poem in about 20 minutes, but tossed it aside because he was dissatisfied with it. The story goes that a soldier later found it and convinced him to send it to a popular British magazine.

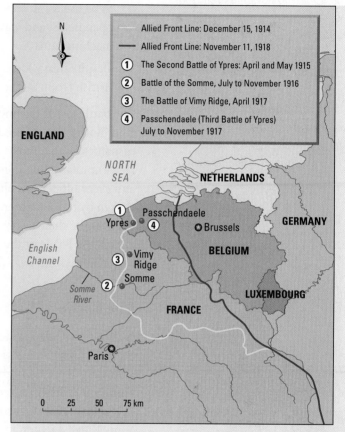

FIGURE 2–13 Map showing the Western Front and major battles

FIGURE 2–14 The Belgian town of Ypres in 1917 showing the massive destruction caused by the war

casualties those injured, killed, captured, or missing in action

I past the worse fighting here since the war started, we took all kinds of prisonners but God we lost heavy, all my camarades killed or wounded.... dear wife it is worse than hell, the ground is covered for miles with dead corpses all over.... pray for me dear wife I need it very bad.... as long as I leave I'll remember it.

–Francis Xavier Maheux, September 20, 1916

Note: The quotation above contains spelling and punctuation errors. It has been reproduced as it was originally written.

FIGURE 2–15 The Canadian National Vimy Memorial in France commemorates Canadian soldiers who were killed during the First World War.

Thinking Critically Do you think that war memorials are important? Why or why not?

What If...

Imagine that Canada had lost at Vimy Ridge. How might that have affected Canada's identity?

The Battle of the Somme

In July 1916, the Allies launched a massive attack against a line of German trenches near the Somme River in France. The attack failed because

- The Allies shelled the German lines for days before the attack began, but the shells did not destroy the Germans' defences or the barbed wire around their trenches.
- The commanders used tactics that, though previously successful, proved to be useless in trench warfare. Troops were ordered to march across open fields, and wave upon wave of men were shot down by German machine guns.
- Despite heavy losses on the first day of battle—including nearly 58 000 British troops—the attack continued.

The battle lasted five months and the Allies captured only 13 kilometres of land. Both sides suffered heavy losses. There were more than 1.25 million casualties, with almost 24 000 Canadians among them. The Royal Newfoundland Regiment alone lost approximately 90 percent of its men, and every officer was either wounded or killed. Most soldiers were badly shaken by the slaughter.

Despite their heavy losses, Canadian troops distinguished themselves during the Battle of the Somme and were brought in to lead assaults in several major battles over the course of the war.

The Battle of Vimy Ridge

In 1914, the Germans took control of Vimy Ridge, a key position near the Somme. This vantage point gave a clear view of the surrounding countryside, supply routes, and enemy positions. For more than two years, both French and British forces tried to capture the ridge but were unsuccessful.

Late in 1916, Canadian troops were chosen to lead a new assault on Vimy Ridge. Lieutenant-General Julian Byng, a popular British officer (later appointed a governor general of Canada; see Chapter 3), carefully planned the attack. His troops trained and rehearsed until Byng decided they were ready. In preparation for the attack, artillery bombarded German positions for more than a month. Meanwhile, sappers (army engineers) built tunnels to secretly move troops closer to the ridge. On April 9, 1917, Canadian troops moved into position. The Canadian Corps followed their plan of attack and in less than two hours they had taken their first objective. On April 10, they captured Hill 145, the highest point on the ridge. By April 12 they had taken "the pimple," the last German position.

It was a stunning victory. The Canadians had gained more ground, taken more prisoners, and captured more artillery than any previous British offensive in the entire war. Although the cost was high—more than 3500 men were killed and another 7000 wounded—the losses were significantly lower than in any previous Allied offensive. Byng's meticulous planning and training, and Canadian professionalism and bravery, had paid off. The Battle of Vimy Ridge marked the first time that Canadian divisions attacked together. Their success gave them a sense of national pride and the reputation of being an elite fighting force.

Passschendaele

Byng was promoted for his role at Vimy. His replacement was a Canadian, General Arthur Currie, a former realtor from Victoria, British Columbia. As the first Canadian appointed to command Canada's troops, Currie brought an increasingly independent Canadian point of view to the British war effort. Although he was a disciplined leader open to new strategies, Currie still took orders from General Haig. In October 1917, Currie and the CEF were asked to break through German lines and retake the town of Passschendaele in Belgium.

FIGURE 2–16 Passschendaele; soldiers and horses sometimes drowned in the mud-filled craters which could be more than 30 metres wide.

Haig's earlier assault on Passschendaele had left massive shell craters, which the heavy autumn rains turned into a muddy bog. Currie warned that casualties would be high, but Haig overruled him. Currie was right. The Canadians captured Passschendaele, but the "victory" resulted in more than 200 000 casualties on each side, including more than 15 000 Canadians. The Allies had gained only seven or eight kilometres, and the Germans soon recaptured the town.

Women on the Western Front

More than 2800 women served during the First World War. They were part of the Royal Canadian Army Medical Corps and worked on hospital ships, in overseas hospitals, and in field ambulance units on the battlefields. Many were killed or injured by artillery fire, bombs, and poison gas.

FIGURE 2–17 Edith Anderson, of the Six Nations Grand River Reserve, cared for wounded soldiers in France.

PRACTICE QUESTIONS

1. What was the Schlieffen Plan, and why did its failure result in a stalemate on the Western Front?

2. **Judgements** Discuss whether chemical weapons should be allowed in warfare. The use of gas as a weapon was outlawed by the 1907 Hague Convention. What is the point of an international agreement if, when the time comes, countries do whatever they wish?

3. Make a list of conditions at the front that might have contributed to psychological stress damage. Use the information on pages 35–39 to gather information.

4. How did new technological developments make the First World War a war of attrition? Give specific examples.

©P

Innovations
War Technology

During the First World War, transportation and weapons technology developed rapidly as nations dedicated their resources to the war effort. The result was an industrial war with more casualties than had ever been experienced.

A new type of warfare The machine gun was largely responsible for changing the way wars were fought. Its ability to fire about 400–500 rounds per minute made it an effective defensive weapon. The water-cooled Vickers gun was capable of sustained fire. Both sides lined their trenches with hundreds of machine guns, making infantry attacks across no man's land futile and forcing leaders to develop new strategies.

Lighter than air Dirigibles (inflatable airships) were developed in the late 1800s. Germany's Ferdinand von Zeppelin built huge, rigid dirigibles that were filled with a lighter-than-air gas, such as hydrogen, and propelled by an engine suspended underneath. Germany, France, and Italy used dirigibles for scouting and bombing missions during the First World War.

Deadly fire During the First World War, more powerful and accurate artillery was developed. The British 60-pounder gun used by Canadian gunners was extremely destructive but, like any large piece of artillery, was difficult to move into position. It was not uncommon for field guns to sink out of sight in the muddy battlefields.

©P

Warfare in the air Planes were first used to scout enemy positions. Later in the war, pilots would throw grenades at enemy planes or shoot at them with hand-held guns. Eventually, machine guns were added to planes and both sides engaged in aerial dogfights. The stable but speedy S.E.5a rivalled the Sopwith Camel in reputation.

The silent enemy Although the United States and Britain did much of the work developing early submarines, Germany used them the most. Their U-boats (from Unterseeboot, or "under-sea boat") were armed with torpedoes that could sink large ships. Germany used its submarines to attack the convoys of merchant ships and freighters that carried supplies to Britain in the hopes of starving the British into submission. This German minelaying U-boat was captured by the British.

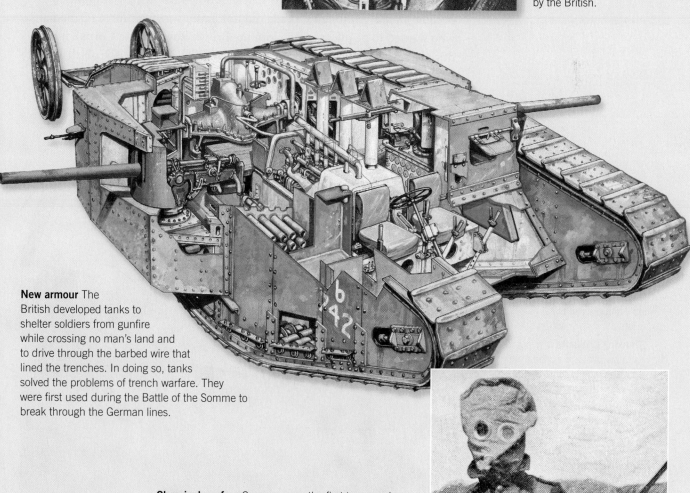

New armour The British developed tanks to shelter soldiers from gunfire while crossing no man's land and to drive through the barbed wire that lined the trenches. In doing so, tanks solved the problems of trench warfare. They were first used during the Battle of the Somme to break through the German lines.

Chemical warfare Germany was the first to use poison gas on the battlefield, releasing clouds of chlorine gas at Ypres in 1915. The gas blinded soldiers and attacked their respiratory systems. Early in the war, the only defence against poison gas was rags soaked in water or urine. Later, anti-gas respirators, or gas masks, made poison gas a less effective weapon.

©P

KEY TERMS

biplane an airplane with two sets of wings, one on top of the body, and one underneath

reconnaissance military search or exploration

sharpshooter a person skilled in shooting

dogfight aerial duels between aircraft

ace a fighter pilot who has shot down five enemy aircraft

The War in the Air

During the First World War, airplanes were still a new invention and being a pilot was very dangerous. Many pilots were killed in training and due to mechanical failure. The average life expectancy of a pilot in 1917 could be measured in weeks. Parachutes were not introduced until late in the war. Thousands of air crew and pilots were killed, many in training.

At the beginning of the war, pilots flew alone in **biplanes** doing aerial **reconnaissance**, photographing and reporting on enemy troop movements. Soon, however, pilots on both sides were armed, dropping bombs on the enemy below and firing guns at each other in the air. Fighter pilots had to be **sharpshooters** with nerves of steel and lots of luck. Aerial **dogfights** were spectacular scenes as pilots used elaborate spins and rolls to avoid enemy planes and stay out of their line of fire.

Air Aces

When a pilot could prove that he had shot down five enemy aircraft, he became an **ace**. Although Canada did not have its own air force (Canadians who wanted to be pilots had to join the British Royal Flying Corps), it produced a number of aces. Among them were Billy Bishop, Ray Collishaw, Billy Barker, William May, and Roy Brown. Some historians credit Brown with shooting down the German flying ace Manfred von Richthofen, who was known as the Red Baron. Because air aces became heroes in their homelands, they were often withdrawn from active duty overseas to promote fundraising and recruitment at home.

FIGURE 2–18 A pair of Canada's ace pilots: Nanaimo's Raymond Collishaw (62 victories) and Arthur Whealy (27 victories). Many air aces were Canadian even though Canada supplied only a quarter of Britain's pilots.

Thinking Critically Why would valuable pilots be pulled from active service to promote the war effort at home? Why were they good for promotion? How do you think they felt about recruiting after they saw so many of their friends killed in battle?

up close and personal | Billy Bishop: War Hero or Cold-Blooded Killer?

 Judgements

Canada's top air ace in the First World War was William Avery "Billy" Bishop, from Owen Sound, Ontario. His record was impressive. He shot down 72 planes, the second highest number of "kills" in the war (Germany's Red Baron had 80). Bishop was the first Canadian pilot to be awarded the Victoria Cross, Britain's most prestigious medal for bravery. He became the toast of Canada because of his success, and toured to promote the war effort and help sell Victory Bonds. In the following passage from his diary, he describes some of his daring adventures:

> He dived for about 600 feet [180 metres] and flattened out. I followed him and opened fire at forty to fifty yards [35 to 45 metres] range, firing forty to fifty rounds. A group of tracers ("visible bullets") went into the fuselage and centre section, one being seen entering immediately behind the pilot's seat and one seemed to hit himself. The machine then fell out of control in a spinning nose-dive. I dived after him firing....
>
> I must say that seeing an enemy going down in flames is a source of great satisfaction. The moment you see the fire break out you know that nothing in the world can save the man, or men, in the doomed machine.

But the life of this Canadian legend was less glamorous than it appeared. In a letter home to his wife, Margaret, he wrote:

> I am thoroughly downcast tonight.... Sometimes all of this awful fighting makes you wonder if you have a right to call yourself human. My honey, I am so sick of it all, the killing, the war. All I want is home and you.
>
> **–Billy Bishop**

In warfare, society's norms are put on hold, as soldiers are often expected to kill, and in some cases are glorified for their number of kills. Many soldiers, past and present, suffer emotional trauma after experiencing the atrocities of war and have difficulty adjusting when they return home. At the time of the First World War, soldiers' battle stress was called shell shock or battle fatigue. It is currently identified as post-traumatic stress disorder.

1. Bishop's diary is his personal account of what happened. His "kill" total has sometimes been questioned because his deeds were not always witnessed. Explain why you think Bishop was given credit for the "kills." Is the diary a primary source? Evaluate it as a historical source.

2. Using the two sources presented here, identify Bishop's personal reactions to killing in warfare. What might account for his conflicting feelings?

3. Bishop most likely killed the pilots he shot down. He needed courage and nerve to do what he did. What do you think the effect of the war would be on someone like Bishop?

4. Do you think soldiers today are encouraged to count "kills"? Why or why not?

5. Are there times when killing is not justified in the heat of battle? Explain.

FIGURE 2–19 A stamp commemorates Canadian air ace Billy Bishop.

KEY TERMS

allegiance loyalty or faithfulness

merchant marine civilian ships and sailors that transported food, weapons, and munitions

convoy a group of ships travelling together protected by an armed force

Victory Bonds bonds issued by the Canadian government to support the war effort

honour rationing a civilian effort to consume less and conserve supplies on the home front

income tax a tax on personal income

corporate tax a tax charged to businesses based on their total revenues

The War at Sea

When war broke out between Britain and Germany, leaders expected that huge battles would be fought at sea. As part of the growing militarism in the years before the war, Britain asked Canada to help contribute to its naval forces. In 1910, Prime Minister Wilfrid Laurier introduced the Naval Service Act, which authorized the building of Canadian warships. The ships would be under Canadian control but could be turned over to Britain if war broke out. Many French Canadians felt that Canada should not automatically support Britain in war. This created tensions with English Canadians, most of whom felt they owed Britain their **allegiance**.

During the war, Britain relied heavily on its own navy to protect the freighters that brought supplies and troops to the Western Front. While Canada's navy was small and unable to contribute much to the war effort, Canada's **merchant marine** played a significant role in the war by doing the dangerous work of ferrying munitions and food to Britain. Although not officially members of the armed forces, many merchant marines lost their lives when their ships were attacked crossing the Atlantic.

Submarine Warfare

Although Germany could not match Britain's navy in size and strength, its U-boat was a dangerous weapon because it could travel under water without being detected. Equipped with torpedoes, U-boats took their toll on Allied warships and merchant ships. Eventually the Allies developed the **convoy** system to help protect their ships from the German U-boats. Freighters travelled together and were defended by armed destroyers. The Allies also developed an underwater listening device that helped them locate and destroy U-boats. Both of these advances helped to greatly reduce the threat of German submarines.

Germany's aggressive use of submarines also contributed to the United States entering the war in 1917. In 1915, a German U-boat sank the *Lusitania*, a British passenger liner, killing close to 1200 passengers. Among the dead were Canadian and American civilians. In February 1917, Germany announced that U-boats would sink any ship within the war zone around Britain—including ships that were not from Allied countries. German leaders believed that this move would put a stranglehold on Britain and help end the war. But this threat also made American ships targets and encouraged the United States to enter the war on the side of the Allies on April 2, 1917.

FIGURE 2–20 The sinking of the *Lusitania*

Thinking Critically Explain why the United States felt justified in entering the war after the sinking of the *Lusitania*. Can you think of any recent events that resulted in political and military conflict? What are some non-military options to resolve disputes between countries?

The Home Front

Canada and many of its citizens were committed to supporting the war effort. Prime Minister Borden replaced Sam Hughes's Shell Committee with the more efficient Imperial Munitions Board, and munitions factories started building ships and airplanes as well as shells. The production and export of Canadian goods reached record highs. Resources such as lumber, nickel, copper, and lead were in high demand. Canadian farmers produced as much wheat and beef as they could to feed the troops overseas. This demand for Canadian goods helped its economy boom during the war.

Most of what Canada produced was exported to Europe, so many goods became scarce within Canada, which caused prices to rise. Some Canadian businesses made enormous profits from the inflated prices. Workers became increasingly frustrated by government controls that kept wages low yet allowed prices to rise. Workers' demands for higher wages and better working conditions became a major issue after the war.

● What was the war's impact on the home front?

Year	Forest Products	Mineral Products	Agricultural Products	Animal Products
1911	$12.0	$6.7	$61.4	$40.6
1912	$11.0	$5.6	$81.8	$36.9
1913	$10.1	$12.1	$106.5	$30.3
1914	$10.6	$16.0	$146.2	$26.7
1915	$9.9	$12.2	$95.8	$38.2
1916	$14.1	$12.4	$196.8	$67.8
1917	$14.9	$15.5	$266.2	$93.3
1918	$4.5	$14.0	$403.5	$112.2

FIGURE 2–21 Value of exports from Canada to Britain during the First World War (in millions)

Using Evidence In which year were Canadian exports to Britain the highest? How significant were the increases in 1916? Why did some exports decrease in 1918?

Supporting the War Effort

By 1918, the war effort was costing Canada about $2.5 million daily. The government launched several initiatives to cover these costs.

- Canadians were urged to buy **Victory Bonds**. The government raised close to $2 billion through these bonds, which Canadians could cash in for a profit when the war was over.

- **Honour rationing** was introduced to help combat shortages on the home front. Canadians used less butter and sugar, and the government introduced "Meatless Fridays" and "Fuel-less Sundays" to conserve supplies.

- In 1917, the Canadian government introduced **income tax**—a measure that was supposed to be temporary. Affluent individuals and families had to pay a tax of between 1 and 15 percent of their income.

- A **corporate tax** was also introduced, charging businesses four percent of their revenues. Many Canadians thought this was too low, considering the profits some companies made during the war.

Despite these efforts, the government still did not raise enough money to cover the costs of the war effort. It had to borrow money from other countries, in particular the United States, to pay its debts.

BUY VICTORY BONDS

FIGURE 2–22 This poster, showing a Canadian nurse, reminded the public of Edith Cavell, a British nurse who was executed by the Germans in 1915 for helping Allied soldiers escape German-occupied countries. The names on the poster represent German atrocities.

Thinking Critically What is the message in this poster?

Getting the Message Out

During the First World War, Canadians were bombarded with **propaganda**. It was everywhere: films, magazine articles, radio programs, political speeches, and posters. Appealing to their sense of patriotism, propaganda encouraged people to join the army, buy Victory Bonds, use less fuel, eat less meat, and support the government. Some of the campaigns used social pressure to encourage men to join the army, contributing to the fact that the majority of Canadians who served in the First World War were volunteers.

Propaganda often distorted the truth. The number of Allied soldiers killed or wounded was minimized, while enemy casualties were exaggerated. British commanders were praised even as they continued to waste lives in futile attacks. When Germany invaded Belgium in 1914, refugees who escaped to England told horrible stories about the invasion. Writers used these stories to portray German troops as barbarians intent on destroying the civilized world. While this propaganda was intended to recruit soldiers, it also fuelled prejudice on the home front. Many Canadian citizens were treated as enemy aliens, subjected to harsh restrictions by the government and violent attacks by angry citizens.

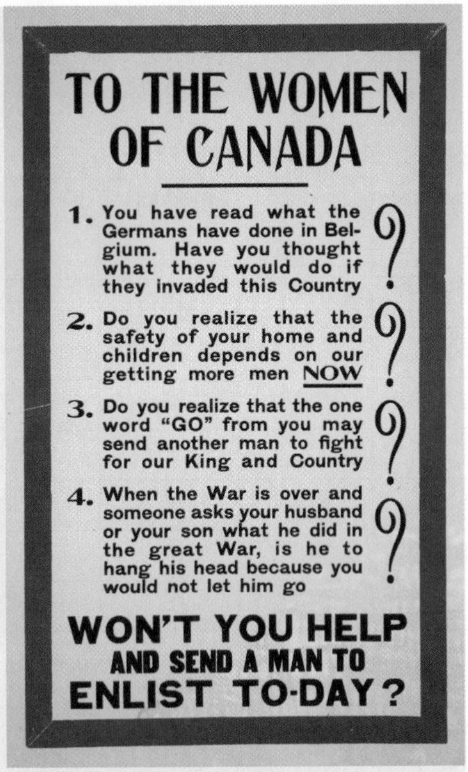

Women and the War

Before 1914, middle-class women had few options for working outside the home. Some became nurses or teachers. Others were employed as domestic servants or worked at low-skill, low-paying jobs in food and clothing industries. During the war, increased industrial production created a demand for labour. Women were hired for all types of work, from operating fishing boats to working on farms. One Toronto woman who worked filling artillery shells described her motivation on the job as follows:

> There was everybody, every single class.... [W]e began to realize that we were all sisters under the skin.... [T]here's nothing that draws people together more than mutual trouble.... [W]e felt, "The boys are doing that for us, what are we doing for them?" You just rolled up your sleeves and you didn't care how tired you were or anything else.
>
> –Tapestry of War, *1992*

TO THE WOMEN OF CANADA

1. You have read what the Germans have done in Belgium. Have you thought what they would do if they invaded this Country ?

2. Do you realize that the safety of your home and children depends on our getting more men **NOW** !

3. Do you realize that the one word "GO" from you may send another man to fight for our King and Country !

4. When the War is over and someone asks your husband or your son what he did in the great War, is he to hang his head because you would not let him go

WON'T YOU HELP AND SEND A MAN TO ENLIST TO-DAY ?

FIGURE 2–23 This recruiting poster was aimed at Canadian wives and mothers.

Thinking Critically Why do you think a war poster targeted women? How effectively does this poster communicate its message to its intended audience? Explain.

● What effect did the war have on the role of women?

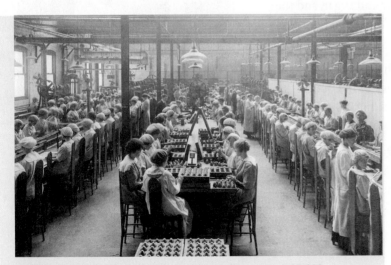

FIGURE 2–24 Munitions assembly, Verdun, Québec. About 35 000 Canadian women worked in munitions factories where shells were manufactured, and thousands more drove delivery trucks.

©P

Suffrage Is Granted to Women

Without women's efforts on the home front, Canada's wartime economy would have collapsed. But when the war ended, most employers assumed that women would return to work in their homes. Many women believed that their contribution to the war effort should allow them to make decisions about how their country was run. During the 1915 provincial election in Manitoba, one of the Liberal Party's campaign promises was to give women the right to vote. They kept their promise, and Manitoban women received this right in January 1916. Thanks to the efforts of suffragists across the country, women in other provinces soon won the right to vote as well. Alberta and Saskatchewan followed Manitoba's example later in 1916, with Ontario and British Columbia following in 1917. In 1918, women were granted the right to vote in federal elections, with the exception of Aboriginal and immigrant women.

KEY TERM

propaganda information, usually produced by governments, presented in such a way as to inspire and spread particular beliefs or opinions

The Halifax Explosion

During the war, Halifax was a valuable base for refuelling and repairing Allied warships. It was also the chief departure point for soldiers and supplies headed to Europe. The harbour was extremely busy, but there was little traffic control and collisions were frequent.

On December 6, 1917, the SS *Mont Blanc*, a French vessel carrying more than 2500 tonnes of explosives, was accidentally hit by another ship. The collision caused an explosion so powerful that it devastated Halifax's harbour and levelled much of the city. More than 2000 people were killed, another 9000 were injured, and thousands were left homeless by the explosion and the fires it caused.

FIGURE 2–25 Halifax Harbour after the explosion, in 1917

Thinking Critically Do you think the Halifax explosion might have made people think differently about the war? Explain.

PRACTICE QUESTIONS

1. How was propaganda used during the war? Discuss whether it is appropriate to manipulate information for patriotic purposes during war. What differences, if any, are there between propaganda and advertising?

2. List specific military contributions made by Canada.

3. Explain how women contributed to the war effort, and describe how their status in Canadian society changed as a result.

4. What contributions did Canadians on the home front make to the war effort?

5. Imagine you are the prime minister and you have received a request for aid from the mayor of Halifax after the 1917 explosion. Write a response explaining why help will be limited.

case study

● What challenges did Aboriginal soldiers face during the war?

Aboriginal Peoples and the First World War

Canada's Aboriginal peoples contributed greatly to the war effort, both by giving money to the cause and by volunteering for the armed forces. This was despite the fact that First Nations' land claims were being brought before the government, and they faced racism, bigotry, and poverty. In fact, at the start of the war, the government discouraged Aboriginal peoples from enlisting. Why, then, did they take part in the conflict?

Many Aboriginal peoples felt strongly about their relationship with the British Crown, with which they had signed important agreements. Many were descended from Loyalists who had fought for Britain in the American Revolution and in the War of 1812. In the words of one Aboriginal soldier:

> ...[T]he participation of Great Britain in the war has occasioned expressions of loyalty from the Indians, and the offer of contributions from their funds toward the general expenses of the war or toward the Patriotic Fund. Some bands have also offered the services of their warriors if they should be needed.
>
> –*Indian Affairs*, **Annual Report,** **1913–1914**

Young Aboriginal men saw the war as a chance to prove themselves. Most came from isolated communities and thought the war would be an opportunity for adventure. Also, soldiers were paid, so there was an economic incentive for volunteering.

The hunting tradition of many Aboriginal peoples was excellent training for the battlefield, where steady nerves, patience, and good marksmanship made them excellent sharpshooters. Francis Pegahmagabow, an Ojibwa, and Henry Louis Norwest, a Métis, both won Military Medals for their exceptional service as snipers and scouts. Inuit soldier John Shiwak compared sniping to swatching, shooting seals in open water as they popped up to breathe. Often, Aboriginal spiritual traditions went to the Western Front, as recounted by Francis Pegahmagabow:

FIGURE 2–26 Francis Pegahmagabow won his Military Medal for bravery at Passchendaele.

FIGURE 2–27 National Aboriginal Veterans Monument in Ottawa

Thinking Critically What do you think the various elements of the monument symbolize?

> When I was... on Lake Superior, in 1914, some of us landed from our vessel to gather blueberries near an Ojibwa camp. An old Indian recognized me, and gave me a tiny medicine-bag to protect me, saying that I would shortly go into great danger. Sometimes [the bag] seemed to be as hard as rock, at other times it appeared to contain nothing. What really was inside it I do not know. I wore it in the trenches, but lost it when I was wounded and taken to a hospital.
>
> –*Francis Pegahmagabow*

In the end, more than 4000 Aboriginal peoples volunteered for service, including nurse Edith Anderson Monture and Boston Marathon winner Tom Longboat, an Onondaga, who served at the Somme.

Looking Further

1. What motivated Aboriginal peoples to enlist in the First World War? What qualities helped them to excel on the battlefield?

2. Do you think Aboriginal peoples' contribution to the war effort would have been featured in a textbook 50 years ago? Why or why not?

The Conscription Crisis

By 1917, thousands of Canadian men had been killed and many thousands more had been seriously wounded. Many men were working in essential industries at home to support the war effort, so there were not enough volunteers to replenish the Canadian forces in Europe.

When the war began, Prime Minister Borden promised there would be no **conscription**, or compulsory enlistment, for military service. But when Borden learned how many men were needed to win the battle at Vimy Ridge, he saw that Canada would have to send more troops to Europe. In 1917, Borden introduced the **Military Service Act**, which made enlistment compulsory. At first, the Act allowed exemptions for the disabled, the clergy, those with essential jobs or special skills, and **conscientious objectors** who opposed the war based on religious grounds. Conscription turned out to be a very controversial and emotional issue that divided the country and left lasting scars.

Opposition in Québec

While Canada had a high overall rate of volunteers, recruitment was uneven across the country, with the lowest levels in Québec. Many French Canadians were farmers and were needed at home. The majority of them did not feel a patriotic connection to either Britain or France because their ancestors had come to Canada generations before. They saw the Military Service Act as a means of forcing them to fight in a distant war that had no connection to them. Relations between Francophones and Anglophones were also strained because French language rights had been lost in many schools outside Québec. When Francophone men did volunteer, there was little effort to keep them together and few officers spoke French. This did little to encourage French Canadians to volunteer to fight overseas and made them feel like second-class citizens on the home front.

Québec nationalist Henri Bourassa was one of the most outspoken critics of conscription. Bourassa believed that the country had lost enough men and spent enough money on a war that had little to do with Canada. Spending more money and sending more troops would bankrupt the country and put a strain on Canada's agricultural and industrial production. He argued that a weakened economy would eventually threaten Canada's political independence. He also believed that conscription would bitterly divide the nation by aggravating tensions between Francophones and Anglophones. Bourassa was right. Violent clashes erupted in Québec between people protesting conscription and those who supported the war.

● What was the war's impact on the home front?

KEY TERMS

conscription forced enlistment in the armed forces of all fit men of certain ages

Military Service Act a 1917 Act that made conscription compulsory for all Canadian men between the ages of 20 and 45, calling up the younger men first

conscientious objector a person who opposes war for religious or moral reasons

● What impact did conscription have on Canadian unity?

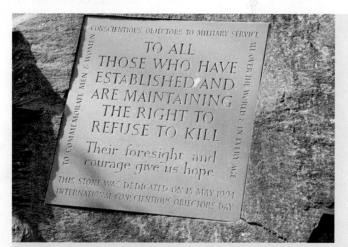

FIGURE 2–28 Stone dedicated to conscientious objectors; thousands of conscientious objectors from the United States took refuge in Canada in the early 1970s to avoid fighting in the Vietnam War (see Chapter 7). They were termed "draft dodgers" (those who wanted to avoid mandatory conscription) or "deserters" (those who abandoned military posts without permission).

Thinking Critically What is your opinion of conscientious objectors? If you were drafted, how would you respond?

labour movement groups organized to improve conditions for workers

Military Voters Act an Act that allowed men and women serving overseas to vote

Wartime Elections Act an Act that gave the vote to Canadian women related to servicemen, but cancelled the vote for conscientious objectors and immigrants from enemy countries

khaki election the name given to the 1917 federal election because of Borden's efforts to win the military vote

Union Government the coalition government formed by Conservatives and some Liberals and independents that governed Canada from 1917 to 1920

The Labour Movement

Farmers, particularly on the Prairies, also opposed conscription because they needed their sons to work the farm at home, not fight a war overseas. Industrial workers felt they were already contributing to the war effort and did not want to give up their jobs to fight in Europe.

In British Columbia, the coal miners of Vancouver Island led the **labour movement**'s opposition to conscription. During the war, miners were urged to increase their output, while wages and working conditions did not improve and the mining companies made more profit. Workers were already finding it difficult to provide for their families because of soaring prices and low wages, and conscription would mean they would earn even less. In 1917, labour leader Albert "Ginger" Goodwin led a group of smelter workers in a strike, demanding an eight-hour workday. During the strike, Goodwin received his conscription notice to report for duty, even though he had been previously excused from active service because he had "black lung" from working in the mines. Goodwin applied for exemption from service. When he was turned down, he hid in the mountains with several other union members and conscientious objectors. He was eventually tracked down and killed by the police.

The Khaki Election of 1917

Prime Minister Borden soon realized that there was strong opposition to conscription in many parts of Canada. To try to strengthen his position, he asked Wilfrid Laurier and the Liberals to join his Conservatives to form a union or coalition government. But Laurier was firmly against conscription, believing the "law of the land... declares that no man in Canada shall be subjected to compulsory military service except to repel invasions or for the defence of Canada...."

Failing to get the Liberal leader's support, Borden passed two pieces of legislation to try to ensure he would win an election. He introduced the **Military Voters Act**, which allowed men and women serving overseas to vote. He also passed the **Wartime Elections Act**, which gave the vote to all Canadian women related to servicemen, but cancelled the vote for all conscientious objectors and immigrants who had come from enemy countries in the last 15 years. The 1917 election became known as the **khaki election** because of these attempts to win the support of people serving during the war.

Before the election, Borden was able to sway some Liberals and independents who favoured conscription to join him in forming a wartime **Union Government**. In addition, the Liberals lost much support outside Québec because of Laurier's position on conscription. As a result, the Union Government won the majority of votes in the 1917 election.

FIGURE 2–29 Prime Minister Borden gave Canadian men and women serving overseas the right to vote in the federal election of 1917. For the women in this photograph, it was their first time voting in a federal election.

Conscription Divides the Country

The Union Government won the election with strong support from the armed forces and women, but the anger and resentment stirred up by the conscription debate did not subside. In Québec, people continued to demonstrate against conscription even after the election. Crowds in Montréal marched through the streets shouting "*À bas Borden*" ("down with Borden"). Canadian troops were pelted with rotten vegetables and stones when they taunted French Canadians for refusing to enlist. Tensions finally erupted at anti-conscription riots in Québec City during the Easter weekend of 1918. On April 1, four demonstrators were shot and killed by soldiers. Ten soldiers were wounded over that weekend as well.

Nevertheless, conscription took place. Of the 401 882 men across Canada who were called up, only 125 000 were enlisted and about 25 000 conscripted soldiers reached France before the end of the war.

	Union Government (Borden)	Liberals (Laurier)
Atlantic Canada	21	10
Québec	3	62
Ontario	74	8
Western Canada	55	2
Total	153	82

FIGURE 2–30 Results of the 1917 election by region; number of seats in Parliament

Using Evidence Find evidence to support the view that the 1917 election divided the country.

FAST FORWARD

CRITICAL INQUIRY Judgements

Conscription Around the World, 2009

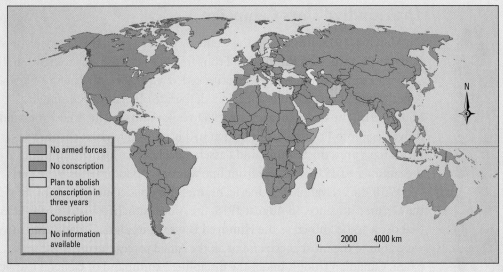

1. No armed forces
2. No conscription
3. Plan to abolish conscription in three years
4. Conscription
5. No information available

0   2000   4000 km

FIGURE 2–31 Mandatory military service in countries around the world in 2009

1. Why do you think some countries have conscription while others do not?

2. Do you think that there should be mandatory military service in Canada? Explain your thinking.

PRACTICE QUESTIONS

1. Why did Prime Minister Borden believe that conscription was necessary? Who was opposed to conscription and why?

2. Write a letter to the editor of the *Vancouver Sun* from Henri Bourassa explaining why conscription was not good for the country.

3. In pairs, create small election posters for the khaki election. Aim your advertising at two of the following groups: soldiers, women, French Canadians, or English Canadians.

4. Why do you think Borden did not allow conscientious objectors or recent Canadian immigrants from enemy countries to vote in the 1917 election? Why did he not give the vote to all women in 1917?

5. By 1917, Canadian soldiers were being used as "shock" troops, leading the attacks in battles. Imagine you are in the position of Robert Borden. Make a list of pros and cons for sending more troops.

KEY TERMS

abdicate to give up a position of authority

socialist a believer in a political and economic system in which the means of production and distribution in a country are publicly owned and controlled for the benefit of all members of a society

Central Powers the German Empire, the Austro-Hungarian Empire, the Ottoman Empire, and the Kingdom of Bulgaria

Hundred Days Campaign the final Allied offensive against the Central Powers on the Western Front, from August 8 to November 11, 1918

armistice an agreement by warring parties to end hostilities

Paris Peace Conference a meeting in Paris in 1919 to discuss the terms of a peace agreement after the First World War

Treaty of Versailles one of the treaties that ended the First World War; it imposed strict sanctions on Germany

FIGURE 2–32 Workers march with banners of the Russian Revolution, 1917

The End of the War

After three long years in a stalemate on the Western Front, two important events in the spring of 1917 changed the direction of the war. Like the other members of the Triple Entente, Russia dedicated its resources to the war. Thousands of soldiers died fighting along the Eastern Front. At home, supplies and food were limited and prices soared. People became increasingly frustrated, and a series of revolutions forced Czar Nicholas to **abdicate** in March of 1917. The Provisional Government was formed, but the Russian people were still dissatisfied with it and the war. In October 1917, **socialist** revolutionaries, called Bolsheviks, overthrew the Provisional Government, promising the war-weary public "peace and bread." They began negotiating with the **Central Powers** to end the war.

While Russia's internal politics weakened the Allies on the Eastern Front, another important event of early 1917 shifted power on the Western Front. The United States, still angered by the sinking of neutral ships such as the *Lusitania*, learned that Germany promised to support Mexico if it attacked the United States. On April 2, 1917, the United States declared war on Germany. In eight months, American soldiers reached the Western Front.

The Hundred Days Campaign

On March 3, 1918, Russia and the Central Powers signed the Treaty of Brest-Litovsk. This truce on the Eastern Front freed German troops to fight on the Western Front. Germany knew that it needed a quick victory before American troops reached France. In a desperate offensive beginning in March 1918, the German army struck at weak points in the Allies' lines and drove deep into France. Positions that had been won at great cost in lives, including Ypres, the Somme, and Passchendaele, were lost within weeks. By the summer of 1918, the new front line was only 75 kilometres from Paris.

With the arrival of the Americans, the Allies rallied and were able to stop the German advance. In August 1918, the Allies launched a series of attacks that came to be known as the **Hundred Days Campaign**. Canada's offensives were among the most successful of all the Allied forces during this campaign. Canadian troops, under the disciplined command of General Currie, broke through German lines and won important battles at Arras, Cambrai, and Valenciennes.

The Central Powers Collapse

Their final offensive in France and the battles of the Hundred Days Campaign exhausted the Germans and the rest of the Central Powers. They had no reserves and could not continue without fresh troops, food, and supplies. The Central Powers collapsed one by one. In November 1918, the German Kaiser abdicated and fled to Holland and Austria-Hungary agreed to a ceasefire. An **armistice**, or truce to end the war, on the Western Front was finally signed in a railway car in France at 5:00 a.m. on November 11, 1918. The war was to stop at 11:00 a.m. This corresponds to the date and time of our modern-day Remembrance Day ceremonies.

Canada's Emerging Autonomy

● What factors contributed to Canada's emerging autonomy?

After signing the armistice, the leaders of the Allies and the other countries that won the war met in Paris in 1919 to discuss the terms of a peace agreement. The **Paris Peace Conference** lasted for six months and resulted in a number of treaties that defined new borders and compensation for losses suffered during the war. More than 30 countries attended the conference, each with their own agenda. Germany and its allies were not allowed to participate. Russia, which had already negotiated the Treaty of Brest-Litovsk with Germany in 1918, was not invited.

> *What If...*
>
> Imagine Canada had not been given a separate seat at the Paris Peace Conference. How might that have affected Canadian autonomy?

Participating in Peace

The Paris Peace Conference marked an important moment in Canada's emerging autonomy from Britain. Because Canada had contributed so much to the war and its soldiers had fought under Canadian leaders on the battlefields, Prime Minister Borden demanded Canada have its own seat at the conference. U.S. President Woodrow Wilson opposed Canada's participation. He thought that Britain should vote on behalf of the British Empire and that a separate vote for Canada was really just another vote for Britain. But British Prime Minister Lloyd George reminded Wilson that Canada had fought longer and supplied more troops than other countries. In the end, Canada won a seat at the conference and Borden insisted that he be included among those leaders who signed the Treaty of Versailles. For the first time, Canada gained international recognition as an independent nation.

	Dead	Wounded	Missing	Total
Canada	57	150	unknown	207
Britain	659	2032	359	3050
France	1359	4200	362	5921
Germany	1600	4065	103	5768
Russia	1700	5000	unknown	6700
Austria-Hungary	922	3600	855	5377
United States	58	190	14	262

FIGURE 2–33 Approximate* number of military casualties of the First World War (in thousands)

* Although precise casualty numbers for the First World War are not available, these numbers can be considered a reliable estimate of the casualties incurred by these countries.

The Treaty of Versailles

One of the treaties that came out of the Paris Peace Conference was the **Treaty of Versailles**. This document laid out the terms of peace between Germany and the Allies. Initially, U.S. President Wilson proposed a 14-point plan for "just and lasting peace" that emphasized forgiveness and future international cooperation. But some Allied leaders wanted to shame Germany and make it pay for the damage their countries had suffered during the war.

FIGURE 2–34 Leaders from around the world gathered in Versailles, outside of Paris, to negotiate a peace agreement, which became known as the Treaty of Versailles.

KEY TERM

War Guilt Clause an article in the Treaty of Versailles that made Germany responsible for starting the First World War

In the end, the Treaty of Versailles included the following terms:

- Germany had to agree to a **War Guilt Clause**, meaning that it had to accept sole responsibility for causing the war.
- Germany's territory would be reduced. Alsace-Lorraine would be returned to France. Rhineland, on the west bank of the Rhine River, would remain part of Germany but would be demilitarized. Some of Germany's land would be given to Poland so it would have a corridor to the sea. Germany also had to give up control of its colonies.
- Germany had to pay war reparations totalling approximately $30 billion.
- The German army was to be restricted to 100 000 men. Germany also had to surrender its navy—including its U-boats—and much of its merchant fleet. It was not allowed to have an air force.
- Austria and Germany were forbidden to unite.

The Treaty of Versailles was signed on June 28, 1919. Naturally, Germany was reluctant to agree to such punishing terms, but it submitted because the Allies threatened to resume fighting. The reparation terms were particularly harsh. Like other European countries, Germany's economy was in ruins after the war and it could not make full reparation payments. Under the Treaty of Versailles, different ethnic and cultural groups were combined to create new nations, which left many people without a homeland. This meant that the feelings of nationalism that helped fuel the war were still unresolved. Many historians believe that, instead of lasting peace, the treaty brought the certainty of renewed war. Even British Prime Minister Lloyd George later found the terms too harsh. He observed that, "We shall have to fight another war all over again in 25 years at three times the cost."

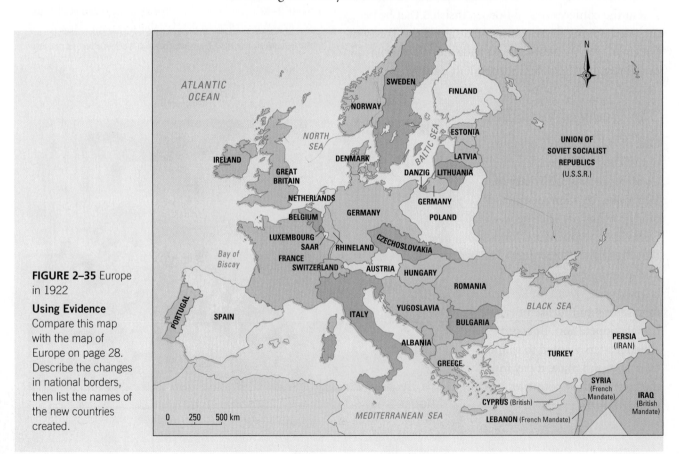

FIGURE 2–35 Europe in 1922

Using Evidence
Compare this map with the map of Europe on page 28. Describe the changes in national borders, then list the names of the new countries created.

©P

Did the war have a positive or negative effect on Canada?

The First World War brought profound changes to Canada. It changed the way we see ourselves as a nation. Canadian troops fought well as a united force and their victories at Vimy Ridge and Passchendaele distinguished them as disciplined and courageous fighters. The need for war supplies stimulated the economy, resulting in major growth in Canadian industry. Women won the right to vote for the first time. The First World War marked Canada's coming of age as it moved from a collection of disparate communities to a nation united by a sense of pride and identity. Canada gained international status by participating at the Paris Peace Conference, and Canadians began to see themselves less as colonials in the British Empire and more as citizens of an independent country. According to Canadian historian George Woodcock,

> ...the emergence of Canada... as a nation among nations within the broader world context, caused people to think less of what divided them than of what united them. They shared a single, if immense, geographical terrain, a common historical tradition in which their various pasts intermingled of necessity, and an identity in which the sense of being colonial—and therefore being linked irrevocably to a land far away— metamorphosed into a sense of being Canadian.
>
> –George Woodcock

A Country Divided

The war had a very negative effect on the solidarity of Canada. The issue of conscription and the bitterness of the debate between Anglophones and Francophones have never been completely forgotten. Those who spoke out against conscription were accused of being unpatriotic and labelled cowards. Such accusations isolated many French Canadians from the federal government that had broken its promise not to impose conscription. The War Measures Act also caused problems in many communities where immigrants from Eastern European countries suffered racial discrimination even after the war. Aboriginal leaders, who hoped their peoples' contributions to the war would ensure them a better situation, were disappointed. If anything, Canadian society was more discriminatory than ever.

The Cost of War

The losses both at home and throughout the world were staggering. Approximately 13 million people were killed during the First World War, and millions more were psychologically or physically wounded. The economic costs of the war in destruction and lost productivity were enormous. Between 1914 and 1918, Canada sent many millions of dollars worth of materials overseas, creating a debt that took decades to pay off. Some historians challenge the idea that the First World War marked Canada's coming of age. Historian Jonathan Vance asks, "How could a war that saw the deaths of 60 000 Canadians and the wounding of 170 000 others become a constructive force in the nation's history?" Vance believes that Canada's "coming of age" was a myth that developed during the 1920s and 1930s to transform the horrors of the war into a more positive experience. The maturity myth was meant to help heal the country, Vance says, because believing in it meant wartime losses had served a real purpose for Canada.

Analyzing the Issue

1. Define "coming of age." How did the First World War help bring about Canada's "coming of age"?

2. Make a study tool on the theme of Canadian unity and the effects of the First World War. Which events enhanced Canadian unity and which diminished it?

3. You and a partner have been chosen to be on a panel to discuss the impact of the First World War on Canada's development. One of you will defend George Woodcock's position, the other, that of Jonathan Vance. Prepare your arguments and present them to the class for further discussion.

Prime Minister
Robert Laird Borden

- born 1854, Grand Pré, Nova Scotia
- teacher, lawyer
- first elected to Commons in 1896
- prime minister 1911–1920

Domestic Record

- passed the War Measures Act (1914) during the First World War
- introduced income tax as a "temporary" measure in 1917
- made conscription mandatory in 1917 by passing the Military Service Act
- won the 1917 khaki election by passing the Military Voters Act and the Wartime Elections Act
- sent federal troops to break up the Winnipeg General Strike (1919)

International Record

- led the Canadian delegation at the Paris Peace Conference in 1919
- fought to allow Canada to sign the Treaty of Versailles
- won Canada a place in the League of Nations
- was lead author of Resolution IX at the Imperial War Conference (1917), arguing that Canada deserved recognition as an autonomous nation

The League of Nations

The Treaty of Versailles included the formation of the League of Nations. The League was Woodrow Wilson's brainchild—as the idea of international cooperation was one of the most important elements of his 14-point plan for lasting peace. The League was based on the principle of collective security. If one member came under attack, all members united against the aggressor, much as the forging of alliances hoped to accomplish at the beginning of the war. As part of his struggle to be included in the Paris Peace Conference, Prime Minister Borden also won the right for Canada to become a member of the newly formed League. The League's 42 founding nations first met in Paris on January 16, 1920.

The idea of a League of Nations was not welcomed by everyone. Britain and France had doubts about it and wanted the freedom to pursue their imperialist ambitions. But their leaders realized that Wilson's proposal had propaganda value, so they agreed to the basic concept, at least in principle. Smaller nations, always concerned about becoming victims of the great powers, eagerly looked forward to a new era of peace. Ironically, the United States refused to join the League. Wilson had powerful opponents who rejected the principle of collective security, which would involve the U.S. in world affairs.

The League's Limitations

In many ways, the League of Nations proved to be a more idealistic vision than a practical solution to world problems. The refusal of the United States to join the League greatly undermined its effectiveness to resolve disputes in the years after the First World War. It required the nations of the world to cooperate with one another, which was not something they had done very well in the past. The League could punish an aggressive nation by imposing economic sanctions against it, thus restricting trade with the offending nation. But the League did not have a military force of its own to impose its decisions on aggressor nations. Nor was it easy to impose sanctions.

PRACTICE QUESTIONS

1. With a partner, prepare briefing notes for the Canadian delegation to the Paris Peace Conference. Emphasize Canada's status as a nation, its contributions to the war, and the costs of the war to Canada.

2. Research the terms of the Treaty of Versailles. Make a PMI chart on the treaty's terms and their possible consequences.

©P

Canada After the War

● What challenges did Aboriginal soldiers face upon their return home?

After four long years of fighting, Canadian soldiers were finally on their way home. Most returned to Canada in early 1919 only to find that there were no steady pensions for veterans, no special medical services for those wounded in the war, and above all, few jobs. To make matters worse, many employers had grown rich during the war. The veterans had made the sacrifices, but it seemed that others were reaping the rewards.

Aboriginal soldiers returning to Canada faced even greater disappointments. During the war, they benefited from some of the social changes that took place, including gaining the right to vote under the Military Voters Act. Aboriginal peoples also believed that their contributions to the war effort would be acknowledged. But they found that nothing had changed. They still faced prejudice, and Aboriginal soldiers received even less support and opportunities than other veterans after the war.

Flu Pandemic of 1918

During the winter of 1918 to 1919, a deadly influenza virus (called Spanish Flu) swept across Europe, killing millions. Many returning soldiers carried the virus to North America. Young people were especially susceptible to the virus, which caused the deaths of an estimated 21 million people worldwide, more than the war itself. From 1918 to 1920, approximately 50 000 Canadians died during the epidemic. Many small Aboriginal communities were almost wiped out. Schools and public places were closed for months in an effort to stop the spread of the virus, and in some communities, people were required to wear breathing masks in public.

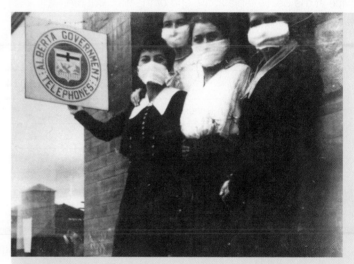

FIGURE 2–36 After the devastation of the First World War, conditions were right for the flu virus to spread rapidly.

Developing Understanding Why are these people wearing masks?

FASTFORWARD

Worldwide Pandemics

When an infectious disease spreads rapidly across a continent or the whole world, it is called a pandemic. The World Health Organization (WHO) is an agency of the United Nations that coordinates international efforts to monitor outbreaks of infectious diseases. It has three criteria to determine whether a flu outbreak is a pandemic:

- It is a new flu germ to which humans did not have immunity.
- Infected people can become very ill or even die.
- It is contagious and spreads easily.

Today, pandemics can spread more rapidly due to increased mobility of the global population. The SARS outbreak of 2003 demonstrated how air travel could help spread disease across continents. H1N1, or Swine Flu, which was first identified in Mexico in 2008, rapidly spread around the globe. H1N1 is a very similar strain to the Spanish Flu, which caused the pandemic of 1918 that killed millions.

CHAPTER FOCUS QUESTION — What effect did Canada's participation in the First World War have on Canadian society and its status as a nation?

The First World War influenced many events throughout the 20th century. It was also Canada's "baptism of fire" and helped create a Canadian identity. Before the war, Canada was part of the British Empire. Many Canadians identified with Britain as much as they did with Canada. The First World War changed that. Men from across the country trained together and then fought together far from home. Canadian troops proved themselves at Ypres, Vimy Ridge and other battles, and Canada won a place at the peace table at the end of the war. But the war also exposed a deep divide in the land: the different goals and aspirations of French and English Canadians

were dramatically at odds, as the conscription crisis of 1917 had shown. On the positive side, women, working in factories and fields and doing jobs formerly reserved for men, saw their roles in society differently as a result. In 1917, women voted for the first time in a federal election. Although the cost in lives was great, the First World War helped transform Canada into a modern industrial nation with international standing.

1. Complete the following organizer to show how Canada changed over the course of the First World War.

	August 1914	November 1918
Relations with Britain		
Status of women		
Feelings of national identity		
Role of government		
French–English relations		

Vocabulary Focus

2. Review the Key Terms listed on page 25 to help you understand the nature and progress of the First World War and its effects on Canada. Learn the key terms of the chapter by using the method of key term review presented in Question 2 of the Chapter Review in Chapter 1. Alternatively, use the key terms in a letter that Robert Borden might have written to explain why and how the war started, how it was progressing, and why it was good or bad for Canada.

Knowledge and Understanding

3. Create an annotated timeline showing steps to Canadian autonomy. This will be an ongoing assignment throughout the history section of this course. Start at 1914 and add dates to the timeline as you progress through each chapter. Provide the date and name of the event, and explain how the event contributed to Canadian autonomy.

4. Create a bubble diagram, or flow diagram, around the assassination of Crown Prince Franz Ferdinand in Sarajevo. Link events that led up to the assassination and what resulted from it. Try to show cause and result where possible.

5. You have the opportunity to accompany either Robert Borden or Henri Bourassa during the weeks when conscription was a national issue. Write a series of blogs on your experience. Be sure to mention the Wartime Elections Act, the Military Service Act, and the election of 1917.

6. In a small group, discuss the following: Without the support received from the home front, Canadian soldiers would not have been as successful on the battlefields of Europe. Write down your group's responses so you can share with the rest of the class.

7. Review the descriptions of technology and trench warfare. In a letter home from a First World War nurse or soldier, explain why you think so many soldiers are being killed or wounded. When you have finished your letter, bracket any parts that the wartime censors would have "inked out" of your letter.

8. Write a paragraph explaining the concept of total war. Provide specific examples from Canada during the First World War.

Critical Thinking

9. In a small group, discuss the wartime internment and monitoring of "enemy aliens." Record your thoughts on display paper and present the results of your discussion to the class. In what ways was the treatment of these immigrants unjust? Do you think immigrants could be treated this way today in a similar situation? Can you think of modern parallels?

10. Use the organizer you developed in the Chapter Focus section to help you answer the following:

    • Assess Canada's contributions to the First World War. Provide specific examples of Canadian contributions and evaluate how important that contribution was to the war effort.

    • Explain the social, political, and economic impacts of the war on Canada.

11. **Cause and Consequence** How did each of the technologies in the innovations feature help to change the nature of war?

Document Analysis

12. Primary sources give us glimpses into what people of a certain period were thinking about, and into the issues that were important to them. At the beginning of the war, being part of the British Empire meant that Canada almost automatically went to war when Britain was threatened by a powerful enemy. Most Canadians of British origin accepted this but feared that Canadians would lose their identity by being put into British army units to fight as "British" soldiers. Consider this excerpt from a 1916 letter to Prime Minister Robert Borden from his Minister of Militia, Sam Hughes:

I do recall my visit to... Britain in the autumn of 1914. I did expect... that I would have been permitted to exercise some "control and direction" over our gallant Canadian boys... But there had evidently been some communication... that "control and direction" of this magnificent Force should be under the British government direct. The then Mr. George Perley, Acting High Commissioner, implied such in the following words; — "You do not pretend surely to have anything to do with the Canadian soldiers in Britain."

–Excerpt from letter, November 1, 1916

As you read through the excerpt, consider the following questions.

• What surprised Hughes on his 1914 visit?

• What was the heart of the issue for Hughes and other Canadians?

• Knowing what you know about Sam Hughes, why do you think he would call the first Canadian volunteers a "magnificent force"?

• How important was it to Canadian identity that Canadians fight as part of their own army?

3

Canada in the 1920s

GUIDING QUESTIONS

Society & Identity

● How did new technologies influence society in the 1920s?

● How does the United States influence Canadian identity?

● How did women advance their status during the 1920s?

● In what ways was Aboriginal identity threatened in the 1920s?

● Why was there labour unrest after the First World War, and how did people try to improve their working conditions?

Politics & Government

● What is regionalism, and how was it expressed in the 1920s?

Economy & Human Geography

● What was the impact of American investment on the Canadian economy?

Autonomy & World Presence

● What factors contributed to Canada's emerging autonomy?

TIMELINE

1919

Winnipeg General Strike gives voice to post-war dissatisfaction

League of Nations established, with Canada as a full member

1920

British Columbia votes against Prohibition

1921

Minority government elected

Agnes Macphail becomes first woman elected to Parliament

Frederick Banting and Charles Best discover insulin

1922

Prime Minister Mackenzie King refuses to send troops to support Britain during the Chanak Crisis

1923

Mackenzie King signs the Halibut Treaty with the United States and refuses to let Britain sign

Foster Hewitt gives play-by-play for first radio broadcast of a Canadian hockey game

©P

CHAPTER FOCUS QUESTION

How did Canada adjust to political, social, and economic changes following the First World War?

The 1920s are generally thought of as a decade of prosperity, fun, and wild living. To some extent this was true. The end of the war released an emotional flood of relief. Prompted by the horror and exhaustion of war, young people in particular tried to sweep away the remnants of the old world. This was the "Jazz Age." Bold new music, shocking fashions, and crazy fads quickly spread across the United States and into Canada.

This 1927 editorial from *Canadian Homes and Gardens* may give a false picture of what life was really like for most women, but it certainly catches the optimism of the age:

> *There is a certain magic to housekeeping these days—the magic of electricity—over which I confess I never cease to marvel. Your modern housewife leaves the dishes within a machine, pops the dinner into an oven, laundry into a washer, and jumps into a roadster [car] with never a thought except for... the round of golf which she is away to enjoy for an afternoon. She returns to find the washing done, her china and crystal sparkle, a six course dinner is ready for serving.*
>
> –Canadian Homes and Gardens, *May 1927*

Life did improve for many people in the 1920s. For many more, however, the prosperity of the decade was merely an illusion. Life continued as before, filled with discrimination, poverty, and lack of political power.

KEY TERMS

communism
Winnipeg General Strike
collective bargaining
Prohibition
Persons Case
Famous Five
Canadian Constitution
regionalism
Old Age Pension Act
Chanak Crisis
Halibut Treaty
King-Byng Crisis
Imperial Conference
Balfour Report
Statute of Westminster
Depression

1924

Revised Red Ensign approved for use on Canadian government buildings abroad

1926

King-Byng Crisis illustrates Canada's need for autonomy from Britain

Imperial Conference leads to publication of the Balfour Report

1927

Federal government introduces old-age pensions; first government-run assistance program in Canada

1929

Persons Case opens way for Canadian women to be appointed to the Senate

Stock market crashes

● Why was there labour unrest
after the First World War, and
how did people try to improve
their working conditions?

FIGURE 3–1 English translation of a 1919 Russian Communist publication

Analyzing Images What do you think the chains represent? What message is being conveyed?

KEY TERMS

inflation the rise in prices for goods and services that increases the cost of living and triggers demand for higher wages

communism a social and economic theory that property, production, and distribution of goods and services should be owned by the public, and the labour force organized for the benefit of all members of society

socialist believing in a system in which the government controls the economy so that everyone benefits equally

branch plants factories, offices, or other operations set up in Canada but owned or controlled by U.S. or other foreign companies

tariffs taxes on imported goods

primary industry an industry that deals with the extraction or collection of raw materials, such as mining or forestry

secondary industry an industry that deals with manufacturing or construction

An Uneasy Adjustment

In November 1918, Canadians celebrated the end of the First World War. Soldiers returned home to find that there were few support services for them, and few jobs. Many Canadians who had jobs were also dissatisfied. During the war, workers had reluctantly agreed to lower wages as part of their patriotic duty. After the war, **inflation** made it difficult for many people because wages no longer covered the cost of rent and food. Workers demanded more money, and confrontation with employers was inevitable.

The Rise of Communism

At the end of the First World War, many people around the world were dissatisfied with governments and the disparity between rich and poor. As you read in Chapter 2, the Bolsheviks established a communist regime during the violent 1917 Russian Revolution. Under **communism**, all the means of production (such as factories and farms) and distribution (transportation and stores) are publicly owned. There is no private or individual ownership of business or land. The Bolsheviks encouraged workers around the world to join this revolution. Communism never gained widespread support in Canada, but the ideas of these revolutionaries inspired workers in Canada to try to improve working conditions.

Workers Respond

Workers' demands for higher wages, better working conditions, and the right to join unions resulted in numerous strikes across Canada. Many strikes were long, bitter disputes. Standoffs between workers and employers, for example, led to four years of labour wars in Eastern Canada. Most communities in the Maritimes depended on a single employer for jobs: the British Empire Steel Corporation. When demand for wartime industries declined after the war, the company tried to save costs by reducing wages. The workers responded by reducing their output and striking. When the strikes turned violent, the company looked for support from provincial police and federal troops. In 1926, a Royal Commission criticized the labour practices of the British Empire Steel Corporation, but the Commission's findings did little to ease suffering and poverty in the Maritimes.

There were also many strikes over wages and working conditions in western Canada. Some western union leaders were more **socialist** in their policies, believing as the Bolsheviks did, that ordinary people should be more involved in government. At the Western Labour Conference in March 1919, union leaders from Western Canada founded One Big Union (OBU), which would represent all Canadian workers. The OBU's goal was to help workers gain more control of industry and government through peaceful means. The main weapon would be the general strike, a walkout by all employed workers.

Canada's Changing Economy

Canada began the 1920s in a state of economic depression. By the middle of the decade, however, the economy started to improve. Wheat remained an important export for Canada, but there was also enormous growth in the exploitation of natural resources and manufacturing. The demand for Canadian pulp and paper grew, and new mills were built in several provinces. Mining also boomed. Record amounts of lead, zinc, silver, and copper were produced for export. These minerals were used to produce consumer goods such as radios and home appliances. The expanding forest and mining industries increased demand for hydroelectric power and several new hydro-generating stations were constructed to provide Canadian industries with cheap energy.

● What was the impact of American investment on the Canadian economy?

The United States Invests in Canada's Economy

Before the war, Canada traded mainly with Britain. After the war, Britain was deeply in debt, and the United States emerged as the world's economic leader. During the 1920s, American investment in Canada increased. American companies invested in pulp and paper mills and mines across Canada. The majority of these resources were then exported to the U.S. Almost 75 percent of the newsprint produced in Canada was exported to the U.S. Most of the metals mined in Canada were used in American-made products, such as cars and radios.

American Ownership of Canadian Businesses

Rather than lend money to Canadian businesses the way the British had, most American investors preferred to set up **branch plants**. By manufacturing cars in Canada for the Canadian market, American car makers avoided having to pay Canadian **tariffs**. By the end of the 1920s, the Canadian auto industry had been taken over by the "Big Three" American automobile companies—General Motors, Ford, and Chrysler. American companies also owned a large proportion of Canada's oil business, nearly half the machinery and chemical industries, and more than half the rubber and electrical companies.

Many Canadians were so pleased with American investment that they did not question the long-term consequences. It was true that the United States enriched Canada's economy by extracting or harvesting raw materials (**primary industries**), but these materials were transported to the U.S. for processing and manufacturing (**secondary industries**). It was the American economy that benefited most from this development.

FIGURE 3–2 Logging in British Columbia continues to be the province's major industry.

The Winnipeg General Strike: Labour Unrest or Communist Conspiracy?

In 1919, the labour movement grew across Canada. Workers formed trade unions in many different industries. These groups usually demanded higher pay, better working conditions, and an eight-hour workday. Scores of workers took action by walking off the job. It is said that more workdays were lost to strikes and lockouts in 1919 than in any other year in Canadian history.

Post-war tensions between labour and business boiled over in Winnipeg, at that time the financial centre of Western Canada and its largest city. The city's metal and building trades workers demanded higher wages, a shorter workweek, and the right to **collective bargaining**, which would allow union leaders to negotiate with employers on behalf of the union members. Labour and management negotiated for months. Finally, in May 1919, negotiations broke down and the Winnipeg Trades and Labour Council voted for a general strike. Up to 30 000 people walked off the job, crippling the city.

The strike closed factories and retail stores. Many people sympathized with the striking workers and joined their strike, including firefighters and postal workers. There were no streetcars or deliveries of bread or milk, and no telephone or telegraph services. Winnipeg was paralyzed. The Strike Committee, which coordinated the strike, bargained with employers and allowed essential food items to be delivered. Opponents of the strike felt that this showed that the strikers were running Winnipeg, instead of the legally elected civic government.

Not everyone sympathized with the strikers. Many people in Canada worried that the formation of trade unions might lead to the same violent uprisings that happened in Russia. The **Red Scare** contributed to an anti-communist sentiment that made people nervous about unions. In response to the strike, business leaders, politicians, and industrialists formed the Citizens' Committee of 1000. The committee saw the union leaders as part of a communist conspiracy to overthrow the government. They urged Winnipeg's leaders to restore order. The city responded by firing the entire police force, who sympathized with the strikers, and replacing them with a special force to contain the strike. The mayor of Winnipeg also had many civic workers and the strike leaders arrested.

FIGURE 3–3 Strikers attacked this streetcar as it moved through the crowd because it was operated by the Citizens' Committee of 1000.

Thinking Critically What does the photograph tell you about the Winnipeg General Strike? How does the information in the photograph compare with the Workers' Liberty Bond?

The federal government decided to intervene because it feared that the disruption and protest could spread to other cities. It changed the Criminal Code so that foreign-born union leaders—and anyone whom it believed was trying to start a revolution—could be arrested and deported without trial. The federal government also sent troops to Winnipeg to try to restore order.

On June 21, strikers held a parade to protest the mayor's actions. The parade turned violent when the Royal North-West Mounted Police and the city's special force, armed with clubs and pistols, charged the crowd. In the resulting clash, one striker died, 30 were injured, and scores were arrested. This event became known as **Bloody Saturday**. Defeated, the strikers returned to work after a 43-day protest.

● Why was there labour unrest after the First World War and how did people try to improve their working conditions?

What did the strike achieve? In the short run, the union movement suffered a setback. Seven of the arrested leaders were convicted of conspiracy to overthrow the government and served between two months and two years in prison. Many striking workers were not rehired; others were taken back only if they signed contracts vowing not to join a union. Distrust and divisions between the working class and businesses grew deeper.

In the long run, the verdict is less clear. A Royal Commission set up to examine the strike found that the workers' grievances were valid. Gradually, much of what they fought for was achieved. Some of those involved in the strike took up political positions in which they could work toward social reform. For example, J.S. Woodsworth (a well-known social reformer who was arrested during the strike) went on to found the Co-operative Commonwealth Federation (see Chapter 4), which later became the New Democratic Party.

KEY TERMS

Winnipeg General Strike massive strike by workers in Winnipeg in 1919

collective bargaining negotiation of a contract between unions and management regarding such things as wages and working conditions

Red Scare the fear that communism would spread to Canada

Bloody Saturday June 21, 1919, when the Royal North-West Mounted Police charged a crowd of protesters during the Winnipeg General Strike

Looking Further

1. Write a newspaper headline to explain the reaction of the Citizens' Committee of 1000 to the Winnipeg General Strike. Remember the attitudes and values of the times.

2. Write a letter to the editor of a newspaper to explain why you think the Winnipeg strikers were, or were not, justified in their actions.

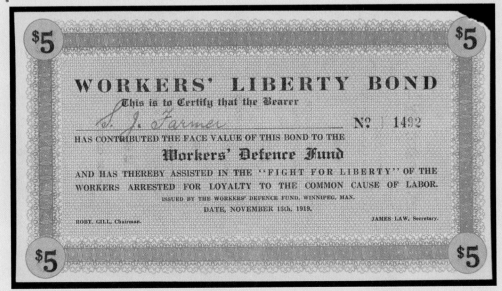

FIGURE 3–4 Canadians were able to show their support for the strikers in Winnipeg by buying bonds to assist in the "fight for liberty." The Workers' Defence Fund used the bonds to help pay for the legal costs of those arrested.

FIGURE 3–5 This young woman with a liquor flask in her garter reflected the carefree attitude toward alcohol that was at odds with those who supported Prohibition.

Thinking Critically In what ways would this young woman have outraged the older generation? What comparisons can you make with the attitudes of young and old today?

Bootlegging Across the Border

There was one product that Canada exported in large quantities to the United States: illegal alcohol. Although organizations such as the Woman's Christian Temperance Union succeeded in bringing about **prohibition** during the First World War, alcohol was still available for those with money. People could get it as a "tonic" from a doctor, or from a "bootlegger"—someone who made or sold alcohol illegally. By 1920, the provincial governments had to admit that Prohibition was not working: it was too unpopular with most Canadians. From 1921 on, most provincial governments regulated the sale of alcohol rather than ban it. In a series of **plebiscites**, Canadians eventually adopted government-controlled liquor outlets.

In the United States, Prohibition continued until 1933. Canadians took advantage of this golden opportunity to supply the U.S. with illegal liquor. Rum-running—smuggling alcohol into the U.S.—became a dangerous but profitable business. Ships from ports in the Maritimes and Québec, speedboats from Ontario, cars and trucks from the Prairie provinces, and salmon trawlers from British Columbia transported alcohol to the U.S. as fast as they could. Although it was dangerous, rum-running was extremely profitable. Many Canadians tolerated rum-runners and admired how they flouted the U.S. authorities. Canadian governments seemed content to close their eyes to the practice.

PRACTICE QUESTIONS

1. Explain the terms *communism, general strike,* and *collective bargaining*.

2. **a)** What was the effect of the 1917 Communist (Bolshevik) Revolution in Russia on Canada?

   b) Why was the One Big Union seen as a threat?

3. Review the concept of perspective and understanding bias in Building Your Skills – Analyzing Evidence: Primary and Secondary Sources (pages 14 to 15). In a two-column organizer, list reasons why the views from the following two newspaper sources would differ.

Source 1

...this is not a strike at all, in the ordinary sense of the term—it is a revolution. It is a serious attempt to overturn British institutions in this Western country and to supplant them with the Russian Bolshevik system of Soviet rule....

–Winnipeg Citizen, *May 17, 1919*

Source 2

It must be remembered that [Winnipeg] is a city of only 200 000, and that 35 000 persons are on strike. Thus it will be seen that the strikers and their relatives must represent at least 50 per cent of the population. In the numerical sense, therefore, it cannot be said that the average citizen is against the strike... there is no soviet [revolutionary council]. There is little or no terrorism.

–Toronto Star, *May 23, 1919*

©P

The Roaring Twenties

The upswing in the economy meant that many Canadians could afford more luxuries and leisure time. The decade became known as the "Roaring Twenties," reflecting the general feeling of indulgence. The misery of the First World War was over and people enjoyed the new forms of entertainment that were available. The "flapper" look dominated women's fashion. "Bobbed" hair, hemlines above the knees, and silk stockings outraged the older generations. Young people also scandalized their parents with dances such as the Charleston, the Shimmy, and the Turkey Trot.

Increased Mobility

In the 1920s, the automobile was beginning to change the landscape of the country. The invention of the assembly line in 1913 by Henry Ford meant that cars could be mass produced inexpensively and quickly. The most popular automobile was the Model T Ford. By the late 1920s, 50 percent of Canadian homes had an automobile. Its popularity prompted more and better roads to be built, making it easier for people to travel.

Aviation expanded rapidly in the years after the war. Airplanes helped to make the rugged coast of British Columbia and Canada's remote northern regions more accessible. Many veteran pilots became "bush pilots" who flew geologists and prospectors into remote areas to explore mining opportunities. Wilfrid "Wop" May was one of the best-known bush pilots who became famous for his daring exploits. In 1929, he and another young pilot tackled dangerous flights from Edmonton to help save the people of Fort Vermilion from a contagious outbreak by delivering serum. May's most famous adventure was his participation in the RCMP hunt for Albert Johnson, the "Mad Trapper" of Rat River. May's flight made Canadian history due to the duration of the chase and because it was the first time two-way radios and aircraft were used in pursuit of a criminal.

FIGURE 3–6 Jack Bowen, Frank Riddell, and Wilfrid "Wop" May, (far right)

Improved Communications

By the 1920s, the telephone had become a standard household appliance. Telephone lines were shared by many neighbours, which meant anyone could listen in on your conversation. Widespread use of the radio began to break down the isolation between far-flung communities. It soon became a necessity, bringing news as well as popular culture and entertainment into Canadian homes across the country. The radio was a revolutionary development. Smaller Canadian stations, however, soon found it difficult to compete with bigger, more powerful stations from the United States. By the end of the 1920s, nearly 300 000 Canadians were tuning in to American stations for their news and entertainment. Canada would move to introduce legislation to ensure Canadian content, which you will learn about in Chapter 6.

● How did new technologies influence society in the 1920s?

KEY TERMS

prohibition the banning of the sale and consumption of alcohol

plebiscite a direct vote by electors on an issue of public importance; the outcome of the vote may not be binding on the government

WEB LINK ●
Read more about Wop May on the Pearson Web site.

Innovations
Canadian Inventions and Inventors

During the 1920s, Canadians witnessed rapid changes in technology. Many innovations occurred in household appliances, and inventors from Québec made surviving the Canadian winter a little easier.

An alternative to the snow shovel Born in Québec, Arthur Sicard responded to Canadian winters by inventing the snow blower in 1925. The difficulty of travelling on snowy roads in early automobiles led him to find a way to efficiently remove snow. He adapted a four-wheel-drive truck to carry a snow-scooping section and a snow blower that would clear and throw snow up to 30 metres away from the truck.

A vehicle of necessity Armand Bombardier of Valcourt, Québec, was only 15 years old when he developed the snowmobile in 1922. Over the next few years, he improved on the first machine and designed vehicles that could travel on snow-covered roads. His invention helped people in rural and remote areas of Canada overcome the isolation of winter.

A medical breakthrough In 1921–1922, Frederick Banting, assisted by Charles Best, discovered insulin. This discovery continues to help millions of people suffering from diabetes. In 1923, Banting won the Nobel Prize in Physiology or Medicine.

Rogers hits the airwaves

In 1925, Edward Rogers of Toronto invented the world's first alternating current (AC) radio tube, replacing the noisy, battery-operated model. The AC radio tube allowed radios to be powered by ordinary household electric current. In 1927, he launched the world's first all-electric radio station, called Canada's First Rogers Batteryless (CFRB). In 1931, he was granted Canada's first television licence.

©P

Arts and Leisure

With the Roaring Twenties and new-found prosperity, people sought out different forms of entertainment. Canada began to find its voice as a nation with a distinct culture. As a result, several new forms of distinctly Canadian art and entertainment emerged in the 1920s.

Moving Pictures

Soon radio entertainment was rivalled by moving pictures—the movies. At first, movies were silent. An orchestra or piano player would provide sound effects to accompany the silent screen, while subtitles conveyed the messages and dialogue. The "talkies" arrived in 1927 with comedians such as Laurel and Hardy and the Marx Brothers.

Movies about Canada were made here during the early days, but Canadian-made films could not compete with productions from the big studios in the United States. Eventually Hollywood came to dominate the industry. In the absence of a home-grown industry, many Canadian actors, writers, and technicians were drawn to the glitter and glamour of Hollywood. Many were very successful. Movie star Mary Pickford, born in Toronto, became known as "America's Sweetheart."

FIGURE 3–7 The Mounties as a symbol of Canada were a favourite topic with Hollywood. In true Hollywood style, the Mounties always caught the villain and got the girl.

Using Evidence What stereotypes are used in this photo to portray the RCMP? Do these stereotypes still hold for the Mounties today?

● How does the United States influence our Canadian identity?

KEY TERM

Group of Seven group of Canadian landscape painters in the 1920s

WEB LINK •
Read more about the Group of Seven on the Pearson Web site.

A New Canadian Art

The increased American influence on Canada's culture coincided with the development of a new Canadian art movement. In 1920, the **Group of Seven** held an exhibition in Toronto that broke with traditional Canadian art. These painters were in tune with the new post-war national confidence. Rather than imitate realistic classical styles, members of the group sought to interpret Canada's rugged landscape as they saw it, using broad, bold strokes and brilliant colours. Although criticized by some critics in the early years as the school of "hot mush" painting, the Group of Seven had gained wide acceptance by the end of the 1920s.

FIGURE 3–8 Stamp commemorating the Group of Seven

Canada's Growing National Identity

The emerging sense of independence and identity was also reflected in Canadian literature. The political magazine *Canadian Forum* first appeared in 1920. Political debates and works of Canadian poets and writers appeared regularly on its pages. As well, *Maclean's* magazine published Canadian stories and articles from across the country, being careful to use only Canadian spellings. Canadian novelists R.J.C. Stead, F.P. Grove, Martha Ostenso, and Morley Callaghan wrote novels about Canadians and their experiences. And poets A.J. Smith and Frank Scott wrote passionately about Canada and Canadian issues. Yet Canadian magazines and writers found it difficult to compete with American magazines and books.

Sports as Popular Entertainment

The thirst for entertainment led to tremendous interest in spectator sports. Hockey came into Canadian homes across the country when sportswriter Foster Hewitt made the first play-by-play radio broadcast in 1923. Canadian athletes also succeeded on the international stage, including two notable athletes who excelled in several sports. Lionel Conacher was a baseball player, a star at lacrosse, a football player, and an NHL all-star. Nicknamed the "Big Train," Conacher was known for his power, stamina, and speed. One day in 1922, he hit a triple in the last inning of a baseball game to win the championship for his team and then later the same day he scored four times and assisted once in lacrosse, bringing victory to that team as well. Fanny "Bobbie" Rosenfeld is one of Canada's greatest female athletes. She was a star at basketball, softball, hockey, and tennis, as well as track and field. In the 1928 Olympic Games in Amsterdam, she won a gold and a silver medal for Canada, becoming a national hero and the best-known Canadian woman of her time.

FIGURE 3–9 Bobbie Rosenfeld (number 677). At the Amsterdam Olympics, Rosenfeld won a silver medal in the 100-m dash and a gold in the women's relay team. She was at one time the joint holder of the world record for the 100-yard [91-metre] dash, which she ran in 11 seconds.

PRACTICE QUESTIONS

1. What evidence is there that the 1920s were the beginning of the modern "consumer age"?

2. a) Which innovations made the 1920s a period of great change in communications.

   b) Beside each development, make short notes on how the change affected Canadian society.

   c) **Patterns and Change** How did these technological developments make Canada a "smaller" country?

3. How did new technology contribute to the spread of American popular culture in Canada?

4. What does the interest in professional sports tell you about leisure time and the standard of living for Canadians in this period?

5. Compare and contrast Bobbie Rosenfeld's and Lionel Conacher's achievements as athletes with those of popular sports heroes of today. How would you account for the differences?

©P

Emily Carr was a unique Canadian artist and writer. Born in 1871 in Victoria, B.C., she trained in the United States, England, and France at a time when new trends in twentieth-century art were developing. She was also inspired by the Group of Seven. She was moved by their bright, powerful images and inspired by their uniquely Canadian vision and commitment to their art. Lawren Harris, one of the Group, became her mentor and helped her develop her artistic style.

Carr seemed to thrive in the isolation of British Columbia's wilderness and drew her themes from First Nations culture and the raw power of nature. She painted scenes of West Coast forests and Aboriginal cultures. Carr made many journeys to sketch at isolated villages in coastal B.C. She described her work as follows:

> *Local people hated and ridiculed my newer work.... Whenever I could afford it I went up to the North, among the... woods and forgot all about everything in the joy of those lonely wonderful places. I decided to try and get as good a representative collection of those old villages and wonderful totem poles as I could.... Whether anybody liked them or not I did not care a bean. I painted them to please myself in my own way.... Of course nobody wanted to buy my pictures*
>
> *–Emily Carr*

At first, Carr gained little recognition for her work. She had almost abandoned hope of making a living from painting when the National Museum in Ottawa organized a showing of West Coast art built around her work. Carr eventually had shows at the Vancouver Art Gallery and in Eastern Canada.

Emily Carr's expression also took the form of writing, publishing journals and five books. She won a Governor General's Literary Award for *Klee Wyck*, a collection of stories about her life with British Columbia First Nations peoples. Another well-known book is her autobiography, *Growing Pains.*

1. To what degree did the isolation of Victoria and B.C. influence the art of Emily Carr?

2. Would you consider Emily Carr's art to be uniquely Canadian? Explain your answer.

3. How important is art like that of Emily Carr and the Group of Seven in developing a Canadian identity? Explain.

4. Why are her paintings so popular today? Explain your answer.

FIGURE 3–10 Totems and Indian Houses

Using Evidence How representative of Canada at the time was Emily Carr's painting?

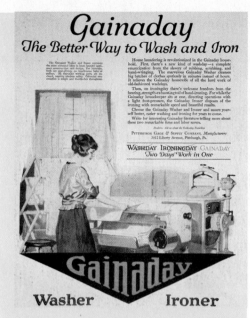

Gainaday
The Better Way to Wash and Iron

Washer   **Ironer**

FIGURE 3–11 New labour-saving devices—such as the washing machine, refrigerator, vacuum cleaner, and electric iron—became more afford-able to middle-class women. But this often meant that women were expected to maintain higher standards of cleanliness in the home.

● How did women advance their status during the 1920s?

Missing the Roar

Not everyone benefited from the social and economic changes of the Roaring Twenties. Many Canadians still battled discrimination, lack of political representation, and poverty.

The Role of Women

In the 1920s, hopes were high for reforms in health, education, and the working conditions for women and children. Women were gaining more control of their lives and were taking on roles traditionally held by men, such as factory workers, politicians, and even sports stars. Despite these gains, women still faced many social and political restrictions.

Women's Social Status

The main role of women was as wives and mothers. Married women were expected to stay at home and raise a family. Single women had limited career opportunities. They could be nurses or teachers, but these jobs paid very poorly. A few women became doctors, lawyers, professors, or engineers, but most women who worked in business or industry held jobs as secretaries, telephone operators, or sales clerks. Women usually earned much less than men for doing the same job.

Women in Politics

Although most women had won the right to vote in federal elections in 1918, only four women ran for office during the 1921 election. Only one, Agnes Macphail, won her seat. Macphail was the only woman in the House of Commons until 1935. The four Western provinces elected nine women to their legislatures, but the federal and provincial governments remained firmly male dominated. Although progress for women at the political level was slow, they made gains in social reform. Mary Ellen Smith, British Columbia's first female Member of the Legislative Assembly (MLA), and reformer Helen Gregory MacGill fought to expand rights for women and children. By the end of the 1920s, an Equal Rights measure was passed in the B.C. legislature. It reversed most of the laws restricting the political and legal rights of women.

TIMELINE	The Advance of Women's and Children's Rights in B.C.			
1917	**1918**	**1920**	**1921**	**1922**
Equal Guardianship of Infants Act gives women same rights to their children as men	The Women's Franchise Act passed, allowing most women to vote in federal elections	Mothers' Pensions Act	Mary Ellen Smith appointed first female Cabinet minister	Jury duty for women approved
Helen Gregory MacGill appointed British Columbia's first female judge	Mary Ellen Smith becomes B.C.'s first female Member of the Legislative Assembly			Maternity Protection Act prohibits the employment of women until six weeks after delivery
	Minimum Wage Bill for Women passed			Fathers made responsible for the maintenance of their children

©P

The Persons Case

The **Persons Case** of 1929 brought the issue of women participating in politics to a head. Emily Murphy, a well-known suffragist, was appointed a magistrate in Alberta. Her appointment was challenged on the basis that only "persons" could hold this office under the BNA Act, and that women were not "persons" in the eyes of the law. The Supreme Court of Alberta ruled that Murphy did, indeed, have the right to be a judge, but the matter did not stop there. Emily Murphy and four other women activists, known as the **Famous Five**, challenged Prime Minister Mackenzie King to appoint a woman senator and to clarify the definition of "persons." In April 1928, the Supreme Court of Canada decided that women were not "persons" under the **Canadian Constitution**. Murphy and her associates appealed to the Judicial Committee of the Privy Council in Britain. On October 18, 1929, the Judicial Committee declared its support for the women:

FIGURE 3–12 The Famous Five were Nellie McClung, suffrage activist and writer; Emily Murphy, writer and the first female magistrate in the British Empire; Irene Parlby, the first female cabinet minister in Alberta history; former Alberta MLA Louise McKinney; and Henrietta Muir Edwards, who helped found the National Council of Women of Canada and the Victorian Order of Nurses.

Thinking Critically How do the backgrounds of the Famous Five represent the changing roles of women in the early 20th century?

> *[The exclusion] of women from all public offices is a relic of days more barbarous than ours.... To those who would ask why the word "person" should include females, the obvious answer is, why should it not?*
> *–Privy Council Judgement, October 18, 1929*

Following the decision, Henrietta Muir Edwards wrote:

> *Personally I do not care whether or not women ever sit in the Senate, but we fought for the privilege for them to do so. We sought to establish the personal individuality of women and this decision is the announcement of our victory. It has been an uphill fight.*
> *–Quoted in* A Harvest to Reap: A History of Prairie Women, *1976*

The struggle for equality was far from won. The economic upheaval of the next decade would threaten the Famous Five's hard-earned gains.

KEY TERMS

Persons Case a court case in which the Famous Five successfully fought to have women declared "persons" under Canadian law in 1929

Famous Five five Alberta women who fought for the political status of women

Canadian Constitution the document that describes the powers and responsibilities of the government and its parts, and the rights of citizens

1923
Factory Act amendment prohibits children under 15 from working

1925
Equal inheritance approved for boys and girls

1928
Mary Ellen Smith appointed the first female speaker of the B.C. legislature

1929
Women declared "persons" under Canadian law

● In what ways was Aboriginal identity threatened in the 1920s?

Aboriginal Peoples: The Struggle to Preserve an Identity

Aboriginal peoples saw little of the good life in the 1920s. As you read in Chapter 2, Aboriginal veterans returning from the battlefields of Europe found that their contribution to the war effort did little to change their situation at home. Aboriginal peoples were still not classified as "persons" under the law. They could not vote in provincial or federal elections. In British Columbia, Aboriginal people did not win the right to vote in provincial elections until 1949. It was not until 1960 that all Aboriginal peoples across Canada could vote in federal elections.

A Policy of Assimilation

The government continued to use residential schools in an attempt to assimilate Aboriginal children. First Nations peoples were instructed by the government to replace traditional or family leaders with graduates of residential schools. This practice often divided the community between those who supported traditional leaders and those who sought to replace them.

FIGURE 3–13 In 1920, attendance at residential schools was compulsory. Instruction was in English and children were not allowed to speak their first language, at the risk of being severely punished.

Using Evidence Use the diagram on page 82 in Building Your Skills: Establishing Cause, Effect, and Results to create a cause and effect diagram dealing with residential schools. `Cause and Consequence`

In the early 1920s, First Nations peoples in British Columbia challenged the federal and provincial governments by fighting for the right to hold potlatches, an important cultural ceremony among certain peoples of the Pacific Coast. At this ceremony, births, deaths, marriages, and other significant events were recorded in the oral tradition. Potlatches involved families and even entire villages and was a way of establishing status in tribes.

The government viewed potlatch ceremonies as an obstacle to assimilation. The practice was forbidden in 1884. The ban was vigorously enforced after the First World War when the Kwagiulth people decided to hold several potlatch ceremonies in 1921. The provincial government arrested the chiefs responsible, and many were sentenced to jail terms.

The Struggle for Land

Aboriginal peoples in British Columbia continued to struggle for land claims, or **Aboriginal title**, in the 1920s. Only a few First Nations peoples on Vancouver Island had negotiated land treaties. The federal government had set aside large tracts of land as reserves, but it had been taking some of this land without the consent of the Aboriginal bands involved. These were known as **cut-off lands**. Aboriginal leaders wanted their claims to the land recognized by the federal government. As you read in Chapter 1 (page 13), Joe Capilano travelled to London, England, in 1906 to present a land claim petition to King Edward VII. Several years later, the Allied Tribes of British Columbia appealed the federal government taking cut-off lands. They claimed the government had gone against the Indian Act, which regulated relations between the federal government and the Aboriginal peoples. The federal government responded by changing the Indian Act so that Aboriginal consent was not needed to transfer reserve lands to the government. The Act was also amended to prevent anyone from raising money to pursue land claims without special permission. This made it virtually impossible for First Nations peoples to fight for Aboriginal title.

The Road to Self-Determination

In addition to residential schools and cut-off lands, Aboriginal peoples also fought against the federal government's use of **enfranchisement** to try to enforce assimilation. In 1920, the Indian Act was changed to allow the government to enfranchise people without their consent. This meant that the government could take away a person's Indian status and land. Aboriginal peoples resisted the government's policy of involuntary enfranchisement and it was given up two years later. But Aboriginal women who married men who were not status Indians were still forced to give up their Indian status (see Chapter 10).

Cayuga Chief Deskaheh (Levi General), a leader of the Six Nations Council of the Iroquois Confederacy, took the issue of Aboriginal **self-determination** to the League of Nations in 1923. He wanted international recognition of the Six Nations as an independent state and to end ties with Canada and the Indian Act. The Six Nations would have their own laws, financing, employees, and police. In a radio talk in 1925, Deskaheh explained the rationale behind the Six Nations' fight for self-determination. Unfortunately, Britain blocked Deskaheh's efforts for the League of Nations to hear the Six Nations' claims. Self-determination for Aboriginal peoples in Canada is still an issue today.

> *This story comes straight from Deskaheh, one of the chiefs of the Cayugas. I am the speaker of the Council of the Six Nations, the oldest League of Nations now existing. It was founded by Hiawatha. It is a League which is still alive and intends, as best it can, to defend the rights of the Iroquois to live under their own laws in their own little countries now left to them, to worship their Great Spirit in their own way, and to enjoy the rights which are as surely theirs as the white man's rights are his own.*
>
> *–Chief Deskaheh*

KEY TERMS

Aboriginal title claims by Aboriginal peoples to lands that their ancestors inhabited

cut-off lands lands taken from reserves without consent of the Aboriginal peoples

enfranchisement giving up one's status as an Indian

self-determination the freedom for a group to form its own government

African Canadians: Undisguised Racism

The Canadian government discouraged the entry of African Americans into Canada during the heyday of immigration before the First World War. Those who managed to move to Canada faced blatant discrimination. In Nova Scotia, the Education Act of 1918 allowed separate schools for "Blacks" and "Europeans," a policy that remained unchanged until 1954. Racial segregation was openly practised and, in some instances, supported by the courts. For example, in 1921, the Superior Court of Québec ruled in favour of racially segregated seating in Montréal theatres.

There were also instances of tolerance. In 1919, the Brotherhood of Railway Employees accepted black porters as members. In 1924, Edmonton City Council refused to support an attempt to ban African Canadians from public parks and swimming pools.

FIGURE 3–14 The Ku Klux Klan, founded in the southern United States, promoted fanatical racial and religious hatred against non-Protestants and non-whites. In the 1920s, the Klan established short-lived local branches in Canada, such as this one in Vancouver in 1925.

Thinking Critically What does the existence of the Ku Klux Klan in Canada say about the attitudes of the time?

Immigrants

After the First World War, the Canadian government adopted immigration restrictions, giving preference to applicants from Britain and the United States. Some Canadians did not want restrictions on immigration for selfish reasons and others welcomed immigrants because they would work for low wages in jobs that Canadian workers did not want. Labour groups, however, supported the restrictions because unions saw the willingness of some immigrants to work long hours for low wages as "unfair competition."

Restrictions on Asian immigrants were particularly severe. In 1923, the federal government passed a law that virtually excluded Chinese immigrants to Canada until 1947 (see Chapter 1). A Canada-Japan agreement in the 1920s restricted immigration from Japan to 150 servants and labourers per year.

In 1925, as the economy improved, the government relaxed restrictions on immigration. Thousands of immigrants landed monthly at Canada's ports looking for jobs and security. Many were forced to work in terrible conditions for pitiful wages.

PRACTICE QUESTIONS

1. **Perspectives** What does it mean to be a "person" in a legal sense? How did the idea of not being a person affect women, Aboriginals, and visible minorities?

2. What was the attitude toward women in positions of authority in Canada during the 1920s?

3. Give examples to show that the federal government was pursuing a policy of cultural assimilation of Aboriginal peoples. What responses show that Aboriginal peoples were prepared to defend their rights?

4. With a partner, list the issues and criticisms faced by women in the 1920s and women of today. Which are most similar and most different?

5. How were blacks treated in Canada during the early 20th century?

6. Which groups supported immigration and which did not? Explain.

©P

A New Challenge to Federalism: Regionalism

● What is regionalism, and how was it expressed in the 1920s?

After the war, **regionalism**, or the concern of the various regions of the country with their own local problems became more pronounced in Canadian politics.

KEY TERMS

federalism a political system that divides power between federal and provincial legislatures

regionalism a concern for the affairs of one's own region over those of one's country

free trade trade between countries without tariffs, export subsidies, or other government intervention

The Maritimes

During the 1920s, the Maritime provinces (Nova Scotia, New Brunswick, and Prince Edward Island) found that their influence in national politics was declining. The population in the Maritimes was small, which meant it had fewer seats in Parliament. Some businesses and banks moved to Ontario and Québec, while others suffered because their products (such as coal) were no longer in demand. Prominent business and political leaders formed the Maritime Rights movement and urged politicians to promote policies that would benefit the Maritimes.

The Prairies and Rural Ontario

Other regional challenges came from farmers on the Prairies and in rural Ontario. They were frustrated by the National Policy of 1878 that placed tariffs or duties on foreign goods imported into Canada. These tariffs made foreign goods more expensive, encouraging people to buy goods produced in Canada. Western farmers felt alienated by this policy because they had no such protection. They were forced to buy Canadian-made machinery, but their agricultural products were sold on the open world market. Farmers wanted **free trade**, abolishing tariffs and allowing them to buy cheaper American-made machinery. They also wanted lower freight rates and storage fees.

When neither the Liberals nor the Conservatives met their demands, farmers formed their own political parties. By the early 1920s, Ontario and the Prairie provinces had all elected members of United Farmers' parties to their legislatures. In some provinces, these parties formed the government. In 1920, the federal Progressive Party was created, led by Thomas Crerar, a former Minister of Agriculture in Robert Borden's Union Government. The Progressive Party wanted a new National Policy based on free trade and public ownership of the railways.

FIGURE 3–15 In 2001, Manitoban farmers demanded more financial aid from the government by driving their vehicles to the legislature in a national day of protest.

Thinking Critically How effective do you think this protest was in getting support for the farmers? In what ways was this protest the same as and different from protests of the 1920s?

KEY TERMS

nationalize move from private to government ownership

minority government a government in which the ruling party has less than half the total number of seats in the legislature

Old Age Pension Act an Act passed in 1927 to provide social assistance to people over 70

Québec

The economic boom in the 1920s, and Québec's proximity to the United States, led to rapid growth in many Québec industries. Cheap labour and vast forests resulted in the expansion of the province's pulp and paper industry to feed the U.S.'s demand for newsprint. Increased manufacturing in Canada and the U.S. during this decade helped to expand Québec's mining industries. To provide power to its growing industries, Québec took advantage of the hydroelectric potential of its many rivers. The abundant hydroelectric resources attracted the aluminum industry, and the Aluminum Company of Canada opened several plants.

As Québec's industries expanded, so did its desire to protect its own interests. Hostility to the Conservative Party because of conscription and language rights helped the Liberals sweep all 65 seats in Québec in the 1921 federal election. Provincial politics were dominated from 1920 to 1936 by Premier Louis-Alexandre Taschereau's Liberal Party.

Western Interests

For most of the 1920s, British Columbia was led by Liberal John Oliver, who often attacked the federal government for favouring the interests of Eastern Canada. B.C.'s growing economic strength during the 1920s meant its politicians had a stronger voice in federal politics. The products of B.C.'s forests and mines were in demand. Communities grew around the new pulp and paper mills and mines. After the war, the port of Vancouver began to benefit from the Panama Canal that had opened in 1914. More importantly, Pacific Coast ports could challenge Eastern Canada's dominance in shipping Western grain. Premier Oliver went to Ottawa three times to demand railway freight rates be reduced, a fight he won each time. As a result, annual shipments of grain from B.C. ports increased throughout the 1920s. By the end of the decade, 40 percent of Canada's grain was exported through B.C.

FIGURE 3–16 Cow East and West

Interpreting a Cartoon What point is being made by the cartoon? How effective is the cartoon in explaining its message? Why?

Canadians Choose a New Government

Regionalism and the Progressive Party greatly influenced the results of the 1921 federal election, effectively upsetting the balance of power between the Liberals and Conservatives.

In the 1921 election, both the Liberals and the Conservatives had new leaders. William Lyon Mackenzie King was chosen to lead the Liberals in 1919. He had a reputation as a reformer and was an authority on social and economic issues. Arthur Meighen, a brilliant debater and long-standing Member of Parliament, was chosen to replace Borden as the leader of the Conservatives. While King always tried to find the middle path that would offend the fewest people, Meighen believed in principles over compromise and did not care who might be offended by his stand on issues. Meighen's hard line alienated many groups before the election. His involvement in creating the Conscription Act and the new electoral laws of 1917 meant he had little support in Québec. His harsh treatment of the leaders of the Winnipeg General Strike also provoked the hostility of the labour movement.

The Progressive Party's election platform was based on their proposed National Policy, calling for free trade and to **nationalize** the railways. In the election, the Progressives managed to win an astonishing 64 seats, mostly in Western Canada. This made it the second largest party in Parliament, giving the Liberals a **minority government**. Because they were not the majority, the Liberals needed the support of some of the opposition members to pass legislation.

Despite its initial success, the Progressive Party did not last very long. However, it was influential in bringing about changes to Canada's social policy. In 1926, for example, King was challenged by the Progressives to set up an old age pension. The **Old Age Pension Act** was passed in 1927. The Act was an acknowledgement that government had a role to play in providing a network of social services for its citizens. The Progressive Party lost public support in the 1925 and 1926 elections, and it eventually dissolved. But it did manage to change Canadian politics by helping to create Canada's first minority government.

Prime Minister
Arthur Meighen

- born 1874, Anderson, Ontario
- lawyer
- first elected to Commons in 1908
- prime minister 1920–1921, June–September 1926

Domestic Record

- helped write and pass the Military Service Act and Wartime Elections Act
- created the Canadian National Railways in 1919 by nationalizing several transportation companies
- played a prominent role in ending the Winnipeg General Strike in 1919
- formed a minority government during the King-Byng Crisis in 1926

International Record

- successfully argued against an Anglo-Japanese alliance at the 1921 Imperial Conference

FIGURE 3–17 In a 1920 speech, Arthur Meighen said, "Thousands of people are mentally chasing rainbows, striving for the unattainable, anxious to better their lot and seemingly unwilling to do it in the old-fashioned way by honest intelligent effort. Dangerous doctrines taught by dangerous men, enemies of the State, poison and pollute the air...."

Using Evidence What groups was Meighen referring to? How would they have reacted to his speech?

PRACTICE QUESTIONS

1. List the concerns expressed by each region during the 1920s: Maritimes; Québec; Prairies and rural Ontario; Western Canada. To what extent were the concerns resolved?

2. Why was the Progressive Party so successful during the 1921 election? What impact did this have on the federal government from 1921 to 1926?

©P

● What factors contributed to Canada's emerging autonomy?

Prime Minister
William Lyon Mackenzie King

- born 1874, Berlin (Kitchener), Ontario
- author, editor, journalist, lawyer
- first elected to Commons in 1908
- prime minister 1921–1926, 1926–1930, 1935–1948

Domestic Record

- created the Industrial Disputes Investigation Act in 1907
- helped create Canada's first old-age pension program in 1927
- fought for Canadian autonomy during the King-Byng Crisis (1926) and in signing the Halibut Treaty with the United States (1923)
- appointed Cairine Wilson as the first woman senator in 1930
- commissioned the Rowell-Sirois Report of 1937
- introduced unemployment insurance in 1940
- held national plebiscite on conscription in 1942
- passed the Family Allowance Act in 1945
- helped create the Canadian Citizenship Act in 1947, which was the first statute to define Canada's people as Canadians
- longest-serving prime minister in Canadian history

International Record

- defended Canada's autonomy during the Chanak Crisis (1922)
- helped create the definition of Dominion status at the Imperial Conference of 1926
- insisted that Parliament decide if Canada would become involved in international conflicts

Canada's Growing Independence

After the First World War, Prime Minister Borden took a number of important steps that raised Canada's profile internationally, including participating in the Paris Peace Conference and signing the Treaty of Versailles (see Chapter 2). Mackenzie King, once he became prime minister, continued to push for greater independence from Britain.

The Chanak Crisis

In 1922, Mackenzie King refused Britain's call for support when British occupation troops were threatened by nationalist Turks during the **Chanak Crisis**. Chanak was a Turkish port controlled by Britain as a condition of one of the treaties signed at the Paris Peace Conference. If Turkey regained this port, it would have clear access to Europe through the Black Sea to the Mediterranean. Britain saw this as a threat and sent a telegram to King, asking him to send Canadian troops to support the Empire. Instead of automatically granting Britain's request, King brought the issue to Parliament. By the time the issue was debated in the House of Commons, the crisis in Turkey had passed. The Chanak Crisis marked the first time that Canada did not automatically support the British Empire in war.

The Halibut Treaty

The following year, Canada negotiated a treaty with the United States to protect halibut along the coasts of British Columbia and Alaska. Mackenzie King insisted that Canada be allowed to sign the **Halibut Treaty** without the signature of a British representative. Britain wanted to maintain its imperial right to sign international agreements on Canada's behalf. When Britain tried to pressure King into letting their representative sign the treaty, King insisted that it was a matter between Canada and the U.S. He threatened to set up an independent Canadian representative in Washington, and Britain backed down. The Halibut Treaty was the first treaty negotiated and signed independently by the Canadian government.

The King-Byng Crisis

In 1926, Mackenzie King publicly challenged Britain over the role of the **governor general** and Britain's influence on Canada's internal politics in what became known as the **King-Byng Crisis**. During the election of 1926, King was able to avoid the issue of the scandal and appeal to nationalist sentiments. He claimed that it was undemocratic for the Governor General, an official appointed by Britain, to refuse to take the advice of the prime minister, who was elected by Canadians. Since the King-Byng crisis, no Governor General has acted against the wishes of an elected prime minister.

1925 Election. Prime Minister Mackenzie King's Liberals win fewer seats than Meighen's Conservatives.

King wishes to remain prime minister. King asks Governor General Viscount Byng to let him remain in power because he has the support from the Progressives in Parliament. (The prime minister and Cabinet can stay in power if they maintain the majority of votes in the House of Commons.)

Governor General Byng grants King's request. The governor general is responsible for making sure that the Canadian prime minister and government have the confidence of Parliament.

Byng refuses. He argues that the vote of censure has to be completed first. King resigns.

King asks for another favour. King asks Governor General Byng to dissolve Parliament and call an election. King knows he will lose the Parliament vote but that he will win a general election.

A customs scandal erupts in 1926. The Conservatives call for a motion of censure—a vote of strong disapproval—against King's government. The scandal weakens the Progressive Party's support for King's Liberal government.

Meighen gets the boot. Governor General Byng appoints Meighen, the leader of the Conservatives, to be prime minister. Meighen's government is ousted from Parliament three days later after a non-confidence vote.

Another election. Byng is forced to dissolve Parliament and call an election in September 1926.

King returns to power. King and the Liberals win a majority government in the 1926 election.

FIGURE 3–18 After the King-Byng Crisis, King gained national support by claiming it was undemocratic for the governor general, a British representative, to go against the wishes of a prime minister elected by Canadians.

KEY TERMS

Chanak Crisis the Canadian government's refusal in 1922, lead by King, to support British troops in defending the Turkish port of Chanak; the first time the Canadian government did not support the British military

Halibut Treaty a 1923 treaty between Canada and the U.S. to protect halibut along the Pacific Coast; the first treaty negotiated and signed independently by the Canadian government

governor general the person who represents the British crown in Canada

King-Byng Crisis a situation that occurred in 1926 when Governor General Byng refused Prime Minister King's request to dissolve Parliament and call an election

coalition a formal alliance of political parties

confidence in politics, it means support

prorogue to postpone or suspend, as in Parliament

FAST FORWARD

King-Byng Revisited in 2008?

In 2008, Prime Minister Stephen Harper faced a crisis similar to that of Mackenzie King in 1926. The three opposition parties (Liberal, New Democrat, and Bloc Québécois) were dissatisfied with the minority Conservative government's financial policies and formed a **coalition** to oust the government. They asked Parliament to hold a non-**confidence** vote against Harper's government. Before the vote took place, Harper asked Governor General Michaëlle Jean to **prorogue**, or suspend, Parliament for a month so the government could bring in a new financial policy. Governor General Jean agreed. During the month Parliament was suspended, Harper managed to convince the Liberal leader to accept the Conservatives' new financial plan and support them in the non-confidence vote. With the Liberals' support in Parliament, Harper's Conservative government stayed in power.

FIGURE 3–19 This cartoon shows the three opposition leaders, Stéphane Dion, Gilles Duceppe, and Jack Layton, pointing at Stephen Harper.

Using Evidence How would you have advised Governor General Jean regarding Harper's request to suspend Parliament?

©P

How many times have you been asked to discuss the causes of an event on an exam? As you probably know, it is much easier to describe *what*, *where*, and *when* an event happened than to explain *why* it happened. For example, there is no disagreement that the First World War (what) began in Europe (where) in 1914 (when). Explaining the causes, effects, and results of the war is not so straightforward. Was one country more responsible than others? Why did countries declare war? Why did the generals continue to use outdated tactics? What future events resulted from the decisions made at the Paris Peace Conference?

Events in history are the result of many other events that directly or indirectly caused that incident to happen. This is called causality. Understanding causality helps us to see the relationship between one event (the cause) and another event (the effect). The effect then leads to long-term results or consequences that in turn lead to more effects (see Figure 3–20). Some of the results of the First World War still affect us today. For example, the location of boundaries in the Balkans, and in Middle East countries such as Iraq, established by the treaties of 1919, are still a source of conflict today. Historians (and geographers) use cause-effect-results organizers to explain change.

People often have different perspectives and world views. Few people will understand events in exactly the same way. They will explain the causes, effects, and results of an event in different ways, and their differing viewpoints will often lead them to different conclusions about the same event.

Although the discussion on this page deals with history, you will find examples of cause and effect throughout this textbook. Issues related to politics, human rights, population, and the environment all raise questions about cause-effect-result relationships. Is the drop in voter turnout in elections related to demographics? What impact did the atrocities in the Second World War have on the development of human rights legislation? What changes in the environment can be directly related to global warming?

Applying the Skill

1. Referring to Figure 3–20, create a cause-effect-results organizer for the Winnipeg General Strike.

2. Identify the background causes of regionalism in Canada during the 1920s.

3. Note the immediate and longer-term effects of closer relations between Canada and the United States in the 1920s.

4. Record the effects of discrimination on one or more of the following groups during the 1920s: Aboriginal peoples, African Canadians, or immigrants.

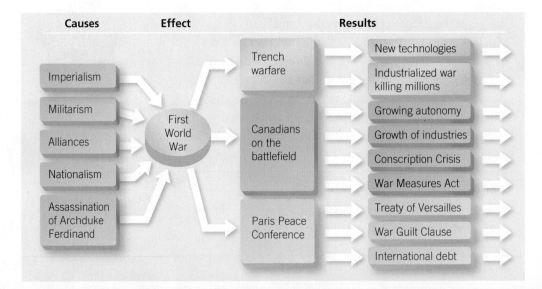

FIGURE 3–20
Cause-effect-results organizer for the First World War

Causes: Imperialism, Militarism, Alliances, Nationalism, Assassination of Archduke Ferdinand

Effect: First World War

Effects: Trench warfare, Canadians on the battlefield, Paris Peace Conference

Results: New technologies, Industrialized war killing millions, Growing autonomy, Growth of industries, Conscription Crisis, War Measures Act, Treaty of Versailles, War Guilt Clause, International debt

The Imperial Conference and the Balfour Report

It was at the **Imperial Conference** of 1926 that Canada made the greatest progress toward changing its legal dependence on Britain. At this conference, the dominions of the British Empire (Canada, Australia, New Zealand, South Africa, and the Irish Free State) requested formal recognition of their autonomy, the freedom to govern themselves. A special committee under the leadership of Lord Balfour, a respected British politician, examined the request. The committee's findings, published as the **Balfour Report**, supported the dominions' position:

> ...[We] refer to the group of self-governing communities composed of... Britain and the Dominions. Their position and mutual relation may be readily defined. They are autonomous communities within the British Empire, equal in status, in no way subordinate one to another in any aspect of their domestic or external affairs, though united by a common allegiance to the Crown....
>
> –Summary of Proceedings at the Imperial Conference, 1926

KEY TERMS

Imperial Conference a meeting of the leaders of the countries in the British Empire

Balfour Report the conclusions of the 1926 Imperial Conference that acknowledged that Canada was an autonomous community within the British Empire

Statute of Westminster the law that changed the British Empire into the British Commonwealth; all commonwealth countries to be considered equal in status with Britain and able to make their own laws

British Commonwealth an association of nations that were formerly colonies of the British Empire

amending formula the process by which changes can legally be made to the Canadian Constitution

The Statute of Westminster

The recommendations of the Balfour Report became law in 1931, when the **Statute of Westminster** was passed by the British government. This statute formally turned the British Empire into the **British Commonwealth**. The commonwealth countries were considered free and equal states that shared an allegiance to the British Crown. Canada was now a country equal in status with Britain and could make its own laws. There were, however, two remaining restrictions on Canada's independence. Canada's constitution, the British North America Act (BNA Act), remained in Britain because the Canadian federal and provincial governments could not agree on an **amending formula**, the procedure for changing the Act. As well, the Judicial Committee of the Privy Council, a court of final appeal for Canadians, resided in Britain until 1949.

PRACTICE QUESTIONS

1. What was the significance of each of the following for Canada: Chanak Crisis, Halibut Treaty, Statute of Westminster?

2. How was King able to turn an election defeat in 1925 into an election victory?

3. Explain the challenges faced by minority governments.

4. **Patterns and Change** Review the Fast Forward. Which elements of the King-Byng Crisis and Harper's prorogation of Parliament are the same? What is the key difference between the two events?

5. What restrictions to Canadian autonomy remained after the Statute of Westminster was passed?

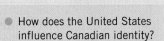

● How does the United States influence Canadian identity?

Was Canada more or less independent by the end of the 1920s?

While Canada gained greater political independence from Britain in the 1920s, it developed much closer economic and cultural ties to the United States. In 1922, U.S. investment in Canada topped that of Britain's investment for the first time. By 1930, 61 percent of foreign investment in Canada was from the U.S. During the same period, close to a million Canadians moved to the U.S. in search of better jobs and higher pay.

Despite a growing cultural industry in Canada, most Canadians listened to American radio stations, watched Hollywood films, and drove American-designed Model T Fords. Even Canadian sports teams were being bought up by U.S. interests. The National Hockey League became Americanized as smaller Canadian cities were unable to compete following the inclusion of U.S. teams.

One historian described the close ties between Canada and the United States in the 1920s:

> ...in the immediate aftermath of the war, the United States had a... depression and Canada had a... depression too. Coal strikes broke out in the United States; coal strikes broke out in Canada. The United States embarked on Prohibition; so... did almost all the provinces of Canada. The United States spawned the Prohibition gangster; Canada spawned the Prohibition rum-runner to keep him supplied.
>
> –*Ralph Allen*, Ordeal By Fire: Canada, 1910–1945

Year	Britain %	U.S. %	Other %
1910	77	19	4
1918	60	36	4
1920	53	44	3
1922	47	50	3
1925	41	56	3
1926	44	53	3
1930	36	61	3

Figure 3–21 Percent of foreign investment in Canada

Interpreting the Table In what year did U.S. investment in Canada overtake that of Britain? What are some reasons that might account for this change?

A Separate Identity

Had the U.S. simply replaced Britain in controlling Canada's development? On the one hand, Canada's economy was very dependent on that of the U.S. Canada was also awash in American popular culture. But it is hard to say how much the exposure to American entertainment diminished Canadian identity in the 1920s. For example, the people of Québec remained relatively untouched by the influence of American culture in Canada. A different language and a protective church helped to ensure that most French Canadians remained beyond American influence.

On the other hand, concern about American cultural and economic domination made Canadians determined to protect their identity. A Royal Commission in 1928 recommended that the government regulate private radio to ensure Canadian content. Although Canadians benefited from having a larger, more prosperous neighbour to the south, they never showed interest in becoming part of the U.S. J.A. Stephenson, a British correspondent in Canada during the 1920s, observed:

> The people of Canada are imbued with... a passion to maintain their own separate identity. They cherish the rooted belief that they enjoy in their existing political and social order certain manifest advantages over their neighbours.
>
> –*Quoted in* Contemporary Review, *October 1931*

Analyzing the Issue

1. In Vancouver in 1923, U.S. President Warren Harding made the following statement about the interdependence of Canada and the U.S: "We think the same thoughts, live the same lives, and cherish the same aspirations...." Do you think many Canadians would have agreed with Harding? Why or why not?

2. Write a letter to the editor of a newspaper, explaining why you agree or disagree with President Harding's statement. Give examples of Canada's dependence or independence to support your argument.

©P

The Stock Market Crash

In the latter half of the 1920s, the North American economy was booming. In 1929, the president of the Vancouver Board of Trade, Robert McKee, reflected a sense of optimism in the financial community when he told a business audience that "prosperity was so broad, so sound, [and] so hopeful" that it inspired confidence in the future.

However, as you will see in the next chapter, the prosperity soon came crashing to an end. On Tuesday, October 29, 1929, the New York Stock Exchange collapsed. On that day, prices of all stocks fell dramatically. The order to traders was to "Sell, sell, sell!" More than 16 million shares changed hands, but prices continued to fall. Everyone knew a disaster had occurred. As you will read in the next chapter, the stock market crash marked a shift from the prosperity of the 1920s to the crushing poverty of the **Depression** of the 1930s.

KEY TERM

Depression a severe economic downturn in the global economy in the 1930s

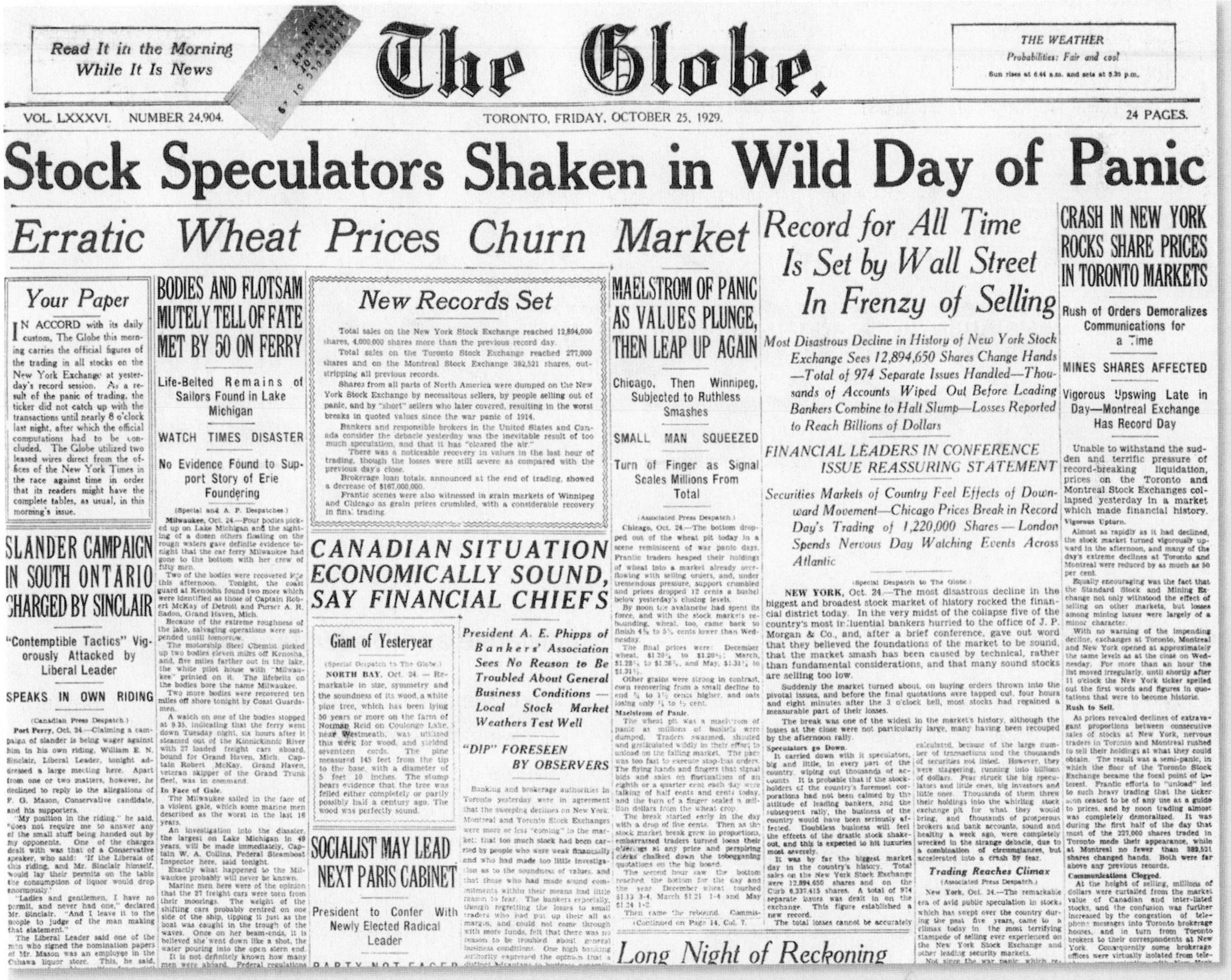

Read It in the Morning While It Is News

The Globe.

THE WEATHER
Probabilities: Fair and cool
Sun rises at 6.44 a.m. and sets at 5.30 p.m.

VOL. LXXXVI. NUMBER 24,904. TORONTO, FRIDAY, OCTOBER 25, 1929. 24 PAGES.

STOCK SPECULATORS SHAKEN IN WILD DAY OF PANIC

Erratic Wheat Prices Churn Market

Your Paper

IN ACCORD with its daily custom, The Globe this morning carries the official figures of the trading in all stocks on the New York Exchange at yesterday's record session. As a result of the panic of trading, the ticker did not catch up with the transactions until nearly 8 o'clock last night, after which the official computations had to be concluded. The Globe utilized two leased wires direct from the offices of the New York Times in the race against time in order that its readers might have the complete tables, as usual, in this morning's issue.

SLANDER CAMPAIGN IN SOUTH ONTARIO CHARGED BY SINCLAIR

"Contemptible Tactics" Vigorously Attacked by Liberal Leader

SPEAKS IN OWN RIDING

(Canadian Press Despatch.)

Port Perry, Oct. 24.—Claiming a campaign of slander is being wager against him in his own riding, William E. N. Sinclair, Liberal Leader, tonight addressed a large meeting here. Apart from one or two matters, however, he declined to reply to the allegations of F. G. Mason, Conservative candidate, and his supporters.

"My position in the riding," he said, "does not require me to answer any of the small stuff being handed out by my opponents. One of the charges dealt with was that of a Conservative speaker, who said: 'If the Liberals of this riding, and Mr. Sinclair himself, would lay their permits on the table the consumption of liquor would drop enormously.'

"Ladies and gentlemen, I have no permit, and never had one," declared Mr. Sinclair. "And I leave it to the people to judge of the man making that statement."

The Liberal Leader said one of the men who signed the nomination papers of Mr. Mason was an employee in the Oshawa liquor store. This, he said,

BODIES AND FLOTSAM MUTELY TELL OF FATE MET BY 50 ON FERRY

Life-Belted Remains of Sailors Found in Lake Michigan

WATCH TIMES DISASTER

No Evidence Found to Support Story of Erie Foundering

(Special and A. P. Despatches.)

Milwaukee, Oct. 24.—Four bodies picked up on Lake Michigan and the sighting of a dozen others floating on the rough waters gave definite evidence tonight that the car ferry Milwaukee had gone to the bottom with her crew of fifty men.

Two of the bodies were recovered late this afternoon. Tonight, the coast guard at Kenosha found two more which were identified as those of Captain Robert McKay of Detroit and Purser A. R. Sadon, Grand Haven, Mich.

Because of the extreme roughness of the lake, salvaging operations were suspended until tomorrow.

The motorship Steel Chemist picked up two bodies eleven miles off Kenosha, and, five miles farther out in the lake, the white pilot house with "Milwaukee" printed on it. The lifebelts on the bodies bore the name Milwaukee.

Two more bodies were recovered ten miles off shore tonight by Coast Guardsmen.

A watch on one of the bodies stopped at 9.35, indicating that the ferry went down Tuesday night, six hours after it steamed out of the Kinnickinnic River with 27 loaded freight cars aboard, bound for Grand Haven, Mich. Captain Robert McKay, Grand Haven, veteran skipper of the Grand Trunk fleet, was in command.

In Face of Gale.

The Milwaukee sailed in the face of a violent gale, which some marine men described as the worst in the last 16 years.

An investigation into the disaster, the largest on Lake Michigan in 49 years, will be made immediately, Captain W. A. Collins, Federal Steamboat Inspector here, said tonight.

Exactly what happened to the Milwaukee probably will never be known.

Marine men here were of the opinion that the 27 freight cars were torn from their moorings. The weight of the shifting cars probably centred on one side of the ship, tipping it just as the boat was caught in the trough of the waves. Once on her beam-ends, it is believed she went down like a shot, the water pouring into the open stern end.

It is not definitely known how many men were aboard. Federal regulations

New Records Set

Total sales on the New York Stock Exchange reached 12,894,000 shares, 4,000,000 shares more than the previous record day.

Total sales on the Toronto Stock Exchange reached 277,000 shares and on the Montreal Stock Exchange 382,521 shares, outstripping all previous records.

Shares from all parts of North America were dumped on the New York Stock Exchange by necessitous sellers, by people selling out of panic, and by "short" sellers who later covered, resulting in the worst breaks in quoted values since the war panic of 1914.

Bankers and responsible brokers in the United States and Canada consider the debacle yesterday was the inevitable result of too much speculation, and that it has "cleared the air."

There was a noticeable recovery in values in the last hour of trading, though the losses were still severe as compared with the previous day's close.

Brokerage loan totals, announced at the end of trading, showed a decrease of $167,000,000.

Frantic scenes were also witnessed in grain markets of Winnipeg and Chicago as grain prices crumbled, with a considerable recovery in final trading.

CANADIAN SITUATION ECONOMICALLY SOUND, SAY FINANCIAL CHIEFS

Giant of Yesteryear

(Special Despatch to The Globe.)

NORTH BAY, Oct. 24. — Remarkable in size, symmetry and the soundness of its wood, a white pine tree, which has been lying 50 years or more on the farm of Norman Reid on Coulonge Lake, near Westmeath, was utilized this week for wood, and yielded seventeen cords. The pine measured 145 feet from the tip to the base, with a diameter of 5 feet 10 inches. The stump bears evidence that the tree was felled either completely or partly possibly half a century ago. The wood was perfectly sound.

SOCIALIST MAY LEAD NEXT PARIS CABINET

President to Confer With Newly Elected Radical Leader

PARTY NOT EAGER

President A. E. Phipps of Bankers' Association Sees No Reason to Be Troubled About General Business Conditions — Local Stock Market Weathers Test Well

"DIP" FORESEEN BY OBSERVERS

Banking and brokerage authorities in Toronto yesterday were in agreement that the sweeping declines on New York, Montreal and Toronto Stock Exchanges were more or less "coming" to the market; that too much stock had been carried by people who were weak financially and who had made too little investigation as to the soundness of values, and that those who had made sound commitments within their means had little reason to fear. The bankers especially, though regretting the losses to small traders who had put up their all as margin, and could not come through with more funds, felt that there was no reason to be troubled about general business conditions. One high banking authority expressed the opinion that a

MAELSTROM OF PANIC AS VALUES PLUNGE, THEN LEAP UP AGAIN

Chicago, Then Winnipeg, Subjected to Ruthless Smashes

SMALL MAN SQUEEZED

Turn of Finger as Signal Scales Millions From Total

(Associated Press Despatch.)

Chicago, Oct. 24.—The bottom dropped out of the wheat pit today in a scene reminiscent of war panic days. Frantic traders heaped their holdings of wheat into a market already overflowing with selling orders, and, under tremendous pressure, support crumbled and prices dropped 12 cents a bushel below yesterday's closing levels.

By noon the avalanche had spent its force, and with the stock markets rebounding, wheat, too, came back to finish 4⅞ to 5⅞ cents lower than Wednesday.

The final prices were: December wheat, \$1.20¼ to \$1.20½; March, \$1.28¼ to \$1.28⅜, and May, \$1.31¼ to \$1.31½.

Other grains were strong in contrast, corn recovering from a small decline to end ¾ to 1½ cents higher, and oats losing only ¼ to ½ cent.

Maelstrom of Panic.

The wheat pit was a maelstrom of panic as millions of bushels were dumped. Traders swarmed, shouted and gesticulated wildly in their effort to unload on the falling market. The pace was too fast to execute stop-loss orders. The flying hands and fingers that signal bids and sales on fluctuations of an eighth or a quarter cent each day were talking of half cents and cents today, and the turn of a finger scaled a million dollars from the wheat crop.

The break started early in the day with a drop of five cents. Then as the stock market break grew in proportions, embarrassed traders turned loose their offerings at any price and perspiring clerks chalked down the tobogganing quotations on the big board.

The second hour saw the bottom reached, the bottom for the day and the year. December wheat touched \$1.13 3-4, March \$1.21 1-4 and May \$1.24 1-2.

Then came the rebound. Commis-

(Continued on Page 14, Col. 7.

Long Night of Reckoning

Record for All Time Is Set by Wall Street In Frenzy of Selling

Most Disastrous Decline in History of New York Stock Exchange Sees 12,894,650 Shares Change Hands —Total of 974 Separate Issues Handled—Thousands of Accounts Wiped Out Before Leading Bankers Combine to Halt Slump—Losses Reported to Reach Billions of Dollars

FINANCIAL LEADERS IN CONFERENCE ISSUE REASSURING STATEMENT

Securities Markets of Country Feel Effects of Downward Movement—Chicago Prices Break in Record Day's Trading of 1,220,000 Shares — London Spends Nervous Day Watching Events Across Atlantic

(Special Despatch to The Globe.)

NEW YORK, Oct. 24.—The most disastrous decline in the biggest and broadest stock market of history rocked the financial district today. In the very midst of the collapse five of the country's most influential bankers hurried to the office of J. P. Morgan & Co., and, after a brief conference, gave out word that they believed the foundations of the market to be sound, that the market smash has been caused by technical, rather than fundamental considerations, and that many sound stocks are selling too low.

Suddenly the market turned about, on buying orders thrown into the pivotal issues, and before the final quotations were tapped out, four hours and eight minutes after the 3 o'clock bell, most stocks had regained a measurable part of their losses.

The break was one of the widest in the market's history, although the losses at the close were not particularly large, many having been recouped by the afternoon rally.

Speculators go Down.

It carried down with it speculators, big and little, in every part of the country, wiping out thousands of accounts. It is probable that if the stockholders of the country's foremost corporations had not been calmed by the attitude of leading bankers, and the subsequent rally, the business of the country would have been seriously affected. Doubtless business will feel the effects of the drastic stock shake-out, and this is expected to hit luxuries most severely.

It was by far the biggest market day in the country's history. Total sales on the New York Stock Exchange were 12,894,650 shares and on the Curb 6,337,415 shares. A total of 974 separate issues was dealt in on the exchange. This figure established a new record.

The total losses cannot be accurately calculated, because of the large number of transactions and the thousands of securities not listed. However, they were staggering, running into billions of dollars. Fear struck the big speculators and little ones, big investors and little ones. Thousands of them threw their holdings into the whirling stock exchange pit for what they would bring, and thousands of prosperous brokers and bank accounts, sound and healthy a week ago, were completely wrecked in the strange debacle, due to a combination of circumstances, but accelerated into a crash by fear.

Trading Reaches Climax

(Associated Press Despatch.)

New York, Oct. 24.—The remarkable era of avid public speculation in stocks which has swept over the country during the past five years, came to a climax today in the most terrifying stampede of selling ever experienced on the New York Stock Exchange and other leading security markets.

Not since the war panic, which re-

CRASH IN NEW YORK ROCKS SHARE PRICES IN TORONTO MARKETS

Rush of Orders Demoralizes Communications for a Time

MINES SHARES AFFECTED

Vigorous Upswing Late in Day—Montreal Exchange Has Record Day

Unable to withstand the sudden and terrific pressure of record-breaking liquidation, prices on the Toronto and Montreal Stock Exchanges collapsed yesterday in a market which made financial history.

Vigorous Upturn.

Almost as rapidly as it had declined, the stock market turned vigorously upward in the afternoon, and many of the day's extreme declines at Toronto and Montreal were reduced by as much as 50 per cent.

Equally encouraging was the fact that the Standard Stock and Mining Exchange not only withstood the effect of selling on other markets, but losses among mining issues were largely of a minor character.

With no warning of the impending decline, exchanges at Toronto, Montreal and New York opened at approximately the same levels as at the close on Wednesday. For more than an hour the list moved irregularly, until shortly after 11 o'clock the New York ticker spelled out the first words and figures in quotations that were to become historic.

Rush to Sell.

As prices revealed declines of extravagant proportions between consecutive sales of stocks at New York, nervous traders in Toronto and Montreal rushed to sell their holdings at what they could obtain. The result was a semi-panic, in which the floor of the Toronto Stock Exchange became the focal point of interest. Frantic efforts to "unload" led to such heavy trading that the ticker soon ceased to be of any use as a guide to prices, and by noon trading almost was completely demoralized. It was during the first half of the day that most of the 227,000 shares traded in Toronto made their appearance, while at Montreal no fewer than 382,521 shares changed hands. Both were far above any previous records.

Communications Clogged.

At the height of selling, millions of dollars were curtailed from the market value of Canadian and inter-listed stocks, and the confusion was further increased by the congestion of telephone messages into Toronto brokerage houses, and in turn from Toronto brokers to their correspondents at New York. Consequently some brokerage offices were virtually isolated from tele-

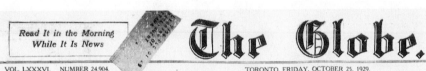

FIGURE 3–22 Front page of Toronto's *The Globe* just days before the stock market crash

Using Evidence How does this front page show the different opinions on the state of the stock market prior to the crash? What words express concern? Confidence?

©P

CHAPTER FOCUS QUESTION How did Canada adjust to political, social, and economic changes following the First World War?

Canadians in the 1920s began to develop a distinct sense of identity from Britain. Events and developments following the First World War at times encouraged and at other times hindered this trend.

1. **a)** Complete the organizer below, gathering examples of events from the chapter that helped in the growth of a Canadian identity and examples of events that worked against developing an identity.

   b) Which of the examples do you think had the greatest impact on the growing sense of Canadian identity? Which examples most hindered the growth of a Canadian identity? Give reasons for your choices.

   c) How many of the examples affect your sense of identity as a Canadian today? Explain.

   d) Pretend you are in a foreign country and are mistaken for an American by someone you meet. How would you explain the difference? What makes us Canadian?

Events helping to promote a Canadian identity

GROWING SENSE OF CANADIAN IDENTITY

Events hindering the growth of a Canadian identity

Vocabulary Focus

2. Review the Key Terms listed on page 61. Create a three-column organizer for the key terms in this chapter using the following headings: social; political; and economic.

   Place each term into the category you think is correct. If a term fits in more than one category, place it in all columns you think are appropriate. Make a note about the terms you are having difficulty understanding and review them.

Knowledge and Understanding

3. Continue the annotated timeline begun in Chapter 2 showing steps to Canadian autonomy. Review the events that are covered in the chapter. Write the name and date of each event on the timeline and explain how the event contributed to Canadian independence.

4. List the advantages and disadvantages of foreign investment and branch plants in Canada. Use your list to determine whether the positive impacts of foreign investment outweigh the negative impacts.

5. Discuss why the 1920s are described as the "Roaring Twenties." Do you agree with this name? Explain your answer. If you do not agree, decide on another name.

6. What do the immigration policy, Aboriginal policy, and treatment of African Canadians reveal about the attitudes and values of Canadian authorities in the 1920s?

7. What current political parties offer a change from traditional parties? How effective are these alternative parties at influencing government policy?

8. What was the long-term impact of the King-Byng Crisis?

Critical Thinking

9. Compare the struggle of women and Aboriginal peoples during the 1920s. In your opinion, which group was more successful in the short term and long term? Provide specific evidence to support your opinion.

10. Rank the following from most to least important for their impact on Canada's independence. Provide information to support your ranking.

   Chanak Crisis
   Halibut Treaty
   King-Byng Crisis
   Imperial Conference
   Balfour Report
   Statute of Westminster

11. Debate: Prime Minister Mackenzie King did more for Canadian autonomy than any other Canadian prime minister.

Document Analysis

12. What point is the cartoon below making about Canadian identity? WASP stands for White Anglo-Saxon Protestants and refers to Canadians of British descent. United Empire Loyalists fought for Britain during the American Revolution and, after the war, settled in what is now Canada.

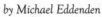

BETWEEN POLLS *by Michael Eddenden*

FIGURE 3–23

©P

4

The 1930s: A Decade of Despair

GUIDING QUESTIONS

Society & Identity

- What were the effects of the Great Depression on Canadians?

- How did minority groups fare during the Depression?

- How did the Depression affect women?

- How did Canadian social programs evolve?

- How was Québec nationalism expressed in the 1930s?

- What was the government's response to the Great Depression?

Politics & Government

- What new political parties appeared in response to the Depression?

Economy & Human Geography

- What were the causes of the Great Depression in Canada?

- How involved should the government be in the economy during a depression?

Autonomy & World Presence

- What were the effects of the Depression on the global community?

TIMELINE

1929

New York Stock Exchange crashes on Wall Street

1930

Severe drought devastates the Prairies (1930–1937)

R.B. Bennett becomes prime minister

1931

City dwellers outnumber rural population in Canada

Statute of Westminster is passed by the British government, making Canada an autonomous state within the British Commonwealth

1932

Co-operative Commonwealth Federation (CCF) established

Federal relief camps established

1933

Unemployment hits highest level

Hitler comes to power in Germany

CHAPTER FOCUS QUESTION

What were the causes, effects, and responses to the Great Depression?

James Gray was a young man at the beginning of the Depression. This account of his family's struggle to survive those difficult years is a vivid picture of the hardships endured by ordinary Canadians in the bleakest decade of the 20th century:

> *For two months, half a million farm people huddled around stoves and thought only of keeping warm. If food supplies ran low, they ate less. Only when fuel reached the vanished point would they venture to town for a load of relief coal.... Winter ended with a thaw... and presently we were into summer which was much worse.... There was no escape from the heat and wind and dust of the summer of 1936.... From Calgary to Winnipeg there was almost nothing but dust, in a bowl that extended clear down to Texas. Within the bowl was stifling heat, as if someone had left all the furnace doors open and the blowers on.*
>
> *–James Gray, The Winter Years, 1976*

For most Canadians, the 1930s was a decade of despair. In this chapter, you will learn about the causes, effects, and government's response to the Great Depression.

KEY TERMS

recession
depression
supply and demand
prosperity
recovery
overproduction
tariffs
protectionism
On-to-Ottawa Trek
Regina Riot
New Deal
laissez-faire
welfare state
Co-operative Commonwealth Federation (CCF)
capitalism
Regina Manifesto
Social Credit Party
Union nationale
Québec nationalism
equalization payments

1935	1936	1937	1938	1939
On-to-Ottawa Trek	Canadian Broadcasting Corporation established	Royal Commission on Dominion-Provincial Relations created	"Sitdowners" occupy Vancouver Post Office and Art Gallery	Second World War begins
Mackenzie King becomes prime minister	J.M. Keynes publishes *General Theory of Employment, Interest and Money*			

Causes of the Great Depression

The end of the prosperity of the 1920s came as a surprise to many Canadians. The stock market crash on October 29, 1929 marked the beginning of a **recession**, which progressed to a decade-long **depression** in Canada and around the world. Prior to examining the causes of the Great Depression and what was happening in the economy at the time, a basic knowledge of economic principles is necessary.

KEY TERMS

recession less severe than a depression, a recession is a downturn in economic activity in which the value of goods and services declines

depression a long period of severe economic and social hardship, massive unemployment, and suffering

market economy an economic system in which individuals produce goods and prices are determined by supply and demand

mixed economy an economic system in which both individuals and the government produce and sell goods

supply and demand the quantity of a product that is available and the market's desire for that product; the price of the product varies based on supply and demand

prosperity in the economic cycle, the period of economic growth and expansion

recovery in the economic cycle, the period following a recession during which the value of goods and services rises

overproduction more goods being produced than being sold; leads to a decrease in production, which leads to increased unemployment

tariffs taxes on imported goods

protectionism a system of using tariffs to raise the price of imported goods in order to protect domestic producers

FIGURE 4–1 People flood the streets of New York after the stock market crash.

Basic Economic Principles

In a **market economy**, or free enterprise system, the means of production—factories, machinery, and land—are owned by individuals, not the government. Individuals decide what types of goods and services they produce and the prices for their products. People are free to buy what they like from whomever they choose. Canada has a **mixed economy**, meaning that the government has some involvement in the economy, including the creation of government-owned industries (for example, Canadian National Railways), limitations on workers' rights to strike, and subsidies to support certain industries.

In a market or mixed economy, production and prices are determined by **supply and demand**. Supply refers to how much of a product is available. Demand refers to how much people want that product. Usually, when the supply of a product is low, demand makes the price higher; when there is a great supply, the price is lower. For example, at the beginning of the 1920s, a shortage of wheat as a result of the First World War led to a higher price for Canadian wheat. As other countries began producing wheat after the war, increased supply lowered wheat prices.

Market economies regularly go through cycles of growth and decline (see Figure 4–2). Expansion in many economic activities results in a period of **prosperity**. This eventually is followed by a slowdown in the economy, called a recession. If the slowdown is longer and more severe, it is called a depression. **Recovery** is when the economy begins to grow again.

FIGURE 4–2 In the economic cycle, market economies have ups and downs.

Thinking Critically How would governments try to alter this cycle? Provide specific examples.

©P

Overproduction

During the 1920s, many industries in Canada expanded as demand for their goods was high. But when the economy slowed down, many companies faced **overproduction** as they produced more goods than they sold. At first, manufacturers lowered prices and stockpiled goods. Eventually, they cut back and produced fewer goods. This decrease in production led to layoffs in factories, which meant people could not afford to buy consumer goods, so sales slowed down even more.

Economic Dependence on Exports

The Great Depression exposed a major weakness in the Canadian economy: its heavy dependence on the export of primary resources. Two exports in particular—wheat from the Prairie provinces, and newsprint from British Columbia, Ontario, and Québec—made Canada extremely vulnerable to changes in world markets. Eighty percent of Canada's production on farms, and in forests and mines was exported.

In the early 1920s, wheat farmers in Canada and the United States produced record quantities of crops and sold them at record prices. But as more countries, including Argentina and Australia, produced wheat crops, there was more competition on the international market. Wheat was being overproduced and the price of wheat began to fall. As international sales decreased, farmers' incomes dropped. Soon, many were unable to meet their mortgage and loan payments.

Tariffs and U.S. Protectionism

Canada's economy was hit particularly hard because of its close ties to the U.S. economy. The United States had become Canada's biggest trading partner and largest investor. Consequently, when the U.S. economy "crashed," Canada's economy was bound to feel the effects.

Since the United States did not need raw materials from other countries, it imposed high **tariffs** on foreign goods. These tariffs were meant to protect the U.S. domestic market by making foreign items, such as Canadian wheat, more expensive. However, this **protectionism** led other countries to impose their own tariffs in response to the United States' actions. Tariffs caused a slowdown in world trade as opportunities for export shrank. Canadian exports decreased substantially as the U.S. and other countries stopped buying Canadian products.

FIGURE 4–3 Increased U.S. protectionism as a response to the recession of 2008–2009

Interpreting a Cartoon How does the cartoonist portray Canada's response to U.S. protectionism?

reparations compensation from a defeated enemy for damages caused by war

speculation buying shares "on margin" with the expectation that the value of the shares will increase enough to pay back the loan and make a profit

Black Tuesday October 29, 1929, when the New York Stock Exchange collapsed

Debt from the First World War

The United States lent several countries money during and after the First World War. Many of these countries relied on trade with the U.S. to raise money to pay these debts. But as protectionism grew, international trade decreased and several countries were unable to pay back the loans. Britain and France in particular relied on German **reparations** to pay their war debts. After the First World War, Germany's economy was in ruins. The enormous reparations it was obligated to pay Britain and France under the Treaty of Versailles further stunted its ability to recover (see Chapter 5). Because Germany could not make its reparation payments, Britain and France in turn could not pay their war debts.

Speculation and the Stock Market Crash

Business was booming in the early 1920s. Companies wanted to expand, and in order to raise money, they would issue shares (or stocks). Investors bought these shares believing that the company would do well and the value of the stocks would rise. Between 1922 and 1926, Canadian companies issued $700 million worth of new shares.

During the 1920s, many investors were buying "on margin." This meant buying shares with only a 10 percent down payment, assuming that when the prices of the stocks increased the remaining 90 percent would be paid. This process is called **speculation**. Loans for stocks were easy to obtain, and high demand had driven the price of stocks up beyond their real value.

When some investors started selling their stocks in order to cash in on high profits, others rushed to follow their lead. As a result, stock prices fell. People panicked and began to sell off huge volumes of stocks, making prices drop even further. On **Black Tuesday**, October 29, 1929, the New York Stock Exchange collapsed, followed by the Toronto and Montréal Stock Exchanges.

Falling Off the Economic Edge

The effects of the stock market crash were devastating. Investors who had borrowed heavily to buy shares went bankrupt in a single day. While few Canadians actually invested in stocks, the crash affected millions of people. Many companies cut back on production or closed their doors when the prices of their goods dropped. More and more people lost their jobs and could not find work. Without jobs, they could no longer afford to buy such items as cars, radios, or telephones. Without customers, the people who worked in the factories producing these goods also lost their jobs. Within a year, millions of Canadians were out of work.

	1928–1929 Average $ per Capita	1933 $ per Capita	Percentage Decrease
Canada	471	247	48
Saskatchewan	478	135	72
Alberta	548	212	61
Manitoba	466	240	49
British Columbia	594	314	47
Prince Edward Island	278	154	45
Ontario	549	310	44
Québec	391	220	44
New Brunswick	292	180	39
Nova Scotia	322	207	36

FIGURE 4–4 Average per person income, 1928/1929 and 1933. Note that these numbers represent the average Canadian; many Canadians fell well below this average and many had no money at all.

Using Evidence Which province do you think was hardest hit by the Depression? Explain.

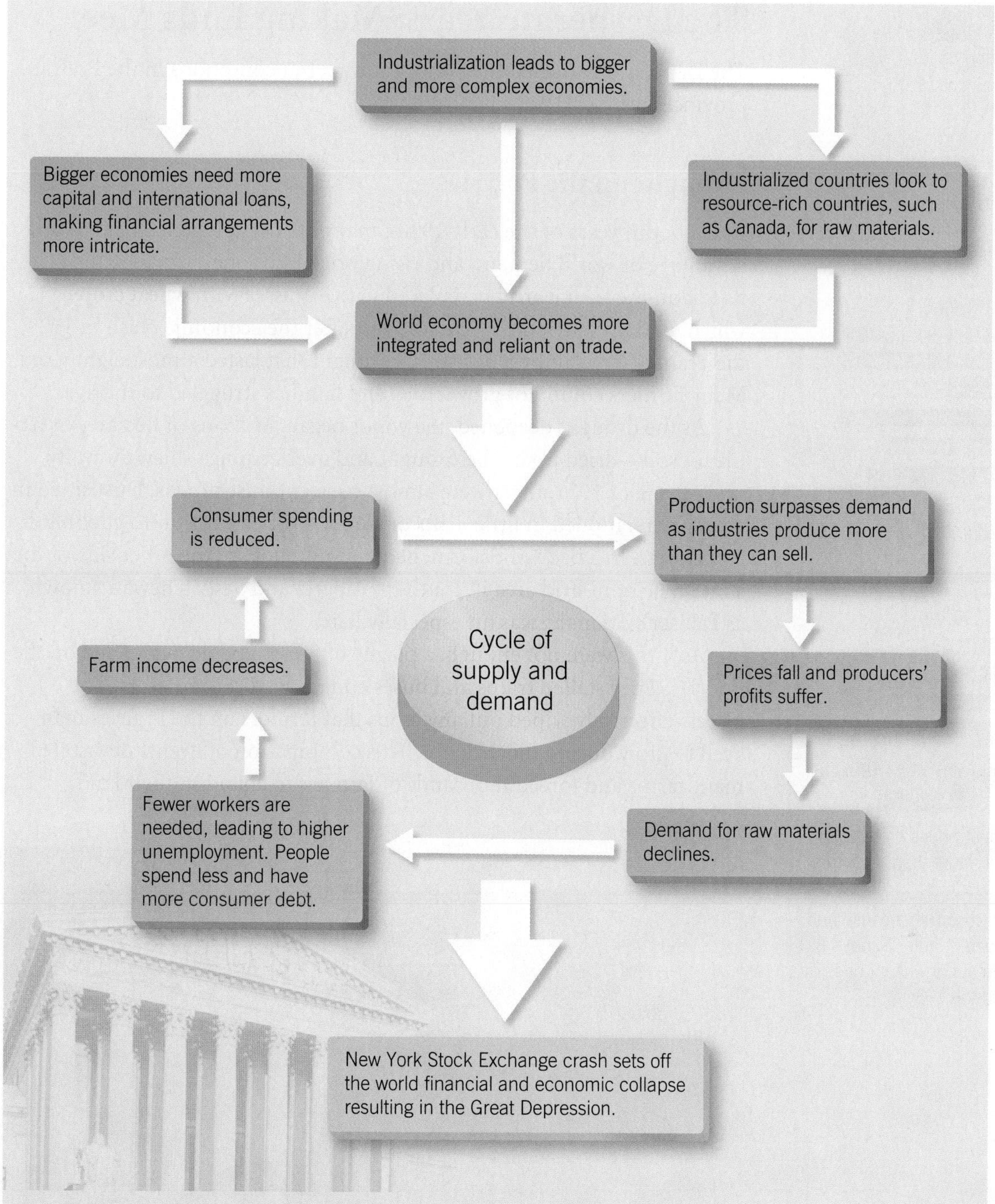
Industrialization leads to bigger and more complex economies.
Bigger economies need more capital and international loans, making financial arrangements more intricate.
Industrialized countries look to resource-rich countries, such as Canada, for raw materials.
World economy becomes more integrated and reliant on trade.
Consumer spending is reduced.
Production surpasses demand as industries produce more than they can sell.
Cycle of supply and demand
Farm income decreases.
Prices fall and producers' profits suffer.
Fewer workers are needed, leading to higher unemployment. People spend less and have more consumer debt.
Demand for raw materials declines.
New York Stock Exchange crash sets off the world financial and economic collapse resulting in the Great Depression.

FIGURE 4–5 Causes of the Great Depression

PRACTICE QUESTIONS

1. **a)** What factors contributed to the Depression?

   b) Explain how a reduction in consumer spending can result in a slowdown in the economy.

2. Why was the Depression so severe in Canada? What part of the country was hardest hit? Why?

3. Explain why Canada's close economic ties to the U.S. contributed to the Depression.

4. Why were so many people able to invest in the stock market?

5. **Patterns and Change** How was the financial collapse of 2008–2009 similar to and different from the 1929 crash?

©P

The Desperate Years: Making Ends Meet

The Depression affected the entire country, but conditions in the Prairie provinces were particularly severe.

Drought on the Prairies

In the boom years of the early 1920s, many farmers planted wheat to take advantage of world demand and rising prices. But one-crop farming takes its toll on the land. Farmers replaced native grasses with wheat crops, which used up nutrients in the soil. Just after the economic crash in 1929, the Prairies were hit by a disastrous drought that lasted almost eight years. Many farmers could not grow crops and families struggled to survive.

As the drought deepened, the winds began. Millions of hectares of fertile topsoil—dried up by the drought and overfarming—blew away. By mid-spring of 1931, there were almost constant dust storms. Dust sifted in everywhere. It piled in little drifts on windowsills, and got into cupboards and closets. In a bad windstorm, people could not see the other side of the street. The semi-arid area in southern Alberta and Saskatchewan, known as Palliser's Triangle, was hit especially hard.

As if this were not enough, a plague of grasshoppers descended on the Prairies. They stalled trains and buses and clogged car radiators. The insects effectively wiped out any crops that farmers on the Prairies managed to grow during the drought. This combination of events devastated many farms and forced thousands of families to abandon their land.

KEY TERM

pogey relief payments by a government, sometimes in the form of vouchers for food and other essentials

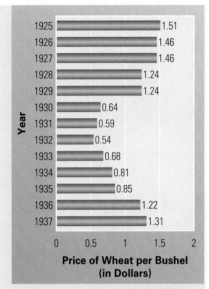

FIGURE 4–6 Wheat prices dropped to the lowest level in more than a century in 1932.

Using Evidence Construct a cause and effect diagram (see Chapter 3, page 82) to explain the impact of wheat prices on Prairie farmers in the 1930s.

FIGURE 4–7 Windstorms such as this one turned the Prairies, already suffering from years of drought, into a dust bowl during the Depression years. Overcultivation of fields and poor land-use practices prior to the 1930s contributed to the erosion of the soil.

Using Evidence Describe the impact of the storm on the community in the photograph.

FIGURE 4–8 Unemployed men of all ages line up at a soup kitchen in Vancouver, for food provided by a private charity.

Thinking Critically How would you describe this scene? How do you think these men felt? Explain.

Unemployment

As the Depression deepened, more and more factories and businesses closed their doors and people lost their jobs. In a population of more than 11 million, only about 300 000 Canadians earned enough money to pay income tax in 1939. At that time, married people earning more than $2000 and single people earning more than $1000 paid tax. People were evicted from their homes because they could not afford to pay rent. The loss of a job also meant the loss of respect, as this man explained:

> I never so much as stole a dime, a loaf of bread, a gallon of gas, but in those days I was treated like a criminal. By the twist in some men's minds, men in high places, it became a criminal act just to be poor, and this percolated down through the whole structure until it reached the town cop or railway bull and if you were without a job, on the roads, wandering, you automatically became a criminal.
>
> –*Quoted in* Ten Lost Years, *1997*

Collecting Pogey

Thousands existed on "**pogey**," government relief payments given to those who did not have an alternative source of income, similar to welfare today. The government did not make getting relief easy. The payments were purposely kept low—$60 per month in Calgary to $19 per month in Halifax for a family of five—to encourage people to look for work rather than depend on the payments. People had to wait in line for hours and then publicly declare their financial failure. They also had to swear that they did not own anything of value and prove that they were being evicted from their home. If the applicants met these requirements, they received vouchers that could be exchanged for food and other essentials. The vouchers were never enough to cover expenses, and getting them was a humiliating experience.

Private charities helped by providing used clothing and meals, while soup kitchens were set up to help the hungry and homeless. For some people, the hardships were too much to bear. One Winnipeg man came home to discover that his wife, who had been living on relief, had drowned their son, strangled their daughter, and poisoned herself. The note she left said, "I owe the drugstore forty-four cents. Farewell."

FASTFORWARD

Permanent Food Banks

In 2008, Food Banks Canada helped more than 700 000 Canadians in an average month. They reported a 20 percent increase in this number during the recession of 2008–2009. The two largest groups accessing food banks are those living on social assistance and those with low-paying jobs.

While some food banks are government funded, most rely on the generosity of Canadians. People donate money, food, clothing, and their time. Their contributions are an example of active citizenship and help to support the less fortunate.

1. What do permanent food banks reveal about the Canadian economy and the lives of many Canadians?

FIGURE 4–9 As the Depression grew worse, more and more people found themselves destitute and out of work.

Developing Understanding Why was unemployment a humiliating experience for many Canadians? What does the sign in the photograph mean? Can you think of a similar situation today?

Riding the Rails

By the winter of 1933, more than one quarter of Canada's workforce was unemployed. The country was filled with young, jobless, homeless men drifting from one place to another, looking for work. They travelled across the country by "hopping" freight trains. Some men even rode on the roof or clung to the rods underneath the train.

After "riding the rails," the men would stay a day or two in the many shantytowns that had sprung up in and around cities. These sprawling shantytowns were often referred to as "jungles." Sydney Hutcheson, a young unemployed man in the summer of 1932, recalls what life was like during these years:

> ...I made Kamloops my headquarters as there were hundreds of men in the jungles on the north side of the Thompson River right across from town.... I made three round trips across Canada that summer by boxcar.... I carried my packsack with a change of clothes, razor, a five pound pail and a collapsible frying pan that a man made for me in the jungles in Kamloops in exchange for a pair of socks. I also had a little food with me at all times such as bacon ends, flour, salt, baking powder and anything else I could get my hands on.
>
> –*Sydney Hutcheson*, Depression Stories, *1976*

● How did minority groups fare during the Depression?

The Disadvantaged

Canadians who had difficulty earning a decent wage when times were good suffered even more during the Depression. Even with emergency assistance payments, there was discrimination. City families received more than country families because it was assumed that country families had livestock and a big garden. Some groups of people, including immigrants, Aboriginal peoples, and women, were particularly disadvantaged.

New Canadians

The Canadian government had previously supported immigration because it served the economic interests of Canada. During the Depression, however, immigrants were viewed with hostility when they competed for scarce jobs. Many immigrants who were already employed lost their jobs because they had been the last to be hired. By 1935, more than 28 000 immigrants were **deported** from Canada.

©P

The Chinese population in Vancouver suffered greatly. Already at a disadvantage due to immigration policies and social prejudice, many Chinese people did not qualify for relief payments. By 1932, many were starving.

> By [1932] destitute Chinese men, most of them elderly, were begging in the street.... The first... Chinese deaths from starvation finally forced the provincial government to show some concern. It funded the Anglican Church Mission's soup kitchen..., but it expected a Chinese to be fed at half of what it cost to feed a white man on relief. Some destitute Chinese said they'd rather starve than accept relief.
>
> **–Denise Chong,** The Concubine's Children, 1994

Jewish people in particular were targeted and they faced blatant **anti-Semitism**. Many professions were closed to them; employers often posted signs forbidding them to apply. Across Canada, many clubs, organizations, and resorts barred Jewish people. These barriers made it particularly difficult for Jewish people to make ends meet during the Depression.

KEY TERMS

transient an unemployed person who moves from place to place in search of work

deport to send back to one's country of origin

anti-Semitism discrimination or hostility toward Jewish people

FIGURE 4–10 The Lions Gate Bridge was built to provide access to the expensive development on the north shore of Burrard Inlet. A similar plan had been rejected in 1927 because a road would have had to be built through Stanley Park to access the bridge. The proposal to build the road and bridge was approved in 1933.

Thinking Critically Why do you think the proposal was approved in 1933 when it had previously been rejected? What considerations would developers have to make today to get a project similar to this one approved? Why might governments overlook these considerations?

Aboriginal Peoples

Aboriginal families on relief were given only $5 a month, compared to the $19–$60 received by non-Aboriginals. They were expected to live off the land, even though conditions on the reserves were so poor that they had been unable to do so for decades. The government continued to take cut-off lands from the reserves, further limiting Aboriginal peoples' resources. In one particular case, the government transferred land from the Squamish Capilano Indian Reserve to the company that was building the Lions Gate Bridge without consulting or compensating the First Nation. While visiting Canada in 1939, King George VI and his wife Queen Elizabeth drove over the completed bridge to honour it. A request by the Squamish First Nation that the Royals stop, receive gifts, and meet Mary Agnes Capilano (see Chapter 1) was ignored. Later they were assured that "Their Majesties took particular pains to acknowledge the homage of their Indian subjects, and that in passing them the rate of speed was considerably lowered."

Faces of Despair: Women in the 1930s

In the 1930s, the primary responsibility of women was seen to be the maintenance of the home and family. Most women were expected to get married and leave the labour force as soon as they could. There were a limited number of jobs considered acceptable for middle-class women. Most were clerical, "pink collar" sector jobs for which women earned 60 percent of men's wages. The garment industry, involving long hours of piece work, was one of the few occupations open to minority and working-class white women. One woman who had a job at that time remembered:

> My family were very unhappy with my having a job on the [Victoria] Times.... They didn't feel that either my sister or I should be working in the first place. My father got poison pen letters from people saying "What are your daughters doing taking the bread out of the mouths of starving people."
>
> –Illustrated History of British Columbia, *2001*

During the Depression, many women who did have jobs were forced into unwanted retirement and married women were fired from their jobs. Most were told that these measures were taken to provide jobs for men supporting families. But Agnes Macphail, the first female Member of Parliament in the House of Commons, claimed that in taking employment, women were doing what they could to ensure the survival of themselves and their families.

Most families suffering economic hardship relied heavily on women's capacity to find ways to cut household costs. They gave up commercially prepared foods and kept bees to cut down on sugar costs, expanded gardens, and picked wild berries. They found ways to reuse everything, such as transforming old coats into quilts. Flour bags were particularly useful, as this mother recalled: "You'd take an empty sack of flour... give it a good wash and bleach out the lettering... cut two holes for the arms and one at the top for the neck.... You had a dress for a nine-year-old girl."

For women on the Prairies, the dust bowl added another problem on washday:

> I could never get my laundry white. I'd try and try. The children's things, the curtains and the sheets, why they all looked as grey as that sky out there. I'd work my fingers to the bone scrubbing.... We were lucky to have a deep well and good water but even down that well... the water came up with dirt and dust in it.... The wind blew that dust all the time. It never stopped.
>
> –Ten Lost Years, *1997*

FIGURE 4–11 The poster on the left encouraged women to come to Canada in the 1920s. The photograph on the right shows the great deal of physical labour required on washday, particularly the constant hauling of water from a well (most homes did not have running water) and the tiring scrubbing on a washboard.

Thinking Critically Compare and contrast the depictions of a farm woman's life in these images. Think of a present-day example where the media's portrayal of a situation differs from reality.

©P

Suffragist Nellie McClung lamented the effect of constant work on women:

> *On the farms before electricity and labour saving devices lightened their loads, women's work obsessed them. Their hours were endless.... Many broke under the strain and died, and their places were filled without undue delay. Some man's sister or sister-in-law came from Ontario to take the dead woman's place.*
>
> **–The Stream Runs Fast, *2007***

Pregnancy and the young offspring it brought added to the household's difficulties. The sale and advertisement of birth control information and abortion were offences under the Criminal Code, yet couples managed to have fewer children as the Depression deepened. The general fertility rate (the annual number of births per 1000 women) went from 128 in 1921 to 99 in 1931 and to 89 by the end of the decade.

Many single and married women in desperation wrote to Prime Minister Bennett. Barbara Harris, a young woman from Moose Jaw, explained her difficult situation:

> *Dear Sir-*
> *I am 19 yrs. of age Mr. Bennett, but it really is impossible for me to get work. I haven't got any shoes to wear & no coat & so I haven't any home or any relatives here, Im all alone as it were. Now I tho't perhaps you could help me a little.... Here... it just seems impossible to get relief unless you go & work for your board & room & I can't work like that as I need clothes so badly. It's even a fact that not only haven't a coat to wear but I haven't any stockings either. Mr. Bennett if you could just help me out a little bit I would be very pleased & would appreciate it very much & would you kindly give me an answer.*
> **–The Wretched of Canada, *1971***

Note: The last two quotations on this page contain spelling and punctuation errors. They have been reproduced as they were originally written.

A young mother from Manitoba described her dilemma:

> *Dear Sir-*
> *I am a young mother of two small children a girl (6) and a boy (4) now in worst of hard times an accident happend, my girl was playing & fell and cut her face very badley, so out off this got a blood poison in her face, she's in hospital now. Just at present I have no money to pay the doctor or fare for the train to go and see her.... Now Mr. Bennett what I want to say is if you can lend me some money for a period of 3 or 4 months when my cows will come fresh I'll turn you the money, everybody here is broke and no where to get.... So please lend me some money... and a couple of dollars wouldn't mean as much as one cent means to me. I'd make you a mortgage for horses and cattle.*
> **–The Wretched of Canada, *1971***

Bennett responded to many of these women by sending them $2–$4 of his own money. This was a lot of money at the time, considering that government relief was $10–$15 a month. Despite this aid, women and their families suffered greatly during the Depression.

Looking Further

1. What were the social attitudes toward women during the 1930s? What were the objections to women working during the Depression?

2. Evaluate the impact of the Depression on married women compared to married men, and on single women compared to single men.

3. Make a list of three to five lessons that we should learn from the difficulties faced by women and families during the Depression. Share your list.

4. What roles do you think women would have preferred during the 1930s?

KEY TERMS

deflation the opposite of inflation, deflation occurs when the price of goods and services falls

majority government a government in which the ruling party has more seats in the House of Commons than all other parties combined

The Plight of Women

For women, there were few jobs other than domestic work, which paid just a few dollars a week. Some critics believed working women actually contributed to the Depression. Médéric Martin, a former mayor of Montréal, summed up the attitude of many toward working women:

> *Wouldn't national life be happier, saner, safer if a great many of these men [the unemployed] could be given work now being done by women, even if it meant that these women would have to sacrifice their financial independence? Go home to be supported by father, husband, or brother as they were in the old pre-feministic days?*
>
> –Chatelaine, *September 1933*

Most unemployed single women did not qualify for government relief and had to rely on charities to get by. In Vancouver, women's groups such as the Women's Labour League campaigned for more support. As a result, the city provided milk for babies, clothing allowances for women and children, and medical care for pregnant women during the Depression.

The Fortunate Minority

While the majority of people suffered during the Depression, wealthy Canadians with secure jobs noticed little change in their lifestyle. Gray Miller, for example, earned $25 000 a year as chief executive officer of Imperial Tobacco. In contrast, clerks in the company's United Cigar Store earned only $1300 a year working 54 hours a week. As **deflation** led to falling prices, money was worth more and the living conditions for those with secure jobs improved. A young reporter in Victoria who was paid only $15 a week found that he could live well. Saturday night dances at the Empress Hotel were easily affordable. "For two dollars a couple, a three-course dinner was served with full valet service at tables arranged in cabaret style around a magnificent ballroom." For the majority of Canadians, however, this lifestyle was an impossible dream.

PRACTICE QUESTIONS

1. What part of Canada was hardest hit by the Depression? Explain.

2. **a)** What seemed to be the government's attitude toward people who had lost their jobs? Why do you think this was the case? Do you think this attitude exists today toward the unemployed?

   b) Compare the possible attitudes of people who received social assistance in the 1930s and those who receive assistance today.

3. What did people have to do to qualify for "pogey"? Why do you think people were given vouchers instead of cash?

4. Reread James Gray's description of the 1930s on page 89. Write a first-person account of the summer of 1936 on the Prairies.

5. Write a paragraph describing conditions in Vancouver's Chinese district during the Depression. Explain why conditions were so harsh. Include information you have learned from previous chapters.

6. Provide specific evidence explaining how minority groups fared during the Depression.

©P

Responding to the Depression

● What was the government's response to the Great Depression?

● How did Canadian social programs evolve?

Prime Minister Mackenzie King was unprepared to deal with a crisis on the scale of the Depression. He believed the situation was temporary and that, in time, the economy would recover. When desperate Canadians turned to the federal government for financial help, King told them this was the responsibility of municipal and provincial governments. The financial strain of the Depression, however, had bankrupted many municipalities. When the Conservative Opposition asked why some provincial governments were not being helped by the federal government, King said he would not give "a five-cent piece" to a Conservative provincial government.

King never lived down this impulsive remark. The Conservatives used his statement to build support during their 1930 election campaign. King lost to Richard Bedford Bennett and his Conservative **majority government**.

The Government's Response

Prime Minister Bennett was no more in favour of government relief than Mackenzie King had been. He once told a group of students that "one of the greatest assets a man can have on entering life's struggle is poverty." Nevertheless, Bennett's Conservative government introduced several measures to help Canadians through the Depression.

- Bennett's government introduced the Unemployment Relief Act, which gave the provinces $20 million for work-creation programs. In spite of this spending, the economy did not improve.

- Bennett tried to "use tariffs to blast a way" into world markets and out of the Depression. He raised tariffs by an average of more than 50 percent to protect Canadian industries, which provided protection for some businesses. In the long run, it did more harm than good, as other nations, in turn, set up trade barriers against Canada.

- The Prairie Farm Rehabilitation Act was introduced in 1935 to help farmers build irrigation systems and reservoirs. But by this time, drought and poverty had forced many families to leave their farms and move elsewhere.

FIGURE 4–12 As the situation in Canada grew worse, Prime Minister Bennett became a target for people's anger and frustration. A deserted farm was called a "Bennett barnyard"; a newspaper was a "Bennett blanket." Roasted wheat was "Bennett coffee." A "Bennett buggy" was an automobile pulled by horses when the owner could no longer afford the gas to run it.

©P

KEY TERMS

On-to-Ottawa Trek a 1935 rail trip from Vancouver to Ottawa (stopped at Regina) by unemployed men to protest conditions at employment relief camps

Regina Riot a riot that occurred when police attempted to clear On-to-Ottawa trekkers from a stadium in Regina

New Deal a series of programs, such as social assistance for the aged and unemployed, introduced by U.S. president Roosevelt in the 1930s to deal with the Depression

The growing number of jobless, homeless men drifting across the country frightened many middle-class Canadians. The "Red Scare" was still dominant in Canada, and Prime Minister Bennett feared these men would come under the influence of the Communist Party. In 1931, Bennett introduced a law outlawing communist agitation. Communist Party leader Tim Buck was convicted in defiance of this law, and spent two years in prison.

Working for Twenty Cents a Day

In addition to relief payments and soup kitchens, Bennett created a national network of work camps for single men in an attempt to provide relief from the Depression. In British Columbia, the provincial government had already established work camps, and these were absorbed into the federal camps. Work camps were usually located deep in the woods, so the men were completely isolated. Men worked on projects such as building roads, clearing land, and digging drainage ditches. They were paid $0.20 a day and given room and board. The food was terrible, and the bunks were often bug-infested. More than 170 000 men spent time in these camps.

The On-to-Ottawa Trek

In 1935, more than a thousand men left the relief camps in the interior of British Columbia in protest against camp conditions and to demand higher pay. They gathered in Vancouver, holding rallies and collecting money for food. Under the leadership of the Relief Camp Workers' Union, the men decided to take their complaints directly to the prime minister in a protest that became known as the **On-to-Ottawa Trek**. Crowding into and on top of freight cars, the trekkers rode through the Prairies. Many people supported them by donating food and supplies, while others joined the trek. By the time they reached Regina, Saskatchewan, there were more than 2000 trekkers and their protest had gained national attention.

Bennett responded to the trekkers by calling in the RCMP to stop them in Regina. The protesters were confined in a local stadium, and only the leaders were allowed to continue on to Ottawa. The union leaders who met with Prime Minister Bennett had great hopes of being heard, but Bennett attacked the leaders as communist radicals and troublemakers.

Back in Regina, the RCMP were ordered to clear the trekkers from the stadium. The trekkers resisted, battling the RCMP and the local police for hours. The incident became known as the **Regina Riot**. One officer was killed, many were injured, and 130 men were arrested.

FIGURE 4–13 Relief Camp Workers' Union newsletter

Thinking Critically Make a list of information that might have been found in this newsletter. What use could a historian make of a source such as this one?

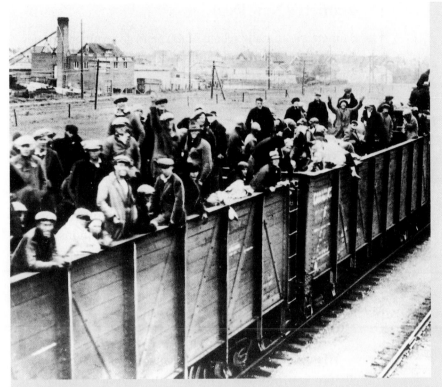

FIGURE 4–14 The On-to-Ottawa Trekkers

Gathering Information How would protests of today differ from the On-to-Ottawa Trek? How might the government response be similar or different today? Explain.

Prime Minister
Richard Bedford Bennett

- born 1870, Hopewell, New Brunswick
- teacher, lawyer, businessman
- first elected to Commons in 1911
- prime minister 1930–1935

Domestic Record

- established relief camps for unemployed single men during the Depression

- created the Canadian Radio Broadcasting Commission (CRBC) in 1932, which regulated broadcasting in Canada; the CRBC became the Canadian Broadcasting Corporation (CBC) in 1936

- passed the Bank of Canada Act in 1934, creating a central bank that issues currency, sets the bank rate, and helps decide banking policies

- helped create the Canadian Wheat Board, which works to control the prices and marketing of Canadian wheat

International Record

- persuaded the British Empire to give Canada preferential tariffs, which helped the Canadian economy during the Depression

Trouble in Vancouver

When the federal government closed relief camps in 1936 and the provincial government reduced relief payments, many men were left destitute. In protest against the lack of government support, these men would conduct "sit-ins" at various buildings until the government responded to their complaints. In April, 1600 protesters occupied the Vancouver Art Gallery, the main post office, and the Georgia Hotel. Most of the protesters were convinced to end their sit-in without incident. At the post office, however, the men refused to leave; they were eventually evicted with tear gas.

Roosevelt's New Deal

When Franklin Roosevelt became the U.S. president in 1933, he introduced a "**New Deal**" that created public work programs for the unemployed and for farmers. His most drastic action was the introduction of the Social Security Act. This Act provided several social assistance programs, such as old age pension, unemployment insurance, and financial assistance for dependent mothers and children. Under the New Deal, the U.S. federal government spent billions of dollars to get the economy working again. The New Deal did not pull the United States out of the Depression. It did, however, help millions to survive, and it gave hope for the future in a time of national despair.

FIGURE 4–15 U.S. President Franklin Roosevelt priming the New Deal pump

Interpreting a Cartoon What is the message of this cartoon? Why has the cartoonist chosen the image of priming a pump to describe Roosevelt's New Deal?

KEY TERMS

laissez-faire an economic condition in which industry is free of government intervention

welfare state a state in which the government actively looks after the well-being of its citizens

Bennett's New Deal

Bennett was initially reluctant to spend government money on relief. But in his radio addresses prior to the 1935 election campaign, Bennett surprised listeners and his Cabinet colleagues by introducing his own version of Roosevelt's New Deal which included

- fairer, progressive taxation so that people who earned more money paid more tax
- insurance to protect workers against illness, injury, and unemployment
- legislation for workplace reforms that regulated work hours, minimum wages, and working conditions
- revised old-age pensions to help support workers over 65 years of age
- agricultural support programs to help farmers and the creation of the Canadian Wheat Board to regulate wheat prices

Many voters saw Bennett's change in policy as a desperate attempt to win votes and not as a true shift in his views. They questioned the value of social insurance programs for people who did not have a job and so could not make a claim. For most people it was too little and far too late.

FIGURE 4–16 To combat U.S. influence on Canadians, a public radio service was created, which became the Canadian Broadcasting Corporation (CBC) in 1936. The CBC ran Canadian-produced music and entertainment programs in French and English. French programming in Québec was very popular, but many English-speaking listeners still tuned in to popular U.S. shows.

PRACTICE QUESTIONS

1. What actions did governments take to deal with the Depression? Explain.

2. What were the main complaints of relief camp workers?

3. Do you think the On-to-Ottawa Trek was a success or failure? Provide evidence to support your opinion.

4. Which three of Bennett's New Deal proposals do you think had the greatest impact on Canadians? Support your choices.

©P

How involved should the government be in the economy during a depression?

Before the Great Depression, governments generally did not interfere in the economy. Instead, they relied on a **laissez-faire** approach, letting the free enterprise system regulate itself. During the 1930s, the public pressured governments to create work programs and to provide money for those who could not help themselves. Some governments, most notably the U.S., followed the advice of British economist John Maynard Keynes who believed that governments needed to jump-start the economy. He supported spending money on programs that would put people back to work. Once they were working, people would spend money. The increased demand for goods would mean more jobs and more spending.

Opposition in the U.S. criticized Roosevelt's New Deal as a "...frightful waste and extravagance.... It has bred fear and hesitation in commerce and industry, thus discouraging new enterprises, preventing employment and prolonging the depression." In Canada, Prime Minister Bennett's campaign during the 1935 election promised his version of the New Deal. He said, "In my mind, reform means Government intervention. It means Government control and regulation. It means the end of laissez-faire." Mackenzie King, who won the election, believed that the economy would improve on its own in time. He warned that

> *A house is not built from the top down. It is constructed from the ground up. The foundation must be well and truly laid, or the whole edifice will crumble. To seek to erect an ambitious program of social services upon a stationary or diminishing national income is like building a house upon the sands.*
>
> *–W. L. Mackenzie King, 1935*

Many of the social programs created by the New Deal are part of today's "social safety net" in Canada and the U.S. These programs help to protect people and businesses during an economic crisis. Since the Depression, people have debated the role of the government in Canada's economy. Most Canadians believe that even if the country is not experiencing a depression, it is the government's duty to provide basic services, such as education, health care, unemployment benefits, and other kinds of social assistance. This is referred to as a **welfare state**. Other people support a competitive state in which the government creates an atmosphere of competition for businesses by cutting spending on social programs and reducing taxes. Most Canadians believe in a mixed economy, where the government provides a certain level of social services, but is not overly intrusive in planning and running the economy (see Figure 4–17).

During the 2008 economic crisis, many governments referred to the lessons learned during the Depression to support intervention in the economy. With little opposition, the Canadian government provided $12 billion of economic stimulus. In the U.S., which was harder hit by this recession, the government supplied $787 billion to bail out failing industries and curb rising unemployment.

Communism	Government involvement in the economy	Capitalism
State control	Mixed economy	Laissez-faire

FIGURE 4–17 Economic systems based on the level of competition and government control

Analyzing the Issue

1. Draw a flow chart to illustrate Keynes' theory of how government spending could lift a country out of a depression.

2. In a two-column organizer, summarize the arguments for and against government intervention in the economy during an economic slowdown and during a period of economic growth.

3. Why do you think there was little opposition to government intervention in the economy during the 2008 recession?

Politics of Protest

As Ottawa struggled to find ways to cope with the Depression, some Canadians looked to new political parties for solutions.

The Co-operative Commonwealth Federation (CCF)

The **Co-operative Commonwealth Federation** (**CCF**), founded in the Prairie provinces in 1932, was Canada's first socialist party. The CCF believed that **capitalism** breeds inequality and greed and had caused the Depression. The CCF supported a socialist system in which the government controlled the economy so that all Canadians would benefit equally. Their ideas appealed to a wide variety of people who were dissatisfied with the government's response to the Depression. At the CCF's convention in Regina in 1933, J.S. Woodsworth was chosen as party leader. The party platform, known as the **Regina Manifesto**, opposed free-market economics and supported public ownership of key industries. It advocated social programs to help the elderly, the unemployed, the homeless, and the sick. Woodsworth also urged the government to spend money on public works to create employment. By 1939, the CCF formed the Opposition in British Columbia and Saskatchewan.

The Social Credit Party

The **Social Credit Party** was another political party from Western Canada that offered an alternative to Canadian voters. The party's leader, William "Bible Bill" Aberhart, was a charismatic preacher. Social credit was based on the belief that capitalism was a wasteful economic system. Under capitalism, banks hoarded money, preventing customers from buying goods that capitalism produced. Aberhart felt that the government should release money into the economy so that people could spend it. The theory of social credit appealed to many people from Alberta because the Depression had devastated their economy and they resented the power and control of the banks in Central Canada. Under Bible Bill's leadership, the Social Credit Party won 17 seats in the federal election of 1935 with nearly 50 percent of the popular vote in Alberta.

Aberhart promised each citizen a "basic dividend" of $25 a month to buy necessities. The federal government challenged the right of a province to issue its own currency, and social credit was disallowed by the Supreme Court. Despite this setback, the Social Credit Party remained in power in Alberta until 1971 under Aberhart's successors, Ernest Manning and Harry Strom.

FIGURE 4–18 William Aberhart came to power based on the popularity of his theory of social credit.

Interpreting a Cartoon What is this cartoonist's opinion of the soundness of social credit?

Union nationale

In Québec, Maurice Duplessis, a former Conservative, joined forces with some disillusioned Liberals to form the **Union nationale**, a party that supported **Québec nationalism**. The Union nationale relied heavily on the support of the Roman Catholic Church and rural voters. Duplessis blamed many of Québec's social and economic problems on the English minority in Québec, which controlled the province's economy. The Union nationale's political platform was based on improved working conditions, social insurance programs, publicly owned power companies, and a system of farm credits. During his first term, however, Duplessis' promises of reform evaporated, and he did little to improve economic and social conditions in Québec. Despite this, he remained premier until 1959 with the exception of one term from 1939 to 1944 (see Chapter 6).

● How was Québec nationalism expressed in the 1930s?

FIGURE 4–19 Hon. Maurice Duplessis (second from right) pictured here in August 1946

Provincial Solutions

During the Depression, voters expressed their dissatisfaction with government inaction by voting out ruling provincial parties. As the CCF and Social Credit parties gained momentum in Western Canada, and the Union nationale gained power in Québec, voters in other provinces also made their voices heard by electing new governments.

In Ontario, the provincial Liberals came to power in 1934 for the first time in 29 years. The Liberal leader was a populist farmer, Mitchell Hepburn, who won wide support by championing the causes of "the little man." He railed against big business and was fond of flamboyant gestures, such as auctioning off the provincial government's fleet of limousines. Although Hepburn tried to improve Ontario's economy, he did little to help the unemployed and was against **unionization**.

In British Columbia, Dufferin Pattullo was elected premier in 1933, returning the Liberals to power in that province. Pattullo was a strong believer in greater provincial spending power. He introduced reforms to shorten the workday, increase the minimum wage, and increase relief payments by 20 percent. Public works projects were launched, most notably the Fraser River bridge at New Westminster and a new city hall for Vancouver. Pattullo's projects were short-lived, however, as the federal government challenged his authority to introduce programs that were considered to be in the federal domain.

KEY TERMS

Co-operative Commonwealth Federation (CCF) Canada's first socialist party founded in the Prairies in 1932; advocated government control of the economy

capitalism an economic system in which the production and distribution of goods are owned privately or by shareholders in corporations who have invested their money in the hope of making a profit

Regina Manifesto platform of the Co-operative Commonwealth Federation party; it supported public ownership of industry and social programs to assist those in need

Social Credit Party political party founded in Western Canada; opposed to capitalism

Union nationale nationalist French-Canadian political party led by Maurice Duplessis

Québec nationalism a movement advocating for the protection and development of Québécois culture and language

unionization the formation of labour unions

Photographs convey information and provide insights into many areas of study in this textbook. Historical photographs are a useful primary source of information about past events. To make use of a photograph as a historical source, you must do more than look at the photograph; you need to interpret the information it provides. This is called decoding.

A photograph is an image created by a photographer. As such, it reflects that person's world view. In the same way, any meaning you take from it will be influenced by your world view (see Chapter 1, Chapter Review). It is important that you try to be open-minded when looking at photographs.

Paintings do not claim to represent reality. Photographs do, but they can be manipulated. Images can easily be altered with today's digital technology, so you must be aware of the intention of the photographer and how the photograph is being used when you try to decode its meaning.

Steps to Decoding Photographs

1. Examine the photograph carefully and describe what you see. Does the image have clues as to when it was taken and where? Who is in it? What is happening? Why was the image taken? Does the caption help to answer these questions?

Examine Figure 4–20. How many of the previous questions can you answer?

2. Analyze the image and ask questions. It may help to divide the image into sections to examine details. What are people in the image doing? Do their facial expressions and body language suggest anything? Are there signs, buildings, landmarks, or other clues visible? Analyze Figure 4–20 using these questions and any others you think are relevant.

3. Evaluate the photograph as a source of information. Do not simply accept the image as showing what happened. Is it reliable and credible? Is there bias in the presentation? (Review Building Your Skills, Chapter 1.) What is your evaluation of Figure 4–20?

4. Draw conclusions based on the information you have collected and consider what information is missing. The photographer frames the image and the story by focusing only on a part of what he or she can see. Does outside information help you to better understand the contents of the picture? Read about the circumstances of the On-to-Ottawa Trek on page 102. Does this change your interpretation of the picture? Why or why not?

FIGURE 4–20 Police and On-to-Ottawa trekkers during the Regina Riot of July 1, 1935

©P

Applying the Skill

1. Apply the four-step decoding process to the images below and then answer the questions accompanying each image.

FIGURE 4–21 Relief camp in the 1930s. Compare and contrast the description of relief camps on page 102 with this photograph. Do you think the picture was staged? Which details do you consider most significant and why? Is it a fair representation of a bunkhouse in a 1930s relief camp? Why or why not?

FIGURE 4–22 Protesters at the free-trade Summit of the Americas held in Québec City, 2001. What point of view does this photograph represent? Why do you think so? What evidence is there in the image that the protesters were aware that the media were covering the event? Compare and contrast this image with Figure 4–20. Which image is a better source of information? Why?

KEY TERMS

Rowell-Sirois Report report of the Royal Commission on Dominion-Provincial Relations, a commission set up in 1937 to examine the Canadian economy and federal-provincial relations

equalization payments a federal transfer of funds from richer to poorer provinces

A Change in Federal Government

By 1935, five years after Bennett was elected prime minister, voters were frustrated by his inability to deal with the crisis of the Depression. In the federal election, they returned Mackenzie King to power.

King did not support government intervention in the economy. He believed that in time, the economy would improve on its own. King also felt that spending money on social programs during a depression did not make economic sense, and that it was better to wait until the economy was strong before introducing these expensive programs.

King's views clashed with the findings of the National Employment Commission, which he had set up in 1936 to examine the state of unemployment in Canada. The commission recommended the federal government spend millions of dollars on job creation and training programs. King ended up spending only a fraction of what was recommended.

Federal-Provincial Tensions

In 1937, King created the Royal Commission on Dominion-Provincial Relations to examine the thorny issue of federal-provincial relations and to look into the responsibilities of the different levels of government. The unemployment crisis of the Depression had caused a great deal of tension between the federal and provincial governments. There was disagreement over which government had the right to collect tax money and which government should pay for social and unemployment assistance.

The Commission's findings, referred to as the **Rowell-Sirois Report**, recommended that the federal government give the poorer provinces grants, or **equalization payments**, to ensure that every province was able to offer its citizens the same level of services. The Commission also recommended that the federal government bear the responsibility for unemployment insurance and other social benefits such as pensions.

The wealthier provinces did not like the idea of equalization payments because they did not want their tax dollars going to other provinces. The provinces also felt that many of the Commission's recommendations would mean a loss of provincial power. By the time the Commission made its report, the economy had started to turn around. More people were finding jobs, and there was a mood of cautious optimism. Canada's involvement in the Second World War meant most of the Commission's recommendations were either pushed aside indefinitely or adopted later.

PRACTICE QUESTIONS

1. List the political parties that were started during the Depression. Identify the supporters, leader, and policies of each party. Where on the political spectrum would each party sit?

2. What difficulties did provincial governments encounter in dealing with the problems of the Depression? Give examples from British Columbia and Alberta.

3. What were Mackenzie King's views on government involvement in the economy?

4. What were the main recommendations of the Rowell-Sirois Report? Why did the wealthier provinces dislike these recommendations?

©P

Medical Advances

During the 1930s, a number of Canadians pushed the boundaries of science and technology. As the government looked for ways to ease the economic suffering, Canadians tried to find ways to improve the lives of others, especially in the areas of health and medicine.

Pablum stands the test of time In 1930, doctors at Toronto's Hospital for Sick Children created Pablum, the first pre-cooked, vitamin-enriched cereal for infants. For 25 years, the hospital received a royalty for every package sold. In 2005, H.J. Heinz Company acquired the Pablum brand. How does the development of Pablum reflect the social conditions of the Depression?

A revolutionary brainwave Canadian doctor Wilder Penfield founded McGill University's Montréal Neurological Institute in 1934, which became an international centre for education and research on the brain. Penfield is most known for developing a surgical treatment for epilepsy known as the "Montréal Procedure." He used a local anesthetic so patients remained conscious during the operation, and then probed their brains to locate the site of the seizures. Doctors today still use maps of the sensory and motor sections of the brain that were drawn from these operations.

Saving lives on the front lines Norman Bethune was a Canadian doctor, inventor, and political activist. As a dedicated physician in Montréal during the Depression, Bethune provided free medical care to the poor and advocated for a social system of health care. He also volunteered for the Spanish Civil War (see Chapter 5). He was the first to set up a blood bank close to the front lines and organize a mobile blood-transfusion team.

up close
and personal

Mackenzie King and Bennett:
Public Persona vs. Private Life

During the turbulent years of the 1930s, Canada was led by two men who were studies in contrast. William Lyon Mackenzie King and Richard Bedford Bennett both had a profound effect on Canada. Yet history's judgement of each man has been vastly different.

King, one of the most dominant political leaders in Canadian history, was prime minister of Canada for almost 22 years, from 1921 to 1930, save for a few months in 1926, and from 1935 to 1948. One historian has called him the "...greatest and most interesting of prime ministers." Bennett led Canada for five years going from landslide victory in 1930 to disastrous defeat in 1935 after one term in office. Bennett's negative historical reputation comes from what was seen as his failure to find a solution to the Depression. He eventually left Canada and died in England as a member of the House of Lords, forgotten by Canadians and generally ignored by historians.

Bennett's One-man Show

In 1930, there were high hopes that the energy and competence Bennett displayed as leader of the Opposition would help the new prime minister find solutions to the economic crisis. However as the Depression worsened, so did his reputation. Bennett lacked the common touch and never wavered in his conviction that he was right. Even his supporters agreed that he liked to hear himself speak, paying little attention to the opinions of others. Members of his Cabinet accused him of running a one-man show, seldom informing them of important decisions. It was joked that when Bennett was mumbling to himself, he was holding a Cabinet meeting. This insensitivity toward the opinions of others and his unwillingness to compromise hindered Bennett's efforts to deal with the worsening Depression.

FIGURE 4–23 Bennett as a one-man government

Interpreting a Cartoon What is the cartoonist trying to say about Bennett? What techniques does the cartoonist use to convey his message?

Bennett was a millionaire bachelor who made his home in Ottawa in a suite occupying a whole floor of the luxurious Château Laurier Hotel. It was small wonder that poverty-stricken Canadians felt little affection for him. However, they did not see the private man who, according to Bennett, between 1927 and 1937 gave nearly $2.5 million to charities from his own income. Sometimes this was in response to the many letters he received from Canadians asking for his help (see the letters on page 99). Bennett secretly sent many of these people money. His generosity was uncovered in his private papers after his death.

King: The People Pleaser

King was a pragmatic and cautious politician who avoided making decisions if he could. He had a feel for the mood of the country and unlike Bennett, he was patient, willing to wait for events to unfold. He claimed that "it is what we prevent, rather than what we do that counts most in Government."

"My Government"

King was notorious for dull and ambiguous speeches that blurred the issues and seemed to promise everything to everyone. These speeches infuriated many listeners. In fact, King was a skilled negotiator who wanted desperately to keep Canada united—French and English, the different regions and social classes—and his vague manner was a deliberate technique to try to please everyone. His successes seemed to result from being the leader who divided Canadians the least.

After King's death, it was discovered that this apparently colourless man had, as he wrote in his diary, "a very double life." He had kept a detailed personal diary from his student days in the 1890s to his death in 1950. The nearly 30 000 pages in the diaries revealed that King was a believer in spiritualism, obsessed with clocks and mystical numbers. He held seances in which he communicated with the dead, especially with his mother, Wilfrid Laurier, and others.

1. Why was King a more successful politician than Bennett? Do you think his reputation as an effective leader is justified? Explain.

2. What were the strengths and weaknesses of each leader?

3. How was Bennett perceived by Canadians during the Depression? Do you think this image of him was justified? Explain your answer.

4. Is it necessary to know private details of the lives of our politicians to evaluate their role in Canadian history?

5. Should we judge politicians based on their accomplishments or personalities?

WEB LINK
You can read King's diaries at the Pearson Web site.

FIGURE 4–24 King as Wobbly Willy

Interpreting a Cartoon Mackenzie King was known for his reluctance to make decisions. Is the cartoonist effective in conveying this idea? Why or why not?

The Depression and Global Politics

During the 1930s, many countries around the world were suffering from an economic slowdown. As in Canada, many people lost their jobs and were destitute, and governments looked for solutions to the economic crisis.

Germany After the War

Germany, in particular, suffered the effects of the Depression. Since the end of the First World War, Germany had grown increasingly unhappy with the terms of the Treaty of Versailles. It bitterly resented the "war guilt" clause that required it to pay $32 billion in reparations to other countries. These payments put a great strain on the German economy, which had been ruined by war. To meet the payments, the government printed large amounts of money in the 1920s, which in turn lowered the value of the German currency. As German money became worth less and less, the price of basic goods continued to rise.

To control this inflation, Britain, France, and the United States agreed to give better terms for Germany's reparation payments. Germany made a modest recovery. However, when world stock markets collapsed in 1929, the weakened German economy was affected more than most countries. As you read at the beginning of this chapter, Germany's inability to make its reparation payments affected the economies of other countries and contributed to the causes of the global Depression.

FIGURE 4–25 This photograph, taken in 1923, shows a German woman using several million marks to fuel her stove.

Using Evidence What can you conclude about the value of German currency from this photograph?

©P

The Depression in Asia

The Empire of Japan, the only independent Asian nation with a colonial empire, developed a strong manufacturing industry after the First World War. Tariff barriers and the decline of international trade during the Depression greatly affected Japan's economy, which relied on raw materials from the United States and other countries. To deal with the slowdown, Japan adopted **Keynesian economics** and increased government spending to stimulate the economy. It also put into action an aggressive plan to expand its territory to gain resource-rich lands by invading China's northern province of Manchuria in 1931 (see Chapter 5).

KEY TERM

Keynesian economics an economic theory named for John Maynard Keynes (1883–1946) who advocated government intervention in the economy, especially during economic downturns

Russians Embrace Communism

After the Bolshevik Revolution in 1917, Russia experienced a series of political upheavals that led to a civil war. In 1922, Russia joined with several other communist countries to form the Union of Soviet Socialist Republics (U.S.S.R.) or Soviet Union. During the Depression, the Soviet Union's communist economic system insulated it from the economic slowdown experienced by other countries. It appeared to many as though the communist system worked, while the capitalist system had failed. This in turn increased people's interest in communism. But the people of the Soviet Union paid a price for their economic progress. Joseph Stalin's ruthless dictatorship robbed the Soviet people of their political and social freedom, and his economic and agricultural policies led to the deaths of millions of people (see Chapter 5).

Prelude to War

The economic crisis of the 1930s resulted in social and political instability around the world. As you will learn in Chapter 5, this instability was the perfect breeding ground for dictators who gained power by offering solutions and hope to desperate people. Ambitious plans to expand territories and resources led to a global military conflict, which had a profound impact on Canada's development and its reputation on the world stage.

PRACTICE QUESTIONS

1. Explain why Germany was affected so deeply by the Depression.

2. How did other countries try to help Germany during the Depression?

3. What effect did the Depression have on Japan? How did Japan respond?

4. Why did communism gain attention during the Depression?

CHAPTER FOCUS QUESTION   What were the causes, effects, and responses to the Great Depression?

For most people, the Great Depression of the 1930s was a decade of hardship and despair. Formative historic events such as the Great Depression often lead to conflict. As you have seen in this chapter, the Depression highlighted weaknesses in the Canadian economy and its close ties to the United States. As the government struggled to provide relief to many suffering Canadians, regional political parties were created that offered new ideas and hope to Canadians. The Great Depression was a national crisis that, in many ways, divided the country: the rich and poor, the immigrants and non-immigrants, men and women, and Western and Central Canada.

1. Create an organizer such as the one below. Provide as many examples as possible for each category.

Causes	Effects	Responses
Economic Cycle	New Political Parties	New Social Programs

Vocabulary Focus

2. Review the Key Terms on page 89. Then, go to the Pearson Web site and complete the activity.

Knowledge and Understanding

3. Continue the ongoing timeline assignment. Write the name and date of each event that occurred in this chapter on the timeline, and explain how the event contributed to Canadian independence.

4. What were the major weaknesses in the Canadian economy from 1919 to 1939? How did these weaknesses make the Depression in Canada particularly severe? How did Canada's economic problems compare to those of other countries? Why was there a reluctance on the part of many governments to take aggressive action to correct these problems?

5. a) In what ways did the federal and provincial governments respond to the needs of Canadians during the 1930s?

   b) What does this response say about the values that were held by society at the time? Use the personal memories in this chapter to support your answer.

   c) How successful were the government responses?

6. Suggest three actions that could have been taken to prevent the Depression. Why do you think these were not done?

7. Why were Aboriginal peoples, Asian men, and women in a particularly desperate situation in the 1930s?

8. In your view, which political party would each of the following have supported during the Depression? Explain your choice.

   a) owner of a small business

   b) single unemployed person

   c) farm wife

   d) hourly paid worker

Critical Thinking

9. Construct a cause and effect diagram for the Great Depression. Refer to Building Your Skills on page 82. Use your diagram to list and explain three key lessons that today's governments should learn from the Great Depression.

Evidence

10. Choose three images from the chapter that you think best illustrate the impact of the Great Depression on Canadians. Explain your reasons for choosing each of the photographs.

Judgements

11. With a partner or in a small group, imagine you are the founding members of a new political party in the 1930s. Your party is dedicated to solving the economic and social problems of the Depression. On a single page, write your party's name, a summary of the country's major problems, and a five- to ten-point declaration of your party's program. Include a catchy slogan or statement that sums up what your party stands for.

Document Analysis

12. Use Figure 4–26 and Figure 4–27, and the content of this chapter, to answer the following:

    a) Which were the two worst years of the Depression? List and explain the evidence you used to reach your decision.

    b) What might explain Saskatchewan and Alberta's steep decline in per capita incomes from 1928 to 1933?

    c) Which provinces do you think were least affected by the Depression? Explain your response.

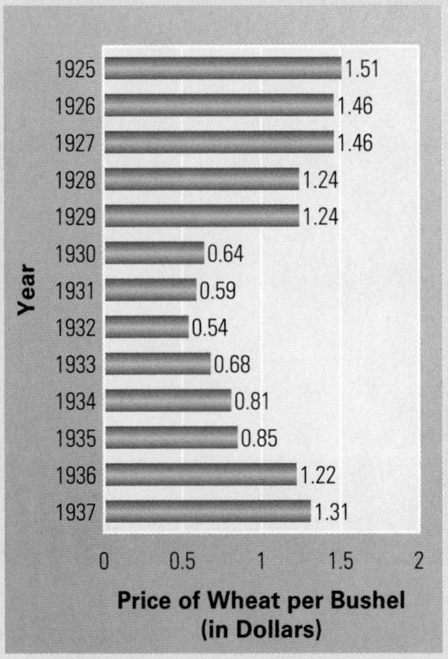

FIGURE 4–26

	1928–1929 Average $ per Capita	1933 Average $ per Capita	Percentage Decrease
Canada	471	247	48
Saskatchewan	478	135	72
Alberta	548	212	61
Manitoba	466	240	49
British Columbia	594	314	47
Prince Edward Island	278	154	45
Ontario	549	310	44
Québec	391	220	44
New Brunswick	292	180	39
Nova Scotia	322	207	36

FIGURE 4–27 Average per capita incomes, 1928/1929 and 1933

5 Canada and the Second World War

GUIDING QUESTIONS

Society & Identity

- What effect did the war have on the role of women?

- What impact did conscription have on Canadian unity?

- What effect did the War Measures Act have on the legal rights of Canadians?

Politics & Government

- Why were totalitarian leaders able to gain power in Europe and Asia?

Autonomy & World Presence

- How did the war raise awareness of human rights issues?

- How did Canada get involved in the Second World War?

- What was the war's impact on the home front?

- Describe Canada's military role in the Second World War.

- What factors contributed to Canada's emerging autonomy?

TIMELINE

1939

Germany invades Poland

Britain and France declare war on Germany

Canada declares war on Germany

1940

Germany invades Denmark and Norway

Germany invades the Netherlands, Belgium, Luxembourg, and France

Evacuation of Dunkirk

National Resources Mobilization Act

France surrenders to Germany

The Battle of Britain

1940–1943

North African Campaign

1940–1944

Battle of the Atlantic

1941

Germany invades the Soviet Union

Japan bombs Pearl Harbor

U.S. declares war on Japan

Battle of Hong Kong

China officially declares war on Japan

©P

CHAPTER FOCUS QUESTION

How did the Second World War impact Canada socially, politically, and economically?

On the Sunday of Labour Day weekend in 1939, Canadians gathered around their radios to hear King George VI address the rumours of war that had been heard across the country.

> *For the second time in the lives of most of us we are at war. Over and over again we have tried to find a peaceful way out of the differences between ourselves and those who are now our enemies. But it has been in vain. We have been forced into a conflict. For we are called, with our allies, to meet the challenge of a principle which, if it were to prevail, would be fatal to any civilised order in the world.*
>
> *–Historical Royal Speeches and Writings*

Once again, the world was at war. What would war mean to Canadians? How was this war different from the First World War? How was Canada different as a nation at the beginning of the Second World War? In this chapter, you will learn about the events of the Second World War and the contributions made by hundreds of thousands of Canadians during its course.

KEY TERMS

totalitarian state
Nazis
Holocaust
policy of appeasement
British Commonwealth Air Training Plan (BCATP)
total war
Allies
Axis
Dunkirk
Battle of Britain
Pearl Harbor
Battle of Hong Kong
Battle of the Atlantic
Bomber Command
Dieppe Raid
Italian Campaign
D-Day
Liberation of the Netherlands
genocide
enemy aliens
arsenal of democracy

1942
Internment of Japanese Canadians
Canadians vote in support of conscription
Allied raid on French port of Dieppe

1943
Allies begin bombing German cities
Sicily and mainland Italy invaded
Canadians win Battle of Ortona, Italy
Axis forces defeated in Stalingrad

1944
D-Day

1945
The Netherlands liberated
Germany surrenders
Bombing of Hiroshima and Nagasaki, Japan
Japan surrenders; war ends

KEY TERMS

dictator a ruler with unrestricted power, without any democratic restrictions

totalitarian state a dictatorship in which the government uses intimidation, violence, and propaganda to rule all aspects of the social and political life of its citizens

five-year plans Stalin's plans for economic development in the Soviet Union over five years

fascist a form of authoritarian government that is totalitarian and nationalistic

Weimar Republic the democratic government in Germany after the First World War

Nazis members of the National Socialist German Workers' Party; the Nazis were extreme nationalists who took power in 1933 and controlled every aspect of German life through a police state

The Rise of Totalitarianism

As you learned in Chapter 4, the economic crisis of the 1930s led to social and political upheaval in countries around the world. During the Depression era, several charismatic leaders promised solutions to their citizens' woes, but soon emerged as powerful **dictators**.

The term *totalitarian* describes political philosophies that put the state above all else, including the rights of the individual. In a **totalitarian state**, the government has total control over all aspects of politics and society. It uses violence and intimidation to gain power, and then relies on its police force to maintain its control. Usually, the ruling party bans other political parties and does not tolerate any opposing ideologies. Propaganda and censorship reinforce the party message and control society. The government controls the economy and all the resources of the state, and uses these to further its goals. The state has one leader who has absolute power. In the 1930s, different forms of totalitarian states arose in Germany, Italy, Spain, the Soviet Union and, in a different way, Japan.

Stalin's Soviet Union

By 1917, the Communists had taken control of Russia. In 1924, Joseph Stalin became the leader of the Communist Party in what was now the Soviet Union. By 1928, he had gained total control of the Soviet Union and began to implement a series of **five-year plans** to industrialize the country and give the government complete control of the economy. The first step of Stalin's plan was to collectivize agriculture, which meant seizing all privately owned land. Next he created industrial projects, including building coal and steel mills, roads, and railways. Stalin focused on building industry and the military, practically ignoring the needs of the people. The government controlled all media and imposed strict censorship and travel restrictions on everyone. The secret police arrested anyone deemed to be a threat, and the government controlled the courts. During the Great Purge of the late 1930s, Stalin eliminated anyone he believed opposed the communist government or his power. Millions of people were convicted of crimes against the state and hundreds of thousands were executed. Many more Soviet people died of exhaustion or starvation in Gulags, labour camps that Stalin established in Siberia.

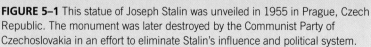

FIGURE 5–1 This statue of Joseph Stalin was unveiled in 1955 in Prague, Czech Republic. The monument was later destroyed by the Communist Party of Czechoslovakia in an effort to eliminate Stalin's influence and political system.

Gathering Evidence What does Stalin's statue reveal about his personality and his views on leadership?

Mussolini's Italy

After the First World War, Italy suffered from chaotic economic and political conditions. Benito Mussolini took advantage of the situation. He established the **Fascist** Party, which emphasized nationalism and challenged Italy's democratic government. His new political movement found support in the government and with the middle class. Mussolini created the Blackshirts, gangs of fascists who intimidated their opponents by attacking communists and socialists in the streets. Their favourite tactic was forcing bottles of castor oil, a laxative, down a victim's throat. Promising to revitalize Italy and to restore Italian pride, the increasingly militaristic National Fascist Party won 35 seats in the election of 1921. Although the Fascists were anti-communist, Mussolini used the totalitarian model of the Soviet Union as a blueprint for his own plans to rule Italy. In 1922, Mussolini led the March on Rome: he gathered 26 000 Blackshirts outside the city and demanded that the government be turned over to him. Soon after taking power, Mussolini—who was called *Il Duce* ("the leader")—brought all communications, industry, agriculture, and labour under fascist control and turned Italy into a totalitarian state.

FIGURE 5–2 Fascist leader Mussolini (seen on left) and his Blackshirts march in Rome

Fascist Germany

Like Italy, Germany was politically and economically unstable at the end of the First World War. The kaiser had abdicated and a democratic government, the **Weimar Republic**, was set up. But the German people distrusted the government since it had signed the Treaty of Versailles, which had added to the country's economic struggles after the war. Many Germans wanted a leader who could solve the country's problems.

Hitler Comes to Power

In 1920, Adolf Hitler joined the National Socialist German Workers' Party, also known as the **Nazis**, and by 1921 he was the leader of the party. The Nazis gathered support throughout the 1920s by criticizing the Weimar Republic and the humiliating terms of the Treaty of Versailles. Hitler persuaded Germans that he could save the country from the Depression and make it a great nation again. In 1932, the Nazis became the largest party in the *Reichstag*, the German parliament, and in 1933 Hitler became chancellor of Germany.

Once in power, Hitler—called *Führer* ("the leader")—ruled his country through intimidation and fear. He banned all political parties other than the Nazis and used the Gestapo, a secret police, to enforce his rule. Hitler's government defied the terms of the Treaty of Versailles by stopping all reparation payments and rebuilding Germany's military. It also subsidized farmers and poured money into public projects. To the delight of the German people, unemployment went down and the economy improved.

Kristallnacht a coordinated attack against Jewish people and their property carried out by Nazis in Germany on November 9, 1938

persecution to oppress or ill-treat because of race, religion, gender, sexual orientation, or beliefs

Holocaust the Nazi imprisonment and murder of 6 million Jewish people and 5 million other peoples during the Second World War

FIGURE 5–3 Under the Nazi regime, the Jewish Star of David was to be worn by all Jewish people for easy identification.

The "Master Race"

The Nazi Party believed that the German people were a "master race" of Aryans, a supposedly "pure" race of northern Europeans. Non-Aryans, including Jewish people, Roma ("Gypsies"), and Slavs, were considered inferior. People with mental or physical disabilities were despised because they destroyed the image of the master race. Communists and homosexuals were also targeted as undesirables. The Nazis banned non-Aryans and undesirables from teaching or attending schools and universities, holding government office, or writing books. As early as 1933, the Nazis set up concentration camps to isolate these people from German society.

Hitler's regime of hatred targeted Jewish people in particular. During his rule, he passed the Nuremberg Laws, which forced Jewish people to wear the Star of David at all times, banned marriages between Jews and Aryans, and made it illegal for Jewish people to be lawyers or doctors. The Nazi government also encouraged violence against Jewish people. On the night of November 9, 1938, Nazi mobs attacked Jewish homes, businesses, and synagogues across Germany. Many Jewish people were terrorized, beaten, and imprisoned for no reason. The attack was called ***Kristallnacht*** or "Crystal Night" because sidewalks in many parts of the country were covered with broken glass from windows. Their **persecution** escalated even more after that night. More laws were introduced which made it illegal for them to own businesses and restricted their travel. Eventually, Hitler and Heinrich Himmler, the head of Hitler's elite police unit, instituted the "Final Solution" and the **Holocaust**, which you will learn about later in this chapter.

FIGURE 5–4 The Nazis were brilliant propagandists, presenting selected information and using symbolism and pageantry to appeal to the emotions of the public.

©P

Fascism in Spain

As in Germany and Italy, Spain struggled with economic and political strife after the First World War. During the Depression, Spain's democratic government was unable to prevent widespread poverty, and people became more and more dissatisfied. Led by General Francisco Franco, fascist rebels—called Nationalists—tried to overthrow the elected socialist government in 1936. This rebellion resulted in a brutal civil war that lasted three years. Although democratic governments around the world chose not to get involved in the conflict, socialist supporters from several countries went to Spain to join in the fight against Franco and fascism. More than 1200 Canadian volunteers, called the Mackenzie-Papineau Battalion (the Mac Paps), fought in the Spanish Civil War. They went to Spain even though the Canadian government passed a law that made it illegal for them to fight in foreign wars. One of the volunteers was Dr. Norman Bethune, a Canadian surgeon and political activist (see Chapter 4).

FIGURE 5–5 Francisco Franco ruled Spain for 36 years.

Despite their efforts, Franco—with military support from Hitler and Mussolini—won the war and became the ruler of Spain in 1939. Once in control, Franco proved to be a brutal totalitarian dictator who ruled by intimidation and violence. Thousands of people were imprisoned in concentration camps or executed, and many others were used as forced labour to build railways and dig canals. Franco ruled Spain until he died in 1975.

Totalitarianism in Japan

Japan also became a totalitarian state in the 1930s, but there were important differences between Japan and the fascist states in Europe. Japan had all the elements of a totalitarian state. Many people had strong nationalist sentiments and notions of racial superiority. Japan had a government loyal to a single leader, the emperor. The country's parliament, called the Diet, had little power because government ministers answered only to the emperor. Much of the power rested with the military and the Zaibatsu, large family-run corporations, such as Mitsubishi. These groups took advantage of the political and economic problems of the Depression to gain control of the country. Influenced by European fascism, Japan took on many of its characteristics, including a Gestapo-like police force, the Kempeitai, which had the power to arrest, torture, or kill anyone thought to be an enemy of the state. Militarists took control of Japan in the 1930s and began strengthening the empire by conquering other countries and seizing their resources.

FIGURE 5–6 Hirohito, the 124th emperor of Japan, reigned from 1926 until his death in 1989.

PRACTICE QUESTIONS

1. In your own words, explain the term *totalitarian*.

2. **Cause and Consequence** What common conditions led to totalitarianism in Italy, Germany, and Spain?

3. List the ways in which Stalin, Mussolini, and Hitler each made his country a totalitarian dictatorship.

4. How did the Nazis try to accomplish their goal of a "master race" in Europe?

5. What was Canada's involvement in the Spanish Civil War?

6. How were totalitarian leaders able to gain power in Europe and Asia?

Causes of the Second World War

As you have read, different forms of totalitarianism took hold in Europe, the Soviet Union, and Japan during the 1930s. Like the colonialist leaders of pre–First World War empires, the totalitarian leaders of these states had nationalistic ambitions to expand their territory and resources. Germany and Italy felt that they had been cheated by treaties at the end of the First World War and wanted to right these wrongs. Japan wanted access to more resources to help support its industries. In other countries, leaders were conscious of the sacrifices their citizens had made during the last war and wanted to avoid another conflict at all costs. All these factors contributed to the Second World War.

Hitler's Imperialistic Ambitions

When Hitler came to power in 1933, he intended to make Germany a powerful nation again. Part of his plan involved uniting the "master race" of Germanic people and taking back territory that he believed belonged to Germany. In the years leading up to the Second World War, Hitler put his plan into action.

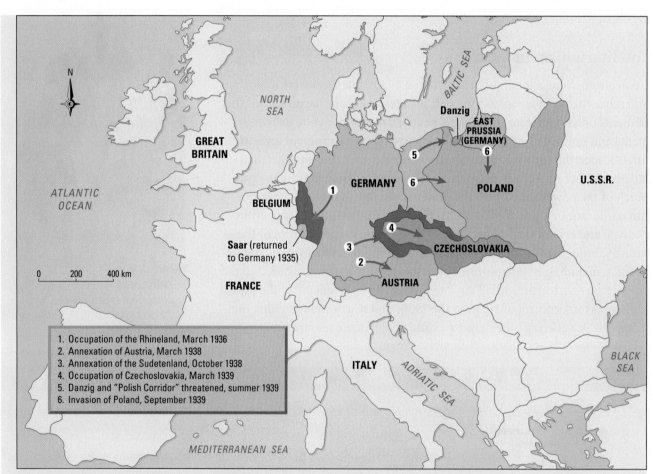

1. Occupation of the Rhineland, March 1936
2. Annexation of Austria, March 1938
3. Annexation of the Sudetenland, October 1938
4. Occupation of Czechoslovakia, March 1939
5. Danzig and "Polish Corridor" threatened, summer 1939
6. Invasion of Poland, September 1939

FIGURE 5–7 Hitler's aggression in Europe, 1936–1939

Thinking Critically Which countries might have felt threatened by Germany's actions? Why? Italy, also ruled by a fascist government at the time, was Germany's ally. What difference might this alliance have made to the countries of Europe?

©P

Appeasing Hitler

In 1936, Hitler ordered his troops into the Rhineland, an area along Germany's western border that had been demilitarized and put under French protection by the Treaty of Versailles. Although this was a violation of the treaty, Britain and France chose not to act at the time. Two years later, Germany annexed, or took over, Austria. Again, this was another breach of the treaty, but Britain and France chose not to act. They were willing to make concessions to maintain peace. However, their weakness made Hitler bolder.

Next, Hitler set his sights on the Sudetenland, a territory populated by ethnic Germans given to Czechoslovakia at the Paris Peace Conference. When Hitler threatened to invade this territory, British and French leaders met with him in Munich to try to negotiate. In exchange for the Sudetenland, Hitler promised not to invade the rest of Czechoslovakia. British Prime Minister Neville Chamberlain announced to the world that the Munich Agreement and their **policy of appeasement** would secure "peace for our time." Only six months later, in March 1939, Hitler broke his promise and Germany invaded Czechoslovakia. Hitler's actions made it clear that the policy of appeasement had failed. Another war in Europe was looming.

The Nazi–Soviet Non-aggression Pact

After taking over Czechoslovakia, Hitler planned to unite East Prussia with the rest of Germany. This territory had been separated from Germany when the map of Europe was redrawn at the Paris Peace Conference, giving Poland a strip of land so it had access to the Baltic Sea and making Danzig an independent state under the protection of the League of Nations. Before Hitler could act, he had a problem to solve. If Germany invaded Poland, the Soviet Union would likely regard Germany's actions as a threat to its own security. In August 1939, Hitler stunned the world by signing a **non-aggression pact** with Joseph Stalin, leader of the Soviet Union, even though the Nazis hated communists and vice versa. Both countries pledged not to fight each other if one of them went to war, and they agreed to divide Poland between them. Germany was now free to make its move.

On September 1, 1939, German troops invaded Poland, and bitter fighting followed. This time, Britain and France responded immediately. They ordered Germany out of Poland by September 3, 1939. When Germany ignored this deadline, Britain and France declared war.

Failure of the League of Nations

While the policy of appeasement failed to prevent German aggression, the League of Nations was not effective in preventing nationalistic aggression in other parts of the world. The League was supposed to help maintain world peace, but it was too weak and did not have a military to enforce its decisions. The League's ineffectiveness in the following two military conflicts helped pave the road to war.

Japan Invades Manchuria

As part of its plans to expand its territory and influence, Japan invaded the Chinese province of Manchuria in 1931. The Chinese government appealed to the League of Nations to take action against Japan. The League condemned Japan's action and tried to negotiate. Japan merely withdrew from the League and continued with its policy of aggression. In 1937, it expanded its invasion of China and the two countries were at war.

Italy Invades Abyssinia

Like Hitler in Germany, Mussolini wanted to expand Italy's territory and power. Still bitter that Italy had not received more land in Europe after the First World War, Mussolini wanted to expand Italy's resources by adding to its African colonies. In the spring of 1935, Italy attacked Abyssinia (now Ethiopia). Abyssinia had never been colonized and was one of the few independent African nations. It fought hard against the Italian invasion and won support around the world. The League of Nations immediately voted to impose trade sanctions against Italy. But this action was not very effective because oil, a crucial import for Italy, was not included in the sanctions. At this point, the League still hoped for Italy's support if there was a new war with Germany.

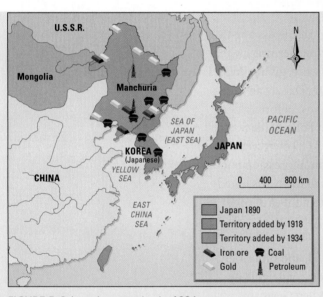

FIGURE 5–8 Japan's aggression by 1934

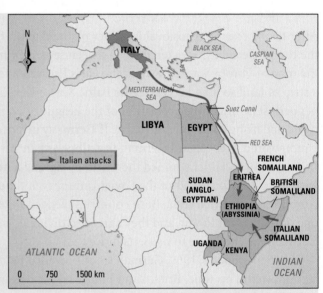

FIGURE 5–9 Route of Italians invading Ethiopia (Abyssinia), 1935

PRACTICE QUESTIONS

1. **Cause and Consequence** Use a graphic organizer to show the causes of the Second World War (similar to the one on page 82 in Chapter 3). Explain the effect and result for each cause of the war.

2. Explain why appeasement was used by Britain and France toward Germany.

3. Why was the non-aggression pact important to both Germany and the U.S.S.R.?

4. Why was the League of Nations unable to stop the aggression of Japan and Italy? How did this failure encourage Hitler?

©P

Canada's Response to the Threat of War

As events escalated in Europe, with Hitler's aggressive policies and the civil war in Spain, many Canadians asked why lives should be risked in another European war when Canada itself was not threatened.

Canada's Policy of Isolationism

Throughout the events of the 1930s, Canada practised **isolationism**, keeping out of affairs outside its borders. Prime Minister William Lyon Mackenzie King did not want Canada to become involved in another world conflict and had hoped that Britain's policy of appeasement toward Hitler would be successful. The First World War had deeply divided Canada on the issue of conscription, and Canadians had made many sacrifices in that overseas conflict. King knew that if he imposed conscription in this war, he and the Liberal Party would lose support in Québec. Besides, Canada was just starting to come out of the dark years of the Depression. The economy was slowly improving and King did not want the country plunged back into debt.

Canada's Response to Jewish Refugees

While King knew that the Nazis were tyrannizing people, he maintained Canada's isolationist policy. Like King, many Canadians believed that what was happening in Germany was a domestic issue that should not affect them. This attitude influenced Canada's immigration policies and attitudes toward Jewish **refugees** fleeing persecution in Europe.

KEY TERMS

isolationism the policy of remaining apart from the affairs of other countries

refugee a person displaced from his of her home and territory by war and other acts of aggression

> [N]othing is to be gained by creating an internal problem in an effort to meet an international one.... We... must seek to keep this part of the Continent free from unrest.
>
> –*Diary of Mackenzie King, Tuesday, March 29, 1938*

WEB LINK • • • • • • • • • •
Read more from King's diary on the Pearson Web site.

FIGURE 5–10 After meeting Hitler in Germany, Mackenzie King (centre) wrote the following in his diary on June 29, 1937: "[Hitler] smiled very pleasantly and indeed had a sort of appealing and affectionate look in his eyes. My sizing up of the man as I sat and talked with him was that he is really one who truly loves his fellow-men...."

Anti-Semitism in Canada

Some Canadians supported the dictators who had seized power in Europe or approved of Hitler's policies and hatred of Jewish people. In Québec, some nationalists called for an independent Québec with a pure French-Canadian population. **Anti-Semitism** in Canada during the 1930s was not restricted to extremists. It was shared by many in mainstream society, and was reflected in newspapers and in general conversation.

Anti-Semitism and isolationism influenced Canada's immigration policies in the 1930s. After *Kristallnacht* in November 1938, Liberal Cabinet Minister Thomas Crerar recommended that 10 000 Jewish people be allowed to immigrate to Canada, but the Cabinet refused his suggestion.

Jewish refugees were seen as a burden on the state. As you read in Chapter 4, due to rising unemployment, Canada was reluctant to accept immigrants other than those from Britain or the United States who could support themselves. The government restricted immigration in the 1930s. As a result, the number of immigrants to Canada fell from 166 783 in 1928 to 14 382 in 1933. The number of **deportations** also increased to nearly 30 000 by 1936.

The SS St. Louis

Canada's immigration policy and refusal to accept Jewish refugees had tragic consequences in 1939. The S.S. *St. Louis* left Hamburg, Germany, in May with 907 Jewish passengers desperately trying to escape persecution. The *St. Louis* was denied entry in Cuba, South America, and the United States. Canada was the passengers' last hope. The Canadian government refused to let the *St. Louis* dock in any port because the passengers did not qualify for entry as immigrants. The ship was forced to return to Europe. Tragically, many of the people aboard later died in concentration camps during the Holocaust.

FIGURE 5–11 Passengers aboard the S.S. *St. Louis* looked to the Canadian government to accept them as refugees.

Using Evidence At what stage of the journey was this photograph probably taken? Explain.

©P

Canadians Speak Out

Many Canadians did not share the government's anti-Semitic views. Cairine Wilson, Canada's first female Senator and chair of the Canadian National Committee on Refugees, spoke out against the banning of Jewish refugees from Canada. Prime Minister Mackenzie King was urged to offer the Jewish refugees sanctuary. In 1938, there were more than 150 000 Jewish people living in Canada. Rallies were held in many parts of the country in support of a more humane immigration policy. When the S.S. *St. Louis* was turned away and its passengers sent back to Nazi Germany, newspaper editorials also lashed out at the government:

> This country still has the bars up and the refugee who gets into Canada has to pass some mighty stiff obstacles—deliberately placed there by the government.... Immigration bars... are undesirable.... We are deliberately keeping out of this country [people] and money who would greatly add to our productive revenues. We are cutting off our nose to spite our face.
>
> –Winnipeg Free Press, *July 19, 1939*

Despite these objections, Canada still admitted only about 5000 Jewish refugees between 1933 and 1945.

● How did the war raise awareness of human rights issues?

FIGURE 5–12 This sign in Québec reflects the anti-Semitism found in many parts of Canada during this time. Discrimination took many forms, including restricting admittance to certain faculties at universities and membership in clubs.

FASTFORWARD

Changing Attitudes

The Canadian Charter of Rights and Freedoms, enacted in 1982, guarantees that every Canadian has the right to live "without discrimination based on race, national or ethnic origin, colour, religion, sex, age, or mental or physical disability." Due in large part to the Charter, discrimination of any form is unacceptable in Canada today. You will read more about the Charter in Chapter 10.

PRACTICE QUESTIONS

1. Why were many Canadians isolationist in the 1930s?

2. What reasons were given for Canada's admitting so few Jewish refugees fleeing persecution in Europe? Do you think that official reasons were the real reasons? Explain.

3. How do you think Prime Minister Mackenzie King could form such a misguided opinion of Adolf Hitler?

4. Why were the Jewish refugees so desperate to leave Germany? Provide specific information from this chapter.

5. Why do you think discrimination like this was considered acceptable by many people in the 1930s and is not acceptable today?

6. **Judgements** To what extent should Canadians be responsible for trying to stop human rights abuses in other countries?

©P

● How did Canada get involved in the Second World War?

KEY TERM

British Commonwealth Air Training Plan (BCATP) a program to train pilots and aircrew during the Second World War; it produced half of all Commonwealth aircrew and is the largest air training program in history

Canada Declares War

On September 1, 1939, Germany invaded Poland. Two days later, Britain and France declared war on Germany. In the First World War, when Britain declared war on Germany, Canada was automatically at war. But, in 1939, Canada was an autonomous country with no such obligation. Prime Minister Mackenzie King knew that once Britain became involved in such a major conflict, Canada would almost certainly support it, but the decision to join the war had to be a Canadian one, decided by Canada's Parliament.

Parliament Votes for War

On September 8, King called a special session of Parliament to decide whether Canada would join the war. He gave a strong speech in favour of declaring war. His Minister of Justice, Ernest Lapointe from Québec, also spoke in favour of the war. But Lapointe spoke bluntly about what conscription would do to Liberal supporters in Québec: "I am authorized by my colleagues in the Cabinet from Québec, to say that we will never agree to conscription and will never be members or supporters of a government that will try to enforce it." This statement helped win support for the war in Québec and convinced voters that Canada's involvement in the war was necessary. Conscious of how conscription had divided the country during the First World War, King assured Parliament, and Québec, that "So long as this government may be in power, no such measure [conscription] shall be enacted."

King's position on joining the war was supported by the opposition Conservative Party. Only J.S. Woodsworth, leader of the Co-operative Commonwealth Federation (CCF), argued against going to war. He believed that nothing could be settled by war and tried to convince the government that Canada should remain neutral. But Woodsworth did not find support for his pacifist position, and Parliament voted in favour of going to war. On September 10, 1939, Canada declared war on Germany.

FIGURE 5–13 Troops departing from Winnipeg

Using Evidence Carefully examine this photograph. How do you think most Canadians felt about going to war? Consider the feelings of those who were staying home as well as those who were going to fight.

©P

Mobilizing Canada's Resources

● What was the war's impact on the home front?

Despite its willingness to join the war, Canada was not prepared for it. Its armed forces were small and unfit for combat. The Canadian army had only 4300 troops, a few light tanks, and no modern artillery. The air force and the navy were small with outdated equipment.

Unlike the First World War, there were no crowds cheering on the streets when Canada declared war in 1939. Many Canadians vividly remembered the horrors of the last world conflict. Still, Canada had no trouble finding volunteers. In September 1939, more than 58 000 people volunteered for service. The Canadian army initially rejected African-Canadian volunteers because of racist attitudes. As the war continued, however, African Canadians were encouraged to join the regular army and the officer corps. As in the First World War, Aboriginal peoples volunteered at a higher percentage of their population than any other group in Canada. Among them was Thomas Prince, a Brokenhead Ojibway from Manitoba. Prince became a sergeant and served in Italy and France as part of an elite unit. One of Canada's most decorated soldiers, he received ten medals, including the Military Medal for bravery given to him by King George VI.

Many people still felt strong ties to Britain and volunteered from a sense of duty. Others were driven by a sense of new-found national pride. After years of economic hardship, some Canadians were attracted by the lure of a steady income. The first Canadian troops sailed from Halifax on December 10, 1939.

FIGURE 5–14 This Vancouver Board of Trade poster encouraged forest workers to contribute to the war effort.

The British Commonwealth Air Training Plan

Mackenzie King hoped that Canada's contribution to the war effort would be mostly supplies and training, rather than troops, so that he could avoid the issue of conscription. In December 1939, Canada agreed to host and run the **British Commonwealth Air Training Plan (BCATP)**. Pilots and other flight personnel from all over the Commonwealth came to Canada to train with British instructors. Airfields were built on the Prairies and in other locations near small towns and villages. Old aircraft were refitted and returned to service for training purposes. The program was a major Canadian contribution to the war effort. The BCATP trained more than 130 000 pilots, navigators, flight engineers, and ground crew. The total cost was more than $2.2 billion, of which Canada paid more than 70 percent. Contrary to King's hopes, however, Canada's role in the war went far beyond its involvement in the BCATP.

FIGURE 5–15 A propaganda poster commissioned by the **Wartime Information Board**

Analyzing Images What three sectors of the workforce are represented here? How would this poster encourage the policy of total war?

Total War

The demands of **total war** meant that the federal government became more involved in planning and controlling the economy. In April 1940, the Department of Munitions and Supply was created and industrialist C.D. Howe was put in charge. Howe, whom you will learn more about in Chapter 6, was given extraordinary authority to do whatever it took to gear up the economy to meet wartime demands. He told industries what to produce and how to produce it. He convinced business leaders to manufacture goods they had never made before. Soon, Vancouver was building ships for the navy, Montréal was constructing new planes and bombers, such as the Lancaster, and Canada's car industries were producing military vehicles and tanks. Munitions factories opened in Ontario and Québec. If the private sector could not produce what Howe wanted, he created **Crown corporations** to do the job. Even farmers were told to produce more wheat, beef, dairy products, and other foods. Under Howe's leadership, the government ran telephone companies, refined fuel, stockpiled silk for parachutes, mined uranium, and controlled food production. Some called him the "Minister of Everything."

FIGURE 5–16 *Maintenance Jobs in the Hangar* by Paraskeva Clark (1898–1986)

Analyzing Images Paraskeva Clark was a feminist whose painting conveyed a strong social message. How do this painting and the poster above it illustrate Canada's commitment to total war? What social message do they convey? How do you think more traditional artists and critics might have reacted to this type of painting in the 1940s?

PRACTICE QUESTIONS

1. What assurance did Mackenzie King give Canadians during the debate on Canada's involvement in the war? Why did he do this?

2. What was the British Commonwealth Air Training Plan? Why was Canada chosen to host it? Why did King support the plan?

3. Compare Canadians' reaction to the announcement of the First World War with that of the Second World War. Why did many people still volunteer?

4. How did Canada's policy of total war change the economy? Why was the policy necessary?

©P

Axis Advances

With the declaration of war in September 1939, the **Allies** (Britain, France, and Commonwealth countries including Canada, Australia, and New Zealand) raced to get their forces organized. The alliance of Germany, Italy (1939), and Japan (1940) became known as the **Axis**. Allied troops were quickly stationed along France's border with Germany, where they waited for Germany's next move. But for seven months, from October 1939 to April 1940, nothing happened. This period became known as the "phony war," and many people started to believe there might not be a war.

These illusions were shattered when Germany renewed its *blitzkrieg* ("lightning war"), attacking Denmark and Norway in April 1940. The *blitzkrieg* was an extremely successful war tactic that used surprise, speed, and massive power to quickly overwhelm the enemy. War planes would often lead the attack, knocking out key enemy positions and supply lines. With lightning speed, German panzers (tanks) would crash through enemy lines, driving forward as far as they could. Soldiers would also parachute into enemy territory, destroying vital communication and transportation links. The attacks left the defending army confused and, eventually, surrounded.

Using these tactics, Germany quickly conquered Denmark and Norway. Germany then attacked the Netherlands, Luxembourg, and Belgium. Within weeks, all three countries were overrun. Hitler then set his sights on France.

Evacuation at Dunkirk

Within days of launching an attack on France through Belgium, German panzers reached the English Channel and surrounded Allied forces in the French port of **Dunkirk**. If the Allied troops surrendered, Britain would lose the bulk of its army. They had to escape before the Germans captured the town. In an act of desperation, the British navy rounded up every boat capable of navigating the English Channel. Hundreds of fishing boats, pleasure crafts, and ferries joined navy and merchant ships as they headed across the Channel for Dunkirk. The evacuation began on May 26. Two days later, the German **Luftwaffe** bombed the port of Dunkirk. The evacuation was finally completed on June 4, 1940.

It was a dramatic rescue. Nearly 340 000 Allied soldiers, thousands more than originally anticipated, were brought to safety in Britain. This could have been a disastrous loss for the Allies. Instead, the evacuation of Dunkirk was seen as a "miracle" and helped boost morale.

After the evacuation at Dunkirk, the German army continued to sweep through France. The French army proved to be no match for the German troops, and on June 22, 1940, France surrendered. Britain and the Commonwealth now stood alone against Germany.

KEY TERMS

Wartime Information Board board established in 1942 to coordinate wartime propaganda in Canada

total war the mobilization of the entire resources of a nation for war

Crown corporations businesses and industries owned by the Canadian government

Allies countries fighting against Germany during the Second World War, including Britain, France, Canada, Australia, New Zealand, and after 1941, the United States and the U.S.S.R.

Axis alliance between Germany, Italy, and Japan

blitzkrieg German war tactic of surprise attacks by tanks and fighter planes

Dunkirk port town in France from which a massive Allied evacuation took place in May 1940, when German forces conquered France

Luftwaffe the German air force

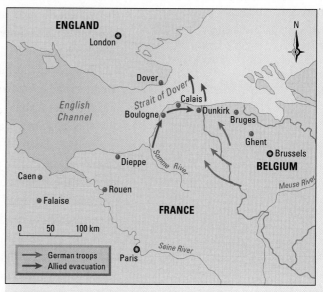

FIGURE 5–17 The Allied evacuation at Dunkirk

KEY TERMS

the Blitz the heavy, frequent bombing attacks on London and other British cities by Nazi Germany

Battle of Britain an air campaign launched
in 1940 by the Royal Air Force to stop the Germans from achieving air superiority

Operation Barbarossa Germany's unsuccessful invasion of the Soviet Union in 1941–1942, which broke the non-aggression pact and ultimately led to the Soviet Union joining the Allies

FIGURE 5–18 For almost two months, the German Luftwaffe bombed London day and night.

Developing Understanding What is the likely target in this photograph? Where could people find protection from such attacks?

Battle of Britain

Once France fell, Hitler launched "Operation Sea Lion," his plan to invade Britain. For this scheme to succeed, the Royal Air Force (RAF) had to be defeated so that German forces could cross the English Channel and land in Britain. In July 1940, the Luftwaffe started a massive bombing campaign, aimed at destroying harbours and shipping facilities in southern England. In August, the Germans targeted airfields and aircraft factories. On August 24, German planes bombed several areas of London (some historians believe that this was accidental, while others claim it was a deliberate attack). In retaliation, the RAF bombed the German city of Berlin. This attack enraged Hitler. He ordered the Luftwaffe to bomb London and other British cities. These raids, which become known as "**the Blitz**," took place over many weeks, destroying buildings and terrifying and killing civilians.

Although the Germans had more aircraft than the British, they were unable to defeat the RAF. One reason was that the British had a very advanced radar system that warned them of German air raids. The British also used Spitfires and Hurricanes, two extremely effective fighter planes. In addition, the RAF was reinforced with pilots, planes, and supplies from Canada and other Commonwealth countries. In September 1940, as the RAF shot down more and more German bombers, Hitler finally gave up on his plans to invade Britain. During the **Battle of Britain**, more than 23 000 people, mostly civilians, were killed.

North-African Campaign

Once Hitler was certain of victory in France, and days before the German Luftwaffe attack on Britain, Axis forces began what would become a three-year campaign in the deserts of North Africa. This campaign, known as the Desert War, was a struggle for the control of valuable resources and strategic positions.

As you read earlier, Italy wanted to increase its territories in Africa. Its first move had been to invade Abyssinia in 1935. Once Italy formally entered the war on the side of the Axis in June 1940, British cavalry and tank regiments immediately invaded Libya (an Italian colony). Italy, in turn, invaded Egypt with its sights on the Suez Canal, a major strategic point.

To have any hope of victory, the Axis had to dominate the Mediterranean by controlling its two access points: the Strait of Gibraltar and the Suez Canal (see map on page 135). Holding these waterways would give the Axis armies access to the oil-rich Middle East.

By December 1940, the British Commonwealth forces had all but destroyed the Italian army. German forces were dispatched to the area to support the Italians and to prevent an Allied victory in North Africa. Germany had hoped their Italian allies would quickly overrun Allied forces in the region. Instead, it now found its forces engaged on a second front.

Over the next three years, neither side won decisive victories. The tide turned in 1942 with a final Allied victory in North Africa in May 1943. The Allied forces could now focus on their next objective: the invasion of Sicily and the liberation of Italy, which you will read about later in this chapter.

Operation Barbarossa

After Germany's defeat in the Battle of Britain, Hitler launched "**Operation Barbarossa**" ("red beard") on June 22, 1941. This massive attack on the Soviet Union broke the non-aggression pact that Hitler had signed with Stalin in 1939. Hitler saw the Soviet Union as a source of raw materials, agricultural land, and labour for the German army, and conquering the Soviet Union was part of his long-term plans for a new German Empire.

The Soviets were unprepared for the attack, enabling the German army to strike deep into Russian territory. By autumn, they had reached the outskirts of Moscow and Leningrad (now St. Petersburg). But the Germans were ill-equipped for the long and bitterly cold Soviet winter and soon lost their advantage. In 1942, Germany launched another offensive in the Soviet Union, this time focused on the rich oil fields in the south. The German troops got as far as Stalingrad, but were stopped once again by the severe winter. The Germans could not turn back. Nor could they hope for reinforcements, since the Axis powers were also engaged in North Africa. After suffering more than 300 000 casualties, the German army surrendered in early 1943.

After the German surrender, the Soviet army went on the offensive, retaking much of the territory it had lost. Hitler's aggression also assured that the Soviets joined the war on the Allies' side.

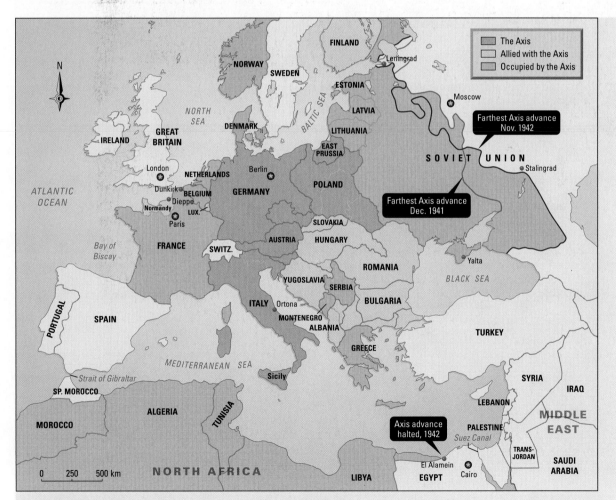

FIGURE 5–19 Extent of Axis control in Europe and North Africa, 1942

Reading a Map Use this map and the text in this section to understand the scope of Axis control in Europe and North Africa.

KEY TERMS

Pearl Harbor the Japanese bombing of the U.S. naval base in Hawaii

Battle of Hong Kong Japan's attack on the British colony of Hong Kong in which there were heavy Canadian losses

Black Christmas December 25, 1941, the date Hong Kong fell to the Japanese

The War in the Pacific

As you read earlier, Japan began a campaign to expand its territory in the 1930s. By 1941, it was prepared to invade American and European colonies in Southeast Asia to gain control of valuable resources such as oil, rubber, and tin. Japan knew such action would almost certainly involve the United States, which had thus far remained neutral in the war.

Japanese strategy depended on a quick and decisive strike against the United States. In a surprise attack on December 7, 1941, Japanese planes bombed the U.S. naval base in **Pearl Harbor**, on the island of Hawaii. More than 2400 people were killed and much of the American fleet was destroyed. Japan then bombed the U.S. territory of the Philippines. The surprise bombings stunned the Americans. On December 8, the U.S. joined the Allies and declared war on Japan. Japan's allies—Germany and Italy—then declared war on the United States. The whole world was now at war.

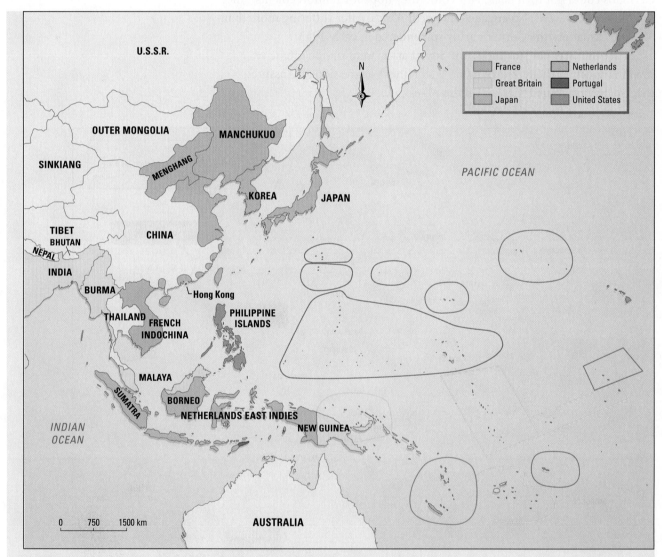

FIGURE 5–20 Control of the Pacific area in 1939

©P

Battle of Hong Kong

Only hours after bombing Pearl Harbor, Japan attacked Hong Kong, a British colony. Weeks earlier, Canada had sent two battalions, from Winnipeg and Québec, to reinforce the British and Commonwealth forces in Hong Kong. The Canadians were inexperienced and the 20 000 Allied soldiers were no match for the skilled Japanese soldiers. After 18 days of bitter fighting, Hong Kong fell to the Japanese on what would be known as "**Black Christmas**," December 25, 1941. Every Canadian was either killed or taken prisoner.

Nearly 1700 Canadian prisoners of war (POWs) faced brutal conditions and were later used as slave labour. More than 260 of these POWs died during three and a half years of imprisonment. Canadians at home were horrified to learn the fate of the soldiers and angry that troops had been sent to Hong Kong. The Japanese treatment of Allied troops may have encouraged the anti-Japanese sentiment that culminated in the internment of Japanese Canadians. You will read about this later in the chapter.

● Describe Canada's military role in the Second World War.

FIGURE 5–21 A recruitment poster issued after Canadian forces were defeated at Hong Kong

Expressing Ideas What is this poster's message?

PRACTICE QUESTIONS

1. Explain why German forces needed to invade Britain if they were to hold Western Europe. What efforts did they make to do this?

2. How did Canada contribute to the Allied victory in the Battle of Britain?

3. What strategic benefit was there to controlling the Mediterranean? Why would the Axis have needed to control this area?

4. Do you think it was an error on Germany's part to invade the U.S.S.R.? Explain.

5. Using the information about each of the major battles in this section, explain the strategic advantages of the Axis forces as well as how these eventually led to the major turning point that occurred in Stalingrad.

6. Why did the Japanese attack the U.S. navy at Pearl Harbor? How did this attack change the course of the war?

7. Why would Canada send troops to Hong Kong? Why were Canadians angry when they learned the fate of troops in Hong Kong?

● Describe Canada's military role in the Second World War.

The Battle of the Atlantic was the dominating factor all through the war. Never for one moment could we forget that everything happening else-where—on land, at sea or in the air—depended ultimately on its outcome, and amid all other cares we viewed its changing fortunes day by day with hope or apprehension.

—*Winston Churchill*

Canada's Contribution to the War Effort

Canadians contributed to the war effort on all fronts. Over the course of the war, Canada expanded its navy and air force to help reinforce the Allies.

Battle of the Atlantic

When war broke out, the Royal Canadian Navy (RCN) had only 13 ships and 1819 sailors. Desperately short of equipment and personnel, Canada embarked on a massive building and training program so that by the end of the war, the RCN had grown to 400 vessels and more than 100 000 sailors. By 1941, the **Battle of the Atlantic** was in full swing and Canada's contribution was much needed. As in the First World War, Britain was almost completely dependent on food and military supplies from Canada and the United States. But the Allied supply ships bound for England were being attacked by "wolf packs" of German U-boats patrolling the Atlantic. Germany was trying to starve Britain by cutting off vital shipping routes.

The Allies Gain Momentum

For the first three years of the war, it seemed that the Allies would lose the Battle of the Atlantic. German submarines pounded convoys, sinking hundreds of ships. Some German submarines even sailed into the Gulf of St. Lawrence and up the St. Lawrence River to attack ships there. Gradually, the situation started to turn around. The British had cracked the German naval code, allowing the Allies to track German submarine movements more easily. As well, the Allies were building more ships than were being destroyed.

Canada's War at Sea

Canada also helped turn the tide. The RCN is credited with providing about half the escorts across the Atlantic. Better training of Canadian navy personnel and more sophisticated equipment contributed to the Allies' success. The Women's Royal Canadian Naval Service was created in 1942. Most "WRENs" were limited to shore-based jobs, and worked as wireless operators, coders, drivers, and operational plotters.

To protect supply ships from German torpedoes, the Allies sailed in convoys so warships could help to protect vessels carrying vital supplies. But even convoys did not stop the attacks. German U-boats destroyed hundreds of supply ships, sinking millions of tonnes of cargo. In response, Canada started building small warships, called **corvettes**, to escort convoys across the ocean. The corvette was quick and manoeuvred well, but it was not a very stable vessel. Nevertheless, the corvette was the best ship that could be built in such a short time. The corvettes were helped by long-range Liberator bombers, which could fly from bases in Britain and Canada to protect much of the convoy's route. By May 1943, the Allies believed they had won the Battle of the Atlantic.

FIGURE 5–22 This convoy, assembled in Bedford Basin, Nova Scotia, was transporting war supplies to Europe.

Thinking Critically Identify the smaller ships in the photograph. What might be the nature and function of these vessels?

©P

War in the Air

Like the RCN, the Royal Canadian Air Force (RCAF) grew quickly once the war began. More than 215 000 people enlisted in the RCAF and, at one point, 35 Canadian squadrons were posted overseas. Canadian aircrews participated in bombing raids in North Africa, Italy, Northwest Europe, and Southeast Asia.

The Women's Division (WD) of the RCAF was created in 1941. Women trained as clerks, cooks, hospital assistants, drivers, telephone operators, welders, instrument mechanics, and engine mechanics. The RCAF refused to let licensed female pilots fly until later in the war. Women ferried bombers to Britain, but they never took part in combat.

Bomber Command

The RCAF also participated in one of the most controversial missions of the war: night bombings over Germany. As part of Britain's **Bomber Command**, Canada's Bomber Group pounded German cities, including Dresden and Cologne, night after night. These cities were targeted for a number of reasons: to retaliate for the German air raids on English cities, to diminish German morale, and to destabilize German industrial centres. Tens of thousands of civilians were killed by these air raids. One of the worst attacks was on the city of Hamburg in July 1943. Relentless bombing by the Allies created a firestorm and the city was engulfed in flames. The city was practically destroyed and more than 40 000 civilians were killed.

The casualty rate for the RCAF aircrew was as high as seven out of ten. Nearly 10 000 Canadian Bomber Group members lost their lives during the war.

KEY TERMS

Battle of the Atlantic the struggle between the Allies and the Axis powers to control the Allies' shipping route across the Atlantic Ocean

corvettes small, fast, warships built in Canada to help protect convoys in the Atlantic Ocean

Bomber Command the section of the RAF that directed the strategic bombing of Germany

FIGURE 5–23 Bombing raids on German cities, like Hamburg, killed thousands of civilians.

Making Generalizations What would you say was the effect of bombing raids on Germany, based on this photograph?

PRACTICE QUESTIONS

1. How did Canadian sea and air forces change over the course of the war?

2. Explain why the corvette and the convoy system were so important to the Allied war effort.

3. What did Winston Churchill mean when he said everything in the war depended on the outcome of the Battle of the Atlantic?

4. Describe the contributions of women in the navy and air force.

5. Why do you think the casualty rate for the RCAF was so high?

6. Is the bombing of civilian targets ever justified? Explain your position.

Advances in War Technology

Technology played an important role in the Second World War and in many ways determined its outcome. Major technological advances were made in weaponry, communications, intelligence, and medicine.

Peril of the seas Both the Allies and the Axis powers used submarines, which were much more efficient than in the First World War. The Germans invented a snorkel that made it possible for U-boats to recharge batteries underwater, reducing the time on the surface, where it was vulnerable to attack.

A new type of terror weapon The German V-2 rocket had a range of 350 kilometres. V-2s were used with deadly effect against London in the closing days of the war. Wernher von Braun, the designer of the V-2, moved to the United States after the war. After becoming a U.S. citizen, he designed the *Gemini* and *Apollo* rockets that eventually led to the U.S. moon landing in 1969.

Finding the enemy Radar (radio detection and ranging) is an electronic system that uses radio waves to detect objects beyond the range of vision. It gives information about the distance, position, size, shape, direction, and speed of approaching aircraft. Radar was a deciding factor in the Battle of Britain.

The deadliest weapon The United States developed the atomic bomb, which permanently changed warfare. In this weapon, a sphere of concentrated radioactive material about the size of a baseball could easily destroy a city.

©P

Technology in the air The first jet-propelled airplanes were used in the Second World War. Because jets could fly higher and faster than propeller-driven planes, both the Axis powers and the Allies worked around the clock to produce as many jets as they could. However, jets were not perfected until after 1945. Not enough were produced to affect the outcome of the war.

Treating the wounded Great advances were made in medical technology as doctors tried to repair the hideous wounds of war. Penicillin, an antibiotic, was first isolated in 1929 by British scientist Alexander Fleming and was used to treat infections in humans in 1941. Recovery rates for wounded soldiers increased significantly due to penicillin. Below, a Canadian doctor treats a German soldier in 1944.

Secret codes The Germans developed a coding machine, known as "Enigma," which converted radio messages into code. This machine spurred the development of an early computer that could decode German signals.

©P

KEY TERM

Dieppe Raid the 1942 trial raid by Canadian troops against Germany's occupation of Dieppe; Canada suffered heavy losses

*We were sacrificial lambs...
They were there waiting for
us—they knew it was just a
matter of time. In fact, one
German at Dieppe actually
asked us: "What took you so
long?"*

—*Thomas Hunter*

The Tide Turns

In 1942, the tide of the war finally began to turn. The Allied forces became stronger when the United States entered the conflict in December 1941. With the Americans' help, the Allies started to gain ground in North Africa. They were more and more successful against U-boats in the Atlantic and made important advances in the Pacific.

The Dieppe Raid

By the middle of 1942, the Soviet Union, now one of the Allied powers, had lost close to a million soldiers in its desperate fight against invading German troops. Stalin demanded that the Allies invade Europe from the west to weaken Germany by forcing it to fight the war on two fronts.

The Allies had hoped to postpone the full invasion of Europe, but they felt ready for a trial run. A smaller raid would allow them to test new techniques and equipment, and serve as a scouting mission for a future invasion. The 2nd Canadian Division was chosen to be the main attack force in a raid on the French port of Dieppe. The plan was to launch four pre-dawn attacks along the coast, followed by the main attack on Dieppe. Air force bombers and tanks brought in by ship would support the troops.

On the morning of August 19, 1942, one of the ships carrying Canadian soldiers to Dieppe met a small German convoy. The two sides engaged in a brief sea battle, and the noise alerted German troops on shore. To make matters worse, the ships were delayed and the troops landed in daylight. They were easily machine-gunned by waiting German soldiers. Allied tanks were ineffective because they could not get enough traction to move on the steep, pebbled beach. Communication between the ships and troops on land was poor. Believing the first wave of soldiers had reached the town, commanders sent reinforcements ashore. These troops, too, became trapped on the beaches. Unable to retreat or advance, they were easy targets for the German soldiers on the cliffs along the coastline.

FIGURE 5–24 Dead Canadian soldiers and tanks on Dieppe beach, August 19, 1942

Using Evidence Canadian troops were supported by tanks that arrived in transport ships, but most never advanced far from the shoreline. Find evidence in this photograph to suggest why tanks were useless in this attack.

TIMELINE	Major Canadian Battles, 1939–1945		
September 1939–May 1943 Battle of the Atlantic	**May 26–June 4, 1940** Battle of Dunkirk	**August–October, 1940** Battle of Britain	**December 7–25, 1941** Battle of Hong Kong

©P

Disaster or Learning Experience?

The Dieppe Raid was a terrible failure. Casualties were high. Of the nearly 5000 Canadian soldiers involved in the nine-hour battle, 907 were killed. Almost 600 were wounded and another 1946 were taken prisoner. Ross Munro, the Canadian war correspondent who accompanied the troops to Dieppe, described the raid and its devastating results:

FIGURE 5–25 Ross Munro, Second World War correspondent for the *Canadian Press*

> For eight hours, under intense Nazi fire from dawn into a sweltering afternoon, I watched Canadian troops fight the blazing, bloody battle of Dieppe. I saw them go through the biggest of the war's raiding operations in wild scenes that crowded helter skelter one upon another in crazy sequence. There was a furious attack by German E-boats while the Canadians moved in on Dieppe's beaches, landing by dawn's half-light. When the Canadian battalions stormed through the flashing inferno of Nazi defences, belching guns of huge tanks rolling into the fight, I spent the grimmest 20 minutes of my life with one unit when a rain of German machine-gun fire wounded half the men in our boat and only a miracle saved us from annihilation.
>
> *–Ross Munro,* The Windsor Daily Star, *1942*

Opinion is divided as to whether Dieppe was a valuable learning experience or a complete disaster. Some historians claim that the Allies were later able to launch a successful invasion based on what they had learned at Dieppe. Others maintain that the raid was poorly planned and taught the Germans more than it taught the Allies.

FASTFORWARD

CRITICAL INQUIRY Judgements

Reporting War

Today, news reports make it possible for us to see what is happening on a battlefield almost instantly. Many have argued, however, that what we see on the news is not always an accurate report of what is happening in a war zone. Several factors can influence what is reported on the news. For example, reporters "embedded" with combat units are often sympathetic to the young soldiers they live and work with. Back home, newspaper editors and television directors choose stories that will attract viewers so they can sell advertising. The government may also censor news reports to prevent security risks or to put their own slant on events. Some people argue that improved coverage of war is positive because it keeps us informed of what is happening in distant parts of the world. Others maintain that this coverage is negative because it hardens us to images of war so that we are no longer shocked by what we see.

1. Can a news broadcast ever completely avoid bias and show viewers the "truth"?

2. Should reporters tell us everything they see on the front lines?

August 19, 1942
Dieppe Raid

July 1943–February 1945
The Italian Campaign

June 6, 1944
D-Day

September–November, 1944
Battle of the Scheldt

February 8–March 10, 1945
Battle of the Rhineland

©P

KEY TERMS

Italian Campaign 1943 Allied battles to recapture Europe from the south, through Sicily and Italy

The Italian Campaign

After the failure at Dieppe, British Prime Minister Winston Churchill felt that the best way for the Allies to recapture Europe was through what he called the "soft underbelly" of Europe: Sicily and Italy. The Allied victory in North Africa made it possible for forces to launch their attack from the south. The invasion ended up lasting almost two years and cost thousands of lives. The "underbelly" proved anything but soft.

Battle of Sicily

On July 10, 1943, Allied forces invaded Sicily. Once again, the Canadians proved themselves to be fierce opponents. They fought Italian and German soldiers through 240 kilometres of mountainous terrain, losing 562 soldiers in the battle. The Allies captured the island after 38 days.

This victory quickly led to Mussolini's downfall. He was overthrown and the new Italian government surrendered. The Germans, however, continued to defend their Italian territory.

Battle of Ortona

The Allies followed the Germans as they retreated to mainland Italy. Canadians were given the task of capturing the medieval town of Ortona on the Adriatic Sea. Before they could reach the heavily fortified Ortona, the Canadians had to capture several smaller villages, cross the river Moro, and fight across several kilometres of German-occupied territory. The regiment describes the battle:

> *Throughout the night of December 8th–9th the RCR [Royal Canadian Regiment] maintained its position on the feature which came to be known... as "Slaughterhouse Hill." The fighting was most confused, the enemy appearing on several sides of the perimeter as well as within it... the incessant shellfire from both sides turned the night into pandemonium.*
>
> **–A Regiment at War,** ***1979***

Once they reached Ortona, advances were slow and battles were often fought house by house on the town's steep, rubble-filled streets. Canadians captured the town on December 28, 1943, but lost 1372 soldiers before the Germans withdrew. After capturing Ortona, Canadian troops advanced through Italy until they were sent to join the campaign in France. Nearly 6000 Canadians were killed in Italy.

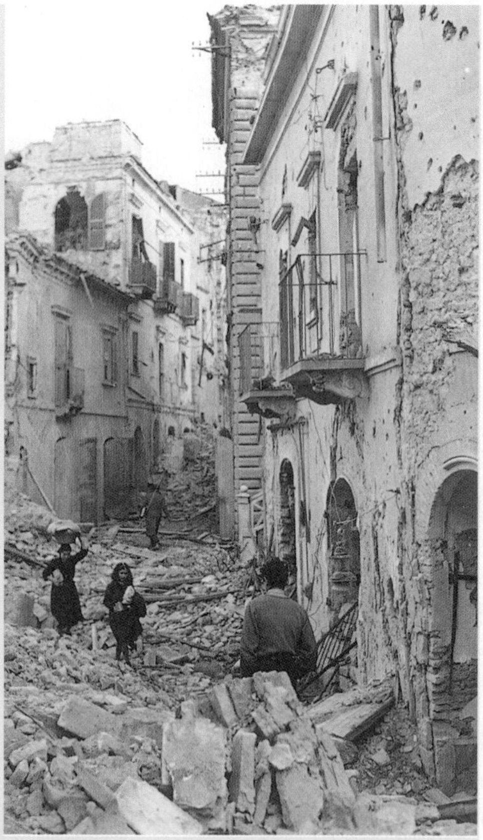

FIGURE 5–26 Ortona after the Canadian advance

PRACTICE QUESTIONS

1. Why was the Dieppe Raid unsuccessful? Do you think it was a disaster or a learning experience? Support your opinion.
2. Explain why the Italian Campaign was strategically important to the Allies.
3. In your own words, describe the Battle of Ortona.

©P

Historical maps are useful documents that give specific information. They are a visual way of conveying facts as well as concepts. As with other historical documents, the information included in these types of maps is selective, so you must examine them carefully.

Steps to Reading a Map

1. Look at the title and legend of the map below. These should tell you the historical period of the map, its main purpose, and the other kinds of information that the map is meant to convey.

2. Examine the names (or symbols) closely. Look for patterns in the information. Why, for example, are some names bigger or bolder than others? Certain colours may be used to illustrate similarities in or differences between regions.

3. Now read the map by analyzing the information. Ask yourself: What is this map about? How is the information being communicated? What conclusions can be drawn from this map?

Applying the Skill

As you read about the events that occurred in Europe between 1942 and 1945, refer to Figure 5–27. Go through the three steps in reading a historical map, and answer the questions below.

1. What is the map about? What are the six pieces of information given in the legend?

2. The cartographer (map-maker) has shown a limited number of cities. How would you explain the choice of Dunkirk, Stalingrad, and Palermo?

3. What ideas does this map convey about

   a) the importance of the success of the North African campaign to the Allies?

   b) the role of the U.S.S.R. in defeating Germany?

   c) the importance of supremacy in naval forces for the Allies?

   d) the importance of an effective air force?

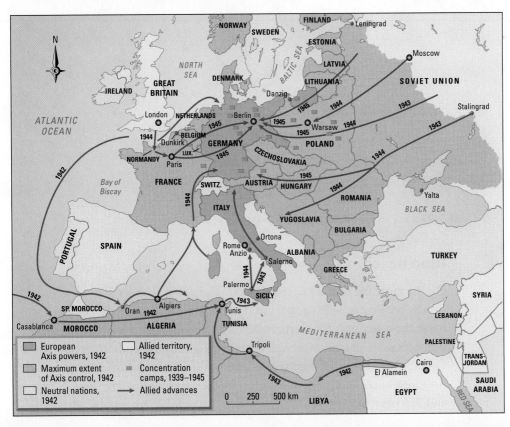

FIGURE 5–27 Allied advances on Germany, 1942–1945

D-Day: The Normandy Invasion

The Allies immediately followed their success in Italy with the biggest Allied invasion of the war. On **D-Day**, June 6, 1944, the Allies launched a full-scale invasion of Europe called "Operation Overlord." To avoid a disaster like Dieppe, the Allies planned and rehearsed the invasion down to the smallest detail.

The Allies launched their attack by landing their troops on five beaches along an 80-kilometre stretch of the Normandy coast in northern France. The beaches were code-named Sword, Juno, Gold, Omaha, and Utah. The soldiers on the beaches had massive air and naval support. The Allies were able to disrupt transportation and communication lines before the attack by dropping **paratroopers** behind enemy lines and bombing targets on the beaches. Their naval support also allowed the Allies to bring in more than a million troops, along with military vehicles and supplies, after the initial landing.

The D-Day invasions were also successful because the Allies had managed to keep the details of the attack a secret from the Germans. Although the Germans had anticipated an attack, they thought it would come from the north. The weather also helped the Allies. A storm delayed the initial attack and the Germans believed that the Allies would not attempt a landing in bad weather. As a result, the German defence was poorly coordinated.

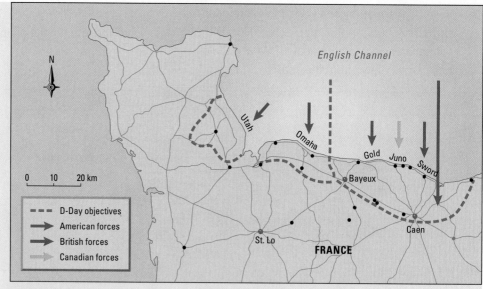

FIGURE 5–28 Allied invasion of Normandy on D-Day, June 6, 1944

Juno Beach

On the morning of June 6, 1944, 14 000 Canadian soldiers arrived at Juno Beach (see Figure 5–28) as part of the first wave of the attack. They had to make their way past the German defences, including concrete barriers, barbed wire, and land mines, to take the beach. By the end of the day, the Canadians had fought their way inland by about nine kilometres. Although they were successful, casualties from the day were high—359 Canadians died and 715 were wounded.

Battle of the Scheldt

It took the Allies weeks of constant fighting to expand their territory before they could begin an advance through France and Belgium toward Germany. The 11-month campaign was exhausting and there were several moving moments in which the Allies were welcomed as the liberators of Europe. In September 1944, for example, Canadians marched triumphantly through Dieppe where only two years earlier they had suffered a terrible defeat.

In October, Canadians were given the task of clearing enemy troops from the Scheldt River in Belgium. This river was important because it connected Antwerp to the North Sea. Although the Allies had already liberated Antwerp, German forces controlled the river and access to the sea. The Canadians achieved their goal after a month of bitter fighting, allowing the Allies to bring in supplies for their final advance into Germany.

Battle of the Rhineland

On February 8, 1945, the Allies—including approximately 175 000 Canadians—began their attack to drive the Germans back over the Rhine River and out of the Netherlands. The fighting was slow as soldiers struggled through mud and flooded fields against fierce German resistance. Nearly 23 000 Allied soldiers were killed, including more than 5300 Canadians. The Germans lost about 90 000 men, including 52 000 who were taken prisoner. On March 10, the German army withdrew to the east bank of the Rhine River, allowing the Canadians to continue north to liberate Holland.

Liberating the Netherlands

Once the Allied forces had reached the Rhine River and Germany, the Canadians were given a separate task: liberating the Netherlands. This was a difficult job. An earlier Allied attempt to free Holland had failed and German troops had practically destroyed the port cities of Amsterdam and Rotterdam and flooded much of the countryside. By the end of 1944, food and fuel supplies to the Dutch had been cut off and many were starving to death. The bitter winter of 1944–1945 made difficult conditions even worse.

KEY TERMS

D-Day June 6, 1944; the day Allied armies, including Canada, invaded France; the biggest Allied invasion of the Second World War

paratroopers soldiers trained to parachute from airplanes onto combat areas

Juno Beach the nine-kilometre stretch of beach in France where Canadian troops landed on D-Day

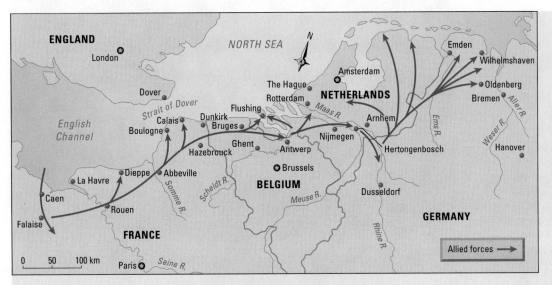

FIGURE 5–29 Allied liberation of France, Belgium, and the Netherlands, and invasion of Germany

Reading a Map Use the text and the map to determine what route the Canadians used in their attack in the Netherlands.

Lasting Gratitude

After reaching the Rhine, it took another month of fighting to drive the Germans out of the Netherlands. On April 28, 1945, the Allies negotiated a truce with Germany, allowing them to bring much needed supplies to the Dutch people. Convoys of trucks carrying food and fuel eventually delivered thousands of tonnes of supplies to civilians.

As they liberated towns and cities throughout the Netherlands, Canadians were hailed as heroes in victory parades. Percy Loosemore, who travelled with Canadian soldiers, wrote:

FIGURE 5–30 Celebrating the liberation of Utrecht, in the Netherlands, by the Canadian Army, May 7, 1945

Analyzing Evidence Use the quotation and image to understand why Canadian troops were hailed as heroes in Holland.

> *When we entered Holland from Belgium, the Dutch people seemed overwhelmed with joy at their deliverance and the end of the war; for while the Belgians had been liberated for some time, the Dutch were celebrating both the end of the war in Europe and their own immediate liberation. Bunting hung everywhere; people cheered as we drove by... Once, when I stopped my car, children gathered around and proceeded to decorate our vehicle with flowers and coloured streamers. To witness the enthusiastic joy and happy faces of these people was a [great] pleasure to me... I was deeply moved.*
>
> *–Quoted in* A Soldier's View, *2005*

Victory in Europe

While the Allies invaded Germany from the north and west, the Soviet Union attacked from the east. Facing certain defeat, Germany surrendered to the Allies on May 7, 1945. Hitler committed suicide in a bunker in Berlin before he could be captured. The war in Europe was over and the Allies declared May 8 as Victory in Europe (VE) Day.

WEB LINK ●

To this day, the Dutch continue to show their appreciation to Canada for liberating the Netherlands. Visit the Pearson Web site to find out more.

FIGURE 5–31 At the Yalta Conference in February 1945, with an Allied victory only months away, Winston Churchill, Franklin D. Roosevelt, and Joseph Stalin (front row, from left to right) discussed the reorganization of post-war Europe, including occupation zones and new borders.

Japan Surrenders

After the Allied victory in Europe, the war in the Pacific intensified. By mid-1945, most of the Japanese air force and navy had been destroyed, but the army was still strong. In March 1945, the Americans, the main Allied force in the Pacific, had begun fire-bombing Japanese cities trying to force them to surrender. Although these bombing raids destroyed cities and killed thousands of people, the Japanese declared that they would "fight to the last person" and not surrender.

The Atomic Bomb

For some time, American and British scientists had been working on the **Manhattan Project**, a top-secret plan to develop an **atomic bomb**. In 1942, Canada was notified of the project and asked to contribute uranium, an important component of the bomb. The Canadian government agreed, and secretly bought the Eldorado mine at Great Bear Lake, Northwest Territories, to produce the uranium.

On August 6, 1945, an American bomber plane (named "Enola Gay" after the pilot's mother) dropped an atomic bomb over the Japanese city of Hiroshima. The destruction unleashed by the bomb had never been experienced before. Three days after the bombing of Hiroshima, a second atomic bomb was dropped on the city of Nagasaki. While precise casualty numbers are not available, it is estimated that the two bombings killed approximately 100 000 people and wounded another 100 000. Long-term effects, such as cancer, affected many more Japanese citizens.

The War Ends

The Japanese, realizing that they could not withstand the awesome power of the new U.S. weapon, surrendered on August 14, 1945. Finally, after six long years and the loss of millions of lives, the Second World War was over.

KEY TERMS

Manhattan Project the code name during the Second World War for the American plan to develop the first atomic bomb

atomic bomb a bomb containing radioactive material, capable of destroying an entire city or region

FIGURE 5–32 The nuclear detonation at Nagasaki on August 9, 1945, created a mushroom cloud that rose many kilometres into the air.

PRACTICE QUESTIONS

1. What was D-Day? Why was it necessary? In what ways did the D-Day invasion differ from the raid on Dieppe? What role did Canadian troops play in both of these invasions?

2. In your own words, describe the situation in the Netherlands in the spring of 1945. Why were Canadian troops considered heroes in the Netherlands?

3. Compare and contrast how the war ended in Europe and Asia.

Are weapons of mass destruction ever justified?

On July 16, 1945, a group of American scientists tested the first atomic bomb—the most powerful weapon ever built until that time. The scientists who witnessed the test were awestruck by the power of what they had created.

> *We knew the world would not be the same. A few people laughed. A few people cried. Most people were silent. I remembered the line from the Hindu scripture—the Bhagavad-gita. Vishnu is trying to persuade the prince that he should do his duty and to impress him, takes on his multi-armed form and says, "Now I am become Death, the destroyer of worlds." I suppose we all felt that, one way or another.*
>
> *–Robert Oppenheimer,*
> *scientific director of the Manhattan Project*

> *Personally I recoiled at the idea and said to Roosevelt: "Mr. President, this would violate every Christian ethic I have ever heard of and all known laws of war. It would be an attack on the non-combatant population of the enemy...."*
>
> *It was my opinion that the use of this barbarous weapon at Hiroshima and Nagasaki was of no material assistance in our war.... The Japanese were already defeated and ready to surrender.... My own feeling was that in being the first to use it, we had adopted an ethical standard common to the barbarians of the Dark Ages. I was not taught to make war in that fashion, and wars cannot be won by destroying women and children....*
>
> *–I Was There, 1950*

Two atomic bombs, dropped on the Japanese cities of Hiroshima and Nagasaki, ended the war, but controversy regarding their use continues to this day. Was it necessary to use such a deadly weapon? Even before the atomic bomb was dropped, there were those who believed its use could never be justified. Admiral William Leahy, an advisor to U.S. President Harry Truman, opposed the bomb. In 1944, he advised Truman's predecessor, Franklin Roosevelt, not to use the bomb.

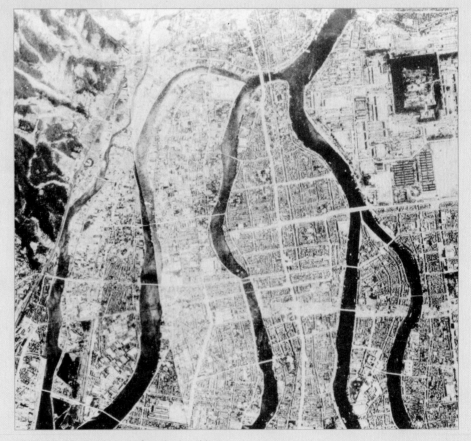

FIGURE 5–33 Hiroshima before the bombing

Colonel Paul Tibbets, commander of the air force squadron that dropped the bombs on Japan and pilot of the plane that dropped the bomb on Hiroshima, rejected such criticism because he felt it failed to take into consideration the "context of the times":

As for the missions flown against Japan on the 6th and 9th of August, 1945, I would remind you, we were at war. Our job was to win. Once the targets were named and presidential approval received, we were to deliver the weapons as expeditiously as possible, consistent with good tactics. The objective was to stop the fighting, thereby saving further loss of life on both sides. The urgency of the situation demanded that we use the weapons first—before the technology could be used against us.

–Quoted in news release by
Airmen Memorial Museum, 1994

For almost 200 years, war strategists have been influenced by the writings of Carl von Clausewitz, a Prussian general and military theorist. In his book *On War*, he writes about his theory of absolute war:

To introduce into a philosophy of war a principle of moderation would be an absurdity. War is an act of violence pushed to its utmost bounds.
–Quoted in Gwynne Dyer, War, 1985

Weapons now exist that have the potential to destroy all life on Earth. Nations have stockpiled thousands of warheads hundreds of times more powerful than the first atomic bombs. Arsenals and laboratories store biological weapons designed to spread diseases. Governments maintain stores of deadly chemical weapons. Von Clausewitz could never have envisioned destruction on such a scale.

Thankfully, some nations have agreed to treaties that limit the testing of nuclear weapons and that reduce the arsenal of nuclear weapons. Still, both the United States and Russia have the capability to destroy the world several times over. Many other nations also have nuclear arms and large quantities of chemical and biological weapons.

Analyzing the Issue

1. What reasons did Admiral William Leahy give against using the atomic bomb?

2. What three arguments did Colonel Paul Tibbets give to support the use of the atomic bomb on Japan?

3. What do you think Robert Oppenheimer meant by "We knew the world would not be the same"?

4. Do you think there are any circumstances in which weapons of mass destruction can ever be justified? Explain your answer.

FIGURE 5–34 Hiroshima after the bombing

©P

Crimes Against Humanity

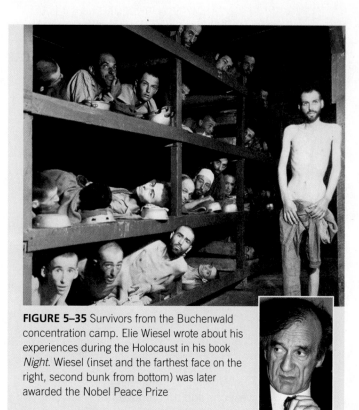
● How did the war raise awareness of human rights issues?

Atrocities inflicted upon civilians and POWs during the Second World War brought the issue of human rights to the world's attention, and ultimately led to the Universal Declaration of Human Rights (see Chapter 10).

The Holocaust

The anti-Semitic and racist views of Hitler and the Nazi government were well-known in the 1930s. By 1941, the Nazi government adopted the "**Final Solution**"—a horrifying plan of **genocide**. Hitler ordered all Jewish people and "undesirables" to be shipped to concentration camps, such as Bergen-Belsen and Buchenwald in Germany, and Auschwitz and Treblinka in Poland. Upon arrival, guards stripped them of their clothes and valuables, shaved their heads, and separated families. The weak, the old, and the young were immediately killed in gas chambers. Healthy people worked as slave labourers. When overwork, starvation, and disease weakened them, they too were murdered. By 1945, the Germans had killed more than 6 million Jewish people and another 5 million Roma, Slavs, and other "undesirables." Though the Allies had known about German concentration camps, they did not realize the full extent of the horrors of the Holocaust until they pressed closer to Germany and saw the Nazi atrocities.

FIGURE 5–35 Survivors from the Buchenwald concentration camp. Elie Wiesel wrote about his experiences during the Holocaust in his book *Night*. Wiesel (inset and the farthest face on the right, second bunk from bottom) was later awarded the Nobel Peace Prize

The Nuremberg Trials

In 1945, the Allies established an International Military **Tribunal** in Nuremberg, Germany, to prosecute prominent Nazi leaders and many others for atrocities committed during the war. Twelve defendants were sentenced to death and others were imprisoned. This is the first time in history that leaders of a country were charged for immoral acts during wartime. The Nuremberg Trials became a model for prosecuting war criminals in Rwanda and the former Yugoslavia (see Chapter 10).

Atrocities in Asia

Liberators of Japanese POW camps also encountered terrible **war crimes** committed during the war. Mass killings, human experimentation, famine, torture, and forced labour were a few of the hardships suffered by POWs and civilians alike. Since many of Japan's wartime acts violated international law, the alleged crimes were subject to trial in international courts of justice, similar to the Nuremberg Trials. The Tokyo Trials heard these cases and passed sentence on military personnel found guilty of war crimes and **crimes against humanity**.

A Canadian soldier at Bergen-Belsen wrote:

Tonight I am a different man. I have spent the last two days in Belsen concentration camp, the most horrible festering scab there has ever been on the face of humanity....

You have seen pictures in the paper but they cannot tell the story. You have to smell it and feel it and keep a stern look on your face while your heart tears itself into pieces and the tears of compassion drench your soul...

–*King Whyte,* Letters Home, 1944–1946, *2007*

©P

The War at Home

Canadians at home made enormous contributions to the war. Under the policy of total war, many Canadian factories were dedicated to producing supplies and war materials. In 1944, Canada produced 14 000 tanks and personnel carriers, more than 4000 aircraft, and 16 000 artillery pieces. Factories operated non-stop, and Canadians worked long hours to run them.

Women and the War Effort

As in the First World War, women joined war industries in roles that were unusual for them at the time. They worked as welders, drillers, and punch-press or machine operators. "Rosie the Riveter" became a popular nickname for these working women. Women were in high demand as factory workers and many moved from rural areas to industrial centres. With government funding, some companies built dormitories close to their factories to house workers.

Canada's Wartime Economy

With so much increased production and employment, people suddenly had more money to spend. At the same time, there were fewer goods to buy as most of what was produced was shipped to Britain. Prime Minister Mackenzie King wanted to avoid soaring inflation and hoped to prevent the massive debt that had burdened Canada after the First World War so the government took the following steps:

- As Minister of Finance, James Ilsley enthusiastically encouraged Canadians to buy Victory Bonds. The government used the money to help finance the war, and people cashed in the bonds for profit after the war.

- Ilsley increased income taxes for added revenue.

- In 1941, the Wartime Prices and Trade Board, which had been set up in 1939, froze all wages and prices to try to prevent inflation.

- In 1942, King introduced food rationing, limiting the amounts of certain goods that Canadians were allowed per week. Each Canadian adult was limited to about 1 kilogram of meat, 220 grams of sugar, 250 grams of butter, and about 225 grams of coffee. Canadian rations were generous compared with those in England and the United States.

● What was the war's impact on the home front?

KEY TERMS

crimes against humanity widespread attacks against civilians, including murder, enslavement, deportation, and torture

Final Solution the Nazis' plan to systematically kill all European Jews

genocide the systematic extermination of a religious or ethnic group

tribunal court of justice

war crimes the killing, torture, and hostage-taking of civilian populations, or the deliberate and extensive destruction of their property

FIGURE 5–36 Women were employed in non-traditional roles during the Second World War.

©P

Women and the War Machine

The Second World War changed Canadian society. Most young men joined the military and many went overseas. At the same time, industrial production greatly increased, meaning that more workers were needed. Although women in poorer families and on farms had always worked, the middle-class ideal was that women looked after the home and men went out to work. This pattern was so engrained that middle-class men resisted even the idea that their wives would go to work, believing that it would indicate, among other things, that the men could not provide for their families. During the Depression, governments wanted women to stay at home to keep more men employed. When the war changed everything, attitudes had to change too.

The National Selective Service Program

During the war, the National Selective Service program registered women for work in factories and established daycare centres in Ontario and Québec, where industry was concentrated. Women also joined the Canadian Women's Army Corps (CWAC), serving mostly as clerks, drivers, and nurses. By 1945, almost one-third of all Canadian women were employed in the war effort.

Ronnie, the Bren Gun Girl

Governments used propaganda and created stereotypes to mobilize the home front and to change the public's mind about women in the workforce. Working in the war effort had to seem glamorous, exciting, and patriotic. The Americans created Rosie the Riveter to idealize the working woman. Her posters show her with sleeves rolled up, ready to pitch in and help her country. Canada's stereotypical working woman was Ronnie, the Bren Gun Girl, who was, as opposed to Rosie, a real person working in a munitions factory.

Looking Further

1. In your own words, describe how the role of Canadian women changed from the Depression to the end of the Second World War.

2. Examine, describe, and compare the images of Rosie the Riveter and Ronnie, the Bren Gun Girl. What do they tell us about the societies they represent?

3. Describe social controls that might be used against a woman who chose to live independently rather than participate in the war effort.

FIGURE 5–37 Ronnie, the Bren Gun Girl—a real Canadian woman named Veronica Foster

FIGURE 5–38 Rosie the Riveter represented the idealized American woman contributing to the war effort.

©P

The Growing Demand for Social Change

The federal government's Wartime Prices and Trade Board was also established to help reduce social unrest. It limited the power of trade unions by controlling wages so that striking would be less effective. The shortage of labour, however, often worked to the unions' advantage, and many ignored restrictions on the right to strike. Workers wanted higher wages but they also demanded the right to bargain. The board was unable to prevent steel workers in Nova Scotia and coal miners in Alberta and British Columbia from going on strike in 1943. In 1944, the federal government softened its policy, allowing workers the right to join a union and forcing employers to recognize their workers' unions.

The war also brought changes to the role of government. The wartime government had been involved in almost every aspect of Canadians' lives, and many Canadians wanted some of this involvement to continue. The Co-operative Commonwealth Federation party and its platform of social reform was becoming increasingly popular at both the national and provincial levels, a fact that was not lost on Prime Minister Mackenzie King. In 1943, the CCF made up the Opposition in Ontario. In 1944, it formed the government in Saskatchewan under T.C. "Tommy" Douglas. Mackenzie King had already brought in an unemployment insurance program in 1940. In 1945, he expanded Canada's social assistance by bringing in the Family Allowance program, which helped families cover the cost of child maintenance. Canada's policy of "**cradle to grave**" **social security** had begun.

The Conscription Crisis

Prime Minister Mackenzie King had promised there would be no conscription when Canada declared war in 1939. But the speed with which the Germans occupied Europe in 1940 stunned Canadians and made it clear that thousands of soldiers would be needed to fight against the Nazis. Canadians, including the opposition Conservative Party, demanded that their government do more for the war effort. In response to these demands, King's government quickly brought in the **National Resources Mobilization Act** (NRMA). This Act gave the government special emergency powers to take over the nation's resources. Most significantly, the NRMA allowed for conscription, although only for home defence.

KEY TERMS

"cradle to grave" social security social assistance provided by the government, from birth to death

National Resources Mobilization Act an Act passed in 1940 enabling the government to do whatever was necessary for the war effort; it was amended in 1942 to allow conscription

FIGURE 5–39 The government reminded Canadians that everyone was involved in the war effort—and to be aware of possible spies in their midst.

Identifying Viewpoints How serious does the danger of spying and sabotage appear to be from this poster? What course of action does it suggest citizens take? What techniques does it use to create an impact on the viewer?

- What impact did conscription have on Canadian unity?

KEY TERMS

plebiscite a vote on a particular issue

enemy aliens nationals living in a country that is at war with their homeland

Canadians Vote on Conscription

As the war progressed, the Conservative opposition continued to pressure Mackenzie King to bring in conscription. But the prime minister knew that there would be strong resistance to conscription in Québec. As in the First World War, many Québécois did not feel connected to a war in Europe that did not directly affect Canada.

King decided to hold a **plebiscite** to get Canadians' views on conscription. He used the slogan "Not necessarily conscription, but conscription if necessary" to describe the government's position on the issue. On April 27, 1942, voters were asked whether they would release the government from its promise not to send conscripts overseas. In all provinces but Québec, the majority voted "yes." Once again, the issue of conscription divided the nation.

"Yes" to Conscription

Mackenzie King finally allowed conscription for overseas service by amending the National Resources Mobilization Act in August 1942. Many Québécois felt betrayed by King's actions. There were riots in Montréal to protest King's decision. The Québec legislature passed a motion condemning the federal government's actions.

King managed to avoid the issue of conscription for the next two years. But after heavy Canadian casualties during the campaigns in Italy and northwest Europe, there was a severe shortage of trained infantry. King could no longer avoid the issue and agreed to send conscripts overseas.

In 1944, King conscripted 15 000 men for active service under the NRMA. In the final months of the war, 12 908 NRMA conscripts were sent to Europe. Only 2463 of these Canadian conscripts ever reached the front.

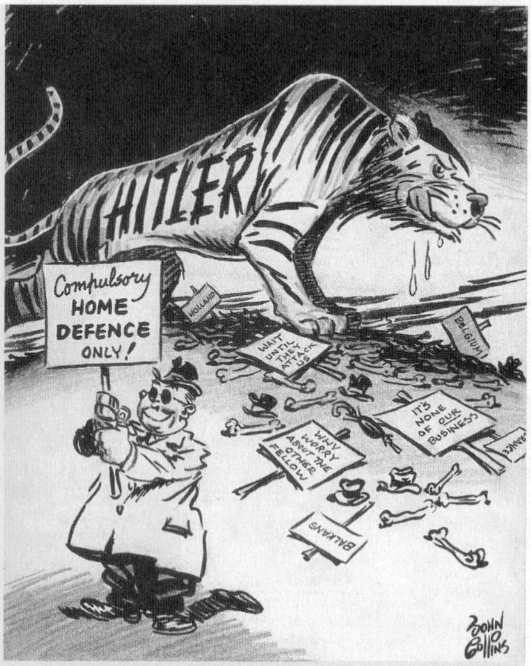

FIGURE 5–40 Cartoon published in the *Montreal Gazette* in 1941

Interpreting a Cartoon What is the cartoonist's message?

Province	Yes (%)	No (%)
Ontario	84.0	16.0
Prince Edward Island	82.9	17.1
British Columbia	80.4	19.6
Québec	27.9	72.1

FIGURE 5–41 Plebiscite results for selected provinces, 1942

PRACTICE QUESTIONS

1. What three initiatives did the Canadian government undertake to prevent inflation and pay for the war? How successful were these initiatives?
2. What social changes took place in Canada during the war? What demands were unions making?
3. **Cause and Consequence** What unintended consequences do you think were caused by women being a major part of the war effort?
4. Explain how Mackenzie King managed to avoid sending conscripts overseas. Why did he eventually have to send conscripts overseas?
5. Why was Québec so opposed to conscription? What had changed between 1917 and 1944? How do you think people felt about conscripts? Why?

©P

● What effect did the War Measures Act have on the legal rights of Canadians?

Racism and Japanese Canadians

When war broke out, more than 22 000 Japanese Canadians were living in British Columbia. No evidence indicated that they supported Japan in the war, nor did the government consider these **enemy aliens** a security risk. But anti-Japanese sentiment grew in Canada after the bombing of Pearl Harbor and the invasion of Hong Kong in 1941. In early 1942, the Canadian government caved in to public pressure. For the second time in its history (see Chapter 2), the War Measures Act was invoked. All Japanese Canadians living near the British Columbia coast were "invited" to move to the Okanagan Valley. They would be settled in temporary "relocation centres." In the wake of anti-Japanese marches in Vancouver, about 750 people moved voluntarily. Soon, the government forced all Japanese Canadians, regardless of how long they had lived in Canada, to leave the coast.

Government officials separated families, sending members to different internment camps in the interior of British Columbia where they were held until the end of the war. David Suzuki, a famous Canadian environmentalist and broadcaster, was interned with his sisters and mother when he was six years old, while his father worked at a labour camp. Some families chose to go to Alberta or Manitoba. These locations were farther away, but at least families were allowed to stay together.

The situation worsened in January 1943. Federal government officials, called Custodians of Enemy Property, were given the power to confiscate and sell Japanese Canadians' property. People who had been relocated inland lost everything. Possessions were auctioned off and the owners received almost nothing.

In 1945, the federal government offered Japanese Canadians a choice: they could apply to be sent to Japan, which had been devastated by war, or they could agree to permanently settle east of the Rocky Mountains. Some people challenged Canada's right to deport innocent citizens, but the Supreme Court upheld the government's position. In all, 3964 Japanese Canadians were deported—2000 were Canadian citizens. Thousands of other Japanese Canadians were relocated to other parts of Canada.

In 1947, the government finally cancelled the policy. It was not until 1988 that the federal government apologized for its actions. As compensation, it agreed to pay the people still living who were affected by the policy $21 000 each. It also agreed to restore Canadian citizenship to any person who had been deported to Japan.

Looking Further

1. Why were Japanese Canadians relocated and detained during the Second World War?

2. How would posters like Remember Hong Kong (on page 137) contribute to these attitudes?

3. In your opinion, what would be just compensation for Japanese Canadians interned during the war?

4. Canadian veterans who were POWs in Asia were not compensated for being starved or used as slave labour in Japanese factories, even though their mistreatment violated the rules of war. People often cite the compensation given to Japanese Canadians as a reason why the Canadian government should negotiate with the Japanese for compensation for these veterans. Do you agree with this reasoning? Explain your thinking.

FIGURE 5–42 A Japanese Canadian family awaits relocation from Vancouver, 1942. Many families were separated, with men being interned separately.

Thinking Critically Why do you think the men were interned separately?

©P

● What was the war's impact on the home front?

KEY TERMS

arsenal of democracy a slogan coined by President Franklin D. Roosevelt in December 1940 promising to help the Allies fight the Germans by providing military supplies while staying out of the actual fighting

war brides foreign women who married Canadian troops serving overseas and then immigrated to Canada after the war

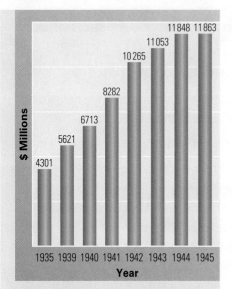

FIGURE 5–43 Value of Canada's gross national product (GNP), 1935–1945. GNP is a measure of the value of all goods and services produced by a nation.

Gathering Evidence Why did Canada's GNP increase significantly during the war?

What the War Meant to Canada

The Second World War had many long-lasting economic, social, and political effects on Canada. As you will read in the next chapter, these effects ushered in tremendous changes in post-war Canadian society.

Economic Growth

Arsenals supply armies with weapons. In 1940, before the United States entered the war, President Roosevelt called the United States the "**arsenal of democracy**." Roosevelt promised to arm and support the Allies, while staying out of the actual fighting. Canada, as part of the Empire, supplied both soldiers and an arsenal, providing Britain with the weapons and resources it needed to resist Germany from 1939 onwards.

Under its policy of total war, Canada provided major military and economic support to the Allies. The value of goods it produced rose from $5.6 billion in 1939 to $11.8 billion in 1945. During the war, Canada gave the Allies billions of dollars in financial aid.

Virtually every sector of the Canadian economy boomed. There was a rapid increase in the production of aluminum, which was used in the manufacture of aircraft. Wood and paper production rose, as did mining and smelting. There was also a great increase in the demand for petroleum to fuel tanks, trucks, and airplanes. A wave of exploration led to discoveries of new oil fields in Alberta. Many jobs were created in production, transportation, processing, and providing services for the new industries.

The wartime boom brought another important change to the Canadian economy. Agriculture, once the most important sector of Canada's economy, was overtaken by manufacturing. Canadian cities and the industrial areas around them became much more important contributors to the economy after the war. During the period from 1939 to 1949, Canada had transformed itself from a rural economy to a modern industrial nation.

Societal Changes

The Second World War changed Canadian society in several ways. Women were employed in great numbers during the war. Their contribution helped to raise their profile in society and promote their rights as workers. There was a significant wave of immigration as about 48 000 **war brides**— along with approximately 21 000 children—arrived from Europe to join their soldier-husbands after the war. The government encouraged war brides to come to Canada by paying for their trip. Once they arrived, many faced a difficult adjustment as they became members of a new culture and society.

In addition to war brides, thousands of people displaced by the war came to Canada to start a new life. After the war, Canada eventually loosened some of its immigration restrictions to allow more people to come to Canada to meet the growing demand for labour. But, for the most part, Canadian immigration policy remained unchanged. It allowed mainly immigrants from preferred countries in Europe to enter Canada.

©P

Building an Identity

Canada's enormous contribution to the war, in both human and economic terms, gave it a new role on the world stage. Just two decades earlier, Canada had been a colony in the British Empire. By the end of the Second World War, Canada had emerged as a major player in a global conflict, with one of the world's largest navies and fourth-largest Allied air force. Once again, Canadian troops proved themselves on the battlefields, and were recognized for their contribution to the Allied victory. In addition, the efforts of Aboriginal, Asian, and black soldiers—along with those from other minority groups—during the war helped further civil rights for all Canadians. Although many Canadians were killed, wounded, and captured, the Second World War became a defining event in the development of Canada's identity.

> *But it was a good war for Canada too, because it made us a great nation. I mean... it showed us what we could do. We just weren't a bunch of wheat farmers and Nova Scotia fishermen and lumbermen in B.C. We were a nation. A big and tough and strong nation.*
>
> *–Quoted in Barry Broadfoot, Six War Years, 1974*

● What factors contributed to Canada's emerging autonomy?

Country	Casualties
Canada	42 000
Britain	326 000
France	340 000
Germany	325 000
Soviet Union	8 668 000
Japan	1 506 000
United States	295 000

FIGURE 5–44 Allied and Axis military casualties

Thinking Critically Casualty numbers for the Second World War vary widely depending upon their source. Give some possible explanations.

FIGURE 5–45 In May 1946, more than 100 black veterans attended a welcome home banquet in their honour.

PRACTICE QUESTIONS

1. **a)** How did the war end the Depression?

   b) What were the major changes in Canada's economy during this period?

2. In what ways did the war change the social make-up of Canada? In what ways was it unchanged?

3. In your opinion, which branch of the armed forces had the greatest impact on the outcome of the war? Provide evidence from the chapter.

4. Do you agree that "it was a good war"? Explain.

5. **Significance** What were the three most significant ways that the Second World War changed Canada?

CHAPTER FOCUS QUESTION How did the Second World War impact Canada socially, politically, and economically?

Unlike in the First World War, Canada entered the Second World War as a recognized and independent nation. Even so, ties to Britain were still very strong. After Britain declared war on Germany in September of 1939, Canada almost immediately followed suit. The war put the development of Canadian industry into overdrive. On the home front, women took over many of the jobs formerly done only by men and everyone had to adjust to rationing and the rigours of a war economy. Canadians fought in Hong Kong, Dieppe, Italy, Normandy, and Holland. The Canadian navy grew enormously during the war, protecting the sea lanes over which the products of Canadian forests, farms, and factories travelled to Britain and Russia to help the war effort. Canadian pilots and crews fought in the Battle of Britain and flew thousands of missions over Europe. The need for more personnel brought back conscription, which again threatened to split the nation. Canada's participation was critical to the war effort and won the nation increased status in the post-war world.

1. Complete the following organizer to show the impact of the Second World War on Canada.

Event	Description	Significance of the Event	Long-lasting Effects

Vocabulary Focus

2. Review Key Terms on page 119. Then go to the Pearson Web site and match the terms with their definitions.

Knowledge and Understanding

3. Continue the annotated timeline showing steps to Canadian autonomy that you started in Chapter 2. Review the events that are covered in this chapter. Write the name and date of each event on the timeline and explain how the event contributed to Canadian independence.

4. Outline the causes of the Second World War.

5. Describe how the war changed women's roles and how you think this may have changed Canadian society.

6. Explain the significance of each of the following to Canada:
   a) Battle of Hong Kong
   b) Dieppe Raid
   c) Battle of Britain
   d) Battle of Ortona
   e) Battle of the Scheldt
   f) Battle of the Atlantic
   g) Liberating the Netherlands
   h) D-Day

7. The Nazis killed millions of Jewish people in the Holocaust during the Second World War, but their anti-Semitism became official government policy in the 1930s. What position do you think the Canadian government should have taken toward Germany before the war? Might the war have been prevented if other countries had protested? Explain.

8. Find examples in the textbook of divisions within the country that were exacerbated by the war.

Critical Thinking

Significance

9. Use the organizer you created in Question 1. Which three events had the greatest impact on Canada? Provide evidence to support your opinion.

Cause and Consequence

10. Could war have been avoided if Britain, France, and their allies had stood up to Hitler's demands earlier than they did? Why do you think politicians were so ready to appease Germany in 1939? Prepare reasoned arguments for both sides of these questions.

11. During the Second World War, Canada and its allies practised "total war." Explain how this contributed to the Allied victory. How successful would Canada have been if it had participated in the war on a limited basis, such as with the war in Afghanistan?

12. Discuss with a partner how the following countries and groups might have viewed Canada at the end of the Second World War. Be prepared to discuss your ideas with the class.

    a) Britain

    b) the Netherlands

    c) United States

    d) Japanese Canadians

    e) Canadian women

Document Analysis

13. Read the quotations on the bombing of Hiroshima on pages 150–151, keeping in mind that quotations must always be understood in context.

    a) What moral question is raised here?

    b) Briefly summarize the arguments presented and rank them by how strong you think they are.

    c) Do you think photos of the bombing victims have influenced the use of nuclear weapons? Explain.

    d) In your opinion, where does the responsibility for the bombings of Hiroshima and Nagasaki chiefly lie? Explain.

    e) Faced with the same factual information as Truman, would you have decided to use the atomic bomb?

Having found the bomb we have used it. We have used it against those who attacked us without warning at Pearl Harbor, against those who have starved and beaten and executed American prisoners of war, against those who have abandoned all pretense of obeying international laws of warfare. We have used it in order to shorten the agony of war, in order to save the lives of thousands and thousands of young Americans.
—Harry S. Truman, 1945

FIGURE 5–46 A woman and child who survived the atomic bomb dropped on Nagasaki, Japan, on August 9, 1945. Their faces are burned from the heat of the explosion.

Use this Study Guide to synthesize your learning about Canada's development as a country. As you work through the following steps, refer back to the Focus Questions for Chapters 1 to 5. Look for evidence in your understanding to answer these questions.

STEP 1 Unpacking Knowledge

Use a chart to record information you learned in Unit 1. Your information may include events, key terms, individuals, or concepts.

Chapter 1	Chapter 2	Chapter 3	Chapter 4	Chapter 5
A Different Canada, 1900–1914	First World War, 1914 to 1919	The Twenties, 1919 to 1929	Great Depression, 1929 to 1939	Second World War, 1939 to 1945

STEP 2 Organizing Your Understanding

Using the information you recorded in Step 1, complete a chart, grouping your items into course topics. You do not need to use every item from Step 1. Focus on the key items. Many items can and will fit into multiple categories. Explain this in the Significance column.

Sample Topics	Event/Person/Date/Key Term	Significance
What steps did Canada take to become an autonomous nation?		
What was Canada's role in the First World War? How did the war affect developments in Canada?		
What were the labour and social impacts of economic cycles and changes between the wars, especially the Great Depression?		
What is regionalism and in what ways was it expressed in Canada from 1900 to 1945?		

☐ Society & Identity   ☐ Politics & Government   ☐ Economy & Human Geography   ☐ Autonomy & World Presence

STEP 3 Making Connections

Complete a mind map for one of the main course themes using the items from the chart you created in Step 2. The four main themes are
☐ Society & Identity, ☐ Politics & Government, ☐ Economy & Human Geography, and ☐ Autonomy & World Presence.

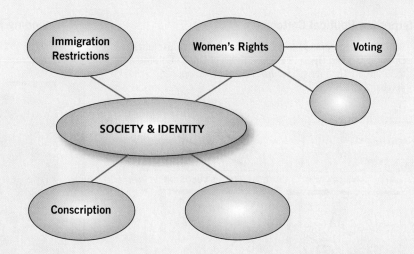

Immigration Restrictions

Women's Rights

Voting

SOCIETY & IDENTITY

Conscription

STEP 4 Applying Your Skills

Analyzing Evidence

Examine the images in the Unit Opener (pages 2–3) and the following sources and discuss how they connect to the material you have covered in this unit. Identify what each source is about, what is its message, and how it is evidence for one of the course themes. Remember to apply the skills you have learned including looking for bias and assessing reliability.

SOURCE 1: *The Battle of Vimy Ridge,* ▶
Richard Jack, 1918

▼ SOURCE 2: Lord Sankey, Privy Council Judgement, October 18, 1929

[T]he exclusion of women from all public offices is a relic of days more barbarous than our.... To those who would ask why the word "person" should include females, the obvious answer is, why should it not?

▼ SOURCE 3: Mr. MacInnis, Debate in the House of Commons, June 26, 1935

The easiest way to provoke a person into taking action which possibly he should not take is to ignore his rightful claims. I contend that these men in the camps have rightful and just claims which have been ignored by this government.

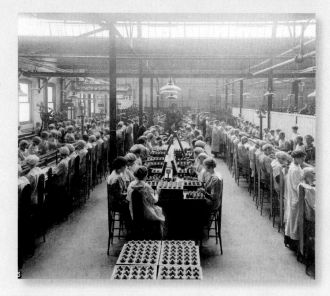

▲ SOURCE 4: Canadian women worked in munitions factories during the First World War.

Interpreting Political Cartoons

▼ **SOURCE 5:** Hawkins, N. H. "The Same Act Which Excludes Orientals Should Open Wide the Portals of British Columbia to White Immigrations." *Saturday Sunset*, Vancouver, August 24, 1907

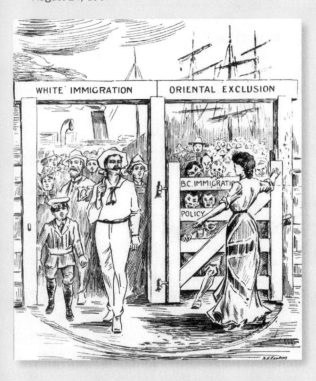

▼ **SOURCE 6:** "Equal Partners All." The Imperial Conference, held in London in 1926, resulted in the Balfour Report. *The Grain Growers' Guide,* Winnipeg, December 15, 1926

Decoding Photos

▼ **SOURCE 7:** During the Second World War, Ronnie, the Bren Gun Girl represented the war machine on the home front.

SOURCE 8: ▶ Unemployment during the Depression

▲ **SOURCE 9:** An automobile pulled by horses was called a "Bennett buggy" in the 1930s.

Gathering Information

▼ **SOURCE 10:** Women with jobs in Canada, 1939–1945

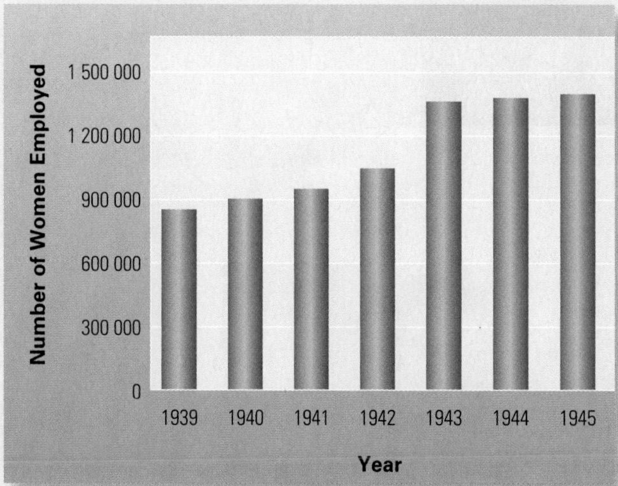
Number of Women Employed
1 500 000
1 200 000
900 000
600 000
300 000
0
1939
1940
1941
1942
1943
1944
1945
Year

▼ **SOURCE 11:** Alaska boundary dispute

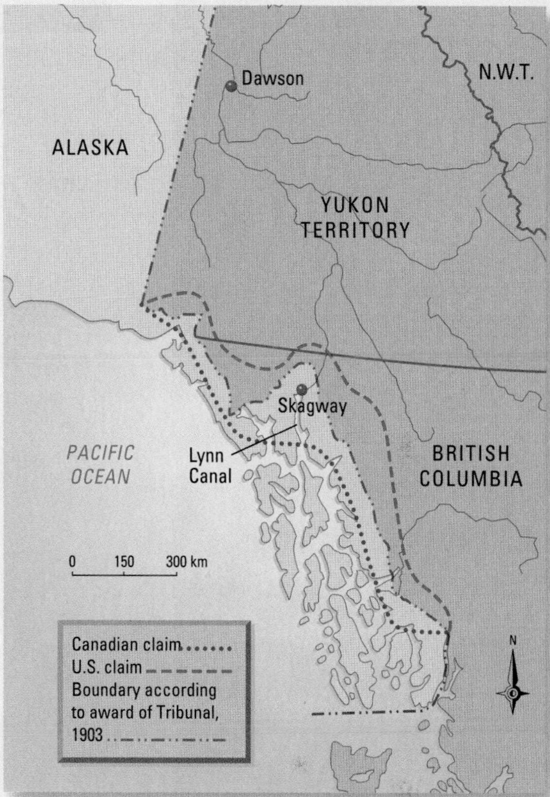
Dawson
N.W.T.
ALASKA
YUKON TERRITORY
Skagway
PACIFIC OCEAN
Lynn Canal
BRITISH COLUMBIA
0 150 300 km
Canadian claim
U.S. claim
Boundary according to award of Tribunal, 1903
N

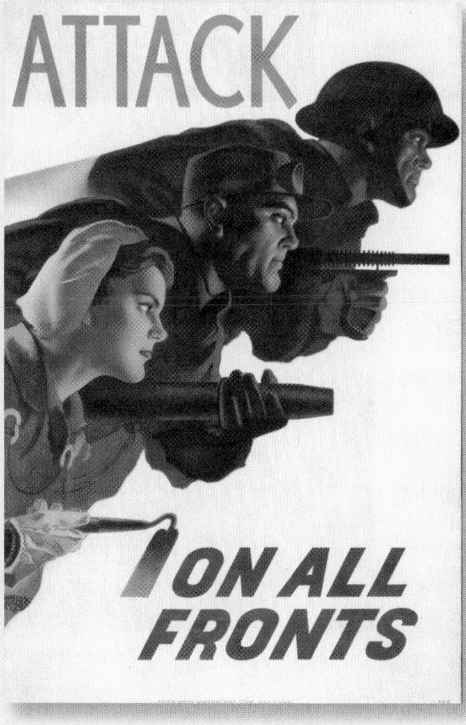
ATTACK
ON ALL FRONTS

◀ **SOURCE 12:** Second World War propaganda poster

STEP 5 **Thinking Critically**

Now that you have reviewed Unit 1 content, practised skills, and explored evidence and themes, it is time to synthesize your learning.

In a well-organized, multi-paragraph essay, discuss the accuracy of Laurier's quote from Chapter 1:

> *...the twentieth century shall be the century of Canada and of Canadian development. For the next seventy-five years, nay for the next one hundred years, Canada shall be the star towards which all men who love progress and freedom shall come.*

CHECK the Pearson Web site for additional review activities and questions.

©P

UNIT

2

Refining an Identity: Canada in the Post-War Years

Nuclear tensions and a Cold War during the post-war years saw Canada's role in the world evolve. Attitudes, economy, and national identity were reshaped as Canada struggled to find its place as a neighbour to one of the world's military and economic superpowers. Canadian society and identity were impacted by renewed questions regarding the role of Québec, immigration and multiculturalism, Aboriginal rights, and the status of women.

CHAPTER 6

During the 1950s, Canada experienced a boom in both its economy and population. Cities expanded into suburbs due to post-war immigration and a baby boom. Teenagers embraced new rock'n'roll music.

CHAPTER 6

The Cold War became a reality for Canadians in 1945 when a Soviet spy ring was uncovered in the country. Canada struggled to remain independent of its superpower neighbour, the U.S., during the Cold War years.

SOUTH AMERICA

CHAPTER 7

During the 1960s and 1970s, the huge youth population engendered a culture of activism and protest that challenged social norms and government policies. A separatist crisis also divided the country.

ATLANTIC OCEAN

CHAPTER 8

Communist countries experienced sweeping reforms in the 1980s. The Berlin Wall fell in 1989, marking the end of the Cold War.

©P

CHAPTER 7

The Canadian government did not support the U.S. in the Cuban Missile Crisis, thereby widening the gap between Canada and the U.S. during the continuing Cold War.

CHAPTER 8

In the final decades of the 20th century, Canada experienced major political and economic changes. Québec sovereignty tested Canadian unity, and our economy became more closely tied to that of the U.S. Advances in technology resulted in globalization and at home, progress was made in Aboriginal rights.

PACIFIC OCEAN

NORTH AMERICA

ARCTIC OCEAN

EUROPE

ASIA

AUSTRALIA

AFRICA

INDIAN OCEAN

	U.S.S.R. and Warsaw Pact
	Eastern bloc allies (Communist)
	U.S. and NATO
	Western bloc allies

The World in 1960: Alliances of the Cold War ▶

0   1500   3000 km

6

Canada in the Post-War World: The 1950s

GUIDING QUESTIONS

Society & Identity

- In what ways did Canadian society change after the Second World War?

- How was the role of women redefined during the 1950s?

- What measures has Canada taken to promote a distinct Canadian identity?

- What challenges did Aboriginal people face in the 1950s?

- How was Québec nationalism expressed in the 1950s?

- How did people improve their working conditions after the Second World War?

Economy & Human Geography

- What were the characteristics of the post-war economic boom?

- How does industrial development affect the environment?

- What was the impact of American investment on the Canadian economy?

Autonomy & World Presence

- What factors contributed to Canada's emerging autonomy?

- What was Canada's involvement in the Cold War?

- Describe Canada's involvement in the UN.

- What was Canada's response to modern conflicts?

TIMELINE

1945

Second World War ends

United Nations created

1947

Immigration of displaced persons from Europe begins

Oil discovered at Leduc, Alberta

1948

Louis St. Laurent becomes prime minister

1949

Newfoundland becomes Canada's 10th province

NATO formed

Communists take over China

1950

Korean War begins

CHAPTER FOCUS QUESTION

How did Canadian political decisions reflect a concern about the growing influence of the United States over Canada?

CRITICAL INQUIRY

Significance

Patterns and Change

Evidence

Perspectives

Cause and Consequence

Judgements

KEY TERMS

Massey Commission

Canada Council for the Arts

Canadian Radio-television and Telecommunications Commission (CRTC)

Cold War

communist

capitalist

superpowers

middle power

North Atlantic Treaty Organization (NATO)

Warsaw Pact

North American Aerospace Defence Command (NORAD)

Distant Early Warning (DEW) Line

United Nations (UN)

Avro Arrow

Korean Conflict

Suez Crisis

On August 31, 1957, Elvis Presley arrived in Vancouver to perform at Empire Stadium. With eight number one singles in two years, Elvis was one of the hottest rock 'n' roll performers of the 1950s and he epitomized the energy and attitude of the era. As soon as Elvis and his band began performing, screaming fans ran onto the field—breaking through security to get closer to their idol. The show was stopped and the fans ordered to return to their seats. But the teenagers refused, and eventually the show went on anyway.

The next day, *Vancouver Sun* reporter John Kirkwood described the concert this way: "It was like watching a demented army swarm down the hillside to do battle when those frenzied teenagers stormed the field... Vancouver teenagers [were] transformed into writhing, frenzied idiots of delight by the savage jungle beat music... [It was] the most disgusting exhibition of mass hysteria and lunacy this city has ever witnessed."

Why might John Kirkwood and many other adults have been so hostile to 1950s teenagers' love affair with rock 'n' roll? How did popular culture in the 1950s reflect a society turning away from the tough times of the war years?

As you will see in this chapter, the 1950s brought new lifestyles, new products, and new values to Canadian society. At the same time, the Canadian economy boomed and consumerism grew in importance—factors that favoured the growth of youth culture. People were also on the move. Cities grew larger and hundreds of new suburbs were developed. Economic growth attracted many new immigrants to Canadian cities. With few environmental protections, industry often polluted the environment without consideration for the long-term effects of development. Internationally, Canada sought a middle path, maintaining strong relations with Britain and the Commonwealth and good, but independent, relations with the United States. Carving out an independent foreign policy for Canada was a challenge during the period known as the Cold War, but Canadian governments successfully maintained our independence.

mission	**1952** First CBC Television broadcast	**1955** Warsaw Pact formed	**1956** Lester Pearson helps to defuse the Suez crisis	**1957** John Diefenbaker becomes prime minister

● In what ways did Canadian society change after the Second World War?

KEY TERM

baby boom the increase in the birth rate that occurred after the Second World War

The Changing Face of Canada

The end of the Second World War marked the beginning of a population boom in Canada. Those who had postponed marriage because of the war began to start families. Generally, families were larger than they are today—three or four children was the average. In all, 6.7 million children were born in Canada between 1946 and 1961, making up almost one third of the population. The increase in the birth rate that took place in Canada as well as Australia and the United States became known as the **baby boom**. For a time Canada's birth rate was the highest in the industrial world, peaking in 1959. The baby boom among the First Nations population also peaked in the late 1950s. In addition, post-war immigration brought thousands of new Canadians into the country—people eager to take part in the prosperity of the post-war years.

The Rise of the Suburbs

After the war, developers began building thousands of new homes for Canada's growing population. Many were in the outlying areas of cities, the suburbs, where land was less expensive. Cheap land encouraged low-density building: big houses on large lots with lawns, patios, even swimming pools. In time, suburban subdivisions became "bedroom communities" with their own schools, parks, and churches. Commuters travelled to work in the cities and returned home to the suburbs at the end of the day.

Increased economic development supported suburban life. Both business and manufacturing were booming and fewer than six percent of Canadians were unemployed throughout the decade. It was also a time of tremendous technological innovation, as you will see later in the chapter.

FIGURE 6–1 Throughout the 1950s, cars were made longer, lower, and wider than previous models. Every fall, manufacturers unveiled new models with eye-catching improvements.

Using Evidence What does this design suggest about the importance of the automobile at this time?

The Age of the Automobile

In the 1950s, Canadians fell in love with cars and bought 3.5 million of them. Automobile culture changed Canada's neighbourhoods. For people living in the suburbs, a car was a great convenience. Although suburban houses were often plain and functional, cars grew steadily fancier with lots of chrome, fins, and fancy tail lights.

The automobile represented all the elements of the post-war era: fascination with technology, progress, and personal freedom. Few thought of the downside costs. Enormous V8 engines needed lots of fuel, which increased society's dependence on oil. Atmospheric pollution, in the form of smog, also became a problem.

Women in the Fifties

● How was the role of women redefined during the 1950s?

Suburban life was centred on the traditional middle-class family, with a stay-at-home mother at its heart. The father's role was to be the breadwinner, supporting the family on his earnings. Popular women's magazines denounced working mothers as the cause of delinquent children. This was a far cry from the propaganda during the war that had urged women to work outside the home.

Fashions of the day emphasized femininity: long, full skirts; narrow waists; and high heels. New gadgets such as electric floor polishers, pop-up toasters, and electric food mixers promised to make housework seem less like drudgery. Women were encouraged to beautify themselves and their homes by consuming new products.

Many women came to resent suburban life. They felt isolated and trapped in a role that did not allow them to develop their potential. By the mid-1960s, many women were looking for a different way of life.

FIGURE 6–2 Not all women in the 1950s lived the suburban dream. Many urban women, particularly immigrants, worked in low-paying factory jobs or as domestic help.

Thinking Critically Compare the situation of women in the 1950s with women you know today.

The Birth of Teen Culture

Because the "boomer" generation is the largest age group in Canada, it influenced Canadian culture and the economy for decades to come. Boy Scouts, Girl Guides, and other youth organizations flourished, as did minor sports. Governments built thousands of new schools, arenas, and playgrounds to accommodate the needs of "boomers." Manufacturers developed and made new products for the baby-boomer market.

Baby boomers spent more time in school than earlier generations. Before the war, the average Canadian child received only eight years of schooling and only one in ten students finished high school. For the boomer generation there were no wars or economic hardships to force students out of school and into the adult world. The result was the invention of the "teenager." Rock 'n' roll, a musical style developed in the mid-1950s, soon became the favourite of many teenagers. The roots of rock 'n' roll were in African-American music from the southern United States. Rock 'n' roll's strong rhythms and sometimes rebellious teen-centred lyrics shocked some members of the older generation. It was banned in many places, and Elvis Presley's onstage hip-swivelling was called obscene. TV producers banned camera shots below his waist. The attacks on rock 'n' roll with its close connection to African-American culture revealed the racism at the heart of society in the 1950s.

FIGURE 6–3 With lots of leisure time and money to spend from part-time jobs, teenagers in the 1950s developed a new sense of independence and group identity.

Gathering Information What hair and clothing styles that you identify with the 1950s do you see in this photograph?

©P

Television and the Consumer Society

In the early 1950s, a television set cost about 20 percent of an average annual income. Neighbours and relatives would gather to watch at the homes of those lucky enough to own a set. But television quickly became something of a necessity, especially for families with children. The first shows were in black and white; colour TV did not come to Canada until 1966. And what were Canadians watching? American programs topped the list. The kids tuned in to *Howdy Doody, Roy Rogers, Lassie,* and *The Mickey Mouse Club.* Families came together to watch game shows, comedies, Westerns, and variety shows like *The Ed Sullivan Show,* a Sunday night institution that featured everything from comedy, classical music, and circus acts to teen pop stars.

The scrimping and saving of the 1930s and the rationing of the war years were now left far behind. The advertisers that sponsored television shows were sending the powerful and appealing message that consumption was the road to happiness. They were selling the good life: bigger cars, more household appliances, new "improved" products. TV also encouraged youngsters to become consumers, introducing them to sweetened cereals, Barbie dolls, and Davy Crockett hats. Advertising was one of the biggest areas of economic growth during the decade—with companies doubling their spending to $11.9 billion by 1960 in the United States.

WEB LINK • ·
Read more about Canadian consumerism on the Pearson Web site.

FIGURE 6–4 Television shaped the values of the time. American shows promoted the ideal of a traditional, wholesome, family-centred lifestyle.

Identifying Viewpoints What values are evident in this still from the show *Father Knows Best*?

PRACTICE QUESTIONS

1. How did the automobile culture change neighbourhoods? What businesses developed because of the automobile culture?

2. Describe the roles of women and men in the 1950s. Discuss reasons why you think many accepted these roles.

3. What effect did television have on many people's buying habits in the post-war period?

4. **Patterns and Change** How would being a teenager in the 1950s be similar to and different from being a teenager today?

The age of the consumer really began in the 1950s when the economy was prospering. People had jobs and they had more access to credit cards than ever before. As a result, they were able to buy the goods that factories were gearing up to produce. Vast numbers of new gadgets and inventions were introduced into the marketplace during this period.

Advertisements were an important part of this process. They created powerful messages to make people want to buy things that would make their lives better, easier, and more glamorous.

Some people would argue that advertisements are, in fact, a form of propaganda. Both advertisements and propaganda try to influence people's emotions in order to make them think and act in certain ways. During the First and Second World Wars the Canadian government used propaganda posters to create support for the war across the country and to encourage people to purchase war bonds. After the war, advertisers continued to use similar techniques to create a need for the products and lifestyle they were selling.

Analyzing Ads and Propaganda

Here are some questions to consider when you are looking at advertisements and propaganda.

1. What product or viewpoint is being sold?

2. What mood is created and why?

3. What is the relationship between the image and the written material?

4. Does the written material provide information or is it there to generate an emotional response?

5. If there are people in the image, what are they like? What message do they convey?

6. What social attitudes are directly or indirectly reflected?

FIGURE 6–5 This advertisement is not only selling a brand of refrigerators, but it is also selling a lifestyle. Why might women find this ad appealing?

FIGURE 6–6 What message does this propaganda poster convey?

FIGURE 6–7 Effective advertising targets specific audiences by portraying people and situations with which the target audience can identify. In addition to telephones, what more is this ad selling? Who is the target audience?

Why you <u>need</u> a kitchen extension phone

First, it's a great help in running the house—near shopping lists and at your finger tips for calls to the plumber or other repairmen.

Next, it saves you trouble. Biscuits won't burn, or a pot boil over, because a telephone call took you out of the kitchen. And you can still keep a watchful eye on playing children.

It saves you lots of steps, too. Your husband,

like you, will find it one of the most useful phones in your house.

And when all your work is done, it's easy and fun to take a break and chat with a friend on your handy kitchen extension.

Fact is, extension phones in the places your family works, sleeps and plays help so much and cost so little.

SPRING-A-LING!
IT'S KITCHEN TELEPHONE TIME!

Drop in soon at your local Bell Telephone business office and see the colorful kitchen phones on display there. One of them will be just right for *your* kitchen!

BELL TELEPHONE SYSTEM

Applying the Skill

1. How do the advertisements and the poster appeal to the viewer's emotions?

2. Evaluate how effectively these three images deliver their messages. Explain.

3. Compare the way women are portrayed in the advertisements and the propaganda poster.

4. Select several contemporary advertisements that contain images of women. Compare and contrast the images to the ones on pages 174 to 175. Analyze what message these contemporary images intend to convey. How does this message help to sell the product?

Protecting Canadian Culture: The Massey Commission

Television was a powerful cultural influence. Many Canadians saw world events unfolding through an American lens as they watched popular newscasts from the United States. Children of the 1950s grew up identifying more with American culture and values than any generation before them. In 1949, the Liberal government of Louis St. Laurent established the **Massey Commission** to investigate the state of Canadian culture. When the Commission reported in 1951, it suggested that Canadian culture needed to be protected from U.S. influences. Measures taken as a result of its recommendations included the following:

- Canadian television would be used to promote national communication and for cultural education in drama and music. The CBC, which already had a national radio network, was put in charge of the development of television. It opened its first two stations in Toronto and Montréal in 1952. Two years later, four more cities were added. By 1960, 90 percent of Canadian homes had a television and access to the CBC.

- The National Film Board (NFB) would be strengthened.

- The government would become involved in funding universities and the arts. Consequently the **Canada Council for the Arts** was created, which awarded grants to writers, artists, and theatres.

Another important step in the protection of Canadian culture was the creation of the **Canadian Radio-television and Telecommunications Commission (CRTC)** in 1968. This agency would regulate the amount of foreign material broadcast over the airwaves and impose rules requiring Canadian content.

Each of these measures encouraged the growth of arts and culture in Canada and had a profound effect on Canadian identity in the post-war years.

What If...

Imagine that measures had never been put in place to protect Canadian culture. To what extent do you think that Canadians' choices in the books they read, the music they listen to, and the movies and television shows they watch would be different today? Give examples from your own experience to support your answer.

FIGURE 6–8 The National Ballet of Canada was established in 1957. This photograph shows Canadian ballet stars David Adams and Lois Smith in a 1950s National Ballet of Canada production of *Swan Lake*.

TIMELINE	Protecting Canadian Culture					
1936 CBC Radio begins broadcasting	**1939** National Film Board established		**1951** Massey Commission report	**1952** CBC Television begins broadcasting	**1957** Canada Council for the Arts established	**1968** CRTC formed

Post-War Immigration

From 1905, when Clifford Sifton's "open-door policy" ended, up until the 1960s, Canada had a somewhat restrictive **immigration policy**. Immigrants of British and European origin, especially northern Europeans, were preferred because it was thought that they would adapt the most easily to the Canadian way of life. Immigrants of other origins did arrive, but the government limited their numbers. After the Second World War, nearly 1 million veterans returned to Canada. Not all of them came home alone: many Canadian bachelors serving overseas married there.

War brides formed just part of the wave of immigrants that arrived in Canada after the Second World War. Millions of refugees were stuck in camps across Europe at the end of the war. They included concentration camp survivors and others uprooted by the war. Canada accepted 165 000 such **displaced persons**, settling them in communities across the country.

Other immigrants were attracted by new possibilities in Canada and wanted to escape war-torn Europe. Unable to practise their former trades or professions in Canada, some of these newcomers had a hard time. Nevertheless, refugee children absorbed English quickly at school, and their parents found that a job, any job, opened up new opportunities. More than 2 million immigrants arrived between 1945 and 1960.

Unlike immigrants before the First World War, who had settled largely on farms in Western Canada, post–Second World War immigrants usually settled in the cities of Central Canada where their cultures and hard work enriched Canada in many ways. Older areas of larger cities, vacated as veterans and their families moved to the suburbs, became home to vibrant new communities.

In 1956 when a violent revolution broke out in Hungary, federal and provincial governments relaxed entry requirements in order to allow Hungarians wanting to escape communism to immigrate to Canada. More than 37 000 Hungarians came to Canada. Many Czechs and Slovaks came to Canada from Czechoslovakia in 1968–1969 under similar circumstances. (You will read about communism in eastern Europe later in this chapter.)

KEY TERMS

Massey Commission a body set up by the federal government to study the state of Canadian culture

Canada Council for the Arts the group that funds Canadian artists and supports the arts in Canada

Canadian Radio-television and Telecommunications Commission (CRTC) the agency that regulates the amount of foreign material broadcast over the airwaves in Canada and imposes rules requiring Canadian content

immigration policy a nation's regulations surrounding immigration

displaced persons those who are forced to leave their native home because of war or for political reasons

FIGURE 6–9 Most war brides were British, although some came from France and the Netherlands.

Expressing Ideas What challenges do you think these women might have faced in their new homeland?

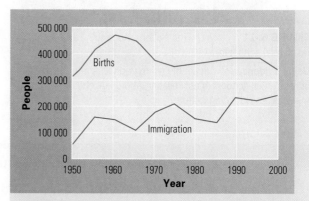

FIGURE 6–10 Immigration and births in Canada from 1950 to 2000

Gathering Information What trends in birth and immigration rates can you see on this graph? To what extent do they match up? What might account for this?

What challenges did
Aboriginal people face in the
1950s?

Aboriginal Communities in Transition

The post-war years were times of transition for Aboriginal communities. Those who had served in the military during the war—3000 status Indians and thousands more non-status Aboriginal people and Métis out of a total population of 166 000—still faced institutionalized racism and other barriers when they returned home. Aboriginal soldiers were denied the same benefits as other veterans.

Education Issues

Education was always a concern for Aboriginal people. For many decades, Aboriginal children were forced to leave home to attend residential schools. Here they were isolated from their home communities and families and forced to abandon their culture and language. The purpose of the schools was the assimilation of Aboriginal children into mainstream Canadian culture.

Although compulsory attendance in residential schools ended in 1948, many remained in operation during the 1950s. In fact, as a result of the baby boom, the 1950s were peak years in the residential school system—with 76 schools in operation. The last residential school did not close until 1996. Residential schools were underfunded and relied on the forced labour of their students. Students in many facilities received a poor education.

In response to the demands of Aboriginal parents, the federal government began to fund off-reserve education. By 1960, thousands of Aboriginal youth were attending provincial schools with certified teachers and modern equipment. However, teachers were often not trained to meet the needs of Aboriginal students. This, and the fact that many students had to commute long distances by bus or board far from home, worked against their academic success.

Changes to the Indian Act

In 1951, a number of changes were made to the Indian Act that governed the lives of First Nations peoples. Women gained the right to vote in band elections, and potlatches and wearing traditional regalia were no longer illegal. However, the Indian Act maintained the federal government's power to define Indian status and band membership and continued to control the political and economic lives of Aboriginal people.

FIGURE 6–11 A class of First Nations students at an Alberta residential school in 1950

Using Evidence How does this photograph illustrate the role of residential schools in assimilating Aboriginal children into mainstream Canadian culture?

PRACTICE QUESTIONS

1. Make a web diagram showing social changes in Canada after the Second World War. Be sure to include the following, and show relationships among them, where possible: war brides, immigration, the baby boom, suburbs, youth culture, and Aboriginal communities.

2. What is the role of the CRTC? Do any media threaten Canadian identity today? Explain.

3. What challenges did Aboriginal people in Canada face during the 1950s?

The High Arctic Relocation

FIGURE 6–12 The Inuit community of Qausuittuq (Resolute) in 1956. It was formerly in the Northwest Territories and is now part of Nunavut.

FIGURE 6–13 The new territory of Nunavut was created in 1999.

Governments around the world have sometimes arbitrarily relocated Aboriginal people with little consideration of their needs and rights. The resettlement in 1953–1955 of Inuit families to the High Arctic almost 2000 kilometres away from their former homes was such a case.

In the summer of 1953, the Canadian government relocated several Inuit families from Inukjuak (formerly known as Port Harrison) in northern Québec and Pond Inlet in Nunavut (formerly the Northwest Territories) to Grise Fjord and Resolute Bay. A second group of families was moved from Inukjuak two years later.

The families volunteered for the move because hunting in their area was poor, but they were not told about conditions in the Arctic or about how difficult it would be to return to Québec if they wished to do so. Families were dropped off without firewood or housing at the onset of the Arctic's four-month winter darkness. Survivors today still talk about their struggles: hunger, defending themselves from polar bears, and living in igloos until they could get wood to build houses.

In the 1980s, a suit was initiated against the federal government arguing that the relocation was done to assert Canadian sovereignty in the Far North rather than to benefit the Inuit. The Arctic had become strategically important for defence during the Cold War. (You will read about the Cold War later in this chapter.)

In 1989, the federal government created a program to help those relocated (and their descendants) who wished to return south. In 1996, the government offered cash compensation to the survivors but did not offer an apology. Today their descendants are bitter, claiming that people were promised abundant game and fish, but instead faced cold, disease, hunger, and poverty.

Looking Further

1. Look up the term "paternalism." Was government action in the High Arctic relocation program paternalistic? Explain.

2. Compare the actions of the 1950s government that relocated the Inuit to the way governments operate now. Would such a program be possible today? Explain.

● What measures has Canada taken to promote a distinct Canadian identity?

● What factors contributed to Canada's emerging autonomy?

KEY TERMS

populist someone who appeals to the concerns of ordinary citizens

referendum the process of referring a political question to the people for a direct vote

New Times, New Leadership

Canada's leadership changed little during the early post-war years. Mackenzie King, who had guided the country through the war, retired and his successor, Louis St. Laurent, pursued very similar policies. The Liberals were finally put out of office when the Progressive Conservatives formed a minority government headed by John Diefenbaker in 1957. Diefenbaker called a snap election in 1958 and won the largest majority government in Canadian history.

The Changing Face of Federal Politics

When Mackenzie King retired in 1948 at the age of 73, he had been in power longer than any Canadian prime minister before him. He was succeeded by Louis St. Laurent as a new age of politics was born. King had governed in the days before television. Today's television commentators would probably have focused on his personal life or pompous speeches, but during his years in power such things were not considered important. By the early 1950s, however, the media was playing a much larger role in Canadian life.

St. Laurent entered politics late in life and during the 1949 election campaign, the Liberal Party election organizers worried about how they could sell this rather shy, reserved, elderly man to the Canadian public. Then, during a campaign stop at a railway station, a reporter noticed St. Laurent, who was a father of five and grandfather of twelve, chatting with a group of children. Newspapers soon began referring to St. Laurent as "Uncle Louis." The media thus created the image of St. Laurent as a kindly relative. The Liberal advertising agency made sure the nickname stuck. From that time on, the media has played an influential part in Canadian politics.

Louis St. Laurent and Canadian Autonomy

Louis St. Laurent was born in Compton, Québec, to an English-speaking mother and a French-speaking father. He was nearing retirement after a successful law career when he was approached by Mackenzie King to become Minister of Justice in his government. St. Laurent was elected to the Commons in 1942 and provided key support to King during the conscription crisis of the Second World War. When King retired, St. Laurent seemed to be the right man to take over as prime minister.

St. Laurent led a progressive government that expanded federal social welfare programs, such as old-age pensions and family allowances. He also brought in hospital insurance, another important step on Canada's road to universal health care. His other major domestic contributions were in the areas of protecting Canadian culture (see page 176) and gaining Canada more autonomy from Britain. Measures St. Laurent took as prime minister to increase Canadian autonomy included

FIGURE 6–14 St. Laurent on the campaign trail

Expressing Ideas What impression does this photograph give of St. Laurent? What elements in the photograph suggest that it was carefully posed?

- appointing the first Canadian-born Governor General, Vincent Massey
- making the Supreme Court of Canada the highest court of appeal for Canadian cases rather than the Judicial Committee of the Privy Council, a British legal body
- negotiating with Britain to give the Canadian Parliament the power to amend portions of its own constitution without appealing to the British Parliament. This resulted in the British North America (No. 2) Act, 1949

St. Laurent also played a leading role in Canadian post-war peace and defence initiatives, as you will see later in the chapter.

Election Defeat

Louis St. Laurent fought and won election campaigns in 1949 and 1953. When the next election rolled around in 1957, the 75-year-old St. Laurent was looking tired and depressed. By comparison, the new Progressive Conservative leader, John Diefenbaker, seemed energetic. Used to public speaking as a defence attorney in Saskatchewan, "Dief" proved to be a great campaigner and a witty orator. Television carried his image across the nation, and he led his party to a narrow election victory. Diefenbaker was the first Westerner to become prime minister. St. Laurent resigned and the defeated Liberals chose a new leader, the diplomat Lester "Mike" Pearson.

Of German extraction, Diefenbaker was the first Canadian prime minister whose father was of neither English nor French background. He saw himself as a Prairie **populist**, one who spoke for and listened to ordinary people. Ordinary people, in turn, responded to him. A colleague recalled the 1958 campaign: "I saw people kneel and kiss his coat. Not one, but many. People were in tears. People were delirious."

The Nation Expands

Prime Minister St. Laurent was part of the negotiations that resulted in Newfoundland joining Canada. The process of expanding Canada from sea to sea had been set in motion by Prime Minister King at the end of the Second World War. Until 1932, Newfoundland had been an independent, self-governing dominion within the British Empire. During the Depression, however, the island had suffered so badly that its government had gone bankrupt. Democracy was temporarily suspended and Britain set up a special commission to govern Newfoundland.

In 1948, the islanders were given the opportunity to vote on their political future in a **referendum**. They were offered three options: to continue to be governed by special commission, to be a self-governing dominion within the British Empire, or to join Canada. J.R. "Joey" Smallwood, a skillful Newfoundland politician, argued that union with Canada would bring modernization to the province. Yet, many Newfoundlanders believed the benefits could not make up for the higher taxes and loss of identity that Confederation would bring. Some preferred economic union with the United States.

Prime Minister
Louis St. Laurent

- born 1882, Compton, Québec
- lawyer
- first elected to Commons, 1942
- prime minister 1948–1957

Domestic Record

- negotiated entry of Newfoundland into Confederation
- made Supreme Court of Canada highest court of appeal
- negotiated changes to BNA Act, giving Canadian Parliament authority to amend portions of the Act
- appointed Vincent Massey, first Canadian-born Governor General
- established Massey Commission investigation into protecting Canadian culture
- expanded social welfare programs
- initiated megaprojects such as the Trans-Canada Highway

International Record

- defined Canada as middle power
- supported NATO and UN
- sent forces to UN in Korea
- sent Lester Pearson to defuse the Suez crisis

FIGURE 6–15 Governor General Vincent Massey shakes hands with the newly elected Prime Minister John Diefenbaker.

In a referendum in June 1948, only 41 percent of Newfoundlanders favoured Confederation. A larger number, 44.6 percent, voted in favour of returning to the self-governing dominion status, while 14 percent preferred government by commission. As no option won a clear majority, another vote was scheduled for late July. This time, the commission option was dropped, and the Confederation option won 52 percent of the vote.

The Terms of Union were negotiated with the federal government under Prime Minister St. Laurent, and on March 31, 1949, Newfoundland became part of Canada. That same year, Joey Smallwood was elected premier of the new province, a job he held for more than two decades.

FIGURE 6–16 Resettlement continued in Newfoundland throughout the 1960s and into the 1970s. This house was towed across Inner Tickle of Newtown to its new location.

Thinking Critically How does the resettlement in Newfoundland show the tensions that sometimes exist between progress on the one hand, and cultural and lifestyle traditions on the other?

Resettlement in Newfoundland

Newfoundlanders had joined Canada in the hope that Confederation would bring better health care, education, and employment opportunities. It was difficult, however, to provide these services in Newfoundland's outports— isolated fishing settlements connected to the outside world only by occasional ferry service. In 1954, the provincial government introduced a "centralization" program that offered compensation to people who wanted to move to larger centres. Families were paid an average of $301, which is about $2430 in today's dollars. By 1959, about 2400 people from 29 communities had been resettled. Unfortunately, prosperity did not follow relocation. In fact, Newfoundland's unemployment rate climbed. The social impact of losing homes, traditions, and a unique way of life in the outports could not be measured. Some Newfoundlanders still feel grief and resentment over the resettlement.

Duplessis and the Roots of Québec Nationalism

● How was Québec nationalism expressed in the 1950s?

From 1936 to 1939, and again from 1944 to 1959, Québec was controlled by Premier Maurice Duplessis and his party, the Union Nationale. Duplessis was a strong Québec nationalist who promoted the idea of Québec as a distinctive society, a "nation" rather than just another Canadian province. To emphasize his province's difference from English-speaking Canada, Duplessis introduced a new flag for Québec bearing the French symbol, the fleur-de-lys. He fiercely opposed the growing powers of the federal government in the post-war years.

Under Duplessis, the Roman Catholic Church was the main defender of Québec culture. Priests urged people in Québec to turn their backs on the materialism of English-speaking North America. The Church praised the old Québec traditions of farm, faith, and family. It ran Québec's hospitals and schools. Religion played a role in every part of the curriculum, and the schools taught children to accept authority. The elite few who attended high

©P

school and university received a fine education, but the emphasis was on traditional subjects such as classical languages and philosophy. As a result, Québec produced many priests, lawyers, and politicians, but few scientists, engineers, or business people.

While Duplessis tried to keep out the influence of foreign culture, he encouraged foreign investment in Québec. The province guaranteed cheap labour, since union activity was either discouraged or banned. It also promised low taxes. Québec would benefit from the new investment, but so would Duplessis. In return for favourable business conditions, companies were expected to contribute generously to the Union Nationale.

Bribery and corruption became the trademarks of the Duplessis regime. One of the worst of these was the case of the "Duplessis Orphans." Thousands of children housed in orphanages financed by the province were falsely certified as mentally ill and moved into insane asylums, which were funded by the federal government. For many Québécois, the Duplessis era is *La Grande Noirceur*, the Great Darkness.

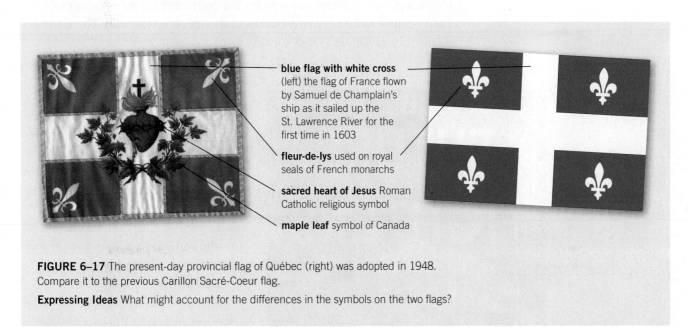

blue flag with white cross (left) the flag of France flown by Samuel de Champlain's ship as it sailed up the St. Lawrence River for the first time in 1603

fleur-de-lys used on royal seals of French monarchs

sacred heart of Jesus Roman Catholic religious symbol

maple leaf symbol of Canada

FIGURE 6–17 The present-day provincial flag of Québec (right) was adopted in 1948. Compare it to the previous Carillon Sacré-Coeur flag.

Expressing Ideas What might account for the differences in the symbols on the two flags?

PRACTICE QUESTIONS

1. **a)** Why was Confederation so hotly debated in Newfoundland in 1949?

   b) Only 52 percent of Newfoundlanders voted to join Canada. Do you think this was enough of a margin to warrant such a huge political change? Should it have been necessary for a greater percentage to support the change? Give reasons for your view.

2. **a)** Explain how the media was important in creating the image of politicians in this period.

   b) How is the current prime minister presented in the media? Use pictures from different sources to compare the images created. Include editorial cartoons.

3. Create a web diagram summarizing Québec society and politics under Maurice Duplessis.

- What were the characteristics of the post-war economic boom?

KEY TERMS

boom town a town that enjoys sudden prosperity or develops quickly

boom and bust cycle a term used to describe a healthy (booming) economy and/or one that is failing (bust)

Post-War Prosperity

The Second World War had transformed Canadian industry and society. As the war ended, the government needed to find ways to ease the transition from a wartime to a peacetime economy. But planning for peace was complicated—a million people who had worked in war-production industries and close to half a million in the armed services were about to lose their jobs.

Veterans returning to Canada were eager to come home but anxious about the future. Would they find jobs? Many had enlisted in the armed forces right out of high school or had been unemployed during the Depression. However, new laws ensured that they got their old jobs back if they wanted them and that the years they had been at war were counted as years of service on the job. Government policy encouraged women to leave factories to make room for men, which freed up many jobs. Veterans who wished to attend university or trade school received free tuition and living allowances. Veterans and war widows got preference for government jobs. The Veterans' Land Act gave veterans mortgages at lower rates. These government interventions saved Canada from economic recession.

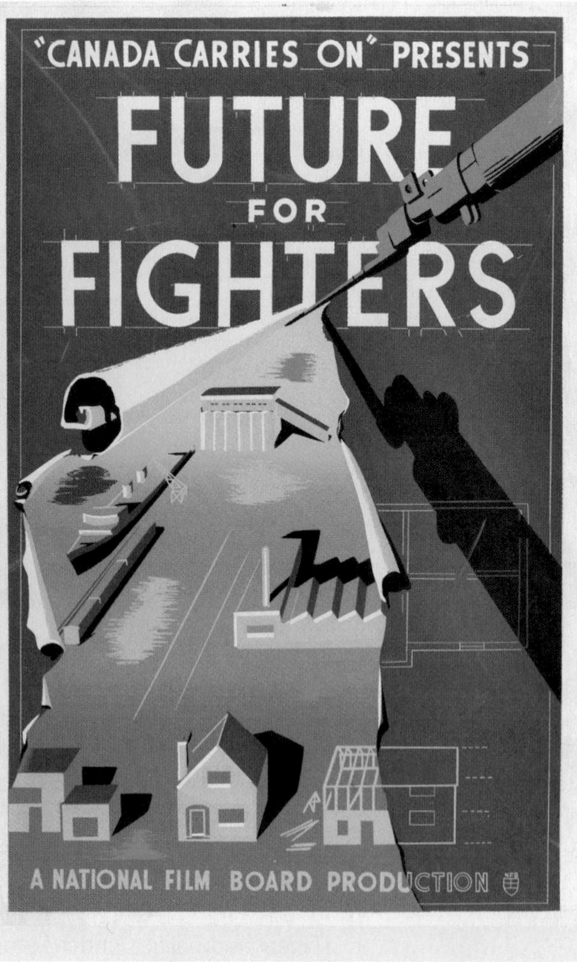

FIGURE 6–18 A 1943 National Film Board poster promoting the "Canada Carries On" series. These films documented Canada's war involvement and sought to inform viewers that the war would bring prosperity to Canada.

Spreading the Wealth

As a wartime measure, the provinces had transferred their economic powers to the federal government. Prime Minister Mackenzie King wanted this to become permanent, but provinces were not willing to give up a power conferred on them at Confederation. In the end, the provinces gave in and transferred taxation powers to the federal government. In return, they received government grants for social services such as health care and education. Through equalization or transfer payments, the federal government would then transfer money to the poorer provinces.

Meanwhile, C.D. Howe, Minister of Reconstruction, Trade, and Commerce, gave economic incentives such as generous tax breaks to private industry. Soon, factories were producing washing machines, automobiles, and other items that were in demand, and Canada's economy was booming.

©P

C.D. Howe was one of Canada's most influential politicians in the post-war period. When the Depression forced him to close his engineering business in 1935, he entered politics as a Liberal MP. Howe rose quickly in government. During the war, he ran the country's economy, and after it he manoeuvred the provinces into giving the federal government more control.

In two decades as a Cabinet minister, Howe was responsible at one time or another for railways, canals, airlines, munitions, war supplies, transition to peacetime, pipelines, trade, and commerce. He was, people said, the "Minister of Everything."

Howe admired the efficiency of the American economy and was impatient with debates over economic issues in Canada's House of Commons. Howe's short temper and determination to force his plans through eventually made him unpopular.

FIGURE 6–19 Howe (second from left) with Winston Churchill and W.L. Mackenzie King, 1944

Rich Resources and New Industries

Traditional industries such as mining and forestry remained at the heart of the Canadian economy. Massive development of mines, forests, smelters, and the like encouraged the economic boom of the post-war period. One of the most important developments was the discovery of oil at Leduc, Alberta, in 1947. It was Canada's entry into the international oil market.

Wherever new mines and wells developed, resource companies carved **boom towns** in the wilderness, sometimes airlifting in heavy equipment, construction material, and other supplies. Employees lived in tents, trailers, and temporary shanties often far from the nearest town or city. Although they were very well paid, many workers—mostly single men—were starved for distractions. Gambling and alcoholism were chronic problems.

While resource industries developed in frontier areas, manufacturing in southern Ontario grew tremendously. By the 1950s, more than half of the nation's factories and plants and 99 percent of its automobile industry were located in Ontario, close to transportation routes and markets.

In later decades, when resource industries in other parts of the country were in the "bust" part of the **boom and bust cycle**, Ontario did well. Those in other provinces deeply resented Ontario's seemingly privileged position and its apparent immunity from economic downturns.

FIGURE 6–20 In the early years of the 21st century, Fort McMurray, Alberta, was called a boom town because of its growth as a result of oil sands development.

Innovations
1950s Technology

Even a famous science fiction writer could not have guessed how much technology would transform life in the decades after the Second World War. H.G. Wells, author of books such as *The Time Machine* and *The Shape of Things to Come*, predicted that by 1950 soldiers would wage war from bicycles and drop bombs from balloons. In reality, the atomic bomb had demonstrated the awesome power of science. It was soon replaced by the even more powerful hydrogen bomb. While military technology was developing rapidly, everyday life, too, was being changed by new inventions.

Ballpoint pen After the war, manufacturers competed to produce the first reliable ballpoint pens.

Satellite The Russians launched the first artificial satellite, Sputnik, in 1957, with the Americans following in 1958. The space race had begun. Today, artificial satellites are used in weather forecasting, television transmission, and supplying navigation data for aircraft and ships. They are also used for military purposes such as surveillance and tracking missile launches.

Television transformed the way Canadians entertained and educated themselves. TV exposure could make or break political careers and start social movements.

Heart pacemaker Technology transformed medicine. In 1957, the first wearable heart pacemaker and artificial heart valves extended the lives of people who, just years before, would not have survived.

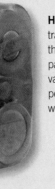

Transistor radio In 1948, Bell Telephone announced the invention of the transistor, an electronic device for amplifying and switching that is durable, small, and inexpensive. In 1955, Sony Corporation sold the first transistor radios, and over the next decades the radios grew smaller and more portable. Radio, which was predicted to die out in the age of TV, was revived, as teens could now take their music with them wherever they went.

Vinyl was invented by the chemist who also discovered bubble gum. This new synthetic product allowed for the invention of many new products in the years after the Second World War. Fire-resistant, waterproof, flexible, and cheap, it was used to make a host of items including long-playing records, convertible automobile roofs, and garden hoses.

©P

Giant Projects for a Giant Land

As towns across Canada grew, governments improved infrastructure—roads, sewer systems, power plants, schools, and hospitals—using taxes from business and workers in the booming economy. The money paid out to construction companies created more jobs and stimulated the economy as workers spent their wages. The federal government under Louis St. Laurent enthusiastically undertook **megaprojects** that changed the face of the Canadian landscape.

Few people realized at the time that many projects and industrial processes had hidden costs. The greatest of these was pollution. Solid industrial wastes were simply buried, creating toxic landfills on which housing, schools, and playgrounds were sometimes constructed. Pulp and paper and petrochemical plants dumped wastes directly into streams, contaminating lakes and rivers. Industry simply wanted high productivity and low costs. Farmers pumped weedkiller and chemical fertilizers into the soil and, indirectly, into the groundwater. Homeowners casually used the insecticide DDT, a contact poison, around their houses and yards. Nevertheless, "pollution" did not become a common word until the late 1960s.

● How does industrial development affect the environment?

KEY TERM

megaprojects large-scale construction projects that require a huge capital investment; the construction of the St. Lawrence Seaway is an example

Trans-Canada Highway	• construction began in 1950 with huge government investment to upgrade and pave roads along the Trans-Canada Route • 7821-kilometre road from St. John's, Newfoundland, to Victoria, British Columbia; would be the longest national highway in the world
Kemano Project	• created to generate hydroelectricity to support aluminum smelting in the town of Kitimat • water of the Nechako River diverted into the Nechako Reservoir behind the Kenney Dam. This resulted in the flooding of land within the territory of the Dakelh First Nation. • dam construction was completed in 1952
Trans-Canada Pipeline	• natural gas pipeline to carry gas east from Alberta all the way to Québec • completed in 1958
St. Lawrence Seaway	• system of locks that would allow large ships from the Atlantic to travel all the way to Lake Superior • built cooperatively by Canada and United States between 1954 and 1959 • benefits: prairie grain could be loaded directly onto Europe-bound ships at Thunder Bay, cutting back on the cost of rail transportation; business increased in inland ports; and hydroelectric power plants were developed at dam sites

FIGURE 6–21 Trans-Canada Highway in Western Canada

What was the impact of American investment on the Canadian economy?

American Investment: A Continuing Issue

In 1945 President Franklin Roosevelt and Prime Minister Mackenzie King discussed economic cooperation between their two countries. King described it to Parliament this way: "It involves nothing less than a common plan [for] the economic defense of the western hemisphere." Canadians regularly debated their economic ties with the United States asking: Is Canada becoming the "49th state"?

The United States, like Canada, had a booming economy in the post-war years. When it began to run short of raw materials, it looked to Canada as a vast storehouse of minerals and other natural resources. Canadians, for their part, recognized that they needed investment to extract resources such as oil, uranium, and iron ore. By 1957, Americans controlled 70 percent of oil and gas investment, 52 percent of mining and smelting, and 43 percent of Canadian manufacturing. In addition, U.S. companies had opened numerous branch plants in Canada.

There were advantages and disadvantages to U.S. investment. Branch plants provided many Canadians with good jobs in manufacturing, and Canadian industries benefited from U.S. technology. However, profits from the branch plants went back to the parent corporations in the United States. To many critics, it looked as though Canada was losing control of its economy. The debate continued for decades, until the North American Free Trade Agreement (NAFTA) brought about a new economic relationship in 1994. (You will read about NAFTA in Chapter 8.)

FIGURE 6–22 Newfoundland lumbermen on strike, March 1959

The Labour Movement in Canada

The wealth of Canada was not entirely in the hands of others. Canadian tycoons built up commercial empires that commanded vast resources and employed many people. On the West Coast, H.R. MacMillan put together one of the world's largest forestry companies. In New Brunswick, K.C. Irving became one of the world's richest men with businesses ranging from gas stations to timber and newspapers. In Central Canada, E.P. Taylor and the Bronfman family controlled the production of many consumer goods and the stores that sold them.

At the same time, members of trade unions fought for a greater share of the country's prosperity. In 1946 and 1947, strikes were frequent as workers fought for the right to form unions and pressed for wages that would support a family. As a result, wages rose, for example, from $0.67 per hour in 1945 to $0.95 per hour in 1948. Workers won a major victory in establishing the 5-day, 40-hour workweek and increasing fringe benefits such as paid vacations. These hard-won benefits eventually became standard for many workers across the country. This meant Canadian workers had more money and more leisure time to enjoy it. Business benefited as well, because consumer spending rose. Non-industrial unions grew rapidly, including organizations for teachers, nurses, civil servants, postal workers, and police.

• How did people improve their working conditions after the Second World War?

The Limits of Prosperity

Some groups did not share the prosperity of the times. The working poor in cities—including many immigrants—washed dishes, cleaned offices, sweated in meat-packing plants, or toiled at sewing machines under miserable conditions. Women who could not afford to be stay-at-home wives and mothers were at a particular disadvantage. They were made to feel guilty by a society that condemned mothers who went out to work. Women were legally discriminated against by their employers, who paid them less than men even if they did the same work.

PRACTICE QUESTIONS

1. Why did the problem of post-war unemployment not arise?

2. What are transfer payments? Why were they instituted?

3. **Significance** Which advances in technology do you think had the greatest effect on society in the short and long term? Which do you think will be the most significant 100 years from now? Why?

4. Explain the importance of one of the megaprojects of the 1950s.

5. List some of the environmental problems that emerged during the post-war period.

6. Which groups were marginalized in the 1950s and 1960s? Why do you think this was so?

7. Why was American investment necessary and controversial?

8. Why were unions important?

9. Why were women workers at a disadvantage in the 1950s?

The Cold War and Post-War Diplomacy

In 1945, a Russian citizen, Igor Gouzenko, was working as a clerk at the Soviet embassy in Ottawa. In September of that year, Gouzenko went to the *Ottawa Journal* with documents proving that a Soviet spy ring was operating within the Canadian government. When no one at the newspaper believed him, Gouzenko took his pregnant wife and child in tow and brought the documents to the offices of the RCMP, the Department of Justice, and the prime minister. Still no one believed him—until Soviet agents broke into his apartment. Finally Gouzenko and his family got protection from Canadian authorities.

Canadian officials informed the British and American governments of the spy ring. In February, 1946, the RCMP made several arrests. The spy ring was likely trying to discover information about the atomic bomb, but it appeared that the Soviets had learned very little. The Gouzenko affair brought Canadians into the new reality of the post-war world—the period of intense hostility and suspicion known as the **Cold War**.

The Cold War

During the Second World War, the United States and the Soviet Union had been allies even though they had little in common except their opposition to the Axis powers. Once the war was over, tensions between the two countries surfaced. At the heart of the conflict were differences in their political and economic systems. The Soviet Union was **communist**, which meant that the

FIGURE 6–23 The government gave Soviet embassy clerk Igor Gouzenko and his family new identities, after which they settled in Ontario. Gouzenko wrote a book about his experiences and occasionally appeared in public, as in this television interview. He always wore a hood, afraid that the Soviet spy agency, the KGB, would kill him.

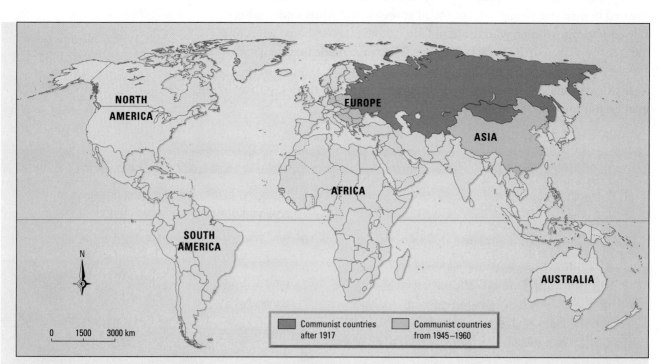

FIGURE 6–24 After the October 1917 revolution in Russia, two countries were recognized as communist. The post-war world, after 1945, saw the addition of 12 new communist countries, most of which were in Eastern Europe.

Developing Understanding How does this map contribute to your understanding of American concerns about the spread of communism?

©P

government controlled all industry and commerce. Under communism, political opposition was not tolerated. The United States and most Western countries were **capitalist**. Their economies were based on private enterprise, with individuals investing in business for profit. Citizens had basic freedoms such as freedom of the press and freedom of speech.

Western countries were suspicious of communism. As in the decades following the First World War, they feared that communists planned to overthrow Western societies in a world revolution. The Soviet Union, for its part, was suspicious that the Western countries might try to invade Soviet territory through Europe. The Soviets took over the countries of Eastern Europe in the years following the Second World War and established communist governments in them. The West, particularly the United States, saw this expansion as proof of Soviet designs on the world.

As a result, the war years were not followed by peace and cooperation, as so many had hoped. Instead hostility increased between the Soviets and the Americans. But this was not traditional warfare; it was a Cold War in which no shots were fired and no battles took place. At the same time, both sides built up huge stockpiles of sophisticated arms, including the atomic bomb and other nuclear weapons and also spied on one another. The rivals became **superpowers**, each capable of inflicting massive destruction.

Canada aligned itself closely with U.S. interests while trying to remain true to the goals and values of Canadians—not an easy task. Through the early part of the 20th century, Canada had achieved independence from Britain; in the latter half, Canada struggled to keep U.S. influences from weakening its national identity.

KEY TERMS

Cold War a period lasting approximately from 1945 to 1989 when there was tension and hostility between the communist Soviet Union and its allies and the capitalist United States and its allies

communist one who believes that property and the production and distribution of goods and services should be owned by the public and that the labour force should be organized for the benefit of all; the application of the theory in the Soviet Union, China, Cuba, and other countries resulted in dictatorships by leaders of communist parties

capitalist one who believes in an economic system in which the production and distribution of goods are owned privately or by shareholders in corporations that have invested money in the hope of making a profit

superpowers the term used to refer to the United States and Soviet Union in the post–Second World War period when both were engaged in building up powerful arsenals of weapons of mass destruction as deterrents against aggression

The Cold War at Home

When the Igor Gouzenko story hit the media, the Canadian public was shocked to learn that a communist spy ring had been operating in Canada. During the early decades of the Cold War, many Canadians worried that an open war between the Soviet Union and the United States would result in a rain of nuclear bombs and missiles on Canada. The federal government in Ottawa developed civil defence plans, and cities prepared to protect their populations. Some cities had nuclear shelters in deep basements or subway tunnels. If an attack were to occur, sirens would sound a warning and people would try to find shelter. Schools ran drills to teach students to "duck and cover" or to lie in ditches. The fear of a nuclear Third World War was very real. Ironically, however, the existence of nuclear weapons—and the threat of mass destruction—probably prevented an all-out war between the superpowers.

FIGURE 6–25 Students doing a duck-and-cover drill

Was the "Red Menace" real?

The "Red Menace" referred to the threat from the communist Soviet Union and its allies. Communists became known as "Reds" because the flags of the Communist International and the Soviet Union are red. The Gouzenko Affair had shown that it was possible for communists to infiltrate democratic governments and institutions in North America.

In the United States, Senator Joseph McCarthy and the House Un-American Activities Committee (HUAC) instituted a "witch hunt" for communists. McCarthy terrified people with secret lists of supposed communists who had, according to him, infiltrated all parts of American society.

The Committee interrogated thousands of suspected communists. For instance, many prominent figures in the entertainment industry, including movie stars, were forced to testify before the Committee because they had once belonged to socialist organizations or had simply attended meetings of such groups.

Many Canadians also feared the spread of communism, as is evident in the following quotation:

> No longer could western governments fail to
> acknowledge that Soviet Russia was conducting
> a gigantic conspiracy for the overthrow of gov-
> ernments throughout the free world.
>
> –Clifford Harvison, RCMP Commissioner, 1950s

The "Red Menace" sometimes became an issue in local elections, as the quotation below and poster on page 193 demonstrate.

> Toronto's Communists took a lacing in the civic
> elections with Ald. Charles Sims and Trustee
> Mrs. Edna Ryerson of Ward 5 remaining as the
> only stooges of Stalin on either city council or
> board of education.... On the Board of Education
> three Communist aspirants fell by the wayside.
> In Ward Four, where Mrs. Hazel Wigdor, a
> Commie, retired, Comrade Samuel Walsh took a
> shellacking....
>
> –Globe and Mail, *January 2, 1948*

Unlike U.S. President Dwight Eisenhower, Prime Minister Louis St. Laurent refused to outlaw communism. He reminded Canadians that such tactics were the trademarks of dictatorships, not democracies. Two of Canada's future prime ministers, Lester Pearson and John Diefenbaker, both supported St. Laurent's moderate approach.

> Let us by all means remove the traitors from
> positions of trust, but in doing so, I hope we
> may never succumb to the black madness of the
> witch hunt.
>
> –Lester Pearson quoted in **The Red Scare**

> I frankly state that in 1948 my own party came
> out in favour of outlawing communism. I was
> the only one to oppose it. I received a very
> unusual lack of welcome. The Conservative Party
> was going to sweep Canada with that policy. I
> said, "You cannot do it. You cannot deny an indi-
> vidual the right to think as he will."
>
> –John Diefenbaker, House of Commons, 1970

FIGURE 6–26 Although Joseph McCarthy had many supporters in the United States, he was feared and hated by many people.

● What measures has Canada taken to promote a distinct Canadian identity?

Nevertheless, injustices did take place in Canada.

- Union leaders who fought for better conditions for workers came under suspicion.

- Defence industries secretly sent lists of their employees to Ottawa for screening and dismissed workers suspected of communist sympathies.

- The RCMP Special Branch put artists, peace activists, union leaders, and intellectuals under surveillance.

- Québec Premier Maurice Duplessis used the so-called "Padlock Law" to shut down organizations and newspapers that criticized his government, and to arrest those who sought better rights for workers.

Analyzing the Issue

1. In the United States, and to some extent in Canada, governments and government agencies used un-democratic tactics and violated the civil liberties of those suspected of communist sympathies. Why do you think the rule of law was broken so often at this time?

2. Maurice Duplessis' government used the so-called Padlock Law to close down newspapers that Duplessis thought were communist or leftist and the publications of other groups he did not like. What fundamental Canadian right does this violate? How would this law stand up against the Canadian Charter of Rights and Freedoms?

3. Find out to what extent anti-terrorist poli-cies after 2001 followed the same pattern as the communist witch hunts of the 1950s.

4. Is banning certain political, social, or economic groups ever justified? Explain.

5. What makes evidence credible? Why is it so important that credible evidence of guilt be established in a democratic society?

GET RID OF THE COMMUNISTS!

Their Loyalty Is to Russia

REMEMBER The Traitorous Spies
REMEMBER The Betrayals

REMEMBER TO VOTE AGAINST COMMUNISM

There is only ONE CANDIDATE for the Board of Education in Ward 5 who is non-Communist. That is HAROLD MENZIES.

Sponsored by the Ward 5 Citizens Anti-Communist Committee.

This advertisement is contributed by J. P. F. Williams.

VOTE FOR THESE:

For Mayor — ROBT. H. SAUNDERS.

For Controllers — McCALLUM, INNES, BALFOUR, McKELLAR

For Aldermen — SAUNDERS, WALTON, WEAVER, SHANNON, FISHLEIGH

FIGURE 6–27 A Toronto municipal campaign poster, 1947

©P

KEY TERMS

middle power a nation that is not a super-power but has international influence

North Atlantic Treaty Organization (NATO) the mutual defence organization set up to protect several Western European countries, Canada, and the U.S. from possible aggression from the U.S.S.R. after the Second World War

Warsaw Pact a post–Second World War military alliance established in 1955 involving the Soviet Union and the Soviet-block countries of Albania, Bulgaria, Czechoslovakia, East Germany, Hungary, Poland, and Romania

North American Aerospace Defence Command (NORAD) a defence agreement signed in 1958 between Canada and the United States (known as the North American Air Defence Agreement until 1981)

Distant Early Warning (DEW) radar stations in northern Canada set up between 1958 and 1960 to detect Soviet activity over the North Pole

NATO and the Warsaw Pact

Prime Minister St. Laurent saw Canada as a "power of the middle rank" and his government expanded Canada's international role accordingly. He believed that although Canada had a close relationship with both the United States and Britain, it could nevertheless act independently of these two nations. As a **middle power**, Canada was in the position of effectively representing the interests of smaller nations. St. Laurent was an enthusiastic supporter of Canada's participation in the **North Atlantic Treaty Organization (NATO)** and the United Nations (UN).

In 1949, Canada joined with the United States, Britain, and other Western European nations to form NATO, a military alliance. An attack on one NATO member was to be treated as an attack on all. NATO members agreed that if conventional weapons were not sufficient, they would use tactical weapons, that is, short-range nuclear weapons such as artillery shells or bombs. As a last resort, they would be prepared to wage total nuclear war.

Since the United States was by far the most powerful member of the alliance, much of NATO's activity served American policy first and foremost. Canada's close ties with the United States made maintaining an independent foreign policy very difficult. When NATO admitted West Germany as a member, the Soviet Union initiated the **Warsaw Pact**, a military alliance with Eastern European communist countries, to counter it.

Much of the northern hemisphere was now effectively divided into two hostile camps. Armies constantly practised for war and added to their arsenals of weapons. Everywhere, spies and counterspies probed for weaknesses in their enemy's security—searching for secrets, carrying out assassinations, and promoting revolutions and counter-revolutions.

Canada's Commitment to NATO

Canada made a serious commitment when it joined NATO. It agreed to keep a full army brigade and several air squadrons in Europe, mostly in West Germany. It built and supplied military bases overseas. Canadian ships and aircraft tracked the movements of Soviet submarines. Canadian forces participated regularly in military exercises with Canada's allies. Perhaps most significantly, by joining NATO, Canada had to adapt its defence policy to those of its allies.

NORAD and North American Defence

In 1958, Prime Minister Diefenbaker signed an agreement with the United States committing Canada to the **North American Aerospace Defence Command (NORAD)**. This meant that Canada and the U.S. had become part of a joint coordinated continental air defence against the threat of attack from the Soviet Union.

Canadian and American fighter forces, missile bases, and air-defence radar were controlled from a command station deep within Cheyenne Mountain, Colorado. NORAD had a force of 1000 bombers at its disposal at any one time, some of which were always in the air armed with nuclear weapons. A Canadian command post, under joint control, was established deep inside tunnels at North Bay, Ontario.

When the Cold War began, it looked like Europe would be the battleground between West and East. However, when long-range bombers were developed that could carry warheads to distant targets, North America also became vulnerable. To protect against direct Soviet attack from the air, the United States built three lines of radar stations across Canada between 1950 and 1957—the Pinetree Line, the Mid-Canada Line, and the **Distant Early Warning (DEW) Line** (see map below). These stations were designed to detect a surprise Soviet attack over the North Pole, giving the United States time to launch a counterattack.

The DEW Line, and other radar stations, compromised Canadian sovereignty. For the first time, the U.S. stationed military personnel in Canada, alarming many Canadians. To visit the DEW Line, Canadian members of Parliament and journalists had to fly to New York and gain security clearance from U.S. authorities.

FIGURE 6–28 The NORAD emblem. What might the elements of this emblem represent?

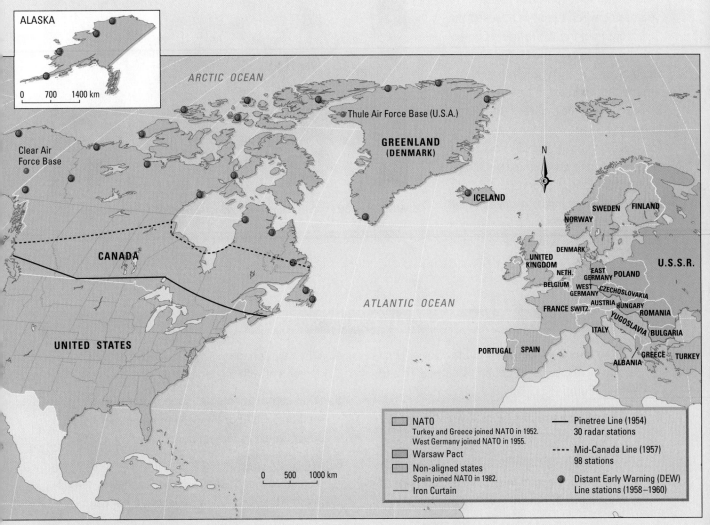

FIGURE 6–29 Countries of NATO and the Warsaw Pact. The dividing line between the Western European and communist countries was known as the "Iron Curtain," and movements of people and information from one side to the other was tightly restricted.

Thinking Critically Why would countries in Western Europe feel threatened by the countries of the Warsaw Pact and vice versa?

intercontinental ballistic missiles missiles equipped with nuclear warheads that have a range of 5500 kilometres

Most Canadians, however, showed little interest in this loss of independence, which the government had "sold" as the price of added security against an attack from the Soviet Union. Soon, the superpowers had developed **intercontinental ballistic missiles** armed with nuclear warheads. Missiles launched from the U.S.S.R. could reach North American cities within 30 minutes, rendering radar stations in Canada less effective.

FAST FORWARD

Terrorist Threats

The Cold War of the 1950s prompted the government to create military alliances and build weapons to protect Canadians from communist spies and attack. Fifty years later, when terrorists attacked the Twin Towers of the World Trade Center and other targets in the United States on September 11, 2001, governments around the world again took strong measures to protect their citizens. In both cases, the threat was real. But were all the security measures really necessary? What price were governments and citizens prepared to pay for security? Critics pointed out the dangers of governments overreacting to threats and sacrificing vital rights and freedoms in the interest of security.

FIGURE 6–30 People around the world were horrified by evidence of torture of terrorist suspects by U.S. military personnel. This 2004 photograph was taken at Abu Ghraib prison in Iraq.

PRACTICE QUESTIONS

1. What was the Cold War? Why did the Soviet Union want to have a buffer of countries between it and Western Europe?

2. **a)** Why was communism considered a threat to democracy?

   b) What groups of Canadians came under suspicion of being communists? What actions were taken against some of these people?

3. Identify a) NATO, b) NORAD, c) the DEW Line.

4. Why was Canada willing to enter an air defence agreement with the United States?

5. What commitments did Canada make as a member of NATO? How did membership in NATO affect Canada's foreign policy?

6. **Significance** Read the feature on the following page. How might Canada's identity have been different if the Avro Arrow project had not been cancelled? What different role might Canada have played in international affairs?

©P

The Avro Arrow: Supersonic Jets

By the end of the Second World War, advances in technology had completely changed aviation. Jet fighters developed by Britain and Germany made propeller-driven warplanes obsolete. Canada, which had many aeronautical engineers in the early 1950s, was a leader in the field. Even though the Avro project was cancelled in 1959, the memory of the Arrow remains.

Delta-winged interceptor By 1958, the A.V. Roe (Avro) Company had developed the Arrow (CF 105), capable of flying at twice the speed of sound (Mach 2). The Arrow was to have exceptionally powerful and state-of-the-art engines and be faster than almost any other interceptor of the day.

Turbojet engine The Arrow, which was to be powered by two huge Iroquois jet engines, had a very specific purpose: to shoot down Russian nuclear-armed bombers.

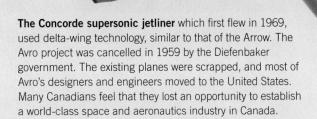

The Concorde supersonic jetliner which first flew in 1969, used delta-wing technology, similar to that of the Arrow. The Avro project was cancelled in 1959 by the Diefenbaker government. The existing planes were scrapped, and most of Avro's designers and engineers moved to the United States. Many Canadians feel that they lost an opportunity to establish a world-class space and aeronautics industry in Canada.

● Describe Canada's involvement in the UN.

KEY TERMS

United Nations (UN) an organization established in 1945 to bring peace and security to the world.

World Health Organization (WHO) the United Nations health organization responsible for providing leadership for global health

United Nations Children's Fund (UNICEF) a UN organization that works to protect children's rights, to make sure the basic needs of children are met and to help children reach their full potential; originally called United Nations International Children's Emergency Fund

Planning for Peace

Despite growing tensions at the end of the Second World War, world leaders began making plans for an international agency that would work to prevent future conflict and alleviate human misery.

Canada and the United Nations

In October 1945, delegates from 51 countries signed a charter that established the **United Nations (UN)**. It was based on the idea of collective security, as the League of Nations had been before it. Canada played an important part in drafting its Charter. Membership in the United Nations is open to all recognized nations. Two bodies govern the United Nations: the General Assembly and the Security Council.

The use of the veto in the Security Council has often prevented the United Nations from taking decisive action. By 1955, as the Cold War escalated, the veto was used 78 times, 75 of which were by the Soviet Union. However, when permanent members agree on a course of action, the United Nations has the potential to implement it.

The founders of the UN also pledged to abolish disease and famine and to protect human rights. Canadian John Humphrey was the leading author of the Universal Declaration of Human Rights. Various agencies such as the **World Health Organization** (**WHO**) and the **United Nations Children's Fund** (**UNICEF**) are designed to accomplish these goals. In addition, the UN established the International Monetary Fund (IMF) to stabilize the world economy by helping countries that face great debt and the collapse of their currencies. The United Nations has benefited millions of people worldwide, especially through its social and economic agencies and peacekeeping operations. As with all international organizations, however, countries pursue their own agenda within it.

Canada has been a strong supporter of the United Nations since its creation and has aided refugees from war or natural disasters and worked on development projects— such as building schools, dams, and roads—in various countries. Canadian peacekeepers have been involved in almost every UN operation since the start of these missions in 1956.

FIGURE 6–31 The UN Security Council is responsible for keeping peace. It issues calls for ceasefires and creates peacekeeping forces. Canada has had a seat on the Council in every decade since the United Nations was formed.

©P

The General Assembly
Seats
• each member nation has a seat
What it does
• provides a forum in which members can debate issues
• has three powers it can use against aggressor nations
– condemn the actions through speeches and resolutions
– use economic sanctions
– deploy armed forces
How decisions are made
• each member nation has the right to vote

The Security Council
Seats
• 5 permanent members, the "Big Five"—Britain, France, the United States, Russia, and China (represented by the government in Taiwan until 1971)
• 10 non-permanent members, each holding a two-year term
What it does
• maintain peace and security
• deploy peacekeeping missions
How decisions are made
• decisions need the consent of 9 members
• each of the "Big Five" has the power of veto—the right to reject actions with which they disagree

The Korean Conflict

Though the threat of nuclear annihilation kept the major powers from open war, both sides supported their own interests in the developing world. The Second World War had left the Asian country of Korea divided. The Soviet Union and communist China supported North Korea, a communist state. The United States supported South Korea which had a fragile democracy. In 1950, war broke out when North Korea invaded South Korea.

The United Nations called on its members to assist South Korea. (The Soviet Union was boycotting the UN at the time because it refused to give communist China a seat. Therefore it could not exercise its right to veto.) Prime Minister Louis St. Laurent sent thousands of Canadian troops and three naval destroyers to Korea. The UN force, led by American General Douglas MacArthur, tried to drive the invaders back over the border into North Korea. Meanwhile, Lester Pearson, Canada's Minister of External Affairs, urged all sides to agree to a ceasefire. At one point, the United States considered using the atomic bomb, but luckily, it did not. In addition, General MacArthur made plans to invade China. Had either of these things happened, a third World War would likely have resulted.

Although a ceasefire was reached in 1953, the war had increased tensions between the West and the communist nations. Global attention returned to this part of the world in the 1960s when American involvement in Vietnam escalated. (You will read about the Vietnam War in Chapter 7.)

Sandwiched between the Second World War and the Vietnam War, the Korean conflict is often called "Canada's forgotten war." Canada sent more than 25 000 soldiers to fight in Korea. More than 1500 were seriously wounded and another 516 died. As of 2009, the Korean War had technically not ended: the Republic of Korea (South) and the Democratic Peoples' Republic of Korea (North) had yet to sign a peace treaty.

● What was Canada's response to modern conflicts?

FIGURE 6–32 Lester Pearson with the Nobel Peace Prize that he won in 1957 for helping to defuse the Suez crisis

WEB LINK ·············

Visit the Pearson Web site to learn more about Lester Pearson's Nobel Peace Prize.

The Suez Crisis

A crisis over the Suez Canal in Egypt gave Canada another chance to take a leading role at the United Nations. The Suez Canal links the Mediterranean and Red Seas and provides the shortest sea route from Europe to the Indian Ocean. It was opened in 1869 and was privately owned by British and French investors.

In 1956, Egypt's president, Gamal Abdel Nasser, took over the canal and threatened to ban ships travelling to and from Israel. In response, Israel, Britain, and France planned "Operation Musketeer" to regain control of the canal. Ignoring a UN Security Council resolution to cease hostilities, they landed troops in the canal zone. The Soviet Union immediately offered Egypt financial and military aid.

The United States was angry with its allies, Britain, France, and Israel, for not consulting the U.S. government before attacking Egypt. Nevertheless, the United States threatened retaliation against any Soviet involvement. Canadian public opinion on the crisis was divided. The Conservative Party and many other Canadians felt it was their duty to support Britain. Liberal Prime Minister Louis St. Laurent, however, denounced the British and French military intervention.

Once again, Lester Pearson went to the United Nations to try to work out a solution. He proposed that a multinational peacekeeping force be created and installed in the war zone to maintain ceasefires and oversee the withdrawal of troops. The United Nations agreed, and the United Nations Emergency Force (UNEF) was formed and sent to the Suez area to bring hostilities to a peaceful end. The force, under the command of a Canadian general, was chosen from countries not directly involved in the conflict. The UNEF remained stationed on the Israel-Egypt border until 1967.

In the following years, Canada gained a reputation as an impartial and peace-loving country, willing to pay the costs of sending peacekeepers to troubled areas of the world. In 1998, the United Nations celebrated 50 years of peacekeeping around the world. During that time there were 49 peacekeeping operations; 36 of which were created by the Security Council between 1988 and 1998.

FIGURE 6–33 Military action during the Suez Crisis

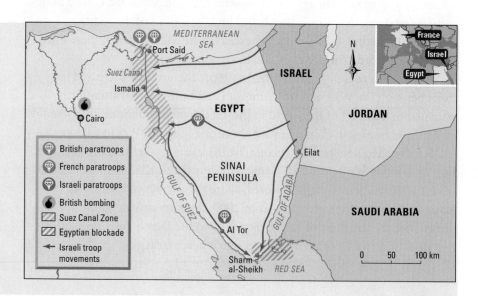

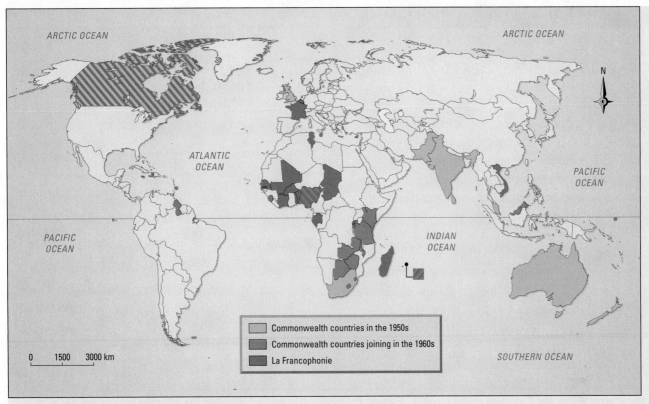

FIGURE 6–34 La Francophonie and the Commonwealth

Map legend:
- Commonwealth countries in the 1950s
- Commonwealth countries joining in the 1960s
- La Francophonie

0   1500   3000 km

The Commonwealth and la Francophonie

Canada was in a good position to build international understanding through its membership in two other organizations, the Commonwealth and la Francophonie. The Commonwealth is made up of countries that had once belonged to the British Empire. La Francophonie is an organization of French-speaking states, many of which are former colonies of France. Both organizations have many members that are less industrialized, and both offer a forum for discussing the economic problems of poverty-stricken countries.

In 1950, Commonwealth countries, including Canada, established the Colombo Plan to provide money and aid to less-developed countries in the organization. Canada contributed in a number of ways, for example, by inviting overseas students to study in Canada and by sending Canadian experts overseas to give technical assistance. Most Canadian aid under the Colombo Plan went to India and Pakistan.

PRACTICE QUESTIONS

1. a) What is the purpose of the UN General Assembly?

b) Why were the five permanent members of the Security Council given veto powers? How did this power create a stalemate in the United Nations?

2. What caused the Korean War? How did Canada participate?

3. What important roles did Canada play in the Suez crisis?

©P

CHAPTER FOCUS QUESTION   How did Canadian political decisions reflect a concern about the growing influence of the United States over Canada?

As you learned in this chapter, the years following the Second World War brought many social, economic, political, and technological changes to Canada. These changes altered the lives of many Canadians and helped to usher in a new era of prosperity and growth. There were also many fundamental shifts in Canada's international focus in the early post-war years, shifts that had a profound effect on the way Canadians viewed themselves and also on the way Canada was viewed by the rest of the world. The transformation in national identity that had begun after the First World War and was strengthened by the Second World War, grew and developed in the second half of the century.

1. Create an organizer such as the one below; provide specific examples of at least three or four decisions made by the Canadian government to limit the influence of the U.S. on Canada. Explain why the decision was made and evaluate its effectiveness at limiting American influence on Canada.

2. Rank the decisions in order from most to least effective. Provide reasons for your rankings.

3. If you had been advising the Canadian government, what other decisions would you have made to limit American influence on Canada? Explain why you would have made these decisions.

Decision made by the Canadian government	Reason for the decision	Explain the effectiveness of the decision
1.		
2.		
3.		
4.		

Vocabulary Focus

4. Review the following Key Terms on page 169. Then, go to the Pearson Web site and match the Key Terms to their corresponding definitions.

Knowledge and Understanding

5. Continue the ongoing timeline assignment. Write the name and date of each event in this chapter on the timeline and explain how the event contributed to Canadian independence.

6. You learned in earlier chapters that Canada began to gain autonomy from the beginning of the 20th century. To what extent did Canada become more independent in the post-war era? In what ways did Canada become less independent during this same period?

7. Explain how the economy of Canada was transformed during the post-war era.

a) How might this transformation have affected the way Canadians viewed themselves?

b) What effect did it have on how other countries viewed Canada?

8. During the late 1940s and early 1950s, a "Red Scare" was alive and well in Canada and the United States. What effect do you think this threat had on Canada's military decisions? Support your opinion with specific examples from the textbook.

9. Complete a PMI chart on the four megaprojects (Trans-Canada Highway, Kemano Project, Trans-Canada Pipeline, and St. Lawrence Seaway). How does each of these projects continue to influence the Canadian economy?

Critical Thinking

Significance

10. Using the information from the Chapter Focus organizer on page 202, list the two political decisions that you believe had the longest-lasting effect on limiting the influence of the U.S. on Canada. Write a paragraph explaining why these decisions were so effective at limiting American influence over Canada.

Evidence

11. What does it mean to be a middle power? Select three examples from the textbook that you think demonstrate Canada's role as a middle power during the Cold War. Support your choices with at least two reasons.

12. How significant was Canada's role in Cold War events? Provide supporting evidence for your opinion.

Document Analysis

Imagine Canada had refused to participate in NATO and/or NORAD. Use the below map, as well as the map showing NATO and Warsaw Pact countries on page 195, to guide your opinion and to formulate answers to the following questions:

13. How might Canada–U.S. relations have been affected if Canada had decided to remain neutral during the Cold War?

14. What do you think the U.S. reaction might have been to such a decision?

15. Did Canada really have a choice on whether or not to join these military alliances?

16. Do your answers to these questions change the views you expressed in Questions 5 and 7?

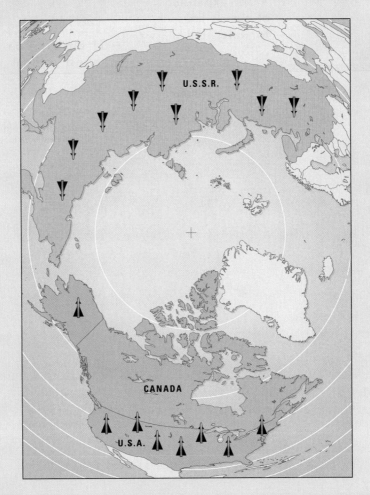

FIGURE 6–35 The United States and the Soviet Union both stockpiled weapons in the years following the Second World War.

Gathering Information Where is Canada on this polar projection? In what way does this projection clarify Canada's decision to join NORAD?

©P

GUIDING QUESTIONS

Society & Identity

- How did Canada respond to changing social values after 1960?

- What measures has Canada taken to promote a distinct Canadian identity?

- How did changes to social policies affect women and minority groups in Canada?

- How did Aboriginal Canadians respond to challenges in the 1960s and 1970s?

- What was the impact of Québec nationalism on Canadian identity?

- What effect did the War Measures Act have on the legal rights of Canadians?

- How did Canadian social programs evolve?

Politics & Government

- How was regionalism expressed in the 1970s?

- How did Canadian voters signal a change in political and social values in the 1960s?

Economy & Human Geography

- How did the Canadian government respond to the economic challenges of the 1970s?

Autonomy & World Presence

- What was Canada's involvement in the Cold War?

- What was Canada's response to modern conflicts?

The Globe and Mail newspaper front page, Toronto, Saturday, October 17, 1970 — "FLQ OUTLAWED — 250 ROUNDED UP"

TIMELINE

1960
Québec's Quiet Revolution begins

1961
Vietnam War begins

Berlin Wall built

1962
Medicare established in Saskatchewan

Cuban Missile Crisis

1963
Federal election over the issue of nuclear warheads on Canadian soil

Lester Pearson elected prime minister

1964
Beatles perform in Montréal, Toronto, and Vancouver

1965
Maple Leaf flag adopted

1966
Canada Pension Plan introduced

Medical Care Act passed

CHAPTER FOCUS QUESTION

How did Canada's political, social, and economic policies reflect a new independence in the 1960s and 1970s?

On the night of March 7, 1963, three Canadian army buildings in Montréal were bombed with Molotov cocktails (homemade firebombs). The mysterious letters "FLQ" were painted on the walls. The next day, a document from an organization claiming responsibility for the bombings was delivered to the news media:

> The Front de libération du Québec is a revolutionary movement of volunteers ready to die for the political and economic independence of Québec. The suicide-commandos of the FLQ have as their principal mission the complete destruction, by systematic sabotage of:
>
> all colonial [federal] symbols and institutions, in particular the RCMP and the armed forces;....
>
> all commercial establishments and enterprises which practise discrimination against Quebeckers, which do not use French as the first language, which advertises in the colonial language [English];
>
> all plants and factories which discriminate against French-speaking workers.
>
> ...INDEPENDENCE OR DEATH
>
> –Revolution by the People for the People

How did this crisis emerge? What had happened between English and French Canadians to make the relationship so strained? How could the crisis be resolved?

The 1960s and 1970s were tumultuous times in Canada and around the world. A culture of activism and protest developed that challenged both social norms and government policies. The continuation of the Cold War brought with it the Vietnam War and the Cuban Missile Crisis. The Canadian government tried to carve out a path of international relations independent of the United States while also dealing with an economic recession at home.

KEY TERMS

Canadian Bill of Rights
White Paper of 1969
Red Paper
Medical Care Act
Quiet Revolution
FLQ
Parti Québécois (PQ)
Royal Commission on Bilingualism and Biculturalism
Official Languages Act
October Crisis
War Measures Act
Bill 101
Bomarc missiles
Cuban Missile Crisis

1967	1968	1969	1970	1971	1972	1973	1976
Canada's centennial, Expo 67	Pierre Trudeau elected prime minister CRTC established	Woodstock	October Crisis Trans-Canada Highway completed	National Action Committee on the Status of Women established Trudeau government restricts foreign ownership of Canadian business	Canada defeats Russian hockey team	Oil crisis in Canada	Montréal Olympics

How did Canada respond to changing social values after 1960?

KEY TERM

counterculture a subculture, especially of young people, with values or lifestyles that are in opposition to those of the dominant, established culture

Toward Social Change

By the early 1960s, Canadians were beginning to accept the teen culture that had evolved after the Second World War. They had very little choice—by 1965, as a result of the baby boom, more than half the population of North America was under the age of 25. The sheer number of young people in North America and Western Europe created a powerful culture of protest—a "youthquake." The young people were joined by other groups calling for change to society, among them members of the women's movement, the environmental movement, and Aboriginal nations.

The "Youthquake"

The transition began with the so-called "British invasion" of pop culture led by four young men from Liverpool—the Beatles. Boys' hair became longer, girls' skirts shorter. This was the start of the hippie phenomenon. Large numbers of young people embraced rock music, new clothing styles, sexual promiscuity, and experimentation with drugs as a protest against mainstream society. With slogans such as "Make love, not war" and "Turn on, tune in, drop out," they strove to be different from earlier generations. Canadian youth participated in these international cultural trends, becoming part of the **counterculture**.

Some young people had aims that went beyond culture. They held strong political beliefs and rejected the consumerism of post-war society in the hope that the world would change for the better. Some became involved in women's, environmental, and Aboriginal rights movements. Others demonstrated to support greater student participation in university affairs. Many joined in protests against the war in Vietnam, demonstrating outside the American embassy in Ottawa and in front of Parliament hoping to persuade Canadian leaders to take a stronger stand against the war. Some joined communes of like-minded people who tried to establish new forms of community living in remote areas.

FIGURE 7–1 Hippies rejected traditional societal values. Their clothes, hair, beliefs, music, and opposition to the Vietnam War were an expression of deep dissatisfaction with their parents' values, particularly materialism and respect for authority. The 1960s term "generation gap" summed up the differences between youth and their parents.

Expressing Ideas Why do you think some members of the older generation might have disapproved of scenes such as this?

Popular music of the day reflected these concerns. Protest songs condemned racism, war, and the devastation of the environment. Protest singers such as Bob Dylan and Joan Baez attracted a wide following. Rock groups such as the Beatles, the Rolling Stones, and The Who captured the mood with songs such as "Revolution," "[I Can't Get No] Satisfaction," and "[Talkin' 'bout] My Generation." Aboriginal singer Buffy Sainte-Marie and African-American artists like Marvin Gaye also used their music to highlight the social conditions of their peoples.

The youthquake showed Canadian governments that young people were becoming more politically aware. Soon, politicians began making an effort to appeal to them by increasing spending on employment and activities for youth. In 1972, the voting age for federal elections was lowered from 21 to 18. Most provinces lowered the voting age around the same time.

As the 1980s approached, baby boomers began moving away from their radical political opinions and lifestyles. They were entering the workforce and starting families. Financial concerns replaced youthful idealism. The social protest movement had all but disappeared.

FIGURE 7–2 "Universal Soldier," a song by Canadian singer-songwriter Buffy Sainte-Marie, expressed the anti-war sentiments of many people, young and old.

Protest and Mockery

Political protests marked the 1960s. Even Woodstock, a huge music festival held in 1969, turned into a kind of protest against the establishment. A new political party, the Rhino Party, which grew out of the protest movement of the 1960s, fielded candidates who made far-fetched promises such as moving the nation's capital from Ottawa to Moose Jaw, Saskatchewan, or making Swedish Canada's official language. The Rhinos made a joke out of politics, but their criticisms were very serious. They used publicity to question and mock the system itself, rather than any one political party or politician.

FASTFORWARD

CRITICAL INQUIRY — Perspectives

Political Protest

Political protests still take place in the tradition of the 1960s and 1970s. The 1990s and 2000s saw an increase in the number of organized protests against economic globalization and human rights abuses. During an Asia-Pacific Economic Cooperation (APEC) summit in Vancouver in 1997, police tore down protest signs and used pepper spray to control students and other protesters. Later, RCMP documents revealed that they had used informants to infiltrate and report on the activities of groups that were acknowledged to be non-violent protest organizations. Many Canadians felt that the authorities' actions were obstructing the expression of free speech.

FIGURE 7–3 Fences were erected to keep hundreds of protesters away from the political leaders attending the Vancouver APEC meeting in 1997.

feminist a person who supports the idea that women are equal to men and deserve equal rights and opportunities

pressure group a group of people who get together around a particular issue to try to influence government policy

civil liberties basic individual rights protected by law, such as freedom of speech

Canadian Bill of Rights a federal document that set out the rights and freedoms of Canadians; it was enacted in 1960 under the leadership of Prime Minister John Diefenbaker

The Women's Movement

Women had been expected to fill men's shoes in industry and manufacturing during the Second World War. However, when veterans returned and women were no longer needed in these jobs, post-war society expected them to return to their traditional role as housekeepers. Many felt isolated in the suburbs and trapped by roles that did not allow them to develop their potential. Many working women continued to hold low-paying jobs such as waitressing, hairdressing, secretarial work, and retail sales. Employers could legally discriminate against them in both wages and benefits. University-educated women were expected to work as either teachers or nurses—other professions were difficult for women to enter.

In 1963, Betty Friedan's book *The Feminine Mystique* became a best-seller. It argued that women were trapped in gender roles that were reinforced by images in the media. Friedan urged women to liberate themselves from these traditional roles and fulfill themselves as human beings by acquiring an education and pursuing careers. Friedan's ideas transformed the lives of many women during this period. Just as they had done during the suffrage movement of the early years of the century, **feminists** joined together to fight for women's rights.

In 1967, responding to pressure from women's groups, Prime Minister Lester Pearson's government set up the Royal Commission on the Status of Women. The Commission thoroughly examined how Canadian women were treated and the problems they faced. It made recommendations that included the following:

- Women should have the right to work outside the home.
- Society in general, as well as parents, should take some responsibility for children; therefore, daycare services should be provided.
- Women should be entitled to paid maternity leave from their jobs.
- The federal government should do all it can to help overcome discrimination against women in society.

Several women's groups joined forces to form the National Action Committee on the Status of Women (NAC) in 1971. This **pressure group** lobbied both federal and provincial governments to act quickly on the Commission's recommendations. One of NAC's key victories was the inclusion of a clause guaranteeing the equality of women in Canada's Charter of Rights and Freedoms, which came into force in 1982 (see Chapter 10).

Canadian feminists demanded that women be promoted to positions of responsibility in government, business, education, and the civil service. They argued against stereotyping women and the kinds of work they do. They also pressed for changes to the education system, under which girls were not encouraged to excel in math and sciences—subjects more likely to lead to well-paying jobs. Soon, more Canadian women were becoming engineers, doctors, politicians, and company presidents—pursuing careers in which they had previously been under-represented. "Sexism," "male chauvinism," and "sexual harassment" became common terms to describe behaviour and attitudes that were no longer acceptable.

FIGURE 7–4 Women burn bras in a protest at Toronto City Hall on International Women's Day, March 8, 1979.

Challenging Social Values

Although there had been groups fighting for **civil liberties** in Canada during the 1930s and 1940s, it was not until the 1960s that there was a dramatic increase in activism for social change. Organizations formed during this time include Human Rights Watch, the Canadian Civil Liberties Association, Amnesty International, and the National Indian Brotherhood.

Diefenbaker and the Canadian Bill of Rights

John Diefenbaker's government set the stage for reform when it introduced the **Canadian Bill of Rights** in 1960 to protect a person's fundamental human rights. These rights included

- freedom of life, liberty, security of person, and the enjoyment of property
- the right to equality before the law and its protection
- freedom of religion
- freedom of speech
- freedom of assembly and association

Although Diefenbaker did not feel he had enough provincial support to make the Bill of Rights part of the Constitution, the fact that it had been passed by Parliament gave it considerable influence. Most of the rights protected by the Bill were included in the Charter of Rights and Freedoms in 1982. (You will read more about the Charter in Chapter 10.)

The Omnibus Bill and Beyond

In 1969, the Liberal government, under Prime Minister Pierre Trudeau, passed Bill C-150, also known as the Omnibus Bill, which made major changes in social legislation. These included

- recognizing the right of women to have access to contraception;
- recognizing the right to abortion (with certain limitations); and
- legalizing homosexuality between consenting adults.

Trudeau was criticized for his progressive social policies, but refused to back down, saying that "There's no place for the state in the bedrooms of the nation." Trudeau also changed Canada's divorce law in 1968, making divorce more freely available to reflect what was happening in society.

In 1970, feeling that the abortion law did not go far enough, women protesters chained themselves inside Parliament, forcing it to close. Dr. Henry Morgentaler also challenged abortion laws. Time after time, juries refused to convict Morgentaler, despite his open admission that he had performed thousands of abortions. The law had become unenforceable.

In 1976, Bill C-84 passed in the House of Commons by a narrow margin (131–124), ending the death penalty. Although Bill C-84 did not have widespread public support, Trudeau and his Cabinet were determined that Canada should join other progressive nations and abolish capital punishment.

> ● How did changes to social policies affect women and minority groups in Canada?

Prime Minister
John George Diefenbaker

- born 1895, Neustadt, Ontario
- lawyer
- first elected to Commons in 1940
- prime minister 1957–1963

Domestic Record
- served as a lieutenant during the First World War
- championed the Canadian Bill of Rights to guarantee certain rights for all Canadians
- appointed James Gladstone, a Blackfoot from the Northwest Territories, Canada's first Aboriginal senator, in 1958
- cancelled the Avro Arrow project in 1959
- extended franchise to all Aboriginal peoples in 1960

International Record
- opposed apartheid and played a role in South Africa withdrawing from the Commonwealth
- signed North American Air Defence Agreement (NORAD) with the U.S. in 1957
- allowed two squadrons of American Bomarc anti-aircraft missiles deployed in Canada (1958)

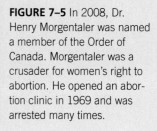

FIGURE 7–5 In 2008, Dr. Henry Morgentaler was named a member of the Order of Canada. Morgentaler was a crusader for women's right to abortion. He opened an abortion clinic in 1969 and was arrested many times.

	Canada	U.S.
Support death penalty	48	64
Support a law banning handguns	52	36
Support public health care	90	59.9
Consider global warming a serious problem	67.7	48.5
Believe religion is very important	32	47.4
Are interested in politics	52.6	59.1
See democracy as absolutely important	56.6	51.9
See self as world citizen	85	68.6

FIGURE 7–6 Canada and the United States: differences and similarities

Women's Rights

Women's rights activists protested against Canadian laws that supported traditional roles for women. The reforms in divorce and abortion legislation were welcomed by many people. These were important steps toward women's equality. Many unions joined the fight for women's rights. For example, the Canadian Union of Postal Workers was the first to win the right to paid maternity leave for its members.

Gay Rights

Before Trudeau's Omnibus Bill was passed, gay people could be arrested and sent to prison, denied employment, and otherwise persecuted. In the 1960s, gay rights activists began to organize to draw attention to these injustices. This took tremendous courage, as the attitudes of many Canadians, churches, and members of governments at all levels were strongly anti-gay. Gay people began to publicly show pride in their sexual orientation and resist persecution.

FIGURE 7–7 Vancouver's first Gay Pride Festival took place in 1973. By 2003, British Columbia had legalized same-sex marriage.

PRACTICE QUESTIONS

1. a) Name two protest movements that emerged in Canada during the 1960s.

b) What kind of impact do you think each of these groups has since had on Canadian society?

2. Many young people of the 1960s and 1970s believed they could change the world. List some of their aims. Do you think they succeeded? Explain.

3. Which group benefited most from the Omnibus Bill? Support your answer.

Immigration and Multiculturalism

By the 1960s, many Canadians had a somewhat more open attitude toward people of other cultures and countries. This was reflected in new immigration regulations as illustrated by the timeline below. In 1971, an official policy of **multiculturalism** was introduced by Prime Minister Trudeau. The policy would

> ...support and encourage the various cultures and ethnic groups that give structure and vitality to our society. They will be encouraged to share their cultural expressions and values with other Canadians and so contribute to a richer life for us all.
>
> –House of Commons

The policy encouraged the country's various ethnic groups to express their cultures. Multicultural activities were organized across the country. For example, heritage language classes were provided to help children learn the language of their parents. Festivals were held for cultural communities to share their music, dances, foods, games, arts, crafts, and stories. Programs were designed to make all residents feel at home in Canada, regardless of their origins. These programs were also intended to prevent racism by promoting respect for all cultures.

● How did changes to social policies affect women and minority groups in Canada?

KEY TERM

multiculturalism a policy of encouraging the expression of the cultures of many ethnic groups that make up a country's population

TIMELINE

Canadian Immigration Milestones

1900 Chinese Immigration Act increases $50 head tax to $100; in 1903 it is raised to $500.

1908 Continuous Passage Act requires immigrants to travel directly to Canada, thus restricting immigration from India.

1919 New Immigration Act excludes people from Canada for reasons of race, culture, and political beliefs.

1923 Law is passed prohibiting almost all immigration from China; this law was revoked in 1947.

1931 Admission to Canada is restricted to American citizens, British subjects, and agriculturalists with economic means.

1939 The *St. Louis*, a ship carrying 930 Jewish refugees from Germany, is turned away from Canadian ports. It returns to Europe where three quarters of the passengers are killed by the Nazis.

1947 Between 1947 and 1952, more than 186 000 displaced persons come to Canada from wartorn Europe.

1962 New regulations eliminate most of the racial discrimination in Canada's immigration policy.

1967 Immigration to Canada becomes "colour blind." The points system is introduced, which assigns potential immigrants points in categories such as education, age, fluency in French or English, and job opportunities in Canada.

1976 Immigration regulations change to allow immigration of family members with relatives already in Canada.

1978 Refugees make up 25 percent of all immigrants to Canada until 1981.

1986 UN awards Canada the Nansen Medal recognizing its contributions to the cause of refugees.

FIGURE 7–8 Language classes and outings were organized to facilitate the integration of newly arrived refugees.

FIGURE 7–9 In 1972, many South Vietnamese people fleeing war sought refugee status in Canada.

marginalized to be pushed aside and made less important in terms of social standing and power

disenfranchised to be deprived of basic legal rights

White Paper of 1969 the government report proposing dramatic changes to the lives of Aboriginal peoples, including the elimination of the Indian Act

Red Paper Aboriginal response to the federal government's White Paper of 1969; the Red Paper caused the government to change its policies

FIGURE 7–10 By the 1960s, racism and neglect had made Africville one of the worst slums in Canada, but its destruction brought an end to a vibrant community. In 2010, the mayor of Halifax apologized to the descendants of the Africville community.

Expressing Ideas What connections can you make between the relocation of people in Africville and the relocations in Newfoundland and the High Arctic that you read about in Chapter 6? What conclusions can you draw from these events?

How did Aboriginal Canadians respond to challenges in the 1960s and 1970s?

The Other Canada

While many Canadians benefited from the booming economic times of the 1950s and 1960s, others were **marginalized**. Governments expropriated properties for the building of freeways and other projects. Citizens sometimes organized themselves to preserve their communities, though this was not always the case—especially when the people affected were poor and not used to speaking out on public issues. In the 1960s, two thirds of Toronto's Chinatown was bulldozed for the construction of a new city hall. In Nova Scotia, officials ordered the destruction of the African-Canadian community of Africville and the forced removal of its residents. The people of these communities were angered at the way they had been **disenfranchised** by government.

Aboriginal Nations: Decades of Action

Governments tend to downplay Aboriginal poverty and other issues. Canada's First Nations had fared badly economically in the boom years following the Second World War. In addition, many had also suffered from environmental damage caused by resource industries. For example, mercury poisoning from a pulp and paper mill contaminated the fish caught and eaten at the Whitedog and Grassy Narrows reserves in Ontario. The development of mines, highways, pipelines, and boom towns disrupted the hunting grounds and way of life of other First Nations.

Organizing for Change

When Aboriginal people living on reserves won the right to vote in 1960, it did little to improve their living conditions. They continued to suffer from serious problems, including poverty, poor health, and inadequate housing and education. Those who left to try their luck in the large cities often faced hostility and discrimination. By the late 1960s, Aboriginal peoples were organizing to pressure Ottawa and the provincial governments to bring about change.

©P

The Liberal government of Pierre Trudeau issued the **White Paper of 1969** to address the issues facing Aboriginal people. The White Paper, prepared by Indian Affairs Minister Jean Chrétien, proposed dramatic changes to the lives of Aboriginal people. Among its recommendations, the White Paper proposed that

- the Indian Act be repealed
- Aboriginal people be given control and ownership of their lands
- the provincial governments take over the same responsibility for Aboriginal people that they have for other citizens
- substantial funds be made available for economic development for Aboriginal people
- the Department of Indian Affairs be closed down

The White Paper would end special status for Aboriginal peoples and place them on an equal footing with other Canadians. Its intent was to encourage Aboriginal people to leave the reserves, seek jobs in the cities, and become part of mainstream Canadian society. Assimilation would supposedly bring an end to their problems.

Aboriginal people were furious. They saw the White Paper as an attack on their right to maintain their unique identity. Harold Cardinal, an Alberta Cree leader, explained their response:

> *The Government believes that its policies must lead to the full, free and nondiscriminatory participation of the Indian people in Canadian society. Such a goal requires a break with the past. It requires that the Indian people's role of dependence be replaced by a role of equal status, opportunity and responsibility, a role they can share with all other Canadians.*
>
> *–Foreword of the White Paper*

> *Ironically, the White Paper concludes by... calling upon Indian organizations... to assist [in the process it recommends].... It is difficult to envision any responsible Indian organization willing to participate in a proposal that promises to take the rights of all Indians away and attempts to... legislate Indians out of existence. It is a strange government and a strange mentality that would have the gall to ask the Indian to help implement its plan to perpetrate cultural genocide on the Indians of Canada. It is like asking the doomed man on the gallows if he would mind pulling the lever that trips the trap.*
>
> *–The Unjust Society, 1969*

The National Indian Brotherhood led the attack. Instead of assimilation into "White" (non-Aboriginal) society, they demanded self-government for Aboriginal peoples and control over their own affairs. When they presented their paper, *Citizens Plus,* which became known as the "**Red Paper**," Trudeau and Chrétien abandoned the White Paper.

FIGURE 7–11 Harold Cardinal speaks to Prime Minister Trudeau and other Cabinet members at an Ottawa meeting in 1970. A delegation of about 200 First Nations peoples representing most provinces attended the meeting.

©P

Save Our Salmon

In the late summer of 2009, it was official: West coast salmon stocks had collapsed. After a poor salmon run the previous year, 2009 was even worse. Some species of salmon simply did not show up. The disaster affected the local economy of B.C. First Nations as well as other commercial and sport fishers. The survival of a number of other species, notably grizzlies, was put at risk by the low fish stocks. Environmentalists believed that power development in fish-bearing streams and commercial fish farming may be responsible for the problem.

Educational Reform

As the residential school system began to wind down by the 1970s, many First Nations took over the education of their children. "Band schools" emerged across the country where Aboriginal children could study their own languages and learn about their own values, cultures, and traditions. The lack of secondary schools near the reserves, however, meant that most Aboriginal children were forced to leave home if they wanted to continue in school. As part of a government-run "boarding home program," some high-school students were sent to live with families and attend school in cities such as Vancouver and New Westminster, British Columbia. But loneliness drove many to return to their reserves before graduating.

Environmental Action

Aboriginal peoples began taking action in another area: the environment. Industries were expanding, some of them in and around reserves. Many Aboriginal groups were concerned that hydroelectric and natural gas projects would jeopardize their hunting, fishing, and trapping activities.

Probably the most significant Aboriginal victory during the 1970s was won by the Inuit, Métis, and Indian Brotherhood (later Dene) of the Yukon and Northwest Territories as they **lobbied** to halt the construction of oil and natural gas pipelines that were to run through their lands in the Mackenzie Valley. They demanded a study to determine its impact on their lands and on the environment.

The federal government agreed to investigate the issue. The Berger Commission conducted hearings all over the North, listening carefully to Aboriginal concerns. In 1977, the commission recommended that construction of the Mackenzie Valley Pipeline be suspended for 10 years pending an in-depth environmental study and negotiations with the Aboriginal peoples about financial compensation, self-government, and other issues.

In fact, construction was suspended for much longer. As of October 2009, the federal government had decided not to invest in the proposed pipeline, jeopardizing the project. By this time, the price tag of the pipeline had risen to $16.2 billion and the **Aboriginal Pipeline Group** (APG) had become a one-third partner in the Mackenzie Gas Project.

PRACTICE QUESTIONS

1. Explain the importance of the following in the development of Aboriginal identity:

   a) the 1969 White Paper and the Red Paper

   b) the Mackenzie Valley Pipeline and the Berger Commission

2. Give examples of the federal government's attempts to assimilate Aboriginal people into Canadian society.

3. What were some of the aims of multiculturalism? How did the government hope to achieve its aims?

4. List three changes that occurred for minority groups in Canada during the 1960s and 1970s.

5. **Perspectives** Write a short paragraph supporting or opposing the following statement: The policy of multiculturalism promoted a shift away from assimilation and toward acceptance of diversity in Canada.

©P

Politics and Government

As the first of the baby boomer generation reached maturity, politicians faced new priorities and demands from Canadians. John Diefenbaker and Lester "Mike" Pearson dominated Canadian politics in the early 1960s. But by 1967, Canada's centennial year, both Diefenbaker and Pearson seemed out of touch with the times. Diefenbaker was defeated in a leadership convention in September 1967, and Pearson announced his intention to retire in December of the same year. Many Canadians wanted a leader who could appeal to a new generation of voters. The answer was the charismatic Pierre Trudeau who came to power on the strength of "Trudeaumania" and the youth vote.

Diefenbaker Versus Pearson

Diefenbaker and Pearson had different styles and visions of Canada. They were bitter rivals, fighting four national elections in 10 years. Diefenbaker was passionately committed to what he called "unhyphenated Canadianism"—a belief in the equality of all Canadians, whatever their heritage. A staunch nationalist, he also believed in preserving Canada's British connections and standing up to the Americans. Diefenbaker championed human rights, introducing the Canadian Bill of Rights. In addition, he was the first prime minister to include a woman in his Cabinet and to appoint an Aboriginal senator. In 1960, his government gave Canada's status Indians living on reserves the right to vote in federal elections. While Diefenbaker's beliefs made him popular among many Canadians, they were also the source of his problems. In particular, French Canadians, who saw their culture as distinct, did not appreciate Diefenbaker's version of "unhyphenated Canadianism."

By contrast, Pearson and his Liberals appealed to younger, urban voters, especially in Central Canada. Pearson's vision of Canada was based on two founding peoples: French and English. He believed that Canadians should sever their British connections and that Canada needed an identity that would be meaningful to all Canadians. Pearson won the election of 1963; Diefenbaker never again led the country. Pearson was responsible for modernizing Canada. His government introduced a trial abolition of capital punishment and easier divorce laws. Above all, he is remembered for introducing Canada's flag in 1965.

The Flag Debate

For some Canadians, the Red Ensign was too British to be the symbol of modern Canada. Still, many opposed a new flag both for reasons of tradition and because they felt that Pearson was giving in to pressure from Québec. An emotional debate split the country. In general, English Canadians wanted to keep the Red Ensign; French Canada wanted a new flag. Finally, after hundreds of suggestions from across Canada, the red-and-white maple leaf design was chosen. On February 15, 1965, Canada's new flag was raised on Parliament Hill for the first time. Ironically, English Canadians have come to regard the flag with pride and affection, while people from Québec, disillusioned by the bitter debate, continue to fly primarily the fleur-de-lys.

● How did Canadian voters signal a change in political and social values in the 1960s?

KEY TERMS

lobby to try to influence the opinions and votes of public officials for or against a cause

Aboriginal Pipeline Group a group formed in 2000 to represent the interests of the Aboriginal peoples of the North in the proposed pipeline

WEB LINK •
Read more about the flag debate on the Pearson Web site.

FIGURE 7–12 Diefenbaker and the Conservatives wanted to keep the Red Ensign (top) with its traditional links to Britain, while the Liberals wanted a new design, favouring the three maple leaf flag (centre). A multi-party committee selected the maple leaf flag we use today, recognized around the world as the symbol of Canada.

Expressing Ideas What do you think might have motivated Pearson to initiate the change of flags in the 1960s?

Social Welfare

Pearson's government continued to build on the social welfare programs started by Mackenzie King. During the war, King was looking for a way to keep the support of voters who remembered the hardships of the Depression and were attracted by the Co-operative Commonwealth Federation (CCF), the political party that stood for social benefits. As a result, he introduced unemployment insurance in 1940 and family allowance, or the "baby bonus," in 1944. In 1966, Pearson's government began the Canada Pension Plan, which improved on existing pension schemes. It also introduced the Canada Assistance Plan to help the provinces finance social assistance programs for people in need. In the same year, Pearson introduced Canada's system of universal health care, the **Medical Care Act.**

---

up close and personal | Tommy Douglas: What Makes Him the Greatest Canadian?

 CRITICAL INQUIRY Significance

Before 1966, most Canadians who fell seriously ill could spend their life savings on medical care. Many had to depend on charity, or face debt or bankruptcy to pay medical bills. Despite bitter opposition from doctors, Saskatchewan Premier T.C. "Tommy" Douglas introduced a complete medicare program that allowed all people in the province to seek medical treatment without paying out of their own pockets. When the bill was finally passed in Saskatchewan in 1962, it illustrated to the rest of Canada that a medicare system was possible.

In the same year, Tommy Douglas left provincial politics to become leader of the New Democratic Party (NDP), which grew out of the CCF. Fearing that the NDP might capture votes with a campaign for national medicare, the Liberals added health care to their party platform. As a result, the national Medical Care Act was passed in 1966. This Act meant that federal and provincial governments would now share the cost of medical care by doctors and hospitals for all Canadians, with funding coming from taxes. Today,

Canadians identify medicare as the social program they value most.

FIGURE 7–13 Tommy Douglas with supporters after winning the New Democratic Party leadership in August 1961

Thinking Critically In 2004, Tommy Douglas was voted the Greatest Canadian of all Time in a nationwide CBC contest. Why might Canadians have such high regard for him?

PRACTICE QUESTIONS

1. List three social changes made by Diefenbaker and three social changes made by Pearson.

2. a) Why did Prime Minister Pearson believe a new flag was necessary?

b) How important do you think a flag is in asserting identity? Should it be a criminal act to show disrespect to a flag? Discuss your views with the class.

©P

Trudeau: A New-Style Politician

Pierre Elliott Trudeau was a French Canadian who was also a strong federalist. He appealed to many young Canadians. Previous leaders had seemed formal and serious; Trudeau was relaxed and witty. He drove a flashy sports car and was a "hip" dresser. A bachelor until 1971, he dated celebrities, went to New York nightclubs, hung out with the rich and famous, and eventually became an international celebrity himself. He delighted in joking with reporters. Crowds of admirers swarmed him at his public appearances. Young people responded to him as though he were a rock star, and "Trudeaumania" gripped the nation. He succeeded Lester Pearson as prime minister in 1968, just as radical separatists were becoming increasingly violent.

Trudeau also had a clear vision of what he thought Canada should be: a "just society" for all Canadians. He believed that government had a duty to protect the rights and freedoms of people and to foster their economic and social well-being. He also supported individual freedom and thought that governments should not interfere with personal liberties.

KEY TERMS

Medical Care Act an Act passed by Parliament in 1966 that provided free access to physician services for Canadians

Quiet Revolution a period of rapid change and reform that modernized Québec society during the years 1960 to 1966 under the Liberal provincial government of Jean Lesage

FIGURE 7–14 Pierre Trudeau stands before a crowd during a visit to Newfoundland in 1971. Trudeau had charisma and used the media very well. Media coverage is a "two-edged sword." The media can bring down a politician as easily as it can raise him or her up.

Expressing Ideas What qualities do you think help politicians to "sell" themselves to a mass audience? Do any contemporary politicians have the mass appeal that Trudeau had?

Québec Nationalism

In 1960, after Duplessis' death in 1959, Jean Lesage and the Liberals came to power with an election slogan that announced it was "Time for a Change." Once in power, Lesage's first step was to stamp out corruption. Government jobs and contracts were now to be awarded according to merit. Wages and pensions were raised, and restrictions on trade unionism were removed.

The government also began to modernize the province's economy, politics, education, and culture. This wave of change became known as the **Quiet Revolution**, and it transformed the face of Québec. It took control of social services and the education system. Students were now required to take more science and technology courses to prepare for the new Québec. Above all, Québécois were encouraged to think of themselves as citizens of the 20th century. As new attitudes began to take hold, the influence of the Roman Catholic Church declined.

● What was the impact of Québec nationalism on Canadian identity?

FLQ (*Front de libération du Québec*) a revolutionary movement founded to work for an independent, socialist Québec

Parti Québécois (PQ) a Québec provincial party that advocates separation from Canada

Royal Commission on Bilingualism and Biculturalism a commission created by the federal government to recommend ways of enhancing and promoting the historically bilingual nature of Canada

Official Languages Act the Act that states that French and English are Canada's official languages, and that all federal institutions must provide services in English and French

WEB LINK • • • • • • • • • • • • • • •
Read more about René Lévesque on the Pearson Web site.

In the 1962 election, the Liberals went one step further. They campaigned, and won, with the motto *Maîtres chez nous*—"Masters in our own house"—with the aim of strengthening Québec's control of its own economy. Among other things, the government bought several hydro companies and turned them into a provincially owned power monopoly, Hydro-Québec.

The Birth of Separatism

Québec nationalism and the separatist movement grew in the 1960s and 1970s. Québécois resented what they perceived as injustices at the hands of English-speaking Canadians. Why was Ottawa, the national capital, so overwhelmingly English speaking? Why did federal politicians from Québec seldom hold key Cabinet posts? Why did Francophones not have the right to their own schools and hospitals in the rest of Canada, even though Anglophones enjoyed those rights in Québec? Why was Québec's Francophone majority expected to speak English in stores and at work?

For some, the only solution lay in a Québec controlled entirely by Québécois—a new country independent of Canada. Some extremists joined terrorist groups such as the **FLQ** (*Front de libération du Québec*) in the name of *le Québec libre*— "a free Québec." The FLQ blew up mailboxes and attacked symbols of English-Canadian power in Québec. Many Québécois supported the aims of the terrorists, if not their methods.

In 1967, Québec Cabinet minister René Lévesque left the Liberal Party and, a year later, formed the **Parti Québécois (PQ)**. Lévesque believed that Québec and Canada would do better to "divorce" peacefully than to continue a "marriage" of two cultures that seemed imposed and unworkable.

FIGURE 7–15 A Canadian army engineer lies injured after an FLQ bomb, which he had removed from a mailbox, exploded in his hands. On May 17, 1963, a total of 13 bombs were placed in mailboxes in the Montréal suburb of Westmount.

Expressing Ideas How might Canadians across the country have responded to images such as these?

A Bilingual Nation

Lester Pearson, who had become prime minister during Québec's Quiet Revolution, was convinced that Canada would face a grave crisis unless French Canadians felt more at home in Canada. In 1963, he appointed the **Royal Commission on Bilingualism and Biculturalism** (the "Bi and Bi Commission") to investigate solutions. The Commission's report called for Canada to become bilingual, with English and French as its two official languages. Perhaps more importantly, it recommended that Canada adopt a bilingual strategy that would promote both languages across the nation, including the protection of French and English linguistic minorities. For example, parents would be able to have their children attend schools in the language of their choice in regions where there was sufficient demand.

When Pierre Trudeau succeeded Pearson in 1968, he was determined to do more to persuade people from Québec that their future lay with Canada. In 1969, his government passed the **Official Languages Act**, making Canada officially bilingual. All federal government agencies were now required to provide services in both languages, and more Francophones were appointed to senior government positions. Trudeau also called on French and English Canadians, especially young people, to increase their understanding of each other's cultures—and provided money to help make this happen.

These tactics were met with mixed reviews. Some loved them, some hated them. Some Canadians embraced the idea of bilingualism with enthusiasm. For example, many parents enrolled their children in French immersion classes. Others, especially Western Canadians, felt that the federal government was forcing French on them. They believed that Ottawa was focusing too much attention on Québec, while the West and its concerns were largely ignored. Francophones in Québec were also unimpressed. They wanted "special status" for Québec in Confederation. Trudeau, however, insisted that Québec was a province just like any other.

**Prime Minister
Lester Bowles Pearson**

- born 1897, Newtonbrook, Ontario
- professor, author, diplomat
- first elected to Commons in 1948
- prime minister 1963–1968

Domestic Record

- served in the Canadian Army Medical Corps and Royal Flying Corps during the First World War
- introduced maple leaf flag in 1964
- established the Canada Pension Plan, universal medicare, and Canada Student Loans Plan

International Record

- Canadian ambassador to the U.S. in 1945 and attended the first conference of the UN
- saw Canada join NATO in 1949
- president of the UN General Assembly (1952–1953)
- won the 1957 Nobel Peace Prize for his part in creating the UN peacekeeping force

BILINGUAL PACKAGING! IN FRENCH!

BILINGUAL PACKAGING! IN ENGLISH!

...same old AMERICAN CONTENT...

Kanada's CORN FLAKES

FIGURE 7–16 This 1976 cartoon shows then B.C. Minister of Human Resources, Bill Vander Zalm, Prime Minister Trudeau, and Québec Premier René Lévesque. Many people in British Columbia, farthest from Québec geographically, opposed the Official Languages Act.

Interpreting a Cartoon What is happening in the cartoon? What is the cartoonist saying about Western Canada's reaction to bilingualism? About regionalism in Canada? About Pierre Trudeau's views?

What effect did the War Measures Act have on the legal rights of Canadians?

FIGURE 7–17 Soldiers patrol the streets of Montréal during the October Crisis.

Expressing Ideas Do you think it was wise to put on a show of force during the Crisis? Explain.

What If . . .

Imagine there was a terrorist threat in your community and the government imposed the War Measures Act. What civil rights would you be prepared to give up? What rights do you think are too important to give up, even in an emergency?

The October Crisis

Trudeau disliked the very idea of separatism and took a forceful stand against Québec nationalists. In October 1970, members of the FLQ kidnapped British diplomat James Cross. In exchange for Cross's safe release, they demanded the release of FLQ members serving prison sentences and a public reading of the FLQ manifesto. Québec Premier Robert Bourassa agreed to most of the demands but refused to release any FLQ prisoners. In response, the FLQ kidnapped Québec Labour Minister Pierre Laporte.

Alarmed by the deteriorating situation in Québec, Trudeau took drastic action. At the urging of Bourassa and Montréal Mayor Jean Drapeau, he imposed the **War Measures Act**. Until then, the Act had only been used in wartime. The Act suspended Canadians' civil rights—anyone could be arrested and detained without being charged with an offence. Membership in the FLQ became a crime. When asked how far he would go to defeat the FLQ, Trudeau replied, "Just watch me."

On October 16, 1970, federal troops patrolled the streets of Ottawa and Montréal, and armouries across the country were locked down. Hundreds of pro-separatist Québécois were arrested and held without charge. Imposition of the War Measures Act was fiercely criticized, but Trudeau was undeterred. After all the rights legislation that had been passed by the Liberals under Trudeau, many people were shocked by this hardline approach.

One day later, police found the body of Pierre Laporte in the trunk of a car. His murder increased pressure on the government to crack down on the FLQ and find the remaining hostage, James Cross. Montréal police located Cross after he was held in captivity for 60 days. His kidnappers negotiated safe passage to Cuba in exchange for Cross's release. The October Crisis was over. Of the 450 people detained under the Act, most were released and only a small number were ever charged.

FIGURE 7–18 On October 16, 1970, several thousand Montréal students protested the imposition of the War Measures Act and showed support for the FLQ.

Robert Bourassa and Bill 22

Premier Robert Bourassa had taken office just months before the October Crisis in 1970. Although most people in Québec did not support radical separatist movements, it was clear Trudeau's Official Languages Act had not gone far enough to satisfy the Francophone majority in the province. In 1974, Bourassa responded with **Bill 22**, the first provincial legislation passed in Québec aimed at protecting the status of the French language. Bill 22 made French the sole official language of Québec. It was to be the language of civic administration and services, and of the workplace.

Bill 22 forced hundreds of thousands of business and professional people in Québec who were not proficient in French to move out of the province. Toronto eventually surpassed Montréal as the business capital of Canada. Many Anglophones were angered by what they saw as the loss of their language rights. Many Francophones, however, did not think that Bourassa had gone far enough. In the next election, Bourassa and the Liberals lost to the Parti Québécois.

The PQ in Power

In 1976, the Parti Québécois won the provincial election. It was a stunning victory for René Lévesque and his party, which had won only seven seats in the 1970 election. Lévesque had reassured voters that a PQ win would not automatically mean separation. He promised that he would hold a province-wide referendum on the issue, and Quebeckers voted in a party dedicated to the goal of separation from Canada.

The separatists had no interest in official bilingualism—their priority was to strengthen the French language. Shortly after taking office, the PQ government passed **Bill 101**, sometimes referred to as the "Charter of the French Language." Its terms specified that

- French was the only official language of the province and government employees had to work in French
- commercial outdoor signs would be in French only
- children of immigrants would be required to attend French schools

The Québécois welcomed the new language law. Many felt that their culture and language were endangered. The birth rate in Québec had fallen, and most new immigrants were educating their children in English. To non-Francophones, however, Bill 101 was a symbol of oppression. Many people in the rest of Canada felt that the PQ's policies were extreme. They looked to the federal government to stand up to the separatists.

KEY TERMS

War Measures Act an Act passed during the First World War giving the government emergency powers in the event of a national crisis

Bill 22 provincial legislation that made French the sole official language of Québec

Bill 101 also called the "Charter of the French Language," Bill 101 strengthened the position of the French language in Québec

FIGURE 7–19 Québec Premier René Lévesque at a PQ rally after his party's victory in the 1976 provincial election

PRACTICE QUESTIONS

1. What did Pearson and Trudeau do to address rising Québec nationalism?

2. Do you think the Official Languages Act was an effective way to address dissatisfaction in Québec?

3. **a)** What motivated the FLQ? What tactics did they use?

   b) Had you lived in Québec in the 1960s, how do you think you would have reacted to the FLQ? Write a letter to the editor explaining your view.

4. Make a timeline of events during the October Crisis. Identify events that you think were most significant. Give reasons for your choices.

5. In Québec elections, the Parti Québécois won 23.5 percent of votes in 1970, more than 30 percent in 1973, and 41 percent in 1976. What do you think accounted for these results in each case?

The use of the War Measures Act by Prime Minister Trudeau remains controversial. Was he justified in invoking such powerful legislation?

The following documents give different points of view. Read each document and identify the circumstances under which the statement was made, and what position was taken.

Source 1

The kidnapping in broad daylight of a Québec Cabinet minister [Laporte] in front of his own... residence had a dramatic effect on [the government's] view of the crisis we were facing. We began to believe that perhaps the FLQ was not just a bunch of pamphlet-waving, bomb-planting zealots after all; perhaps they were in fact members of a powerful network capable of endangering public safety, and of bringing other fringe groups—of which there were a large number at the time—into the picture, which would lead to untold violence. If all these groups coalesced [came together], the crisis could go on for a very long time, with tragic consequences for the entire country.

—Pierre Trudeau, Memoirs, *1993*

Source 2

...[T]he list of people arrested, without warrant, on the strength of suspicions, prejudice, or pure idiocy, exceeded the incredible number of four hundred.... Deprived of all their rights, beginning with habeas corpus, a great many of them were to remain in custody for days and weeks. As much as, if not more than in 1917, when there was at least the excuse... of a real world war, the whole of Québec found itself behind bars as Trudeau and company now attempted to justify their act before Parliament, the existence of which they seemed just to have remembered.

—René Lévesque, Memoirs, *1986*

Source 3

...[T]here were no fine distinctions drawn between separatism and terrorism in the general round-up in October 1970.... After the crisis had passed, rather than issuing an apology for such overzealous police work, the prime minister boasted that separatism was "dead." Other... Liberals agreed: the FLQ crisis had been an opportunity to "smash separatism" and the government had taken it.

—The Structure of Canadian History, 1984

Source 4

As for the objection that Trudeau was acting to squash separatism and... the Parti Québécois, we have the statements of both the prime minister and one of his supporters... during the crisis. On October 17, [Bryce] Mackasey stressed to the House of Commons that the Parti Québécois was "a legitimate political party. It wants to bring an end to this country through democratic means, but that is the privilege of that party." Trudeau... made the same point in November to an interviewer.

—Canada Since 1945: Power, Politics, and Provincialism, 1989

Applying the Skill

1. Are these documents primary sources or secondary sources? Explain in each case.

2. Summarize each document's main argument.

3. Which documents support Lévesque's claims?

4. Which documents do you consider to be the most credible sources? Justify your choices.

5. Write one or two paragraphs giving your view on whether the use of the War Measures Act was justified. Support your view with details from the text and the documents above.

Economic Challenges

When the Trudeau era began, Canadians could look back on nearly two decades of economic growth. People old enough to remember the dark days of the Depression were amazed by the prosperity they were enjoying. Many Canadians believed that the post-war boom would continue indefinitely. High unemployment and poverty were surely problems of the past, never to be seen again. But within just a few years, this optimism was badly shaken.

The Problem of Inflation

A variety of factors caused the economic crisis, but one of the most important was an oil **embargo** imposed in 1973 by the Organization of the Petroleum Exporting Countries (OPEC). In that year, war broke out in the Middle East between Israel and its Arab neighbours. Many Western countries, including Canada, supported Israel. In retaliation, OPEC, which included Saudi Arabia, Kuwait, and other Arab oil-producing countries, refused to sell oil to these countries. Almost overnight, oil and gas prices jumped about 400 percent.

The huge increase in oil prices started a round of **inflation** that would last most of the 1970s. The prices of all manufactured products went up sharply, and Canadians found that the purchasing power of their dollar fell steadily. Suddenly, they were heading for tough economic times.

As prices rose, Canadian workers began to demand higher wages; but as their wages increased, so did prices, and inflation spiralled. At the same time, businesses were failing. Their energy and labour costs had soared while the demand for their products was down. Unemployment rates rose from the average of 3 to 5 percent during the 1950s and 1960s to a high of 12 percent by 1983.

For the average Canadian family, the 1970s were unsettling times. Inflation stretched household budgets and increased the need for women to enter the workforce. Dual-income families became common. By 1978, the average family's buying power had fallen for the first time since the end of the Second World War.

● How did the Canadian government respond to the economic challenges of the 1970s?

KEY TERMS

embargo the prohibition by a government or organization that prevents certain goods from being shipped in or out of a country

FIGURE 7–20 Canada's high rate of inflation in the 1970s was tied to massive oil price increases generated by the oil crisis of 1973.

Thinking Critically What would it mean if prices went up more than 14 percent a year, but your income remained the same?

● How was regionalism expressed in the 1970s?

KEY TERMS

regional disparity differences in income, wages, and jobs in one area compared with another

Western alienation the feeling on the part of Western Canada that federal policies favour Central Canada; it has led to the rise of several regional parties, including the Canadian Alliance Party

Regionalism

To make matters worse, two economic problems that had plagued Canada in the past resurfaced. Both were the result of regionalism. The first of these problems was **regional disparity**, or the economic gap between the poorer and more prosperous regions of Canada. As in the Depression of the 1930s, industries based on natural resources were hit the hardest in the recession of the 1970s. The fishing industry in Atlantic Canada and the forestry, mining, and fishing industries in British Columbia suffered massive layoffs. Ontario and Québec were less affected, and the other provinces resented them. The Trudeau government increased transfer payments to the provinces to be used for social services. It also spent millions of dollars on regional projects to help economic development in certain areas, especially the Atlantic provinces.

The second problem of **Western alienation** had long existed. Many Westerners believed that Ottawa's policies favoured Central Canada at the expense of the West. In the 1970s, Westerners were shocked when, in response to the oil crisis, the federal government froze the price of domestic oil and gas and imposed a tax on petroleum exported from Western Canada. The money raised by the tax would subsidize the cost of imported oil in the East. These actions infuriated Albertans. Along with their premier, Peter Lougheed, they felt that Alberta had the right to charge world prices for its oil:

> *The Fathers of Confederation decided that the natural resources within provincial boundaries would be owned by the citizens through their provincial governments.... We view the federal export tax on Alberta oil as contrary to both the spirit and the intent of Confederation.*
>
> *–Federal–Provincial Conference on Energy, 1974*

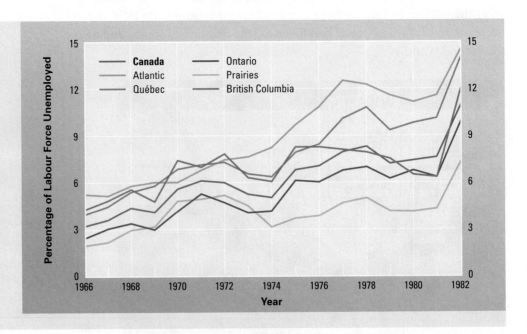

FIGURE 7–21 Regional unemployment rates, 1966–1982

Reading a Graph Which regions had the highest unemployment rate? Which had the lowest? How did the rate in British Columbia vary in relation to other provinces? What might account for the difference?

To deal with a renewed oil crisis and rising gas prices, the Liberals also brought in the National Energy Program (NEP). The NEP aimed to

- reduce the consumption of oil
- protect Canadians from rising oil prices
- make Canada self-sufficient in oil

The program provided funding to Canadian petroleum companies to drill for oil in promising sites in the Arctic and off the coast of Newfoundland. It also encouraged consumers to switch from oil to gas and electric sources of power. Alberta, once again, reacted angrily. By 1984, oil prices had fallen and the NEP had been dismantled, but the bitterness it caused in the West would linger for years to come.

FAST FORWARD

The Future of Energy

The energy crisis of the 1970s resulted from the Arab world's response to Western support for Israel in the 1973 Arab–Israeli War. Today's energy crisis is caused by a vastly increased world demand for hydrocarbons. To meet demand, and to diminish the climate-changing effects of burning petroleum and coal, new technologies are now in widespread use. Many governments actively promote energy conservation; some even use tax incentives. In January 2010, the government of Ontario signed a $7 billion deal with Korean technology company Samsung to develop green energy technology and to construct solar and wind power facilities in that province. Selling the green technology developed under this scheme is expected to create jobs and bring financial benefits.

FIGURE 7–22 Solar collectors like this one may soon be a common sight in some areas of Canada. Wind turbines also produce energy and are situated in areas with consistent strong winds, such as in the Prairies or on coastlines.

Expanding Horizons

During the 1970s, Canadians were again asking themselves whether the United States had too much influence over the Canadian economy. Prime Minister Trudeau was particularly interested in finding new trading partners so that Canada would no longer depend so heavily on the U.S. as the major customer for its exports. Trudeau tried to interest the European Economic Community in expanding trade with Canada. Those countries, however, were more eager to strengthen trade links among themselves. And the newly industrialized countries of Southeast Asia, the so-called "Asian tigers," showed little interest in a special agreement with Canada.

Reluctantly, the Trudeau administration accepted the reality of Canada's continuing economic dependence on the United States. The government tried to strengthen its control over the economy and culture through programs and agencies such as the NEP, the CRTC (see Chapter 6), and the Foreign Investment Review Agency (FIRA), which reviews all major proposed foreign investments to determine whether they serve Canada's national interest.

● What measures has Canada taken to promote a distinct Canadian identity?

Innovations
The Information Age

The Second World War spurred a wave of new technology that continued into the 1960s and 1970s. Computers and other communications technologies were revolutionizing the way Canadians worked, played, and communicated. Canada had entered the information age. With satellite broadcasting, Canadians had access to hundreds of television stations. Satellite links also allowed for cheap long-distance telephone calls, making it easier for Canadians to communicate with family or friends and businesses abroad.

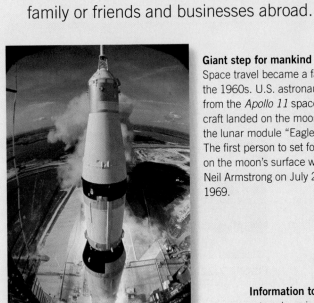

Giant step for mankind
Space travel became a fact in the 1960s. U.S. astronauts from the *Apollo 11* spacecraft landed on the moon in the lunar module "Eagle." The first person to set foot on the moon's surface was Neil Armstrong on July 21, 1969.

Happy baby, happy mom
Disposable diapers hit the marketplace in 1961. The first Pampers were marketed for use during special away-from-home outings. Sales of disposable diapers increased dramatically over the next few decades and greatly reduced women's work around the home.

Information to go The first computer microchip, invented in 1971, revolutionized computer technology. Computers had been in use since the end of the Second World War, but they were very big and slow at processing information. The microchip made computers smaller, more portable, and cheaper. The first flexible disk drive was invented in 1976.

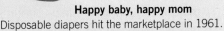

Information at your fingertips The Internet was formed in 1969 when the U.S. Defence Department and four U.S. universities linked their computers to create the Advanced Research Projects Agency Network (ARPAnet). Its aim was to decentralize the Defence Department's computer system and make it less vulnerable to attack by the Soviet Union.

Transplanting futures
The 1960s and 1970s saw dramatic advances in medicine. The first successful heart transplant took place in 1967.

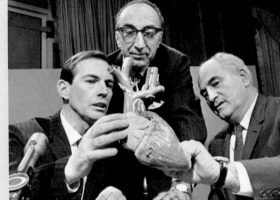

©P

The Environmental Movement

Canada's prosperity was won at a great cost. Many environmental challenges facing the world today had their roots in this period. It was not until 1962 that North Americans began to be aware of the extent of environmental damage. In that year, an American scientist, Rachel Carson, published a widely read book titled *Silent Spring*. In it, she warned that pollution of air, water, and soil was threatening life on Earth. She criticized the chemical industry for producing toxic pesticides such as DDT and claiming that they were safe.

At first, business and governments resisted any attempts to limit pollution, but public concern over the environment rose steadily. Environmental groups were established to lobby governments to control pollution and as awareness grew, legislation changed. Greenpeace was created in 1970 by a small group of activists in British Columbia to draw attention to environmental concerns.

FIGURE 7–23 Initially, little was done to address the issues raised in Rachel Carson's groundbreaking book, *Silent Spring*.

up close and personal ◯ Greenpeace: Warriors for the Environment

In the fall of 1971, 11 people with a shared vision of a green and peaceful world set sail from Vancouver on an old fishing boat. They were headed toward Amchitka Island, Alaska, to "bear witness" to underground nuclear testing by the United States. Not only were they concerned about the immediate effects on the region's ecology, including the possibility of earthquakes and tsunamis along Pacific coastlines, but they also had a strong anti-nuclear message to spread.

Although their mission was unsuccessful, and the U.S. detonated its bomb, it was that country's final nuclear test in the area. Some believe that this voyage and the global environmental awareness that resulted was the beginning of the end of the Cold War. Today, Greenpeace is an international organization with more than 40 offices, and 2.8 million members around the world. Through direct action, Greenpeace seeks to

- protect biodiversity in all its forms
- prevent pollution and abuse of Earth's oceans, land, air, and fresh water
- end all nuclear threats
- promote peace, global disarmament, and non-violence

FIGURE 7–24 Crew of the boat *Phyllis Cormack*, also known as Greenpeace; inaugural protest mission

PRACTICE QUESTIONS

1. What economic problems arose in the 1970s? How did Trudeau propose to deal with them? What was the outcome?

2. What would be the effect of high inflation on
   a) people on fixed incomes and pensions?
   b) workers who were not in unions?
   c) a family seeking a loan to buy a house?

3. How did the problems of this period influence the growth of regionalism and Western alienation?

4. **Perspectives** How do you think space travel changed people's perspective about planet Earth?

● What was Canada's involvement in the Cold War?

KEY TERM

Bomarc missiles nuclear missiles that Canada agreed to accept from the U.S. during the Cold War; led to a rift in Canada/U.S. relations

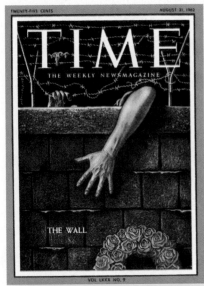

FIGURE 7–25 For many people, the 1961 construction of the Berlin Wall to separate the German city into two zones—one communist and one capitalist—was a frightening symbol of Soviet power and aggression. It appeared that the Cold War was still going strong.

A More Independent International Policy

As the Cold War intensified during the early 1960s, tensions developed between Canada and the United States. Even at the personal level, the leaders of the two countries did not get along: Prime Minister John Diefenbaker and U.S. President John Kennedy strongly disliked each other; President Johnson treated Lester Pearson with contempt; Trudeau had nothing but scorn for President Richard Nixon. These differences were particularly obvious during the most serious crisis of the Cold War: the Cuban Missile Crisis, which took the world to the brink of nuclear war. Later, the Vietnam War further strained Canada's relations with the United States.

The Nuclear Issue in Canada

The Cuban Missile Crisis caused a debate about Canada's defence policy and the government's stand on nuclear weapons. Should Canada accept nuclear weapons on its territory, as the United States wished? When the Avro Arrow was scrapped (see Chapter 6), Canada accepted U.S. **Bomarc missiles** that were capable of carrying nuclear warheads. The years that passed before the missiles were actually installed, however, allowed time for second thoughts.

In 1963, the ruling Conservative Party was divided on the issue. The Minister of External Affairs felt Canada should be a non-nuclear nation. He argued that it was hypocritical to urge the United Nations to work for disarmament while accepting nuclear weapons. The Defence Minister, in contrast, insisted that nuclear weapons were vital in protecting Canada against communist aggression. Meanwhile, the anti-nuclear movement was growing among Canadian citizens. Many were starting to realize that nuclear war would amount to global suicide.

During the election campaign of 1963, the Liberals, under the leadership of Lester Pearson, proposed that Canadian forces accept nuclear weapons under certain conditions. Prime Minister Diefenbaker and the Conservatives, however, appealed to Canadian nationalism, including Canada's right to decide for itself on international matters. Many business leaders and influential newspapers supported the Liberals, fearing that Diefenbaker's anti-Americanism would injure trade with and investment from the United States. The nuclear issue split the country. Diefenbaker was narrowly defeated in the election of 1963, and the Liberals formed a minority government. This federal election was the first to be fought over Canada–U.S. relations since 1911.

FIGURE 7–26 Prime Minister Trudeau and American President Richard Nixon are smiling in this staged photograph. In reality, Nixon and Trudeau disliked one another. Nixon particularly resented Trudeau's support of Cuba, which ran counter to American policy.

case study

The Cuban Missile Crisis: Canada–U.S. Relations Deteriorate

In 1959, Cuban rebels led by Fidel Castro overthrew Cuba's pro-U.S. dictator, Fulgencio Batista. The United States reacted angrily, imposing trade and economic sanctions on Cuba. In 1961, a group of Cuban exiles, supported by the U.S., landed in Cuba with the aim of overthrowing the Castro government. The "Bay of Pigs" invasion was a failure, which encouraged Cuba to turn to the Soviet Union for support.

In October 1962, U.S. surveillance showed that the U.S.S.R. was installing offensive nuclear missile bases in Cuba. Missiles launched from these sites were a direct threat to U.S. security. President Kennedy announced a naval and air blockade of Cuba. U.S. forces and NORAD were readied for war. Armed B-52 bombers were constantly in the air. The world seemed to be poised on the brink of war.

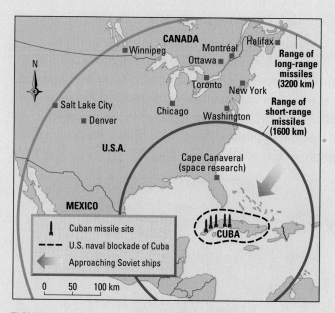

FIGURE 7–27 Projected range of Cuban missiles

At first, Soviet Premier Nikita Khrushchev refused to remove the missiles. He put the armed forces of the U.S.S.R. on full alert and Soviet ships steamed toward U.S. ships blockading Cuba. At the last minute, Khrushchev agreed to dismantle the missile bases in exchange for a promise that the U.S. would not invade Cuba.

FIGURE 7–28 On October 22, 1962, U.S. President John F. Kennedy gave a dramatic radio and television address explaining his position on the Cuban Missile Crisis to the American public.

After the Missile Crisis ended, relations between the U.S. and Cuba continued to be difficult. The U.S. tightened its economic embargo and restricted its citizens from doing business with or visiting Cuba. As of 2009, the embargo was still in place.

During the crisis, the United States expected Canada, its partner in NORAD, to provide unconditional support of its policies. Prime Minister Diefenbaker, however, preferred that the United Nations send a fact-finding mission to Cuba to verify the U.S. surveillance.

Diefenbaker was reluctant to have Canada drawn into a major conflict that seemed largely rooted in U.S. policy and interests. At first, the Canadian government refused to place Canada's NORAD forces on alert. Nor did it allow U.S. planes with atomic weapons to land at Canadian bases. The Americans were furious.

Diefenbaker believed he was defending Canada's independence, but a poll later showed that 80 percent of Canadians thought he was wrong. Canadian troops were eventually put on alert but the damage to Canada–U.S. relations had already been done.

Looking Further

1. The Monroe Doctrine is a policy enacted by the U.S. government in 1823, which gives it the right to intervene if foreign governments interfere in countries in the Americas. Was President Kennedy justified in using the Monroe Doctrine to support his actions during the Cuban Missile Crisis? Explain.

2. In your opinion, should Canada have supported the United States during the Cuban Missile Crisis? Give reasons for your answer.

3. "At the time of the Cuban Missile Crisis, the U.S. had missiles of its own in Europe that were capable of striking Soviet targets." To what extent does this statement affect your thinking about the crisis?

● What was Canada's response to modern conflicts?

KEY TERM

draft resisters citizens who refuse to join the army to fight in a war during conscription

The Vietnam War

The war in Vietnam profoundly affected politics and society in the United States and Canada. Vietnam was divided, almost in half. North Vietnam had a communist government. The government in South Vietnam, more a dictatorship than a democracy, was supported by the United States. The Americans felt that if the south fell to communism, then it would not be long before other Asian states fell, a sort of domino effect. At first, the United States sent military advisors and economic help to the South Vietnamese, but by the 1960s it was sending troops as well. By 1966, there were 317 000 U.S. soldiers in Vietnam, and the number kept growing. At the same time, the U.S.S.R. and communist China supplied weapons and aid to North Vietnam.

Vietnam was the first war recorded by television cameras. Nightly newscasts brought the events of the war into the living rooms of millions of Americans. In 1968, the public was horrified to learn of a massacre of Vietnamese civilians by U.S. troops in the village of My Lai. That same year, North Vietnamese forces simultaneously attacked cities throughout South Vietnam during the Tet Offensive. They even briefly seized the U.S. embassy in the capital city of Saigon (today's Ho Chi Minh City). Americans, who had been assured that they were winning the war, were stunned.

As Americans watched Vietnamese villages being bombed, and their own young men returning home disabled or in body bags, many began questioning the war. As more and more Americans disagreed with their government's actions, massive anti-war protests swept across the country.

Canada's Reaction to the War

Canadians were divided in their response to the war in Vietnam. Many people still saw communism as a real threat to Western security. However, as the war raged on, more and more Canadians turned against American policy. Until 1968, most opponents of the war were students, but opposition soon came from a much wider group of Canadians.

FIGURE 7–29 Images of American soldiers in Vietnam encouraged anti-war sentiments.

Identifying Viewpoints How might seeing images such as this one in newspapers and on television influence young people to oppose the war? Why do you think today's wars do not generate so much interest from young people?

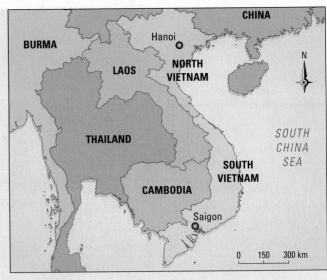

FIGURE 7–30 Southeast Asia

During the Vietnam War, the U.S. drafted young men to serve in the armed forces. Beginning in 1965, thousands of American **draft resisters** and deserters who were opposed to the war came to Canada. Anti-draft groups were established in many cities to help them get settled and support their protests against the war. The U.S. government was unhappy about Canada accepting resisters.

The Canadian government tried its best to stay neutral during the Vietnam War, but its close relationship with the U.S. made this complicated. Canada did not send troops to fight in the war, although thousands of Canadians did join the U.S. forces voluntarily. Some Canadian companies benefited from the war by selling goods such as berets, boots, airplane engines, and weapons to the U.S. Defense Department. In 1965, when Prime Minister Pearson spoke out against a U.S. bombing campaign in North Vietnam, he was severely reprimanded by President Lyndon Johnson.

FIGURE 7–31 This demonstration was one of hundreds of anti-war protests in Canada.

Expressing Ideas Do you think Canada was right to offer American draft resisters and deserters a safe haven?

The Vietnam War Ends

In 1969, President Richard Nixon took office in the United States, with a pledge to pull American troops out of Southeast Asia. By 1972, the Americans began to withdraw. The last American combat forces left South Vietnam in 1973. Less than two years later, a massive North Vietnamese military offensive crushed the South Vietnamese army. Vietnam, ravaged by decades of war and destruction, was unified under communist rule. Those who did not support the new regime were stripped of their property and forced into "re-education" camps, where they were pressured to support their new leaders.

Many anti-communist Vietnamese fled. They took to the seas in boats hoping to find freedom. These "boat people" made their way to refugee camps in Malaysia and Hong Kong where they applied for refugee status. Thousands of Vietnamese were accepted into Canada and became citizens.

PRACTICE QUESTIONS

1. Identify the following and explain the role each played in the Cuban Missile Crisis: a) Nikita Khrushchev, b) Fidel Castro, c) John F. Kennedy, d) John Diefenbaker.

2. What questions about nuclear weapons did the Cuban Missile Crisis raise in Canadians' minds? Why did these questions divide Canadians?

3. What effect did the Cuban Missile Crisis and the Vietnam War have on Canada–U.S. relations?

4. How did U.S. policy deal with Cuba after the Cuban Revolution? How did Canada's policy differ?

5. How would you explain the war in Vietnam to someone who knew nothing about it? Answer the following questions: What? Where? When? Why?

6. List the ways in which Canada asserted its independence from the U.S. in the 1960s.

Should Canada's foreign policy be independent of the United States?

As you learned in Chapter 6, Canada has a long history of international involvement and the Canadian military has been in many places in the world. Mostly, our troops have been part of United Nations peacekeeping missions, in Cyprus and Suez, for example. Peacekeeping allowed us to actively participate in international conflict while still maintaining a non-combative role—and a largely independent foreign policy. We were not directly involved in either the Cuban Missile Crisis or the war in Vietnam, even though both were very important to our superpower ally, the United States. However, in 1990, we joined the U.S.-led coalition against Iraq and sent ships and planes into that conflict. Although our commit-ment was relatively small, it represented a shift in Canada's foreign policy. Lately, as part of NATO, Canada has taken on a more active combat role, particularly since the 9/11 attacks and the beginning of America's "War on Terror."

At the time of writing, Canadian troops are fighting in Afghanistan as part of the NATO force there. This is a significant departure from peacekeeping. Defeating the Taliban in Afghanistan is an important NATO goal, but it is also fundamental to the geopolitical goals of the United States. Is Afghanistan important to Canada? Should we be involved? Are we helping the U.S. achieve its goals rather than our own? In today's world, with the

FIGURE 7–32 Two images of Canadian forces: above, combatants in Afghanistan, and left, under a UN peacekeeping mandate in Haiti

Analyzing Images Compare these images. What differences do you see in the soldiers? How might these differences be interpreted by citizens of the countries in which they are stationed?

● What measures has Canada taken to promote a distinct Canadian identity?

threat of international terrorism, is it really possible for a middle power closely allied to a superpower, as Canada is, to have an independent foreign policy?

Consider these opinions for and against Canadian participation in Afghanistan. The first is from an article in the Tyee newspaper, published in October, 2006. Byers argues that following the American lead has meant that Canada's peacekeeping reputation has been sacrificed. The second is from an interview in *Maclean's* magazine with commentator Andrew Coyne. Coyne thinks Canada's mission in Afghanistan is necessary. He also makes the point, in this excerpt, that helping the U.S. has other benefits.

Against:

Wrapped up in the distinction between the peacekeeping opportunities in Lebanon and Darfur and the counter-insurgency mission in Afghanistan is the additional issue of reputation costs, most notably the cost to Canada's international reputation for independence and objectivity, and thus our ability to lead and persuade on a wide range of issues. Where would we gain the most in terms of our international reputation: continuing with a failing counter-insurgency mission in Afghanistan, or leading a humanitarian intervention to stop the genocide in Darfur?

For:

There's a crasser, more self-interested reason for why we should stay. Just now we're having a devil of a time convincing the Americans we're as serious about fighting terrorism as they are. The issue has all sorts of obvious implications for our trade relations. Sticking it out in Afghanistan would be a fine way to prove our credentials. Whereas clearing out before the job's done risks giving aid and comfort, not just to the enemy, but the French and Italians.

FIGURE 7–33 Canadian peacekeeping missions

Analyzing the Issue

1. In your opinion, does Canada have an international role that is different from, and independent of, that of the U.S.? How would you define that role?

2. Summarize Coyne's argument in a sentence and support it with two examples of Canadian military action from the 20th century. Do the same for Byers' argument.

3. Research Canada's participation in the Gulf War. Compare this with Canada's participation in the Afghan operation in terms of length of commitment, military resources provided, cost of the war, and casualties.

4. A Nanos poll in November 2009 showed that at least 60 percent of Canadians wanted troops withdrawn from Afghanistan. In your opinion, does this mean that the mission needs to be better explained to Canadians? Write a brief description of Canadian foreign policy goals as you see them and include an explanation of why or why not the Afghan mission fits the goals.

KEY TERMS

trade and aid the process of stimulating the economies of developing countries with aid so that they can access global markets and trade with developed nations

tied aid aid given to a foreign country with conditions attached

Trudeau's Foreign Policy

The Vietnam War and the Cuban Missile Crisis highlighted the differences between American and Canadian foreign policy. As prime minister, Pierre Trudeau reflected the changing attitudes of the time. One of his goals was to chart a course in foreign policy that was less dependent on U.S. approval.

This intention was clearly signalled in 1970, when Canada officially recognized the communist government of the People's Republic of China. Even though Trudeau defied U.S. policy, his decision made sense to most Canadians. Mainland China was a great power, a major purchaser of Canadian wheat and other goods, and potentially a significant trading partner.

At the same time, Trudeau did not wish to anger the U.S. Neither did he think Canada could act on foreign or economic affairs without considering the U.S. to some extent. He explained his views in a now famous speech:

> *Let me say that it should not be surprising if these policies in many instances either reflect or take into account the proximity of the United States. Living next to you is in some ways like sleeping with an elephant. No matter how friendly or even-tempered is the beast... one is affected by every twitch and grunt.*
>
> *–Speech to the National Press Club, Washington, 1969*

FIGURE 7–34 In 1976, Trudeau became the first leader of a NATO country to pay a state visit to Fidel Castro's communist Cuba. At the end of a speech, he surprised and delighted the audience by proclaiming "Viva Cuba" and "Viva Castro."

Expressing Ideas Why would his words be controversial in Canada and the United States?

Defence Revisited

Trudeau's approach to national defence was a sharp departure from that of previous governments. Lester Pearson had referred to Canada and the United States as "defence partners." Trudeau believed that Canada needed to re-evaluate this policy. He took steps to scale back Canada's participation in the nuclear arms race with the Soviet Union in the hope that this would ease Cold War tensions. These steps included the following:

- From 1970 to 1972, Canada's NATO forces gave up their nuclear missiles in Europe.
- The Bomarc missile sites that Pearson had accepted in 1963 were dismantled. A new jet fighter, the CF-18 Hornet, was armed with conventional rather than nuclear warheads.
- The national defence budget was cut by 20 percent and Canada's NATO contingent in Europe was reduced to half its former strength.

Military officers, diplomats, and officials from the U.S. embassy in Ottawa were outraged, but the government pursued its new course.

At the same time, Canada continued to participate in NATO and NORAD, alongside the United States. American vessels and submarines armed with nuclear missiles were permitted to dock in Canadian ports. American branch plants in Canada accepted contracts from the U.S. Defence Department to develop nuclear technology or other war materials, sometimes over strong protests from Canadian pacifists.

Canada's International Profile

Throughout Trudeau's period in office, the Cold War continued to dominate international affairs. The world remained divided between the West (the U.S. and its allies) and the East (communist China, the Soviet Union, and countries friendly to it). Trudeau wanted Canada to be a middle power, strong enough and respected enough to chart an independent foreign policy.

Outside the two rival power blocs, most of the world's people lived in countries not officially allied with either superpower. African and Asian nations emerging from colonial rule after the Second World War tried to remain detached from Cold War rivalries—at least for a time. But other divisions were emerging. Most new nations were located in the southern hemisphere. They were also, for the most part, far less industrialized than countries in the northern hemisphere. So, while the Cold War split the world politically between East and West, a huge economic gap separated the rich North from the poor South.

The Trudeau government aimed to bridge both gaps in order to promote world peace and understanding among nations. As a middle power, Canada could build links between East and West and North and South. Trudeau's efforts to reduce nuclear weapons and to establish trade and sporting links with communist states were part of this plan. Trudeau called for more aid for the poor countries of the world. He believed that the prosperous nations of the North should be helping the poverty-stricken countries of the South to develop their economies and improve the living conditions for their people. This policy of "**trade and aid**" became the cornerstone of Trudeau's foreign policy in bridging the North–South gap.

In 1968, a new government body known as the **Canadian International Development Agency (CIDA)** was formed. CIDA's responsibility was to boost foreign aid to less industrialized countries. Countries receiving aid would have to agree to use it to buy products manufactured in Canada. In this way, Canada would benefit as well. This was known as **tied aid**, and it made up more than half the total development aid Canada extended to less industrialized nations. During Trudeau's administration, the total amount of aid Canada extended to developing countries increased from $278 million in 1969 to more than $2 billion in 1984.

FIGURE 7–35 Paul Henderson celebrates after scoring the winning goal for Canada in the Canada–U.S.S.R. hockey series in 1972. This popular event was one of many steps taken by Canada to lower Cold War tensions. Why do you think winning the series meant so much to Canadians?

What If...

Imagine Canada had taken a stronger military stance during the 1960s and 1970s. How might Canada's image as a middle power have been affected? Would the Canada–U.S. relationship have been different?

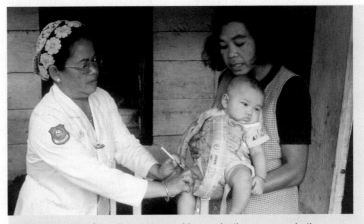

FIGURE 7–36 Canadian-sponsored immunization program in the Philippines

Developing Understanding How would Canadian programs, such as immunization, improve living conditions for less industrialized countries? How would improved living conditions promote peace?

©P

KEY TERM

Anti-Ballistic Missile Treaty (ABMT) an agreement between the U.S. and the U.S.S.R. limiting strategic offensive weapons and defensive systems

The Cold War Renewed

While Trudeau was trying to bridge the economic gap among countries during the early 1970s, tension between the United States and the Soviet Union eased, and the two countries agreed to reduce the number of their nuclear weapons. In 1972, at the Strategic Arms Limitation Talks (SALT I), the U.S. and the Soviet Union signed the **Anti-Ballistic Missile Treaty (ABMT)** and an interim agreement on strategic offensive arms. This marked a breakthrough in relations between the two superpowers.

In 1979, however, the Soviet Union invaded Afghanistan. It also sent medium-range missiles to Eastern Europe. In response, NATO announced that it, too, was deploying more advanced missiles in Europe. In protest against the Soviet occupation of Afghanistan, many Western nations, including Canada, boycotted the 1980 Olympic Games held in Moscow.

Sovereignty in the Arctic

Canada and the United States were soon drawn into a confrontation over territory. Canada claimed sovereignty, or possession, of the islands of the Arctic and the waterways between them, including the Northwest Passage. In 1968, oil was discovered at Prudhoe Bay in Alaska, and American oil companies were interested in establishing a regular tanker route through the Northwest Passage to the east coast of the United States—in other words, through an area Canada believed was its own. The following year, an American oil tanker, the *Manhattan*, travelled along this route without Canadian approval. The Canadian government became alarmed that the U.S. was treating the Northwest Passage as an international waterway, rather than as part of Canada's Arctic possessions.

Canada was also concerned about the fragile Arctic ecosystem. Greater tanker traffic through the Northwest Passage increased the likelihood of an oil spill that could spell environmental disaster. The government announced it was extending Canada's territorial limit from 3 to 12 miles (about 5 to 19 kilometres) offshore. In addition, it passed the Arctic Waters Pollution Prevention Act, creating a 100-mile (160-kilometre) pollution-free zone around the islands of the Canadian Arctic. Within this zone, strict environmental regulations would be enforced, and oil tanker traffic would be controlled. Despite protests from Washington, the oil companies involved in the Alaska development agreed to respect Canada's rules.

Canada won support for its moves in the Arctic region from a number of nations with Arctic territories. At the United Nations, a conference on a "Law of the Sea" was suggested, endorsing the idea that the nations of the world should act together to protect the oceans as "the common heritage of mankind." Canada renewed talks about a 12-mile territorial sea and a further 200-mile economic zone for every country whose land mass faced an ocean. Canada also suggested that oil or mining companies active in environmentally sensitive areas should pay a special tax and channel some of their revenues into local economic development. To date, these suggestions have been adopted by more than 160 nations as part of the Law of the Sea Convention.

Prime Minister Pierre Elliott Trudeau

- born 1919, Montréal, Québec
- lawyer, law professor, author
- first elected to Commons in 1965
- prime minister 1968–1979, 1980–1984

Domestic Record

- changed the Criminal Code to decriminalize homosexuality, make it easier to divorce, and legalize abortions
- passed the Official Languages Act in 1969 to officially make Canada bilingual
- invoked the War Measures Act during the October Crisis in 1970
- campaigned against Québec separatism during the 1980 referendum
- passed the Constitution Act in 1982, which entrenched the Canadian Charter of Rights and Freedoms in the Canadian Constitution
- appointed Jeanne Sauvé Canada's first woman Governor General in 1984

International Record

- won the Albert Einstein Peace Prize in 1984 for negotiating the reduction of nuclear weapons and easing Cold War tensions

The Politics of Global Warming

In recent years, global warming has severely weakened Arctic ice and made the region easier to navigate. Canada now faces a serious threat against what some see as its sovereign territory. Many countries lay claim to the region—and the seabed—of the Arctic Circle. At stake is the Arctic's many important resources: oil, natural gas, diamonds, gold, and silver.

The Northwest Passage is enormously beneficial to Canada as well. Prime Minister Stephen Harper announced that Canada will build a deep-water port in the High Arctic. Will this be enough to protect Canada's sovereignty in the Arctic? Though Inuit governments and organizations are generally positive, the Inuit have mixed feelings about these developments, which will significantly change their lives. Paul Kaludjak of the Arctic Athabaskan Council (AAC) expressed the council's view:

> The Canadian government does not have a strategy to assert our sovereignty. Instead, individual departments have reacted to events. We need a long-term plan that knits together federal and territorial agencies and Inuit organizations. We all have roles to play. Asserting Arctic sovereignty is a national, not a federal, project.
>
> –*Arctic Athabaskan Council Newsletter,*
> *November 2006*

Canada has until 2013 to submit evidence to the UN to support its claim to the Arctic.

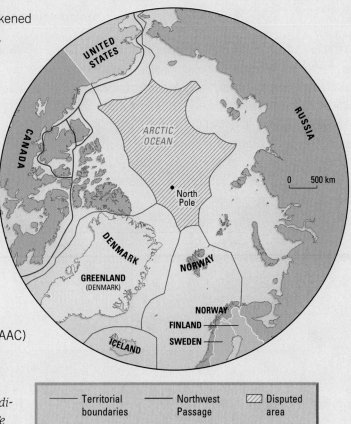

FIGURE 7–37 How might the extension of territorial limits affect Canadian sovereignty in the Arctic? Do you think Canada should defend its claims to the region?

PRACTICE QUESTIONS

1. What do you think Trudeau meant when he said that living next to the United States is like sleeping next to an elephant?

2. List the ways in which Trudeau distanced Canada's foreign policy from that of the U.S. in the 1970s.

3. How did Trudeau try to bridge the gap between rich and poor countries?

4. In what areas of the world did Cold War tensions increase from 1979 to 1984? What was Canada's response?

5. What steps did Canada take in the 1960s and 1970s to uphold its rights in the Arctic? Have these efforts been effective?

CHAPTER FOCUS QUESTION

How did Canada's political, social, and economic policies reflect a new independence in the 1960s and 1970s?

By 1967, Canada had a population of 20 million people, half of whom were under 25 years of age. The needs, views, and priorities of youth affected everything from politics to social priorities. In politics, Pierre Trudeau and his policies seemed to reflect the times. The country experienced a separatist crisis to which Trudeau responded forcefully. Canadians also thought a lot about their ties to the United States, particularly after Americans became involved in the unpopular Vietnam War. And, perhaps for the first time, the environment became an important national and international issue.

1. Make a three-column chart like the one shown below for the key people, events, and ideas of the 1960s and 1970s. Use the information in the chapter to fill in the chart, including a brief explanation of each item and a sketch to help you visualize the concept.

Key People	Key Events	Key Ideas

Vocabulary Focus

2. Create a series of study cards, one for each of the following terms. Write a definition for each term and then pass the cards to two other students, each of whom will add another layer of meaning to the definition by linking the term to two other terms on the list.

Québec nationalism
October Crisis
Flag Debate
hippy
Cuban Missile Crisis
draft dodger
NATO
Red Ensign
NORAD
War Measures Act
Vietnam War
Canadian nationalism

Knowledge and Understanding

3. Continue the ongoing timeline assignment for the history section of this course. Review the events that are covered in the chapter. Write the name and date of each event on the timeline and explain how the event contributed to Canadian independence.

4. What was the October Crisis? Why was this event a challenge to Canadian unity? How did Trudeau respond?

5. What efforts were made to celebrate Canada's identity in 1967?

6. How successful was the Canadian government in dealing with the economic challenges of the 1960s and 1970s? Provide evidence from the textbook.

7. What is inflation? What caused the inflation of the 1970s? Why would inflation affect Canadian unity? (Hint: Think about regionalism.) How did the National Energy Program add to the problem?

8. Write a summary explaining the Vietnam War to modern newspaper readers who know little about it. Answer the following questions: a) Who? b) What? c) When? d) Where? e) Why?

9. "The Vietnam War helped define Canada as a nation since it encouraged Canadian leaders to distance their country from U.S. foreign policy." Explain this statement in your own words.

10. How successful was Canada at keeping its independence from the U.S. during the 1960s and 1970s? Create a two-column chart like the one below. Provide examples of independence and rate their success.

Evidence of Canadian Independence from the U.S.	Success Rate (high/moderate/low)

Critical Thinking

11. Using the chart from Question 1, select at least five events that you think were the most significant to Canada's independence during the 1960s and 1970s. Provide evidence to support your opinion.

Significance

12. Assess the impact of Québec nationalism both on Québec and on the rest of Canada.

13. List and then rank Trudeau's largest national and international challenges. Provide evidence from the textbook to support your choices.

Judgements

14. Trudeau was right to impose the War Measures Act in 1970. Present a reasoned argument for or against this statement.

Document Analysis

15. The 1960s and 1970s were decades of varied and widespread social activism. Look at the photos in the collage below and respond to the following:
    - How might these images influence other groups or individuals?
    - Analyze the photos and explain why each group was protesting.
    - Is there a common theme or goal for the groups?
    - Describe some of the methods used by the groups to achieve their goals.
    - Evaluate which methods were the most successful in drawing attention to the groups' causes and explain why this was the case.
    - Which of these methods are still used today?
    - From your knowledge, how successful were the groups in achieving their goals?

8 Canada Shifts Focus: 1980 and Beyond

GUIDING QUESTIONS

Society & Identity

- In what ways did Canadian society change after 1980?

- How did Canada's multiculturalism policy affect minority groups?

- How did changes to social policies affect women and minority groups in Canada?

- How did Aboriginal Canadians respond to challenges in the late 20th century?

- What was the impact of Québec nationalism on Canadian unity?

- What measures has Canada taken to promote a distinct Canadian identity?

Politics & Government

- How did changes to the Constitution impact Canadian society?

Economy & Human Geography

- How did the Canadian government respond to economic challenges after 1980?

- How does globalization affect living standards?

Autonomy & World Presence

- What factors contributed to Canada's emerging autonomy?

- What was Canada's involvement in the Cold War?

- What was Canada's response to modern conflicts?

- Describe Canada's involvement in the UN.

TIMELINE

1980	1982	1985	1987	1990	1990s	1992
First Québec referendum on sovereignty-association	Constitution patriation	Peak of the debt crisis	Meech Lake Accord signed	Meech Lake Accord dies Oka Crisis in Québec	Asian countries become major sources of immigration	Charlottetown Accord rejected

How did Canada and Canadian identity change as a result of social, economic, and cultural trends at the end of the millennium and beyond?

In the summer of 1990, events in the Québec town of Oka made headlines across the nation. The town council decided to expand a golf course into long-disputed land that Mohawks at the nearby Kanesatake reserve considered sacred.

The Mohawks decided to stop construction of the golf course by blockading the land. In response, the mayor of Oka called in Québec's provincial police. On July 11, the police advanced on the Mohawk lines, gunfire broke out, and an officer was killed. It was not clear which side had fired the fatal shot.

From that point, events snowballed. The police blockaded Kanesatake. Mohawks from the nearby Kahnawake reserve barricaded the road to a bridge that ran through their reserve, blocking motorist access to part of Montréal. There were nightly violent confrontations involving the population of nearby Québec communities, the police, and the Mohawks. Across Canada, other Aboriginal groups demonstrated their support by blockading highways and railway tracks that ran through their reserves.

As the tense standoff continued, Québec Premier Robert Bourassa called in the Canadian Forces. Troops with heavy weapons moved into the area. Negotiations to end the crisis were tense. Toward the end of September, members of other bands persuaded the Mohawks of Kanesatake to end the standoff. Eventually, the disputed land was purchased by the federal government and given to Kanesatake.

KEY TERMS

Multiculturalism Act
self-government
sovereignty-association
distinct society
amending formula
notwithstanding clause
Meech Lake Accord
Bloc Québécois
Free Trade Agreement (FTA)
North American Free Trade Agreement (NAFTA)
Rwandan genocide

1993
B.C. Treaty Commission established
Collapse of the Conservative Party

1994
Widespread access to Internet

1995
Second Québec referendum

1997
Delgamuukw decision regarding Aboriginal land claims

1999
Nunavut created

2000
Nisga'a Treaty given royal assent

2001
Terrorist attack on New York's World Trade Center (9/11)
Canadian Forces at war in Afghanistan

Popular Culture and the Spirit of the Age

As the millennium approached, popular culture—which for the most part mirrored what was happening with young people—reflected some of the cynicism and confusion that seemed to characterize the era. The revolutionary optimism of the 1960s seemed almost naïve from the perspective of the 1980s, 1990s, and 2000s. Environmental disasters, economic shocks such as the stock market crash of 1987 and the economic crisis of 2008, and perennial high unemployment among young workers made for an uncertain future.

FIGURE 8–1 Canadian rap artist k-os. Rap and hip-hop culture, which emerged in the 1980s, incorporates music, language, and dance as well as fashion.

Youth culture tended to fragment into subgroups—each identifying with a style of music, a way of dressing, and an attitude toward life. The list of musical styles that came and went included new wave, punk, glam rock, heavy metal, grunge, alternative, pop, house, rap, hip hop, and gangsta. Fashionable looks ranged from mullets to big hair to neon-dyed buzz cuts, from dancewear to ripped jeans to belly shirts. Body piercing and tattoos became popular with everyone from punks to preppies.

These decades saw a huge rise in consumerism and materialism. Brand names and designer labels became extremely powerful marketing tools. Yet at the same time, people became more aware of the social and environmental costs of their consumption. Some refused to buy products such as running shoes because they were produced in sweatshops, often by children, in developing countries. Naomi Klein's book *No Logo: Taking Aim at the Brand Bullies*, which criticized branding and globalization, became a best-seller.

FIGURE 8–2 *The Simpsons*, which began its phenomenally successful run in 1989, had an anti-establishment message. It mocked the lifestyle of the boomers.

The Boomers and After

Most baby boomers were between the ages of 20 and 40 in the 1980s. They were still the largest demographic group in history, and eventually became the holders of power and wealth. As their parents retired, boomers moved into influential positions in government and business. The huge growth in the economy since the 1990s is due, in large part, to the fact that these were the peak earning and spending years of the boomers. Their comparative wealth changed the way people expected to live their lives. Travel had become less expensive and the price of consumer goods relative to wages dropped.

Financially secure boomers became known as "yuppies," which stood for young urban (or upwardly mobile) professionals. Yuppies were not afraid to spend their money. They took expensive holidays, bought the latest electronics, fancy cars, and expensive houses. The opening decade of the 21st century saw a huge explosion in goods and services aimed at aging boomers, including retirement communities, health and anti-aging products, and cosmetic surgery.

Aging Boomers

The disproportionately large size of the baby boomer generation, the increased longevity of the population, and declining birth rates all add up to problems for Canada in the future. As the boomers retire in large numbers, there will not be enough workers entering the workforce to replace them. Some experts predict that by 2020, Canada will face a labour shortage of 1 million workers. The skills and talents of the boomers will be sorely missed. In addition, pension costs, health services, and old-age benefits required by aging boomers will put huge pressure on the Canadian economy. The rising costs of these social programs will force young Canadians to pay higher taxes than previous generations.

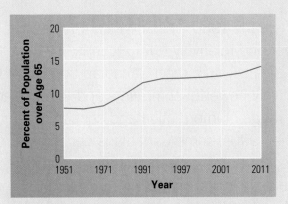

FIGURE 8–3 This graph shows the number of Canadians over age 65 as a percentage of the total population.

Interpreting a Graph What trend do you notice on this graph? What factors do you think might account for this trend?

1. What are some of the negative aspects of an aging population?

2. How might the large number of aging baby boomers impact your life?

Generations X and Y

The generation immediately following the baby boomers was much smaller than its predecessor. Called Generation X, or the Gen Xers, they were the first of the so-called "latchkey kids," children of single working parents or those who lived in households in which both parents worked. Canadian author Douglas Coupland, who wrote a novel called *Generation X*, described them as "underemployed, overeducated, intensely private and unpredictable." Gen Xers were not, generally, as interested in politics and social change as the boomers. They came of age during times of economic difficulty when all the good jobs seemed to be taken. As a result, they tended to be more cynical and less optimistic about the future. The widespread introduction of computers and the Internet had a huge effect on the lifestyles of the Gen Xers. Popular television shows, such as *Seinfeld* and *Friends*, made fun of the supposed self-centredness of Gen Xers.

Generation Y, made up of people born between the mid-1970s and the end of the 1990s, was even more heavily influenced than the Gen Xers by new technologies such as computers, video games, and cellphones. The buying power of Generation Y forced manufacturers to keep up with its demands for better and faster computing and networking products, and these have fundamentally changed the way society operates.

Generation X, also known as Gen Xers	Generation Y, also known as Baby Boom Echo, Millennials
• born between 1965 and 1976	• born from the mid-1970s to the late 1990s
• latchkey kids of working parents	• born into nurturing, child-centric times
• comfortable with technology	• most technologically literate generation in history, plugged in 24/7
• comfortable with diversity	• celebrate diversity
• over-educated, underemployed	• success-oriented
• independent, individualistic	• confident, ambitious
• cynical, pessimistic outlook	• fun-loving outlook

FIGURE 8–4 Characteristics of Generations X and Y

Innovations
The Wave of the Future

In the early 1980s, personal computers had limited power and relatively few functions. By the end of the 20th century, most Canadian homes had relatively powerful computers and Internet access to a range of information and consumer services. In the 1990s, some Canadians began to "telecommute": to work from their home or car, keeping in touch with the office via computer. In many industries, computers displaced humans. A new knowledge-based economy emerged, one in which knowledge, skills, and the ability to adapt to new situations became more important than ever before.

Not pocket size Cellphones were first made commercially available in 1983. The first cellphone cost nearly US$4000. Early models were large and needed to be recharged frequently.

Getting smaller Today, cellphones are smaller and have more capabilities. Many people use them as personal organizers to store contact information, photographs, music, and videos. Many cellphones also have Internet capabilities.

What came before One of the first home computers, the Commodore 64 (1982), had no hard drive, a very slow 1-MHz processor, and limited software. Nevertheless, it showed that desktop computers in homes were practical.

At home, at work Laptop computers were introduced in 1981. As they improved over the years, they gave people more freedom by allowing them to take their work with them wherever they went.

Home viewing Video cassette recorders (VCRs), microwave ovens, and cable television came into widespread use in the 1980s.

Easy listening CDs were introduced in 1984 and largely displaced vinyl records.

What's next? Over the past few decades, computers and other communications technologies have revolutionized the way Canadians work, play, and communicate. The widespread use of the Internet has important social implications. People network with new friends, new social groups emerge, tastes in music and art shift rapidly, and notions of personal privacy change.

Canada reaches out The first *Canadarm* was designed and built by Spar Aerospace in 1981. The remote arm that is attached to NASA's space shuttles allows crews to launch and recapture satellites. Without this technology, much of the world's satellite communication would be impossible.

Hello Dolly Scientists announced the first cloning of a mammal, a sheep named Dolly, in 1996. This technological breakthrough raised ethical questions about human cloning.

- How did Canada's multiculturalism policy affect minority groups?

KEY TERM

Multiculturalism Act or Bill C-93, was adopted in 1988 and provides a legal framework for multiculturalism in Canada

Multiculturalism Becomes an Issue

During the 1980s, Canada became more multicultural than ever before. Government policies encouraged immigrants with money and business skills to create jobs by investing in existing companies or starting new ones. Figures 8–5 and 8–6 show how the countries of origin of immigrants changed over the years.

Unlike immigrants who had arrived earlier in the century in search of good farmland, later immigrants were drawn to Canada's cities. For instance, in 2006, 94.9 percent of Canada's foreign-born population and 97.2 percent of recent immigrants who had landed in the previous five years, lived in urban communities. This compared with 77.5 percent of the Canadian-born urban population.

As new cultures took root in British Columbia, some issues were raised. For example, traditional Canadian holidays, such as Easter and Christmas, are rooted in the Christian faith and culture. These holidays presented a challenge for schools with large multicultural populations. One solution was to highlight the festivals of groups represented in sufficient numbers in the school. For example, Chinese New Year, the Muslim holy month of Ramadan, and Sikh holy days such as Baisakhi were celebrated in some schools. These festivals offered students a better understanding of the beliefs and customs of Canada's multicultural society.

Multiculturalism Act

The Canadian Multiculturalism Act (Bill C-93) was enacted by Parliament in 1988, to provide a legal framework for existing multiculturalism policies across Canada. In the spirit of the Bill of Rights and the Canadian Charter of Rights and Freedoms (see Chapter 10), the Multiculturalism Act aimed to reinforce racial and cultural equality with legal authority. The Act ensured that all federal institutions took into account the multicultural reality of Canada.

The federal government further recognized the growth of Canada's multicultural communities by establishing the Department of Multiculturalism and Citizenship. Supporters say the government's multiculturalism policy helped strengthen national unity by drawing all Canadians closer together in mutual respect.

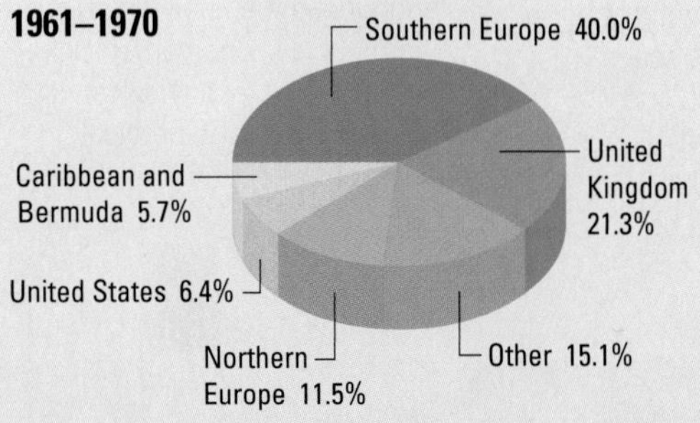

FIGURE 8–5 Immigration to Canada by region of birth (leading regions) from 1961 to 1970

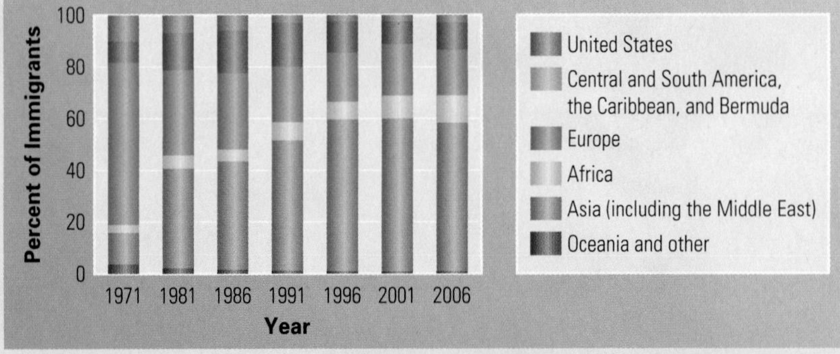

FIGURE 8–6 Immigration to Canada by region of birth from 1971 to 2006

Using Evidence Based on these graphs, find evidence to support the following conclusion: The sources of Canadian immigration changed almost completely between 1961 and 2006.

 ©P

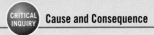
Does Canada need a multiculturalism policy?

The federal government established the Department of Multiculturalism and Citizenship in 1989 with the aim of promoting multiculturalism in all areas of government policy. Despite this initiative, Canadian attitudes toward multiculturalism are complex. Canada's official multiculturalism policy has fierce defenders and critics. Many Canadians believe the policy benefits Canada. They feel multiculturalism plays a positive role in the nation's development, and that it helps create national unity, as Pierre Trudeau had claimed it would in 1971. Supporters also feel that multiculturalism allows people of all ethnic, racial, religious, and cultural backgrounds to feel welcome here, and to play a positive role in the development of the nation. It gives Canadians an awareness of other cultures, an asset when dealing with problems that may arise in various communities. Furthermore, they say the policy helps promote values such as tolerance, equality, and support of diversity.

Opponents of multiculturalism claim that it is not good for the country to promote differences in cultures. They say this approach weakens the country's unity. Others feel that ethnic groups should maintain their own cultures in Canada if they wish but that the government should not provide financial support to these groups. As examples, they point to countries such as Rwanda and the former Yugoslavia, where ethnic diversity has ripped communities and families apart. It would be better, they say, to follow the "melting-pot" model of the United States, where cultural groups were encouraged to assimilate—that is, to give up their identities and take on the mainstream culture to a greater extent.

For:

Hedy Fry, the Member of Parliament for Vancouver Centre, has expressed the following view:

> *Multiculturalism is the key to Canadian unity. We must understand that people of different races can have a strong sense of belonging to one nation while maintaining their original cultural identities.... Multiculturalism and respect for our differences are important reasons why this country has been ranked as the best nation in the world by the United Nations.*

Against:

During a House of Commons debate in 1994, Saskatchewan Member of Parliament, Lee Morrison, said:

> *Every few years a politician will stop in your community... and patronizingly solicit your votes... to preserve cultural diversity. Now lest any hon. member dismiss my deeply held convictions... as the insensitive views of one white guy in a suit... I would like to [quote]... Dr. Rais Khan... a very wise new Canadian... "I did not come here to be labelled as an ethnic or as a member of the multicultural community or to be coddled with preferential treatment, nurtured with special grants and then sit on the sidelines and watch the world go by.... If I want to preserve my cultural heritage, that is my business. If I want to invite you into my home to eat some spicy traditional food, that is our business. If I expect you to pay for my cultural activities, that is your business."*

Analyzing the Issue

1. In a group, survey a variety of Canadian newspapers, magazines, and television programs to determine the extent to which they reflect Canada's multicultural nature. Use a three-column chart to record your findings, according to the media types surveyed. Summarize your findings, and present them to the class.

2. Why do you think views differ on multiculturalism?

3. Imagine you are the federal minister responsible for multiculturalism. Prepare a speech announcing that you are going to do one of the following:

   a) continue the policy of multiculturalism or

   b) make changes to it

   Justify your decision, taking possible consequences into account.

Toward a More Just World

The rights movements of earlier decades (see Chapter 7) continued to gain strength during the 1980s and 1990s. Equality rights for women were enshrined in the Constitution in 1982. In 1985, Aboriginal women won the right to Aboriginal status even if they married non-Aboriginals. Tests for job suitability, such as height and strength requirements that favour men, were challenged in the mid-1990s. Gay rights activism also accelerated during this period. Although some bills that prohibited discrimination based on sexual orientation failed to pass the House of Commons in the 1980s, such discrimination was outlawed by the mid-1990s. In 2005, Canada had become the fourth country in the world to legalize same-sex marriage through the passage of the Civil Marriage Act. You will read more about each of these rights in Chapter 10.

A Spirit of Generosity

A renewed sense of responsibility to help out those in need became part of the world view of many Canadians in the 1980s. In 1984, CBC reporter Brian Stewart brought the world's attention to the famine in Ethiopia. Canadian recording stars such as Neil Young, Bryan Adams, Joni Mitchell, and Robert Charlebois got together to form the supergroup Northern Lights and recorded the song "Tears Are Not Enough" to raise money for famine relief. Proceeds from the recording eventually raised more than $3 million. American musicians also created a similar supergroup. USA for Africa recorded "We Are the World" in 1985. Bob Geldof founded Band-Aid in 1984—comprised of Irish and British musicians—and recorded "Do They Know It's Christmas?" This recording, along with the Live-Aid concerts that followed, each raised money for international aid efforts. Similar concerts continued into the next century.

FIGURE 8–7 The Northern Lights

up close and personal ○ Terry Fox: Running for Your Life

In 1978, 21-year-old Terry Fox, who had lost a leg to cancer, decided to run across Canada. The goal of his run, which he called the Marathon of Hope, was to raise money for cancer research. Terry started his run by dipping his leg into the Atlantic Ocean in St. John's, Newfoundland, on April 12, 1980. He intended to run all the way to the Pacific Ocean on the west coast of Vancouver Island.

Terry set himself a gruelling pace—42 kilometres per day. By the time Terry reached Southern Ontario, crowds of people were lining his route cheering him on.

When Terry was approaching Thunder Bay, he was forced to stop his run due to pains in his chest. He went to the hospital where doctors discovered that the cancer had spread to his lungs. He died in 1981, and was mourned across the country.

Canadians honour Terry Fox with annual Terry Fox runs and have donated hundreds of millions of dollars to the cause he championed. He is considered one of Canada's heroes.

1. Terry Fox hoped to raise $21 million for cancer research. So far, his organization has raised more than $400 million worldwide. Why do you think his goal has been surpassed on such a grand scale?

FIGURE 8–8 Terry Fox had a special brace fitted for his run but endured pain and discomfort nevertheless.

PRACTICE QUESTIONS

1. How did Canadian immigration policies and patterns develop between 1960 and 2000? Present your answer in the form of a timeline or chart.

2. Explain how the Canadian model of a "cultural mosaic" differs from the American model of a "melting pot."

3. Québec has long pressed for a greater share of immigrants to Canada and a greater say on who can enter. Why do you think this is so?

4. **Cause and Consequence** What impact has computer technology had on Canadian society?

5. How did Canadian youths express their individuality during the late 20th century?

6. Describe the lifestyle of many baby boomers.

7. Which technological innovation has had the most impact on your life? The least? Might this change in the future? Explain.

8. Why do you think Canada introduced an official policy of multiculturalism? Do you think the policy had its intended effect? Support your views with examples.

The Fight for Aboriginal Rights

The crisis in Oka, Québec, which you read about at the beginning of the chapter, ended after about two and a half months of tense and sometimes violent confrontation. Oka served as a wake-up call to the government and people of Canada. Canada's Aboriginal peoples had demonstrated again that they were prepared to fight for their rights.

The Legacy of Residential Schools

Even though the residential school system had been dismantled by the final decade of the 20th century, its effects continued to haunt Aboriginal people who had lived through it. In 1990, a new aspect of the residential school legacy was brought to light. The Grand Chief of the Assembly of Manitoba Chiefs, Phil Fontaine, spoke out about the physical and sexual abuse he suffered at a residential school. Others soon came forward with horrifying stories of abuse. Eighteen years later, Prime Minister Stephen Harper read an official apology to Aboriginal people in the House of Commons. It said, in part:

> *The treatment of children in Indian residential schools is a sad chapter in our history.... The government now recognizes that the consequences of the Indian residential schools policy were profoundly negative and that this policy has had a lasting and damaging impact on Aboriginal culture, heritage and language. While some former students have spoken positively about their experiences at residential schools, these stories are far overshadowed by tragic accounts of the emotional, physical and sexual abuse and neglect of helpless children, and their separation from powerless families and communities.... The Government of Canada sincerely apologizes and asks the forgiveness of the Aboriginal peoples of this country for failing them so profoundly.*
>
> *–Stephen Harper, 2008*

Prime Minister
Stephen Joseph Harper

- born 1959, Toronto, Ontario
- author, economist
- first elected to Commons in 1993
- prime minister 2006–

Domestic Record

- helped found the Reform Party of Canada in 1987
- co-founded the Conservative Party of Canada in 2003
- in 2006, proposed to reform Senate so positions were elected rather than appointed
- tabled the "Québécois nation motion" in 2006, recognizing that "the Québécois form a nation within a united Canada"
- officially apologized to Aboriginal peoples for the Canadian government's residential schools in 2008

International Record

- launched plans for a strong military presence in the North to protect Canadian sovereignty in the Arctic

FIGURE 8–9 Assembly of First Nations National Chief Phil Fontaine is presented with a citation by Prime Minister Stephen Harper (left) at a ceremony in the House of Commons on June 11, 2008, where the Canadian government officially apologized for more than a century of abuse and cultural loss involving Indian residential schools.

©P

1850s–1860s	Assimilation of Aboriginal people through education becomes official policy.
1892	Federal government and churches officially partner in operation of residential schools.
1920	Indian Affairs Minister Duncan Campbell Scott makes residential school attendance mandatory.
1958	Indian Affairs inspectors recommend abolition of residential schools.
1970s	Residential schools begin to be transferred to Indian bands.
1986	United Church apologizes for its role in residential schools. Eventually Anglican, Presbyterian, and some Catholic churches also offer apologies.
1996	Last government-run residential school closes.
2006	Government, Assembly of First Nations, and churches sign $4-billion residential schools settlement agreement.
2008	Residential schools Truth and Reconciliation Commission launched to examine claims of abuse at residential schools.
	Prime Minister Stephen Harper apologizes to former students of the residential schools.

KEY TERMS

self-government the right of a colony or cultural group to define the structure, laws, and policies that will govern its affairs

specific claims First Nations' claims to land based on the belief that the government did not fulfill its obligations under a treaty or other agreement related to money, land, or other assets

comprehensive claims the assertion of the right of Aboriginal nations to large tracts of land because their ancestors were the original inhabitants

WEB LINK • • • • • • • • • • • • • • • •
Visit the Pearson Web site to find out more about residential schools.

The Path to Self-Government

In 1982, the Assembly of First Nations was formed to represent Aboriginal peoples in their dealings with the federal government. During the constitutional negotiations (see Chapter 10), the Assembly pressured political leaders for legal recognition of Aboriginal rights. As a result, Aboriginal rights were entrenched in the Charter of Rights and Freedoms. In 1985, Parliament also passed Bill C-31, which gave Aboriginal band councils the power to decide who had the right to live on Aboriginal reserves. Previous decisions of this sort had been made by the federal government's Department of Indian Affairs.

The increase in band council powers raised the question, "What other powers should be transferred from the federal government to the band councils?" The stage was set for discussions about **self-government**. Aboriginal peoples argued that self-government would give them the right to manage resources and gain control of their education, culture, and justice systems. This would then give them the tools needed to tackle social and health concerns in their communities.

But how would self-government work in practice? Should reserves be run as municipal or town governments by the band members? Or would Aboriginal lands and reserves across Canada eventually join together to form something like a province? Furthermore, by what means could Aboriginal nations lay claim to lands that they considered to be theirs?

Aboriginal land claims have been of two types. **Specific claims** have arisen in areas where treaties between Aboriginal peoples and the federal government have been signed, but their terms have not been kept. For example, the agreed-upon size of a reserve may have decreased as land was taken away to build highways or other projects. **Comprehensive claims** have questioned the ownership of land in large parts of Canada that were never surrendered by treaty.

FIGURE 8–10 The eagle and the bear in the logo of the Assembly of First Nations are symbols of strength.

WEB LINK • • • • • • • • • • • • • • • •
Visit the Pearson Web site to find out more about Aboriginal self-government.

Land Claims in British Columbia

Most land claims in British Columbia have been comprehensive, as Aboriginal nations never officially gave up their claims to most of what is now British Columbia. In addition, when the British took over Canada, the Royal Proclamation of 1763 declared that "any lands whatever, which, not having been ceded to or purchased by us, ...are reserved to the ...Indians." Treaties were not signed except in a few areas, such as the province's northeast corner and parts of Vancouver Island.

Opponents of comprehensive claims argue that the 1763 proclamation cannot be valid in parts of Canada, such as the North and British Columbia, that were not known to the British at that time. They assert that Canada exercised the traditional rights of "discoverers and conquerors." In any case, without written records, it is difficult for some First Nations to prove continuous occupation of the land.

FIGURE 8–11 Prime Minister Jean Chrétien congratulates Joseph Gosnell, president of the Nisga'a Tribal Council, on the passage of the Nisga'a Final Agreement Act in the House of Commons. Assembly of First Nations Chief Phil Fontaine (second from right) and Indian Affairs Minister Robert Nault look on.

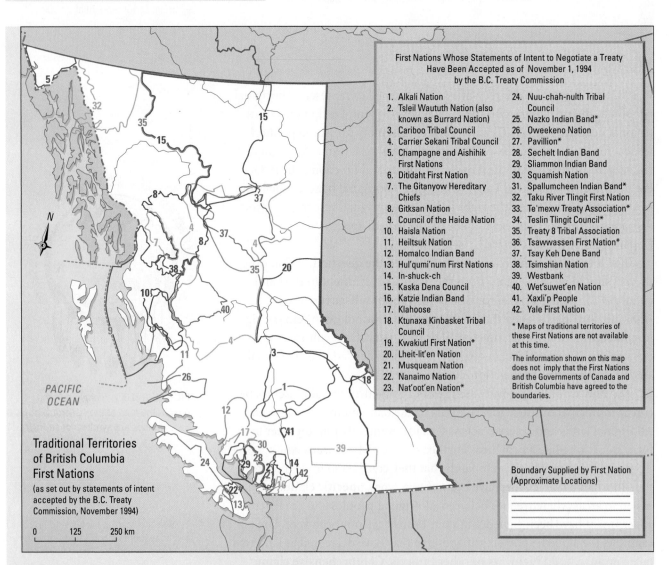

First Nations Whose Statements of Intent to Negotiate a Treaty Have Been Accepted as of November 1, 1994 by the B.C. Treaty Commission

1. Alkali Nation
2. Tsleil Waututh Nation (also known as Burrard Nation)
3. Cariboo Tribal Council
4. Carrier Sekani Tribal Council
5. Champagne and Aishihik First Nations
6. Ditidaht First Nation
7. The Gitanyow Hereditary Chiefs
8. Gitksan Nation
9. Council of the Haida Nation
10. Haisla Nation
11. Heiltsuk Nation
12. Homalco Indian Band
13. Hul'qumi'num First Nations
14. In-shuck-ch
15. Kaska Dena Council
16. Katzie Indian Band
17. Klahoose
18. Ktunaxa Kinbasket Tribal Council
19. Kwakiutl First Nation*
20. Lheit-lit'en Nation
21. Musqueam Nation
22. Nanaimo Nation
23. Nat'oot'en Nation*
24. Nuu-chah-nulth Tribal Council
25. Nazko Indian Band*
26. Oweekeno Nation
27. Pavillion*
28. Sechelt Indian Band
29. Sliammon Indian Band
30. Squamish Nation
31. Spallumcheen Indian Band*
32. Taku River Tlingit First Nation
33. Te'mexw Treaty Association*
34. Teslin Tlingit Council*
35. Treaty 8 Tribal Association
36. Tsawwassen First Nation*
37. Tsay Keh Dene Band
38. Tsimshian Nation
39. Westbank
40. Wet'suwet'en Nation
41. Xaxli'p People
42. Yale First Nation

* Maps of traditional territories of these First Nations are not available at this time.

The information shown on this map does not imply that the First Nations and the Governments of Canada and British Columbia have agreed to the boundaries.

PACIFIC OCEAN

Boundary Supplied by First Nation (Approximate Locations)

Traditional Territories of British Columbia First Nations
(as set out by statements of intent accepted by the B.C. Treaty Commission, November 1994)

0   125   250 km

FIGURE 8–12 Aboriginal land claims in B.C. amount to 110 percent of the province. The B.C. government stated that it favours a total land settlement of approximately 5 percent, reflecting the Aboriginal percentage of the population of the province.

©P

TIMELINE

Nisga'a Land Claims in British Columbia

1887	The Nisga'a, the original occupants of the Nass Valley in the northwest, begin asserting their land rights.
1912	The Nisga'a become the first group to make a land claim against the Canadian government.
1927–1951	Although the Indian Act makes it illegal for the Nisga'a to raise funds for land claims, they continue their struggle.
1968	The Nisga'a take their land claim to court.
1991	The B.C. government recognizes Aboriginal title and the Nisga'a right to self-government; tripartite framework agreement is signed.
1996	The Nisga'a are offered a settlement that entitles them to a very small percentage of their original claimed land, ownership of the forests, and partial profits from salmon fisheries and hydro development. The Nisga'a also win the right to develop their own municipal government and police. The government offers to pay the Nisga'a $196 million for lost land. The Nisga'a agree to become taxpayers, giving up their tax-exempt status under the Indian Act.
1997	The Supreme Court of Canada defines Aboriginal title in its ruling on the Delgamuukw case. It rules that Aboriginal groups could claim ownership of land if they can prove that they occupied the land before the Canadian government claimed sovereignty, and that they occupied it continuously and exclusively. This was a landmark ruling that would have application in other parts of the country.
1999	The Parliament of Canada passes the Nisga'a deal.

Today, the Nisga'a people become full-fledged Canadians as we step out from under the Indian Act—forever. Finally, after a struggle of more than 130 years, the government of this country clearly recognizes that the Nisga'a were a self-governing people since well before European contact. We remain self-governing today, and we are proud to say that this inherent right is now clearly recognized and pro-tected in the Constitution of Canada.

–Nisga'a Chief Joseph Gosnell on the Nisga'a deal receiving royal assent in 2000

Nunavut

Self-government and land claims continue to be important issues in many other parts of Canada. The creation of the territory of Nunavut in 1999 resulted from the largest treaty ever negotiated in Canada. It gave the Inuit of this northern area political control over 2 million square kilometres of the eastern Arctic. Aboriginal land claims and self-government will continue to be a powerful force for change in shaping the nation into the 21st century.

What If...

Opponents of the Nisga'a settlement demanded that a provincial referendum be held on the issue. But the government refused, arguing that the rights of a minority can never be fairly decided by a vote of the majority. What do you think the outcome would have been if the government had not made this decision?

FIGURE 8–13 Celebrating the creation of Nunavut in Iqaluit, the territory's capital, in April 1999

Aboriginal art is an important part of Canadian culture, and Aboriginal writers and artists are recognized and have won acclaim around the world.

Tomson Highway (born 1951) is a Cree from Manitoba. After studying music and literature in Ontario and in England, he joined a performing arts company. He is a playwright whose works include *Dry Lips Oughta Move to Kapuskasing* and *The Rez Sisters*. He became Artistic Director of Native Earth Performing Arts in Toronto, one of only a few Aboriginal theatre groups in North America.

Daphne Odjig was born in 1919 on Manitoulin Island, Ontario. Her grandfather was a stone carver who told her about the history and legends of her people. Odjig later moved to British Columbia, where her paintings were inspired by the landscape of the B.C. interior and the West Coast islands. She published her memoirs, *A Paintbrush in My Hand*, in 1992, and in 1998 received the Achievement Award in Arts and Culture from the National Aboriginal Achievement Foundation.

Joseph Boyden (born 1966) is a highly acclaimed Canadian novelist and short story writer of Irish, Scottish, and Ojibwa descent. His first novel, *Three Day Road*, is about two young Cree, Xavier and Elijah, who sign up for the military during the First World War. It is inspired by Ojibwa Francis Pegahmagabow, the legendary First World War sniper. Boyden's second novel, *Through Black Spruce*, follows the story of Will, son of one of the characters in *Three Day Road*, and his niece, Annie, who has returned to the bush from the city where she has been searching for her missing sister. Joseph Boyden won the prestigious Scotiabank Giller Prize for *Through Black Spruce* in 2008.

I ask Elijah where I can find rounds for the Fritz rifle. Elijah'd promised me more a while ago, and only a handful is left now. I think he is holding out. Elijah covets this gun, but I am responsible for taking down the Hun sniper who loved the dead. The night of the day I killed my first human was the first time I felt like an ancestor, an awawatuk raider and warrior. I prayed to Gitchi Manitou for many hours on that day and the following day, thanking him that it was I who still breathed and not my enemy. Since that time I am able to shoot at other men and understand what I do is for survival, as long as I pray to Gitchi Manitou. He understands. My enemy might not understand this when I send him on the three-day road, but maybe he will on the day that I finally meet him again.

Excerpt from Three Day Road

FIGURE 8–14 *The Indian in Transition* by Daphne Odjig. Painted in the late 1970s, the mural outlines the history of Aboriginal peoples in Canada.

FIGURE 8–15 Douglas Cardinal designed the First Nations University of Canada, in Regina.

Douglas Cardinal (born 1934) is a distinguished architect from Calgary, Alberta. He is best known for designing the Canadian Museum of Civilization. In his words, "the Museum will speak of the emergence of man from the melting glaciers; of man and woman living in harmony with the forces of nature and evolving with them."

Bill Reid (1920–1998) discovered in his teens that his mother was Haida. He became interested in traditional Haida carving techniques and began to create wooden masks and totem poles using traditional techniques. Reid's work inspired other Aboriginal artists to return to traditional art forms.

John Kim Bell (born 1952) was born on the Kahnawake Mohawk reserve in Québec. He studied violin and piano as a youth. In 1980, he was appointed apprentice conductor of the Toronto Symphony Orchestra. He went on to devote his time to promoting opportunities for Aboriginal artists and, in 1993, he established the National Aboriginal Achievement Award.

Susan Aglukark (born 1967) was raised in Arviat, Northwest Territories, now part of Nunavut. She has developed a distinctive musical style, fusing traditional Inuit chants with modern pop melodies.

1. What themes and concerns are evident in the works of the Aboriginal artists featured here?

2. Explain the importance of these artists to young Aboriginals in Canada.

FIGURE 8–16 One of Bill Reid's most famous works, *The Spirit of Haida Gwaii*, sits in the foyer of the Canadian Embassy in Washington.

The Royal Commission on Aboriginal Peoples

In 1991, one year after the Oka Crisis, the federal government launched an extensive study of the issues that affected Aboriginal peoples. The Royal Commission on Aboriginal Peoples travelled across the country for five years, gathering information and talking to Aboriginal and non-Aboriginal Canadians. It released a five-volume report of its findings in 1996. The report concluded that sweeping changes were needed to help mend the relationship between Aboriginal peoples and the government. The report also presented strategies to close the economic gap between Aboriginal and non-Aboriginal peoples and improve social conditions.

Ten years later, the Assembly of First Nations put out a "report card" describing the progress that had been made on the recommendations of the Royal Commission. The report card stated the following statistics:

- One in 4 First Nations children live in poverty compared to 1 in 6 Canadian children.
- Life expectancy for First Nations men is 7.4 years less, and 5.2 years less for First Nations women, compared to Canadian men and women respectively.
- Unemployment is over 50 percent, and rises to over 60 percent for those without high school completion.

The report card also noted that Canada was one of two countries that voted against the UN Declaration on the Rights of Aboriginal People in June 2006. The report card concluded that "Canada has failed in terms of its action to date."

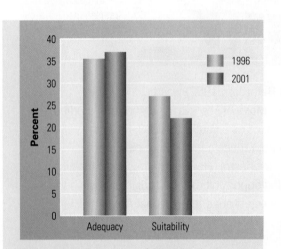

FIGURE 8–17 Percentage of Aboriginal homes meeting Canada's standards for adequate housing and suitable living conditions

---

PRACTICE QUESTIONS

1. What was the government's response to demands that it acknowledge its part in the ill treatment of Aboriginal children in residential schools? Do you think this response was adequate? Give reasons.

2. Explain the importance of
   a) the Assembly of First Nations
   b) specific land claims
   c) comprehensive land claims
   d) the Nisga'a Treaty
   e) the Delgamuukw decision

3. **Evidence** What percentage of British Columbia land do Aboriginal groups claim? What Aboriginal land settlement percentage does the B.C. government favour? What issues do these percentages raise?

4. a) Why do you think the creation of Nunavut is significant?

   b) What challenges do you think are posed for Nunavut by having 29 000 people politically control 2 million square kilometres of land? How do you think e-mail and other modern technologies can help?

5. Summarize the contributions of Aboriginal artists to Canadian society.

6. What were the conclusions of the Royal Commission on Aboriginal Peoples? Does this surprise you? Explain.

7. Make a list of at least five events that contributed to Aboriginal Canadians affirming their identity and position in society. Explain why you chose each item.

©P

Constitution and Discord

In the 1970s, the October Crisis and the election of the Parti Québécois (PQ) made it clear that the threat of Québec separatism was very real. Concerns about separatism contributed to Prime Minister Trudeau's determination to **patriate** Canada's Constitution. He hoped that a "made in Canada" Constitution would make Québécois feel more comfortable about their position. Québec discontent and the Constitution continued to define Canadian affairs well into the 1990s. Twice during this time, PQ governments tried and failed to win referenda that would have separated Québec from the rest of Canada.

The 1980 Referendum

In 1980, the PQ government of René Lévesque called a referendum on Québec sovereignty. Lévesque asked Québécois to give his government a mandate to negotiate a new agreement with Canada based on what he called **sovereignty-association**. Québec would become politically independent, or "*maîtres chez nous*," yet maintain a close economic association with Canada. This partnership would include

- free trade between Canada and Québec
- a common currency for the two nations
- common tariffs against imported goods

Prime Minister Trudeau asked Québec to remain part of a strong, united, and forward-looking Canada. He promised to negotiate a new Constitution, which proved popular among Québécois who wanted a Constitution that recognized Québec as an equal partner in Confederation and as a **distinct society** within Canada.

In the referendum, only 40 percent of Québécois voted "yes" to sovereignty-association. Lévesque accepted defeat but promised that, one day, they would realize their dream of a sovereign Québec.

KEY TERMS

patriate to take control of power over a document from a former colonial government

sovereignty-association a proposal by Québec nationalists that Québec have political independence yet retain close economic ties or association with Canada

distinct society a phrase that refers to the recognition of the unique nature of Québec within Canada; it often has the sense that Québec should have special powers and privileges to protect its language and culture

● What was the impact of Québec nationalism on Canadian unity?

NOW REMEMBER, I'VE CHANGED THE OPERATION FROM COMPLETE SEPARATION TO SOVEREIGNTY ASSOCIATION... THAT MEANS WE'LL BE COMPLETELY SEPARATE ... EXCEPT FOR WHERE I'M ATTACHED TO YOUR WALLET...

The Canadianese Twins

FIGURE 8–18 This cartoon showing Prime Minister Trudeau and Premier Lévesque offers one view of sovereignty-association.

Interpreting a Cartoon According to the cartoonist, how did sovereignty-association differ from separation? What was this cartoonist's view of Lévesque? How do you know?

● What factors contributed to Canada's emerging autonomy?

● How did changes to the Constitution impact Canadian society?

KEY TERMS

amending formula a process by which changes can legally be made to the Canadian Constitution

notwithstanding clause a clause in the Canadian Constitution (Section 33[1]) that enables Parliament or the legislature of a province to allow an Act to stand even though it contravenes the Charter of Rights and Freedoms

WEB LINK ● · · · · · · · · · · · · · · · ·

Visit the Pearson Web site to find out more about the Constitution debates.

Patriating the Constitution

The British North America (BNA) Act had been Canada's Constitution since 1867. The Act set out the powers of the federal and provincial governments and guaranteed the language and education rights of Québec's Francophone majority. Since the BNA Act fell under British jurisdiction, no changes could be made without the British Parliament's approval.

Amending the Constitution

Prime Minister Trudeau wanted to patriate the Constitution so that the Canadian government would have sole authority to make changes to it. Trudeau hoped, above all, to include in the Constitution a clear statement of the basic rights to which all Canadians were entitled. You will read more about the Charter of Rights and Freedoms in Chapter 10.

As a first step, Trudeau needed to come up with a formula for amending, or making changes to, the Constitution. Questions such as the following needed to be considered: How many provinces need to be in agreement to make a change to the Constitution? Should Québec, as the Francophone partner in Confederation, be given veto power? Getting both the federal and provincial governments to agree to an **amending formula** was difficult.

While Québec pushed for more power, the Western provinces saw patriating the Constitution as a way to have more say in affairs that affected them. Most of the provincial premiers outside of Québec felt that the Charter would make the courts more powerful than provincial legislatures. In Québec, Lévesque feared that the Charter could be used to override his language laws or any other legislation that might be passed to protect Québec's distinct society.

A series of meetings failed to resolve the concerns that divided the provinces and the federal government. In a final attempt to reach an agreement, the prime minister and the premiers met in Ottawa on November 4, 1981. Over late-night cups of coffee in the kitchen of the National Conference Centre, federal Justice Minister Jean Chrétien and the justice ministers from Saskatchewan and Ontario hammered out what came to be called the "Kitchen Accord." The provincial premiers were awakened in their rooms at the Château Laurier Hotel and asked to approve the deal.

Including a Notwithstanding Clause

The premiers agreed to accept the Charter if an escape clause were added. This was the **notwithstanding clause**, which allowed the federal government or any of the provinces to opt out of some of the clauses in the Charter. An agreement on the amending formula was also reached. Changes to the Constitution could be made only with the agreement of "seven out of ten provinces representing 50 percent of Canada's population." This meant, in effect, that Québec could be excluded as long as Ontario was included.

René Lévesque argued against the deal but Trudeau accepted the compromise. He maintained that the federal government had so many members from Québec that it could speak for that province. Lévesque and the people of Québec felt that the federal government and the other provincial premiers had ganged up to deny Québec recognition of its distinct status. The Québec provincial government refused to sign the proposed Constitution.

Trudeau went ahead without Québec's agreement. On April 17, 1982, Queen Elizabeth II and Prime Minister Trudeau signed the new Constitution Act into law. As the rest of Canada celebrated, flags in Québec flew at half-mast and Premier Lévesque led an angry demonstration through the streets of Québec City. The last step toward making Canada a completely independent nation had been taken, but the process had revealed cracks in national unity that would continue to trouble Canadians in the years that followed.

Trudeau Steps Down

Trudeau's dream of a Canadian Constitution had become a reality. He felt he had played his part and was growing tired of politics. On February 28, 1984, he left his official residence at 24 Sussex Drive in Ottawa for a walk through the snowy streets of the capital. It was then that he decided to retire from politics. The Trudeau era had come to an end.

John Turner, who had served in the Cabinet under both Pearson and Trudeau, won the leadership of the Liberals. He called an election soon after, and the Liberals suffered a disastrous defeat to Brian Mulroney's Progressive Conservatives, winning only 40 seats in the House of Commons. When the Liberals under Turner lost the next election as well, Turner resigned his position and was replaced by Jean Chrétien.

FIGURE 8–19 Queen Elizabeth II arrives to sign Canada's Constitution Act, April 17, 1982.

Thinking Critically Why would the Canadian government want to have the Queen sign the Act in Canada?

Building Your Skills

Defending a Position on an Issue

When you defend a position on an issue, you present arguments that you hope will persuade others. Argument and persuasion are important components of many forms of communication, including opinion pieces, essays, editorials, speeches, and debates. When you prepare an argument to defend your position on an issue, you need to use facts and anecdotes that support your position. Remember that a well-structured argument is very different from simply expressing opinions or ideas on a subject.

Defending a position on an issue means that you must do the following:

Know what you are talking about. Understanding the basis for your argument is the key to defending it. Do research to gather facts and evidence to support your position.

Clarify your position. You should begin by clearly stating your point of view. This statement is the thesis of your argument and needs to be as specific as possible.

Understand the terms. Learn the meaning of the terms that you are using. The proper use of terminology is fundamental to defending your position.

Anticipate objections. Knowing your position well means that you also know what objections might be raised by those who disagree with you. Be ready to counter objections with well-reasoned and well-supported points.

Practising the Skill

Québec separation has been a major issue in Canada for many decades. Below are three positions on separatism: the first by a Grade 11 student from Kitchener, Ontario; the second from a Québec sovereigntist group's Web posting; and the third from a grand chief and chairman of Québec's Grand Council of the Crees. Summarize the position each writer has taken on the issue of separatism and describe how you would defend it.

1. *The separation of Québec would have a large impact on our lives as Canadians, perhaps not directly, but indirectly. If Québec were to separate, we would have to take many things into account, such as how we would connect with the eastern provinces, how to organize trade with Québec, and how the rest of the world will view us if Québec does secede.*

    It is my belief that as citizens in this country, we must be conscious of this movement and take action to convince Québec to stay. We have so far spent billions of dollars on protecting the French language and the Québec way of life.

    We have even let the rights of Anglophone citizens (English-speaking people in Québec) be violated for the sake of the French culture in acts such as Bill 101.

    There is evidence to show that if Québec ever did separate, its language and culture would be even more at risk than it is now. Canada is one of the main reasons that the French language is as strong as it is today. We have passed many laws to protect it and provided funding for the spread of the French language throughout the rest of the country.

    –Claire Lehan, "Separatism is an issue for all of Canada, not just Québec," 2006

2. *French is Québec's official language. Nevertheless, Québec's English-speaking community has always had the right to maintain and develop its own institutions, especially in the fields of health and education, and it is quite possible for an English-speaking person to live and even work in Montréal in English. Despite these guarantees, some people regard the measures taken to protect French as excessive and systematically fight against it with the aid of the Canadian government. It is our view that all citizens, regardless of their origins or the communities they belong to, are entitled to freedom of expression; and indeed Québec's Bill of Rights is among the most progressive on that score. This individual freedom of expression can, in our view, coexist harmoniously with the legitimate promotion of the French language which, in the North-American context, requires appropriate legislation.*

–Québec Sovereignty: A Legitimate Goal posted on the Internet by Intellectuals for the Sovereignty of Québec (IPSO)

3. *In the past few years, Québec secessionist leaders have stated that their right to separate from Canada is based on a right of self-determination under international law. When faced with the issue of the Crees' competing right of self-determination as a First Nation and a people, Lucien Bouchard, now the Premier of Québec, resorted to a blatant double standard. He simply declared that the right of self-determination belonged to the "Québec people," but not to the Indians.*

   The fundamental and constitutional rights of Aboriginal peoples in Québec are clearly a major obstacle for the secessionists. They claim that they have a historic right to determine their future on the basis of a distinct language, history, and culture. On what ground can they possibly deny, as they do, that we too have this right? The separatists claim that they have the right to choose to end their ties with Canada. On what basis can they possibly claim, as they do, that the Crees and the Inuit do not have the right to choose instead to maintain and renew our relationship with Canada?

–Grand Chief Matthew Coon Come, speech at the Canada Seminar, Harvard Center for International Affairs and Kennedy School of Government, October 28, 1996

Applying the Skill

1. **Evidence** Which opinions in each argument could be strengthened by citing specific, credible evidence?

2. Explain why knowing your subject and knowing the meaning of terms is important to defending a position on an issue.

3. With a partner, scan blogs, newspaper or magazine articles, or TV news shows for issue statements that you think state a position that needs to be defended or is being defended. Assess the strengths and weaknesses of each statement.

4. Pick a Canadian issue that you think is important and develop a position on that issue that is clearly stated and defensible. Use the guidelines for defending a position to help you. Share your work with others in a small group and get feedback. Use your fellow students' comments to strengthen and further clarify your position.

KEY TERMS

Meech Lake Accord a package of constitutional amendments that would define Québec as a distinct society within Canada

Bloc Québécois a federal party dedicated to Québec separation from Canada

WEB LINK ●
To learn more about these constitutional debates, visit the Pearson Web site.

Mulroney and the Constitution

By 1984, most Canadians outside Québec felt that the issues of the Constitution and Canadian unity had been settled. Yet, when John Turner called an election later that year, Brian Mulroney, the leader of the Progressive Conservatives, returned to the issue of the Constitution. To build support from separatists in Québec during the election campaign, Mulroney promised to repair the damage of 1982 by obtaining Québec's consent to the Constitution "with honour and enthusiasm."

Once elected, Mulroney looked for an opportunity to make good on his promise. The time seemed right when René Lévesque retired and the pro-federalist Liberal Party, led by Robert Bourassa, took office in Québec. Mulroney's first priority was to negotiate an agreement to have Québec sign the Constitution. But by then, other provinces had their own demands. For example, Newfoundland and Alberta wanted more control of their resources—Newfoundland of its fisheries, and Alberta of its oil industries. As well, both Alberta and Newfoundland demanded reforms to the Senate that would give them a stronger voice in Ottawa.

Western alienation, which had grown through the oil crisis of the 1970s, had come to a head once again over a government contract to repair air force jets. Ottawa awarded the multibillion-dollar contract to the Bombardier company of Montréal, even though Bristol Aerospace of Winnipeg had made a better proposal. Westerners were convinced that the contract went to Bombardier just to "buy" Conservative votes in Québec.

The Meech Lake Accord

Prime Minister Mulroney called the premiers to a conference to discuss the Constitution at Meech Lake, Québec, in 1987. He proposed a package of amendments that included an offer to recognize Québec as a distinct society. The package also included giving more power to the other provinces. All provinces, for example, would have the power to veto constitutional change. In a radio discussion, Premier Bourassa announced Québec's support for the accord:

> History will say... that [the] Meech Lake Accord was a unique chance for Canada. If it is accepted Canada will be and could be a great country. If it is rejected, it is hard to predict what will be the future.
>
> –Robert Bourassa

FIGURE 8–20 Some critics thought Mulroney had made a mistake in reopening the Constitution debate.

Interpreting a Cartoon What point of view about Mulroney and the Meech Lake Accord is this cartoonist expressing? Do you find the cartoon effective? Explain.

TIMELINE	Québec Nationalism				
1960	**1963**	**1968**	**1969**	**1970**	**1974**
Jean Lesage elected premier; Quiet Revolution begins	Royal Commission on Bilingualism and Biculturalism	Founding of Parti Québécois	Official Languages Act	October Crisis	Bill 22

However, the accord had many critics. Former Prime Minister Pierre Trudeau argued that the designation of Québec as a distinct society would create "two solitudes" in Canada. It would, he said, simply isolate the Francophones of Québec and make them less, rather than more, a part of Confederation. Many Québécois, on the other hand, saw this clause as a way of protecting French culture and language. Other critics also focused on the "distinct society" clause. They worried that it might be used in Québec to override the Charter and deprive specific groups of their rights. Aboriginal peoples pointed out that they too had a distinct society that needed to be recognized and protected. Others argued that Canadians had not been given enough opportunity to have their say on the issue.

Two provinces, Manitoba and Newfoundland, withheld their support from the Meech Lake Accord, and it died in June 1990. The failure of the accord was seen as a rejection of Québec itself, even a "humiliation." Support in Québec for separation had soared to 64 percent. Lucien Bouchard, a powerful Québec member of Mulroney's Cabinet, resigned in protest and formed a new national party, the **Bloc Québécois**. The Bloc would run in federal elections but it remained committed to Québec separation.

The Charlottetown Accord

Prime Minister Mulroney was not willing to let the Constitution debate end. He appointed a "Citizens' Forum," a committee that travelled across the nation to hear the views of Canadians on the Constitution. Eventually, Mulroney and provincial premiers proposed a package of constitutional amendments called the Charlottetown Accord. It answered Québec's concerns in ways similar to the Meech Lake Accord, but it also advocated the principle of Aboriginal self-government. In addition, the Charlottetown Accord proposed reforming the Senate. In response to pressure from the Western provinces, the Senate would become an elected body with equal representation from all parts of the country.

The Charlottetown Accord was put to a national referendum in October 1992. Although Mulroney warned that rejection of the accord would endanger the very future of the nation, 54.3 percent of Canadian voters rejected it. The greatest opposition came from British Columbia, where 68.3 percent voted "no." B.C. voters felt that the accord gave Québec too much power and they objected to the guarantee that Québec would always have 25 percent of the seats in the House of Commons, regardless of the size of its population. Many voters in Québec, on the other hand, believed that the Charlottetown Accord did not give them enough power because most of the Senate seats would go to the West. They also objected to Aboriginal self-government because it would affect a large portion of northern Québec.

FIGURE 8–21 Elijah Harper, a Cree member of the Manitoba legislature, opposed the Meech Lake Accord because it did not recognize Canada's Aboriginal nations as a distinct society.

● How did Aboriginal Canadians respond to challenges in the late 20th century?

1976	1977	1980	1982	1991	1995
Parti Québécois under René Lévesque elected	Bill 101	Referendum on sovereignty-association	René Lévesque rejects the Constitution	Founding of the Bloc Québécois	Referendum on separation

Referendum of 1995 and After

Perhaps angered by events in the Constitution debates, Québécois again elected the separatist Parti Québécois in 1994. In 1995, Premier Jacques Parizeau called a provincial referendum on full sovereignty. The "yes" forces reminded Québécois of their "humiliation" in the rejection of the Meech Lake Accord. On October 30, 1995, the nation held its breath as the referendum votes were counted. The results: 49.4 percent of the people of Québec had voted "yes" to sovereignty. The close vote shocked Canadians.

The threat of separatism lessened somewhat in the following years. Lucien Bouchard, who became Québec's premier in 1996, talked periodically of a new referendum, and the federal government under Prime Minister Jean Chrétien prepared guidelines for any future vote, stressing that the costs of sovereignty would be high for Québécois. Chrétien also sent the question of how Québec might separate to the Supreme Court of Canada and followed up on the Court's ruling with his controversial **Clarity Act**. This set down in law, for the first time, Ottawa's insistence on a clear question in any future referendum. Also, Ottawa would only negotiate Québec separation if a substantial majority of Québécois voted for it.

As the century closed, support for separatism appeared to decline. Liberal gains in Québec in the 2000 federal election and the resignation of Premier Bouchard seemed to support Chrétien's tough stand on separation.

Chrétien to Martin to Harper

In 2002, Jean Chrétien announced that he would not seek a fourth term as prime minister. In 2003, the new leader of Canada's Liberal Party, former finance minister Paul Martin, became prime minister. Martin called an election and the Liberal Party won, although it lost its majority.

In 2005, a scandal involving the misappropriation of government funds by the Chrétien government threatened the stability of the Martin government. Martin himself was not involved in the scandal, but Canadians had lost confidence in the Liberal Party. In the 2006 election, the Conservatives won 36 percent of the vote and Stephen Harper became prime minister.

FIGURE 8–22 In 1995, people came to Québec from across Canada to tell the people of Québec that they wanted them to stay in Canada.

Using Evidence How does this photograph demonstrate support for the "no" side? How does a symbol such as the Canadian flag play a part in national events such as the referendum campaign?

PRACTICE QUESTIONS

1. Would you describe Lévesque's plan for sovereignty-association as a plan for separation from Canada? Why or why not?

2. Why was it difficult to patriate the Constitution?

3. Why do you think that it was so difficult for the provinces and the federal government to agree about the Constitution?

4. Do you think Lévesque was betrayed by the Kitchen Accord? Why or why not?

5. Why did Brian Mulroney reopen the Constitution debate? Why did the Meech Lake Accord fail? Why did the Charlottetown Accord fail?

6. How did the Québec referendum of 1995 differ from that of 1980?

7. Why did the results of the 1995 Québec referendum shock Canadians? What action did the federal government take?

8. **Cause and Consequence** How might the rest of Canada have changed if the 1995 referendum had passed?

New Economic Ideas

By 1981, the oil crisis, inflation, and high interest rates had all taken a toll on Canada's economy. As the world slipped into an economic recession, many Canadians faced serious financial difficulty. The recession meant more unemployment and poor job prospects for young people. Canadians looked back wistfully on the confident 1950s and 1960s.

During the boom years, Canada had been a nation of savers. Now it was becoming a nation of spenders. But there was an important difference. In the past, Canadians had bought most of their goods with cash. Now they were experiencing the credit-card revolution, and consumerism was to become a way of life for the next decades. At the same time, governments cut public services and transfer payments to the provinces to deal with the national debt. Such measures dramatically changed Canadians' expectations.

An Uncertain Future

When Trudeau decided to retire in 1984, the government faced huge economic problems. Years of high unemployment and interest rates had resulted in a faltering economy. The National Energy Program (NEP), which was intended to shelter Canadians from soaring world oil prices, had failed.

High unemployment meant that government revenues fell as fewer people paid income tax and more required government assistance. The government had to borrow money to pay for social services, and the **national debt** grew tremendously. Both provincial and federal governments often ran a **deficit** as government expenditures (the amount of money spent) were greater than revenues (the amount of money taken in, mostly through taxes). Although reluctant to do so, the Trudeau government had begun to cut social programs and offer tax breaks to corporations to help stimulate the economy.

Mulroney and the Debt Crisis

Brian Mulroney's Progressive Conservatives came to power in 1984 with a promise to address Canada's economic problems. Mulroney's approach was inspired by conservative governments in the United States and Britain, which were cutting back on the role of government in the economy. President Ronald Reagan thought the solution to economic problems lay in the hands of corporations and wealthy citizens. He believed that if they were given large tax breaks, they would reinvest in the economy and create new jobs for everyone else. This became known as the "trickle-down effect." In Britain, Conservative Prime Minister Margaret Thatcher took a similar line. She lowered taxes and drastically cut spending on social benefits.

Mulroney planned to use this approach to cut the debt. He would save money by trimming social programs, and the savings would help to pay off the debt. He would also stimulate the economy by cutting taxes. At the same time, the Mulroney government tightened economic links with the United States. Over the years, some Canadians continued to express concern that U.S. companies controlled too much of the Canadian economy. Some measures had been put in place to limit U.S. investment, such as the Foreign

● How did the Canadian government respond to economic challenges after 1980?

KEY TERMS

Clarity Act (Bill C-20) legislation passed by the Chrétien government requiring separatist referendums to pass with a "clear majority" rather than 50 percent plus 1, before Québec could negotiate separation

national debt the amount of money owed by a federal government; most of Canada's national debt money is owed to Canadians who hold Government of Canada savings bonds, treasury bills, and so on

FIGURE 8–23 Brian Mulroney built close ties with the U.S. and shared the economic and political ideals of President Ronald Reagan. The Mulroney government reversed many of the programs previously enacted by Trudeau's Liberals.

What If...

Imagine the federal government had not cut transfer payments to the provinces. Would supporting Canada's social safety net be worth running a deficit?

KEY TERMS

Free Trade Agreement (FTA) the agreement that came into effect in 1989 between Canada and the United States to allow goods produced in each country to cross the border tariff-free

North American Free Trade Agreement (NAFTA) the agreement signed in 1992 and implemented in 1994 between the United States, Mexico, and Canada to create a free trade zone among the countries

Investment Review Agency (FIRA), which was formed by the Trudeau government in 1973 to block any foreign investment that seemed not to be in Canada's interest. Now Mulroney announced that Canada was "open for business." He dismantled FIRA and replaced it with Investment Canada, a body that would encourage suitable foreign investment. Mulroney also came to believe that free trade with the United States would help businesses to thrive, raise the employment rate, and increase government revenues.

Mulroney's plan to cut the debt did not work as planned. Canada was hit by a recession in 1990. Businesses failed and workers lost their jobs. Once again, the debt increased and the government was forced to increase, rather than cut, taxes. Failure to tackle the debt contributed to the defeat of the Conservative Party in 1993, when only two Tories won seats in Parliament.

Down the Road to Free Trade

In 1987, Mulroney started negotiations that led Canada into the **Free Trade Agreement (FTA)** with the United States. The agreement removed tariffs on goods crossing the border, and opened Canada to U.S. investment as well as opening the United States to Canadian investment.

Free trade proved to be a very controversial issue for Canadians. Supporters of free trade made arguments that included the following:

- By eliminating tariffs, Canada would attract more U.S. investment. This would help Canadian industry grow and benefit the whole economy.

- Free trade would give Canada access to the larger U.S. market, which would increase our productivity and growth. With more demand, Canadian products could be sold at lower prices to compete with imports.

- A free trade agreement would attract U.S. firms to Canada to take advantage of our natural resources, skilled workers, and well-planned transportation system.

People who were against the Canada–U.S. Free Trade Agreement put forward arguments that included the following:

- Once protective tariffs were removed, U.S. branch plants that had moved to Canada to avoid paying tariffs would simply return to the U.S. As a result, hundreds of thousands of jobs would be lost.

- Canadian businesses could not compete against giant U.S. companies that would flood the Canadian market with cheap goods and services.

- Free trade threatened Canada's independence. Economic union would also lead to pressure for political union.

FIGURE 8–24 Free trade was a popular topic for cartoonists.

Interpreting a Cartoon What opinion about free trade does the cartoonist express? How do the relative sizes of the hands help to put across this message?

©P

After much heated debate, the FTA was established in 1989. It included the following points:

- Tariffs between Canada and the U.S. would be eliminated. Complete free trade would be achieved by 1999.

- Cultural industries were exempt from the agreement, allowing Canada to retain protection for publishing, television and films, and the arts.

- The agreement included mechanisms to ensure fair competition between the two countries and fewer conditions on investment.

In 1992, the Mulroney government expanded the free trade zone by signing the **North American Free Trade Agreement (NAFTA)**, which included free trade with Mexico. This agreement also proved to be controversial. The major fear of NAFTA's opponents was that companies operating in Canada would move to Mexico to take advantage of the low wages and less strict anti-pollution laws. Those who supported NAFTA argued that while a few companies might move to Mexico, most would remain in Canada because Canadian workers are better educated and skilled. Canada had other attractions, such as transportation and communication systems, social services, and social stability. Although the Conservatives were defeated in 1993, their policies linked Canada's political and economic fortunes much more closely to those of the United States.

FIGURE 8–25 Protests against NAFTA continued into the new century. This protester holds a sign outside the B.C. Supreme Court in Vancouver in 2001.

Prime Minister
Martin Brian Mulroney

- born 1939, Baie-Comeau, Québec
- lawyer, author
- first elected to Commons in 1983
- prime minister 1984–1993

Domestic Record

- passed the Multiculturalism Act in 1985 to recognize and promote multiculturalism as an essential part of Canadian heritage and identity

- launched the Meech Lake Accord (1987), which proposed giving the provinces more say in federal matters and declaring Québec a distinct society within Canada

- apologized in 1988 to Japanese Canadians for their internment during the Second World War

- introduced the Goods and Services Tax (GST) in 1991

- tried to pass the Charlottetown Accord (1992), which proposed that provinces have more power, that the Senate be reformed, and advocated Aboriginal self-government

International Record

- negotiated the Free Trade Agreement with the U.S. in 1987

- expanded free trade to include Mexico in the North American Free Trade Agreement (NAFTA) in 1992

PRACTICE QUESTIONS

1. How did Mulroney's ideas about government differ from those of the Liberals? What other politicians inspired Conservative policies?

2. **Evidence** Describe the FTA and NAFTA. Why are these agreements controversial? Find evidence to show that NAFTA has benefited or damaged the Canadian economy.

● How did the Canadian government respond to economic challenges after 1980?

Prime Minister
Joseph Jacques Jean Chrétien

- born 1934, Shawinigan, Québec
- lawyer
- first elected to Commons in 1963
- prime minister 1993–2003

Domestic Record

- first prime minister to win three consecutive terms since Mackenzie King
- supported federalism during the referendum on Québec sovereignty in 1995
- appointed Beverley McLachlin as the first female Chief Justice of the Supreme Court of Canada in 2000
- passed the Youth Criminal Justice Act, which came into effect in 2003, creating a separate criminal justice system for youths between the ages of 12 and 18

International Record

- led a series of "Team Canada" missions to improve international relations and trade
- supported Canadian involvement in NATO's campaign in Yugoslavia (1999)
- refused to send Canadian troops to support the U.S. invasion of Iraq in 2003

The Liberals Tackle the Debt

When Jean Chrétien and the Liberals came to power in 1993, they inherited a staggering national debt of close to $459 billion. Their solution was to inject $6 billion into the economy through public works such as road repairs and new bridges. These projects would create jobs, and workers would then spend their earnings and boost the economy.

Chrétien's Liberals had little opportunity to judge the effectiveness of their policy. At the end of 1994, interest rates shot up. Provincial and federal governments used 43 percent of revenues to pay interest on the debt. Martin announced that Canada could no longer afford "big government" nor could it fund social services as it had in the past. He eliminated more than 40 000 jobs in the federal civil service and drastically reduced money transfers to provinces for post-secondary education, health care, and welfare. The provinces were thus forced to cut programs as well. To try to enhance the effects of the cuts, Martin put extra money into the Canada Pension Plan and Employment Insurance—programs essential to Canada's "social safety net."

The government was reducing the deficit, but Canadians paid a high price. For example, universities and colleges had to raise their tuition fees. Through the 1980s and 1990s, health care costs rose rapidly. New drugs and technologies were expensive and an aging population meant more demand on the system. At the same time as the federal government was cutting transfer payments to the provinces, less money was available for health care. Hospital wards were closed, the length of hospital stays was reduced, staff was cut and registered nurses were replaced by aides with less training. Some patients went to the United States for treatment because the services they needed were not available in Canada.

There were other problems. Growing numbers of Canadian children were living in poverty. More Canadians were homeless, and many had to rely on food banks. Food banks reported that 40 percent of their users were children, although only 26 percent of Canada's population was children (see Chapter 10). In the new millennium, social services were more hard pressed than ever to meet the needs of Canadians.

A New Era of Globalization

When the Liberals came to power in 1993, one of Chrétien's priorities was to expand Canada's trading opportunities. He sent "Team Canada" trade missions to Asia and Latin America to secure deals for Canadian investment and exports. The Canadian government also signed free trade agreements with Chile and Israel, and joined APEC (Asia-Pacific Economic Cooperation) to promote cooperation, freer trade, and economic growth among Pacific Rim countries.

FIGURE 8–26 Prime Minister Jean Chrétien supported Finance Minister Paul Martin's deficit-cutting measures, many of which went against Liberal policies set up while Chrétien was in Trudeau's Cabinet.

Expressing Ideas How might cutting social programs change Canadian expectations and values?

These trade initiatives were part of a **globalization** trend sweeping the world by the end of the 20th century. Globalization was partly the result of rapid changes in communications technology and the fall of communism. Goods could be shipped easily around the world, and the Internet made it possible to do business online from almost anywhere on the planet.

KEY TERM

globalization a process by which the regions and countries of the world are becoming economically and culturally interconnected

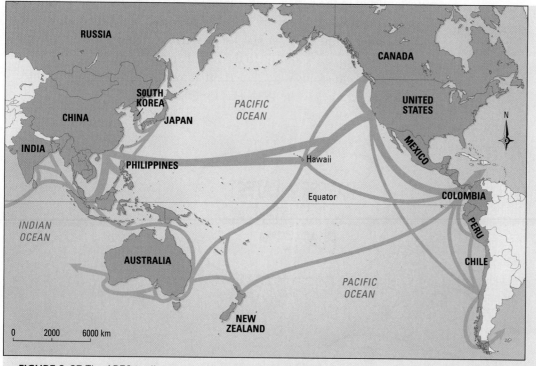

FIGURE 8–27 The APEC trading area, including major ocean trading routes

Globalization as an Issue

People have strong views on globalization and there have been fierce protests against it. Supporters believe that globalization is a powerful trend that will raise living standards for everyone, rich and poor. They argue that when large corporations invest in less-industrialized countries, jobs and economic opportunities are created for people. This, in turn, raises standards of living, which benefits everyone.

Opponents say that globalization makes businesses rich at the cost of workers everywhere. For example, in the 1990s, many multinational corporations moved production away from North America, Europe, and Japan to countries that had lower labour costs and fewer environmental regulations. As the 21st century began, China became the world's leading producer of manufactured goods of all kinds—and this trend continues. Meanwhile, thousands of Canadian factories have closed.

Globalization also raises ethical questions. For example, although no country has a perfect human rights record, should Canada build trade relationships with countries that consistently disregard human rights? Canada has introduced human rights as a topic in some of its trade talks, a move critics believe does little to change conditions in countries with poor human rights records.

● How does globalization affect living standards?

Environmental Action on a Global Scale

Globalization has created strong economic links around the world. At the same time, the global community has come together to work on environmental issues (see Chapter 13). The Kyoto Protocol is an international agreement that sets targets for reducing greenhouse gas emissions. It was an important step in the fight against climate change. The agreement went into effect in 2005 and, by the end of 2009, 187 countries had signed. However, Canada, under Prime Minister Harper's government, did not meet its emission reduction goals. According to the David Suzuki Foundation: "As of 2006, Canada's emissions were 22 percent above the 1990 level. Our Kyoto target is 6 percent below the 1990 level for 2008–2012."

FIGURE 8–28 Canada's record on responding to the crisis of climate change has been highly criticized.

Interpreting a Cartoon What viewpoint does this cartoon express about Prime Minister Harper's action on environmental issues?

PRACTICE QUESTIONS

1. What caused the debt crisis of the 1990s? How did Conservative and Liberal governments deal with debt?

2. How did Paul Martin deal with the deficit?

3. Why did Jean Chrétien organize "Team Canada" trade missions?

4. Why do you think trade with Asian countries is especially important to British Columbia?

5. What is globalization? What are its benefits? What are its disadvantages?

6. What economic reasons might the Canadian government give for not reducing greenhouse gas emissions?

©P

A New Era of International Action

Canada's international role shifted over the decades as world events and government priorities changed. It became increasingly difficult for Canada to maintain its role as a middle-power that gave it the prestige to mediate international disputes. Canadian governments have always been aware of the consequences of close adherence to American foreign policy and of how important it is that Canada pursue its own goals on the world stage.

Canada's relationship with its closest neighbour continued to complicate its foreign policy. The extent of Canada's support for American decisions remained an issue for Canadian leaders. For example, Prime Minister Mulroney generally supported U.S. foreign policy while Prime Ministers Trudeau and Chrétien were much less inclined to do so.

The federal government was often forced to make hard choices. For example, after the events of 9/11, President George W. Bush told the countries of the world that they could either be "with us or against us."

● What was Canada's involvement in the Cold War?

● What measures has Canada taken to promote a distinct Canadian identity?

The Cold War Continues: Canada's Concerns

The Cold War continued to define international relationships throughout the 1980s. In 1981, the United States government announced a massive increase in its defence budget, with most of the money to be spent on modernizing its nuclear arsenal. The U.S. also continued its policy of fighting communism in the Americas and elsewhere. As a result, the U.S. supported numerous right-wing movements and governments that disregarded human rights. The U.S.S.R., on its side, supported pro-communist struggles.

In September 1983, Soviet jets shot down a Korean passenger jet that had strayed into Soviet air space. The next month, U.S. forces invaded the Caribbean nation of Grenada and deposed the pro-Soviet, left-wing government. The two superpowers accused one another of provoking hostilities.

Prime Minister Trudeau appealed to the United States and the Soviet Union to show more restraint. He visited a number of countries to enlist other political leaders in his campaign to mediate between the superpowers. Unfortunately, Trudeau's initiative had little effect.

Let it be said of Canada and of Canadians, that we saw the crisis; that we did act; that we took risks; that we were loyal to our friends and open with our adversaries; that we have lived up to our ideals; and that we have done what we could to lift the shadow of war.

–Prime Minister Trudeau's summary of his peace initiative delivered to Parliament in February 1984

FIGURE 8–29 In 1978–1979, there was a revolution in Nicaragua against a repressive military government. After a left-wing government was established, the U.S. gave support to right-wing, anti-government rebels called Contras. This support undermined American prestige around the world. An 87-year-old man of the first Sandino rebellion, armed with a double-barrelled shotgun, stands with an 18-year-old guerrilla holding an assault rifle in Leon, Nicaragua, June 19, 1979. "I fought against the Yankee invasion in the thirties and I'd like to fight today, but I'm too old," said the old man.

1945	Second World War ends United Nations established Gouzenko Affair
1949	NATO formed
1950– 1953	Korean War
1955	Warsaw Pact established
1956	Suez crisis
1957	Canada and U.S. sign NORAD agreement
1962	Cuban Missile Crisis
1963	Canada accepts Bomarc missiles
1966	190 000 U.S. troops in South Vietnam
1973	Last U.S. combat forces leave Vietnam
1983	Soviet jet shoots down Korean passenger jet U.S. announces "Star Wars" defence shield
1989	Fall of the Berlin Wall
1991	Collapse of Soviet Union

The Mulroney Era: Closer Ties with the United States

Conservative leader Brian Mulroney became Canada's prime minister in September 1984. His approach to international relations was the opposite of Trudeau's. In many ways, Prime Minister Mulroney worked to forge closer links with the United States and developed a close personal relationship with President Ronald Reagan, with whom he shared a conservative philosophy.

In 1983, the U.S. government unveiled an ambitious plan to create a defence shield, part of which would orbit the Earth. This Strategic Defence Initiative (SDI), nicknamed "Star Wars," had an enormous budget. Did Canada's membership in the North American Aerospace Defence Command (NORAD) commit it to Star Wars? Across Canada, anti-nuclear groups protested Canada's possible involvement. These groups believed that Star Wars would provoke other nations to develop similar weapons. Canada eventually declined to participate. However, the door was left open for private Canadian companies to bid on Star Wars contracts.

The End of the Cold War

By the mid-1980s, Soviet leader Mikhail Gorbachev realized that the Soviet Union could no longer afford its costly arms race with the United States. He proposed massive cuts in the arsenal of both superpowers. Gorbachev then began a series of sweeping economic, social, and political reforms that would help the communist countries run more efficiently and create better conditions for their citizens. He also loosened censorship and allowed greater freedom of speech. These policies, called *perestroika* (reconstruction) and *glasnost* (openness), encouraged the people of East Germany, Poland, Czechoslovakia, Hungary, and Romania to demand similar reforms in their countries. By 1991, the Soviet Union had collapsed, and the Cold War was

FIGURE 8–30 The Berlin Wall, a powerful symbol of Cold War tensions, fell in November 1989. A few days before this picture was taken, guards would have machine-gunned anyone who tried to cross the Wall.

Expressing Ideas Why do you think some historians called the end of the Cold War "the end of history"?

over. The various member republics of the Soviet Union regained their independence and a new Russia emerged under the leadership of Boris Yeltsin, an ex-communist who now supported democracy.

Communist China, too, experimented with a kind of *perestroika*, allowing capitalism to flourish in some areas of the economy. However, Chinese citizens' hopes for political freedom were brutally dashed in Tiananmen Square in June 1989. Red Army soldiers and tanks attacked students involved in the democracy movement, killing hundreds, perhaps thousands, of protesters.

FIGURE 8–31 A protester stands in front of tanks approaching Tiananmen Square in Beijing, China, in June 1989.

FASTFORWARD

The Air India Tragedy

Canada's place in the world and international tensions were emphasized by the Air India tragedy. In 1985, a bomb exploded in the cargo hold of Air India Flight 182, causing it to crash into the Atlantic Ocean off the coast of Ireland. The flight was on its way from Montréal to London, England, en route to Delhi and Bombay. All 329 people on board died, including 280 Canadians. At the time, this was the largest number of people killed in an act of air terrorism. The plot to destroy the aircraft was hatched and planned on Canadian soil. The investigation and prosecution of the bomber suspects went on for 20 years, but only one person, Inderjit Singh Reyat, was convicted and imprisoned for five years on the lesser charge of manslaughter. It was not until 2005 that Ripudaman Singh Malik and Ajaib Singh Bagri, the final suspects who were arrested in connection with the bombing, were found not guilty of all charges. There were allegations that the case was mishandled by the RCMP and the Canadian Security Intelligence Service (CSIS).

1. Why was Flight 182 the target of a terrorist attack?
2. Why did the investigation take so long?
3. In what ways did the RCMP and CSIS mishandle the case?
4. Do you think justice was served in this case?

FIGURE 8–32 The Air India memorial in Ireland, unveiled on the first anniversary of the tragedy

WEB LINK • • • • • • • • • • • • • • • • •
Visit the Pearson Web site to find out more about the Air India disaster.

PRACTICE QUESTIONS

1. Contrast Prime Minister Brian Mulroney's approach to foreign affairs with that of Prime Minister Pierre Trudeau. Present your information in the form of a diagram, chart, paragraph, poem, or other representation.

2. What brought about the end of the Cold War?

3. What actions did the Canadian government take during the last years of the Cold War?

4. Use the Cold War timeline. Make a list of the events in which Canada participated. Was Canada's involvement small, medium, or large?

● What was Canada's response
to modern conflicts?

● Describe Canada's involvement
in the UN.

Peacekeeping: A Tradition in Peril?

Many thought the end of the Cold War might bring a new era of world peace. Instead, regional conflicts and ethnic rivalries erupted, most notably in the Persian Gulf, the former Yugoslavia, and Africa. The United Nations looked for ways to solve these problems using its standard methods: negotiation, peacekeeping, and sanctions.

With the end of the Soviet Union, the United States was left as the only world superpower. Now unrivalled, it could enforce its will anywhere on the planet. It was not long before this new reality played out in the Persian Gulf, in the first international crisis of the post–Cold War era.

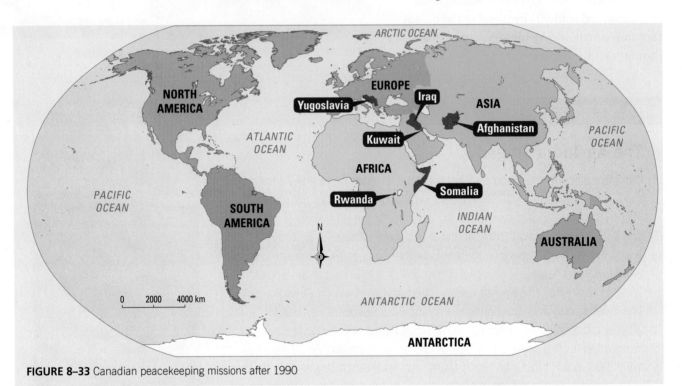

FIGURE 8–33 Canadian peacekeeping missions after 1990

The Persian Gulf War

In August 1990, Iraqi forces under the leadership of Saddam Hussein invaded the oil-rich country of Kuwait. Almost immediately, the United Nations demanded that Iraq withdraw and threatened economic sanctions if it refused. The United States insisted that military force be used to oust Iraqi forces.

For the first time since the Korean War, the United Nations authorized a multinational force against an aggressor nation. As in Korea, the United States would take the lead. The U.S. was joined by a coalition of forces from 35 other countries. Canada contributed two destroyers, a supply ship, a squadron of CF-18 fighter jets, a field hospital, and hundreds of military personnel.

FIGURE 8–34 American marines near a burning oil well in Kuwait during the First Gulf War

Although the Canadian contribution was modest, there was considerable debate in Parliament before forces were sent into combat. Prime Minister Mulroney emphasized that Canada made its commitment to enforce United Nations resolutions against Iraq, not merely to support the United States. Critics argued that sanctions had not been given enough time to work.

In January 1991, U.S. and coalition forces began bombarding targets in an effort to drive Iraqi troops from Kuwait. The use of "smart" weapons, such as laser-guided bombs and cruise missiles launched many kilometres from their targets, significantly changed the nature of the war. By February 27, the Iraqis were overcome by the forces massed against them. The coalition had won a stunning victory, with only a few casualties. Not a single Canadian soldier was killed or injured in the fighting. In the end, the Gulf War destroyed the Iraqi fighting force and much of the country's infrastructure.

After victory in the Gulf War, U.S. President George H. W. Bush proclaimed a "new world order," one in which the United Nations would take a much more active role as a global police force. In the past, the UN had been dedicated to peacekeeping—negotiating settlements and keeping warring factions apart. Now it would have more of a peacemaking role: it would, where necessary, use military force to preserve long-term peace and security. As the only superpower remaining after the collapse of the Soviet Union, the United States would take the lead in this peacemaking role.

Genocide in Rwanda

The population of the central African country of Rwanda is divided into two major groups—Tutsis and Hutus. Colonial administrations had put Tutsis in a position of dominance in the society. In 1994, after an incident in which a prominent Hutu was killed, the Hutus overthrew the Tutsi-led government and began murdering Tutsis and their supporters. France and Belgium, the former colonial powers in the area, sent troops to try to control the slaughter and the UN sent a small detachment of peacekeepers under the command of Canadian Lieutenant General Roméo Dallaire.

Dallaire sent a series of urgent appeals to United Nations headquarters and outlined an ambitious military plan to halt the killing. As he saw it, the UN needed to send a large multinational force to disarm the warring factions. His plan required two things: speed and the support of the United States, the only country that could provide enough troops on short notice. Unfortunately, the response from the UN and Washington was unenthusiastic. The U.S. feared a defeat similar to that in Somalia. Dallaire watched helplessly as close to a million people were murdered in the **genocide** that swept Rwanda.

KEY TERM

Rwandan genocide the 1994 mass murder of nearly one million Tutsis in Rwanda

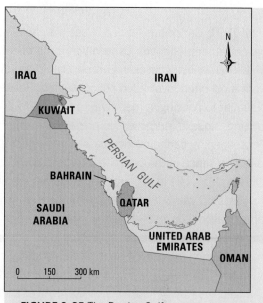

FIGURE 8–35 The Persian Gulf

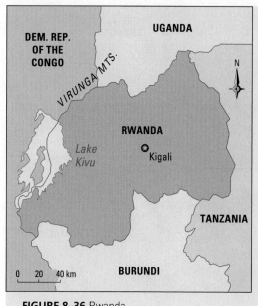

FIGURE 8–36 Rwanda

Disgrace in Somalia

Until 1991, Canadians tended to see their soldiers as peacekeepers. Although Canada was a member of NATO, which had military bases in Europe, Canadian soldiers were most often involved in peacekeeping. Peacekeeping is similar to policing in many ways. It rarely involves fierce fighting, since its purpose is to prevent conflict. Peacekeeping cannot work unless warring parties agree to the presence of the peacekeeping forces.

Canada's role in military conflicts changed with the Persian Gulf War, when Canadian troops were part of a large coalition against Saddam Hussein. Since then, Canadian soldiers have been involved in other conflicts and are sometimes called upon to fight and die in military operations. Changing the mission of the military has changed the way Canadians view themselves and the way the world sees Canada.

Canada's more aggressive stance has had other results, some of which have hurt our international reputation. In 1992, the UN launched "Operation Restore Hope" in Somalia. Somalia, an East African nation, was ravaged by a civil war that broke out in 1991. By 1992, many Somalis were starving. Canadian forces joined those from other countries in distributing food and other essential supplies to the desperate local population. The mission was directed by the U.S. which has important strategic interests in the "Horn of Africa."

One night, members of the Canadian Airborne Regiment arrested a Somali teenager found wandering in the Canadian base camp. During the night, the teen was tortured and beaten to death. At first, a military inquiry found that only a few low-ranking soldiers had committed this terrible, racist crime. As more evidence came to light, however, it became clear that there had been a high-level attempt to cover up the incident.

Canadians were shocked by the brutality of these events and, in 1995, the federal government disbanded the Airborne Regiment. A serious shadow was cast on the international reputation of Canada's armed forces.

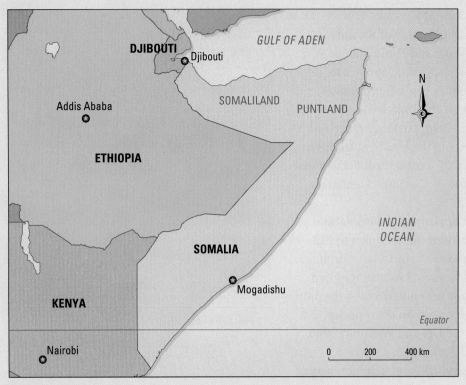

FIGURE 8–37 Somalia

Looking Further

1. How is peacekeeping different from combat? How would you describe the operation in Somalia?

2. How does the way Canada uses its military reflect on Canadians? On Canadian identity?

3. What kind of international operations do you think Canada's military should be involved in?

Civil War in Yugoslavia

After the Second World War, a communist nation called the Federal People's Republic of Yugoslavia was created in Eastern Europe. It was made up of six small republics: Serbia, Croatia, Bosnia-Herzegovina, Macedonia, Slovenia, and Montenegro, as well as two autonomous regions, Kosovo and Vojvodina. Until 1980, Yugoslavia was run by political strongman Prime Minister Josip Tito, but after his death, internal divisions began to appear.

When Slobodan Milosevic became president of Serbia in 1989, tensions among the republics broke out into ethnic conflict. United Nations peace-keeping missions, which included Canadian forces, were sent into the area, but they were unable to control the situation. Eventually, the member countries of NATO threatened to take steps to end the fighting.

FIGURE 8–38 This map of the Balkans shows the political divisions of the former Yugoslavia after the civil war in the 1990s. Although still contested by Serbia, Kosovo has been recognized as an independent nation since 2008.

In May 1995, NATO forces launched a series of air strikes against the mainly Serbian forces of the Yugoslav army, which was perceived as the aggressor. The warring factions eventually agreed to a ceasefire, and American troops were sent to bolster the UN peacekeeping forces.

In 1998, Serbian forces moved into the province of Kosovo to ensure it would remain under Serbian control. The Albanian Muslims who made up the majority of the population in Kosovo were persecuted, murdered, and displaced. In spring 1999, after diplomatic efforts failed to stop the Serbian operations, the U.S.-dominated NATO alliance launched its first-ever military operation against an independent country. Canada, as a NATO member, engaged in the controversial air strikes on the Federal Republic of Yugoslavia.

Canada's participation in the bombings was the subject of heated debate at home. Some Canadians supported NATO's bombings, insisting that NATO was obligated to prevent the Serbian-Albanian conflict from spreading to neighbouring countries. Critics of the bombing argued that NATO should never have interfered in the domestic affairs of a sovereign nation, and that its involvement escalated the conflict. Some Canadians began to question NATO's role in the "new world order" and Canada's role in NATO.

Throughout the developments in the Persian Gulf, Africa, and the former Yugoslavia, the world watched with concern. The failure of UN efforts to keep the peace brought grave doubts as to the effectiveness of the organization.

FIGURE 8–39 A young Muslim girl pats a Canadian peacekeeper on the head as he walks by the front gate of the Canadian base in Visoco, Bosnia, in 1994.

Interpreting a Photograph What impression of the UN mission does this image convey?

The Attacks of 9/11

On September 11, 2001, terrorist attacks of unprecedented magnitude and severity shocked the world. Members of a fundamentalist Islamic group called al-Qaeda hijacked four passenger jets. Two planes flew into the Twin Towers of the World Trade Center in New York City. Another plane was flown into the Pentagon, the headquarters of the United States Department of Defense in Virginia. The fourth plane crashed in a field in Pennsylvania after passengers attacked the hijackers. In all, 2976 people were killed and many more were injured. Billions of dollars worth of property was destroyed or damaged.

In response to the attacks, President George W. Bush declared a "war on terrorism" and promised to strike back. Leaders of NATO countries and others rushed to show their support for the United States. Many Canadians agreed that significant anti-terror measures were necessary. The federal government enacted anti-terrorist legislation and began using security certificates, which allowed people suspected of terrorist activity to be tried in secret hearings and deported.

FIGURE 8–40 On September 11, 2001, terrorists attacked the World Trade Center in New York City.

War in Afghanistan

A month after the 9/11 attacks, the United States, with the support of the United Kingdom, attacked Afghanistan. The aim of the attack was to destroy al-Qaeda and its leader, Osama bin Laden, as well as the Islamic fundamentalist Taliban government that supported and protected the terrorists. The Taliban were soon defeated, and al-Qaeda members were either killed or forced to flee the country. However, the war was far from over. In the years that followed, the Taliban and al-Qaeda launched attacks to try to regain power.

The United Nations had not approved the original attack on Afghanistan. However, by December 2001, the UN Security Council authorized the creation of the International Security Assistance Force (ISAF) to conduct operations in Afghanistan. NATO assumed the leadership of the ISAF in 2003.

©P

Canada's involvement in Afghanistan began in 2001 when it sent a naval task force to the Persian Gulf. A year later, a battle group from the Princess Patricia's Canadian Light Infantry was sent to Kandahar to assist in an offensive against Taliban and al-Qaeda forces. From August 2003 to December 2005, Canada's forces were mainly based in the capital, Kabul, as part of the ISAF. They provided security for elections, which were held in the fall of 2005.

As of the end of 2009, Western forces remained in Afghanistan to help local military and police forces secure the country from internal and external threats. Foreign countries also helped the Afghan government to reconstruct basic infrastructure, promote health and education services, and support other development initiatives. There were approximately 2500 Canadian personnel in Afghanistan, and 138 had died in the fighting.

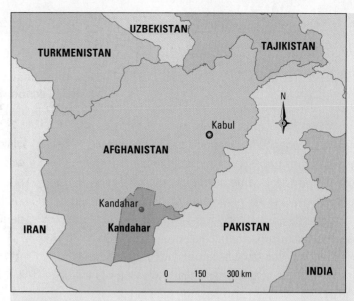

FIGURE 8–41 Kandahar province is close to Taliban strongholds in western Pakistan and, for NATO troops, is one of the most dangerous parts of Afghanistan.

When Canadian soldiers were first sent overseas in 2001, polls showed that about 20 percent of Canadians were opposed to military involvement in Afghanistan. However, as the operation wore on, Canadians became even less supportive. By 2009, 54 percent of Canadians opposed Canadian military participation in Afghanistan, while only 34 percent supported it.

The Iraq War

In 2003, the United States government decided to invade Iraq to "disarm Iraq of weapons of mass destruction (WMD)." The U.S. was joined by forces from Britain, Australia, and Poland. The war was not supported by a broad coalition of nations, and the Canadian government was not convinced that the Iraqis had, and were prepared to use, weapons of mass destruction. As it turned out, no WMD were found in Iraq. The United States and Britain, with some contingents from other countries, defeated Iraq and occupied the country.

The Department of Foreign Affairs and International Trade summed up Canada's role in Afghanistan this way:

Canada's participation is guided by our core values of freedom, democracy, the rule of law, and respect for human rights, especially the rights of women and girls.

PRACTICE QUESTIONS

1. How and why have Canadians participated in conflicts after the end of the Cold War?

2. What did President George H. W. Bush mean when he proclaimed a "new world order"?

3. Is there a difference between using our armed forces for peacekeeping as opposed to peacemaking? Which do you think is more "Canadian"?

4. Why did Canada become involved in the NATO action in Yugoslavia? Why was NATO's involvement controversial? Provide specific examples.

5. Why did the U.S. not respond to Lt. Gen. Dallaire's request for immediate assistance? What was the result due to the lack of U.S. troop support?

6. What was the stated purpose for the wars in Afghanistan and Iraq?

CHAPTER FOCUS QUESTION How did Canada and Canadian identity change as a result of social, economic, and cultural trends at the end of the millennium and beyond?

Canada experienced severe political and economic shocks in the final decades of the 20th century. Our Constitution finally came home, but attempts to bring Québec onside failed—Canadian unity barely survived two referenda on Québec sovereignty. The national debt rose and Canada experienced a severe recession. Gradually, our economy became more integrated with that of the United States, particularly after the signing of NAFTA. Globalization also became a fact of life and manufacturing moved increasingly offshore. At home, women continued to enter the workforce in increasing numbers and Aboriginal peoples began to make significant progress in securing rights that had previously been denied or resisted by governments.

1. Create an organizer such as the one below. Provide as many examples as possible from the text for each category.

Social Trends	Effects on Canadian Identity
. . . . .	
Economic Trends	**Effects on Canadian Identity**
. . . . . .	
Cultural Trends	**Effects on Canadian Identity**
. . . . . .	

Vocabulary Focus

2. To practise your use of the chapter and unit's Key Terms, refer to the Pearson Web site for a crossword puzzle activity.

Knowledge and Understanding

3. This chapter covers the final steps to Canadian autonomy. Complete the timeline by writing the name and date of each event and explaining how the event contributed to Canadian independence.

4. Why do you think the Canadian government has not made more progress in dealing with Aboriginal issues?

5. Provide a list of ideas/solutions on how the issues of child poverty, life expectancy, and high unemployment could be solved in Aboriginal communities.

6. Do you think Canada should have signed NAFTA? Provide support for your opinion.

7. Compare how governments in the 1980s and 1990s dealt with economic crises versus governments during the Great Depression. Which do you think were most effective? Why?

8. How did the UN involvement in the Gulf War, Somalia, Yugoslavia, and Rwanda affect its reputation in the eyes of the world? Why do you think the traditional role of peacekeepers no longer seems to apply?

9. Compare and contrast the wars in Afghanistan and Iraq. Include information on the cause, countries involved in the war, and level of support for the war.

Critical Thinking

10. Use the organizer from Question 1 to help you complete the following task.

Select five different trends and rank them from most impact on Canadian identity to least impact. Provide an explanation for each ranking.

For your top two selections (most impact), explain the long-lasting effects each will have on Canada.

11. "Canadian politicians should make every effort to have Québec sign the Constitution." Create arguments for and against this statement. Prepare to discuss your position with the class.

12. If you lived in a developing country, how might globalization affect you? What would your attitude be toward developed countries?

13. Significance "Canada's role as a peacekeeping nation has changed." Provide specific evidence that would support this statement. Write a paragraph explaining if you think this change is permanent or temporary. Support your viewpoint.

Document Analysis

14. Consider the following copy of a primary source document.

Canada MUST redefine its independence on the world stage, and in particular set a course in foreign policy independent of the United States. There are already welcome signs of this, including... Canada's advocacy role in trying to establish a world ban on the use of land mines.... There is much to recommend the long-standing relationship between Americans and Canadians across the longest undefended border in the world, but lock-step adherence to U.S. foreign (military) policy is not one of them. (A recent example of this kind of concern was provided on the CBC National News..., when the Minister of

Defence, Mr. Art Eggleton, ...opined that Canada should consider contributing to the resurgent, ultimately destabilizing and doomed-to-failure U.S. "Star Wars" missile defence program.)

In this way [by redefining its independence on the world stage], Canada will recover the world respect it deserves from an earlier time, and rediscover its mandate to provide a much needed forum of sober second thought, a necessary counter-measure to those "great powers" too often inebriated by their own self-righteous views....

–Professor Donald Fleming

- When and why was this document produced?

- What is the nature of the document? For example, is it an official government document, a statement of personal opinion, or something else? Does the nature of the document influence how it can be used?

- What is Professor Fleming's thesis and how effectively does he support it?

- Comment on the effectiveness of the language used. Does the professor state his case well? Explain.

- In your opinion, could a historian use this document to assess Canadian public opinion for the years leading up to 2000? Explain.

Use this Study Guide to continue synthesizing your learning about Canada's development as a country. As you work through the following steps, refer back to the Focus Questions for Chapters 6 to 8. Look for evidence in your understanding to answer these questions.

STEP 1 Unpacking Knowledge

Create a triangle chart by writing a chapter focus question in each corner. Look through the unit and within the triangle, list all the items you could use as evidence in answering these questions.

The more specific the evidence is to a question, the closer to the question you will write it down. For example, if an item could be used to answer all three questions, you will write it in the middle of the triangle. If it is an item specifically about Canada/U.S. relations, it will be located closer to the top of the triangle.

How did Canadian political decisions reflect a concern about the growing influence of the United States over Canada?

How did Canada's political, social, and economic policies reflect a new independence in the 1960s and 1970s?

How did Canada and Canadian identity change as a result of social, economic, and cultural trends at the end of the millennium and beyond?

STEP 2 Organizing Your Understanding

Examine your triangle chart from Step 1 and identify trends and themes in the evidence you have listed. What answer is emerging for each chapter focus question?

Using your triangle chart, create a ranking ladder for each question. Select the strongest pieces of evidence for each chapter focus question and write your choices in descending order of importance.

How did Canadian political decisions reflect a concern about the growing influence of the United States over Canada?

STEP 3 Making Connections

Interview someone who grew up in Canada during the Cold War/post-war era (1945–1989). Write interview questions that address any gaps in your understanding of the chapter focus questions. You should have at least one question from each of the four course themes (Society & Identity, Politics & Government, Economy & Human Geography, and Autonomy & World Presence). Be prepared to share interview responses with the class. For sample interview questions, visit the Pearson Web site.

STEP 4 Applying Your Skills

Assessing Viewpoints

Examine the following images and quotations, and discuss the points of view and perspectives reflected in each source. To what events do the sources refer? How might these sources be used as evidence in answering the three chapter focus questions? In what ways do they support or contradict the evidence you have already chosen? Remember to identify who made the statement, the circumstances under which the statement or image was produced, and the position that is being presented.

GROUP A

SOURCE 1: Lieutenant Commander Dr. Lalitha Rupesinghe at a visit to a girls' school in Kabul, Afghanistan

▼ **SOURCE 2:** Roméo Dallaire at the University of Saskatchewan, September 27, 2006

The concept of peacekeeping has failed in this era. The Canadian army hasn't been in peacekeeping for the last 15 years.

©P

▼ **SOURCE 3:** Prime Minister Trudeau's "Just watch me" impromptu interview with Tim Ralfe of the CBC and Peter Reilly of CJON-TV, October 13, 1970

Ralfe: *I still go back to the choice that you have to make in the kind of society that you live in.*

Trudeau: *Yes, well there are a lot of bleeding hearts around who just don't like to see people with helmets and guns. All I can say is, go on and bleed, but it is more important to keep law and order in the society than to be worried about weak-kneed people who don't like the looks of...*

Ralfe: *At any cost? How far would you go with that? How far would you extend that?*

Trudeau: *Well, just watch me.*

Ralfe: *At reducing civil liberties? To that extent?*

Trudeau: *To what extent?*

Ralfe: *Well, if you extend this and you say, ok, you're going to do anything to protect them, does this include wire-tapping, reducing other civil liberties in some way?*

Trudeau: *Yes, I think the society must take every means at its disposal to defend itself against the emergence of a parallel power which defies the elected power in this country and I think that goes to any distance. So long as there is a power in here which is challenging the elected representative of the people I think that power must be stopped and I think it's only, I repeat, weak-kneed bleeding hearts who are afraid to take these measures.*

▼ **SOURCE 4:** Reaction of the FLQ to the invocation of the War Measures Act, October 17, 1970; communiqué released on December 8, 1970

SOURCE 5: Soldiers guard a side entrance to Montréal City Hall, October 15, 1970 ▶

The present authorities have declared war on the Québec patriots. After having pretended to negotiate for several days they have finally revealed their true face as hypocrites and terrorists.

The colonial army has come to give assistance to the "bouncers" of Drapeau the "dog." Their objective: to terrorize the population by massive and illegal arrests and searches, by large and noisy deployments, and by making shattering statements on the urgent situation in Québec, etc.

▼ **SOURCE 6:** Prime Minister Chrétien's remarks on September 6, 2002, to reporters who asked what kind of proof Canada wanted to see before backing a U.S. attack on Iraq.

A proof is a proof. What kind of a proof is a proof? It's a proof. A proof is a proof. And when you have a good proof, it's because it's proven.

▼ **SOURCE 7:** Jean Chrétien commenting on the fact that Canada needs UN approval before going to war in Iraq, House of Commons, March 17, 2003

If military action proceeds without a new resolution of the Security Council, Canada will not participate.

▼ **SOURCE 8:** George Bush Heads off to War

STEP 5 Thinking Critically

Now that you have reviewed the Unit 2 content, practised skills, explored sources, and gathered evidence, it is time to synthesize your learning. Read the following comments from Canada25, a non-partisan organization dedicated to bringing the ideas of young Canadians into public policy debate, and then complete the activity below.

As a relatively young country with a tradition of offering assistance to our allies to attain mutual goals, Canada needs to define its values and objectives, both at home and abroad. Although everyone agreed that our traditional role as peacekeeper and "helpful fixer" was a vital one that we should continue to fill, our international reputation in these areas has clearly suffered over the years, evidenced by our failure to facilitate consensus on important contemporary global issues. Perhaps it is a question of confidence and boldness where Canada has been weak in the past, but what underlies these qualities must be real. Are we hoping to restore the reputation of the Pearson/Trudeau years or create a completely new one… or is the answer somewhere in between? How important is our international reputation—is it really soft power? Is it enough that other nations "like us"?

–David Eaves, Canada25 2004 report,
"From Middle Power to Model Power"

These comments suggest a shift from Canada's role to Canada's goal. How do you think Canada should act on the world stage? On what principles or actions should we base our reputation? Prepare a position statement that clearly states your argument and defends it. Remember to follow the procedure for defending a position as outlined in Chapter 8.

CHECK the Pearson Web site for additional review activities and questions.

UNIT

3

Canadians and Their Government

A well-functioning government requires the active involvement of its citizens. To participate effectively in Canadian society, it is important to understand the workings of the government, and your rights and responsibilities. In Canada, human rights are protected by the Charter of Rights and Freedoms, which guarantees equality "before and under the law" for all Canadians.

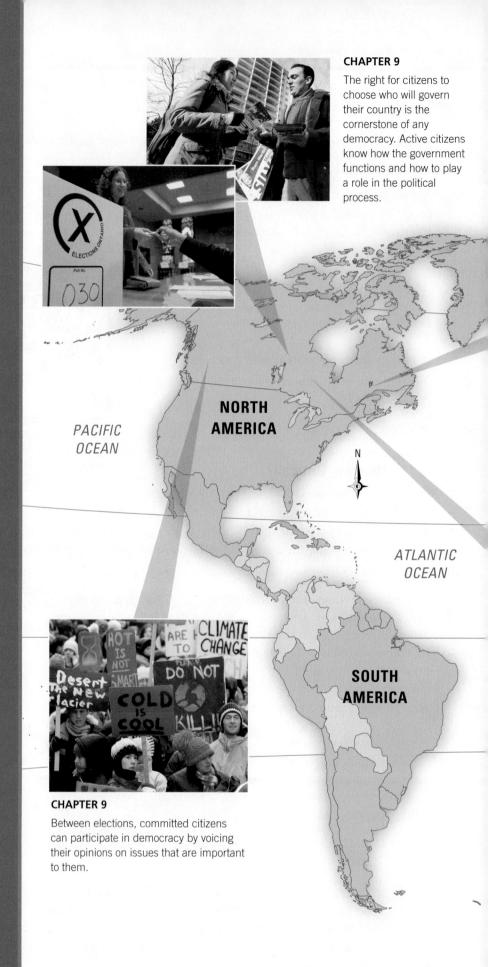

CHAPTER 9

The right for citizens to choose who will govern their country is the cornerstone of any democracy. Active citizens know how the government functions and how to play a role in the political process.

PACIFIC OCEAN

NORTH AMERICA

ATLANTIC OCEAN

SOUTH AMERICA

CHAPTER 9

Between elections, committed citizens can participate in democracy by voicing their opinions on issues that are important to them.

©P

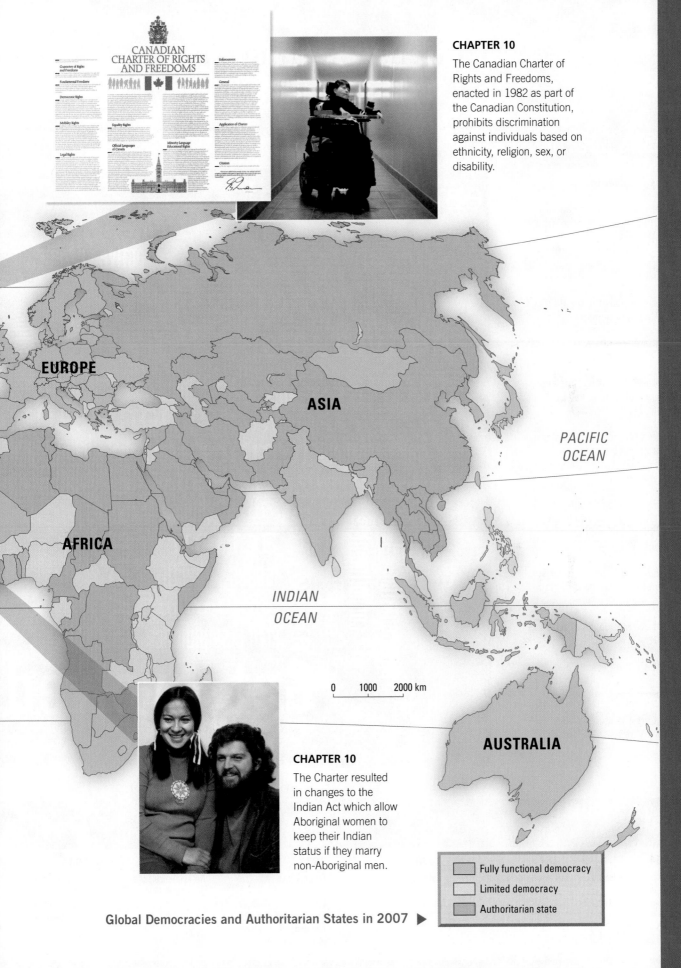

CANADIAN CHARTER OF RIGHTS AND FREEDOMS

CHAPTER 10

The Canadian Charter of Rights and Freedoms, enacted in 1982 as part of the Canadian Constitution, prohibits discrimination against individuals based on ethnicity, religion, sex, or disability.

EUROPE

ASIA

PACIFIC OCEAN

AFRICA

INDIAN OCEAN

0   1000   2000 km

AUSTRALIA

CHAPTER 10

The Charter resulted in changes to the Indian Act which allow Aboriginal women to keep their Indian status if they marry non-Aboriginal men.

	Fully functional democracy
	Limited democracy
	Authoritarian state

Global Democracies and Authoritarian States in 2007 ▶

9 Citizens Effecting Change

GUIDING QUESTIONS

Politics & Government

- What does active citizenship look like in Canadian politics?

- How do lobbyists and pressure groups influence government decisions?

- What role does the media play in effecting change?

- What are the characteristics of civil disobedience?

- What are the similarities and differences among key political ideologies?

- Explain the political spectrum. What characterizes the left, centre, and right portions of the spectrum?

- How do Canada's political parties differ and where do they fit on the political spectrum?

- How do B.C.'s political parties differ and where do they fit on the political spectrum?

- What are the stages of passing a bill?

- What are the benefits and challenges of a minority government?

- What are the steps of the electoral process in Canada?

TIMELINE

1854
Sir John A. Macdonald founds Liberal Conservative Party, known after 1873 as the Conservative Party

1873
The Liberal Party of Canada emerges as a united force under Alexander Mackenzie

1898
National plebiscite on prohibition

1932
Co-operative Commonwealth Federation, Canada's first socialist party, is founded; J.S. Woodsworth is its first leader

1942
National plebiscite on conscription

1944
CCF forms the first socialist government in North America

CHAPTER FOCUS QUESTION

How are governments formed in Canada and how can individuals influence government?

Significance · Patterns and Change · Evidence · Perspectives · Cause and Consequence · Judgements

CRITICAL INQUIRY

Canadian Why bother? freedoms authoritarian referendum rights promises politics accountability free speech election compromise decisions

We are so used to living in a democracy that sometimes we forget the responsibilities that go with our right to choose the people who make the laws and regulations that govern our lives. Sometimes we forget to ask ourselves how we would handle an issue, what we would want to accomplish, and how we can ensure that our government represents our wishes. In democracies, government is not separate from the people. In fact, democracy needs active citizen involvement or it ceases to be democracy.

In this chapter, you will learn how you can make your voice heard in Canada's system of democracy. You will also learn about political ideologies, and where Canada's political parties fit on the political spectrum. This will help you match your own beliefs and values with a political party. You will also learn how the Canadian government works and how political parties try to gain and maintain power.

KEY TERMS

democracy
lobbyist
ideology
socialism
liberalism
conservatism
totalitarian
authoritarian
communism
fascism
political spectrum
party platform
patronage
Senate
Cabinet
House of Commons
Cabinet solidarity
Order-in-Council
royal assent
party discipline
free vote
private member's bill
majority government
minority government
coalition
prorogue Parliament
dissolve Parliament
electoral district, riding, constituency
nomination
enumeration
balloting
tabulating

1948	1961	1983	1987	1992	2000	2003
Racial exclusions are removed from election laws	CCF is disbanded and replaced by New Democratic Party	The Green Party of Canada is founded in Ottawa	The Reform Party of Canada, led by Preston Manning, is founded in Winnipeg	National referendum on the Charlottetown Accord	The Reform Party of Canada becomes the Canadian Alliance	The Canadian Alliance merges with the Progressive Conservative Party of Canada to become the Conservative Party of Canada

KEY TERMS

democracy a system of government in which people freely choose in elections who will govern them; the principles and ideals of such a government, including free speech and the rule of law

civil servant someone who works for a government department

pressure groups organized groups of individuals with common interests and concerns who attempt to pressure political decision makers; also known as interest groups

Democracy Begins with the People

Democracy is a form of government that gives the people who are ruled by its laws and policies certain rights over the actions and careers of those in power. However, democratic governments still do things that people do not like, and making those who rule us answer to us is not often easy. Making government responsive to our needs is important. Active citizenship means that we learn how best to accomplish this.

Suppose you think that government should do more to protect the environment, or that a new social program should be introduced, or you feel that the voting age for elections should be lowered. How could you work to make your goal a reality? Would letters to the editor of a widely read newspaper accomplish anything? Or a letter to the government or opposition? Should you start a blog? Should you speak to somebody who works in a government department? Should you join the youth wing of a political party, or join a group of like-minded people that is pressuring the government? How could you become more involved in the democratic process?

Issues Important to Canadians

The issues important to Canadians change over time. Some make headlines for a time and then fade out of the spotlight. Others, such as whether Canada should go to war, are often time specific. Some issues are so basic to our view of Canada and ourselves that they arise again and again. We expect political candidates to know about important issues and to take positions on them, and we hope to learn, through news reports, editorials, and analysis, that the candidates are working to address these issues. Recurring Canadian issues include Aboriginal rights, Québec and bilingualism, continentalism (how closely we align ourselves with the United States), minority rights, civil liberties, the influence of big business, the environment, defence, spending priorities and taxation, crime, and maintaining social programs. What issues are important to you? Has government addressed these issues? How effective has government action been? Is it possible for ordinary people to have a say on an issue and to influence how government addresses it?

FIGURE 9–1 Protest in Montréal against global warming, 2005
Thinking Critically How effective do you think protests are at getting decision makers to pay attention to an issue? Should there be limits on such protests? Why is media attention important?

©P

Influencing Government

● What does active citizenship look like in Canadian politics?

People can and do participate in democracy between elections. One way is to contact one's Member of Parliament (MP), Member of the Legislative Assembly (MLA), or local representative, which is surprisingly effective. Another is to contact **civil servants**, who conduct the daily business of the government. Writing letters to the editor, e-mailing, blogging, or participating in radio phone-in shows also help citizens communicate their thoughts and ideas to government. While individuals can make a difference, especially at the local level, it is usually more effective to join a group of like-minded people who are committed to a specific goal.

Special interest groups, called **pressure groups**, organize to influence government policies and decisions. Such groups are made up of people who share a certain viewpoint and want to promote their common interest. Institutionalized pressure groups, such as the Assembly of First Nations, are well-established and have formal organizations. Issue-oriented groups are not permanent because their purpose is to accomplish limited aims and they usually disband once their goal is reached. A group that lobbies a local government to have a traffic light installed would be an example of an issue-oriented group.

FIGURE 9–2 The abortion issue produces some of the most passionate pressure groups.

WEB LINK ●
Find out more about Canadian pressure groups on the Pearson Web site.

Organization	Goals	Methods/Outcomes
Spirit Bear Youth Coalition	To protect kermode (spirit) bears and their habitat	Created international youth-led environmental coalition; B.C. government announced plans to protect two thirds of kermode bear habitat
The Wilderness Committee	To protect old-growth forests and the environment	Raises public awareness of environmental issues; lobbies government to protect old-growth forests
B.C. Citizens for Public Power	To prevent privatization of power supplies in B.C.; to promote energy conservation	Lobbies government on power generation and supply issues; organized class-action lawsuit against sale of portion of B.C. Hydro to the private sector
Alliance for Arts and Culture	To protect the arts in B.C.	Raised awareness of effects of cuts to arts programs
United Native Nations	To represent Aboriginal people whose status is defined "solely on Aboriginal ancestry, not on the artificial definitions created by an outdated Canadian Indian Act"	Lobbies and raises awareness on housing and other social issues, particularly for Aboriginal people living in cities

FIGURE 9–3 Canadian pressure groups

Letter-writing campaigns can be very effective. Governments listen to citizen complaints and concerns, and it is a policy of most Canadian government departments to respond to all letters. This does not mean that a government minister will personally respond to every concern. Usually, letters are prepared for the minister's signature by officials who are responsible for the program or issue in question. But letters can have positive results since governments know that for every person who writes a letter, there are likely many more people who share the same view. To be effective, your letter must be directed to the right department or person, and it should also be well thought out, even if it takes the form of an e-mail. You should follow these guidelines when communicating with a politician.

Letter-Writing Tips

Research which level of government deals with the area of your concern. It makes little sense to direct a letter about Canada's defence policy to the provincial government, or a complaint about street cleaning to the federal government. Effective letter writing requires that you target your request or complaint to the appropriate department or person.

Know where to direct your message. Decide whether it would be more effective to direct your letter to the opposition, to the government, or to both. Although all elected representatives will answer your letter and even bring your issue to the attention of the government, it is up to you to decide where your letter will be most effective. If your letter is about a provincial matter, it is also usually better to target your message to a minister rather than to the premier.

Identify yourself. Tell the reader who you are and why you are writing the letter. Tell the politician something about yourself and why the issue is important to you.

Keep it simple. Your letter should address a single issue and you should explain what your concerns are in a straightforward way. Do not confuse the reader or bury your concerns by including off-topic items. Try to limit your letter to one page. Politicians are often very busy and reading long letters is time consuming.

Request that a specific action be taken. Make concrete suggestions as opposed to vague reminders. A request such as "Please pass legislation banning free plastic bags" has more authority than "Please think about the environment."

Be courteous. Always be respectful in letters to politicians. Rude comments or insults will make it less likely that your message will find a sympathetic ear. Always thank the person for taking the time to read your letter.

Make it clear that you expect a reply. Close your letter with "I look forward to receiving your response."

Applying the Skill

1. List issues or problems that might warrant a letter to the government or the opposition. Sort these by level of government and responsibility, and then identify the office holder in each to whom you would address your concern.

2. Pick an issue that is important to you and outline a letter to a newspaper expressing your concern.

3. Summarize a concern in one paragraph that could be included in a letter to a politician. In another paragraph, suggest a solution or strategy that you think might help.

The Controversial Role of Lobbyists

Institutions and groups also use **lobbyists** to deal with lawmakers. Lobbyists are people paid to try to influence key decision makers, such as high-level **bureaucrats** in the **public service** or politicians. In fact, many professional lobbyists are former high-ranking members of the public service and thus have influential connections.

Paid lobbyists get contracts from the companies or groups they serve. Most public interest groups do fundraising and some get funds from government. While receiving government funds is helpful, it can also limit the actions of the group, as in the case of the National Action Committee on the Status of Women. This lobby group had its funding drastically cut in 1988 after it spoke out against government policies.

Lobbyists and the Public Interest

The danger with lobbying is that insiders can persuade governments to put in place policies that are not necessarily in the public interest. For example, prior to the 1997 enactment of the Tobacco Act that regulated the sales and promotion of tobacco products in Canada, the tobacco company lobby long fought government efforts to limit advertising for tobacco products. In 1989, a new law required lobbyists to be registered and new guidelines restricted public servants from lobbying for a year after leaving their positions.

Well-funded, highly organized groups with professional lobbyists can have great influence over government policy. But is lobbying democratic? Some critics argue that if pressure groups are too successful, then democracy is put at risk. They argue that if government is influenced too greatly by well-organized minority interest groups, then the wishes of the majority may not be heard—or even sought.

● How do lobbyists and pressure groups influence government decisions?

KEY TERMS

lobbyist a person hired to represent the interests of a pressure group by influencing policy decision makers in the group's favour

bureaucrats government officials and administrators

public service the government administration

FIGURE 9–4 Alberta oil sands. Environmental lobby groups, including those fighting Alberta oil sands projects, are one of the largest special interest groups in Ottawa. Oil and gas producers form one of the largest industrial lobbying groups.

Thinking Critically What advantages would environmental groups have when lobbying government officials? What advantages would oil and gas lobbyists have? Who do you think will have more influence? Why?

KEY TERMS

brand recognition awareness by the general public of characteristics associated with a particular product, business, or person (in the case of politics)

spin doctors people who publicize in a positive way the words and actions of politicians

civil disobedience the act of intentionally breaking the law while protesting against laws one considers unjust

apartheid an official policy of racial segregation involving political, legal, and economic discrimination against non-whites

● What role does the media play in effecting change?

WEB LINK ●
View campaign ads for Canada's political parties on the Pearson Web site.

The Courts and Democracy

Interest groups and individuals can also use the courts to influence government and effect change, since courts are bound to interpret laws within the context of the Constitution and the Charter of Rights and Freedoms. For example, in 1988 Canada's law prohibiting abortion was struck down by the Supreme Court in a case backed by a coalition of pro-choice groups. The court ruled that anti-abortion laws violated women's Charter rights to "life, liberty and security of person." Court cases, however, can cost a lot of money, and the desired outcome is not guaranteed. Also, while courts can strike down a law, they cannot order that it be replaced by something else. That is up to the government. For those individuals or pressure groups who are hoping to convince the government to create new laws or policies, the best the courts can do is to make governments aware that a new law may be needed.

The Role of the Media

Active citizenship requires you to be aware of the role and power of the media in politics. People often try to get media attention for a cause or to enhance their political profile. Social networking sites such as Facebook have also become a new form of public media. The traditional media (also called mass media)—television, radio, magazines, and newspapers—are still very important. They give politicians and political commentators the chance to establish a presence in people's lives. Without a media presence, a politician would not have the **brand recognition** necessary to gain people's votes. The media also provide feedback that lets politicians know how citizens feel about issues and government programs. The media can also frame an issue or debate by focusing on what generates the most public interest.

For politicians, the popular media are both a blessing and a curse. They give candidates very wide exposure, but they also magnify faults the candidates may have or political gaffes that may occur. For this reason, political parties hire media consultants, or **spin doctors**, to coach candidates on what to say and make sure they look good in the media.

The Internet has opened up a whole new area for political contact and publicity. Blogs and other forms of reporting are probably as important today as the mainstream media. Political parties and candidates have Web sites to get their message out and garner support for their campaign. In other times, people voted the same way their families voted, but now many wait until election day to make up their mind. Sometimes the last powerful message carries the day, which is why media experts are so important to political parties.

FIGURE 9–5 Opposition leader Michael Ignatieff in a Liberal Party attack ad against Conservative leader Stephen Harper

Interpreting a Cartoon What is the message of the cartoonist? How effective are attack ads? Why might politicians use negative ads instead of positive ones?

Civil Disobedience

Citizens can make their voices heard in many ways: with their votes, through individual actions such as letter writing, and by joining pressure groups and using the media. While such actions may not be successful in changing government policies, citizens must have the opportunity to express concerns. Suppose you feel that the actions of the government are unethical or undemocratic. Is it ever acceptable to break the law as a way of protesting government actions?

Civil disobedience is the act of intentionally breaking the law while protesting laws one considers unjust. This form of protest has been used by some of the greatest moral leaders of our time, including Indian political and spiritual leader Mohandas Gandhi, U.S. civil rights activist Martin Luther King Jr., and South-African anti-**apartheid** activist Nelson Mandela. Both Gandhi and King embraced non-violent civil disobedience in their quest for justice, and both ultimately died for their cause. Mandela resorted to violence only as a last resort after many years of peaceful protests with no progress.

During my lifetime I have dedicated myself to the struggle of the African people. I have fought against white domination, and I have fought against black domination. I have cherished the ideal of a democratic and free society in which all persons live together in harmony and with equal opportunities. It is an ideal which I hope to live for and to achieve. But if needs be, it is an ideal for which I am prepared to die.

–Nelson Mandela, 1964

FIGURE 9–6 Gandhi used non-violent civil disobedience to protest unjust taxation of the poor, and discrimination against women and the underprivileged. His theories about non-violence inspired Martin Luther King Jr. and Nelson Mandela.

Of course, if everyone in society disobeyed laws with which they disagreed, the result would be chaos. Civil disobedience is warranted only when the law itself causes significant harm. Relatively trivial matters do not merit breaking the law, as the harm to society could be greater than the benefit. As well, those who choose to practise civil disobedience should be willing to face the consequences of their actions. This gives the act of civil disobedience for a good cause great moral authority.

The Three Principles of Civil Disobedience

1. Civil disobedience should not involve violence.

2. Civil disobedience should be directed against laws that are seriously harmful.

3. Civil disobedience requires taking responsibility for one's actions. Willingness to face punishment shows the strength of one's beliefs.

FIGURE 9–7 Greenpeace activists hang a banner on the Parliament Buildings in Ottawa.

Thinking Critically How could social networking help or hinder civil disobedience?

©P

ideology political and social principles or beliefs

direct democracy a system in which citizens vote directly on every issue

representative democracy a system in which citizens elect a politician who then makes decisions for them

socialism a political and economic system in which the means of production and distribution in a country are publicly owned and controlled for the benefit of all members of a society

liberalism a political philosophy supporting individual freedoms and governmental protection of civil liberties

Clayoquot Sound: Civil Disobedience in Action

Acts of civil disobedience, including blocking logging roads near Clayoquot Sound, British Columbia, brought the issue of clear-cut logging to the public's attention in 1993. In response, the provincial government announced a compromise. It would set aside 34 percent of the area as protected lands, and allowed selective and environmentally sensitive logging of another 21 percent. The government claimed that opinion polls showed a majority of the population was in favour of this solution.

However, opposition to logging intensified and resulted in the largest example of civil disobedience in Canadian history. Protesters organized blockade after blockade, holding "sit-downs" in the middle of roads to prevent loggers from entering the forest. Police were forced to drag people away and arrest them, including Aboriginal Elders well-advanced in years. The arrests generated maximum media exposure and worldwide interest. More than 750 people were arrested in the summer of 1993 alone. Most were given warnings, but some received fines of up to $2000 or jail sentences. Since that time, logging practices in the area have been closely monitored and all decisions regarding the clear-cutting of old-growth forests are closely examined.

FIGURE 9–8 The 1993 anti-logging protests at Clayoquot Sound resulted in the largest mass arrests in British Columbia's history.

Thinking Critically Why would protesters want to be publicly arrested? How would a totalitarian government deal with such protests?

PRACTICE QUESTIONS

1. In what ways have traditional media been replaced or changed by new technologies? In your opinion, will new technology help voter awareness and participation? Explain.

2. What are the three basic guidelines for practising civil disobedience? Why are these guidelines an important part of this approach to changing government policies?

3. Why were blockades more effective at Clayoquot Sound than a violent protest might have been?

4. In your opinion, when should civil disobedience be used? Do you think governments have the right to limit civil disobedience? Explain your position.

5. **Cause and Consequence** With a partner, develop a ten-point strategy for direct political action. Explain how you will use the media to help your cause.

©P

Political Ideologies and Parties

Like all modern nations, Canada is governed by one or more political parties. Political parties are a relatively recent invention and no party is more than a few hundred years old. Most are organized around political and social principles—an **ideology**—that guide them in everything they do. Most of Canada's political parties believe in a balance between the powers of the state and the rights of the individual. They support some form of capitalism and the kind of parliamentary democracy we currently enjoy.

● What are the similarities and differences among key political ideologies?

Democracy: Rule by the People

Canada operates on democratic principles. In Europe, democracy, which means "rule by the people," was first practised by the ancient Greeks. In the Greek city states, every eligible citizen participated directly by voting on all decisions that affected society. This was called **direct democracy**. In modern societies, our large populations make this much involvement by each individual impractical. Instead, citizens in **representative democracies** such as Canada allow elected representatives to make decisions on their behalf.

The main principles of democracy are equality and freedom. All citizens are equal before the law, meaning that everyone is subject to the same laws, and no one is above the law. The rights and freedoms of people living in a democracy are protected by a constitution or other written laws (see Chapter 10). Democracy refers to a very broad form of government, and most countries around the world are democratic. Under the umbrella of democracy, there are various political philosophies, as outlined below.

Socialism

Early **socialism** was a backlash against the industrial revolution and the resulting capitalist laissez-faire economy. Socialism developed when capitalism was causing great social harm and poverty was widespread. Socialists believe that government should control important parts of the economy and major industries. As you learned in Chapter 4, Canada's first socialist party, the Co-operative Commonwealth Federation, was formed during the Depression when people were disillusioned with Canada's capitalist system.

Liberalism

Liberalism began as a political theory that favoured individual freedom above all else. Originally this belief was tied to the right to own property and to the conviction that government should have minimal involvement in the lives of citizens, so as not to infringe on people's liberty. This focus on property rights lost favour in the late 19th century when it became clear that the growing working class had few, if any, property rights. In the 20th century, liberalism shifted its focus from property and individual rights and evolved into a belief that the government should intervene to regulate the economy. On a social level, liberalism supports government intervention to maintain basic standards of living for all people and to protect the rights of individuals and groups.

FIGURE 9–9 A statue depicting Justice

Thinking Critically Why would artists choose to portray Justice with a blindfold and scales? With a sword? As a woman?

©P

conservatism a political philosophy supporting traditional values and institutions and opposing sudden change

fiscal pertaining to money issues

totalitarian a form of government that uses intimidation, violence, and propaganda to rule all aspects of the social and political life of its citizens

authoritarian a form of government in which one individual or small group holds all the power and directs the lives of citizens

communism a social and economic ideology that believes property, production, and distribution of goods and services should be owned by the public, and that the labour force should be organized for the benefit of all members of society

bourgeoisie the ruling or middle class

proletariat the workers or lowest class

fascism an authoritarian system of government that exercises complete power, suppresses opposition, often through use of force, and encourages nationalism and racism

political spectrum a linear visual used to illustrate political ideologies, from left to right

FIGURE 9–10 This statue represents the workers of the Soviet Union, a country that had a totalitarian government.

Thinking Critically Why would totalitarian governments use images of idealized people serving the state and other such propaganda?

Conservatism

Conservatism is less of an ideology than a stance taken against change, innovation and reform, and for maintaining established political and social institutions and values. It supports laissez-faire capitalism, or minimal government intervention in the economy. In the late 20th century, many conservatives came to believe that government has a role in encouraging traditional behaviours and they opposed same-sex marriage and abortion, for example. **Fiscal** conservatives support reductions in government spending and a balanced budget.

Totalitarianism: Total Control

Not all political ideologies are based on democratic principles. **Totalitarian** governments are **authoritarian**, as opposed to democratic, and control every aspect of life within a country—its culture, religion, government, and economy. These regimes use harsh laws and restrictions on freedom to maintain their power.

Communism

Communist ideology is based on the work of Karl Marx and Friedrich Engels, political theorists of the 19th century who believed that the ruling class should be overthrown by the working class. In *The Communist Manifesto*, published in 1848, Marx claimed that capitalism creates a class struggle in which those who own the means of production (the ruling class or **bourgeoisie**) exploit those who work for them (the **proletariat**). Marx believed that a proletarian revolution would result in a classless society in which all property would be collectively owned. Communist governments that developed from Marx's ideology were one-party states, and maintained their power through propaganda, secret police, and government control of its citizens. Until the end of the Cold War, many countries, including the Soviet Union, had communist governments. Today, communist countries include the People's Republic of China, Cuba, Laos, North Korea, and Vietnam.

Fascism

Fascist ideology is about the importance of the state and the responsibility of people to serve it. Fascists believe that a country is an organic community requiring strong leadership, a collective identity, and military strength. Fascist governments emphasize nationalism and militarism; war is glorified and viewed as a means to keep the nation strong. Political opposition or individual freedom is forbidden in fascist states. **Fascism** was born after the First World War, a period of time that was particularly unstable. It originated in Italy under the leadership of Benito Mussolini. Germany under the Nazis was another fascist state (see Chapter 5).

©P

The Political Spectrum

A **political spectrum** is a visual used to illustrate how various political ideologies relate to one another. The linear left–right spectrum is the most common (see Figure 9–11), with totalitarian ideologies at the extreme left and right. Socialism is left of centre and commonly referred to as "left wing." Liberalism is generally considered to be slightly left of centre on the spectrum, with conservatism situated right of centre. Many political theorists believe that the traditional left–right spectrum is too simplistic and have added other axes (see Figure 9–12).

● Explain the political spectrum. What characterizes the left, centre, and right portions of the spectrum?

WEB LINK ● • • • • • • • • • • • • •
To find your own position on the political spectrum, visit the Pearson Web site.

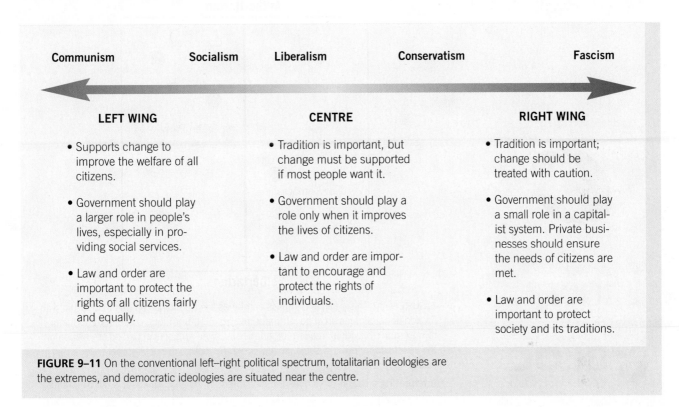

FIGURE 9–11 On the conventional left–right political spectrum, totalitarian ideologies are the extremes, and democratic ideologies are situated near the centre.

Canadian Politics and Ideology

In Canadian politics today, the major political parties cluster around the centre of the political spectrum. The lines between them are somewhat blurred. You cannot equate the Liberal Party of Canada too closely with liberalism, nor the Conservative Party of Canada with conservatism. The Liberals adopted some of the progressive social policies of the socialists, such as universal health care and other social programs, place less emphasis on the military, and provide more support for arts and culture. Conservatives, however, are more likely to support tradition and business interests, such as tax breaks for large corporations. They tend to be nationalistic and pro-military.

The New Democratic Party (NDP) supports social assistance programs and government-funded health care and education, and is against privatization of Crown corporations. Of the major political parties in Canada today, the NDP is the most socialist. The Bloc Québécois is the third-largest party in the House of Commons today. Its main objectives are to protect the

● How do Canada's political parties differ and where do they fit on the political spectrum?

WEB LINK ● • • • • • • • • • • • • •
Read more about Canada's political parties on the Pearson Web site.

interests of Québec and to support **Québec sovereignty.** The Green Party of Canada is devoted to green politics, which focuses on achieving environmental goals through grassroots democracy.

If a shared ideology is a major reason for forming and maintaining a political party, how do Canada's major parties differ? The best way to understand a party's ideology is to look at its stated positions on important issues. What political parties state in their election platforms about these issues helps us to understand their ideology.

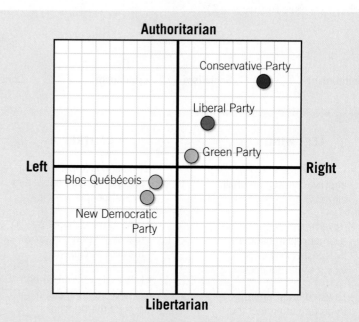

FIGURE 9–12 This political compass combines the traditional left–right spectrum with an additional dimension of government involvement, from total control (authoritarian) to maximum individual freedom (libertarian). Canadian political parties are placed on the spectrum in terms of social policy, economic policy, the environment, and other issues.

Interpreting a Graph What does the placement of the Bloc Québécois tell you about its ideology?

FIGURE 9–13 Party platforms are greatly publicized and debated during election campaigns, but are difficult to find once elections are over.

Thinking Critically Why do you think political parties do not keep their party platforms easily accessible between elections?

Party Platforms

A **party platform** is a list of priorities and a plan for governing published by a political party. This platform helps the public to understand what the party stands for and it reminds party members about goals and core beliefs. In the 2008 election campaign, the Liberals promised to encourage a green economy and reduce the number of people living below the poverty line by 30 percent. Conservatives promised to lower both the Goods and Services Tax (GST) and taxes paid by lower-income families and seniors, and to establish sovereignty over the Arctic. The New Democratic Party also promised a new green energy economy and to train and hire more doctors and nurses. On the environment, all parties promised new greenhouse gas emissions targets. Other federal political parties, such as the Bloc Québécois and the Green Party, also included statements about these issues in their platforms.

©P

Party Membership

Many people join political parties because they believe strongly in the ideology of the party and share values with members of the party. Others want to serve the public and bring about change. Still others are attracted to the power and influence that politics generates. Perhaps the real question is, But why do so few people—only about two percent of the population—join political parties? Individuals are far more likely to seek change by participating in a special interest group or a **non-governmental organization (NGO)** than by joining a party. Even so, joining a party and becoming involved in the political process is also a very effective way of gaining a voice on issues.

Party Politics and Accountability

As in all modern democracies, Canada's political parties dominate government and there is little room for independent politicians. For this reason, those interested in political life usually decide which party they want to join, and which ideology they feel comfortable with. Parties have their own power structures, with the leader at the top. The strength of a party and its leader help it win elections and form governments. But this also makes it difficult, sometimes, for party members to know whether their first loyalty lies with the party or with the people. For this reason, citizens must be vigilant. Once a party is in power, it is very difficult to keep it accountable. Strong leadership and good party discipline, the very qualities that help it win power, help the party stay in power. The prime minister or premier also has great executive power, and the advantage of the rules and procedures of parliament, that can also make the governing party less accountable.

Patronage

Patronage refers to the giving, by premiers and prime ministers particularly, of offices and rewards in return for loyalty or favours to the party. Although opposition parties always criticize patronage and promise to avoid it if they form the government, the practice continues. A large part of government is deal making, and it is very difficult to make deals with others if you have nothing to offer in return. Also, powerful party members need to be rewarded and appeased. A prime minister has a lot to offer in the way of patronage, such as Senate seats, ambassadorships, and committee chairpersonships. In some cases, patronage serves more than one purpose. For example, appointing a long-time party supporter to the Senate not only rewards the supporter but also adds to the number of senators loyal to the party, which makes implementing policies easier.

KEY TERMS

Québec sovereignty a movement advocating that Québec separate from the rest of Canada and become a country of its own

libertarianism a political ideology that supports maximum individual freedom and minimal government involvement in the lives of its citizens

party platform a list of priorities and a plan for governing published by a political party

non-governmental organizations (NGOs) local, national, or international groups that work independently of government on issues such as health, the environment, or human rights

patronage a favour, often a government position, given in return for political support

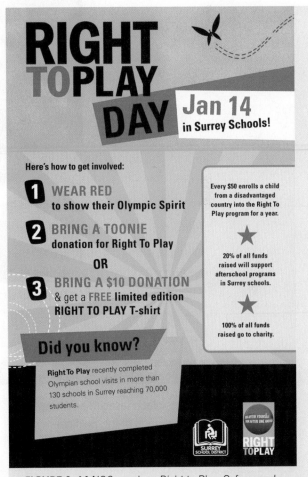

FIGURE 9–14 NGOs such as Right to Play, Oxfam, and World Wildlife Fund are non-profit organizations that work to change unfair laws or policies or to better people's lives.

©P

● How do B.C.'s political parties differ and where do they fit on the political spectrum?

KEY TERMS

populism a political movement that advocates the interests of ordinary people

elite a group of people who hold power

polarize to go in opposite directions

partisan loyal to a party or cause

B.C. Politics

Politics in British Columbia has always been intense and proceedings in the legislature are very combative. **Populism**—a style of politics that pits the people against the **elite**—has always been important in B.C. Also, at least within the past 50 years, B.C. politics has been **polarized**. Two parties on opposite sides of the political spectrum, the socialist NDP and the "free enterprise" party represented first by the Social Credit Party and, later, by the B.C. Liberals, have alternated in power. The members of both parties are intensely **partisan** and there often seems to be little room for compromise. Although other parties exist, it has proved extremely difficult for them to make inroads because many people think that voting for a minor party is, in essence, throwing away a vote. Although the Green Party—the largest of the other parties—has increased its presence and fielded strong candidates, it has, at time of writing, yet to seriously contest a riding.

FIGURE 9–15 B.C. Liberal Finance Minister Carole Taylor delivers her budget, February 2008. B.C. Premier Gordon Campbell is seen on the bottom right.

PRACTICE QUESTIONS

1. What characteristics place fascism and communism on the extreme ends of the political spectrum?

2. List Canada's main political parties. What are their main policies and priorities? State where each party is located on the political spectrum.

3. Why do political parties that are in the middle of the political spectrum do better in elections?

4. Explain the term *patronage*. Why is it controversial?

5. **Patterns and Change** Which socialist ideas of the 1930s and 1940s do all parties now consider essential social services?

©P

Canadians regularly revisit the issue of Senate reform. Some claim that the Senate should be abolished altogether, since patronage has weakened its original purpose and lowered its prestige. Many people feel that Senate positions have been given to people who are not necessarily best qualified for the position. Given that a senator's role is to give legislation "sober second thought," the assumption is that he or she is qualified to do so. Senators should be exemplary and highly experienced individuals capable of examining legislation in detail and holding the government to account.

Some appointments seem to revive the idea that senators ought to be exceptional citizens with a lot to offer the country. This is the case with Roméo Dallaire, a former general who led the United Nations force during the Rwandan genocide in 1994 and later wrote about the tragedy in his book *Shake Hands with the Devil*.

Rwanda will never ever leave me. It's in the pores of my body. My soul is in those hills, my spirit is with the spirits of all those people who were slaughtered and killed that I know of, and many that I didn't know.... Fifty to sixty thousand people walking in the rain and the mud to escape being killed, and seeing a person there beside the road dying. We saw lots of them dying. And lots of those eyes still haunt me, angry eyes or innocent eyes, no laughing eyes. But the worst eyes that haunt me are the eyes of those people who were totally bewildered. They're looking at me with my blue beret and they're saying, "What in the hell happened? We were moving towards peace. You were there as the guarantor"—their interpretation—"of the mandate. How come I'm dying here?" Those eyes dominated and they're absolutely right. How come I failed? How come my mission failed? How come as the commander who has the total responsibility—We learn that, it's ingrained in us, because when we take responsibility it means the responsibility of life and death, of humans that we love.

Deeply affected by the experience of the genocide and the failure of UN peacekeeping, Dallaire is now a human rights activist, speaking out on issues such as genocide and child soldiers. Dallaire has also been a senior civil servant and has received a number of honorary degrees and prizes. General Dallaire was appointed to the Senate as a Liberal in 2005 by Prime Minister Paul Martin.

1. In what ways does Roméo Dallaire represent the ideal senator?

2. In your opinion, does the appointment of Senator Dallaire, or other prominent citizens, make reform or abolition of the Senate less of an issue? Explain.

3. Outline your own view of what should, or should not, happen to the Senate.

Senate the second legislative body in Parliament consisting of appointed members whose role is to give sober second thought to the passage of bills

Cabinet the group of ministers chosen by the prime minister who decide government policy; each Cabinet minister has a responsibility for a particular department

House of Commons the first legislative body of Parliament whose members are elected

WEB LINK •
For more information on Canada's Parliament, visit the Pearson Web site.

A Guide to Government

Active citizens need to know how governments operate. As you know, Canada's government operates as a federal system—an organization of provincial governments each acting on behalf of its own residents, with a central government in Ottawa responsible for matters vital to the nation as a whole. There are also municipal governments and Aboriginal governments. Knowing which level of government is responsible for a particular matter is very important. Federal and provincial governments also have legislative, executive, and judicial branches and bureaucracies to carry out the policies and responsibilities of government.

The executive and legislative branches of the federal government make and administer the laws and regulations of the country, and the judicial branch administers the courts and interprets and enforces the law. The provinces have the same branches of government, with similar powers and responsibilities over those areas for which they have jurisdiction.

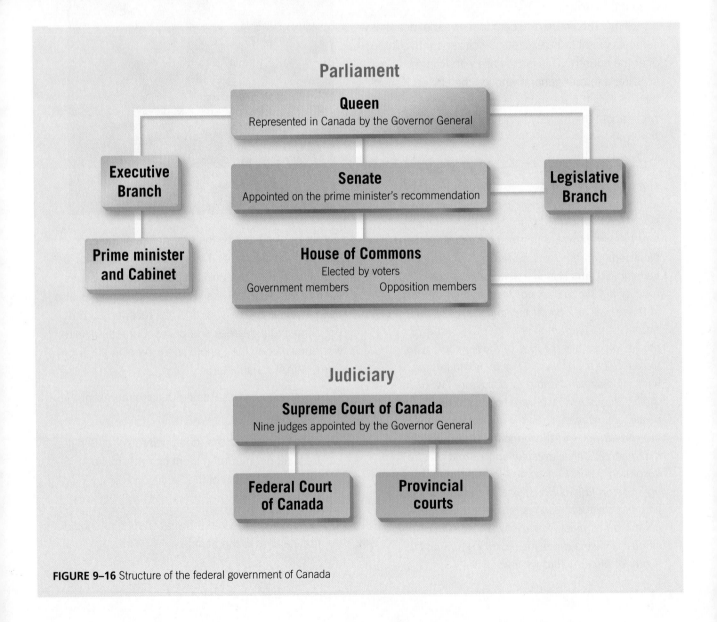

FIGURE 9–16 Structure of the federal government of Canada

What Government Does

In general, we expect government to do things that keep Canada safe, prosperous, and strong. Beyond these basics, Canadians are often divided about how much of a role government ought to play in our lives. Think back to what you learned about ideology. Political parties often identify themselves by describing what they think government should do, and what the relationship between citizens and government ought to be. Usually this means that they think government should do more, including enhancing social services, or less. They also have plans for spending and taxation. In Canada, parties to the right of centre want less government involvement and lower taxes, while those on the left want more government involvement and think that taxes should pay for needed services.

Taxes and Spending

It is always important to know how much government takes in taxes, its methods and sources, and the ways it spends the money it collects. Federal and provincial governments collect corporate taxes, income taxes, *ad valorem* **taxes** such as the HST, **excise taxes** such as taxes on alcohol and gas, payroll taxes, and fees on services, which some people think are also a form of taxation. Municipalities rely mostly on property taxes. In Canada, income taxes are graduated—how much a person pays relates to income level. The amount governments take in taxes seldom matches the amount they spend. When a government takes in more than it spends, it has a **surplus**; when it takes in less, it runs a **deficit**. When the deficit increases beyond what a government can repay easily, it borrows money and adds to its debt, on which it pays interest. Money is the lifeblood of government and knowing where it comes from and where it goes is very important to the citizens who, by and large, supply it.

How Government Works

The actual work of government is carried out by the **civil service**, also called the **bureaucracy**. Ideally, the civil service is non-political. Civil servants are organized into ministries, each headed by a minister who, in turn, relies on a deputy minister to oversee the administration of the ministry's work. The government will also have an information office, which will review anything bureaucrats want to report to the public and answer controversial queries. When a citizen has a complaint and writes to the government about it, or when the Opposition has a question, bureaucrats supply the answer. Typically, a response will begin with someone low down in the hierarchy of a ministry, be "signed off" by superiors, and end up with the minister who will answer the question.

KEY TERMS

ad valorem **tax** a tax that is proportional to the value of goods

excise tax an added tax on certain goods produced or sold in the country, for example, alcohol, gas, and tobacco

surplus the amount of money remaining when a government takes in more than it spends

deficit the amount of money a government owes when it takes in less money than it spends

civil service the body of people who work in government administration

bureaucracy officials and administrators who carry out the work of government

FIGURE 9–17 The British Columbia legislative buildings. Like all provinces, British Columbia has a parliament, usually called a legislature, where government ministers have their offices. Bureaucrats in their ministries occupy buildings in cities and towns throughout the province.

Thinking Critically Do you think government services should be centralized in major centres, or located close to where services are needed? Why?

Office of the Prime Minister (PMO) the prime minister's political advisors and staff

Privy Council Office (PCO) the office that organizes the work of the Cabinet

Cabinet solidarity the custom that Cabinet members must not show disagreement with government policies

Order-in-Council an order signed by the Governor General (or the Lieutenant-Governor in the provinces) on the advice of the prime minister (or premier) and Cabinet; allows laws and regulations to be passed without a parliamentary vote

Political parties are fundamental to our parliamentary system, and much of what happens in government relates to party politics. Many of the things done by the party with the mandate (the right to form a government) help the party to keep that mandate. The government party leader at the federal level, the prime minister, has enormous executive power that, in principle, he or she shares with Cabinet. Neither the prime minister nor the Cabinet are directly chosen by the people. Committees play a very important role too, as does the **Office of the Prime Minister (PMO)** and the **Privy Council Office (PCO)**.

The Executive Branch: Consolidating Power

The prime minister, or premier in the provinces, is the chief minister of the Crown and the head of the Cabinet. Together, the prime minister and Cabinet form the executive branch of government. In practice, due to tradition, the prime minister has considerable powers. The prime minister can choose and discipline Cabinet members, directs the activities of the legislature, has the right to be consulted on all important Cabinet decisions, controls appointments to the Senate and to the judiciary, and can recommend that Parliament be adjourned or dissolved and an election called. Publicly, Cabinet ministers must display full support for the prime minister and the decisions of the government. This show of strength is called **Cabinet solidarity**.

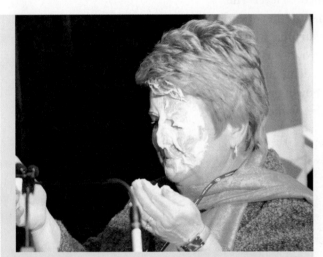

FIGURE 9–18 Federal Fisheries and Oceans Minister Gail Shea received a pie in the face from an animal-rights activist protesting the annual seal hunt, January 2010.

The Cabinet initiates laws, and its ministers are responsible for the smooth running of government and the spending of public money. Usually, but not always, Cabinet ministers are part of the governing party and have a seat in the House of Commons. Members of Cabinet are chosen by the prime minister and are called ministers. Each is responsible for a department of the government, called a portfolio. We have a Minister of Fisheries and Oceans, a Minister of Justice, a Minister of Foreign Affairs, and so on. Once appointed, the minister is held responsible for everything that happens in his or her department. This is called ministerial responsibility, and the minister is expected to resign if certain serious breaches of office take place. The minister introduces new legislation pertaining to the ministry and guides it through the House.

The PMO and the PCO

In the past, the Cabinet was the most powerful part of the federal government next to the prime minister. This has changed as the executive power of the prime minister has grown. The Office of the Prime Minister consists of the prime minister's political advisors and staffers. The Privy Council Office is used by the prime minister to set the agenda for Cabinet meetings and to organize its work. Both the PMO and the PCO are at the service of the prime minister and are staffed by his or her appointed and unelected officials. Some think that these two bodies have too much power.

©P

Orders-in-Council

Orders-in-Council make laws or regulations without the necessity of a parliamentary vote. At the federal level, they are signed by the Governor General on the advice of the prime minister and Cabinet. Orders-in-Council are used for Senate appointments, for necessary changes in law, and in the case of real or perceived emergencies. Although they may seem undemocratic, Orders-in-Council are part of parliamentary tradition, and governments are generally wise to use the power sparingly.

1. Speaker
2. Pages
3. Government Members
4. Opposition Members
5. Prime Minister
6. Leader of the Official Opposition
7. Leader of the Second-Largest Party in Opposition
8. Clerk and Table Officers
9. Mace
10. Hansard Reporters
11. Sergeant-at-Arms
12. The Bar
13. Interpreters
14. Press Gallery
15. Public Gallery
16. Official Gallery
17. Leader of the Opposition's Gallery
18. Members' Gallery
19. Members' Gallery
20. Members' Gallery
21. Speaker's Gallery
22. Senate Gallery
23. TV Cameras

FIGURE 9–19 House of Commons floor plan

PRACTICE QUESTIONS

1. Create a three-column chart showing the three branches of government. For each branch, list the positions and their roles.

2. How does the government pay for its programs?

3. Explain the role of the civil service.

4. What are the responsibilities of Cabinet ministers?

5. Explain the term *Order-in-Council*. Why is it seen as being undemocratic?

KEY TERMS

royal assent the final stage a bill must complete before it is passed into law in which the Governor General (or Lieutenant-Governor in the provinces) signs or grants approval for the bill

Lieutenant-Governor the provincial representative of the Crown appointed by the Governor General

party whip a member of the legislature assigned the specific role of ensuring all members of his or her party are present in the legislature to support party interests

party discipline all party members voting the same way, as one voice

free vote members voting according to their own conscience

backbenchers members of a legislature who are not Cabinet ministers, party leaders, or opposition critics

private member's bill a bill introduced into the legislature by a member of the legislature who is not a member of the Cabinet

Passing Legislation

One of the most significant tasks of parliament is making and passing laws. A bill becomes law in the federal parliament after it goes through three readings in the House of Commons, is amended by a committee, has three readings in the Senate, is signed by the Governor General (referred to as **royal assent**), and is proclaimed. Bills introduced in the provincial legislature must also undergo three readings and are passed into law by the **Lieutenant-Governor** who represents the monarch in the provincial executive.

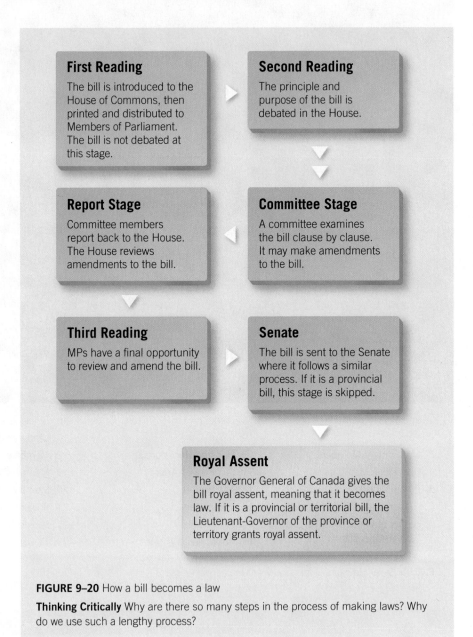

First Reading
The bill is introduced to the House of Commons, then printed and distributed to Members of Parliament. The bill is not debated at this stage.

Second Reading
The principle and purpose of the bill is debated in the House.

Report Stage
Committee members report back to the House. The House reviews amendments to the bill.

Committee Stage
A committee examines the bill clause by clause. It may make amendments to the bill.

Third Reading
MPs have a final opportunity to review and amend the bill.

Senate
The bill is sent to the Senate where it follows a similar process. If it is a provincial bill, this stage is skipped.

Royal Assent
The Governor General of Canada gives the bill royal assent, meaning that it becomes law. If it is a provincial or territorial bill, the Lieutenant-Governor of the province or territory grants royal assent.

FIGURE 9–20 How a bill becomes a law

Thinking Critically Why are there so many steps in the process of making laws? Why do we use such a lengthy process?

©P

Party Loyalty and Party Discipline

Parties make sure their members vote as the party wishes in the legislature. Often they do this through the whip system. The **party whip** makes sure that members of his or her party are in the House of Commons (or legislature in the provinces) for important votes and vote as the party requires. This almost always guarantees that MPs (and MPPs and MLAs at the provincial level) vote as part of a block. In the past, some parties have campaigned against this and promised not to follow the tradition—notably the Progressive Party in the early part of the 20th century and later the Reform Party. Unfortunately for such parties, lack of **party discipline** seriously weakens them and they either break up or change. Whips have various ways to enforce discipline, but mostly they persuade their fellow party members to put the interests of the party first. The party leader, especially as prime minister, has the greatest disciplinary powers.

Free Votes and Private Members' Bills

Some parliamentary procedures seem, on the surface, to be more democratic than others. For example, **free votes** allow members to vote on legislation according to their own conscience, but party leadership will only allow a free vote if it is in the interest of the party for this to happen. For example, in 1987, Prime Minister Brian Mulroney allowed a free vote on reintroducing capital punishment. Mulroney, knowing that a free vote would fail anyway, apparently used it to placate Conservative **backbenchers** who were pressuring the government on the issue.

Most bills are introduced by Cabinet ministers. At the federal level, any member of the House of Commons or the Senate may introduce a bill. If the member is not in the Cabinet, the bill is referred to as a **private member's bill**. Many private members' bills do not get passed. Passing a law requires a great deal of party support, which is rarely the case for a private member's bill. Some federal private members' bills passed in 2008 include an Act respecting a National Peacekeepers' Day, an Act to protect heritage lighthouses, and an Act to increase the criminal penalty for animal cruelty.

FIGURE 9–21 NDP MP Peter Stoffer is known as the King of the Private Member's Bill. In 2009, he introduced a total of 24 bills to the House, including one to remove the GST from funeral costs and another to designate April 6 as Tartan Day. Stoffer states, "If I do have to introduce them to the end of time, that means I'm going to be a very old MP."

PRACTICE QUESTIONS

1. At which stage of passing a bill is it most heavily debated?

2. How do political parties ensure support among their members?

3. When might free votes occur in the House of Commons?

4. Why are private members' bills seldom passed?

Minority Governments: Advantages and Disadvantages

The first goal of a political party is to gain power and the second is to keep it. When a party wins a general election and becomes a **majority government**, hanging onto power is much easier since the party holds more than half the total number of seats in the House of Commons. A majority government can implement its policies and can govern without much compromise. But parties do not always win majorities. **Minority governments** have to compromise to stay in power.

A minority government is one in which the governing party has more seats than any other party, but the other parties combined have more seats than the government. When this happens, the governing party has to be careful not to introduce legislation that will not pass. Votes on budgets and other money bills are votes of confidence and the government traditionally resigns when it loses such a vote. Canada has had a number of minority governments and some people think they are more democratic than majority governments because they are more responsive to the public. However, a party in minority cannot fully implement its policies or make important changes because to do so would risk defeat. Minority governments tend to maintain the **status quo** even if change would be better for the country.

KEY TERMS

majority government a government in which the ruling party has more than half of the total number of seats in the legislature

minority government a government in which the ruling party has more seats than any other party, but the other parties combined have more seats than the government

status quo the existing order of things

coalition a formal alliance of political parties

prorogue Parliament to suspend Parliament for a period of time upon the prime minister's request to the Governor General

dissolve Parliament to call an end to a sitting Parliament, at the request of the prime minister (or premier) to the Governor General (or Lieutenant-Governor in the provinces); followed by a general election

Minority Government 40th Canadian Parliament November 2008 to Present (2010)		
Conservative	143	**143**
Liberal	77	
Bloc Québécois	49	**165**
New Democratic	37	
Independent	2	
Total	308	308

FIGURE 9–22 In the general election of 2008, the Conservatives won more seats than any other party, but not more than the other parties combined. In other words, the Conservatives did not win more than half the total number of seats in the House of Commons, making them a minority government.

Coalitions and Mergers

Ideally, a political party has a platform that represents the pure political views of its members and never compromises these views. In reality, sticking to principles can mean that the party never forms a government, or even becomes significant in opposition. Sometimes, several small parties oppose the government but, individually, none is strong enough to threaten it. When this occurs, parties have two options: they can form a **coalition** in which each party maintains its identity, or they can merge and become a new political party. Canada has had coalition governments in the past, as in the First World War. Parties also merge. In 2003, the Canadian Alliance merged with the Progressive Conservative Party of Canada to form the Conservative Party of Canada, with Stephen Harper as its first leader.

©P

Proroguing Parliament

To **prorogue Parliament** means to suspend it for a period of time until the opening of another session. Members are released from their duties until the next session of Parliament begins. All bills, other than private members' bills, are dropped from the agenda and all committees are dissolved. A government can use prorogation to get itself out of a jam on a particular issue, to kill legislation it has problems with, to shuffle the membership of committees, and to otherwise keep itself in power. Although it is a legitimate use of parliamentary procedure, proroguing often seems undemocratic. Nevertheless, it is part of the gamesmanship of parliament and all governments will use it if it helps them stay in power. Liberal Prime Minister Jean Chrétien prorogued Parliament four times from 1996 to 2003, the last time to allow a new Liberal Party leader, Paul Martin, to be appointed prime minister. The opposition, however, suggested it was done to avoid a sponsorship scandal.

FIGURE 9–23 Citizens protest Prime Minister Harper's proroguing of Parliament, January 2010. The government claimed it needed time to consult with Canadians on their economic action plan. Opposition parties claimed the prorogation was undemocratic and that the prime minister was using it to avoid dealing with difficult issues.

Dissolution

A parliament ends when the Governor General (or Lieutenant-Governor in the provinces) **dissolves** it, which is always done at the prime minister's (or premier's) request. This happens when the government loses a vote of non-confidence or when the prime minister wishes to call a general election. The ability to ask for dissolution, and thus call an election, at a time of its choosing gives the governing party the huge advantage of being able to avoid elections when it is weak and to hold them when it is strong. The prime minister can also use the threat of an election to discipline backbenchers who are rebelling against his or her leadership. In any case, once a parliament is dissolved, an election campaign officially starts.

PRACTICE QUESTIONS

1. Define *majority* and *minority governments*. Describe the benefits and challenges for each of these types of governments.

2. Explain the term *prorogue*. Why is it seen as undemocratic?

3. Under what circumstances might Parliament be dissolved?

● What does active citizenship look like in Canadian politics?

Can citizens have more input in the processes of government?

In our parliamentary system, new policies and laws originate within the caucus of the governing political party and the Cabinet. In other words, relatively few people set the country's agenda during the government's time in office. This is reasonable when electors know and understand the platform of the governing party. They, in a sense, have given approval for its policies by electing it. What happens when policies or new initiatives are introduced without consulting the public? Or when the party that won the most seats, but not a majority of the popular vote, takes power? Should citizens then have more input into government? Or would this be counter-productive and make government more difficult?

Earlier in this chapter, you learned about ways to provide feedback to your government representative. But expressing an opinion is different than having a direct say in what happens in government. Does it make sense to give people a more direct say in decision making?

Would it help if parties allowed more free votes so that legislators could vote as their **constituents** directed? In practice, parties rarely allow free votes. Former NDP MLA Dennis Streifel in British Columbia once suggested that the public should be allowed to participate in question period, and that new legislation be publicly debated before it is even introduced.

Referendums and Minority Rights

In theory, using a **referendum** seems like a very democratic way to involve the general public in decision-making. In fact, governments hold very few referendums, since they can cost millions of dollars and voters usually have to respond with a simple "yes" or "no" to complex issues. Also, while it might be fair to ask all people in the country to approve or reject some measure that affects everyone more or less equally, is the same true for measures that deal with minority rights? What happens when a referendum is based on minority rights?

In 2002, British Columbia held a referendum on eight principles designed to guide the Liberal government in Aboriginal treaty negotiations. People voted either yes or no for each principle.

Aboriginal leaders and other critics protested that the referendum questions were simplistic and misleading, and that the voting process was too complicated. More than 80 percent voted yes to all eight principles, which the government promised to use to guide it in treaty negotiations. Many Aboriginal peoples, who represent less than 5 percent of the population of the province and could not possibly carry the vote, boycotted the process.

More input into government means more direct democracy, which requires people to accept their responsibilities as active citizens. This means actively learning about legislation and policy and about how government operates. Would this happen? Only two percent of people actually join political parties and a large sector of the population does not even vote in elections. Voter apathy has important ramifications. When large numbers of voters do not participate, the influence of those that do is magnified. The issue of increasing citizen input into the processes of government is complicated and it is debatable whether it is desirable.

Analyzing the Issue

1. Create an organizer to show the pros and cons of each of the reforms suggested.

2. a) Should the general public be able to participate during question period? Why or why not?
   b) Draw up a plan for allowing citizens to participate in question period. Consider, for example, who would choose the questions, how many citizen questions would be asked, and if the government would be made aware of the questions beforehand.

3. Do you think that citizens should have more say in deciding government policy? Consider the pros and cons and explain your answer.

4. Why are so few referendums held?

5. Was the 2002 referendum on B.C. treaty negotiations fair or unfair? Explain. Why might such a referendum cause anger among minority groups?

Choosing the Government

As you saw in Figure 9–16, the federal Parliament of Canada consists of the Senate and the House of Commons. Members of the Senate are appointed by the Governor General on the recommendation of the prime minister. Members of the House of Commons are elected by citizens in general elections. Representation in the House of Commons is based on geographical divisions known as **electoral districts**, commonly called **ridings** or **constituencies**. Since Canada's population is spread over an immense area, some electoral districts are very large and sparsely populated. Nunavut is a good example, covering 2 million square kilometres and serving approximately 29 000 people. Papineau in Québec, Canada's smallest riding, covers only nine square kilometres and serves a population of almost 104 000.

KEY TERMS

constituent a voter in a riding

referendum a direct vote in which everyone is asked to either accept or reject a particular proposal

electoral district, riding, constituency a geographical area of a given size or population used as a unit in elections

Chief Electoral Officer an independent officer of Parliament responsible for federal elections

voter apathy reluctance or lack of interest in voting

Election Basics

The **Chief Electoral Officer** is an independent officer of Parliament who is responsible for managing federal elections and referendums in Canada. Elections are held at least every five years for federal and provincial parliaments. In British Columbia, election days are set for every four years and municipal elections are held on the same day every three years. All Canadian citizens over 18 years of age are eligible to cast a ballot in an election.

Voting in elections is how citizens choose the government. Provincial voter participation varies from election to election and from province to province. Participation in municipal elections also varies considerably, but is usually lower than in provincial or federal elections. Depending on the size of the municipality and the election issues, voter turnout can range from 20 to 70 percent.

FIGURE 9–24 Democracy requires active citizens to take part in the electoral process.

Those who choose not to vote make the votes of others more important. Some say that not voting means that one has no right to criticize the policies or conduct of the ruling party. Certainly, it is less likely that whoever forms the government will share one's views if one does not vote for the candidate who does. In some elections, fewer than half of eligible voters cast a ballot. The successful candidate may represent the views of a minority of eligible voters. Low voter turnout or **voter apathy** is a real problem for Canadian democracy (see Case Study on page 318).

Party Mechanics

Political parties regularly hold conventions to discuss the party platform and other important issues, such as the need to pick or change a party leader. Traditionally, leadership races were held at conventions and generated a lot of publicity for the party. Currently all parties have adopted a "one-member, one-vote" system to choose a new party leader, which means that each registered member of the party has one vote, thereby having a direct say in who will lead their party. The winning candidate must receive a majority of votes, either through multiple ballots or a preferential ballot.

WEB LINK •

For more information on Canada's electoral system, visit the Pearson Web site.

● What are the steps of the electoral process in Canada?

Choosing Candidates

Political parties always wish to pick the best candidates to run in elections. Whether the chosen person can win the riding or constituency is important but there are other qualities to consider. The person must be loyal to the party and be able to take on the responsibilities of an elected member, perhaps even of a Cabinet minister. In addition, the person should not be an embarrassment or have a personal history that might harm the party.

Parties have their own ways and criteria for choosing candidates. Sometimes leaders personally choose the candidate to run in a riding. Others are chosen by riding associations. Since the person's **nomination** papers must have the leader's signature, all candidates must be acceptable to the party leadership. Becoming a candidate gives a person an opportunity to become a member of the federal parliament or the provincial legislature. When a party has held a riding for a long time, election of its candidate is somewhat guaranteed. It may be very difficult for other parties to get elected in that riding. Why, then, do people run when they are likely to lose? Sometimes, it is a matter of political presence. The candidate hopes to show, through effort and loyalty, that he or she has a place in the party. This allows the person to gradually build a reputation and gain influence.

Most of the major political parties have special youth wings that allow young people under 18 to have input into policies and future directions for the party. Youth wings often have considerable influence over party policies, because they ensure the party's survival in the future.

Articulating the Party Platform

A political party crafts its platform very carefully as it contains the party's central message in an election campaign. The platform tells voters what to expect if the party is elected and outlines its political philosophy. There is no guarantee, voters realize, that the party's platform will be realized should it gain power. But the platform is important as a statement of intent. Candidates and party spokespeople must know the platform by heart and be consistent with its message, even if they do not agree with some features. Parties also employ spin doctors who make sure news that is bad for the party is "spun" in the media so that it seems less important or misunderstood.

1. Dissolution	2. Enumeration	3. Nomination	4. Campaigning	5. Voting or Balloting	6. Tabulating
The Governor General dissolves Parliament; a federal or general election is called.	A national list of voters is compiled.	Political parties choose candidates to run in each constituency or riding.	Parties seek to increase public awareness and support, as well as to raise money.	Eligible voters visit polling stations to register and cast their vote.	Votes are counted and a winning candidate is declared for each constituency or riding.

FIGURE 9–25 Steps to a federal election in Canada

©P

Public Opinion Polls

During elections, parties and others poll public opinion, and the media report the results. Parties allocate a small percentage of their campaign budget to polling. Polling companies contact people from a statistical cross-section of the population that represents the views and opinions of voters. **Pollsters** ask about candidates, party leaders, party positions and statements, the issues, and other things. Then they tabulate and interpret the results, which they give to party strategists. Campaign organizers will often change candidate speeches, ads and commercials, debate responses, blogs, and even the candidate's appearance to reflect what they have learned from the polls.

Public opinion polls published during election campaigns can affect voter choices. Voters may believe their vote is unnecessary, even wasted, if one party seems to have a large lead just prior to an election. Or they may switch their vote to be with the winner. For this reason, the results of public opinion polls cannot be published or broadcast on election day.

Election Campaigns

The prime minister calls an election by asking the Governor General to dissolve Parliament. This is usually done near the end of his or her five-year term when public opinion polls show that the ruling party is popular, but there are strategic reasons to consider as well. In 2000, Prime Minister Jean Chrétien called an election less than three and a half years into his term—before the new, untried leader of the Canadian Alliance Party, Stephen Harper, could garner wide public support. Where possible, a party will look for a chance to split the vote that might go to a rival. For example, many of the people who support the Green Party might also support the NDP. It is therefore in the interests of the B.C. Liberals, for example, to provide an issue that will polarize the vote for these parties, while not affecting its own core vote.

Most candidates in federal and provincial elections are members of political parties, although some run as independents. A candidate needs money and plenty of volunteers to run an election campaign. Citizens often become actively involved at this stage, answering phones, distributing campaign literature, putting up signs, canvassing for support from door to door, driving voters to polling stations, and raising money.

Political parties usually pay for their campaigns with donations from individuals. Campaigning costs are high. Some candidates have lots of money to spend, while others do not. This can distort the election process, giving an advantage to the candidate who can pay for an image or presentation that attracts voters. Some believe that expensive advertising and other campaign tactics divert attention from real issues and problems, which are glossed over or ignored.

FIGURE 9–26 Volunteers on the campaign trail

Gathering Information
Why are volunteers necessary to a democracy? What jobs do they do?

The Voting Process

Polling stations have nothing to do with voter opinion polls. They are the places where citizens in a riding cast their ballots on election day. (People who are unable to vote on election day may cast their ballots earlier at **advance polls**.) Polling stations are often in schools or public buildings. Voting is not complicated. When you arrive at a polling station, your name is crossed off the **voters list** and you are given a ballot. Voting, putting an X in the circle beside the candidate's name on the ballot, takes place behind a privacy screen. No campaign signs or literature are allowed at or around the polling station. When the polls close, **electoral officers** count the votes. The candidate with the most votes in a riding wins the riding and a seat in the legislature.

What happens when a seat is vacated in the middle of a legislative session, for example, if a Member of Parliament passes away? A smaller **by-election** is held to fill the vacant seat.

Voter Apathy

One of the most worrying trends in Western democracies is that voter apathy, the reluctance of people to vote, is increasing. Voter turnout has also declined in France, Britain, the United States, and other countries. Even in the 2008 election in the United States that brought Barack Obama to power, only about 60 percent of the population voted. In Canada, voter turnout has declined from around 75 percent in 1988 to around 59 percent in 2008. The problem is even greater in British Columbia where the voting rate is only 50 percent (2009). The causes of voter apathy are not well understood, but it is a serious problem for democracy. In Canada, as in other countries, the relationship between age and interest level seems to be a factor, as the following chart shows.

WEB LINK • ·
For more information on voter apathy among adults and youth, visit the Pearson Web site.

Importance of reason for not voting (% very or fairly important)	68+	58–67	48–57	38–47	30–37	25–29	21–24	18–20	Total
Just not interested	31.4	34.0	46.4	50.6	51.8	59.3	57.0	59.1	52.9
Didn't like parties/candidates	41.7	40.8	56.0	50.9	46.9	43.2	50.7	45.3	47.6
Vote wouldn't matter	30.6	37.5	47.1	37.9	41.1	36.7	34.3	30.4	37.1
Didn't care about issues	42.9	28.0	35.7	37.3	36.6	32.8	37.7	36.5	36.0
Busy at work	16.7	14.3	16.5	24.8	36.9	33.9	38.6	40.9	32.2
Out of town	19.4	34.7	16.7	19.3	18.3	21.5	25.1	24.8	21.8
Didn't know where or when	28.6	12.2	12.9	9.4	19.2	24.4	28.5	28.4	21.1
Not on the list	25.7	16.3	15.5	16.8	16.0	20.3	18.4	24.2	18.7
Too many elections	26.2	24.5	20.0	18.5	21.4	16.5	13.0	9.5	17.3
Illness	41.7	20.4	11.9	11.8	8.5	10.7	9.2	10.8	11.7

FIGURE 9–27 Reasons given for not voting in a federal election, by age group

©P

FPTP Versus STV

Canadian elections are decided by the **first-past-the-post (FPTP)** system. The winner does not necessarily have to win a majority of the votes cast; he or she simply has to win more votes than any of the other candidates. This system has the virtue of being simple and straightforward. Its supporters also argue that it means there is usually a clear winner of elections and that minority governments do not often happen. However, the result does not always represent the wishes of the majority of voters.

In 2004, the Citizens' Assembly on Electoral Reform recommended that British Columbia replace FPTP with **single transferable vote (STV)**, which would have allowed a form of proportional representation. That is, parties would gain seats by the proportion of votes they received in a large electoral district rather than having a single party win a riding by simple majority. British Columbians overwhelmingly rejected STV in a referendum in 2009.

KEY TERMS

polling stations locations where citizens in a riding vote

advance polls locations where people can vote in advance of election day

voters list a list of persons eligible to vote

electoral officers Elections Canada officials who count the votes

by-election an election held in a riding to fill a vacancy

first-past-the-post (FPTP) an electoral system in which the candidate who has more votes than any other candidate wins

single transferable vote (STV) an electoral system in which parties gain seats by the proportion of votes won in large electoral districts

FASTFORWARD

Electronic Voting

Can technology increase the effectiveness of democracy? Various democratic countries around the world are exploring electronic voting via electronic kiosks, the telephone, or the Internet. In Canada, electronic voting has occurred at both provincial and municipal levels, but not yet at the federal level. Electronic voting has resulted in increased voter participation.

1. What are other advantages of electronic voting? What are some disadvantages?

2. **Cause and Consequence** How might electronic voting, especially by telephone or on the Internet, change voter participation for different age groups?

FIGURE 9–28

PRACTICE QUESTIONS

1. Do you think the voting age should be lowered to 17? Why or why not?

2. How are constituencies determined?

3. How often are elections held? Be specific.

4. How are candidates selected by their parties?

5. What is meant by the term *party platform*? Why is it important?

6. Why are public opinion polls valuable to political parties?

7. What is the purpose of election campaigns? How are they funded?

8. Explain the term *voter apathy*. What are the main reasons people do not vote?

9. Explain the positives and negatives for FPTP and STV.

Compulsory Voting in Australia

FIGURE 9–29 Australians at the polls

What is democracy worth? Should we allow uninterested people in one or two generations to throw away rights that have taken centuries to achieve simply because people are not interested enough to vote? Voter apathy is a serious problem for democracies such as ours, but it is one that is difficult to solve. Some countries, such as Australia, make voting compulsory. In fact, many other countries require citizens to vote, although some do not enforce the law. Would compulsory voting be a good idea for Canada? Is compulsory voting, a measure designed to ensure citizens accept their responsibility to maintain democracy, actually undemocratic?

How Compulsory Voting Works

By law, Australians over the age of 18 must register to vote. Votes are always held on Saturdays when all voters must attend a polling station and vote in private "without delay." Since the vote is secret, officials do not check to see whether the ballot is marked correctly or even marked at all. Electors who fail to vote must satisfactorily explain themselves to the Returning Officer or face a $20 fine or be jailed. About five percent of voters either accidentally or deliberately spoil their ballot.

Compulsory voting is, surprisingly, not very controversial in Australia (almost 60 to 70 percent are in favour). Those who oppose it say that compulsory voting denies people their democratic right not to vote, that it penalizes those who cannot find a candidate or party to vote for, that it makes things easy for political parties, and so on. Supporters claim that, among other things, compulsory voting is no more undemocratic than serving on juries or paying taxes, that it makes certain that all parts of the electorate are represented, and that it increases interest in the issues and in politics in general.

Countries with compulsory voting (CV) that is enforced	
Argentina	Australia
Austria	Belgium
Brazil	Chile
Cyprus	Ecuador
Fiji	Greece
Lichtenstein	Luxembourg
Mexico	Nauru
Peru	Singapore
Switzerland (one canton only)	Turkey
Uruguay	

Countries with compulsory voting that is not enforced	
Bolivia	Costa Rica
Dominican Republic	Egypt (male voters only)
France (Senate only)	Gabon
Guatemala	Honduras
Italy	the Netherlands
Paraguay	Philippines
Thailand	

©P

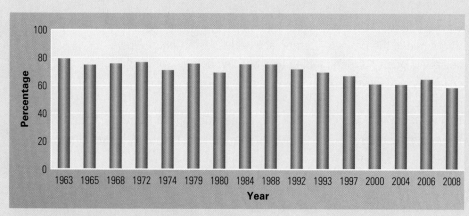

FIGURE 9–30 Voter turnout, Canada, 1963–2008

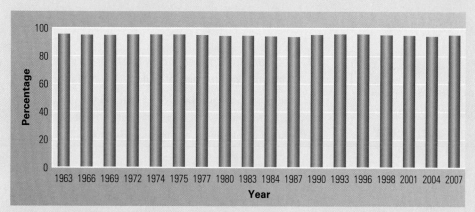

FIGURE 9–31 Voter turnout, Australia, 1963–2007

Looking Further

1. Why do you think some countries with compulsory voting do not enforce the practice?

2. Compare the graphs above. What conclusion can you draw from them?

3. Create a PMI chart on compulsory voting in Canada.

4. People criticize the referendum process because a referendum on issues may result in the "tyranny of the majority." Should issues be resolved through compulsory voting in referendums? Explain your position.

5. Review Figure 9–27. What were the major reasons for each age group not voting? Do you think that compulsory voting might change their attitudes? Why or why not?

CHAPTER FOCUS QUESTION   How are governments formed in Canada and how can individuals influence government?

To be effective and active citizens, we need to know about ideologies, alternative systems of government, how our own system works, and our role in the process. Democracy works best when groups of people join together to try to achieve certain goals. Understanding how our democracy works and taking part in the process are essential features of active citizenship.

1. Create a mind map for the unit. Use each of the guiding questions as a category for your mind map (see the Chapter 9 opening spread). Your mind map should do the following.

   • Convey a clear central idea. Use graphics, humour, or metaphor to communicate the idea.

   • Show ideas moving out from the central idea, from most to least complex. Include images to add visual interest.

   • Use colours to make connections between ideas.

   • Cover all guiding questions and Key Terms and demonstrate your understanding.

Vocabulary Focus

2. Check your knowledge of the Key Terms on page 289 by forming pairs and then writing the terms and their meanings on separate index cards. Shuffle both piles and exchange them with another pair of students. Match the terms with their meanings as quickly as possible and check your results. Reshuffle the cards and hand them on to another team and repeat the exercise until all teams have matched all terms and meanings.

Knowledge and Understanding

3. Why do you think so few people join political parties in Canada? What advice would you give to party organizations to help them recruit members from your age group?

4. Describe the role of the media in the democratic process.

5. Describe how professional lobbyists, pressure groups, and polls influence government.

6. Do you think it is appropriate for lobbyists to do favours or raise money for politicians? Explain.

7. You have just formed a new provincial (or federal) party, the Youth Party of British Columbia (or Canada). Develop policy statements covering at least three different areas of government. What issues would you want to see on the political agenda?

8. Make a list of suggestions for increasing voter turnout in federal and provincial elections. How might you persuade students to vote in school elections? Would you use similar or different techniques to promote voter turnout?

9. How might social networking make participating in the democratic process more appealing to youth?

10. Why do you think voters are hesitant to change from the FPTP to STV?

Critical Thinking

11. You may work in small groups to create a graphic organizer, such as a flow chart, with the individual as the focus. Consider important national, provincial, or municipal issues and use the organizer to describe how citizens can take action to address those issues. Consider the role of the media, government, pressure groups, individual citizens, and the private sector.

Evidence

12. Why do you think the majority of Canadian citizens do not make the effort to vote in elections? If this trend continues, what effect might it have on our government?

13. How legitimate is a government that is established when voter turnout is less than 60 percent?

14. How do you think people in non-democratic countries might view Canada's government?

15. People who live in democracies often criticize governments where citizens' rights are not respected. In what ways could those countries be critical of Canada and its government selection?

Document Analysis

16. View the cartoon in Figure 9–32 and answer the following questions.

a) What does the term *prorogue* mean?

b) Describe how Prime Minister Harper is being portrayed by the cartoonist. What message is being sent by this portrayal?

c) Describe the way Canada has been illustrated. Why did the cartoonist choose to show Canada in this way?

d) Is there evidence of bias on the part of the cartoonist? Provide examples.

e) Explain the play on words used by the cartoonist.

FIGURE 9–32

10 Protecting Human Rights

GUIDING QUESTIONS

Society & Identity

- How are minority rights protected in the Canadian Charter of Rights and Freedoms?

- How have affirmative action programs affected the workplace and why are they controversial?

- What human rights apply to children?

Politics & Government

- How does the Canadian Charter of Rights and Freedoms protect human rights in Canada?

- Are there any limits to our rights and freedoms?

- What is the significance of the notwithstanding clause?

- What are the fundamental rights and freedoms defined in the Charter?

- How are human rights protected in British Columbia?

- Why is the amending formula important?

Autonomy & World Presence

- What is the role of the United Nations in protecting human rights?

- How does Canada participate in human rights issues?

TIMELINE

1941
U.S. President Roosevelt calls for the right of peoples everywhere to four basic freedoms: freedom of speech and expression, freedom of religious worship, freedom from want, and freedom from fear

1945
The United Nations forms with Roosevelt's four basic freedoms as the basis of its charter

1948
The United Nations adopts the Universal Declaration of Human Rights

UN Convention on the Prevention and Punishment of the Crime of Genocide

1949
Four Geneva Conventions establish rules for the humane treatment of military personnel, prisoners of war, and civilians

©P

CHAPTER FOCUS QUESTION

What are human rights and how are they protected in Canada?

Living in Canada today, you enjoy the guarantee of rights and freedoms that are denied to people in many countries. It is hard to imagine that these rights and freedoms were not always a part of life in Canada. In previous chapters, you have read about how Aboriginal peoples, women, and minorities in Canada have struggled to achieve their political and civil rights. The ongoing struggle of Aboriginals for self-determination, the fight for women's suffrage, and the forced internment of Japanese Canadians during the Second World War are part of Canada's human rights history.

Canada's laws reflect our common values. As a society, we choose to have laws that protect children, workers on the job, the aged, and minorities. Our laws also recognize and protect basic rights and freedoms. Perhaps most important, we have the right to oppose laws that we feel are unjust and to work to change established laws by legal means.

In this chapter, you will explore human rights and how they are defined by the United Nations. You will learn about Canada's efforts to guarantee human rights for all its citizens, in particular Aboriginal peoples, women, children, and visible minorities.

> *Peace, in the sense of the absence of war, is of little value to someone who is dying of hunger or cold. It will not remove the pain of torture inflicted on a prisoner of conscience. It does not comfort those who have lost their loved ones in floods caused by senseless deforestation in a neighboring country. Peace can only last where human rights are respected, where the people are fed, and where individuals and nations are free.*
>
> *–The Dalai Lama, 1989*

KEY TERMS

Universal Declaration of Human Rights

Canadian Bill of Rights

Canadian Charter of Rights and Freedoms

notwithstanding clause

democratic rights

language rights

fundamental freedoms

mobility rights

equality rights

affirmative action

minority rights

legal rights

amending formula

employment equity

1959	1960	1965	1981	1982	1989	2007
UN Declaration of the Rights of the Child	Canada passes the Bill of Rights	International Convention on the Elimination of All Forms of Racial Discrimination	UN Convention on the Elimination of All Forms of Discrimination Against Women comes into force	Canadian Charter of Rights and Freedoms	UN Convention on the Rights of the Child	UN adopts the Declaration on the Rights of Indigenous Peoples

KEY TERMS

Universal Declaration of Human Rights
the United Nations outline of the rights to
which all human beings are entitled

ratified approved

What Are Human Rights?

The term *human rights* is used so frequently, and in so many different situations, that a simple definition is hard to find. Many believe that human rights are rights that are considered basic to life in any human society. They include the rights to adequate food and shelter and protection from abuses such as torture. But we often use the term *human rights* to describe other rights—such as freedom of speech, thought, expression, and religion, or the political and legal protections outlined in Chapter 9. Other people would add to the list the rights to adequate health care, a basic education, and freedom from economic bondage.

The concept of human rights can vary from culture to culture. In some cultures, women must be completely covered in public and remain separated from men, except in the privacy of their home. Is this an infringement of their human rights? To some people, these cultural practices seem unfair; yet members of this culture would argue that North American society places too much emphasis on the individual and not enough on society as a whole.

Despite these different points of view, many people believe that some moral values are, or should be, universal. These are the foundation for human rights around the world.

The Global Movement for Human Rights

Concern for the protection of human rights became a global issue after the atrocities committed during the Second World War. The timeline below outlines some human rights abuses that have taken place in the last 100 years. These and other atrocities have strengthened the resolve of the United Nations and human rights organizations to protect the basic rights of all people, regardless of where they live. This global movement for human rights has become increasingly influential in bringing about change in some countries. For example, pressure from human rights organizations helped end the racist system of *apartheid* in South Africa.

Human rights organizations have also helped expose the issue of child labour in many countries. Even governments have started including human rights abuses as topics for discussion with other governments. Rights groups have pressured successive Canadian governments to link human rights with trade talks, hoping to persuade some of Canada's trading partners to improve human rights in their countries.

FIGURE 10–1 Amnesty International is an organization working to protect human rights around the world. It is particularly concerned with violations of freedom of speech and religion and the imprisonment and torture of people who speak out against their government.

Interpreting an Image What does the candle wrapped in barbed wire symbolize? Why do you think the logo is effective?

TIMELINE	Human Rights Abuses							
1870–1996	**1900–1969**	**1924–1953**	**1939–1945**	**1948–1994**	**1959–**	**1971**	**1971–1979**	**1973–1990**
Indian Act and residential schools, Canada	Australia's "Stolen Generation"	Millions executed or died of starvation in Soviet Union under Stalin	Holocaust, Europe	Apartheid, South Africa	Chinese occupation of Tibet	Bangladesh Liberation War	Idi Amin's dictatorship in Uganda	Pinochet government in Chile

The Universal Declaration of Human Rights

The **Universal Declaration of Human Rights** was proclaimed at the United Nations General Assembly in 1948. The Declaration is based on the belief that "all human beings are born free and equal in dignity and rights." It condemns the "barbarous acts which have outraged the conscience of mankind," a reference to the horrors of the Holocaust of the Second World War. This document is significant because it was the first international statement recognizing that all human beings have specific rights and freedoms.

The Declaration was adopted unanimously by UN member states. The Canadian federal and provincial governments have signed and **ratified** the Declaration, and it is now binding on Canada in international law. This means that individuals in Canada can complain to the UN's Human Rights Committee if they believe the Canadian government is not meeting UN standards.

The United Nations has succeeded in getting most countries to agree with the general principles of the Universal Declaration of Human Rights. Non-governmental organizations (NGOs) have also played a role in promoting acceptance of the UN Declaration in developing countries. Yet, the only power the United Nations has to enforce the provisions of the Declaration is to draw world attention to abuses, putting pressure on offending countries. The Declaration is not part of binding international law. However, its acceptance by most countries around the world gives great moral weight to the fundamental principle that all human beings—rich and poor, strong and weak, male and female, of all races and religions—are to be treated equally and with respect for their natural worth as human beings.

● What is the role of the United Nations in protecting human rights?

● How does Canada participate in human rights issues?

WEB LINK ●

The full text of the Universal Declaration of Human Rights and more information on the human rights abuses in the timeline can be found on the Pearson Web site.

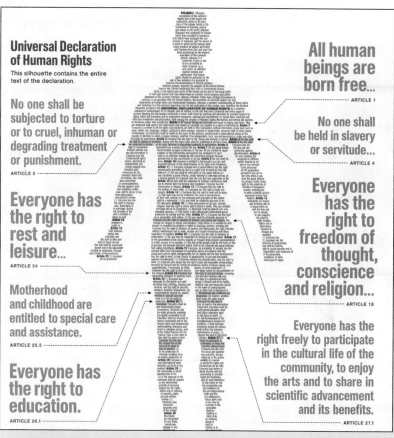

FIGURE 10–2 This silhouette contains the entire text of the Universal Declaration of Human Rights.

Thinking Critically What is the intended purpose and audience for this poster? How could the poster be more effective at getting its message across to the audience? What title would you give this poster?

1975–1979	1975–	1989	1991–1999	1992–1995	1994	1997–1998	1999	2004
Cambodian genocide by Khmer Rouge	Civil war (1975–1990) and ongoing abuses of freedoms in Lebanon	Tiananmen Square Massacre, China	Civil war in Sierra Leone kills more than 50 000 people, including child soldiers	Bosnian War	Rwandan genocide	Burmese army tortures and kills civilians of Shan State, Myanmar	Violence against supporters of independence from Indonesia in East Timor	Darfur genocide

cultural exceptionalism the belief that human values vary by culture and that human rights should be interpreted according to ethnic, cultural, or religious traditions

International Courts and Tribunals

Who makes sure that human rights are protected? In 1946, the United Nations established the International Court of Justice (ICJ) at The Hague, Netherlands, to settle disputes between countries based on international law. But this court becomes involved only if both sides agree to ask for its help. The UN also establishes temporary courts, or tribunals, to deal with specific events. Examples of tribunals include the Nuremberg and Tokyo trials, which dealt with atrocities committed during the Second World War in Europe and the Pacific.

During the Cold War, the protection of human rights was left to individual countries and violations often went unpunished. With the end of the Cold War came a renewed effort to bring those who are responsible for gross violations of human rights and humanitarian law to justice. In the 1990s, temporary tribunals were set up to investigate war crimes in Kosovo, part of the former Yugoslavia, and the genocide in Rwanda. International criminal tribunals have also been established to deal with human rights violations in Cambodia, Sierra Leone, Lebanon, and East Timor.

Many agencies, including Amnesty International, called for a permanent international court to deal with human rights abuses. By 2002, 60 countries established a permanent International Criminal Court (ICC) that would have the power to investigate and prosecute individuals, including political leaders, who commit war crimes, genocide, or crimes against humanity. Some countries, such as the United States and China, were against the creation of the ICC. Opponents say they are not willing to let an international body interfere in areas of law affecting their citizens. Despite this opposition, convictions have occurred in various international tribunals established to deal with individual cases.

FIGURE 10–3 Louise Arbour is the Canadian judge who was appointed as the chief UN war crimes prosecutor at the ICJ and later as UN High Commissioner for Human Rights. Here she tours Bosnia as part of her investigation into war crimes in the former Yugoslavia.

Using Evidence How might visits to the sites of atrocities help judges decide cases involving genocide and war crimes?

PRACTICE QUESTIONS

1. In your own words, define the term *human rights*.

2. Look at the timeline on pages 324–325. How many of these human rights abuses have you heard about? Which did you find the most disturbing? Are you surprised by the number of incidents around the world? Why do you think that we hear more about some atrocities and not others?

3. What is the significance of the Universal Declaration of Human Rights? Why did the members of the United Nations feel it was necessary to prepare the Declaration?

4. What are the problems of enforcing the Declaration?

5. What is the purpose of the ICC? Name a case that has been heard by the court.

Are universal standards for human rights possible in a world of diverse cultural and religious beliefs?

As you read earlier, the UN adopted the Universal Declaration of Human Rights (UDHR) in 1948 in response to the atrocities of the Second World War. Since then, it has added conventions to deal with specific issues, such as economic or social rights, genocide, children, and women. Most countries in the UN have signed the UDHR, but not all of them follow its provisions.

UN Diversity

Since 1948, the world and the UN have changed. In 2010 the UN had 192 member states representing diverse cultures and ideas. This diversity has made agreement on human rights difficult, as some of the UDHR's ideals do not fit with all cultural traditions.

People who object to a universal definition of human rights claim that: rights are specific to a culture; the community comes before individuals; and rights are a matter of national sovereignty. Some people believe that applying universal standards to developing countries hinders their development. They argue that human values vary by cultural perspectives and human rights should be interpreted according to ethnic, cultural, or religious traditions. According to this view, called **cultural exceptionalism**, human rights are cultural rather than universal. While the condemnation of

wide-scale violence or genocide is generally approved, it is harder to deal with human rights violations that fall into the category of cultural practices, such as female genital mutilation (a traditional or religious practice in which the external female genitalia are partially or totally removed).

Tension in a Digital Age

The recent growth of the Internet, blogs, and social networking sites has made society increasingly global and multicultural. Some people embrace the digital revolution and global culture. Others resent its influence and see it as a means of promoting Western culture. For example, men and women can interact openly in Western societies, but this clashes with cultural and religious conventions in some Islamic states where the morality police can arrest a man and woman out in public if they cannot prove they are related.

The West is not immune to cultural exceptionalism. Canada, for example, sees the treatment of Aboriginal peoples as a domestic issue. In 1981, the UN Human Rights Committee found Canada in breach of the International Covenant on Civil and Political Rights over sexual discrimination in the Indian Act. More recently, Canada refused to sign the UN Declaration on the Rights of Indigenous Peoples. The United States also claims exemption from many international treaties in the interests of its national security and human rights covenants. For example, the U.S. and Somalia were the only two countries that did not sign the Convention on the Rights of the Child.

FIGURE 10–4 A girl performs domestic labour in a rural Mauritanian encampment. The International Labour Organization estimates there are at least 80 million working children in Africa.

Thinking Critically Assess the extent to which the labour of these children should be considered a human rights issue. What would be the effect on these nations if child labour were forbidden?

Analyzing the Issue

1. What are the principal problems in having all countries accept the UDHR?

2. To what extent do you think universal human rights can exist in a culturally diverse world?

3. To what degree do you think the communications revolution will help in the acceptance of universal standards for human rights?

KEY TERMS

rule of law the principle that laws apply to all members of society equally; no one is above the law

Canadian Bill of Rights a bill passed in 1960 that outlined human rights for Canadians

Human Rights Legislation in Canada

In Canada, we are governed by a fixed set of laws that apply to all people equally, regardless of their position in society. This **rule of law** helps to protect our rights and prevent those in authority from abusing their power. It also means that police can only charge an individual for a specific offence, and then only by following proper legal procedures.

Before the Second World War, there were few laws to protect human rights apart from some individual property, criminal, and civil laws. Attitudes began to change after 1945, and the rights of minority groups in particular gradually improved. In 1947, Canadians of Chinese and East Indian descent won the right to vote, and Canadians of Japanese origin won this right in 1948. But it was 1960 before Aboriginal peoples on reserves could vote. Even after gaining the right to vote, many Canadians of non-European descent still faced racism and discrimination:

> The postwar trend in Chinatown was for anyone who could afford better accommodation to move out. Like other Canadian families, Chinese families had aspirations to own their own homes. However, they did not necessarily have their choice of neighborhood. Mr. Gee had put down a deposit on a house in Kitsilano, a crowded middle-class neighborhood that rose up the slope from English Bay. When white neighbors got wind that a Chinese family wanted to move in, they amassed a petition against him. He walked away, losing his deposit.
>
> –**Denise Chong**, The Concubine's Children, *1994*

FIGURE 10–5 The Magna Carta is a symbol of the rule of law. In 1215 CE, King John of England approved this document, which stated that the law applies to everyone equally, including the ruler.

The Canadian Bill of Rights

Since signing the Universal Declaration of Human Rights in 1948, the Canadian government has taken steps to protect human rights in Canada. When he became prime minister, John Diefenbaker made the passing of a bill of rights a priority. In 1960, Diefenbaker's government passed the **Canadian Bill of Rights**. This bill formally outlined and recognized rights already held by Canadians under common law. However, as an act of Parliament, the Bill of Rights could be amended or changed like any other piece of legislation, and it did not override other federal or provincial laws. Human rights in Canada were not solidly entrenched in our legal system until 1982, when the Canadian Charter of Rights and Freedoms became part of the new Canadian Constitution.

The Evolution of Human Rights in Canada

1900 — Dominion Elections Act makes the qualifications for voting in federal elections the same as for the provinces. In B.C., visible minorities, Aboriginals, and women are excluded from voting in federal elections.

1903 — Chinese Immigration Act is amended, increasing head tax to $500.

1914 — Continuous Passage Act and *Komagata Maru* incident

1917 — B.C. follows Manitoba, Saskatchewan, and Alberta in granting most white women the right to vote in provincial elections.

1927 — Indian Act makes it illegal for Aboriginal peoples to hire lawyers to pursue land claims without the permission of the Superintendent of Indian Affairs.

1928 — Alberta passes Sexual Sterilization Act requiring patients in psychiatric wards to be sterilized.

1929 — Women are ruled to be "persons" by the Privy Council in England.

1940 — Government uses War Measures Act to ban a number of organizations, including the Communist Party and Jehovah's Witnesses.

1942 — Canadians of Japanese origin are relocated and interned, and their property is confiscated. Doukhobors, Hutterites, and "enemy aliens" are barred from buying land in Alberta.

1948 — Canadian Federal Elections Act is amended to ensure a person's race cannot be a reason to deny the vote in federal elections, excluding Status Indians.

1960 — Status Indians are granted the right to vote in federal elections.

Prime Minister Diefenbaker passes the Canadian Bill of Rights.

1969 — Prime Minister Trudeau's Omnibus Bill decriminalizes homosexuality and makes it legal for women to have an abortion in certain situations.

1970 — War Measures Act is invoked during the October Crisis (see Chapter 7).
Canadian Criminal Code makes it a crime to advocate genocide or publicly incite hatred against people because of their colour, race, religion, or ethnic identity.

1973 — Calder case is seen to be the basis for contemporary Aboriginal law in Canada.

1974 — Thirty-two women are sworn in as the RCMP's first female recruits.

1976 — Capital punishment is removed from the Criminal Code as a penalty for crime in Canada; it is still permitted in the military for treason until 1998.

1977 — All restrictive regulations based on nationality, citizenship, ethnic group, occupation, class, or geographical area of origin are removed from the Canadian Immigration Act.

Canadian Human Rights Act guarantees equal opportunity in areas affecting the federal government; it exempts all decisions and actions taken under the Indian Act.

1982 — Canadian Charter of Rights and Freedoms sets out the basic rights to which all Canadians are entitled and is enshrined in the Constitution Act.

1985 — Indian Act is amended to allow Aboriginal women who married non-Aboriginal men to reclaim their status.

1988 — Canadian government apologizes to Japanese Canadians for internment during Second World War.

1990 — Federal government removes the ban preventing Sikhs in the RCMP from wearing turbans.

1995 — The Supreme Court of Canada rules that sexual orientation is to be judged in the same way as other protected personal characteristics.

1996 — B.C. Human Rights Code becomes law, protecting areas such as employment, housing, and services and facilities customarily available to the public.

1999 — The Supreme Court recognizes same-sex relationships.

2003 — British Columbia becomes the second province, after Ontario, to legalize same-sex marriages.

2006 — Canadian government apologizes for Chinese Head Tax and Chinese immigration exclusions.

2008 — Prime Minister Harper apologizes for the treatment of Aboriginal children in residential schools.

WOMEN   VOTING   ABORIGINAL   IMMIGRATION   OTHER

● How does the Canadian Charter of Rights and Freedoms protect human rights in Canada?

KEY TERMS

Canadian Charter of Rights and Freedoms the bill identifying human rights that are guaranteed to everyone in Canada; enacted in 1982 and embedded in the Constitution of Canada

notwithstanding clause a clause in the Canadian Constitution that enables Parliament or the legislature of a province to allow an Act to stand even though it contravenes the Charter of Rights and Freedoms

democratic rights Charter rights to participate in a democratic society, including voting in elections, guaranteed by the Canadian Charter of Rights and Freedoms

language rights Charter rights to receive government services in English or French and to be educated in either English or French

● Are there any limits to our rights and freedoms?

● What is the significance of the notwithstanding clause?

The Canadian Charter of Rights and Freedoms

Few laws have had as profound an effect on the life of Canadians as the **Canadian Charter of Rights and Freedoms**. As you read in Chapter 8, Prime Minister Pierre Trudeau spearheaded the campaign to amend the Canadian Constitution in 1982 to include the Charter. The Charter protects the fundamental freedoms of Canadians and guarantees their democratic, mobility, equality, legal, and language rights. The Charter gives Canadians the right to challenge in court any law they believe violates their Charter rights. The courts do not always agree with the challenges made, but Canadians generally believe that the Charter offers them a chance to stand up for their rights, even against powerful government interests.

Limiting the Charter

The Charter sets limits on some rights to make sure that one person's rights do not take precedence over someone else's. The Charter also allows the federal and provincial governments to have the final say in which laws are passed.

Reasonable Limits

Section 1 of the Charter contains this limiting clause: "the Canadian Charter of Rights and Freedoms guarantees the rights and freedoms set out in it subject only to such reasonable limits prescribed by law as can be demonstrably justified in a free and democratic society." This means that the government can limit a person's rights or freedoms, but it must show that the limit is necessary. This clause was tested in 1990 when James Keegstra, an Alberta high-school teacher, was charged with promoting hatred by making anti-Semitic statements in his classes. Keegstra argued that the Charter protected his right to express his opinion, but the Supreme Court ruled that his teachings went beyond his right to freedom of expression and that it was reasonable to limit his right in this case.

The Notwithstanding Clause

As you learned in Chapter 8, the **notwithstanding clause** (section 33 of the Charter) allows the federal and provincial or territorial governments to pass a law even if it violates a specific freedom or right in the Charter (see Figure 10–7). This clause was a compromise. Some provincial politicians felt the Charter, which would be interpreted by justices, would weaken their power as elected lawmakers. The notwithstanding clause allowed legislatures to have the final say.

Section 33 can be applied to	Section 33 cannot be applied to
fundamental freedoms (section 2)	**democratic rights** (sections 3–5)
legal rights (sections 7–14)	mobility rights (section 6)
equality rights (section 15)	**language rights** (sections 16–23)

FIGURE 10–6 Application of the notwithstanding clause

Thinking Critically Which of the sections of the Charter would you move from one category to the other and why?

©P

The federal government has never used the notwithstanding clause. Saskatchewan used it to protect a law that ordered striking workers back to work. Québec protested the patriation of the Constitution in 1982 by withdrawing all its laws and re-enacting them with the notwithstanding clause included. The same was done with all laws passed in the next three years. Since then, Québec governments have used the notwithstanding clause 15 times, dealing with issues such as the language on signage, pensions, and same-sex marriage.

WEB LINK ● · · · · · · · · · · · · ·

The Constitution Act, the Canadian Bill of Rights, and the Charter of Rights and Freedoms, along with some examples of key court decisions in the Charter's history, are available on the Pearson Web site.

Section	Rights	What does this mean to me?
1	Guarantee of rights and freedoms	• I can live as a free citizen in a democratic nation, with certain legal limitations.
2	Fundamental freedoms of conscience and religion; thought, belief, opinion, expression, and the press; peaceful assembly; association	• I can follow any religion I choose. • I can believe what I want. • I can express my opinions openly without fear. • I can associate with whomever I choose. • I can meet with others peacefully.
3–5	Democratic Rights	• Once I am 18, I can vote in elections at least once every five years. • Once I am 18, I can run as a candidate in elections.
6	Mobility Rights	• I can enter, remain in, or leave Canada. • I can live, work, or study wherever I wish in Canada.
7–14	Legal Rights	• I have a right to life, liberty, and security of person. • I have the right not to be arbitrarily arrested and detained. • I have the right to a fair trial if I am accused of a crime. • I have the right to humane treatment.
15	Equality Rights	• I can live, study, and work regardless of my race, religion, national or ethnic origin, colour, sex, age, and mental or physical ability. • I have the right to be treated as "equal before and under the law."
16–22	Official Languages of Canada	• I can communicate with and receive federal government services in English or French. • I can use French or English in any federal court.
23	Minority Language Educational Rights	• I can have my children educated in either French or English where sufficient numbers of students exist.
24	Enforcement	• I can take the matter to court should any of the above rights and freedoms be denied.
25–31	General	• Aboriginal peoples of Canada retain any rights previously established. • Charter to be interpreted consistent with the preservation and enhancement of multiculturalism. • Rights under the Charter are guaranteed equally to both sexes.

FIGURE 10–7 Some of the human rights protected by the Canadian Charter of Rights and Freedoms

PRACTICE QUESTIONS

1. What are the Canadian Bill of Rights and the Canadian Charter of Rights and Freedoms? How do they help protect the rights of all Canadians?

2. Do you think section 1 of the Charter is necessary? Why or why not?

3. Why was the notwithstanding clause included in the Charter? To which section of the Charter can it be applied? Why do you think the notwithstanding clause has not been used more often?

The Charter in Action

As you have read, the Canadian Charter of Rights and Freedoms defines the basic rights and freedoms that individuals and groups are entitled to in Canada. We will now explore these rights and freedoms in more detail and see how the Charter helps to protect them.

Fundamental Freedoms

Section 2 of the Charter protects the **fundamental freedoms** of conscience, religion, thought, belief, opinion, expression, peaceful assembly, and association. These are the political civil liberties at the core of Canada's democratic society ensuring individual Canadians freedom from fear and persecution. They are at the heart of what it means to be a citizen of Canada. These freedoms are, however, subject to reasonable limits (see Case Study: Human Rights and Freedom of Expression on page 338).

In the past, the federal government has restricted or denied these freedoms. For example, in 1907 it passed the Lord's Day Act, which restricted activities such as shopping on Sundays. This Act was overturned in 1985 as contrary to freedom of religion. In 1970, during the October Crisis, the government invoked the War Measures Act, the first time it was applied in peacetime, restricting people's freedom of assembly, association, and expression.

case study

Religious Freedom in a Multicultural Society

In 2001, when he was 12, Gurbaj Singh Multani's ceremonial dagger, his kirpan, fell out of its cloth holder in the schoolyard. The school board in Montréal banned Gurbaj from bringing his kirpan to school because it was considered a weapon. Gurbaj argued that it was not a weapon but a religious symbol, which he as an orthodox Sikh was required to wear at all times. After numerous court cases, the Supreme Court of Canada ruled unanimously that the ban on kirpans was a violation of Gurbaj's religious freedom as guaranteed by the Canadian Charter of Rights and Freedoms. "Religious tolerance is a very important value of Canadian society," wrote Justice Louise Charron. The decision, however, does allow school boards to impose restrictions on how kirpans can be worn to protect the safety of students.

FIGURE 10–8 Gurbaj was 17 when the Supreme Court made its ruling. In the meantime, he had transferred to a private school for his education. Do you think his family should be compensated for the cost of his private schooling? Explain.

©P

Mobility Rights

Section 6 of the Charter gives citizens the right to remain in and leave Canada, and to move and live within the country. **Mobility rights** have been brought to the public's attention since the 9/11 attacks in 2001 because heightened security has led to a number of cases in which Canadians were refused admission to Canada. Most mobility cases are concerned with **extradition** of Canadians accused of a crime by another country. The Supreme Court has ruled that people may not be extradited for crimes that might result in the death penalty. Subjecting a Canadian citizen to a possible death penalty in another country would contradict section 7 of the Charter, which entitles each Canadian the right to life, liberty, and security.

Equality Rights

Section 15 of the Charter guarantees **equality** "before and under the law." "Before the law" means everyone must have access to the courts, which is why we have legal aid programs to make sure that those who cannot afford a lawyer are represented fairly. "Under the law" means that laws passed by the government must treat everyone equally. The courts cannot favour the rights of one group over another. Section 15 prohibits anyone, including the justice system or any other branch of government, from discriminating against individuals based on race, national or ethnic origin, colour, religion, sex, age, or mental or physical disability. Some exceptions are allowed if they aim to improve the conditions of "disadvantaged individuals or groups." Similarly, **affirmative action** programs are recognized under subsection 15(2) of the Charter to ensure **minority rights** for disadvantaged individuals and groups.

One of the most significant cases decided by the Supreme Court confirmed the equality rights of gays and lesbians. In 1991, Delwin Vriend, an instructor at a private religious college in Alberta, was fired because the school discovered he was gay. The Alberta Human Rights Act did not cover discrimination based on sexual orientation, so the Alberta Human Rights Commission would not hear Vriend's case. When the matter reached the Supreme Court, it ruled that exclusion on the basis of sexual orientation violated section 15 of the Charter.

You will read more about three different types of equality rights—Aboriginal, gender, and child—later in this chapter.

KEY TERMS

fundamental freedoms freedoms in the Charter that guarantee citizens are free to worship and believe what they wish, to express their opinions freely, to associate with whomever they wish, and to gather together peacefully with others

mobility rights Charter rights that guarantee people the ability to move around or in and out of the country

extradition the surrender of a person accused of a crime from one country to another

equality rights Charter rights that guarantee people will not be discriminated against based on race, national or ethnic origin, colour, religion, sex, age, or mental or physical disability

affirmitive action programs that are designed to help disadvantaged individuals or groups achieve equity

minority rights legal rights to ensure that specific groups which are vulnerable or disadvantaged are protected and able to achieve equality

WEB LINK •
You can read the decision of the Supreme Court in the Vriend case on the Pearson Web site.

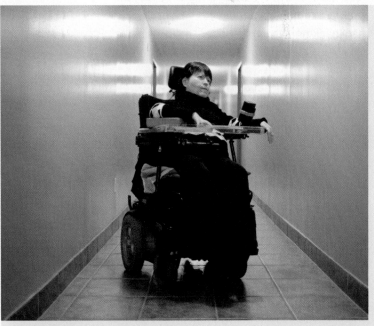

FIGURE 10–9 In 2007, Bobby Sarlina claimed that a Toronto hospital denied her right to make decisions about her treatment because of her disability. The UN adopted the Convention on the Rights of Persons with Disabilities in 2006 to help ensure that their rights and dignities are protected.

Legal Rights

Canadians have their legal rights guaranteed by sections 7 to 14 of the Charter. These rights cannot be taken away without proper legal process. Many of the Charter cases before the courts are attempts to settle situations in which the Criminal Code conflicts with individual rights and freedoms.

The powers of police to arrest and question suspects, seize evidence, and conduct searches have been steadily reduced since the introduction of the Charter in 1982. Some people argue that this is necessary to protect the rights of citizens. Others maintain that it severely restricts the ability of the police to carry out their duties. The courts have also strongly upheld the rights of those held or arrested by the police. Prisoners have the right to know the reason for their arrest and to have a judge decide whether they are being held legally. They also have the right to contact a lawyer, and the right to a speedy trial.

FAST FORWARD

An Illegal Search

In 2002, at St. Patrick's High School in Sarnia, Ontario, police used a sniffer dog to search back-packs while the students were kept in their class-rooms. During the search, the dog reacted to one of the backpacks. Without getting a warrant, the police opened the backpack, found illicit drugs, and charged the student. At both the trial and appeal, judges dismissed the charges, finding both the search with the sniffer dog and the search of the backpack unreasonable under section 8 of the Charter. When the case reached the Supreme Court, six of the nine judges supported these findings, noting that students can "...expect the contents of their backpacks not to be open to the random and speculative scrutiny of the police." The other three judges disagreed, saying that students were warned before and at the time about the zero-tolerance policy of drugs in the school.

WEB LINK •·····························

You can read the transcript of this and a similar case decided at the same time on the Pearson Web site.

PRACTICE QUESTIONS

1. Create a three-column chart with the following headings: Right or Freedom; Explanation; Examples. In your own words, give a brief explanation of the rights and freedoms on pages 332–334 and give specific examples from the textbook.

2. What is the purpose of affirmative action programs? Why are these programs "technically" against the Charter of Rights and Freedoms?

3. Would you agree with the majority or minority view of the Supreme Court for the search described in the above Fast Forward? Explain.

4. **Judgements** Where would you draw the line between personal privacy and public safety? Explain.

©P

Advocating for Your Rights

Imagine you are 19 years old and looking to rent an apartment with two friends. Your mother was shown a suitable apartment, but when you call to set up an appointment to view the rental unit with your friends the landlord coldly tells you the unit is taken. Is this age discrimination, you wonder. Human rights abuses such as this take place across the country. Fortunately, we can seek help from the legal system to resolve these types of issues.

● How are human rights protected in British Columbia?

KEY TERM

legal rights Charter rights that guarantee people will be treated fairly by the legal system, including knowing why they were arrested, having access to a lawyer, and getting a fair and speedy trial

Federal and Provincial Human Rights Legislation

The federal and provincial governments have passed specific laws to deal with particular cases of discrimination. These laws are administered by human rights commissions that investigate complaints and attempt to find solutions. The Canadian Human Rights Act covers all federally regulated businesses and agencies including banks, the major airlines, Canada Post, and the national media. The Canadian Human Rights Commission administers this Act. Provincial human rights codes clarify people's rights in areas such as employment, tenancy, and institutions, and are interpreted by provincial bodies.

The British Columbia Human Rights Code

Most human rights complaints in British Columbia fall under the British Columbia Human Rights Code. The Code protects citizens against discrimination on the grounds of age (19 to 65), ancestry, colour, family or marital status, physical or mental disability, place of origin, political belief, race, religion, sex, or sexual orientation. It covers employment, tenancy and property purchases, accommodation, services, facilities usually available to the public, and hate propaganda. The British Columbia Human Rights Tribunal deals with complaints and hearings.

In 2009, over 1100 complaints were filed with the British Columbia Human Rights Tribunal. The majority of the complaints dealt with employment, followed by services and tenancy. Of the cases that appeared before the Tribunal, 607 were settled, withdrawn, or abandoned.

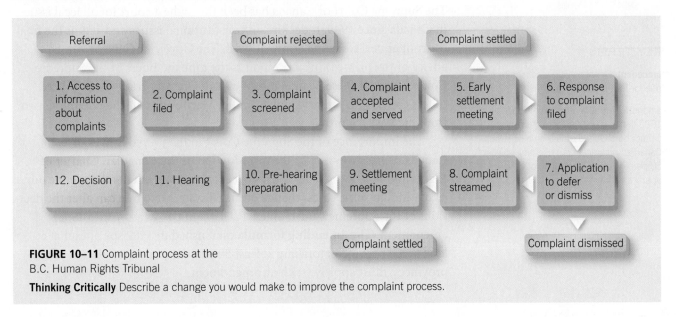

FIGURE 10–11 Complaint process at the B.C. Human Rights Tribunal

Thinking Critically Describe a change you would make to improve the complaint process.

©P

Employment	• You cannot be refused work or a promotion because of your age, or any of the other grounds listed in the Code.
	• Employers cannot refuse to hire an applicant because of a criminal record if the crime is unrelated to the job.
	• Job ads cannot exclude any category of persons except on the basis of occupational requirements.
Tenancy	• Offer tenants same protection as employees.
	• Landlord cannot refuse to rent to you based on your source of income.
	• Landlord can determine whether you can afford to pay the rent, except in the case of older people and those with disabilities.
Accommodation, service, or use of facilities	You cannot be unfairly denied accommodation, service, or use of a public facility, with two exceptions:
	• In matters of public decency (public washrooms and change rooms), discrimination on the basis of sex is allowed.
	• Insurance companies are allowed to take sex and physical and mental health into account when calculating insurance costs.
Hate propaganda	A person cannot publish or display any notice, sign, symbol, or emblem that is likely to expose a person or class of persons to hatred or contempt.

FIGURE 10–12 Some of the protections provided by the B.C. Human Rights Code

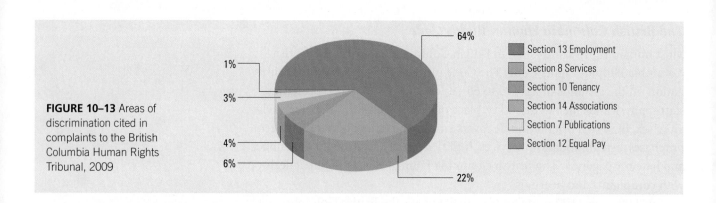

FIGURE 10–13 Areas of discrimination cited in complaints to the British Columbia Human Rights Tribunal, 2009

64%
1%
3%
4%
6%
22%

Section 13 Employment
Section 8 Services
Section 10 Tenancy
Section 14 Associations
Section 7 Publications
Section 12 Equal Pay

● Why is the amending formula important?

KEY TERMS

precedent a legal decision that serves as a rule for future cases

amending formula a rule established in 1982 that states Canada's Constitution cannot be changed unless at least seven Canadian provinces, representing at least 50 percent of the population of Canada, approve

The Supreme Court and the Charter

The Supreme Court of Canada has been the highest court for all legal issues in Canada since 1949. It decides on constitutional issues and acts as the final court of appeal for some criminal cases. The Governor General, on the advice of the prime minister, appoints the nine members of the Supreme Court. Three of these justices must be from Québec. Traditionally, three others come from Ontario, one from the Maritimes, and the remaining two from the Western provinces.

The importance of the Supreme Court in the everyday lives of Canadians has grown since the introduction of the Canadian Charter of Rights and Freedoms. The Court's decisions set **precedents** that define our rights and, in some cases, change our legal system. No one can alter the decisions of the Supreme Court, unless Parliament passes a constitutional amendment. The **amending formula** established in 1982 specifies that at least seven provinces, totalling at least 50 percent of the population of all provinces, must approve such an amendment.

©P

Charter Appeals

When an appeal involving a Charter right reaches the Supreme Court, the justices consider three questions:

1. Did the government or one of its agencies restrict a right or freedom?

2. Is the right or freedom protected by the Charter?

3. Was the restriction reasonable under the limits of section 1?

The media regularly report on Charter decisions made by the Supreme Court. Since 1982, some of the Court's most newsworthy judgements included decisions to strike down a government abortion law, uphold cruise missile testing, condemn unfair treatment on the basis of pregnancy, affirm Aboriginal rights, and grant survivor benefits to same-sex couples.

FASTFORWARD

Rewriting History

In 2008, several female lawyers and scholars established the Women's Court of Canada (WCC). Their goal is to challenge conventional thinking and highlight what they see as problems with Supreme Court equality decisions under section 15 of the Charter. The WCC see themselves as part of the long tradition of Canadian women, such as those in the Persons Case (see Chapter 3), refusing to accept decisions of the Supreme Court as the last word. Adopting the declaration of the writer Oscar Wilde that "the only duty we owe to history is to rewrite it," the WCC set itself the task of rewriting a number of Supreme Court cases to reflect equity as they see it.

WEB LINK • ·
Read about the WCC on the Pearson Web site.

PRACTICE QUESTIONS

1. Both the Canadian Charter of Rights and Freedoms and the B.C. Human Rights Code restrict age discrimination to those between 19 and 65. What problems might occur if this age restriction were removed?

2. Which of the following situations violate human rights, and under which category might they fall in the B.C. Human Rights Code?

   a) A person in a wheelchair is denied access to a sporting event because the wheelchair cannot fit in the space designated for wheelchairs.

   b) An advertisement for a house rental says that only non-smoking women need apply.

   c) A woman is refused an interview for a job as a security guard in a mall because the company says it finds men are more effective at controlling groups of young people.

   d) A group puts up posters for a dance that include some racist lyrics from the songs that will be played.

3. How does the Supreme Court decide whether it will hear a Charter challenge? How has the Charter changed the role of the Supreme Court in the lives of Canadians? What problems are associated with this new role?

4. **Perspectives** How might the WCC's decisions differ from the Supreme Court's on major issues? Explain.

©P

case study

Human Rights and Freedom of Expression

Canada guarantees its people equality and inclusion in society. Federal and provincial human rights laws protect our right to equality as well as our right to be different. The Criminal Code of Canada protects minority groups from those who would incite hatred toward them. In short, Canadian legislation promotes tolerance and open-mindedness, which characterizes our multicultural society.

Yet there are times when multiculturalism is at odds with another Canadian value: free speech. The Charter protects "freedom of thought, belief, opinion and expression, including freedom of the press and other media of communication." Reconciling the ideals of multiculturalism and free speech has become an important public issue in Canada.

Free Speech at All Costs?

This question was at the centre of three cases launched by the Canadian Islamic Congress before the Canadian Human Rights Commission and the human rights commissions in B.C. and Ontario. Dr. Mohamed Elmasry lodged complaints against *Maclean's* magazine after it published an excerpt from Mark Steyn's book *America Alone* in an article entitled "Why the Future Belongs to Islam." The article asserts that Muslims will soon dominate world culture because they have "youth, numbers, and global ambition," while Western culture is in decline because it "is growing old and enfeebled, and lacks the will to rebuff those who would supplant it."

According to section 13(1) of the Canadian Human Rights Act and section 7 of the B.C. Human Rights Code, it is discriminatory to say anything that is likely to expose a person or persons to hatred or contempt. Dr. Elmasry claimed the article was "flagrantly Islamophobic," demonized Islam, and contributed to discrimination. The Canadian Human Rights Commission dismissed his claim without a hearing. At the B.C. hearing, Dr. Faiza Hirji, a university journalism instructor, testified that the

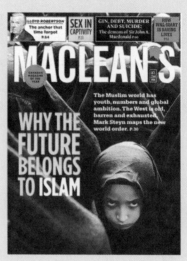

FIGURE 10–14 "Why The Future Belongs to Islam," *Maclean's,* October 23, 2006

article had examples of common stereotypes of Muslims being associated with violence and terrorism. The lawyers for *Maclean's* argued that the hearings "constitute an unjustifiable infringement of freedom of the press." The tribunal ruled that the article did not violate anti-hate laws and was a legitimate subject for public discussion.

Restricting Free Speech

After the judgement, Dr. Elmasry commented that "the state should act to empower those who are disadvantaged by hate speech, and that may mean lowering the voices of some in order that others may be heard." This was echoed by the Ontario Human Rights Commission, which said that the media should try harder to not promote stereotypes.

Many people in the media defended the right to disagree and to offend as part of the price of free speech. They also argued that free speech is the best protection for minorities. The writers' group PEN Canada claimed this case raised "disturbing questions about the degree to which human rights commissions have taken it upon themselves to become [the judges] of what constitutes free speech."

Looking Further

1. How would you have decided Dr. Elmasry's complaint? Explain.

2. Would you support removing section 13(1) of the Canadian Human Rights Act? Why or why not?

WEB LINK •

Read more about this case on the Pearson Web site.

©P

Aboriginal Rights

Rights taken for granted by most Canadians were sometimes denied or only slowly granted to Aboriginal groups. The issue of residential schools is an extreme example of the Canadian government imposing its will on Aboriginal peoples to try to assimilate them into mainstream culture. Even though residential schools and most of the legal restrictions that had been placed on First Nations peoples are now gone, Aboriginal groups still suffer from serious problems, including poverty, poor health, and inadequate housing and education.

The Bill of Rights did not advance Aboriginal rights in Canada, but the Canadian Charter of Rights and Freedoms has helped to eliminate some of the injustices that existed in law before 1982. In July 2000, Aboriginal leaders presented their case at the UN Working Group on Indigenous Populations, claiming Canada had violated their human rights. Despite these efforts, Canada was one of only four countries (Australia, New Zealand, and the United States were the other three) that refused to sign the UN Declaration on the Rights of Indigenous Peoples. Australia endorsed the Declaration in 2009.

> ● How are minority rights protected in the Canadian Charter of Rights and Freedoms?

Our experience with Canada is an ongoing violation of our people's fundamental human rights.... Our people are still confined to tiny portions of Canada's land mass, with few or no resources.... Our peoples still mostly live in desolate communities with unsafe drinking water and inadequate sanitation. Our people are still crowded into unsafe and unhealthy dwellings or live homeless on the streets of the big cities.

–Ashley Iserhoff, a James Bay Cree, to the UN Working Group on Indigenous Populations

---

up close and personal | Jeannette Corbière Lavell: Fighting for Equality

Under the Indian Act, if an Aboriginal woman married a non-Aboriginal, she was no longer considered a status Indian. This meant that she could not live on the reserve, nor receive any of the treaty benefits of her band or nation. She could not participate in band councils. As a final indignity, she could no longer be buried with her ancestors. None of these rules applied to Aboriginal men who married non-Aboriginal women. In those cases, the non-Aboriginal wives gained Indian status for themselves and the children born to the marriage.

In 1970, Jeannette Corbière, a member of the Anishnawbe nation in Ontario, lost her Indian status when she married a non-Aboriginal, David Lavell. She decided to challenge the law. Her case was the first that claimed discrimination on the basis of gender under the 1960 Canadian Bill of Rights. Lavell lost her case in County Court but the Federal Court of Appeal ruled in her favour. The Crown, however, chose to appeal the decision.

In 1973 the Supreme Court ruled against Lavell. The Court found that, as Lavell was being treated the same as other Aboriginal women who had married non-Aboriginals, she had not been discriminated against. It dismissed the argument that treating Aboriginal women differently from Aboriginal men was discriminatory.

However, Lavell did eventually triumph. When the Canadian Charter of Rights and Freedoms was passed, it expanded the equality provisions in the Bill of Rights. The Charter also contained a provision that Aboriginal and treaty rights must be applied equally to men and women. These changes meant that the regulations in the Indian Act were now unconstitutional. In 1985, this part of the Act was changed so Aboriginal women keep their status when they marry non-Aboriginal men.

FIGURE 10-15 Jeannette Corbière Lavell with her husband

©P

KEY TERMS

Human Development Index an index used to rank countries based on life expectancy, adult literacy, and GDP rates

employment equity policies that ensure certain groups are given an advantage by employers, in particular women, people with disabilities, Aboriginal peoples, and visible minorities

WEB LINK •••••••••••••••••••••

To read more about cases involving Aboriginal rights, visit the Pearson Web site.

The Impact of the Charter and the Constitution

Section 25 of the Charter protects the practices and customs of Aboriginal peoples and those outlined in section 35 of the Constitution Act of 1982. The Constitution recognized "the existing Aboriginal and treaty rights of the Aboriginal peoples of Canada." These rights have been in place since the arrival of Europeans and predate the Consitution.

The Supreme Court's recent decisions regarding Aboriginal rights have been among its most controversial. In its decisions, the Court has also considered the historical mistreatment of Aboriginal groups and their existing social and cultural needs. Recent court decisions have defined the nature of Aboriginal and treaty rights and clarified the legal relationship between the governments of Canada and Aboriginal peoples. These decisions are important in British Columbia because of the lack of treaties covering most of the land in the province.

Case	Issue	Summary
Calder vs. B.C. 1969	Aboriginal title to traditional lands	The Nisga'a went to court to establish title to their traditional lands. In 1973, the Supreme Court of Canada (SCC) ruled that the Nisga'a did hold title to their traditional lands before British Columbia was created. Because Native title to land is proclaimed to exist under English law, predating colonization, the decision forms the basis for contemporary Aboriginal law in Canada.
R. vs. Sparrow 1990	Inherent Aboriginal rights	The Supreme Court decision that Aboriginal rights that were in existence in 1982, such as fishing, are protected under the Constitution of Canada and cannot be infringed upon.
Delgamuukw vs. B.C. 1997	Aboriginal title to land	The Supreme Court's landmark decision that Aboriginal title is an ancestral right protected by the Constitution Act. It ruled that Aboriginal title is a right to exclusive use and occupation of land. To claim Aboriginal title, the people must be able to prove that they occupied the land before sovereignty. The Court made another important decision by allowing oral tradition to be used as evidence to prove a claim to Aboriginal title.
R. vs. Kapp 2008	Aboriginal fisheries	A federal government initiative, the Aboriginal Fisheries Strategy, allowed only Aboriginal fishers to catch and sell salmon in a closed fishery on the Fraser River. Non-Aboriginal fishers were excluded and claimed their equality rights under section 15(1) of the Charter were being violated. The Court ruled that the exclusion of non-Aboriginal fishers falls under section 15(2) of the Charter that enables governments to develop programs to help disadvantaged groups improve their situation.

FIGURE 10–16 Supreme Court cases involving Aboriginal rights

PRACTICE QUESTIONS

1. Why do you think the government appealed the Lavell case to the Supreme Court? What was at stake for the government? For Aboriginal women?

2. In your own words, explain the difference between Lavell's view of what constituted discrimination and the Supreme Court's view.

3. Give examples of how the Charter has helped gain human rights recognition for Aboriginals.

4. Why has B.C. been the focus of so many Charter challenges that have appeared before the Supreme Court of Canada? How might these challenges impact future relations between the government and Aboriginal peoples?

Gender Equity

In 2009, the United Nations ranked Canada fourth on the **Human Development Index (HDI)**, down from first place in the 1990s. Less impressive are Canada's efforts to deal with gender equality. The gender-related development index (GDI) measures the same achievements as the HDI but includes data on inequalities between men and women. The gender empowerment measure (GEM) reveals whether women take an active part in the economy and politics of a nation. In 2009, Canada was ranked twelfth out of 109 countries in the GEM. These findings encouraged efforts to enforce the gender equity provisions of the Charter.

FIGURE 10–17 The RCMP was one of the last police forces in Canada to recruit women. The first female Mounties graduated in 1975. Some regulations, however, were different for women than for men. For example, female officers were required to carry their guns in their purses. How have attitudes toward gender equity changed since then?

The Charter and Gender Equity

Though the Charter provides guarantees against gender discrimination, this does not mean that attitudes change quickly. While most Canadians believe in the idea of equality and fairness, opinions differ as to how these goals are realized in the workplace. Women continue to be under-represented in many traditionally male disciplines, and they are often paid less than men when they perform the same type or an equal amount of work.

As Figure 10–18 shows, the average earnings of women have been rising, perhaps partly because the number of women in the labour force has increased. However, in 2006, about 26 percent of the 2 million employed women in Canada were working part-time (less than 30 hours per week). Part-time work generally provides fewer benefits, such as pensions, health coverage, and life insurance.

The Charter allows for special initiatives, such as affirmative action programs, that would improve the situation of those people who have been discriminated against because of "race, national or ethnic origin, colour, religion, sex, age, or mental or physical disability." Just how far should this principle be extended? Two practices designed to improve **employment equity** still cause debate: the principle of equal pay for work of equal value, and the use of preferential hiring practices.

Year	Women's Earnings	Men's Earnings	Women's Earnings as a % of Men's (2007$)
1998	$25 900	$41 300	62.8
1999	$26 400	$42 100	62.6
2000	$26 800	$43 500	61.7
2001	$26 900	$43 400	62.1
2002	$27 300	$43 400	62.8
2003	$26 900	$42 800	62.9
2004	$27 300	$43 100	63.4
2005	$27 900	$43 700	64.0
2006	$28 400	$43 800	64.7
2007	$29 200	$44 400	65.7

FIGURE 10–18 Average earnings by gender, full- and part-time

Thinking Critically Are you surprised by these statistics? Why or why not? What changes might improve women's average earnings?

©P

Equal Pay for Work of Equal Value

Women in the workplace face the challenge of breaking out of traditional "job ghettoes," occupations that usually pay poorly and are dominated by female workers. For example, secretarial and nursing positions were once overwhelmingly held by female workers, and as a result the average wages were lower than for equivalent positions held by males.

KEY TERMS

equity groups certain groups of people who have traditionally been disadvantaged or discriminated against by employers

reverse discrimination discrimination against a majority group in order to give preference to a disadvantaged group

undue hardship financial strain or excessive difficulty

> *Studies have shown that the values attached to various types of work often reflect attitudes based on stereotypes of who does what kind of work and a frequent assumption that the work performed mainly by men is more valuable than work performed mainly by women.*
>
> **–Public Service Alliance of Canada** Pay Equity Bulletin, 2000

To avoid this form of discrimination, the Canadian Human Rights Act, 1986, states the following:

(1) It is a discriminatory practice for an employer to establish or maintain differences in wages between male and female employees employed in the same establishment performing work of equal value.

(2) In assessing the value of work performed by employees employed in the same establishment, the criterion to be applied is the composite of the skill, effort and responsibility required in the performance of the work and the conditions under which the work is performed.

Most people agree that female teachers, police officers, and postal workers should be paid at the same rate as their male colleagues (equal pay for equal work). However, some critics claim that it is impossible to compare the value of jobs, especially when those jobs are as different as clerk and plumber, for example.

FIGURE 10–19 In 2000, Beverley McLachlin became the first female chief justice of the Supreme Court of Canada. She said, "We (Canada) lead other nations in the opportunities we open to women. We have more senior female judges, more female university professors, more practising physicians than many Western countries."

Thinking Critically Do you think the appointment of women to the Supreme Court changed the nature of the Court's judgements? Beverley McLachlin is a very well respected judge. Why do you think some people still hint at gender bias in her appointment as chief justice? Is this view fair or unfair? Support your opinion.

Preferential Hiring Policies

"Universities hiring, but white males need not apply." So read the headline in a Vancouver newspaper in the summer of 1999. The employment advertisements for a number of Canadian universities clearly expressed a preference for **equity groups**—candidates who were female, from a minority, or had disabilities. The universities claimed they wanted to hire instructors who would more accurately reflect the mix of students in university. To receive federal government funding, universities had to set equity hiring targets.

Employment equity or affirmative action policies have become quite controversial. Some critics argue that they amount to **reverse discrimination** and are unfair to qualified applicants who cannot be considered for some positions. Critics feel these hiring policies are unnecessary because existing inequities will correct themselves in time.

©P

In 1994, Tawney Meiorin lost her job as a forest firefighter because she took too long to finish a 2.5-kilometre run. She had been doing the job for three years before she failed the new test, which was based on the aerobic capacity of several dozen elite male firefighters. Meiorin's union brought the case to the courts after a B.C. labour arbitrator's decision was overturned by the B.C. Court of Appeal. At issue was whether the running test was a reasonable occupational requirement.

In a unanimous decision, the Supreme Court ruled that although the province apparently developed its aerobics test in good faith, it failed to take into account the physical differences of males and females. Madame Justice Beverley McLachlin wrote: "If men and women do not have equal ability to meet the excessive standard, the effect may be to exclude qualified female candidates from employment for no reason but their gender."

The Court said that employers can discriminate in hiring standards only if not doing so would impose **"undue hardship"** on the employer and if the standards reflect a legitimate occupational requirement. It ordered the province of British Columbia to compensate Tawney Meiorin for lost wages and benefits.

Some people saw this ruling as a major step in eliminating discrimination that had stopped women from being hired for jobs traditionally dominated by

FIGURE 10–20 Tawney Meiorin, with her lawyer, after the Supreme Court of Canada ruled in her favour

Thinking Critically Do you think there should be different standards for men and women in physical occupations such as firefighting?

men. They said that relaxing such restrictions would give them access to a larger pool of applicants who better reflect the diversity of Canadians. Critics of the judgement claimed that it would compromise safety standards in the name of political correctness. One editorial claimed that "more people will die in burning buildings in order to ensure that more women can become firefighters."

PRACTICE QUESTIONS

1. In your own words, explain the following terms: *preferential hiring policy*, *equity group*, and *reverse discrimination*. Provide specific examples of efforts to minimize these issues.

2. Explain why preferential hiring programs are controversial.

3. **a)** In what areas of Canadian society could the laws still be changed to improve equality in the workplace?

   b) What methods, other than using decisions from the human rights commissions, could be used to promote equality in the workplace?

4. How were Tawney Meiorin's rights under the Charter violated when she was dismissed? Do you agree with the Supreme Court's decision? Why or why not?

5. What occupations do you think would be justified in imposing discriminatory hiring standards, based on the Supreme Court's requirement of "undue hardship" on the employer? What would the standards be?

6. **Evidence** What does the term *glass ceiling* refer to? Which social values and forces do you think created glass ceilings?

How many times have you heard someone say, "Just give me the facts!" It is important to distinguish what is factual from what is simply someone's opinion. When an opinion is passed from person to person, details can often get exaggerated. Even if there is a factual basis to the opinion, the central point is often overlooked and can lead to stereotyping.

In today's world of constant and instant communications, people are bombarded with information from print and electronic sources, including commercial advertising, public service announcements, and social networking sites. It is important to remember that media sources contain both fact and opinion, along with statements that are often controversial.

It is important for courts and tribunals to deal only with statements that can be backed by evidence. Facts contain truths that can be verified by research, while opinions are biased statements based on a person's beliefs and values (see Building Your Skills in Chapter 1). This means that facts are objective (not influenced by personal beliefs) and are as close to the truth as you can get.

Opinions are personal and subjective because they are the result of one's beliefs and perspective on the world. Ideally, your opinion should be supported by facts and not based on only one point of view. This is referred to as an informed opinion. Even if your opinion is informed, it is likely to be influenced by your life experiences and by those around you. You may think your opinion is the right one, but others will likely have contrary opinions that they consider equally valid.

Applying the Skill

The following examples will help you to distinguish between fact and opinion.

1. Read the following paragraph. Indicate and explain which of the sentences are fact, opinion, and informed opinion.

(a) Since it was enacted in 1982, the Charter of Rights and Freedoms has led to an expansion of the basic rights to which all Canadians are entitled and has had a profound effect on Canadian society. (b) Advocates for human rights groups conclude that the expansion of human rights has been a benefit to Canadians and should be expanded further. (c) As the examples in this chapter illustrate, the Charter has been instrumental in defining the rights of Canadians in relation to the police and the courts. (d) On the other hand, representatives of law enforcement agencies conclude that the expansion of rights in some areas has been misdirected, allowing criminals to escape punishment. (e) The powers of the police to question, arrest, and conduct searches have been reduced. (f) Section 8 of the Charter guarantees everyone "the right to be secure against unreasonable search and seizure." (g) It severely restricts the ability of the police to carry out their duties. (h) Police point to cases of drug dealers having charges dismissed on technicalities as a result of the way the police carried out the arrest. (i) However, it is necessary to protect the rights of citizens.

FIGURE 10–21

2. In 2002, the Supreme Court overturned the restriction in the Canada Elections Act prohibiting prisoners from voting in federal and provincial elections as denying a fundamental democratic right guaranteed by the Charter. Use the cartoon on page 344 to answer the following questions.

a) Analyze the cartoon. Select and explain details in the illustration that are based on fact or on opinion.

b) Would you consider the cartoon to be subjective or objective? Why?

3. Read the following excerpt from an article and answer the questions that follow.

Fewer Young Criminals May Face Life-Without-Parole Sentences

Texas joined six other states this year in banning life sentences without the possibility of parole for young offenders.

The legislation reverses a 2005 law that allowed life sentences without parole, under which four juveniles were incarcerated, according to Human Rights Watch. The new law will not retroactively affect those already incarcerated, although... a measure (may be introduced) next year to change existing sentences.

Critics of lifetime incarceration for juveniles have long called for banning the practice because minors often act on impulse, without the same level of emotional control of which adults are capable.

A person's brain is not fully developed until he or she is an adult, said Debra Kowalski, M.D., chair of the Children and Adolescents Committee of the Texas Society of Psychiatric Physicians, in an interview with Psychiatric News.

A growing body of research on adolescent brain development has found that teens do not have the abilities of adults to make sound decisions, control their impulses, resist group pressures, or weigh the long-term consequences of their actions.

The new law "gives [offenders] an opportunity to make these changes and develop a better life," Kowalski said.

Human Rights Watch has found that the numbers of youths receiving such sentences was small until 1982, when the number began to rise until it peaked at 152 in 1996. Although the number of new sentences has declined since 1996, at least 2574 people are serving such sentences for crimes committed before they were 18 years old.

That research has led Congress to consider action on the issue. The Juvenile Justice Accountability and Improvement Act of 2009 (HR 2289) would require states and the federal government to offer youth offenders meaningful opportunities for parole after serving 15 years of a life sentence.

–Rich Daly, Psychiatric News, 2009

a) What is the writer's opinion? Is it an informed or an uninformed opinion?

b) What facts are used to back up the opinion?

c) Opinions are biased in nature. List examples of bias in the article. Do they detract from the opinion offered?

d) Can you find words associated with persuasion and argument?

e) What points would someone who held the opposite opinion to the author make?

f) Indicate whether you agree or disagree with the article and why.

Children's Rights

Children are entitled to all the rights guaranteed by the Universal Declaration of Human Rights and the various treaties that have developed from it. Children are also guaranteed additional rights because they need special protection and care. Children must be able to depend on the adult world to look after them, to defend their rights, and to help them develop and realize their potential.

> *A century that began with children having virtually no rights is ending with children having the most powerful legal instrument that not only recognizes but protects their human rights.*
>
> *–Carol Bellamy, UNICEF executive director*

The UN Convention on the Rights of the Child—the most widely ratified human rights treaty—outlines children's unique rights (see Figure 10–23). This Convention is the first legally binding international agreement to include children's civil and political rights. It also outlines their economic, social, and cultural rights, giving all rights equal emphasis. Work on drafting the Convention began in 1979, the International Year of the Child. Countries that ratify the Convention have a legal and moral obligation to advance the cause of children's rights through administrative, legislative, judicial, and other measures.

FIGURE 10-22 A young student in the Maldives writes on a sand slate. Nearly half of the population of this island republic in the Indian Ocean are, as in most developing countries, under the age of 15.

Non-discrimination	The State must protect children from any form of discrimination and take positive action to promote their rights.
Best interests of the child	All actions concerning children shall be in their best interests.
Survival and development	Every child has the inherent right to life, survival, and development.
The child's opinion	Children have the right to express their opinions freely and to have that opinion taken into account in any matter affecting the child.
Freedom of thought, conscience, and religion	Children have the right to freedom of thought, conscience, and religion.
Health and health services	Children have a right to the highest standard of health and medical care available.
Education	Children have a right to education, and the State must ensure that primary education is free and compulsory. School discipline shall be consistent with the child's rights and dignity.
Child labour	Children have the right to be protected from work that threatens their health, education, or development.

FIGURE 10–23 Some of the substantive provisions of the UN Convention on the Rights of the Child

Thinking Critically Why do you think the UN chose these rights as important for children? Why do you think they included rules on how countries should ensure these rights are protected?

Children's Rights in Canada

Canada has taken a number of steps to protect the rights of children. The British Columbia government established the Ministry of Children and Family Development to help communities and families "care for and protect vulnerable children and youth," as well as "support healthy child and family development to maximize the potential of every child in B.C." Children's rights are considered paramount and social workers have the power—and the obligation—to remove children from unsafe environments. In 2006, Mary Ellen Turpel-Lafond became the first Representative for Children and Youth, a new position created in the B.C. legislature. The representative's role is to act as an advocate for children and youth, protecting their rights and ensuring access to support for those who are vulnerable.

Canadian Coalition for the Rights of Children

Shortly after Canada adopted the Convention on the Rights of the Child in 1989, several organizations decided to form the Canadian Coalition for the Rights of Children (CCRC). The CCRC is a network of Canadian organizations and individuals that monitor how well Canada fulfills its obligation to the UN Convention on the Rights of the Child. The coalition has looked into child abuse and neglect, refugee children, education, health care, and other basic rights and freedoms of Canadian children.

Child Poverty

Child poverty is perhaps the single biggest children's rights issue in Canada. In 1989, the House of Commons passed a resolution "to achieve the goal of eliminating poverty among Canadian children by the year 2000." Almost 20 years later, the number of children in Canada living below Statistics Canada's low income cut-off (LICO)—meaning the family spent more than 70 percent of its income on food, clothing, and shelter—had only decreased to 9.5 percent (637 000 children) in 2007 from 11.9 percent (792 000 children) in 1989. This means that about 1 in 10 children in Canada were living in poverty in 2007. In First Nations communities, 1 in 4 children were living in poverty.

There is significant disagreement about how to eliminate child poverty in Canada. Some activists feel that parents with low income should pay lower taxes. This would give them more income and allow them and their families a better standard of living. Others emphasize the need for governments to invest in programs and services for poor children and their families, such as good-quality and affordable child care, housing supplements, and allowances (such as the Child Tax Benefit Program) paid directly to low- and middle-income families.

As you have read in this chapter, the Canadian Charter of Rights and Freedoms defines what rights Canadians are entitled to, which also helps define living standards. You will learn more about living standards in Canada in Chapter 12.

What If...

MP Marc Garneau tabled a private member's bill (see Chapter 9) in 2009 to establish a Children's Commissioner for Canada. The commissioner would promote and monitor implementation of the Convention on the Rights of the Child in Canada. What if this private member's bill passed? How might it improve the rights of children in Canada?

FIGURE 10-24 Access to shelter is a fundamental human right, yet homelessness is on the rise in Canada today. Young people under the age of 18 make up the fastest growing segment of homeless people.

Developing an Understanding What are some of the factors that might account for the numbers of young people living on the streets in Canadian cities?

PRACTICE QUESTIONS

1. Do you think the UN Convention on the Rights of the Child has made a difference in the lives of children in Canada and other countries? Explain.

2. How are children protected in Canada and B.C.?

3. Is child poverty a human rights issue? Explain your viewpoint with reference to the UN Convention on the Rights of the Child.

4. Why do you think Canada has made so little progress since 1989 in ending child poverty?

5. Do you agree with the definition of poverty used by Statistics Canada in the LICO? In a two-column organizer, list the benefits and drawbacks of using such a definition as a way of helping children living in poverty in Canada.

CHAPTER FOCUS QUESTION   What are human rights and how are they protected in Canada?

We live in what could be called the age of human rights. As Canadians, our rights are protected by international, national, and provincial documents.

1. Define *human rights* in your own words.

2. Create an organizer for human rights issues in each of the following categories: International, Canada, British Columbia. Each organizer will have three columns (see sample below).

a) In the first column, record at least three documents that protect human rights for that category.

b) In the second column, use an "E" to indicate if the protections in the document can be enforced. Use an "N" if the protections are not enforceable.

c) In the third column, describe one or more situations that would be regarded as a violation of human rights related to the document.

Documents	E / N	Examples of violations related to the documents
1.		
2.		
3.		

Vocabulary Focus

3. Review the Key Terms on page 323. Then visit the Pearson Web site to complete a matching activity.

Knowledge and Understanding

4. Explain, using examples from this text or other examples that you are familiar with, how the Canadian Charter of Rights and Freedoms protects the human rights of each of the following: women, Aboriginals, gays and lesbians, Sikhs, persons arrested by the police, persons travelling outside Canada, voters, media sources, and Francophones.

5. Since its introduction, the Canadian Charter of Rights and Freedoms has changed the way Canadians think about their rights. Should its protections be extended to the way parents govern their children at home? Should Charter rights apply to limitations placed on students in the school system?

6. Make a list of exceptions to the equality rights in section 15 of the Canadian Charter of Rights and Freedoms that you would consider reasonable under the age category. Compare your list with others, and discuss areas of disagreement.

7. What is the importance of each of the following cases in expanding the Charter rights of Canadians?
   a) Calder vs. B.C.
   b) R. vs. Sparrow
   c) Delgamuukw vs. B.C.

Critical Thinking

8. Consider the following situations. Explain why each would or would not be considered a violation of human rights.

   a) In an Islamic country, a woman is stoned after being accused of having an affair.

   b) A woman of a visible minority is refused a university teaching post on the grounds that her qualifications are not sufficient for the job.

©P

c) A Canadian citizen is refused entry to Canada after visiting Africa because he or she is considered a security threat.

d) A Sikh employee is refused permission to wear a turban at work.

e) A gay man is called names as he walks down a Vancouver street.

f) A young man is refused the right to vote because he is 16 and not a Canadian citizen.

g) A protest at a trade conference is broken up by the police using tear gas.

h) A prominent Canadian makes derogatory remarks about Aboriginal people.

i) A qualified man is refused a job because the company says it must give the position to a qualified woman.

9. Summarize the achievements of someone who actively supported human rights. You could choose from these examples: Rosemary Brown or John Diefenbaker in Canada, Rosa Parks or Eleanor Roosevelt in the United States, Mohandas Gandhi in India, Aung San Suu Kyi in Myanmar, Nelson Mandela in South Africa, or Andrei Sakharov in Russia. Organize a classroom bulletin board to display the results of the research. The B.C. Human Rights Tribunal's Web site is a good place to start (visit Pearson's Web site).

Document Analysis

10. View Figure 10–25 and answer the following questions:

a) Describe how Neda is portrayed in the poster.

b) What message is being sent by this portrayal?

c) Is there evidence of bias in this photo of Iranian protestors? Provide examples.

d) What freedoms under the Canadian Charter of Rights and Freedoms allow for this type of demonstration?

FIGURE 10–25 Neda, a young girl allegedly killed by the police during the election protests in Iran, became a symbol for rebellion. Her death was filmed by bystanders and broadcast all over the world.

Study Guide

Use this Study Guide to continue synthesizing your learning about Canadian government and human rights. As you work through the following steps, refer back to the focus questions for Chapters 9 and 10. Look for evidence in your understanding to answer these questions.

STEP 1 Unpacking Knowledge

Use a chart to record terms and concepts you learned in Unit 3, classifying them under the following categories. Highlight items that you have forgotten or cannot define, so you can prioritize what you need to study.

Ideologies, Systems of Government, and Political Parties	Canadian Government	Active Citizenship	Elections	Human Rights

STEP 2 Organizing Your Understanding

1. Draw the linear political spectrum. Place major ideologies, systems of government, and major Canadian political parties on your spectrum. Next, draw and label a diagram like the Political Compass on page 300. Which representation do you find more useful? Why?

2. Draw a mind map of the factors that make Canada a democracy. Think beyond voting to consider other workings of government that are also democratic.

3. Create a table such as the one below and list two or three specific rights in each category.

Fundamental Freedoms (Charter)	Democratic Rights (Charter)	Equality Rights (Charter)	Legal Rights (Charter)
Mobility Rights (Charter)	**B.C. Human Rights Code**	**Universal Declaration of Human Rights**	**Children's Rights**

©P

STEP 3 Making Connections

Using a major Canadian national or local newspaper, examine the sections of the paper that deal with national, international, and provincial news. Find and identify as many examples as possible of the following items:

a) Political opinions or government policies that reflect a political ideology. In some cases this will be a direct reference, but in most cases it will be up to you to infer a connection. For example, if you see a statement from the Canadian Taxpayers Federation asking the government to lower taxes, you can write "fiscal conservative."

b) Stories about rights. Identify the type of right, and if possible, the document that protects that right.

c) Examples of active citizenship.

d) Stories about government or elections.

Newspapers represent many various points of view in Canada.

STEP 4 Applying Your Skills

Media Analysis

Every day, newspaper editors make many decisions—picking a top news story, the wording of headlines, the size and placement of stories, the "slant" of stories, and the selection of images. Use your newspaper from Step 3 to analyze the decisions editors made and what impact they may have had on how we viewed the stories of the day.

Political Advertising Analysis

Visit the Pearson Web site for links to some recent and classic television ads from Canadian and American elections. While viewing each ad, consider:

a) Who produced the ad?

b) Is a certain type of voter targeted by the ad?

c) What is the central message of the ad?

d) What methods does the advertiser use to convince the viewer? (For example, consider music, other sound effects, narrator voice, use of lighting and colour, people shown, and clothing worn.)

e) Is this a positive ad, a negative ad, or a combination of the two?

f) How effective do you find the ad?

©P

Study Guide

Active Citizenship Case Study

Choose one of the scenarios below, and create an active citizenship plan to get involved. Use the strategies for active citizenship and your understanding of the workings of Canadian government and human rights protections from Unit 3.

1. Answer the following questions:

   a) What is the nature of your concern?

   b) Who has the power to make a decision in this case?

   c) Who (individuals, groups, bodies) might be willing to help you?

   d) Who might oppose what you would like to do?

2. Create a chart to consider your options.

Strategy	Benefits	Drawbacks	Chance of success with this method

3. Summarize your action plan.

Scenario 1

The Throne Speech announces a plan by the provincial government of British Columbia or the government of Canada to introduce the following legislation (choose one):

a) Ban all commercial ocean fisheries for a 10-year period to allow stocks to rebound.

b) Allow police more power to monitor the Internet sites visited by citizens.

c) Raise the driving age to 21.

©P

Scenario 2

There is a popular local coffee store chain across the street from your school. On television, you see a news report that exposes new evidence that the coffee being sold is sourced in ways you do not support. The coffee beans are treated with chemical pesticides that threaten the water supply where they are grown and can cause illness in coffee workers. Up to 60 percent of coffee workers in that country are children. Coffee workers are paid less than legal minimum wage, with women and children earning less than men.

Making wise choices about products you use and consume could have an impact on child labour.

STEP 5 Thinking Critically

Now that you have reviewed Unit 3 content, practised skills, explored sources, and gathered evidence, it is time to synthesize your learning. As you learned in Chapter 9, young Canadians are the least likely of any age group in Canada to vote. Write and deliver a persuasive speech to your classmates presenting the most compelling arguments for informing themselves and for voting on election day. Your speech should include a minimum of three strong arguments supported with appropriate evidence.

The right to vote at 18 years of age is embedded in the Canadian Charter of Rights and Freedoms.

CHECK the Pearson Web site for additional review activities and questions.

Human Geography: The Future in Balance

As Canada enters the second decade of the 21st century, the global village is larger than ever. The gulf widens between the rich and the poor, and between the living conditions of developed and developing nations. While Canadians worry about an aging population and carbon emissions, nations in sub-Saharan Africa struggle with the HIV/AIDS health crisis and access to clean water. At the same time, the world is shrinking with interdependent economies, global environmental issues, and shared concerns about sustainable development.

CHAPTER 11

As Earth's population nears the 7 billion mark, governments and organizations around the world prepare for the increased pressure on global resources, primarily food and energy. Some governments must concentrate on controlling the number of births in their countries, while others must think of ways to encourage population growth in order to sustain their economies and pay for their aging citizens.

CHAPTER 12

Many people who live in the richer, Western nations of the world have available time to pursue their interests. Some of these individuals use their time to speak out against the injustices experienced by the citizens of poorer nations. Education, poverty, and access to health care are just some of the issues that affect a person's standard of living.

©P

CHAPTER 13

Global warming affects the whole planet but certain regions will feel the effects sooner and harder than others. Although the issues are extensive, there are many practices that individuals and governments can change, in order to make a real difference.

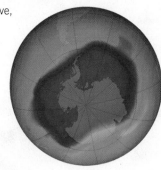

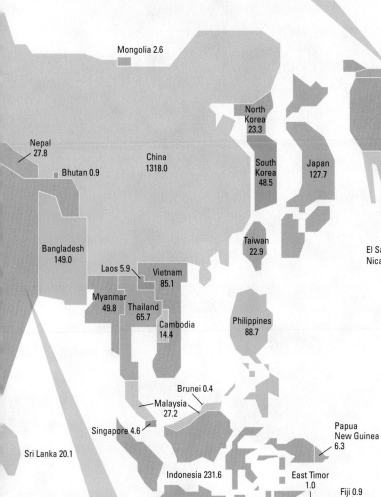

Mongolia 2.6

Canada 32.9

North Korea 23.3

United States 302.2

Nepal 27.8

China 1318.0

Bhutan 0.9

South Korea 48.5

Japan 127.7

Bahamas 0.3

Dominican Republic 9.4

Mexico 106.5

Cuba 11.2

Puerto Rico 3.9

Belize 0.3

Taiwan 22.9

Jamaica 2.7

Haiti 9.0

Bangladesh 149.0

Guatemala 13.4

Laos 5.9

Vietnam 85.1

El Salvador 6.9

Honduras 7.1

Nicaragua 5.6

Myanmar 49.8

Thailand 65.7

Cambodia 14.4

Philippines 88.7

Costa Rica 4.5

Panama 3.3

Colombia 46.2

Venezuela 27.5

Ecuador 13.5

Brazil 189.3

Peru 27.9

Bolivia 9.8

Brunei 0.4

Paraguay 6.1

Malaysia 27.2

Chile 16.6

Uruguay 3.3

Singapore 4.6

Argentina 39.4

Sri Lanka 20.1

Papua New Guinea 6.3

Indonesia 231.6

East Timor 1.0

Fiji 0.9

Australia 21.0

New Zealand 4.2

▼ **The World's Countries Sized According to Population, 2007**

CHAPTER 13

Life on Earth could not exist without air and water, but pollution from industrial activity is damaging these resources in profound ways. Although the extent of the damage is not yet clear, international efforts to reverse climate change have escalated in recent years.

1 Czech Republic 10.3	16 Kyrgyzstan 5.2	31 Burundi 8.5
2 Slovakia 5.4	17 Pakistan 169.3	32 Zambia 11.5
3 Moldova 4.0	18 Jordan 5.7	33 Antigua and Barbuda 0.1
4 Switzerland 7.5	19 Lebanon 3.9	34 St. Kitts-Nevis 0.05
5 Austria 8.3	20 Israel 7.3	35 Guadeloupe 0.5
6 Croatia 4.4	21 Palestinian Territory 4.0	36 Dominica 0.1
7 Serbia 9.5	22 United Arab Emirates 4.4	37 Martinique 0.4
8 Slovenia 2.0	23 Mali 12.3	38 St. Vincent and the
9 Bosnia-	24 Burkina Faso 14.8	Grenadines 0.1
Herzegovina 3.8	25 Niger 14.2	39 Saint Lucia 0.2
10 Albania 3.2	26 Chad 10.8	40 Barbados 0.3
11 Macedonia 2.0	27 Togo 6.6	41 Grenada 0.1
12 Armenia 3.0	28 Benin 9.0	42 Trinidad and Tobago 1.4
13 Azerbaijan 8.6	29 Cameroon 18.1	43 Netherlands Antilles 0.2
14 Turkmenistan 5.4	30 Central African	44 Guyana 0.8
15 Tajikistan 7.1	Republic 4.3	45 Suriname 0.5

20 million

1 million

Size of each nation is proportional to the population
Population figures given in millions for each country
Figures from Population Reference Bureau, mid-2007
Some countries have not been shown because their size would be too small.

©P

11

Population Trends and Issues

GUIDING QUESTIONS

Economy & Human Geography

- What are the components of population change?

- What is the formula used to calculate population growth in a country?

- Explain the stages of the demographic transition model.

- What measures have countries adopted to try to control their population growth, and to what degree have they been effective?

- Identify the different types of population pyramids. What does each type represent?

- What is the dependency ratio and why is it important?

- What effect does an aging or young population have on a country?

- Why is immigration important to Canada's population and economy?

- What problems are associated with population growth?

- What is the difference between population distribution and density?

TIMELINE

1804	1927	1960	1974	1979	1987
World population at 1 billion	World population at 2 billion	World population at 3 billion	World population at 4 billion	One-child policy established in China	World population at 5 billion

CHAPTER FOCUS QUESTION

What is the significance of changes in global population for Canada and the world?

The United Nations declared that the world's population had reached 6 billion in 1999 and estimated it would number 7 billion by 2013. Some people see the growth in population as a contributor to shortages in energy, housing, and food, and to an increase in pollution, unemployment, global warming, and the destruction of the environment. The question such people pose is, At what point will the world's resources fail to support its population?

Others scoff at such a doomsday scenario. According to these optimists, the world's population will increase to 9 billion in 2054 and level off at 10 billion in 2200. By then, they predict, technology will have found ways to provide for the increased numbers of people. Both sides find hope and despair in the United Nations' projections.

The uneven growth of population is also a concern. In some parts of the world the population is in decline, while in others it is increasing. In this chapter, you will learn about the impact population growth has on Canada and the world, and measures governments have taken to control it.

KEY TERMS

demography
developed country
developing country
birth rate
death rate
immigration rate
emigration rate
natural increase
exponential rate
rule of 70
doubling time
net migration
population growth rate
life expectancy
demographic transition model
mortality
family planning
total fertility rate
one-child policy
population pyramid
age cohort
dependency ratio
carrying capacity
population distribution
population density
nutritional density

1999	2008	2013	2028	2054	2200
World population at 6 billion	Half the world's population now lives in urban areas	World population at 7 billion	World population at 8 billion	World population at 9 billion	World population at 10 billion

World Population	When reached?	How long to reach?
1 billion	1804	Human history to this date
2 billion	1927	123 years
3 billion	1960	33 years
4 billion	1974	14 years
5 billion	1987	13 years
6 billion	1999	12 years
United Nations' Estimates of Future Growth		
7 billion	2013	14 years
8 billion	2028	15 years
9 billion	2054	26 years
10 billion	2200	146 years

FIGURE 11–1 World population growth

Making a Graph Make a line graph of the actual growth in population from 1804 to 1999 and the four estimates for 2013 to 2200. Then, brainstorm reasons for (a) the rapid growth in the 20th century, (b) reasons for the different UN estimates, and (c) the possible consequences of rapid growth.

WEB LINK ● · · · · · · · · · · · · · · · ·
You can find population estimates on the Pearson Web site.

World Population Growth

Two thousand years ago, there were about 300 million people on Earth. In 1804, there were 1 billion. From that point on, the rate of increase began to accelerate. The 20th century began with a world population under 2 billion people and ended with triple that number. Today, 76 million people are added to the Earth's population every year. This rate of increase is of greater concern than the numbers themselves.

It is difficult to grasp the difference between large numbers like a million and a billion. How do we understand the difference in size of population between India at over 1 billion and Fiji at nearly 1 million? It might help to understand these numbers by noting that you had lived a *million* seconds when you were 11.6 days old. You won't be a *billion* seconds old until you are 31.7 years of age.

Demography

Demography is the statistical study of the characteristics, trends, and issues of human populations. It helps us understand the causes and consequences of population change. Population change in your community, in Canada, and in the world is an ongoing concern to agencies such as government and business. All levels of government need accurate figures of population change so that they can plan for such things as the numbers of schools and hospitals that are needed. Businesses are interested in information about family size, incomes, and consumer habits as they plan their marketing strategies.

FIGURE 11–2
People fill the platforms of a rail station in Mumbai, India (left) and Vancouver's SkyTrain (right).

Interpreting Photographs What differences do you see between these two photographs? How might these differences affect the lifestyles of people living in either place?

The Census: Counting People

The most complete way to gather information about population is to conduct a population **census**. Censuses go back to the ancient civilizations of Egypt and Rome, when rulers used them to determine the number of people under their rule and to identify taxpayers, labourers, and soldiers.

Since 1871, Canada has had a major census every 10 years. Currently, a less detailed one is also conducted every 5 years. A federal agency called Statistics Canada conducts the census, which provides a snapshot of a particular point in time of the Canadian population. All Canadians are required by law to be counted in the census. A random selection of people is chosen to give more detailed information, such as housing, household contents, income, and buying habits. In 2006, 98 percent of Canadians completed the census questionnaire, and, for the first time, they were able to do so online.

Deciphering Demographic Data

Demographic figures must be treated with caution. A **developed country** such as Canada has the resources to keep its data current, yet its figures will still have a margin for error. For example, it is difficult to ensure all homeless people are counted. In **developing countries**, the census data are usually much less accurate because the registration of births and deaths is not as complete as in developed countries. Census takers may not be able to reach remote areas. People in shantytowns are not counted because they are not considered permanent residents of cities. Some people may also avoid census takers out of fear of authorities, the wish to avoid taxation, or conflicts with governments over population policies.

Making comparisons between countries for such things as literacy or the size of an urban location can be difficult, as definitions may differ. Published numbers of people in fast-growing cities can often vary widely. Figures may be outdated, especially if a country does not have accurate **birth rate** and **death rate** statistics or has not held a recent census.

KEY TERMS

demography the study of population numbers, distribution, trends, and issues

census the process of collecting, compiling, and publishing demographic, economic, and social data about all people living in a particular area

developed country a country with a highly developed economy and infrastructure and high living standards

developing country a country with a less sophisticated economy and lower standard of living than developed countries; may have extensive poverty

birth rate the number of births per 1000 people in a country in a given year

death rate the number of deaths per 1000 people in a country in a given year

WEB LINK •
To read more about the Canadian census, visit the Pearson Web site.

FIGURE 11–3 A census taker fills in a questionnaire for Kenya's 2009 census. Ethnic violence during the 2008 election made the 2009 census controversial due to one question that asked to which ethnic group people belonged.

Graphs are an effective way of analyzing and communicating information. Four purposes of graphs are to show quantities, make comparisons, describe trends, and observe relationships.

- **Showing quantities:** Graphs for this purpose show amounts or values at a specific time and are always expressed in a unit of measurement (number of people, or amount of production, or varying rates). The best graph type shows the amounts most clearly. Line graphs are not usually used for this purpose.

- **Making comparisons:** Graphs can effectively compare sets of data with the same units of measurement, for example comparing levels of foreign investment in Canada in a bar graph. The best graphs show the comparison most clearly.

- **Describing trends:** Graphs can effectively show how data changes over time. Line graphs are particularly good for this purpose. Trends is a term used to describe significant patterns in the data.

- **Observing relationships:** Relationships are links between variables. For example, to look at the levels of development in various countries, we might plot the two variables of income levels and birth rates on the same graph. Scatter graphs are particularly useful for observing relationships.

Try to select the type of graph that best fits your purpose. The following are some examples in this text:

- Line graph – Figure 7–20

- Simple bar graph – Figure 11–6

- Stacked or divided bar graph – Figure 8–6

- Divergent bar graph – Figure 13–30

- Pie or circle graph – Figure 11–25

- Scatter graph – Figure 12–41

Making Graphs that Work

1. Keep content simple and straightforward. Do not try to combine too many ideas in one graph.

2. Place time along the bottom, from left to right.

3. Data that is continuous, such as population growth, can be shown in a line graph.

4. Connect only related events. For example, a graph of life expectancy at birth for different countries should be a series of unrelated points, not a line graph.

5. Liven up charts by adding colour, illustrations, icons, different fonts, and varying types of lines.

Applying the Skill

1. **a)** Examine the data in Figures 11–4 and 11–5, and decide on the type of graph that will most effectively compare and contrast the birth and death rates for Canada and Cameroon in one graph.

   b) Construct an effective graph following the principles outlined above.

   c) Briefly describe why you chose this format and why it is effective.

Period	Birth Rate	Death Rate
1950	43.4	24.9
1965	44.6	20.1
1980	44.8	14.6
1995	37.9	13.6
2010	34.2	13.2

FIGURE 11–4 Birth and death rates in Cameroon (per 1000 people), 1950–2010

Period	Birth rate	Death rate
1950	27.8	8.7
1965	18.4	7.5
1980	14.8	6.9
1995	11.6	7.2
2010	10.8	7.6

FIGURE 11–5 Birth and death rates in Canada (per 1000 people), 1950–2010

2. Figure 11–6 is a simple bar graph showing immigrant arrivals in Canada.

   a) For which of the four purposes was this graph constructed?

   b) Does a simple bar graph show the values clearly? Explain your answer.

   c) Suggest one other type of graph that would show this data equally well or better. Explain why you decided on your choice of graph.

   d) Create the alternative graph.

3. Refer to the table in Figure 11–12. Choose an appropriate style of graph based on the data. You do not need to complete the graph. Simply sketch out how you would construct it for your purpose and explain why.

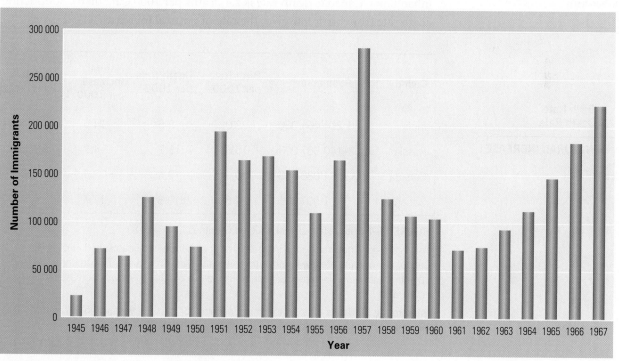

FIGURE 11–6 Immigrant arrivals in Canada, 1945 to 1967

KEY TERMS

immigration rate the number of new arrivals in a country in a given year per 1000 people

emigration rate the number of people leaving a country in a given year per 1000 people

natural increase (NI) the rate at which a population increases (or decreases) in a year expressed as a percentage of the total population; calculated by subtracting the death rate from the birth rate

exponential rate a rapid rate of population growth as each generation doubles in size

rule of 70 the time it takes a country to double its population, approximately 70 divided by the country's growth rate

doubling time the number of years it takes a country to double its population at its current growth rate

net migration the difference between the number of people immigrating to a country and the number of people emigrating

migrant a person who moves from one region to another

Calculating Population Change

Demographers are most interested in statistics that help them predict and explain changes or trends in society. At its most basic level, demography can determine whether a population is growing or shrinking. On another level, demographers study segments of the population. For instance, the number of working women in a society will affect the birth rate. It may also influence the diet of families, increasing the amount of packaged and prepared foods they eat.

The four basic components of population change are how many people are born (birth rate), how many die (death rate), how many move into a region (**immigration rate**), and how many move out of a region (**emigration rate**).

Natural Increase

It is not very useful to compare numbers of births and deaths between countries that have widely differing population sizes. To know that each day almost 1000 children are born in Canada, 73 778 in India, and 106 in Gabon is not very useful unless the total populations of the countries are considered. What really matters is comparing the relationship between the number of births and the size of the population in each country. Demographers do this by using birth rate and death rate statistics.

Birth rate is the number of children born in a region for every 1000 inhabitants. It is calculated by dividing the number of births in one year by the population and then multiplying the result by 1000. Canada's birth rate is 10.6 children per 1000 Canadians.

Death rate is the number of people who die in a region for every 1000 inhabitants. Canada's death rate is 7.4 deaths per 1000 Canadians. Subtracting death rate from birth rate gives the rate of **natural increase (NI)**.

Birth Rate
– Death Rate
_____

= NATURAL INCREASE

Country	Population	Birth Rate per 1000	Death Rate per 1000	Natural Increase per 1000	% Natural Increase
India	1 214 464 000	23.0	8.5	14.5	1.45
Russia	140 367 000	10.8	15.1	−4.3	−0.43
Canada	34 086 245	10.6	7.4	3.2	0.32
Gabon	1 501 000	27.5	9.8	17.7	1.77

FIGURE 11–7 Natural increase of selected countries, 2005–2010

This figure does not include the increase that comes from immigrants. In countries like Gabon, where there are few immigrants, the annual growth rate of 1.77 percent is made up entirely of natural increase. Canada would see its population growth increase by immigration.

Interpreting Statistics What factors might account for the wide variation in the natural increase of these populations?

©P

Exponential Growth

Human populations have the potential to grow at an ever-increasing rate. Suppose that a couple has two children, and each of these grows up to produce two children. By the third generation, the couple will have 14 descendants. This is called an **exponential rate** of increase. A regular arithmetic rate of 1, 2, 3, 4, and so on is quickly overtaken by an exponential rate, which increases by 1, 2, 4, 8. Each generation builds on previous generations in a compound fashion.

A convenient way to express exponential population growth is to use the length of time it would take for a population to double in size. One way of calculating this is to apply the "**rule of 70**," which states that **doubling time** is approximately equal to 70 divided by the growth rate (in percent) per year.

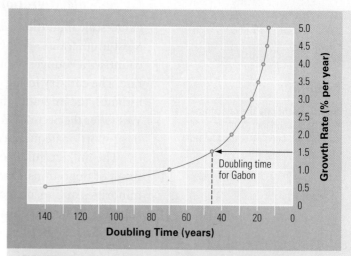

FIGURE 11–8 Population growth rate and doubling times

Reading a Graph Canada's rate of natural increase is 0.32. How many years would it take Canada's population to double if we did not take in immigrants? Use the equation on the left to calculate your answer.

Calculating Doubling Time for Gabon
70 divided by 1.77 (% natural increase) = 39.5 years

Immigration Rate
− Emigration Rate
―――――――――――
= NET MIGRATION

Net Migration

Population increase in some countries, particularly Canada, depends on immigrants. Emigrants leave the country each year, which also affects the demography. A country's **net migration** rate is the difference between its immigration and emigration rates. A combination of the birth rate, the death rate, and the net migration rate gives a complete picture of a country's annual population change.

Canada, the United States, and Australia are among the few countries in which immigration is a significant factor in the growth of their populations. Most immigrants to Canada come as economic **migrants** from developing nations, wanting to better their standard of living. Others come as refugees seeking to escape persecution in their home country. In Canada's 2006 Census, nearly 6.2 million people were immigrants. Between 2001 and 2006, Canada averaged 222 000 international migrants per year.

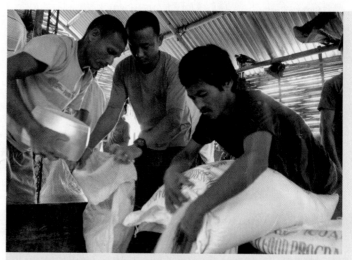

FIGURE 11–9 Food aid is distributed to Bhutanese refugees who have been living in camps in Nepal since the early 1990s. More than 850 Bhutanese refugees have been resettled in Canada to date.

● What is the formula used to calculate population growth in a country?

KEY TERM

population growth rate the rate at which a country's population increases or decreases; calculated by adding natural increase and net migration

WEB LINK ● · · · · · · · · · · · · · · · ·

Visit the Pearson Web site to see a population clock developed by Statistics Canada.

Large-Scale Migrations

Large-scale migrations affect the structure of population by age and gender. Most immigrants are young and generally single males. This gives the host countries a younger population that will eventually result in a higher birth rate. The country losing population experiences the reverse effect. For instance, the migration from Communist-controlled East Germany to the West after the Second World War gave East Germany a population with a disproportionate number of older people.

The multicultural populations of Canada and the United States are the result of migrations. During the last decades of the 20th century, visible minorities in Canada increased dramatically with immigration from Asia and the Caribbean. Canada and the United States have also become home to many Spanish-speaking migrants from Latin America.

Population Growth Rate

Population growth rate is the rate at which a country's population changes per year. It is a country's rate of natural increase plus its net migration, usually expressed as a percentage.

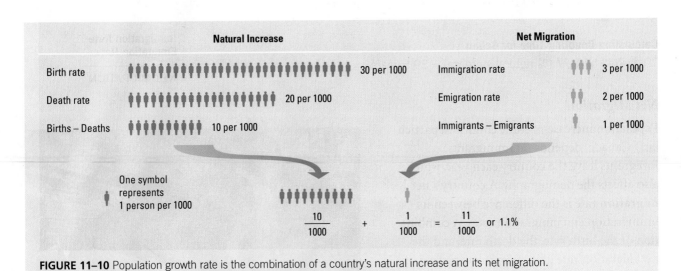

FIGURE 11–10 Population growth rate is the combination of a country's natural increase and its net migration.

PRACTICE QUESTIONS

1. Define *demography, natural increase, emigration, immigration, net migration,* and *exponential growth.*

2. What types of information are collected in a census? Give examples of three uses of this information.

3. What are some reasons why people may be reluctant to provide information in a census?

4. **a)** What are the main components of population change?

   b) What is meant by the rule of 70?

5. Why is immigration more important to Canada's population growth than to some other countries?

6. Why are rates more useful for comparing population growth than raw numbers?

The Demographic Revolution

For most of human history, birth rates have been high. Yet the population grew slowly before the 1700s because death rates were also very high, particularly among infants and young children. People had a **life expectancy** of little more than 30 years. Disease, poor medical care, poor nutrition, and unsanitary living conditions contributed to the high death rate. Families needed to have many children to ensure a few survived. Larger families were also needed to help farm the land and to provide security for parents in old age. This situation is still common today in many developing countries.

The rapid population growth after 1750 was mainly due to falling death rates. Beginning in Europe, then spreading to North America, and then to developing countries, death rates fell much more rapidly than birth rates. The agricultural revolution increased food production so that people had better diets. Clean drinking water, a more varied and nutritious diet, and vaccination against infectious diseases meant that far more children survived to become parents themselves. Birth rates remained high for a number of years, producing a wide gap between birth and death rates and a rapid growth in population.

The Great Depression of the 1930s and the Second World War kept birth rates low in most Western countries. After 1945, there was a rapid and prolonged rise in birth rates, and today Western countries are experiencing lower birth rates and longer life expectancy.

After the Second World War, the World Health Organization (WHO), aid programs, and improved transportation and communications made better health measures available to most countries. The developing world experienced the same changes as the developed world had in the 19th and early 20th centuries. Death rates fell in developing countries, but birth rates have not dropped as rapidly.

KEY TERM

life expectancy the average number of years an individual is expected to live

FIGURE 11–11 Polio, a virus that attacks the nervous system, was rampant in the first half of the last century and crippled huge numbers of children. Today polio has been eradicated in most countries due to a vaccine developed in the 1950s.

Country	1900		1950		2010	
	Males	Females	Males	Females	Males	Females
Portugal	33.3	35.2	56.9	61.9	75.4	81.9
Japan	42.8	44.3	60.4	63.9	79	86
Mali	n/a	n/a	35	36	47.6	49
Canada	47	50	66.8	71.7	78	83
Afghanistan	n/a	n/a	29	28	44	44

(n/a = not available)

FIGURE 11–12 Life expectancy at birth in selected countries for 1900, 1950, and 2010 **Interpreting Statistics** Why has there been an increase in life expectancy in all these countries? Suggest why there are differences in life expectancy. How could a demographer use the statistics for Japan and Canada in 1900 to argue that these were developing countries at that time?

KEY TERMS

demographic transition model a model that shows changes in a population's birth and death rates and growth based on technological development

industrialization the overall change in a society from farm production and crafts-manship to mechanized manufacturing production

urbanization the move of people from farms to cities where jobs are available

mortality deaths in a population

The Demographic Transition Model

Geographers sometimes use models to represent reality or a theory. A model simplifies information to make it understandable. Models must strike a balance between detail and useful generalization.

One useful way of explaining population change is the **demographic transition model**. It shows changes over a period of time in three elements: birth rates, death rates, and trends in overall population numbers. The model assumes that, in any country, high birth rates and high death rates (Stage 1) will gradually fall (Stages 2 and 3) as a result of economic and social development. Because the model is based on what has happened in developed countries, it assumes that countries will pass through periods of **industrialization** and **urbanization** on the way to reduced birth and death rates. The model is useful in showing how the population growth rates of countries that are industrializing are in a state of transition. It seems that this transition period is unlikely in some countries, particularly in Africa, and so the model must be used with caution.

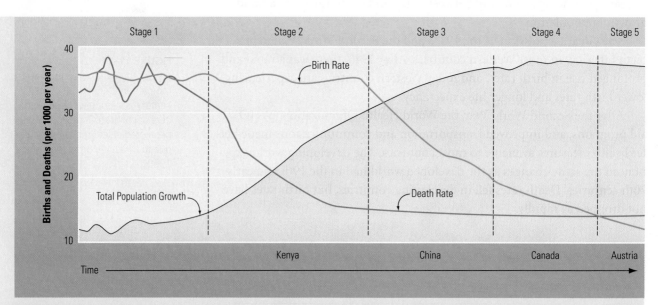

FIGURE 11–13 The demographic transition model showing examples of countries in various stages of demographic transition

Stage 1: Pre-transition: High birth rates and high fluctuating death rates result in small population growth. Plagues, diseases, and poor nutrition keep mortality high.

Stage 2: Early Transition: Improved health care, sanitation, and increased food supplies lead to a rapid fall in death rates. Birth rates are still high, so there is a rapid increase in population numbers.

Stage 3: Late Transition: Birth rates begin to fall, so population growth begins to decline. Industrialization, urbanization, and improved living standards lead to less desire for large families.

Stage 4: Post-transition: The transition is complete. There is a stable or slow population increase with low birth and death rates. The birth rate may fluctuate in special circumstances, such as the post-war baby boom.

Stage 5: Declining Population: Birth rates drop below death rates. Many older people are in the population. This is happening increasingly in European countries and in Japan. It is not known whether this trend will extend to other regions.

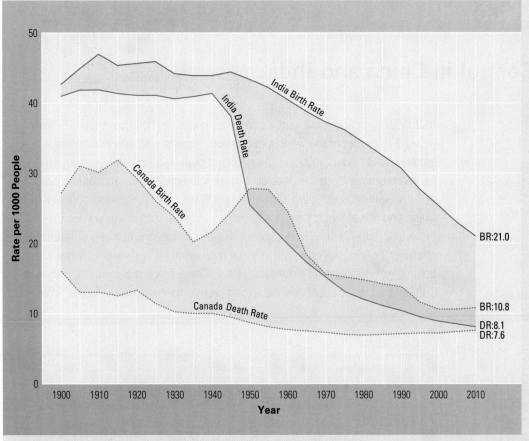

FIGURE 11–14 The population of Canada and India, 1900–2010

1. In which years was the natural increase greatest of each country?

2. Based on the demographic transition model, in what stage is (a) Canada and
   (b) India at present?

3. Predict what will likely happen to India and Canada in the next five decades. Explain
   your answer.

4. Use a three-column organizer to compare Canada and India using the information
   from the graph. In the centre column, note problems that will be common to both
   countries. In the outside columns, note problems that will be unique to each country.

PRACTICE QUESTIONS

1. a) Why was world population growth so slow
   before the 1800s?

   b) What improvements in living conditions led to
   population growth?

2. How do declines in birth rates differ between the
   developed and the developing world?

3. What is the most important factor in starting a
   country to move from one stage of the demographic transition model to the next? Suggest ways
   to influence this factor.

4. What is the second factor in starting a country to
   move from one stage of the demographic transition model to the next? Suggest ways to influence
   this factor.

©P

Population Control in China and India

KEY TERMS

family planning the concept of limiting the size of families

rhythm method a method of birth control in which a couple does not have intercourse during the time when a woman is likely to ovulate

sterilization a procedure by which a person's ability to reproduce is destroyed

vasectomy a form of male sterilization in which the tube carrying sperm from each testis is cut and tied

coercion the use of force

contraception birth control

total fertility rate the average number of children born over the lifetime of a typical woman in a particular country

one-child policy a policy adopted by China to control population growth

infanticide the act of killing an infant

gender selection the choice of whether to keep a fetus based on its gender

In 2008, China and India had a combined population of more than 2.5 billion—nearly 37 percent of the world's population. Experts estimate that this figure will increase to 3 billion by 2050. The issues of population size and growth rate have figured prominently in the development policies of each country since 1950.

The years following the Second World War brought profound changes to China and India. Since then, the government of each country has dealt with its increasing population in very different ways and with dramatically different consequences. Politics played a role in these two countries' approaches to population control, with India being a democracy and China being a communist country. Cultural traditions, especially the strong preference for sons, have also affected the demographic profile of both countries.

TIMELINE

Timeline of India's Policies on Population Control

1952 India became the first developing country to launch a **family-planning** program, focusing on abstinence and the **rhythm method**. Rural India was targeted with little success.

1962 The government launched awareness-building campaigns: "Small family" songs on the radio and posters on walls and buses. The fertility rate remained high while infant mortality and death rates fell rapidly, leading to high population growth.

1970 **Sterilization** programs and targets were established. **Vasectomy** clinics were located in strategic locations, including railway stations. The effort failed, since the poor wanted the economic security of children, especially sons.

1975 Prime Minister Indira Gandhi suspended democratic rights and elections. The Nasbandi program used **coercion** and rewards to promote male sterilization. Children of parents with more than three children were refused schooling, prisoners were not granted parole, and government workers were threatened with firing or demotion if they did not have a a vasectomy. More than 8 million sterilizations were performed in 1975.

1977 An election called by Gandhi led to the defeat of her party, the end of coercive policies, and a backlash against family planning. The new government changed the focus to family welfare, with an emphasis on education, voluntary **contraception**, and child-survival programs.

1983 The National Health Policy stated that replacement levels of **total fertility rate** (TFR) would be reached by 2000. The program did not meet targets.

2000 A new National Population Policy was established to slow population growth. The emphasis was on female sterilization following the UN's urging to reduce the TFR to 2.1 by 2010. India's population passes the 1-billion mark.

2010 The UN estimates India's TFR is at 2.5, down from 5.9 in 1950 but shy of the 2.1 target. The population continues to increase.

©P

TIMELINE

Timeline of China's Policies on Population Control

1949

Population increase was encouraged as a way to make China a great power. When asked how China would feed the growing population, communist leader Mao Zedong responded that "every stomach comes with two hands attached."

1958–1960

A program called "The Great Leap Forward" brought massive instability to food supplies as agricultural land was organized into large collective farms. Famine and food shortages reduced birth rates and increased death rates, which led to population decline.

1970

The growth rate reached 2.61 percent and the population was 816 million. The government reacted with a publicity campaign that encouraged people to have only two children.

1979

The Chinese government launched a population planning policy after Mao Zedong's death in 1976. With just 7 percent of the world's arable land and two thirds of the population entering their reproductive years, the **one-child policy** was established. Cash, free medical care, and improved educational and housing opportunities were offered as rewards. People who did not cooperate were fined for having more than one child, and lost medical and educational privileges.

1980s/1990s

Pressure to be sterilized and have abortions was common in the mid-1980s. Birth rates were less than half of what they had been in the mid-1960s. The one-child policy was more successful in urban than in rural areas. Sons were valued as farm labourers, and they were expected to look after their aging parents. Reports of forced abortions and **infanticide** if the first-born was a girl led the government to relax the policy in the late 1980s. A second child was allowed in rural areas if the first-born was a girl or was born with a disability.

2002

The 2000 census put the population at 1.27 billion. An increasing gender imbalance in favour of males led family planning to focus on education, health, and economic opportunities for women. **Gender selection** was banned and discrimination against female infants forbidden.

2008

The Chinese government estimated that the one-child policy resulted in 400 million fewer people. The population still increased by 800 000 every five weeks.

2009

Concern about an aging population and a shrinking labour force led to relaxing restrictions in many provinces and cities, such as Shanghai and Beijing, allowing two "only-child" parents to have two children.

2011

Many Chinese demographers expect changes in the population policy during the 12th five-year plan for the development of the country from 2011 to 2016.

Looking Further

1. Use a Venn diagram or another organizer to compare and contrast the methods and effectiveness of population control programs in China and India. Explain why China has been more successful in reducing population growth than India.

2. To what extent do you agree or disagree with the following statement: The coercion associated with the Nasbandi program was justified in the face of India's runaway population growth.

3. In the case of China and India, would you agree or disagree with those who claim that the rise from poverty to affluence is the most effective population control? Explain.

4. How accurate do you think the projections are of future populations of China and India? Explain.

5. Imagine that you are either a Chinese or an Indian government official in charge of a billion dollar program to reduce population growth. Identify the two most effective uses of your economic resources to reach this goal. Justify your choices.

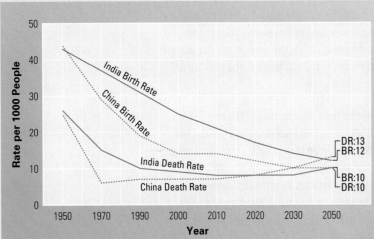

FIGURE 11–15 Birth and death rates for China and India, 1950–2050

FIGURE 11–16 Poster promoting the one-child policy in China

©P

Population Profiles

Demographers use various tools to analyze population information. The population pyramid is a powerful tool that reveals the age and gender structure of a population, and can provide valuable insight into the types of government services that are and will be needed in a region or country.

Population Pyramids

A **population pyramid** is a graph that shows the age and gender structure of a population. A series of horizontal bar graphs for the male and female populations are placed back to back at age intervals of five years, called **age cohorts**. Population pyramids make it easier to see the structure of a population. They are also useful in comparing the population structures of different countries. As the examples in Figure 11–17 show, countries with high birth rates have many children and an expanding population. A stable population will have birth rates and death rates in balance, and a contracting population will have a growth rate below replacement level. In general, the expanding pyramids are representative of developing countries, while the stable and contracting pyramids represent developed countries.

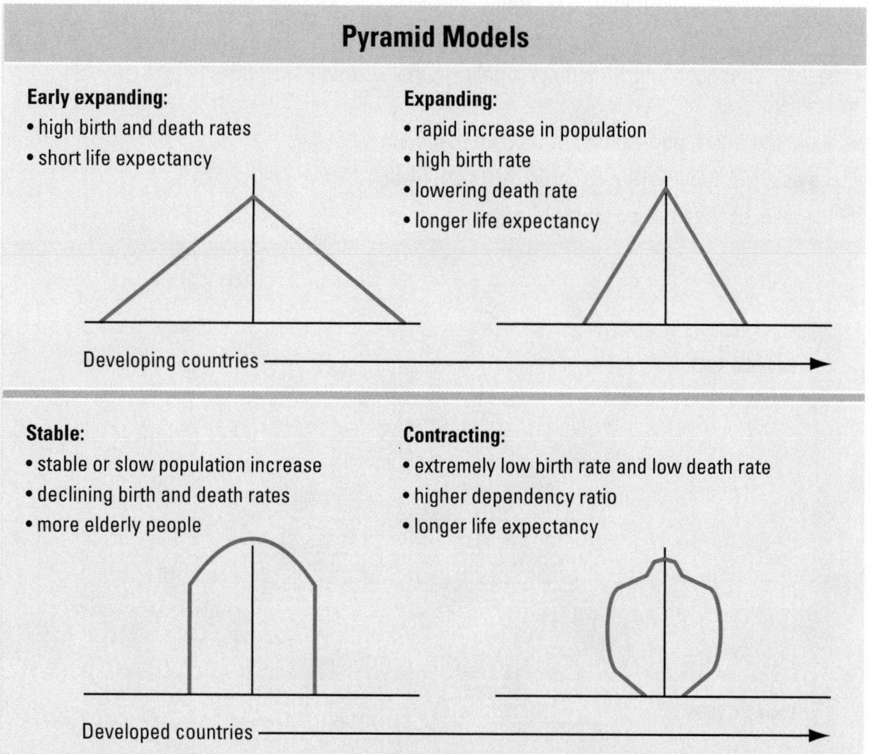

● Identify the different types of population pyramids. What does each represent?

KEY TERMS

population pyramid a bar graph that shows male and female populations back to back at age intervals of five years

age cohort an age group in a population, for example, the number of people between the ages of 10 and 14

Pyramid Models

Early expanding:
- high birth and death rates
- short life expectancy

Expanding:
- rapid increase in population
- high birth rate
- lowering death rate
- longer life expectancy

Developing countries ⟶

Stable:
- stable or slow population increase
- declining birth and death rates
- more elderly people

Contracting:
- extremely low birth rate and low death rate
- higher dependency ratio
- longer life expectancy

Developed countries ⟶

FIGURE 11–17 Model pyramids of populations at different stages of development

Interpreting a Graph Match these models with the population pyramids shown in Figure 11–18.

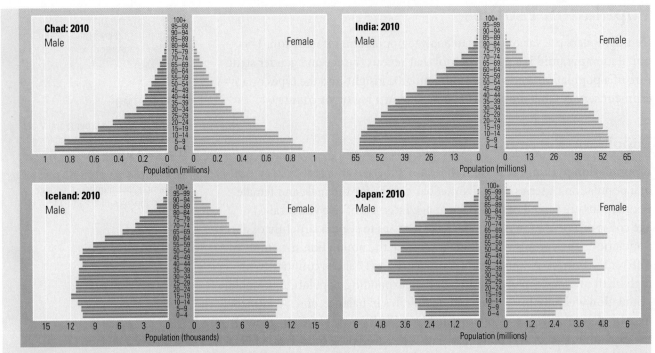

FIGURE 11–18 Population pyramids for selected countries

Thinking Critically

1. What evidence is there that the pyramid for Chad has a very high birth rate? What percentage of the population would you estimate is under the age of 15?

2. What does the shape of the pyramid for India tell you about trends in infant mortality in that country? How does India compare with Chad and Iceland in this regard?

3. What does the pyramid for Iceland tell you about the future population numbers in that country?

4. Suggest a number of problems Japan will face as a result of the age structure of its population.

5. In what state of the demographic transition model is each of the pyramids? Explain.

FIGURE 11–19 Population pyramids for Canada, 1911 and 2006

Reading a Graph

1. Refer to Figure 11–17. At what stage of development—early expanding, expanding, stable, or contracting—would you place each of these pyramids?

2. What impact will the increasing number of older people in 2006 have on the population?

3. What other information can be learned by analyzing these pyramids? Give examples of how government and business might use these pyramids to deal with present and future trends.

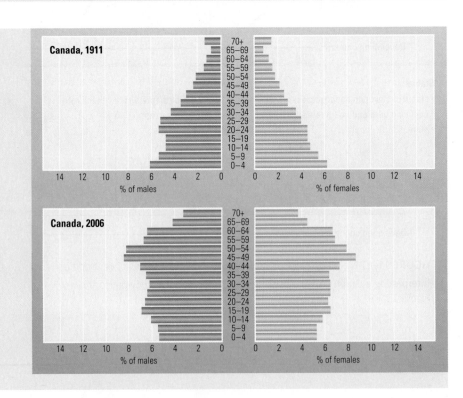

©P

Too Many Men

China's gender imbalance is getting worse. According to a 2009 article, "China has 32 [million] more men aged under 20 than women.... [and] 119 male births for every 100 girls, compared with 107 to 100 in industrialised countries.... The gap is greater in provinces that allow couples to have a second child if the first is a girl. Among second-born children, boys outnumbered girls by 143 to 100."

The gender imbalance is beginning to be recognized as a problem for the future. Many male children will not be able to marry when they are older. These men are referred to as "bare branches." The article also notes that the "[Chinese] government has expressed concerns that too many men could lead to social instability and is expanding programs that encourage people to have female children."

1. What types of social problems may occur in China as a result of the gender imbalance?

2. **Perspectives** Do you think that female children will become more valued in the future in China? Why or why not?

KEY TERMS

dependency ratio the proportion of the population (children and those over 65 years of age) that is being supported by the working age group

dependency load the percentage of a population that is younger than 15 or older than 64 years of age

The Age Structure of Populations

The age structure of a population helps us understand the reasons for changes in population. Demographers divide populations into three age groups: children up to the age of 15, working people from ages 15 to 64, and adults 65 years and older. This gives the **dependency ratio**, which is the proportion of the population that is being supported by the working-age group.

Children and older people put pressure on society for medical, education, housing, and other services. In the 2006 Census, Canada's population included 17.7 percent children and 13.7 percent adults 65 years and older, giving it a **dependency load** of 31.4 percent. A country like Bangladesh has a dependency load of 38.6 percent, made up of 34.6 percent children and 4 percent adults aged 65 years and older. The age structure can give us insights into problems that could arise in the future resulting from a predominantly old or young population.

● What is the dependency ratio and why is it important?

FIGURE 11–20 Japanese seniors (left) pose for a photographer in Yokohama, Japan. Thirteen percent of Japanese are under the age of 15, while 22.8 percent are 65 or older.

On the opposite end of the spectrum, 43 percent of the population in Kenya is under the age of 15 (right), with only 2.6 percent 65 or older.

WEB LINK ●·······················

To read more about the aging of the world population, visit the Pearson Web site.

Dependency: Too Young or Too Old

There has been a major change in the age structure of the world's population as the numbers of people have increased. There have never been so many people in the dependant category. This change will put increasing pressure on the financial resources of countries. In Japan, for example, the life expectancy is 79 for males and 86 for females—the highest in the world. The government has declared the aging population to be its greatest future challenge. If present trends continue, close to one third of the Japanese population will be over 65 by 2025. Years of exceptionally low birth rates mean there are fewer workers to care for them. How and whether Japan can maintain its economic position in the face of these problems remains to be seen.

At the other end of the scale, some developing countries have young dependants under the age of 15 making up almost half of their population. Any fall in birth rates in these areas has been offset by a greater number of women who can bear children, even if families are smaller. These countries remain in a cycle of poverty, as their limited resources and attempts to improve development are swallowed up by young populations. India and sub-Saharan Africa, with a combined population of more than 2 billion people, face a daunting task of providing employment for the increasing numbers of young people entering the labour market. Young men in particular grow restless as they reach working age and find few opportunities to improve their standard of living. This results in an underemployed generation that could threaten the stability of entire regions.

FAST FORWARD

An Aging World

The average age of the world's population is rapidly increasing. By mid-2008, the total number of people 65 and older was approximately 506 million, and will reach 1.3 billion by 2040. A U.S. Census Bureau report on aging states that in just over 30 years, the proportion of older people in the world will double from 7 percent to 14 percent.

1. What parts of the world will be able to deal more effectively with the problem of an aging population? Explain.

2. **Significance** List the three most likely consequences that Canada's aging population will have for you. Justify your answers.

PRACTICE QUESTIONS

1. What information does a population pyramid show about a population?

2. Name the population pyramids that are typical of developing countries.

3. Name the population pyramids that are typical of developed countries.

4. Refer back to Figure 11–13. With which stage of the demographic transition model would each population pyramid be associated? Explain.

5. What is the dependency ratio? Why is it important for a country to know this figure for future planning?

6. Why does an aging population present a serious problem in the developed world?

Canada's Population: Past and Future

Canada's birth and death rates have been dropping steadily in the past 30 years. This means the population is getting older. In 1951, 1 in 13 Canadians was over 65 years of age. In 2020, 1 in 5 will be over that age. Life expectancy in Canada increased from an average of 45 years in 1900 to 65 years by 1950 and to 81 years by the year 2010. This trend is the same for most developed countries.

The increasing number of elderly people puts immense strains on social and medical services. There are fewer children to look after aging parents. This has put pressure on the health care system to provide more long-term care for the elderly. The cost of health services for the aged continues to rise as medical technology becomes more complex.

FIGURE 11–21 The years between 1947 and 1966 are generally referred to as the baby boom years in Canada, with the peak occurring in 1959 when 479 000 babies were born. According to Statistics Canada, baby boomers make up more than 30 percent of Canada's population, which is why much of Canada's population today is aging.

Canada's Immigrant Population

The age structure of Canada's population is one of the main factors the federal government considers when deciding on the number of immigrants Canada will accept each year. Today, immigrants account for a large and increasing proportion of labour force growth in Canada. According to Statistics Canada, "immigrants who arrived during the 1990s accounted for about 70 percent of net labour force growth between 1991 and 2001." This percentage will likely grow substantially over the next decade, partly as a result of low rates of natural increase in the Canadian-born population.

The 2006 census indicates that 1.1 million of the 1.6 million growth in the Canadian population since 2001 was due to immigration. By 2012, all

©P

net growth in Canada's labour force is expected to come from immigration. Without these levels of immigration, the average age of the Canadian population would increase rapidly.

The number of immigrants entering Canada fluctuates above or below the 200 000 level. This is far from the federal government's goal, which is to have annual immigration equal 1 percent of the population. The difference between planned and actual immigration levels is shown in Figure 11–22. Immigration numbers have never come near the record level of 400 870 immigrants in 1913, which represented 5.5 percent of a population of 7.3 million.

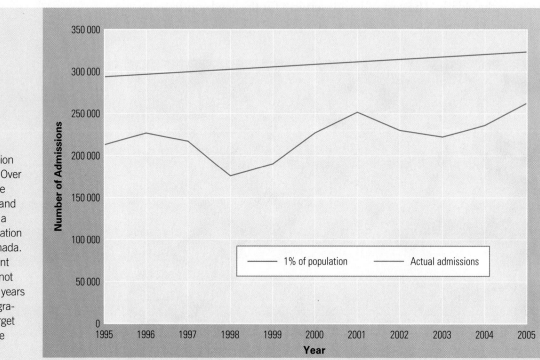

FIGURE 11–22
Immigration admission levels, 1995–2005. Over the years, there have been many reports and alleged promises of a one-percent immigration intake target for Canada. However, government statistics show that not once in the past 13 years has Canada's immigration intake met a target of one percent of the population.

● Why is immigration important to Canada's population and economy?

Canada Looks to Immigrants

As Canada's birth rate remains low and the population ages, the workforce will decline as the number of retirees increases. This will increase demands for government services while the tax base will be shrinking. Immigration provides the only source of replacement workers, ensuring continued economic growth and a sustainable tax base. The main difficulty the government faces is in attracting young, skilled workers and entrepreneurs to offset the aging workforce. Many skilled immigrants, such as those in health care and other professions, find it difficult to get professional **accreditation** in Canada. There is also fierce competition among countries for highly skilled labour. As Industry Canada noted in a 2008 report, "In recent decades, highly skilled workers have become more mobile internationally. Furthermore, high demand for skills in industrialized countries has led to intense international competition for these mobile workers."

©P

Canada accepts approximately 25 000 refugees a year, but increasing numbers of refugees from Eastern Europe and Mexico led the government to impose visa restrictions on those countries in 2009. More money is now spent on handling refugee claims than on processing regular immigration. Critics have claimed budget cuts and the time spent processing refugees are the reasons Canada has not reached its immigration targets.

Canada's Aboriginal People Pass One Million

Data from the 2006 Canadian census shows that the number of people who identified themselves as an Aboriginal person surpassed the 1-million mark. Aboriginal people's share of Canada's total population is on the rise. In 2006, they accounted for 3.8 percent of the total population of Canada enumerated in the census, up from 3.3 percent in 2001 and 2.8 percent in 1996.

Factors Accounting for Growth

Several factors may account for the growth of the Aboriginal population. These include demographic factors, such as high birth rates. In addition, more individuals are identifying themselves as Aboriginal, and population data for Indian reserves has been more complete since 1996. Other highlights from the 2006 census include the following:

- The number of status Indians living off reserves has increased since 1996, from 50 percent to 51 percent.

- Eighty percent of Aboriginal peoples lived either in Ontario or in the four Western provinces in 2006.

- The average age of the Aboriginal population in Canada is 27, compared to 40 for the non-Aboriginal population. Almost half (48 percent) of the Aboriginal population is under the age of 25.

PRACTICE QUESTIONS

1. What information can you discover about a country's past and future by analyzing a population pyramid?

2. **a)** What effects do migrations have on the structure of the receiving country's population?

b) How would the age structure of the population in Canada be different if there had been no immigration?

3. What factors have accounted for the growth of Canada's Aboriginal population since 1996?

©P

Optimists versus pessimists: Are there limits to population growth?

With a United Nations projected world population of 9 billion by 2054, the debate continues as to whether there are limits to the number of people Earth can support. Optimists have focused on humankind's ability to adapt to a growing population, while pessimists highlight the problems that population growth has caused or will cause.

The Pessimists

Thomas Malthus was a British economist who began writing about the risks of population growth in the late 1700s. He claimed that population would soon outstrip food supply, leading to famine, disease, and social disorder. Malthus's predictions were not realized, since he did not foresee the improvements in agriculture, hygiene, and medicine. Also, millions of people migrated to British colonies to cultivate farmlands there, which eased population pressure.

Neo-Malthusians

Some thinkers, called **neo-Malthusians**, predict that disaster will overtake populations in the world's poorest developing countries in the next 50 years due to increasing global warming, shortages of arable land, conflicts over fresh water, declining fish stocks, and the spread of AIDS or other diseases. Africa will be most vulnerable to these threats.

Neo-Malthusians claim that migrations, technology, and new farming lands cannot solve the problems in these countries. A leading neo-Malthusian, Lester Brown of the Worldwatch Institute, says that millions of people will die while the population in the developing world tries to return to a balance with the environment's ability to provide food. By 2050, the populations of many poor countries are projected to double in size. Ethiopia, with 85 million people, will reach a population of 174 million, and the Democratic Republic of the Congo's population will rise to 147 million. Unless there are profound changes, the population in these countries will be checked by famine, disease, and war.

In the 1980s, William Catton modernized and expanded the views of Malthus. He coined the term **carrying capacity** and claimed that Earth has been exceeding its carrying capacity for many years, at the expense of environmental damage. In his book *Overshoot*, he states:

> *If, having overshot carrying capacity, we cannot avoid crash, perhaps with ecological understanding of its real causes, we can remain human in circumstances that could otherwise tempt us to turn beastly.*
> –**William Catton**, Overshoot, 1982

In 1996, William Rees and Mathis Wackernagel from the University of British Columbia published a book in which the term **ecological footprint** was introduced. They pointed out that if all the world's population lived by North American standards, the resources of three Earths would be required.

> *Indeed, we believe that confronting together the reality of ecological overshoot will force us to discover and exercise those special qualities that distinguish humans from other sentient species, to become truly human. In this sense, global ecological change may well represent our last great opportunity to prove that there really is intelligent life on Earth.*
> –**Mathis Wackernagel and William E. Rees,** Our Ecological Footprint, 1996

The Optimists

Those with an optimistic outlook on population growth are called **cornucopians**. They have faith in mankind's ability to find innovations, such as solar and wind energy, that will increase Earth's carrying capacity.

In the 1960s, American demographer D.J. Bogue identified his theory of **demographic regulation**, meaning that as living standards around the world improve, population growth will naturally level off. Many countries, such as Sweden, illustrate this levelling off of population growth. Bogue's theory of demographic regulation is also

©P

supported by the demographic transition model, as well as the measures adopted by China and India to limit population growth (see Case Study on pages 368–370).

Organizations such as the United Nations, the World Bank, and most international aid agencies are also positive in their outlook on population growth. They claim technological developments, increased trade, and more efficient ways of sharing Earth's resources will ease the problems of developing nations. They point to the rapid increases in population in the 20th century that were always matched by increased food production—26 percent since the 1960s. New developments in genetic engineering of crops and animals could repeat this success. Famines in large parts of the world predicted by the pessimists have not happened. Educational programs will increase awareness of the benefits of population control. The programs show that enough food is produced to feed everyone adequately, and it is the distribution system that causes malnutrition in some countries. Increased globalization, optimists believe, will create a more equal distribution of food and resources.

RIBER
SVENSKA DAGBLADET
Stockholm
SWEDEN

CARTOONISTS & WRITERS SYNDICATE

SIX BILLION AND COUNTING

FIGURE 11–23

Interpreting a Cartoon What is the point of view of the cartoonist regarding present world population figures? Is the cartoonist a neo-Malthusian or a cornucopian? Explain.

Analyzing the Issue

1. Explain the concept of carrying capacity.

2. What technological changes in the 20th century increased the carrying capacity of farmland in Canada? Can the example of Canada be duplicated in the developing world in the 20th century? Why or why not?

3. Summarize the viewpoint of each of the following people on world population trends: Malthus, Brown, Catton, Rees and Wackernagel, and Bogue. Which do you find most credible? Why?

4. Use a two-column organizer to compare and contrast the views of optimists and pessimists on the effects of future population growth. Then use the information to determine your viewpoint. Explain why you are an optimist or a pessimist regarding the growth of world population.

5. In what ways might a 16-year-old from the slums of Mumbai, India have a different perspective on the future from you?

KEY TERMS

neo-Malthusians people who share Malthus' pessimistic views regarding population growth

carrying capacity the maximum number of people that can be sustained by an environment

ecological footprint the impact of humans on the environment

cornucopians people who have optimistic views on population growth due to advances in science and technology

demographic regulation the theory that population growth will level off as living standards improve

KEY TERMS

population distribution the pattern of where people live in an area

ecumene the populated area of the world

population density the number of people living in a given area; calculated by dividing the population by its area

Where Do Six Billion–Plus People Live?

Population distribution refers to the way people are spaced over Earth's surface. The Greek fathers of geography studied population distribution. They called their part of the world **ecumene**, and we now use this word to describe permanently inhabited places. As Figure 11–24 indicates, global population is unevenly distributed. The majority of the world's population lives north of the equator in mid-latitudes, with most living close to the world's oceans.

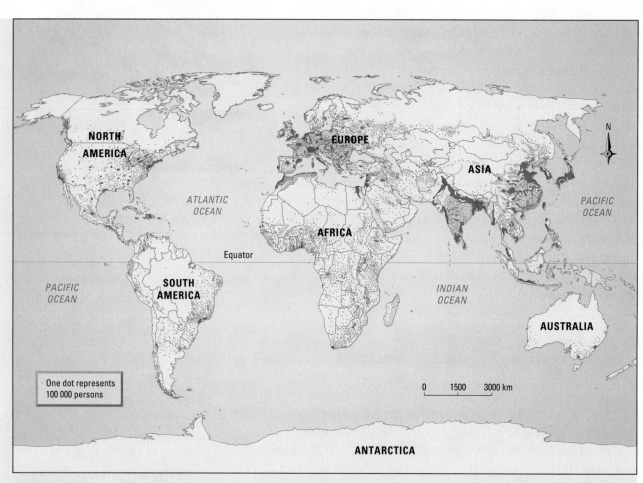

FIGURE 11–24 World population distribution

Reading a Map

1. Why do you think the dot method is used for distribution maps rather than other methods, such as shading?

2. Are the most densely populated areas north or south of the equator?

3. Compare this map with a map showing landforms or relief. What relationship do you see between
   a) densely populated areas and lowlands?
   b) sparsely populated areas and highlands? Identify two highland areas that are densely populated.

4. Compare this map with a map showing climate. What is the relationship between population distribution and areas that are
   a) very cold throughout the year?
   b) very dry?

5. Identify two very dry areas that are densely populated. Refer again to the relief map, and give an explanation for this population density.

6. Which two continents are most densely populated? Make a list of reasons that might account for the density in these two continents.

©P

Population density measures the number of people in a given area. Population densities for the countries of the world are shown in Figure 11–26. These are crude densities. They are calculated by dividing the population of a country by its area. These figures are useful for general comparisons, but do not take into account the wide variations that exist within larger countries. For example, the Canadian population density of 3.5 persons per square kilometre is one of the lowest in the world. Yet with an 80-percent urban population, most Canadians live at far higher densities than those indicated for Canada by calculating the small population against its large size. Rural and urban densities also differ dramatically in most countries. There are many explanations for the different population densities found in countries. The web in Figure 11–27 shows some of the major physical and human factors affecting population density.

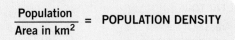

$$\frac{\text{Population}}{\text{Area in km}^2} = \textbf{POPULATION DENSITY}$$

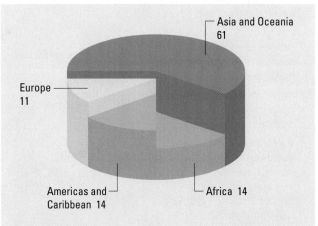

FIGURE 11–25 Earth's population as a village of 100 people

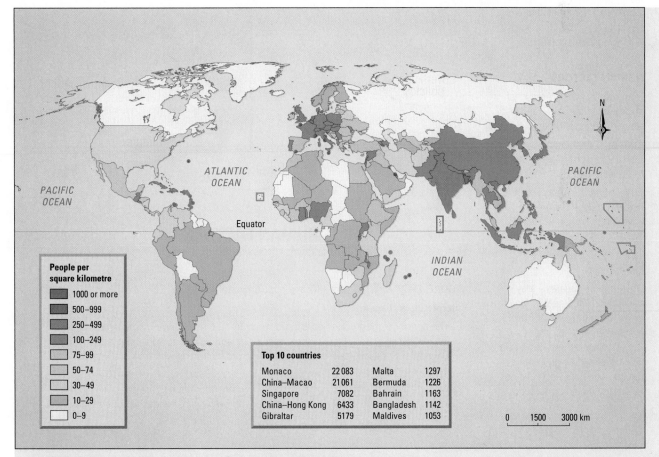

FIGURE 11–26 Population density of the countries of the world, 2008

Reading a Map

1. List a number of uses for a map like this.

2. How does this map reinforce the information in Figure 11–24?

©P

PHYSICAL FACTORS

Climate – Areas that are very dry or very cold generally have lower densities.

Landscape – Lowlands near the rims of continents have the highest densities.

Resources – Areas rich in a variety of resources will attract higher densities.

Soils – Rich river valley and lowland soils result in higher densities.

Vegetation – Areas of very dense vegetation, such as rainforests, have low densities. In temperate zones, former forested areas and grasslands have high densities.

Water – A reliable water supply from rainfall or rivers is necessary for higher densities.

Accessibility – Areas that are easier to reach by land or sea will increase in population.

HUMAN FACTORS

Communications – Areas that are easier to reach by land or sea will increase in population.

Culture – Nomadic or agricultural cultures may determine the level of density.

Development – Areas with a highly developed economy will have much higher densities.

Disease – Areas with a high incidence of disease will have low densities.

Government policies – May encourage settlement in remote areas, as in the case of Brazil and the Amazon basin, the Soviet Union moving workers to new cities in Siberia, or in Canada's eastern Arctic where Innu settlement was forced.

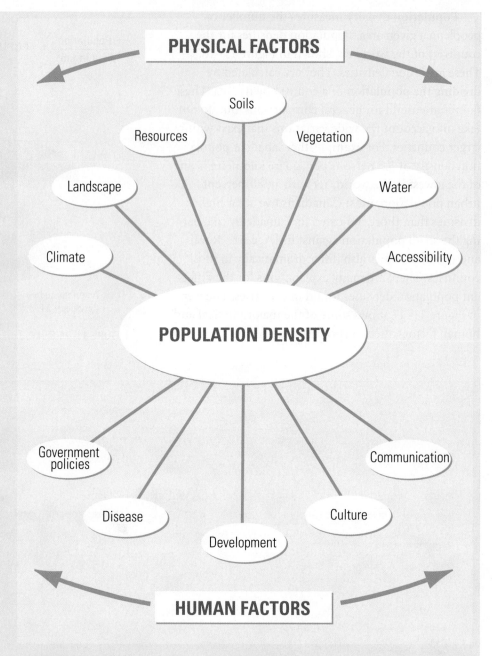

FIGURE 11–27 Major factors affecting population density

Interpreting a Diagram

1. The density of most countries is determined by a combination of some factors shown in the ideas web. Which factors apply best to Canada? Which factors apply best to British Columbia? For each area, rank the factors in order, starting with those having the greatest effect.

2. Working alone or with a partner, choose a country from each of the categories in the legend of Figure 11–26. Use the ideas web to give reasons for each country's inclusion in the category.

©P

Nutritional Density

There are great differences in the productivity of farmlands in different parts of the world. For example, the Fraser Valley in southern British Columbia has exceptionally rich agricultural soils, but its output is restricted by a short growing season. Canadian farms cannot match the output of areas like southern China, where rich soils and ideal climate produce three crops a year. This means that a square kilometre of farmland in southern China can produce far more food for people than a similar area in the Fraser Valley. **Nutritional density** of land is a measure of how much nutrition in calories can be produced from the land. The nutritional density column in Figure 11–28 shows the average nutritional densities for the countries listed.

Country	Densities in km²	
	Crude	**Nutritional**
Australia	3	46
Canada	3	62
Egypt	84	2181
Japan	336	2741

FIGURE 11–28 Crude population densities and nutritional densities for selected countries

Interpreting Statistics Why are the differences between crude and nutritional densities for Canada and Australia lower than for the other two countries? Use a climate map from an atlas to help explain why the nutritional density of Egypt and Japan is so much higher than the crude density.

Earth's Crowded Future

The world's population will continue to grow in the 21st century. What is not certain is how fast it will grow. Given the large populations of China and India, the attempts and varying success of these countries at bringing their population growth under control are important considerations in the overall world population.

Age structure is an important factor in determining how fast a population will increase. Developing countries with high numbers of young dependants will likely experience greater population growth than developed countries. The number of developing countries that will improve their standards of living to a point at which birth rates begin to fall cannot be predicted. Changes in birth rates in the developed world also cannot be foretold. For example, it is possible that a major cultural change in Canada and the United States could change fertility rates and bring about another baby boom.

Birth rates will continue to decline worldwide, but the large base in countries such as India means increases will continue to be too high for their population to be sustained without environmental damage. The future will be determined by the youth of developing nations. The age at which they choose to marry, and the number of children they have, may be the most important deciding factors of the 21st century.

KEY TERM

nutritional density a measure of how much nutrition in calories can be produced from a certain area; an area with fertile soil and adequate temperatures and precipitation will have a higher nutritional density than an area such as Canada's North

PRACTICE QUESTIONS

1. Define population distribution and population density.

2. How useful are crude densities in giving a picture of how many people could live in Canada?

3. Why is nutritional density a more accurate measure of density in the developing world?

©P

CHAPTER FOCUS QUESTION   **What is the significance of changes in global population for Canada and the world?**

Significant changes in world population have occurred in the past 50 years. As you read in this chapter, this has brought benefits to some and problems for others. As the world's population moves toward 7 billion and beyond, a number of issues must be addressed.

1. Use the organizer below to list the five most pressing population issues for the present and future. Beside each issue, note a country or region of the world in which it is a problem or concern and a country or region in which it is not a problem or concern. For each, briefly describe why this is the case.

Issue	A concern or problem	Not a concern or problem
1.	Example of a country or region and explanation	Example of a country or region and explanation
2.		
3.		
4.		
5.		

a) Which of the issues should be of greatest concern to the world? To Canada? Explain.

b) Which issue should be of least concern to the world? To Canada? Explain.

c) If these issues are not dealt with effectively by 2050, what might be the consequences for the world and Canada? What impact might these consequences have on your life?

Vocabulary Focus

2. Define the following terms using an example from the chapter to explain how each provides insights into changes in world and regional populations.

demography
developed country
developing country
demographic transition model
population pyramid
life expectancy
one-child policy
dependency ratio
carrying capacity
birth rate
death rate
net migration
population distribution
population density
nutritional density

Knowledge and Understanding

3. How do each of the following influence populations?
   a) fertility
   b) mortality
   c) migration

4. What role do population structures and characteristics play in population change?

5. How do present rates of world population growth affect the future of people in developing and developed countries?

6. Sketch imaginary population pyramids for the following populations:
   a) expanding rapidly following a lengthy war
   b) expanding after experiencing a devastating famine
   c) stable with an aging population
   d) experiencing a negative growth rate

©P

7. Using three countries from different regions of the world as examples, explain how population density figures for countries can often be deceiving.

Critical Thinking

8. Compare the typical shapes of population pyramids for developing nations and developed nations. Describe the differing dependency problems for these nations.

9. Use Figure 11–23 as a model to draw a cartoon about population growth that might appear in a future year based on the UN estimates of future growth given in Figure 11–1.

10. With a partner, discuss the effects the aging population will have on the workforce in Canada. Prepare to discuss the measures the government should take to deal with this problem. Suggest career choices that they might consider as a result of your discussions.

Evidence

11. Reviewing all you have studied in this chapter, identify the country you feel has the best prospects of successfully coping with problems that will result from world population growth in the next 50 years. Provide evidence to support your choice.

Document Analysis

12. Examine the following images and respond to the questions below.

    a) Describe the methods or techniques used in each poster to encourage people to limit the size of their family. Be specific.

    b) What are some of the similarities or differences between the two posters?

    c) Who is the target audience for each poster? Be specific.

    d) Which poster is more effective in your opinion? Justify your choice.

FIGURE 11–29 Family planning information poster from India

FIGURE 11–30 The Chinese government used posters to promote its one-child policy.

GUIDING QUESTIONS

Economy & Human Geography

- What are the different ways of measuring a country's development?

- What is the impact of population growth on a country's standard of living?

- What are the main causes of poverty?

- What problems are created by high debt in developing countries?

- How does improving the status of women improve a country's economic development?

- What factors contribute to mortality rates?

- What is the relationship between the levels of health of populations and their economic development?

- How do we determine the success of aid programs in assisting developing countries?

Autonomy & World Presence

- What role does Canada play in aiding developing countries?

TIMELINE

1944
UN sets up the World Bank and International Monetary Fund (IMF) to help improve standards of living through economic growth

1948
Marshall Plan created to help rebuild European economy after the Second World War

1949
U.S. President Truman coins the terms "developed" and "underdeveloped" nations

1960s
World Bank, IMF, and OECD loan billions of dollars to developing countries

1968
Canadian International Development Agency (CIDA) created to administer Canada's foreign aid to developing countries

1970
UN sets foreign aid target of 0.7 percent of the loaning nation's GNP

©P

CHAPTER FOCUS QUESTION

How do living standards in Canada compare with those of developing countries and what is being done to close the poverty gap and improve human development around the world?

We live on a planet divided between the rich and the poor. Standards of living vary widely between nations and within nations. In both rich and poor countries, disparities exist between the "haves" and the "have-nots." Some people are very rich, while others try to live on less than $2 a day. This gap in living standards will continue to be one of the most important issues in the 21st century.

While most people in Canada enjoy a comfortable standard of living, people in many parts of the world still struggle to eke out a living. They strive to survive each day and cannot see better lives for their children in the future. According to the United Nations Children's Fund (UNICEF), "Every year, nearly 10 million children die totally preventable deaths."

The international community is hoping to address the problems of developing countries through the United Nations' Millennium Development Goals (MDGs). One of these goals is to halve extreme poverty by 2015. In this chapter, you will learn how the development gap has a profound impact on people's quality of life including their mortality, nutrition, health, education, and general welfare. You will also explore standards of living in various developed and developing countries and consider the problems in comparing standards of living. How and what do we measure? Why is there such a huge gap between the wealth of the "have" and "have-not" countries and what is Canada's policy regarding this gap?

It is now our responsibility to make up lost ground—and to put all countries, together, firmly on track toward a more prosperous, sustainable and equitable world.

–Ban Ki-moon, Secretary-General, United Nations

KEY TERMS

Human Development Index
standard of living
literacy rate
GDP per capita
non-governmental organizations (NGOs)
developed countries
developing countries
mortality
malnutrition
United Nations Children's Fund (UNICEF)
World Health Organization (WHO)
multilateral aid
tied aid
Canadian International Development Agency (CIDA)

1980s–1990s
HIV/AIDS pandemic reaches crisis point in Africa

World Bank and IMF encourage developing countries to adopt Structural Adjustment Programs (SAPs) to pay off their debts

1990
UN publishes first Human Development Report

1996
Heavily Indebted Poor Countries (HIPC) Initiative launched to provide debt relief

2000
UN member states adopt the Millennium Development Goals

2008
Half the world's population live in cities for the first time in history

©P

Measuring Development

Each year since 1990, the United Nations has published a Human Development Report. The report contains the **Human Development Index**, which ranks the **standard of living** in UN member countries according to three indicators: life expectancy, **literacy rate**, and the **GDP per capita**. GDP, or gross domestic product, is the total value of all goods and services produced in a country in one year. Dividing this number by the population gives the average GDP per person, or per capita.

The purpose of the UN index is to give a crude indication of different levels of economic and social development among the countries of the world. As you can see in Figure 12–1, there is a huge gap between the 10 countries at the bottom of the index and the 10 at the top. The 2009 report explored the gap between rich and poor countries, and between rich and poor people in those countries. It showed that people in 85 countries were worse off than they were in the 1980s. In more than 34 countries, life expectancy at birth was still 50 years or younger, a full 30 years less than in Canada. Yet the wealth of the 200 richest people in the world—nearly US$800 billion in 2008—was greater than the combined income of approximately 40 percent of the world's population. Despite the efforts of organizations like the United Nations, along with aid from government agencies and **non-governmental organizations** (**NGOs**) such as Save the Children and Oxfam, the gap between rich and poor continues to grow.

KEY TERMS

Human Development Index the UN's index used to rank standards of living in its member countries

standard of living a measure comparing how well people live in different countries based on three indicators: life expectancy, literacy rate, and gross domestic product (GDP) per capita

literacy rate the percentage of a population that is able to read and write

GDP per capita gross domestic product, or the total value of all goods and services produced in a country in one year, divided by the population

non-governmental organizations (NGOs) non-profit local, national, or international groups that work independently of government on issues such as health, the environment, or human rights

FIGURE 12–1 Top Ten and Bottom Ten Countries, UN Human Development Index, Statistical Update, 2009 (2007 data)

Thinking Critically From your reading of Chapter 11, what are the characteristics of the birth, death, and infant mortality rates in the top and bottom countries? Are these three measures adequate to show human development in a country?

Rank	Country	Life Expectancy at Birth (Years)	Adult Literacy Rate (%)	GDP per Capita (PPP* $US)
1	Norway	80.5	99.0	53 433
2	Australia	81.4	99.0	34 923
3	Iceland	81.7	99.0	35 742
4	Canada	80.6	99.0	35 812
5	Ireland	79.7	99.0	44 613
6	The Netherlands	79.8	99.0	38 694
7	Sweden	80.8	99.0	36 712
8	France	81.0	99.0	33 674
9	Switzerland	81.7	99.0	40 658
10	Japan	82.7	99.0	33 632
173	Guinea-Bissau	47.5	64.6	477
174	Burundi	50.1	59.3	341
175	Chad	48.6	31.8	1477
176	Dem. Rep. of the Congo	47.6	67.2	298
177	Burkina Faso	52.7	28.7	1124
178	Mali	48.1	26.2	1083
179	Central African Republic	46.7	48.6	713
180	Sierra Leone	47.3	38.1	679
181	Afghanistan	43.6	28.0	1054
182	Niger	50.8	28.7	627

*PPP stands for Purchasing Power Parity, which compares the currency of the country to the U.S. dollar to help account for relative cost of living and inflation in the different countries.

The Divided Planet

In 1949, U.S. President Harry Truman referred to a world of "developed" and "underdeveloped" nations. He saw "developed" countries as industrialized, with their people well-housed, healthy, and possessing generally good literacy skills. Their **infrastructure**—such things as transportation and communications links, electric-power distribution systems, schools, and hospitals—was well-developed. "Underdeveloped" countries had few schools, doctors, and hospitals; roads were mainly unpaved; there were few railways; few people had telephones, and only the cities had electrical power.

In the mid-1970s, the geographical location of "developed" and "underdeveloped" countries led some to refer to the industrialized countries as the North and the countries with lower incomes as the South. Today the accepted terms are **developed countries** for the most wealthy countries, **newly industrializing countries** for places like Indonesia and Brazil, which are building up their industries and infrastructure, and **developing countries** for countries that do not have a modern infrastructure or many industries. Most of the countries at the bottom of the UN Human Development Index are in debt to the developed nations, and they are now being called **heavily indebted poor countries (HIPCs)**.

KEY TERMS

infrastructure structures such as roads, railways, power grids, and communications links that are basic to the functioning of a modern economy, as well as buildings such as schools and hospitals

developed countries the world's wealthiest countries; they have well-established infrastructures and their people are well-housed, healthy, and have good literacy skills

newly industrializing countries countries that are experiencing rapid economic and industrial growth; many are switching from agricultural to industrial economies

developing countries countries that have lower standards of living than developed countries; many have extensive poverty

heavily indebted poor countries (HIPCs) countries at the low end of the UN Human Development Index that are in debt to developed nations

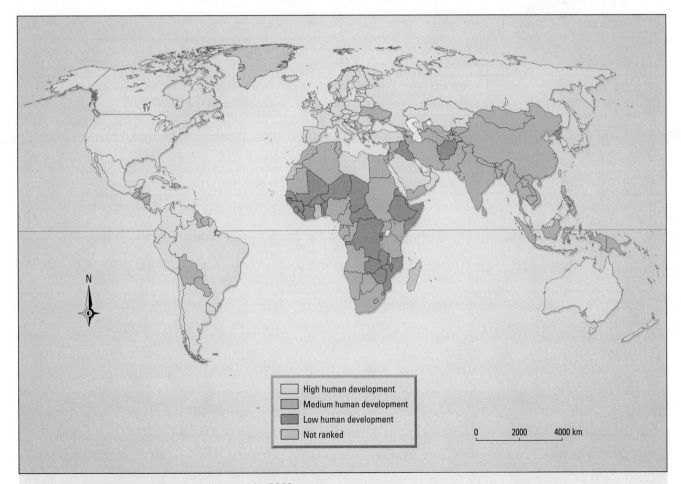

FIGURE 12–2 The Human Development Index for 2009

©P

KEY TERM

Millennium Development Goals (MDGs)
eight goals developed by the member states of the United Nations to close the gap in living standards between developed and developing countries

WEB LINK •·············

Visit the Pearson Web site to find out more about the UN's Millennium Development Goals.

Closing the Development Gap

In 2000, a major worldwide initiative was launched to close the gap in living standards between developed and developing countries. All member states of the United Nations (189 at that time) adopted eight **Millennium Development Goals (MDGs)** targeting the world's main development challenges. By 2015, the world would have less poverty, hunger, and disease, greater survival rates and prospects for mothers and their infants, education for all, equal opportunities for women, an improved physical environment, and a partnership between developed and developing countries to achieve these objectives. These goals are designed to deal with the interdependence between growth, poverty reduction, and sustainable development.

Goal	Targets 1990 to 2015
1. Eliminate extreme poverty and hunger	• Halve the percentage of people whose income is less than $1 (PPP) a day • Achieve full and productive work for all, including women and young people • Halve the proportion of people who suffer from hunger
2. Achieve universal primary education	• Ensure that children everywhere, boys and girls alike, will be able to complete primary school
3. Promote gender equality and empower women	• Eliminate gender inequality in primary and secondary education, preferably by 2005, and in all levels of education by no later than 2015
4. Reduce child mortality	• Reduce by two thirds the under-five mortality rate
5. Improve maternal health	• Reduce by three quarters the number of women who die during pregnancy and childbirth • Make sure every woman has access to reproductive health
6. Combat HIV/AIDS, malaria, and other diseases	• Halt and begin to reverse the spread of HIV/AIDS, malaria, and other diseases • Make sure everyone who needs it has access to treatment for HIV/AIDS
7. Ensure environmental sustainability	• Incorporate the idea of preserving the environment into policies and programs and reverse the loss of environmental resources • Reduce biodiversity loss • Halve the proportion of people without access to safe drinking water and basic cleanliness • By 2020, significantly improve the lives of at least 100 million slum dwellers
8. Develop a global partnership for development	• Address the special needs of the least developed countries, landlocked countries, and small island developing states • Develop an open, rule-based, non-discriminatory trading and financial system • Deal with developing countries' debt • Provide access to affordable essential drugs in developing countries • Spread benefits of new technologies, especially information and communications

FIGURE 12–3 The Millennium Development Goals (MDGs)

Thinking Critically Which three of the MDGs do you think are the most important? Give reasons for your answer. Which of the goals are most likely to be met? Which are least likely to be met? Explain.

PRACTICE QUESTIONS

1. What would Canada have to do to improve its ranking on the UN Human Development Index?

2. Should Canada feel any responsibility to nations at the bottom of the index?

3. What should the UN do to hold nations to their commitments? How can citizens keep their governments accountable to the MDGs?

4. What are the characteristics of "developed" and "developing" nations?

Until recently, researchers could not easily access accurate and up-to-date information on population and living standards. The Internet has made it easier to find these statistics for Canada and the world. However, as with any resource, the World Wide Web should be used with care. Some Web sites may not be reliable sources of information. Because there is no agency to control what is put on the Internet, you must be selective in those sites you choose to use, and all content must be approached with caution.

Steps to Evaluating Web Sites

1. **Authority:** Are the authors or producers of the material clearly identified, and do they have expertise in the subject area? Is the person or organization responsible for the page clearly indicated? Check the site for credentials, a title, or whether it represents an organization or commercial body. Is it from a preferred domain, such as .gov, .edu, or .org?

2. **Accuracy:** Are sources of information credited? Are dates given for current data? Is bibliographic information provided, such as external links, journals, or books? Is the purpose of the site clear? Does the domain name reflect the site's purpose? Is the information verifiable? Are the links appropriate to the content of the site?

3. **Bias:** Does the author or producer of the information have a particular point of view? Is more than one perspective presented? Are facts clearly distinguished from opinions? Use external links and statements of purpose to determine the target audience for the site.

4. **Coverage:** Are all topics that you need to know about covered?

5. **Current:** Is the information up to date? Most Web sites have a copyright date or tell you the last time they were updated. Does the site link to other up-to-date sites?

6. **Usability:** Do you understand the material? Check for spelling, grammar, and consistency. How much advertising is on the site? Does it seem reliable?

How to Decide

What should you do when information on different sites varies? For example, two reliable sources each give different numbers for Mexico City's population in 2005. The UN sets it at 19 million. The U.S. Department of State lists 22 million. So which number do you use? The best advice is to check the source against the six steps and use the figure that seems to come from the most reliable source. If a number of reliable sources agree on the same figure, you can usually assume it is accurate. Be sure to include your source for the information.

The following Web sites are credible sources of particular interest to people studying demographics and living standards. Bookmark these and other sites that are reliable sources of information.

- The United Nations Web site has data from many countries in a variety of formats.
- Statistics Canada gives you access to a wealth of data on Canada's population and social trends.
- For a world perspective, the U.S. Census Web site has links to population and statistics relating to population and development for various countries.
- The Population Reference Bureau is a non-governmental site that has reliable data on population and development.

Applying the Skill

1. Which of the steps listed would you consider to be the most important? Why?

2. Search for Web sites with population and development statistics. Rate the sites as good, fair, or poor based on the evaluation checklist. Compare your findings with other students.

3. Find data for a country of your choice, such as literacy rates or GDP per capita, on several Web sites. Account for any variations you may find.

> **WEB LINK** •·····················
> Visit the Pearson Web site for links to the sites above and checklists for evaluating Web sites.

©P

● What is the impact of population growth on a country's standard of living?

KEY TERMS

mortality death rate, calculated as number of deaths per 1000 people in a population

malnutrition poor, or lack of, nourishment

globalization the spread of ideas, information, and culture around the world through advances in communication, technology, and travel

multinational corporations (MNCs) companies that do business in more than one country

Measuring Living Standards

Levels of economic development are hard to measure accurately. The developed world has accounting systems that can determine such things as the level of industrialization, value of services, and exports and imports. It is much harder to measure these things in developing countries.

Deciding what to measure is another problem when trying to compare levels of development. Developing economies have many people who make goods at home and trade them in local communities. Bartering, rather than currency, may be used in these transactions, making it impossible to measure output. This kind of production is not included in the countries' accounting systems.

If the wealth of a country is not shared among the people, the average income figure does not reflect the standard of living for the majority. In Qatar, for example, the 2009 GDP per capita (PPP) was US$121 400 because of the income from the sale of oil resources. However, the wealth from these sales is in the hands of a few very wealthy families.

FIGURE 12–4 Approximately 1.3 million people live in the 750 slums, or *favelas*, of Rio de Janeiro, Brazil.

Quality of Life

Standards of living are not only measured in incomes people earn. The quality of life includes such things as health, levels of nutrition, life expectancy, literacy rate, and the status of women and children. A person living in poverty in Canada has access to government programs that provide a safety net of services, such as health care and education. In developing countries, a very poor urban family is likely to live in a dwelling made from scrap materials with no electricity, sanitation, or access to safe water. Getting water and basic supplies may take women hours each day.

Quality of life depends on more than meeting the necessities of life. Many people in countries with repressive regimes can be denied freedom of expression, economic freedom, and the right to a safe and clean environment. For example, advocates for the poor in Canada are free to promote their cause. In some developing countries, the homeless and the illiterate may be denied the vote, or may be intimidated by government-hired thugs if they try to improve their conditions. Even in countries that are recognized as democracies, the illiterate may have no way of confirming that their vote is recorded as requested.

©P

An Urban World

More people live in cities than ever before. As Figure 12–5 indicates, people move to urban areas for many reasons. Various factors can push people to leave the land. Others are attracted to cities by the prospect of a better life. Many migrants find themselves in the growing slums of major cities without a significant improvement in their standard of living.

The UN-HABITAT *State of the World's Cities 2006–2007* report found that poor people living in urban areas are as badly off, if not worse off, than rural populations: "...there are two cities within one city—one part of the urban population that has all the benefits of urban living, and... the slums and squatter settlements, where the poor often live under worse conditions than their rural relatives." The urban poor and people in rural environments face similar issues in health, education, employment, **mortality**, and **malnutrition**.

Push Factors	Pull Factors
Underemployment	Labour opportunities
Ethnic or religious tensions	Medical and social provisions
Requisition of land for industrial or other uses	Greater access to food and resources
Droughts or floods	Greater anonymity
Land degradation	Social networks established by migrants attract relatives and friends
Lack of resources	
Environmental impacts, such as deforestation	

FIGURE 12–5 Reasons for rural–urban migration in the developing world

Thinking Critically What do you know about work opportunities and medical or social programs for migrants in your area? Do you think migrants usually find what they expect when they move to the city? Explain.

Globalization

Many people in the developed world believe **globalization** brings freer trade, cheaper goods, and access to technology, which in turn contribute to wealth and improved standards of living. By joining large trading blocs, such as the North American Free Trade Agreement (NAFTA), and the Asia-Pacific Economic Cooperation (APEC), countries create larger markets for their goods and services. These blocs stimulate economic growth, which helps to improve living standards. Opponents of globalization note that these trade agreements limit the control a government has over its trade, economy, and even social policies. Many people in manufacturing see globalization as a threat because their job may be sent to a country with cheaper labour or fewer environmental protection policies.

Some countries, such as China and India, have benefited from globalization and have seen a rise in their standard of living. Other developing countries find it hard to compete in the global economy because they lack a functioning infrastructure. Many developing nations are in debt and their industries and natural resources are controlled by **multinational corporations (MNCs)**. Some developing countries also worry that globalization brings social changes that overwhelm local cultures and traditions. Yet, for countries with expanding populations, globalization promises employment and improved living standards.

The UN defines slums as

Urban households lacking one or more of the following: durable housing; sufficient living area; secure tenure; access to improved water source and sanitation.

–UN Human Settlements Program, *2003*

PRACTICE QUESTIONS

1. Why is it difficult to accurately measure levels of economic development?

2. Compare and contrast the lives of Canadians who live in poverty with those in developing countries.

3. Explain the problems faced by people moving from rural to urban areas in developing countries.

4. Create a Plus-Minus-Interesting (PMI) chart for globalization.

©P

KEY TERMS

World Bank an international group of five financial institutions that provide financial and technical help to developing countries

Organisation for Economic Co-operation and Development (OECD) originally created as the Organisation for European Economic Co-operation (OEEC) to administer the Marshall Plan to rebuild Europe after the Second World War; OECD's mission is to improve living standards in developing countries

Measuring Poverty

Poverty is measured differently in developed and developing countries. The most common measure is the poverty line, which is the minimum income required to pay for basic needs. In developing countries, the absolute poverty line is about $1.25 (2005 PPP) per person per day. Using this measure, the **World Bank**—an international lending agency—estimated that in 2008 approximately 1.4 billion (one in four) people in developing countries were living on less than $1.25 per day, putting them below the poverty line. Yet there are people who earn $2, $3, or even $5 a day in these countries who remain poverty-stricken. Critics of the World Bank's measurement prefer to look at individual countries to determine at what level people are unable to afford a minimum of food, clothing, shelter, health care, and education services. This is closer to the way poverty is measured in Canada and the United States.

FIGURE 12–6 Homeless people and poverty protestors pitched this "tent city" to raise awareness about the plight of the poor in Vancouver, B.C.

Thinking Critically What policies could the various levels of government adopt to improve the standard of living of poor people in Canada?

Category	Number Living in Poverty	Poverty Rate
All persons	2 952 000	9.2%
Adults (18–64)	2 113 000	9.9%
Children (0–17)	637 000	9.5%
Seniors (65+)	201 000	4.8%

FIGURE 12–7 Canadian poverty rates in 2007

Thinking Critically How would the life of a child living in poverty be the same as and different from yours? How do Canada's social services help people living in poverty?

Measuring Poverty in Canada

Until recently, a set income figure was used to measure poverty in Canada. This figure did not take into account the differences in cost of living across the country. Today, Statistics Canada uses a low income cut-off (LICO) to determine those living in poverty. LICO is defined as a household that spends more than 70 percent of its income on food, clothing, and shelter. The National Council of Welfare (NCW), a federal government agency, differs from Statistics Canada in determining LICOs. The NCW uses after-tax income to measure poverty, whereas Statistics Canada uses before-tax income. The difference can be seen by comparing the number of seniors living in poverty using the two approaches. The NCW's after-tax measure shows 201 000 seniors living in poverty (see Figure 12–7), while Statistics Canada's before-tax measure shows 524 000 poor seniors. (See Chapter 10 for a discussion of child poverty in Canada.)

Measuring Poverty in the United States

In the United States, poverty is measured against the cost of a minimum adequate diet multiplied by three to allow for other expenses. In the 1960s, the U.S. government declared a "war on poverty" and chose a set income figure to define poverty. In 2009, it was US$10 830 for a single person, US$14 570 for a family of two, rising to US$37 010 for a family of eight or more. For the family of two, this translates to about US$40 a day.

Human Poverty Index

To accommodate the differing living standards between countries, the UN Human Poverty Index uses different indicators when comparing developing and developed countries. For developed countries, the UN uses data from selected member countries of the **Organisation for Economic Co-operation and Development (OECD)**. Looking at the different indicators may help those in developed countries see the types of advantages that they take for granted.

	Human Poverty Index for developing countries	Human Poverty Index for selected OECD countries
A long and healthy life	• Probability at birth of not surviving to age 40	• Probability at birth of not surviving to age 60
Knowledge	• Adult literacy rate	• % of adults lacking functional literacy skills
A decent standard of living	• % of population not using an improved water source • % of children underweight for age • Deprivation of a decent standard of living	• % of people living below the poverty line
Social exclusion	Not included as a dimension	• Long-term unemployment rate

FIGURE 12–8 The Human Poverty Index

Thinking Critically Which dimension (in blue) do you feel is most significant in determining the level of poverty in the developing countries? In the OECD countries? Would you add or delete any dimensions in either index? Why or why not? Why do you think there are different indicators for developing and OECD countries?

PRACTICE QUESTIONS

1. What is the purpose of the Human Poverty Index? How effective is it in highlighting the differences between rich and poor countries?

2. a) How is poverty defined in Canada?

   b) What difficulties are there in comparing poverty in Canada with poverty in developing countries?

3. a) How useful do you think the terms *developed* and *developing* are in describing the differences in standards of living between countries? Explain.

   b) Brainstorm in a group to think of other terms to describe the differences in standards of living in countries.

4. **Evidence** From what you have learned about measuring poverty levels, what are the five most important basic needs that must be met adequately for a person not to be considered impoverished?

©P

● What are the main causes of poverty?

● What problems are created by high debt in developing countries?

WEB LINK ● · · · · · · · · · · · · · · ·

Visit the Pearson Web site to learn more about the World Bank, IMF, and OECD.

The Poverty Trap

About 1 billion people in developing countries go hungry every day. Yet the world produces enough food to feed all 6.79 billion people on Earth. For many poor people, the problem is that they cannot afford the food that is available. Farmers who do not own their land and migrant labourers are the first to feel the effects of droughts, crop failures, or economic downturns (see Case Study on page 398).

Loans to Developing Countries

At the end of the Second World War, the **International Monetary Fund (IMF)** and the World Bank were set up as agencies of the United Nations. The Organisation for Economic Co-operation and Development (OECD) was also created after the war to help administer the Marshall Plan (an American program for rebuilding Western Europe and its economy). These organizations gave loans and development assistance to help improve standards of living through economic growth. The World Bank, IMF, and OECD encouraged developing countries to engage in **megaprojects** to promote economic growth. Many of these initiatives caused environmental damage and did not improve the countries' economies.

In the 1960s, Western banks loaned billions of dollars to newly independent African countries for megaprojects. These nations' main income came from exporting minerals and agricultural products. A world economic slowdown led to a collapse in prices for these **commodities**, making it difficult for them to repay the debts. Also, some of the loaned money had gone into overseas bank accounts of corrupt dictators.

FIGURE 12–9 Critics of the World Bank and IMF say that the SAPs and strict loan conditions of these agencies add to poverty since some countries need to cut social programs to meet their debt obligations.

The Cycle of Debt

The Western banks and their governments encouraged the IMF and the World Bank to lend countries money to pay off their debts. The lenders had changed, but the debt remained. Today, African countries alone owe $227 billion. Along with the loans, the IMF told these countries to restructure their economies to help repay their debts. The IMF encouraged poor countries to pursue foreign investment, cash crops for export, and private companies to run some government services. These measures are called **structural adjustment programs (SAPs).**

Critics have been quick to point out the negative effects of SAPs. They suggest that poor countries are forced to sacrifice spending on health and education to meet the demands of SAPs and repay their debts. For example, in 2005, the IMF instructed the Niger government to increase taxes on basic goods and services such as milk, bread, water, and electricity. The people of Niger, impoverished by years of bad harvests and SAPs, reacted by taking to the streets in protest. The protesters eventually won a reduction in the proposed tax.

The Burden of Debt

Many countries that are in debt have few natural resources or receive low prices for them on the world market because there is an oversupply. In addition, their resources are under the control of foreign multinational corporations. For example, West Africa produces 70 percent of the world's cocoa, but it must sell its crops to four multinational corporations that control the price. Very little of the profit filters back to the farmers. This makes it very difficult for these countries to earn the money to pay their debts.

The burden of debt for governments in developing countries means they are hard pressed to pay for services that could improve the standard of living of their people. Mozambique, for example, spends 10 times more on debt repayments than on health care. As well, many countries and regions in Africa have suffered natural disasters, such as the devastating floods in Mozambique, drought in East Africa, or brutal civil wars such as those in Rwanda, Sierra Leone, or the Darfur region in Sudan.

Debt Relief

The Heavily Indebted Poor Countries (HIPC) Initiative was launched in 1996 by the International Development Association (IDA) and International Monetary Fund (IMF). The goal of this initiative is to ensure that poor countries are not crippled by their debts. The HIPC Initiative provides debt relief to poor countries with external debts that severely burden export earnings or public finance. In 1999, the initiative was enhanced to help more countries to qualify for debt relief. By the end of 2008, the World Bank and International Monetary Fund had committed more than US$57 billion to help HIPC restructure their debts.

In a 2009 report, the IMF noted that 40 HIPCs were eligible for debt relief under the initiative, and 31 of these nations are in Africa. Of the eligible countries, 35 had qualified for HIPC Initiative assistance. Twenty-six countries have reached the completion point, where the HIPC's debt is forgiven by the governments of developed countries. The IMF notes that some creditors have been reluctant to provide debt relief.

KEY TERMS

International Monetary Fund (IMF) an international organization designed to promote economic stability and development

megaproject a very large-scale, costly project to help develop infrastructure, such as building roads, dams, or irrigation systems

commodities goods or services that are bought or sold

structural adjustment programs (SAPs) programs designed by the World Bank and IMF to adjust the economies of developing countries as a condition of receiving loans

WEB LINK •
Visit the Pearson Web site to find out how citizens can help fight poverty in their own communities and around the world.

©P

Kenya: Trapped in Poverty

Kenya is an example of a country in which most people are caught in the cycle of poverty. This East African country is about 60 percent of the size of British Columbia, but it is estimated to have a population of 40 million in 2010. This represents an increase of nearly 35 million people in 60 years. With a growth rate of 2.7 percent, nearly a million people are added to Kenya's population each year. Economic opportunities are limited: many people cannot afford education, and the country's unemployment rate is 40 percent. According to the 2009 Human Development Report, the per capita income is about US$1542.

Kenya has three main geographical regions. The tropical coast has rainforests and sandy beaches that are now a tourist destination for Europeans. In the central plateau region, there are natural parks with abundant wildlife that form the basis of a tourist industry. About one quarter of the plateau is too dry for farming and has scrub vegetation that is poor grazing land. Another 37 percent of the plateau is tropical grassland, and is traditionally used by nomadic herders for grazing cattle. The highlands in the west are the one good farming area in the country, but represents only about 7 percent of the land. This area produces tea, coffee, and flowers for export. Kenya has suffered from a series of droughts in the past two decades. The most devastating one lasted from 2007 to 2009, drying up 80 percent of the wells, withering crops, and killing cattle.

About 75 percent of the population makes a living from farming. There is now less food produced per capita than 30 years ago, because of the population increase and the use of good cropland to produce cash crops for export. Less than half of the population has access to safe drinking water, and nearly 20 percent of children under 5 are underweight. More than a million people are infected with HIV/AIDS. The median age of Kenya's population is 18 years, compared to 39.4 in Canada.

Drought, floods, and ethnic and political violence have forced many Kenyans to leave the countryside to move to cities. Each day, thousands of people move to Nairobi, the nation's capital, which has industries, services, and is the centre of tourism. More than 60 percent of the population of Nairobi live in slums. In the shantytowns of the Mathare Valley, just outside the capital, one-room shacks made of wood and cardboard are home to an estimated 500 000 people. The settlement has one paved road and no electricity, running water, or sanitation system. People live in a maze of lanes littered with garbage, which turn into rivers of mud in the rainy season. The shantytowns provide a pool of cheap labour for Nairobi.

Ethnic rivalry and government corruption hamper efforts to improve this situation. Transients in the shantytowns have little influence on the government. The new arrivals from the countryside put added pressure on the few services available. All the problems facing Kenya are made worse by a crushing national debt.

FIGURE 12–10 There are several shantytowns like Mathare near Nairobi.

©P

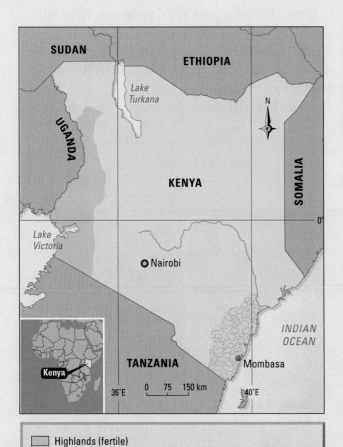

FIGURE 12–12 Dromedary camels in the Koroli Desert

FIGURE 12–13 Sisal fields on the Vipingo Estate

FIGURE 12–14 A lodge on a beach near Kiwayu

FIGURE 12–11 Kenya's geographic regions

Reading a Map Match each of the photographs with the appropriate region on the map. How is Kenya's geography related to its poverty?

	Total Population	Growth Rate (%)	Life Expectancy (Years)	Urban/Rural Population (%)	Number of People with HIV/AIDS	Internet Users	Doctors per 1000 People
Canada	33 890 000	0.8	81	80/20	73 000	28 million	19.0
Kenya	40 863 000	2.6	57	22/78	1.4 million	3.36 million	1.4

FIGURE 12–15 Canada and Kenya: A Comparison, 2005–2010

Looking Further

1. List the principal problems faced by Kenya as a result of the increasing population.

2. Make an illustration modelled on the diagram of the cycle of poverty in Figure 12–22 for people leaving the countryside in Kenya and moving to Nairobi.

3. **Cause and Consequence** What two strategies would you suggest to help Kenya break out of the cycle of poverty?

4. Which two factors in Figure 12–15 do you think most clearly illustrate the differences in development between Kenya and Canada?

©P

KEY TERM

bilateral aid assistance from one country to another

Canada and Debt Relief

Canada has called for an easing of the debts owed by HIPCs. As of 2004, the federal government has spent $312 million on HIPC programs. The goal is to reduce the debt load of HIPCs so their scarce resources can go toward poverty reduction programs rather than paying interest and service charges. Canada has forgiven all overseas development aid debt to all HIPCs except Myanmar, which is governed by a military dictatorship.

Since 1986, all of Canada's **bilateral aid** for development has been in the form of grants, as opposed to loans. Also, 10 Latin American countries have been allowed to repay debts by investing in environmental and other sustainable development projects in their own countries.

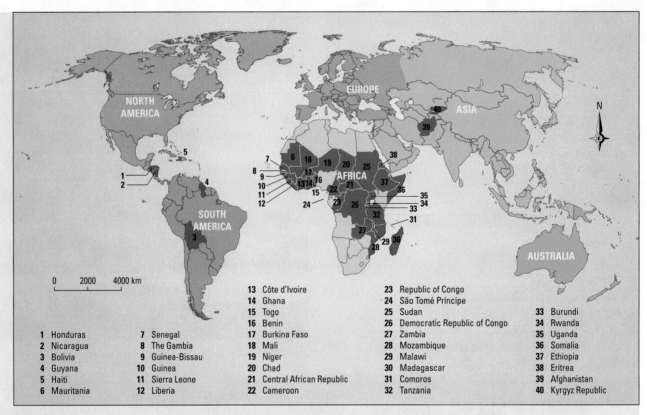

1 Honduras	7 Senegal	13 Côte d'Ivoire
2 Nicaragua	8 The Gambia	14 Ghana
3 Bolivia	9 Guinea-Bissau	15 Togo
4 Guyana	10 Guinea	16 Benin
5 Haiti	11 Sierra Leone	17 Burkina Faso
6 Mauritania	12 Liberia	18 Mali
		19 Niger
		20 Chad
		21 Central African Republic
		22 Cameroon

23 Republic of Congo	33 Burundi
24 São Tomé Príncipe	34 Rwanda
25 Sudan	35 Uganda
26 Democratic Republic of Congo	36 Somalia
27 Zambia	37 Ethiopia
28 Mozambique	38 Eritrea
29 Malawi	39 Afghanistan
30 Madagascar	40 Kyrgyz Republic
31 Comoros	
32 Tanzania	

FIGURE 12–16 The 40 developing countries classified by the International Monetary Fund as HIPC, 2009

Thinking Critically Do you think Canada is right to forgive debts and put money into debt reduction plans for these countries? What might be the positive and negative outcomes for Canada and the countries whose debts we are forgiving?

PRACTICE QUESTIONS

1. How has the debt burden in developing countries prevented governments from looking after the basic needs of their people?

2. In a two-column chart, list the reasons for and against completely forgiving the debt of developing countries with the highest debt loads.

3. How is the HIPC Initiative meant to help the poorest developing countries?

4. Write a letter to your Member of Parliament explaining your point of view on debt forgiveness.

5. What role have the World Bank and IMF played in the economies of developing countries? Explain some of the problems with SAPs.

Offshore farms: Food for whom?

Each day, one in six people—mostly women and children—does not get enough food to be healthy. In poorer countries where most people depend on agriculture to survive, the costs of oil and fertilizer affect food production. In turn, the prices of imported food have soared.

A recent development in world agriculture threatens to put further pressure on food supplies in some of the poorest countries. Wealthy countries with little agricultural land or water purchase or lease farmland from poor countries. Food is grown and then shipped back to the country that owns the land. This practice is called offshore farming.

China began the trend in 2000 when it purchased land in Cuba and Mexico. Saudi Arabia, Qatar, Kuwait, India, and South Korea are some of the countries that have followed China's lead. A research group has estimated that foreigners have bought 15 to 20 million hectares of farmland in poor countries since 2006.

There are concerns that offshore farming threatens the future of food production in many developing countries. In 2009, Saudi Arabia received its first food crop harvested from the farms it owns in Ethiopia. While this food was being exported, the UN World Food Programme helped to feed more than 10 million people in Ethiopia.

FIGURE 12–17 Children in Malawi pump water to irrigate maize. Some experts worry that offshore farming may endanger food security in Africa.

Against Offshore Farming

Opponents of offshore farming accuse wealthy countries of preying on the misfortunes of very poor countries. The UN report *Land Grab or Development Opportunity?* raised a number of concerns: local farmers' ability to prove they own their land, political corruption in many poor countries, and environmental issues (such as the use of herbicides and diverting water resources for irrigation). As another UN report noted: "The sale of farmland to international investors is not without risks for developing countries. Experiences show that they can cause land expropriation or lead to an unsustainable use of resources, thereby undermining the livelihoods of local populations."

For Offshore Farming

Supporters of offshore farming argue that foreign investment in agriculture helps poor countries. It provides export revenues, creates jobs and infrastructure, and gives developing countries access to new agricultural technology. They say that without foreign investment, the land may never be used. According to an investor from Saudi Arabia: "We can become the farmers of the world in terms of food security to Africa. Although we're taking so many hectares, we are actually going to be helping farmers contiguous [next] to our farms, assist them in repairing the land, plant seedlings, and have an agreement if they wish so that we can buy their products."

Analyzing the Issue

1. Do you think the benefits of offshore farming outweigh the drawbacks for the poor country? Explain.

2. **Cause and Consequence** Japan, which owns offshore farms, has suggested that there should be an international code of conduct for foreign farmland deals. What three protections for poor countries would you include in such a code?

3. Canada has vast amounts of farmland, but foreign ownership rules prevent other countries from buying the land. List some reasons for and against selling some of Canada's farmland to other countries.

KEY TERMS

subsistence farming a form of farming in which the crops grown are used to feed the farmer and his or her family, with little or nothing left over to sell or trade

desertification the spread of desert-like conditions in an area, sometimes caused by human activity

● How does improving the status of women improve a country's economic development?

The Vulnerable Ones: Women and Children

The burden of poverty creates particular hardships for women and children. Many developing countries have male-dominated societies in which females and children have lower status than men. Women and children may have no legal rights, or the legal system may allow them to be treated as property. Women may even be killed to satisfy a family's honour. In some tribal societies, women and children may have to eat whatever is left after the men have finished their meals, which can lead to malnutrition.

The Position of Women

Women in developing countries may have to work more than twelve hours each day to ensure the survival of their families (see Figure 12–18). They are responsible for more than two thirds of the food production and are often left to support the family when men migrate in search of work.

In much of the developing world, the literacy rate is lower among women than among men. Education is often a luxury restricted to males. Only one third of girls in rural India go to school compared to more than half of boys. Many families in this area will keep girls at home to look after the younger children and help with chores until they are married and move to their husband's village.

Education Is the Solution

Demographers agree that economic development and the fertility rate of countries are connected. A decline in the number of children a woman has in her lifetime frees her to improve her lot and that of her children. Studies show that better-educated women tend to marry later and have fewer children. Because they are literate, they have a better understanding of contraception, and may be able to resist family pressures to have more children.

The children of educated women are also more likely to survive because their mothers know the importance of immunization, clean water, and good nutrition. A study in Peru showed that the infant mortality rate dropped for every year of schooling the mother had. When mothers are sure that their children will survive, they are less likely to have large families.

8:30 to 9:30 p.m.
Wash children
and dishes

9:30 p.m.
Bedtime

4:45 to 5:00 a.m.
Wake up, wash,
and eat

5:00 to 5:30 a.m.
Walk to fields

6:30 to 8:30 p.m.
Cook dinner
and eat

5:30 to
6:30 p.m.
Collect
water

4:00 to
5:30 p.m.
Pound and
grind corn

3:00 to 4:00 p.m.
Collect firewood

5:30 a.m. to 3:00 p.m.
Work in fields

FIGURE 12–18 The illustration shows how a rural woman typically spends her day in developing countries like Zambia.

Thinking Critically How does this woman's day compare to yours? How would this workload prevent a woman from improving her status?

©P

Women in Niger

The African country of Niger, a landlocked nation almost entirely in the Sahara Desert, is one of the world's least-developed countries (see Figure 12–1). Niger ranked last on the UN's 2009 Human Development Index, with a life expectancy at birth of 50.8 years and a literacy rate of 28.7 percent. As the poorest country in the world, the average income of people in Niger is US$280 per year. A 2010 study estimated that more than half of Niger's population of 15 million face food insecurity, which includes missing meals, malnutrition, or famine. Many people survive by **subsistence farming**, producing enough to feed their families with little left over to sell. Niger's economy centres on exporting livestock and natural resources (it has some of the world's largest uranium deposits). Fluctuations in world prices affect Niger's economic stability. Drought cycles, **desertification**, population growth, and political instability have also undercut the economy. Debt relief provided under the HIPC Initiative significantly reduced Niger's annual debt, freeing government funds for basic health care and primary education.

Women in Developing Countries

Niger is a traditional Muslim society, and women are bound to obey the wishes of their husbands, fathers, brothers, and other male relatives. Polygamy, or the practice of having more than one wife, is widespread, and the average marrying age for women is 17.6. The average number of children per woman is 7.75. In Niger, most of a woman's time is dedicated to raising and feeding her children, and she has little opportunity for education. Because of the prevalence of forced early marriage and violence against women in the country, Niger was criticized for ratifying the UN convention on women's rights. Niger is an extreme example of the situation for women in many developing countries.

Several aid agencies are working to improve the standard of living of women in Niger. Many of their programs focus on women's equality and education for girls. They believe that community-based programs will help women work together to improve their status. As a result of these and other programs, women are taking a larger role in the economy by selling pottery, firewood, cloth, and anything else that they can to keep their families from starving.

Between 20% and 35% of women are literate	Fewer than 20% of women are literate
Benin	Afghanistan
Burkina Faso	Guinea
Central African Republic	Mali
Chad	Niger
Ethiopia	
Mozambique	
Senegal	

FIGURE 12–19 Women's literacy rates in some developing countries

Interpreting Statistics On what continent are most of these countries located? What do the countries with the lowest literacy rates for women have in common?

FIGURE 12–20 Women in Niger, one of the world's least-developed countries, sell what they can at markets like this to support their families.

Thinking Critically Do you think women's larger role in their country's economy might lead to other changes in their lives? Why or why not?

The World's Children
Every six seconds, a child dies because of hunger and related causes.
Worldwide, 148 million children under age five were underweight in 2007. More than 93 percent of underweight children live in Africa and Asia.
In 2007, 9.2 million children under five died worldwide. Malnutrition and hunger-related diseases caused 60 percent of these deaths.
Every year, the World Food Programme (WFP) feeds more than 20 million children in school feeding programs in 70 different countries. In 2008, WFP fed a record 23 million children.

FIGURE 12–21 Snapshot of the world's children

Children in Crisis

Children are often the first victims of underdevelopment. Famine, disease, war, and a host of other problems prey on society's most vulnerable people. Even if they survive the critical first five years, children in some developing nations have few educational opportunities and are often exploited as child labour. Some are even trapped in the sex trade. The high birth rates in many developing areas mean that this problem will continue in the future. In 1992, the **United Nations Children's Fund (UNICEF)** published the Progress of Nations Report (PNR) on the welfare of children. The PNR launched the 21st century with a new index that measures the risk for children in countries worldwide on a scale of 0 to 100. The measure is based on five factors: the mortality rates of children under the age of five, the percentage of children who are moderately or severely underweight, numbers of children who do not attend primary school, risks from armed conflict, and risks from HIV/AIDS.

Canada, the United States, Australia, Japan, and other highly developed nations had risk scores of five or below, which UNICEF considers of no consequence. Africa is the continent where children face the greatest risks. Africa's average score was 61, compared to Europe's average of six, and the world average of 30.

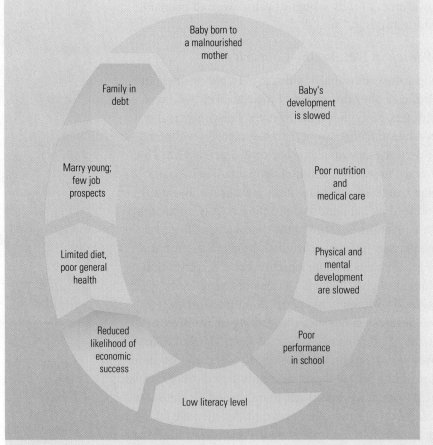

FIGURE 12–22 The cycle of poverty

Thinking Critically At what stage do you think intervention in the poverty cycle would be most effective? How might remedies applied to developing countries differ from those applied to poverty in Canada?

©P

Under-Five Mortality Rate

UNICEF's main measure of human development is the under-five mortality rate (U5MR). Although the difference in U5MR between developing and developed countries is slowly narrowing, children born in developing countries are 13 times more likely to die under the age of five than in developed countries. In addition, 19 of the 20 countries with the highest U5MR are in Africa.

According to UNICEF's 2008 report *The State of the World's Children*, an average of 26 000 children under the age of five die worldwide each day. Almost all of these children are in developing countries, and most of them die of preventable causes. About one third die before they are one month old because they do not have access to basic health care. Up to half of the deaths of children under the age of five are due to undernutrition. Diseases like measles, which is controlled by a vaccine in industrialized countries, are often widespread and contribute to the U5MR. Many children also die of diseases related to poor sanitation, lack of hygiene, and no access to clean water.

● What factors contribute to mortality rates?

KEY TERM

United Nations Children's Fund (UNICEF) a UN organization that works to protect children's rights, to make sure the basic needs of children are met and to help children reach their full potential; originally called United Nations International Children's Emergency Fund

FIGURE 12–23 Save the Children, an international organization working to improve children's lives around the world, helped children in Haiti after the 2010 earthquake that devastated this HIPC.

Thinking Critically What indicators would you use to determine quality of life? How would you measure whether you have a good life?

FAST FORWARD

Controlling the Under-Five Mortality Rate

One of the UN Millennium Development Goals (MDGs) is to reduce the under-five mortality rate by two thirds between 1990 and 2015. In 2009, UNICEF reported that the death rate of children under five years of age continued to decline. Approximately 10 000 fewer children are dying every day compared to 1990.

The under-five mortality rate has decreased over the past two decades, with the highest rate of decline (2.3 percent) between 2000 and 2008. Key health interventions have contributed to the declining mortality rates. Immunizations, including measles vaccinations, the use of insecticide-treated bed nets to prevent malaria, and vitamin A supplements are examples of some of the initiatives that are helping to save children in developing countries. Progress has been made in all parts of the world, including Malawi and some of the other least-developed countries.

While progress has been made, the global rate of improvement is still short of the MDG target. Combined, Asia and Africa account for 93 percent of all under-five deaths that occur in developing countries each year.

1. What measures need to be taken to meet the MDG target to reduce the under-five mortality rate? Do you think it can be achieved?

KEY TERM

ethnic cleansing the elimination of one ethnic group from an area by another ethnic group

Children at War

According to a 2000 UNICEF report, about 540 million children in the world live in dangerous situations. Civil wars, **ethnic cleansing**, land mines, and other dangers threaten children in many countries.

Each year, at least 300 000 children and young adults under the age of 18 are engaged in armed conflicts around the world, many of them in Africa. These children have to fight as soldiers, attack civilians, and even provide sexual services to army commanders. In Uganda, the Lord's Resistance Army forced new recruits to prove themselves by killing their family. War Child International, a network of organizations that helps children affected by war, estimates that children are employed in nearly 75 percent of all armed conflicts worldwide, by both regular armies and rebel groups. Approximately 80 percent of these children are younger than 15.

Amnesty International and other human rights organizations would like to outlaw the participation of children in armed conflict. They want the UN Convention on the Rights of the Child to forbid military recruitment before the age of 18. Countries that have 16-year-old soldiers in their armies oppose this proposal. Other critics point out that the African population is generally younger than 18, and that in many tribal societies a 16- or 17-year-old is not considered a child. In Sudan and Somalia, 11- and 12-year-olds have been involved in battle. The key issue, critics argue, should be whether the involvement of young people in military activity is voluntary.

up close and personal ◯ Emmanuel Jal: Child Soldier to Child Advocate

Emmanuel Jal grew up in Southern Sudan, a country torn apart by civil war. When he was seven years old, his father joined the Sudan People's Liberation Army (SPLA), his mother was killed, and his village was destroyed. Emmanuel was alone in a war zone. Like thousands of other orphans lured by the promise of an education, he decided to flee to Ethiopia. Many of these children, including Emmanuel, were kidnapped by the SPLA and forced to fight.

After enduring the horrors of war for four years, he decided to join a group of child soldiers, or "lost boys," escaping to eastern Sudan. Of the 300 that set out, fewer than 20 survived the journey across the war zone. Emmanuel was lucky. He was taken in by a British aid worker, who smuggled him out of the country.

Once free from the violence of war, Emmanuel turned to music to tell his story. He has become an international star, combining traditional African styles

FIGURE 12–24 In the documentary "War Child," Emmanuel Jal (centre) travelled back to the Sudan to help raise awareness about and help protect child soldiers.

with hip hop. He promotes peace through his songs, and has used his celebrity to help fight violence and raise awareness of the plight of child soldiers. His music has been featured in several films, and a documentary has been made about his experience as a child soldier.

©P

Working Children

In many developing countries, children work to help support themselves and their families. Abandoned children in cities survive by begging, stealing, or selling sex. According to the UN's International Labour Organization (ILO), the root causes of child labour are poverty and no access to education. In response to these causes, the first two Millennium Development Goals (MDGs) aim to wipe out extreme poverty and achieve universal primary education.

Working children generally come from the most vulnerable families. In its 2006 Global Action Plan to eliminate child labour, the ILO asked UN members to work toward eliminating the worst forms of child labour by 2016. A dozen countries, including India, Afghanistan, Sierra Leone, Myanmar, and Somalia, have not signed the agreement. Some developing countries are reluctant to put restrictions on children working because 70 percent of child labour is in the agricultural sector.

Unsafe Working Conditions

Children are often forced to work in unsafe conditions. An article in the *Guardian* states that Plan, a children's aid agency, "cites research showing that Malawi has the highest incidence of child labour in southern Africa, with 88.9 percent of 5- to 14-year-olds working in the agricultural sector. It is estimated that more than 78 000 children work on tobacco estates—some up to 12 hours a day... without protective clothing." According to the article, "child labourers as young as five are suffering severe health problems from a daily skin absorption of up to 54 milligrams of dissolved nicotine," which is "equivalent to smoking 50 cigarettes a day." A Plan spokesperson concludes: "These children are risking their health for 11p [15 cents] a day."

The majority of child labourers are in Asia, where few labour laws regulate safety conditions or the hours that children work. The *Hindustan Times* reported that "children are widely employed in restaurants, canteens, garages, tanneries, and brick kilns where they work for up to fifteen hours a day, without leave for months together. Those working as household help are just slightly better off."

FIGURE 12–25 Young children work alongside adults under the scorching sun baking bricks in Batapur, Pakistan.

KEY TERMS

bonded labour (or debt bondage) paying off a loan with labour rather than money; bonded labourers often work for very little pay and their labour is worth more than the original debt

subsidies grants from the government, intended to help people

World Health Organization (WHO) a UN agency that coordinates international health activities and helps governments improve health services

Bonded Labour

Many children are forced to work as **bonded labour** to help pay off their families' debts. Craig Kielburger, a Canadian children's rights activist, recalled his experiences with children forced to work in a carpet factory:

> *While I was [in India], Kailash Satyarthi, a social activist working to help free children enslaved in bonded labour, led a raid on a carpet factory in which twenty-one children were rescued. These children had been tricked into thinking that they were going to a training school to learn how to make carpets. They were even told that they would be paid while learning this trade. Instead, they were taken to another state far away from their homes and forced to work fourteen hours a day for twenty-five cents a day. They had to give the twenty-five cents back to the carpet owner in exchange for one bowl of rice and dal, which is all that they were fed for the day.*
>
> *–Craig Kielburger*

The Burden for Girls

The ILO estimates there are 100 million girls working as child labourers. Girls are sometimes pulled out of school to earn money so their brothers can get an education. Girls face the double burden of working and completing domestic duties in their own homes.

> *After quitting school, I started to help my parents financially. I collect garbage that can be sold from early morning till afternoon. I give the money I earn to my parents to buy food so we can survive and send my brother to school. When I see my friends go to school, I feel I want to cry. Sometimes, I daydream, imagining myself in school.*
>
> *–A scavenger girl from Pancur Batu, Medan, Indonesia*

FIGURE 12–26 This nine-year-old girl stands in a landfill in Jakarta, Indonesia. Children like her scavenge the piles of garbage for items to sell.

PRACTICE QUESTIONS

1. Why are women and children more likely than men to face hardships in developing countries?

2. **a)** What is the relationship between female literacy and reduced birth rates?

   b) Give three reasons why women's literacy rates in developing countries are lower than men's.

3. Do you think there should be a set age for soldiers? Why?

4. **a)** Choose five abuses of children in the developing world. Match them against the list of rights guaranteed by the UN Convention on the Rights of the Child (see Chapter 10).

   b) How effective do you think the Convention on the Rights of the Child will be in dealing with some of these abuses? Explain your answer.

©P

The Health Crisis

In many developing countries around the world, a lack of clean water and medical care have resulted in a health crisis.

Clean Water: A Basic Human Need

The UN estimates that, in 2002, about 1.2 billion people around the world did not have access to clean or enough water. Climate change, which has contributed to extreme droughts and damaging floods, is adding to the problem. Open water sources are contaminated. Rivers that supply water for human use are also used for washing and disposing of waste. Irrigation for agriculture takes the largest share of water supplies in the developing world. Many developing countries in the tropics have a dry season. The lack of water during this time affects agriculture and, ultimately, people's health. Aid programs and water **subsidies** are often relied upon to help those who can afford to pay, leaving the poor with the filthiest water.

The **World Health Organization (WHO)** estimates that improving drinking water, sanitation, and hygiene could prevent about 10 percent of diseases worldwide. Cholera and typhoid are among the diseases caused by bacteria that breed in unclean water. Almost a quarter of the developing world's population lives without any form of sanitation or sewage system. The WHO believes that a "significant amount of disease could be prevented, especially in developing countries, through better access to safe water supply [and] adequate sanitation facilities." Clean water is such an important factor in living standards that the UN included reducing the number of people without access to safe drinking water and basic cleanliness as one of its Millennium Development Goals.

Canada has an enviable record for providing safe water to its citizens. Yet, in May 2000, an E. coli outbreak in Walkerton, Ontario, showed how the system can fail. The bacteria contaminated wells that supply municipal water, making more than 2000 people ill and killing several others.

> What is the relationship between the levels of health of populations and their economic development?

On average, people in Europe use more than 200 litres [per day]—in the United States more than 400 litres. When a European person flushes a toilet or an American person showers, he or she is using more water than is available to hundreds of millions of individuals living in urban slums or arid areas of the developing world. Dripping taps in rich countries lose more water than is available each day to more than 1 billion people.

–Human Development Report 2006

FIGURE 12–27 Nearly 400 million people live along the Ganges, a sacred river in India. Devout Hindus bathe and pray in the river. The river is also used to wash clothing, water livestock, irrigate and drain cropland, and carry away the cremated remains of the dead. Industrial contaminants also find their way into the river.

Thinking Critically What does the way people treat their rivers tell us about their cultural and economic values? What are the clean water issues in your area?

KEY TERM

malaria a deadly infectious disease common in tropical climates, transmitted to humans by the mosquito

WEB LINK •

Visit the Pearson Web site to learn more about how Canadians can help support initiatives to stop the spread of diseases like malaria.

The Scourge of Epidemics

Despite advances in medicine, epidemics of tuberculosis, sexually transmitted diseases, HIV/AIDS, and **malaria** are widespread in the developing world. These scourges pose a threat to the health of Canadians and fellow citizens of the global village. Tuberculosis and malaria, between them, cause more than five million deaths annually around the world.

Malaria on the Rebound

In northern wealthy countries, malaria is often thought of as a problem that has been solved. Yet malaria affects more people than ever before. It is prevalent in 106 countries, affecting half of the world's population. More than 240 million cases of malaria were diagnosed in 2008, causing untold suffering and loss of productivity in tropical countries. At least a million of these people will eventually die. Many of them will be under the age of five, and the majority of them live in Africa.

Why is malaria an epidemic of the poor in the developing world? For those in remote areas or the slums of cities, help is not readily available. Forest clearing in South America and Asia allows sunlight to warm standing water, creating breeding grounds for mosquitoes in areas that had previously not been affected. Because the incidence of malaria is on the rise around the world, the World Health Organization has made fighting malaria a priority.

Currently, there is no vaccine available, so preventing malaria-carrying mosquitoes from biting people is the the most effective way to fight the spread of the disease. One way to do this is to use insecticide-treated bed nets to protect people from being bitten while they sleep. Another effective remedy is DDT, a chemical that nearly eradicated malaria by the 1960s. Due to its overuse in agriculture, the chemical accumulated in soil and water and was eventually banned. In countries such as Zambia, authorities have begun to spray the inside of houses with DDT to repel and kill mosquitoes in the hopes of reducing the spread of malaria.

FIGURE 12–28 Warm temperatures, humidity, and poor drainage of surface water make slums, like this one in India, the perfect breeding ground for malaria mosquitoes.

Thinking Critically
What measures could be taken to eliminate mosquito breeding areas in tropical cities?

The HIV/AIDS Pandemic

Possibly the most serious epidemic, now and for the future, is the continued spread of HIV/AIDS. The virus that causes HIV/AIDS destroys the immune system, which protects the body from disease. The virus passes from person to person through sexual contact, blood transfusions, sharing hypodermic needles, or from mother to child during birth. While treatments are available, they are often too costly for sufferers in developing countries, making death a certainty in many cases.

The HIV/AIDS pandemic—an epidemic that occurs over a wide geographical area—affects 33 million people worldwide. In 2008, 2.7 million people became infected, and two million died. More than two million children under 15 years of age were living with HIV and 430 000 children became newly infected.

Sub-Saharan Africa remains the centre of this epidemic. Developed countries, such as Canada, have kept their infection rates for HIV/AIDS to less than one percent of the adult population. But in many sub-Saharan countries, the infection rate is out of control. Of the 33 million people living with HIV worldwide, 22 million are from sub-Saharan Africa. Further, 70 percent of those who died and 91 percent of new HIV infections among children were in sub-Saharan Africa (see Figure 12–30).

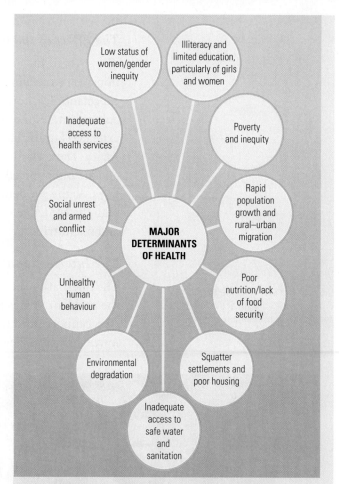

FIGURE 12–29 The major determinants of health in developing countries

Thinking Critically Use what you have learned to identify the causes and effects that are linked on this web.

Region	Adults and children living with HIV	Adults and children newly infected with HIV	Adult prevalence (%)	Adult and child deaths due to AIDS
Sub-Saharan Africa	22.4 million	1.9 million	5.2	1.4 million
Middle East and North Africa	310 000	35 000	0.2	20 000
South and Southeast Asia	3.8 million	280 000	0.3	270 000
East Asia	850 000	75 000	<0.1	59 000
Oceania	59 000	3900	0.3	2000
Latin America	2.0 million	170 000	0.6	77 000
Caribbean	240 000	20 000	1.0	12 000
Eastern Europe and Central Asia	1.5 million	110 000	0.7	87 000
Western and Central Europe	850 000	30 000	0.3	13 000
North America	1.4 million	55 000	0.6	25 000
World	33.4 million	2.7 million	0.8	2.0 million

FIGURE 12–30 HIV/AIDS statistics for different regions in the world, 2008

The Effect of the Pandemic

The effect of the pandemic in Africa is being felt in the structure of populations, as those dying are often the productive workers. In Botswana, life expectancy fell from 59 in 1990 to 53 in 2007. The long-term effects will be cultural and economic. Children have lost parents and members of their extended family. There are at least 1 million AIDS orphans in sub-Saharan Africa. These children may face poverty, homelessness, or loss of education and are often forced to take on the role of parent to younger orphaned siblings. As the pandemic spreads, scarce resources will have to be used to deal with the epidemic, and it is likely to add to problems of poverty, illiteracy, and malnutrition.

WEB LINK • • • • • • • • • • • •
Visit the Pearson Web site to find out more about Canadian activist Stephen Lewis and his foundation.

The International Community's Response

The international community has been slow to react to the seriousness of the problem. Drugs used to treat HIV/AIDS are expensive, and many countries cannot afford them even though drug manufacturers have promised to lower the prices. Few countries in sub-Saharan Africa can afford to provide large-scale programs for their infected populations. For example, AIDS patients occupy 70 percent of the beds in some hospitals in South Africa.

Dealing with the problem of HIV/AIDS requires the cooperation of many national and international agencies. Canada has been one of the leaders in establishing the Joint United Nations Programme on HIV/AIDS (UNAIDS). UNAIDS coordinates the work of such bodies as the World Bank, the World Health Organization (WHO), UNICEF, and the **United Nations Educational, Scientific, and Cultural Organization (UNESCO)**. It helps countries respond to HIV/AIDS and provides health workers to educate people and limit the spread of the disease.

FIGURE 12–31 The Grandmothers' Gathering, hosted by the Stephen Lewis Foundation, took place in Toronto on August 11–13, 2006. Grandmothers and project facilitators from 11 countries in sub-Saharan Africa came to raise awareness of grandmothers caring for children orphaned due to HIV/AIDS.

PRACTICE QUESTIONS

1. Describe three difficulties in providing basic health care in developing countries.

2. Why should people in the developed world be concerned about the health of people in the developing world?

3. Explain why clean water is important.

4. Why is the spread of malaria increasing?

5. Predict how the loss of productive workers from the HIV/AIDS pandemic will affect the future of countries such as Swaziland or Botswana.

6. What actions have the international community taken to fight the HIV/AIDS pandemic? Comment on the success of these actions.

Helping to Improve Living Standards

Since the Second World War, the developed world has been providing aid to the nations of South America, Africa, and Asia. A lack of political and economic stability in most of the former colonies in Asia and Africa made the transition to independence difficult. **Foreign aid** programs were chosen as the way to foster development in these countries, while at the same time countering the growing influence of the communist bloc. As the volume of aid grew, the political and humanitarian motives of aid donors became interconnected.

Foreign Aid

Development assistance, or the foreign aid received by developing countries, takes a number of forms:

- **Official development assistance (ODA)** is delivered by governments.
- Non-governmental organizations (NGOs) give another type of aid.
- **Multilateral aid** is funded by a number of governments, and usually involves large-scale programs like dam building.
- Bilateral aid goes directly from one country to another.

Developing nations receive foreign aid from various sources. It can come through international bodies such as the United Nations or from national government agencies that manage the distribution of foreign aid. It can also come from NGOs representing religious groups, service organizations such as Rotary International, and other non-profit organizations, such as Oxfam.

Tied Aid

Much bilateral aid is often **tied aid**, given with conditions attached. For example, donated money must be spent on goods bought from the donor country. More than 40 percent of Canadian bilateral and multilateral aid has been tied to Canadian purchases. A criticism of Western aid projects is that they have been tied too much to the trade system that benefits the industrialized countries at the expense of the developing world. In 2008, the Canadian government announced that food aid had been fully untied and CIDA's development aid funding would be fully untied by 2013.

KEY TERMS

United Nations Educational, Scientific, and Cultural Organization (UNESCO) a UN organization that helps build peace, fight poverty, and promote sustainable development through education, the sciences, culture, communication, and information

foreign aid aid from rich, industrialized countries to poorer, developing countries

official development assistance (ODA) aid given to developing countries through official government programs to promote economic development and the welfare of the people

multilateral aid aid delivered through international organizations such as the UN and the World Bank

tied aid aid given to a foreign country with conditions attached

FIGURE 12–32 A soldier prepares supplies from the Canadian Red Cross and CIDA to be shipped to Iran following a devastating 2003 earthquake that left thousands dead and injured.

Development Assistance Goals

In the 1960s, a UN commission led by Canadian Prime Minister Lester Pearson set a target for development assistance of 0.7 percent of donor countries' gross national product (GNP). That goal remains today, although countries rarely reach it. Canada's foreign aid has been decreasing for the past two decades. In 1984, Canada pledged to reach the UN aid target by 2000. As Figure 12–33 shows, Canada's aid was at 0.32 of the GNP in 2008, falling short of the 0.7 percent target.

Many UN agencies are dedicated to improving the living standards of people in the developing world. For example, UNICEF has been in the forefront in fighting iodine deficiency disorder, a disease that can stunt growth and brain development. The addition of a few grams of inexpensive iodized table salt to the daily diet prevents this disorder. With UNICEF's help, a campaign to iodize table salt has all but eliminated iodine deficiency in Bolivia. Canada was one of the major supporters of this initiative, which was one of UNICEF's most successful public health programs.

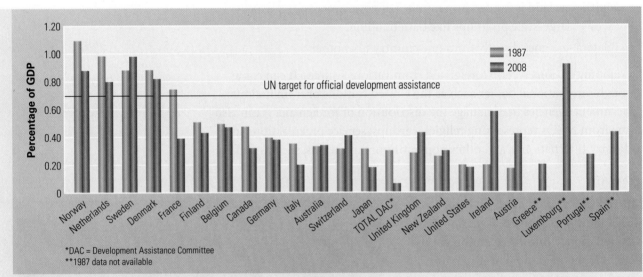

FIGURE 12–33 Official development assistance (ODA) targets in 2008 as a percentage of GNP

Thinking Critically What could be done to ensure Canada meets its target for development assistance? Is there any value in setting these kinds of targets if there is a consistent lack of political, social, and economic will to see them through?

What If...

What if Canada and the United States put all of their military spending for one year into foreign aid? What do you think the results might be?

FAST FORWARD

Foreign Aid Versus Military Spending

Around the world, the money spent on aid is still dwarfed by military spending. In 2008, military spending was an estimated US$1464 billion worldwide, accounting for 2.4 percent of global GDP. UN aid agencies estimate that a fraction of this total would be needed each year to meet the Millennium Development Goals. They believe that the annual cost of meeting all the MDGs would be about US$143 billion in 2010, rising to US$189 billion in 2015.

©P

Canada's Foreign Aid Program

Canada's foreign aid programs began by supporting newly independent Commonwealth countries in Asia, Africa, and the Caribbean. These programs took on greater significance under Prime Minister Pierre Trudeau. In 1968, his government created the **Canadian International Development Agency (CIDA)** to administer Canada's aid to developing countries.

CIDA is responsible for administering much of Canada's foreign aid budget. Like all such organizations, it develops plans and strategies for administering its budget and directing money to areas it deems worthy. CIDA has six priority areas: basic human needs; women in development; infrastructure services; human rights, democracy, and good government; private sector development; and the environment. The agency maintains that its programs

- provide people with access to clean water and sanitation
- improve women's lives by reducing poverty
- promote access to rural services such as rural electricity and communications
- strengthen democratic development and increase respect for human rights
- help to create jobs
- protect the environment

One way that CIDA deals with foreign aid is to find "partners"—universities, non-government organizations (NGOs), and businesses—that will agree to administer programs or otherwise cooperate with the government. These partners help CIDA to run projects in more than 100 of the poorest countries in the world. CIDA is particularly interested in sustainable development, and it also helps groups to upgrade technology, find and train teachers, improve agriculture, and so on. When this book was written, the Canadian government's official position was to promote the use of genetically modified seeds and foods, so CIDA is likely to take a similar position.

> ● What role does Canada play in aiding developing countries?

> **KEY TERM**
>
> **Canadian International Development Agency (CIDA)** Canada's leading development agency for assistance to the developing world

FIGURE 12–34 One of CIDA's projects involves children in Africa. How might making living conditions better for poor children in other parts of the world benefit Canada?

FIGURE 12–35 Women stall owners in Bolivia's Sipe Sipe marketplace have taken classes on women's rights, gender equality, and leadership through the CIDA-funded Centre for the Study of Economic and Social Reality.

Thinking Critically Why would women need to take these various courses in order to run a market stall?

WEB LINK • • • • • • • • • • • • • • • • • •
You can learn more about CIDA and its programs in the 20 countries of focus at the Pearson Web site.

CIDA's Foreign Aid Policy

CIDA distributes aid through UN agencies, directly to governments, and through NGOs. Multilateral programs support efforts such as the Global Fund to Fight AIDS, Tuberculosis, and Malaria and the UN's World Food Programme. Approximately 53 percent of Canada's total aid budget goes to bilateral aid.

In 2009, CIDA announced a change in policy that focuses 80 percent of Canada's bilateral assistance on 20 priority countries and areas, with the goal of getting more resources to those in need. Programs vary by region. For example, aid is focused on combatting poverty and inequity in South America. Under this policy, Canada's largest aid program will help to rebuild and develop Afghanistan with $1.2 billion over 10 years. The focus is on security, education, and humanitarian aid, including food, health care, and clearing land mines.

Critics of CIDA's focus complain that Canada is not sending enough aid to Africa. In a 2002 document, CIDA noted that two thirds of the least-developed countries and two thirds of HIV/AIDS cases worldwide were in Africa. Although this region will still get aid, most of Canada's bilateral aid will now go to countries on the priority list. Less is left for African countries at the bottom of the Human Development Index, such as Niger and Burkina Faso. The government claims that focusing the aid will make it more effective.

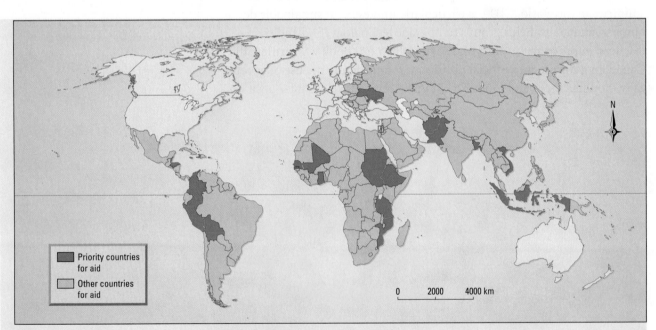

FIGURE 12–36 Countries of focus for Canadian bilateral assistance

Americas: Bolivia, Caribbean Regional Program, Colombia, Haiti, Honduras, Peru; **Asia:** Afghanistan, Bangladesh, Indonesia, Pakistan, Vietnam; **Eastern Europe:** Ukraine; **North Africa and Middle East:** West Bank and Gaza; **Sub-Saharan Africa:** Ethiopia, Ghana, Mali, Mozambique, Senegal, Sudan, Tanzania

Thinking Critically What are the advantages and disadvantages of targeting 80 percent of Canada's bilateral assistance on these 20 priority countries and areas (in dark purple)?

©P

Global Problems, Local Solutions

Non-governmental organizations' aid projects often operate at the grass-roots level, providing help directly to people. Initiatives range from well-known, large organizations, such as the Red Cross and Doctors Without Borders, to smaller groups that deal with local projects. Often, the development assistance of NGOs has been more effective than the large projects sponsored by governments because the aid goes directly to the people who benefit.

In Bangladesh, women—many of them landless labourers or wives abandoned by husbands—work on a CARE scheme repairing dirt roads for a four-year period. A portion of their wages of $1 a day is held back and then given to them as a lump sum to invest. Some women establish small businesses or buy motorized rickshaws or plots of land. Most are able to stop the cycle of poverty, improve their living conditions, and provide for their children's education.

Changes in Aid

Billions of dollars in aid have been spent in developing countries, much of it without improving conditions for the poor. Dictators or local elites are often the winners in the aid sweepstakes. The most successful forms of aid have come from programs that consult the local people and listen to their suggestions.

In recent years, governments have followed the lead of NGOs by promoting small-scale projects that can be maintained locally and are appropriate to the region's environment. Wells with simple pumps replace irrigation projects, tools are made from local or recycled materials, and local people are given the means to sustain their own development initiatives.

It is clear that poverty is at the root of problems in the developing world. Women and children in particular are trapped in a cycle of poverty. High birth rates, high infant mortality rates, low literacy rates, high instances of disease, and other problems are all connected. Too many of the world's people are still poorly housed, malnourished, in poor health, and without a secure economic future.

> ● How do we determine the success of aid programs in assisting developing countries?

FIGURE 12–37 This women's weaving co-operative in Banaue, Philippines, was started with a grant and loan from a local development agency. Members pay a small annual fee, which goes toward the purchase of yarn. The weavers sell their products through local craft shops to tourists. To generate income in the months when there are few tourists, the co-op buys and sells rice. Membership in the co-op entitles weavers to small, low-interest loans.

PRACTICE QUESTIONS

1. In an organizer, list the types of aid Canada sends to developing countries and comment on the pros and cons of each type of aid.

2. Make a list of the top three priorities Canada should follow in distributing aid to the developing world. Support each of your choices.

3. Make a list of reasons for and against a proposal to increase the amount of aid Canada gives to developing countries.

4. Give three reasons for and three reasons against the statement that funding NGOs is the most effective way to get aid to the developing world.

5. In a two-column organizer, list the pros and cons of Canada's official development assistance (ODA) policy of focusing 80 percent of bilateral aid on 20 countries. Do you support this change? Why or why not?

Should Canada link its foreign aid to human rights?

FIGURE 12–38 Since 2003, there have been human rights violations against mostly black, Christian farmers in the south of Darfur, Sudan. When the International Criminal Court issued a warrant for Sudan's president in 2009, he responded by expelling many of the aid agencies helping the refugees who fled their farms. The people of Darfur face continuing government-sponsored violence and are in desperate need of aid.

Most Canadians would likely agree that the 1 billion people living in extreme poverty worldwide should benefit from foreign aid programs. Yet many of these people live under regimes that are regularly accused of abusing human rights. To what extent should Canadian aid be tied to the human rights records of governments receiving help?

As outlined in Chapter 10, the interest in human rights grew in response to wartime atrocities. The Universal Declaration of Human Rights and the agreements that followed have become international benchmarks, and the actions of a state toward its citizens are now measured against these standards. The UN takes the position that official development assistance (ODA) cannot reach its potential where human rights are being violated. Yet places where human rights are abused, such as Zimbabwe, can also be the countries that have the greatest need for humanitarian aid.

It was not until the 1970s that human rights began to feature widely in foreign aid, and Scandinavian countries were the first ones to express their concern. Before 1990, Cold War rivalries meant that foreign aid often propped up dictators and repressive regimes. Following the events of September 11, 2001, the "war on terror" revived support for regimes with poor human rights records, such as Pakistan and Indonesia, in an effort to combat Islamic militants and al-Qaeda.

The Universal Declaration of Human Rights and other UN-sponsored agreements, such as the Convention on the Elimination of All Forms of Discrimination Against Women, call for protection of the political, legal, and social rights of women. Two of the Millennium Development Goals are focused on women and maternity. CIDA's Policy Framework for Women in Development calls for women to be involved in planning and delivering aid programs in countries receiving aid. Should Canada insist that all countries comply with these requirements?

The Case for Denying Aid

Those in favour of denying aid say that it is not enough for Canada just to support UN conventions and formulate policy. The best way to change the practice of these governments is to deny aid whenever human rights are violated. Also, there is no guarantee that the aid will get to the poor and underprivileged. In supporting a strong emphasis on human rights, Lloyd Axworthy,

FIGURE 12–39 Many women in developing countries are denied rights that Canadian women take for granted. In rural societies in India and countries that promote strict interpretation of Islamic law, women have little freedom.

a former Minister of Foreign Affairs, noted that "...respect for human rights is a critical component of the Canadian identity and therefore must play an important role in our foreign policy agenda."

The Case for Giving Aid

Those opposed to denying aid point out that diverse cultures have different interpretations of rights (see the discussion of cultural exceptionalism in Chapter 10). They claim the UN Declaration of Human Rights represents a Western view of rights, a view not all people agree with. Can there be one code of ethics in a world of diverse cultures, languages, values, and religions? People must be allowed to follow their own culture's teachings about rights and tolerance—including the treatment of women.

These critics maintain that good causes are not made better by confusing needs with rights, and dialogue is the key to bringing about change. In practical terms, not addressing poverty in developing nations creates breeding grounds for social unrest, political instability, and terrorism, as seen in Sudan, Ethiopia, and other countries around the world.

The Pragmatic View

Some might argue that aid policies reflect the donor government's political and economic interests, and that these will generally outweigh human rights. With democratic governments facing regular elections, the need to ensure a healthy economy and respond to pressure from business and special interest groups often means that human rights issues are sacrificed. For example, in 2006 Prime Minister Stephen Harper said he would not "abandon important Canadian values" by toning down criticism of China's human rights record to improve trade relations with China. During a visit to China in 2009, Harper noted that "a mutually beneficial economic relationship is not incompatible with a good and frank dialogue on fundamental values like freedom, human rights and the rule of law."

Analyzing the Issue

1. In a two-column organizer, list the reasons for and against giving aid to countries whose governments have poor human rights records.

2. Which side of the debate do you support? Explain.

3. Human rights advocates claim there is a list of basic human rights that could be accepted by all cultures.
   a) If this is true, what rights would that list contain and how might they appeal to all cultures?
   b) If you disagree, explain why.

4. Write a letter to the Minister for International Cooperation outlining the precautions you would advise the ministry to take to ensure that Canada's development aid gets to poor people in need.

5. Humanitarian groups have criticized developed countries for abuses of human rights, such as the disproportionate number of Aboriginal people in Canadian prisons. What is your reaction to the suggestion that Western countries should not impose standards for human rights on developing countries until all human rights claims against themselves have been dealt with? Explain.

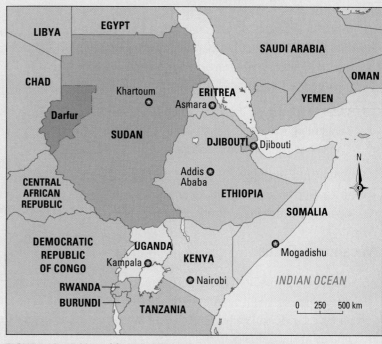

FIGURE 12–40 Map of Somalia, Ethiopia, and other countries in the Horn of Africa

CHAPTER FOCUS QUESTION How do living standards in Canada compare with those of developing countries and what is being done to close the poverty gap and improve human development around the world?

As you read in this chapter, there are great differences in the standards of living of people in developed and developing countries, particularly those in the least-developed countries. There are many factors that contribute to living standards and they contribute to the varying standards in countries around the world.

1. **a)** In an organizer, indicate how each of the factors listed (and others you wish to add) influence living standards in Canada, which is a developed country, and a developing country.

   b) Use the list of factors to create a web or mind map. Connect these factors with lines to show how the factors are related and depend on one another in the developed and the developing world. You could use different coloured lines to distinguish between Canada and developing countries, or make a separate web or mind map for each.

Factors	Canada	A Developing Country
Life expectancy		
GDP		
Employment rates		
Living conditions		
Education/literacy		
Level of health care		
Safe water		
Diseases		
Fertility rates		
Infant mortality		
Gender equality		
Nutrition		
Hygiene		
Sanitation		
Number of young dependants		
Environment		
Land use		
Climate change		
Political system		
Armed conflict		

2. What three factors do you consider most important in determining Canada's standard of living and the standard of living of a developing country? Explain your choices in each case.

3. What factor do you think Canadian governments should target to improve the standard of living of Canadians? Support your choice.

4. What factor would you choose to target if you were to develop an aid program for one of the least developed countries? Explain your choice.

Vocabulary Focus

5. Match five terms from the left column with five terms from the right column. Use a term once only. In each case, explain how each set of two terms relates to standards of living.

Human Development Index	Millennium Development Goals
literacy rate	GDP per capita
heavily indebted poor countries	NGOs
multinational companies	WHO
tied aid	UNICEF
under-five mortality rate	HIV/AIDS
CIDA	World Bank
malaria	infrastructure

Knowledge and Understanding

6. Use a Venn diagram to compare and contrast the life of a child in a developing country involved in civil war with that of a child you know in Canada. Summarize the similarities and differences.

7. Why is the under-five mortality rate so important? How is it used to gauge living standards?

8. List the five most pressing problems facing Africa in the order they need to be addressed to raise the standard of living.

9. The United Nations, International Monetary Fund, World Bank, and Organisation for Economic Co-operation and Development have set a goal of cutting in half extreme poverty in the world by 2015. What steps do you think should be taken to achieve this aim by
 a) these world financial institutions?
 b) the developing countries?
 c) Canada?

10. Discuss the importance of access to clean water.

11. List the arguments a person from one of the least-developed countries might make for the benefits of smaller local development projects over larger projects.

12. Outline the main points of an advertising strategy convincing people that their governments should divert 10 percent of military spending to developing countries for development aid.

Critical Thinking

13. Almost 10 percent of Canada's children are estimated to be living in poverty. With a partner, list in order of priority five steps the government should take to improve their standards of living. Display the list, with appropriate artwork, in a poster.

14. **Judgements** With a partner, develop a Charter of Aid. Include in it the criteria Canada should use in deciding which countries will receive Canadian assistance.

15. Create a cause-effect-results organizer (see Chapter 3) for the causes of diseases, their effects, and how safer water supplies might contain their spread.

16. Why do you think there has been limited progress in achieving the UN's Millennium Development Goals to this point in time? Provide reference to specific goals. Present possible solutions to help increase the likelihood of meeting the goals.

17. Some people believe that giving developing countries money or relieving their debts is the best way to help them. Others argue that sharing technology and teaching them techniques to address their problems will be more beneficial over the long term. Which approach do you think would be more effective in solving the problems of developing countries? Explain.

Document Analysis

18. a) Explain the relationship between women's education and fertility that is evident in the graph below (Figure 12–41).

 b) How would you describe the development level of countries with low secondary school enrolments? With high enrolments?

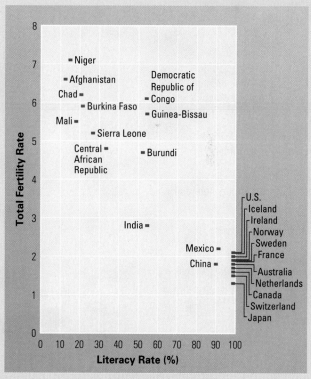

FIGURE 12–41 Women's fertility rates in relation to their literacy rates

13 The Environment: Our Challenges and Responsibilities

GUIDING QUESTIONS

Politics & Government

- How has the international community responded to ozone depletion?

- How has the international community responded to climate change?

- What are the principal international agreements concerning the environment?

Economy & Human Geography

- How are resources, the environment, and human populations interconnected?

- What is sustainable development?

- What are the environmental threats to water resources and how might they be addressed?

- Should Canada treat water as a resource to be traded?

- How is human activity affecting the atmosphere and the ozone layer?

- What is global warming?

- How can we offset environmental threats at the local, national, and international levels?

TIMELINE

1962	1970	1971	1972	1974	1987	1988
Rachel Carson's book *Silent Spring* is published	First Earth Day	Canadian government establishes the Department of the Environment B.C. activists found Greenpeace	UN Conference on the Human Environment is held in Stockholm, Sweden, and leads to creation of the United Nations Environment Programme (UNEP)	Agricultural Land Reserve established in B.C.	The UN report *Our Common Future* urges the developed world to limit the use of resources for a sustainable lifestyle	The UN creates Intergovernmental Panel on Climate Change

CHAPTER FOCUS QUESTION

How is global development causing environmental issues and what challenges do they pose for Canada?

Earth's resources, environment, and human populations are interconnected. As the world's population increases, the scale of human impact on the planet grows. Oceans, fresh water, soil, forests, minerals, and energy resources have been used, and often abused. Our use of fossil fuels has caused the thinning of the ozone layer and the greenhouse effect. We have caused harmful changes in the **biosphere**, the zone of earth, water, and air in which we live. Our livelihoods come from this thin zone, and all things, including people, eventually return to it.

Canada has a unique perspective on the effects of changes to the environment caused by human activities. The impact of global warming is evident in the Arctic's melting ice and permafrost, and in the decreased water flows from retreating glaciers in the Rocky Mountains. Changes to the environment threaten Canada's boreal and temperate forests. The overuse of resources has depleted marine harvests and other food supplies, and our health is compromised by toxins in our rivers and soils. Changes to the environment also cause extreme weather, such as droughts, storms, and floods.

Canada, along with other industrialized countries, must take its share of responsibility for causing problems related to environmental changes. As a major consumer and exporter of resources and fossil fuels, we leave a larger environmental footprint than countries of comparable size. While major decisions are made by government and industry, many individuals and communities have become active in helping to protect the environment. Recycling, composting, and green energy initiatives are all examples of how Canadians can work to preserve a healthy environment.

In this chapter, you will examine some of the changes in our environment, including global warming, the depletion of the ozone layer, and the threats to our water resources. You will also look at some of the solutions proposed and initiatives launched to help address the problems created by environmental changes.

KEY TERMS

deforestation
global warming
acid precipitation
CO_2 emissions
groundwater
aquifer
greenhouse gases (GHG)
ultraviolet radiation (UV)
ozone layer
CFCs (chlorofluorocarbons)
Montréal Protocol
Kyoto Protocol

1992
Earth Summit in Rio de Janeiro, Brazil, calls for a sustainable world economy

1997
Countries signing the Kyoto Protocol commit to cut their CO_2 emissions

2000
Environmental Protection Act comes into force in Canada

2007
Fourth Assessment Report of Intergovernmental Panel on Climate Change

Bali conference held to agree on new treaty to replace Kyoto in 2012

2008
British Columbia government introduces a carbon tax on energy

2009
UN Climate Change Conference in Copenhagen, Denmark

2014
Fifth Assessment Report of Intergovernmental Panel on Climate Change

KEY TERMS

biosphere regions of Earth occupied by living organisms, made up of all the ecozones

stewardship careful management of resources to ensure that they are sustainable

permafrost subsoil that remains frozen all year long

carrying capacity the largest population that an environment can support

deforestation the process of destroying a forest and replacing it with something else

Why Care About the Environment?

People are changing Earth and the effects are seen all over the planet. The world's boreal forests are threatened with increased fire risk, water needs are outstripping supply, flooding and storms are more severe, and tropical diseases are affecting people farther north. For years, there have been warnings about how people's actions affect the environment. In 1992, 1700 concerned scientists from around the globe signed the World Scientists' Warning to Humanity:

> *Human beings and the natural world are on a collision course. Human activities inflict harsh and often irreversible damage on the environment and on critical resources.... A great change in our **stewardship** of the Earth and the life on it is required, if vast human misery is to be avoided and our global home on this planet is not to be irretrievably mutilated.*

FIGURE 13–1 The top photograph shows Arctic ice in September, 1979. The bottom photograph shows the same view in September, 2005.

Interpreting a Photograph What differences do you see between the two photographs? What do the differences mean?

Despite these warnings, people continue to take Earth and its resources for granted. In 2009, the United Nations Environment Programme (UNEP) report on climate change again warned that "serious and irreversible changes in Earth's Ecosystems due to anthropogenic [human] activities are increasingly recognized...."

It can be difficult to convince Canadians that rising temperatures are a problem even though the changes are evident. Extreme weather conditions, such as the ice storm that hit eastern Ontario and Québec in January 1998, are happening more frequently. Warmer weather brings more droughts that make forest fires more likely.

Canada's Arctic regions show some of the most dramatic signs of change. Sea ice is shrinking and the seasonal melt is happening weeks earlier. Polar bears are in danger of extinction as they slowly starve because they cannot use the ice to hunt seals. Arctic communities face sinking shorelines and transport problems as a result of melting **permafrost**. The effects of these climate changes are also political. Some countries, including the United States, Russia, Denmark, and Norway, see the potential for economic wealth from oil and natural gas deposits in the Arctic seabed and shipping lanes through an ice-free Northwest Passage. These nations question Canada's claim to sovereignty over the Arctic, as you read in Chapter 7.

Population Growth and Sustainability

As you read in Chapter 11, Earth is getting more and more crowded every day. Each year, nearly 80 million people are added to the world's population, putting more pressure on Earth's natural systems. Because much of the population increase is in the developing world, the impact is not as great as if it had occurred in the developed world. About 80 percent of the goods and services produced from the world's resources are being consumed by 20 percent of the world's population, mainly in industrialized Western countries. As an increasing number of nations reach the development levels of the industrialized world, pollution and waste levels are rising and threaten to overwhelm Earth's **carrying capacity** and natural systems.

Feeding a Growing Population

The United Nations estimates that the world's population will be close to 8 billion by 2028 (see Chapter 11). Massive amounts of land and water are required to feed all these people. For example, 70 percent of the world's water is used for agriculture. It can take up to 1500 litres of water to produce 1 kilogram of wheat and 500 litres for 1 kilogram of potatoes. As standards of living improve, people are eating more meat and dairy products, which puts the greatest strain on resources. For example, it takes about 1000 litres of water to produce 1 litre of milk, and nearly 16 000 litres to produce 1 kilogram of beef. Added to this are the costs of **deforestation** to create grazing land, energy use to ship food, and depletion of resources. The problem may not only be how to feed the world's growing population, but how to ensure enough resources are available to keep up with the increase.

Agricultural Practices

Soil is one of our primary resources. It is the basis of plant life, which in turn gives us food and other resources. It can take hundreds of years for soil to form in some places. But it can be eroded by wind or water in a fraction of that time. In North America, the "dust bowl" of the 1930s (see Chapter 4) led to improved farming techniques, such as planting trees to form wind breaks, contour plowing, and using wheat stubble and straw to return nutrients to the soil and stop wind erosion.

FIGURE 13–2 The Tata Nano, produced in India, is a compact car aimed at the millions of motorcycle owners in the developing world. It features low emissions, excellent fuel economy, and a starting price of about $2500.

Thinking Critically What impact do you think the Tata Nano will have on the economy, people's lifestyles, and the environment if many people in the developing world drive them?

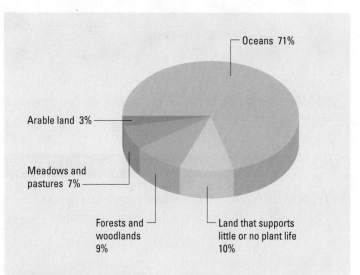

Oceans 71%

Arable land 3%

Meadows and pastures 7%

Forests and woodlands 9%

Land that supports little or no plant life 10%

FIGURE 13–3 Only a small percentage of Earth's surface can be used for growing crops, yet soils are being lost and degraded around the world.

global warming the observed and pro-jected increase in the earth's average tem-perature due to burning of fossil fuels and deforestation

ecology the science concerned with the relationship between living things and their environment

acid precipitation any form of precipita-tion that is high in sulfuric and nitric acids as a result of pollution in the air

Today, Canada's farmers face challenges, such as changes in weather patterns due to **global warming**, urban settlements encroaching on farm-land, competition from giant farms operated by multinational corporations, and genetically modified crops mixing with regular crops. More than 100 genetically modified foods, such as soybeans, corn, and potatoes, have been approved by the Canadian government. Many of these crops rely on herbi-cides, which increase the risk of damage to the environment and possibly lead to long-term effects on people's health.

Making Room for People

Forests are a vital part of world **ecology** because they take in carbon dioxide and give off oxygen. Almost half of the forests that covered Earth before humans began to practise agriculture have been cleared or are in a degraded state. Every day, approximately 350 square kilometres of forest are lost worldwide. These forests are being turned into agricultural or grazing land, harvested for timber, or cleared to make room for human settlements. Many forests and natural areas are also suffering from the effects of industrial pol-lution, such as **acid precipitation**. When the environment can no longer neutralize the acidic content of the soil and water, plants and animals die, and entire ecosystems are ruined.

Without the protection of trees and their roots, wind and rain can erode the soil and leave barren landscapes. This damage is particularly severe on hillsides, where soil erosion and deadly mudslides can silt lakes and rivers, affecting water quality and marine ecosystems. Floods are more common when forests are no longer there to absorb and slowly release rainfall. In Canada, deforestation deprives wildlife of habitat, which may lead to more attacks by bears and cougars as urban settlements encroach on their territory.

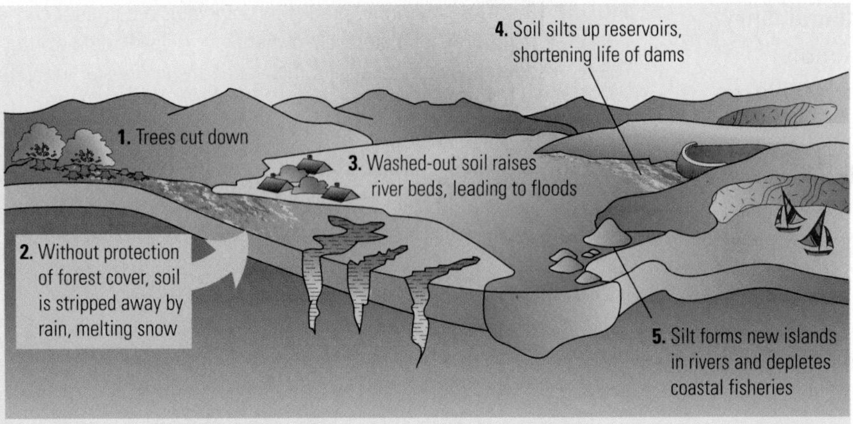

1. Trees cut down
2. Without protection of forest cover, soil is stripped away by rain, melting snow
3. Washed-out soil raises river beds, leading to floods
4. Soil silts up reservoirs, shortening life of dams
5. Silt forms new islands in rivers and depletes coastal fisheries

FIGURE 13–4 The immediate effects of deforestation are dramatic and wide ranging.
Thinking Critically Where in Canada are forests being cleared? What steps could be taken to slow the rate of clearing?

PRACTICE QUESTIONS

1. Write three different headlines, each one summa-rizing one of the concerns in the World Scientists' Warning to Humanity.

2. Provide specific examples of environmental changes in Canada's Arctic.

3. Explain the difficulties of feeding a growing world population.

4. Explain why soil is an important resource.

5. List three farming techniques used to protect soils.

6. Explain the challenges and concerns faced by farmers today.

7. Discuss the environmental impact of deforestation.

Problem solving is the process of figuring out how to reach a desired goal. Decision making is the process of selecting one of two or more possible solutions to a problem.

Steps to Problem Solving and Decision Making

1. **Identify the problem.** Analyze the components of the issue and any relationships among the parts. State the problem clearly and concisely.

2. **Gather all the information you can.** Research the issue. Take note of cause and effect when they apply.

3. **Brainstorm possible options or solutions.** Generate ideas on the subject. Include those you have read about as well as any ideas you come up with. Do not try to evaluate ideas at this stage.

4. **Consider the advantages and disadvantages of each option.** Use organizers or other aids to help you categorize the options and solutions.

5. **Rank the options.** Evaluate the options or solutions and select the top three choices.

6. **Decide on the option you think is the best.** Be able to support your decision with a number of reasons.

7. **Evaluate the effectiveness of your decision.** If you are dissatisfied with the results, return to step five and select from the remaining two choices.

FIGURE 13–5 Some experts estimate that more than 90 percent of waste from Canada's cities ends up in landfills.

Practising the Skill

Canadians are used to discarding their solid waste in landfills. In some large urban centres, landfills are full and there is nowhere for the garbage to go. Some people worry that if landfills are not managed properly, they can pollute groundwater and emit methane gas. What are some possible solutions to the problem of solid waste disposal?

- Many cities encourage people to decrease waste by using the three Rs—reduce, reuse, and recycle. Some cities also restrict the amount of waste they will accept. This approach can be expensive, as cities need to collect, sort, and recycle the materials they collect, as well as promote their programs and convince people to change their habits.

- Other cities incinerate some of their solid waste to keep it out of landfills. This approach has the advantage of producing heat, which in turn can be used to produce electricity. But some people argue that the smoke and ash released into the air contain hazardous chemicals.

- Another option is to ship solid waste to rural areas. While this might solve the problem for one city, it could cause problems where the new landfill is created. It also costs money and uses fuel to ship the waste, which increases the environmental footprint of the landfill.

Applying the Skill

1. Evaluate the solutions presented and look for other options. Decide which option you think is best and support your decision with reasons.

2. Use the steps to problem solving and decision making to examine the following issues.
   a) The Alberta oil sands
   b) Rising water levels in coastal areas
   c) Alternative energy sources in British Columbia
   d) Preserving sufficient natural habitat for wildlife

● What is sustainable development?

KEY TERMS

sustainable development a way to maintain economic growth without damaging the environment

Earth Summit a meeting of world leaders, held in Rio de Janeiro, Brazil, in 1992, to discuss environmental changes and sustainable development

Agenda 21 a statement of environmental action, produced at the 1992 Earth Summit, that outlines actions that should be taken to protect the planet and achieve sustainable development

herbicides substances used to kill plants

pesticides substances used to kill pests such as unwanted plants and animals

organic grown or produced without chemical fertilizers or pesticides

CO₂ emissions carbon dioxide emissions caused by burning of fossil fuels; largest contributor to global warming

biodiversity having a variety of life forms

ecotourism tourism to threatened areas that tries to be low-impact and small-scale

WEB LINK ●

Visit the Pearson Web site to learn more about the Earth Summit and Agenda 21.

Sustainable Development

Although scientists have warned of the harmful effects of environmental change for many years, developed nations have made only moderate progress toward **sustainable development**. Globalization and the emphasis on economic growth have encouraged wasteful consumption habits. One example of the devastating effects of abusing natural resources is the collapse of the cod fisheries off the coast of Newfoundland. Overfishing depleted cod stocks to the point that the Canadian government imposed a moratorium on cod fishing in 1992 and finally banned cod fishing altogether in 2003. This marked the end of an industry that thousands of Newfoundlanders depended on. Future generations depend on today's leaders and individuals to find sustainable ways to support economic growth.

International Efforts

Many international meetings have discussed how to maintain economic growth without damaging the environment so much that it compromises the future of life on Earth. In 1987, the United Nations World Commission on Environment and Development published its report, *Our Common Future*, asking people in the developed world to reduce resource consumption and develop a sustainable lifestyle. In 1992, 172 nations participated in the UN's **Earth Summit** in Rio de Janeiro, Brazil. International leaders looked at various environmental issues that affect people around the world, including toxic chemicals used in production (for example, lead in gasoline and radioactive waste), alternative energy sources to replace fossil fuels, and the scarcity of water. The conference produced a statement of action called **Agenda 21**. This document proposed several actions that should be taken globally, nationally, and locally to achieve sustainable development. Despite having this blueprint for action, there has been little progress in slowing the wasteful consumption that threatens the well-being of the planet.

The First Nations' Approach

Some approaches to sustainable development are modelled on Aboriginal peoples' practice of environmental stewardship and responsibility. On their Web site, the Squamish Lil'wat First Nation says, "Elders teach that we should keep in mind seven generations ahead of us in everything we do, to ensure that we care for future generations in our present decisions." This idea of responsibility has inspired many people to think about how their actions affect others and what they can do today to protect the environment for future generations.

FIGURE 13–6 The Gwa'ni Hatchery, near Alert Bay on Vancouver Island, is part of the Namgis First Nation Project, which helps to ensure that salmon stocks are managed and sustained for future generations.

Thinking Critically What elements of the First Nations' approach to decision making can you see in different environmental protection programs in your school or community?

Farming for the Future

The globalization of agriculture has led to unsustainable practices such as offshore farms (see Chapter 12) and large-scale farming operations (often referred to as "factory farms"). These approaches keep costs down by using large-scale, assembly-line methods to mass produce livestock and crops. Multinational corporations, such as Monsanto and DuPont, have tried to control markets for their seeds, fertilizers, and pesticides by aggressively promoting the genetically modified (GM) seeds they develop. These companies argue that new biotechnologies are necessary to feed the growing world population. Critics point to the environmental effects of using GM seeds. GM crops depend on **herbicides** and **pesticides**, rather than natural defences, and these chemicals can be dangerous as they seep into groundwater and streams.

FIGURE 13–7 The market for natural pest control is growing. One ladybug can eat up to 4000 harmful insects in its lifetime.

Thinking Critically What other activities might use chemicals that would harm the soil and affect the environment?

Becoming more aware of the impact food production has on the environment and their health has prompted many people to adopt a more sustainable diet. This change is reflected in the increase in certified **organic** farms in Canada to more than 3500 in 2006. But organic farms represent only 0.9 percent of Canada's agricultural land, and most of these farms grow cereal crops for export. At the same time, nearly 90 percent of organic food bought in Canada is imported. Concern over the environmental impact of shipping food great distances has led some people to become "locavores," eating foods that are grown or produced locally. Supporters of this diet say it is more sustainable because shorter shipping distances reduce CO_2 **emissions**. Despite this growing demand, many local farmers find it hard to compete with low-priced imported food and must produce crops in demand for export in order to make enough money to get by.

WEB LINK

Visit the Pearson Web site to learn more about foods produced in British Columbia.

Can We Preserve Our Forests?

Around the world, 1.6 billion people depend on forests for food, shelter, and employment. Forests also protect **biodiversity** and remove carbon dioxide from the atmosphere. To emphasize the importance of forests and support efforts to promote sustainable management and conservation, the UN declared 2011 the International Year of Forests.

Several measures have been introduced to preserve and manage the world's forests. Some programs focus on reforestation, replanting trees where they have been cut down for timber or paper. Other programs grow trees specifically for these purposes, thus preserving existing forests. Another approach is to show that there is economic value in preserving forests instead of cutting them down. **Ecotourism** programs allow people to explore threatened natural environments, while the tours raise money for conservation efforts. Individuals can also help to preserve forests by conserving paper. One fifth of wood harvested worldwide ends up in paper, and nearly half of that is used for packaging. In 2003, Canadians used more than 2 million tonnes of paper, which is about 20 000 pages per person.

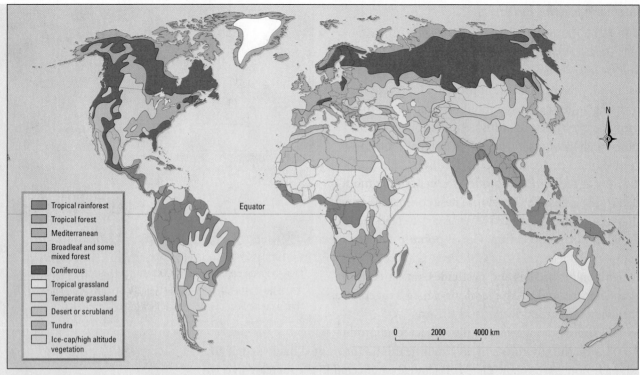

FIGURE 13–8 This map shows forested areas that existed under natural conditions. Much of the forested areas in India, China, Western Europe, and eastern North America have been cleared.

Map legend:
- Tropical rainforest
- Tropical forest
- Mediterranean
- Broadleaf and some mixed forest
- Coniferous
- Tropical grassland
- Temperate grassland
- Desert or scrubland
- Tundra
- Ice-cap/high altitude vegetation

KEY TERMS

Protected Areas Strategy (PAS) a plan to preserve approximately 12 percent of B.C.'s provincial land for parks, recreation, and wilderness

watersheds river basins drained by a river and flowing into the same large body of water

FIGURE 13–9 The Great Bear Rainforest is located on B.C.'s central coast between the northern tip of Vancouver Island and the southern tip of the Alaska Panhandle.

Thinking Critically In what other areas might an agreement to conserve land be used to promote sustainable use of resources? Explain.

Protecting British Columbia's Forests

In 1993, the government of British Columbia launched the **Protected Areas Strategy (PAS)** to preserve about 12 percent of provincial land for parks, recreation, and wilderness. However, the PAS only included a portion of B.C.'s coastal old-growth **watersheds**. Once considered only as a source of revenue, they are now seen as a resource for recreation, research, industry, and—in the case of First Nations peoples—culture. These diverse needs must be balanced with careful management and stewardship to ensure the sustainability of British Columbia's economic and heritage resources.

One example of the clash between these interests is the Great Bear Rainforest. This area is one of the last remaining tracts of unspoiled temperate rainforest left in the world. It is home to thousands of species, including the Kermode (or spirit) bear. These bears are rare, and logging and industrial development in the area threaten their habitat and existence. In a 2006 agreement, First Nations communities, environmentalists, and logging companies agreed to conserve part of the 6.4 million hectares of the Great Bear Rainforest. Two million hectares are protected from logging, with lighter-touch logging outside that area. The agreement supports conservation-based economies in coastal communities and strengthened First Nations involvement in deciding the future of the forest.

©P

When Simon Jackson learned about the plight of the spirit bear, he wanted to do something to help. In 1995, when he was 13 years old, he founded the Spirit Bear Youth Coalition (SBYC) to unite young people to save British Columbia's endangered white bear. He wanted to give young people a voice as the future stewards of the rainforest and get them involved in protecting the environment.

Since it began, the SBYC has reached nearly 6 million young people in more than 70 countries, becoming one of the world's largest youth-run environmental organizations. Today, two thirds of the spirit bear's old-growth rainforest habitat is protected. But the SBYC still has work to do. As part of their efforts to protect the bears' remaining habitat, Simon and the SBYC have helped to produce an animated film called *The Spirit Bear*. This movie will spread the SBYC's message, and all proceeds from the film will go toward saving the rest of the bears' habitat.

Simon works hard to get his message to young people and decision makers alike. He learned from experts in the environmental movement, such as Dr. Jane Goodall, and from people in business, media, and politics. Simon and the SBYC have received various awards, and *Time* magazine named Simon one of its 60 "Heroes for the Planet." Through the SBYC,

WEB LINK •
Find out more about the Spirit Bear Youth Coalition on the Pearson Web site.

FIGURE 13–10 Simon Jackson, shown in 2000 when he was 17 years old, advises young people to "Position yourself so you're ready to take advantage of success when opportunity knocks."

Simon encourages young people to become involved in environmental and social issues, and to use the experiences they gain as a way to make a difference in the world. He says, "I don't really think what I've done is unique or special. Anybody has the capacity to create change."

1. Make a list of environmental issues that concern you. Choose one and outline how you might begin a campaign to create change.

2. How important and necessary are organizations such as SBYC in protecting the environment?

PRACTICE QUESTIONS

1. Which countries or areas of the developed and developing worlds might be most affected by
   a) population growth?
   b) resource use?

2. If the First Nations' approach to decision making were used, do you think there would be so many endangered species? Keeping that approach in mind, how would you respond to the comments in the World Scientists' Warning to Humanity?

3. Explain the issues related to large-scale farming operations.

4. How have some people tried to make food production more sustainable?

5. What strategies are being used to better manage the world's forests?

6. Explain how the Great Bear Rainforest has become an example of environmental stewardship.

Water: The Indispensable Resource

People cannot survive without water. Every person needs at least 1.8 litres of fresh water each day for good health. With water so readily available, Canadians seldom think of it as one of the planet's scarcest resources.

The State of the World's Water

Only 2.5 percent of the world's water is fresh water. About 70 percent of that is in the form of ice caps and glaciers, and most of the remaining amount is **groundwater**. Only 0.3 percent of the world's fresh water is in lakes and rivers. As Figure 13–11 shows, **surface water** is by far the most used source of water.

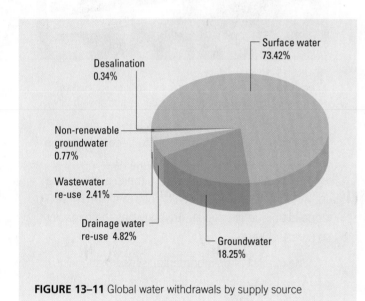

FIGURE 13–11 Global water withdrawals by supply source

In its World Water Development Report (2009), the United Nations World Water Assessment Programme (WWAP) noted that many people still lack adequate access to water. The UN's media release on the report states that freshwater withdrawals from surface and groundwater sources "have tripled over the last 50 years, while the area under irrigation doubled during the same period." The report links this increase to population growth, noting that "demand for freshwater is increasing by 64 billion cubic metres a year." Much of this demand comes from growing populations in the developing world, where water is already scarce.

But water scarcity does not only threaten developing countries. The UN's 2009 report revealed that many sources of fresh water are threatened. Industrialization and rising living standards are rapidly increasing the demand for water. Diets are changing to include more foods, such as meat, that require larger amounts of water to produce. The UN report predicts that if demands for water keep increasing, nearly half of the world's people will face severe water shortages by 2030.

Threats to Our Freshwater Supply

Canada's major water resources contain about 20 percent of the world's total fresh water and 7 percent of the world's renewable freshwater supply. Much of the fresh water is in northern regions, held in glaciers and the polar ice caps, inaccessible to fast-growing urban centres in the south. The Great Lakes contain 18 percent of all the surface fresh water on Earth, but we share them with the United States and they are becoming increasingly polluted. The average Canadian uses about 343 litres of water per day, compared to Germany's 193 and China's 86 litres per person per day (Figure 13–15).

©P

Surface Water Pollution

People often build settlements and cities around sources of surface water, such as lakes, rivers, and coastal waters, but they sometimes neglect to take care of these resources. Surface water can be polluted from municipal, agricultural, and industrial sources. Municipal **wastewater** may contain human waste, detergents, and solvents. Agricultural chemicals like herbicides and pesticides can also make their way into surface water. Industries such as oil refineries, pulp mills, and chemical factories release wastes into rivers and oceans.

The effects of surface water pollution are apparent in Canada. For example, toxic wastes such as mercury have been found in whales and polar bears in the Arctic. Beluga whales in the St. Lawrence River are threatened by water pollution from industrial, agricultural, and human wastes. In British Columbia, sturgeon in the Fraser River are also at risk. Sewage is a major threat to the ecology of the Fraser River. An estimated 90 percent of the municipal waste in the river originates in the Fraser Valley and Vancouver areas. In lakes near populated areas, chemicals and wastes promote the growth of algae and weeds, which can deplete the lakes' oxygen supply, harming other living things, and affect recreational use. In the Okanagan, the spread of **watermilfoil weed** could threaten a multimillion-dollar tourist industry.

Abusing an Underground Resource

Increasing populations are the main threat to the world's freshwater supply. Falling groundwater tables and diversion of surface supplies for crop irrigation are the main causes of shortages. The Yellow River in China, the Ganges River in India, the Nile River in Africa, and the Colorado River in the United States are examples of rivers that run dry, or have little water left when they reach the sea. These shortages threaten world agricultural production. About 36 percent of the world's harvests comes from irrigated croplands. The United States, China, and India are all facing reduced groundwater supplies. These countries produce half of the world's food. In the latter half of the 20th century, the amount of irrigated land increased to more than 250 million hectares. Using new well-drilling technologies and techniques, farmers were able to tap the groundwater in **aquifers** beneath their land. The problem is that, unlike surface water supplies, aquifers are not rapidly replenished.

KEY TERMS

groundwater water beneath Earth's surface in underground streams and other forms

surface water water that is readily available on Earth's surface in streams, rivers, lakes, wetlands, and oceans

wastewater water that has been used in homes or industries and, as a result, contains waste products

watermilfoil weed a plant that grows and spreads quickly, choking out native plants, affecting spawning areas for fish, and posing a safety problem if it grows around public beaches

aquifer an underground layer of rock, gravel, etc., from which water can be drawn for wells and which is a source of springs

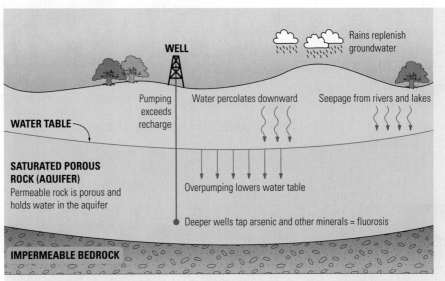

FIGURE 13–12 Groundwater depletion. Overpumping with diesel and electric pumps mines the water faster than it can be recharged by rain or seepage from surface sources. The falling water table means wells must be dug deeper.

Should Canada treat water as a resource to be traded?

As freshwater supplies diminish around the world, business people from Vancouver Island to Newfoundland have been quick to suggest ways to take advantage of Canada's abundant water supply. Although the federal government has officially opposed large-scale export of water since 1987, there have been conflicts over treating water as a sellable resource on the provincial level. In 1996, the government of British Columbia banned the export of bulk water and was sued by a California company under the North American Free Trade Agreement (NAFTA) for compensation for lost opportunity. Public outcry forced the government of Ontario to cancel a deal to export Lake Superior water to Asia. In Newfoundland, a plan to export lake water to the United States and the Middle East raised questions about Canada's water export policies.

Water Exports: Drinking Canada Dry

Some Canadians argue that Canada's fresh water should be treated like other resources exported for profit. They point out that this new industry would increase revenues and create jobs in areas of high unemployment, such as the Maritimes. Opponents claim that water is different from other natural resources. They argue that it is essential to human survival and Canada's supply should be treated as a public resource rather than a commodity sold to profit only a few. Maude Barlow of the Council of Canadians, a nationalist lobby group, strongly opposes exporting water. She believes that "Once you turn on the tap, you can't turn it off again." Nationalists claim that, under the terms of NAFTA, exporting any bulk water will mean that all water can be treated like any other trade good and Canada will lose control of its water.

Some water experts think that the whole issue of bulk water exports is overblown. They claim that transporting bulk water over long distances may not be profitable. A report to the government of Québec pointed out that desalination plants could turn salt water into fresh water for less than the cost of transporting it long distances by tanker. U.S. studies show that conservation

FIGURE 13–13 The southwestern U.S. is an arid region with scarce water resources. All of the surface water is regulated by legislation, and overreliance on groundwater has led to dramatic drops in the water table.

TIMELINE Water Export Decisions in Canada

1967
U.S. Supreme Court authorizes removal of bulk water from Lake Michigan into the Mississippi River system through the Chicago Diversion—the Chicago Shipping and Sanitary Canal. This is the only major diversion out of the Great Lakes Basin.

1970
Canada Water Act does not mention exports of bulk water.

1988
Canada Water Preservation Act introduced but not passed due to election. Would have banned the export of bulk water and large-scale diversions.

1998
A California company, Sun Belt Water Inc., files suit under NAFTA after B.C. government bans bulk water exports.

Public pressure forces Ontario government to cancel permit for bulk water exports from Great Lakes to Asian markets.

©P

methods, such as low-flush toilets and drip irrigation, make far better economic sense than schemes to import large amounts of water. However, rich countries like the United States and Canada do not always adopt the most obvious or lowest-cost solutions to resource issues. The southwestern U.S. sunbelt states are looking for a quick solution to water shortages, and some see Canada's vast freshwater lakes as a resource they are willing to pay for.

Since 2002, the United States has linked a safe and reliable water supply to its national security. Global Water Futures, an American institute contracted by the U.S. government, has noted that "Water issues are critical to U.S. national security and integral to upholding American values of humanitarianism and democratic development. Moreover, engagement with international water issues guarantees business opportunity for the U.S. private sector, which is well positioned to contribute to development and reap economic reward." As a result of this new policy, the U.S. is putting pressure on Canada to give Americans access to Canadian freshwater supplies.

As the population grows and lifestyles put more pressure on water resources, sustainable water supplies may reach a crisis state in North America in the 21st century. In their 2008 report *Climate Change and Water*, the Intergovernmental Panel on Climate Change (IPCC) states, "Climate change will constrain North America's already over-allocated water resources, thereby increasing competition among agriculture, municipal industrial, and ecological uses." The integration of the North American economy and Canada's reliance on U.S. agriculture for much of our vegetables may force Canada to face difficult choices about our water resources.

FIGURE 13–14 While government regulations have prevented the export of bulk water, few Canadians pay attention to the fact that Canada exported about $38 million worth of bottled water in 2008.

Analyzing the Issue

1. Why might Québec be opposed to regulation of the export of water supplies?

2. With a partner, script and act out a short dialogue between a Canadian opponent of water exports and a Texas farmer whose wells are running dry.

3. Do you think Canada should allow the export of bottled water, bulk water, both bottled and bulk water, or no water? Give reasons for your answer.

4. Write a short opinion piece for a blog entitled "Three Good Reasons to (or Not to) Export Canada's Water." Include a suggestion for an appropriate picture to accompany your opinion piece.

5. Debate the pros and cons of bulk water exports.

2001

Canadian government amends the International Boundary Waters Treaty Act prohibiting bulk water removals from boundary water basins within Canada.

Government of Newfoundland and Labrador cancels plans to export water because it is unprofitable.

Government of Québec bans bulk water exports.

2005

Great Lakes Charter Annex Agreement signed by Ontario, Québec, and eight U.S. states that border the Great Lakes, banning the diversion of water other than to communities beside the Great Lakes.

2006

Businessman applies to the B.C. government to export 1 million gallons of water a day from a Kamloops Lake for export to the Middle East. Public opposition forces withdrawal of the proposal.

2007

Closed-door discussions in Calgary between Canada, Mexico, and U.S. on bulk water exports for North American Future 2025 Project.

KEY TERMS

carbon footprint the total amount of carbon dioxide (CO_2) and other greenhouse gases emitted over the full life cycle of a product or service

troposphere the lowest level of Earth's atmosphere

greenhouse gases (GHG) various gases in the atmosphere that absorb and emit radiation, including carbon dioxide, methane, nitrous oxide, and ozone

ultraviolet radiation (UV) invisible rays from the sun that can cause skin cancer

ozone layer a thin layer of ozone in the atmosphere 15 to 30 kilometres above Earth; the ozone layer filters the sun's ultraviolet (UV) rays

CFCs (chlorofluorocarbons) chemicals used in coolants, solvents, and aerosol cans that damage the ozone layer

Montréal Protocol an international agreement signed in 1987 to phase out the ozone-depleting chemicals CFCs

Conserving Our Water Resources

Experience has shown that conserving water by using it more efficiently makes sound economic and environmental sense. Infrastructure costs for water supply and wastewater treatment are reduced. The ecosystem is sustained and improved because less water is withdrawn.

Improving Supply

Water development programs are moving toward conservation and efficient small-scale supply systems. Some experts are optimistic that technology can help us manage our water supplies. Large-scale projects can be replaced by micro-dams, hydro systems that run with a river's natural flow, shallow wells, and more efficient rainwater harvesting. As technologies develop, experts believe we will use more reclaimed or recycled water and, to a lesser degree, desalinated sea water. Low-energy sprinkler systems and drip irrigation, which directs water to plant roots, are reducing agricultural water consumption in water-scarce Israel and could be used worldwide.

Reducing Water Consumption

In developed countries, industrial and domestic water use can be reduced using the same thinking. For example, high-efficiency and low-flow toilets reduce the amount of water needed to flush millions of toilets by 70 percent. Many Canadian municipalities are offering rebates to encourage people to switch to energy-efficient toilets. Taxes or user rates could also be introduced to encourage people to conserve water.

In 2009, the Federation of Canadian Municipalities called on cities to promote municipal drinking water to reduce the consumption of bottled water. Only 5 percent of these bottles are recycled and they leave a **carbon footprint** from processing and distribution. A total of 50 municipalities have voted to introduce restrictions on bottled water.

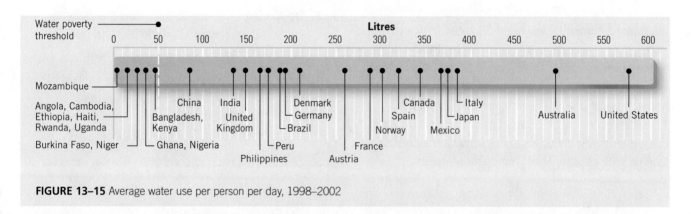

FIGURE 13–15 Average water use per person per day, 1998–2002

PRACTICE QUESTIONS

1. Do you agree that increasing populations are the main threat to the world's freshwater supply? Explain your answer.

2. What are the main threats to surface water in Canada?

3. In a two-column organizer, list the benefits and problems associated with groundwater use.

4. Which of the solutions to water management do you consider to be the most practical? Explain.

Change Is in the Air

The lowest layer of Earth's atmosphere, the **troposphere**, contains most of the atmospheric gases, including **"greenhouse" gases (GHG)**: water vapour, carbon dioxide, methane, nitrous oxide, and ozone. These gases occur naturally and play a vital role in regulating Earth's temperature, but human activities have upset the balance, causing ozone layer depletion and global warming.

The Hole in the Ozone Layer

Ozone, a special kind of oxygen (O_3), is the only gas in the atmosphere that blocks the sun's ultraviolet (UV) rays. **Ultraviolet radiation** can cause skin cancer in humans, and can damage other animal and plant species.

In 1978, satellite observation of the atmosphere revealed that the **ozone layer** was thinning. Ozone depletion is most evident over the polar regions, where seasonal thinning, or a "hole," appears in the ozone layer during winter and early spring each year. As much as 60 percent of the layer disappears over Antarctica in the spring, filling in again over the summer.

The Montréal Protocol

Chemicals, particularly **chlorofluorocarbons** (**CFCs**), destroy the ozone layer. CFCs have been widely used since the 1930s in coolants for refrigerators and air conditioners, and in foams, solvents, and aerosol cans. It is believed that the release of CFCs into the atmosphere has done 80 percent of the damage to the ozone layer.

The United Nations Environment Programme created the **Montréal Protocol** to phase out the use of ozone-depleting chemicals. In 1987, all industrial nations agreed to the protocol, which allowed countries of the developing world to use CFCs until 2000. The Montréal Protocol successfully united countries in the effort to reduce CFCs. In 2009, 97 percent of all the chemicals controlled by the protocol had been phased out.

In 2007, the countries involved in the protocol met again in Montréal to deal with hydrochlorofluorocarbons (HCFCs), the less-harmful replacement for CFCs. With new chemicals available that do not damage the atmosphere, the world agreed to phase out HCFCs in developed countries by 2030 and in developing countries by 2040. Only the complete elimination of HCFCs will begin to halt the damage to the ozone layer. The United States Environmental Protection Agency claims that even when all ozone-depleting chemicals are phased out, it could take a century before the annual thinning of the ozone over Antarctica does not reappear.

● How is human activity affecting the atmosphere and the ozone layer?

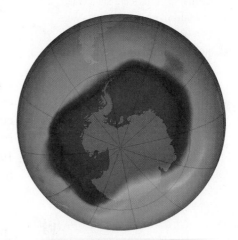

FIGURE 13–16 The hole in the ozone layer above Antarctica on September 24, 2006

● How has the international community responded to ozone depletion?

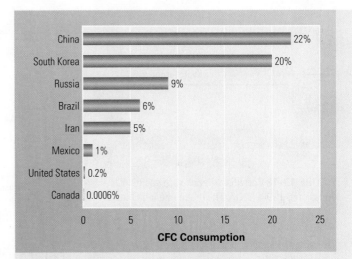

FIGURE 13–17 CFC consumption, 1999 (percentage of world totals)

Thinking Critically What reasons might account for the countries with the top and the bottom CFC emissions?

©P

Greenhouse Gas Emissions

While natural emissions from volcanoes and other processes collect in the atmosphere, the results of human activities have the greatest effect. Since the Industrial Revolution in the 19th century, industrial and chemical contaminants have polluted the air. These pollutants cause smog, acid rain, and the widening hole in the ozone layer.

Fossil fuels—coal, oil, and natural gas—are at the centre of global warming. Coal is widely used outside Canada for heating and energy generation. China and other Asian countries are the world's greatest producers and consumers of coal. As Figure 13–18 shows, greenhouse gas (GHG) emissions in Canada have increased since 1990. Environment Canada reports that there was significant long-term growth in emissions between 1990 and 2007. These emissions came from increases in oil and gas production (much of it for export), motor vehicles, and coal electricity generation.

Canada ranked seventh in the world for carbon emissions from fossil fuels. It will move up on this list if it continues to produce greenhouse gas emissions at the same rate. One reason for increasing emissions is the development of the Alberta tar sands, where natural gas is used to process the tar sands. According to the oil industry, 29.5 megatonnes of greenhouse gases are emitted from the tar sands each year. This accounts for nearly 5 percent of Canada's total emissions. According to Sierra Club Canada, that figure will rise to more than 50 megatonnes by 2015. If that happens, the tar sands would be the single greatest contributor to GHG emissions growth in Canada. Carbon stored in **peatlands** disturbed by tar sands development will also add to the total GHG output.

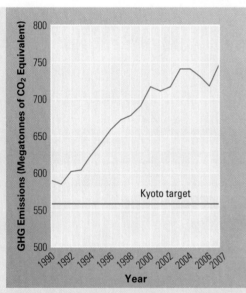

FIGURE 13–18 Canadian greenhouse gas (GHG) emissions, 1990–2007. The green line indicates Canada's GHG emission targets outlined in the Kyoto Protocol (see page 444).

Thinking Critically In 2009, the Conservative government set a target of reducing emissions by 20 percent from 2006 levels. Why do you think they picked 2006 as a baseline date? Do you agree or disagree with this target? Why or why not?

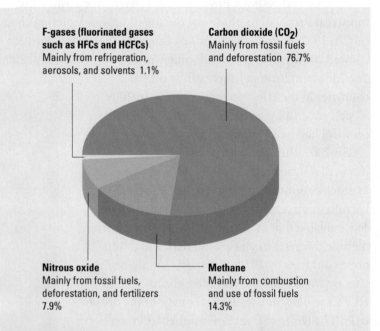

FIGURE 13–19 Greenhouse gases that contribute to global warming

Reading a Graph Which are the two main greenhouse gases? What percentage of greenhouse gases comes from burning fossil fuels and deforestation?

©P

Things Are Warming Up

The gases in the atmosphere work like the glass in a greenhouse. They trap heat energy from the sun, creating our climate and making life on Earth possible. If these gases—especially carbon dioxide—are out of balance, they can cause major changes to our climate. Natural factors, such as volcanic explosions and meteor impacts, have caused dramatic climatic changes in the past. Scientists estimate that carbon dioxide (CO_2) in the atmosphere has increased by 30 percent since the Industrial Revolution and the subsequent burning of massive amounts of fossil fuels. By increasing the heat-trapping gases, we have increased the **greenhouse effect**. The global temperature has risen by about 0.74°C in the past 100 years. Scientists predict that it could rise by an additional 0.2°C every 10 years for the next two decades. Even minor increases in Earth's temperature can have profound effects on life on Earth.

In 2007, the Fourth Assessment Report of the Intergovernmental Panel on Climate Change (IPCC) summarized the state of global climate change:

(1) Warming of the world climate system is undeniable.
(2) The rise in global average temperature is very likely due to increases in greenhouse gases.
(3) Despite present policies, emissions will continue to grow over the next few decades.
(4) Present adaptation strategies do not adequately address the threat of climate change.

● What is global warming?

KEY TERMS

peatlands wetlands with soil formed mostly from decomposing plants

greenhouse effect greenhouse gases trap heat in the atmosphere, causing Earth's temperature to rise

WEB LINK ● ● ● ● ● ● ● ● ● ● ● ● ●

For more information about Earth's temperature increase and a summary of the Fourth Assessment Report of the IPCC, 2007, visit the Pearson Web site.

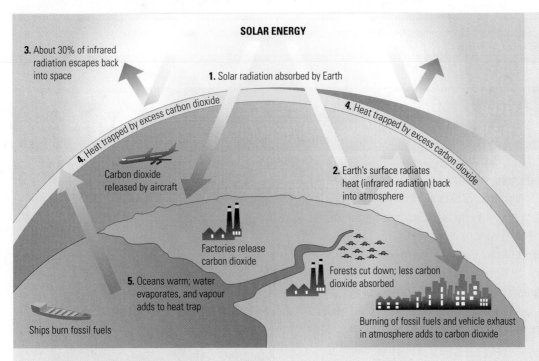

SOLAR ENERGY

3. About 30% of infrared radiation escapes back into space

1. Solar radiation absorbed by Earth

4. Heat trapped by excess carbon dioxide

4. Heat trapped by excess carbon dioxide

Carbon dioxide released by aircraft

2. Earth's surface radiates heat (infrared radiation) back into atmosphere

Factories release carbon dioxide

Forests cut down; less carbon dioxide absorbed

5. Oceans warm; water evaporates, and vapour adds to heat trap

Ships burn fossil fuels

Burning of fossil fuels and vehicle exhaust in atmosphere adds to carbon dioxide

FIGURE 13–20
How the greenhouse effect works. Excess carbon dioxide accumulations trap heat that would otherwise be radiated back into space.

Consequences of Global Warming

Scientists agree that the increased number of heat waves and violent storms in recent years are linked to global warming. Above-average temperatures in polar regions are melting glaciers, and sea levels are rising as a result. Other effects are harder to link directly to global warming. These include diseases extending their ranges because of warmer temperatures, and the earlier arrival of spring in many parts of the world. Plant and animal ranges are shifting as species try to adapt to changing temperatures by moving to different habitats. Coral reefs in more than 30 countries are experiencing coral bleaching as the microscopic algae that give them their colours fail to adapt to warmer water temperatures and die.

WEB LINK
The full UNEP report on climate change is available on the Pearson Web site.

Geographic Area	Results of Climate Change
Arctic regions	Summer sea ice melts, exposing darker ocean, absorbing more heat accelerating melting and increasing sea levels
Greenland and Antarctic Ice Sheets	Ice sheet breakup exposes land accelerating warming and rise in sea levels
Boreal Forests	Dry spells and lengthier cultivation seasons result in a higher susceptibility to pests and fire
Tropical Rainforests	Loss of forest cover affects regional hydrological cycle and climate triggering further forest dieback
Atlantic and Pacific Oceans	Ocean circulation systems of winds and currents destabilized by temperature changes and addition of fresh water from ice sheets
Indian, Saharan, and West African Monsoons	Monsoons, seasonal winds and rain critical to agricultural economies disrupted

FIGURE 13–21 A 2009 UN Environment Programme (UNEP) report on climate change outlined the elements of Earth's system vulnerable to possible change.

---

up close and personal **David Suzuki: Can One Person Make a Difference?** | CRITICAL INQUIRY | Cause and Consequence

Scientist David Suzuki became internationally famous for his commitment to the environment. Suzuki was born in Vancouver in 1936. From an early age, Suzuki's father fostered a love and appreciation of nature in his son. During the Second World War, Suzuki and his family were interned with thousands of other Japanese Canadians. His internment camp was located in a deserted mining town in the Slocan Valley. Later, Suzuki trained as a geneticist, but he has also applied his scientific knowledge to many environmental issues. He has contributed to a growing awareness of environmental issues in Canada and around the world through his popular books and radio and television programs. Today, he continues his role as a warrior for the environment through his speaking engagements and the David Suzuki Foundation. Most recently, he has been focusing on the disastrous effects of climate change.

FIGURE 13–22 David Suzuki

Understanding Significance In what ways might David Suzuki's background have encouraged his commitment to the environment?

Forests and Climate Change

Even small changes in temperature and precipitation can affect forest growth. Although changes in forests will differ regionally, they will affect Canada's economy, society, and culture.

Warmer temperatures have already had damaging effects on British Columbia's pine forests. Warmer winters allowed the mountain pine beetle to survive in previously inhospitable areas and to extend its range. Westerly winds have allowed the insect to migrate over the Rockies and take root in the pine forests of northern Alberta. This has raised fears for the rest of Canada's pine forests. The spruce budworm is also a concern in the boreal forests of Western Canada. The effect of these insects goes beyond the loss of wood. Dead trees act as fuel for wildfires that threaten communities. Once a forest dies, it no longer acts as a **carbon sink**, but emits carbon dioxide into the atmosphere instead.

KEY TERM

carbon sink a reservoir that can absorb and store carbon dioxide from the atmosphere, including forests, peat, and oceans

WEB LINK

For more information about the mountain pine beetle, visit the Pearson Web site.

FASTFORWARD

A Walk in the Arctic Woods

In 2009, the International Union of Forest Research Organizations claimed that, as a result of global warming, trees might someday spread to Canada's Arctic where only tundra now exists. The report says that in areas of northern Canada, Sweden, Finland, and Russia, the evergreen trees of the boreal forests will start to shift northward. By 2070, forests may spread to Baffin Island, the coastline of Hudson Bay, northern Québec, and Labrador. This shift of forests will change the ecology in the new forested areas and in the old areas where different species of plants and animals will now thrive. The authors of the report caution that it will take a long time for new forests to establish themselves in warming areas.

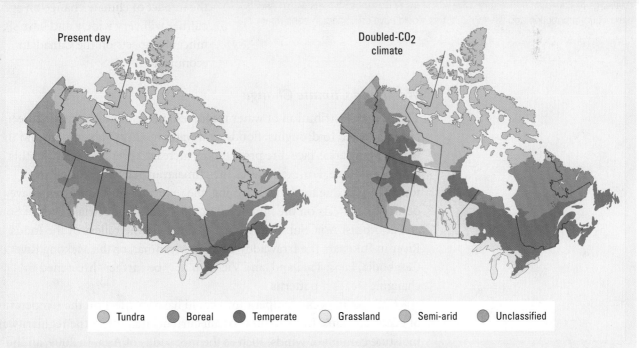

Present day

Doubled-CO_2 climate

○ Tundra   ● Boreal   ● Temperate   ○ Grassland   ● Semi-arid   ● Unclassified

FIGURE 13–23 Projected changes to vegetation boundaries with doubled CO_2 levels

Using Evidence What changes do you see in the forest and grassland boundaries with the doubled CO_2 climate?

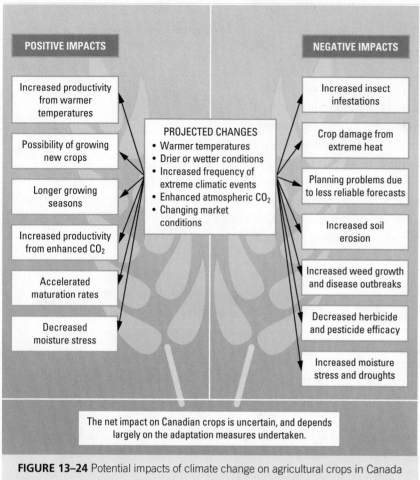

POSITIVE IMPACTS

- Increased productivity from warmer temperatures
- Possibility of growing new crops
- Longer growing seasons
- Increased productivity from enhanced CO₂
- Accelerated maturation rates
- Decreased moisture stress

PROJECTED CHANGES
- Warmer temperatures
- Drier or wetter conditions
- Increased frequency of extreme climatic events
- Enhanced atmospheric CO_2
- Changing market conditions

NEGATIVE IMPACTS

- Increased insect infestations
- Crop damage from extreme heat
- Planning problems due to less reliable forecasts
- Increased soil erosion
- Increased weed growth and disease outbreaks
- Decreased herbicide and pesticide efficacy
- Increased moisture stress and droughts

The net impact on Canadian crops is uncertain, and depends largely on the adaptation measures undertaken.

FIGURE 13–24 Potential impacts of climate change on agricultural crops in Canada

Thinking Critically Natural Resources Canada suggests that, as a result of climate change, extreme events such as floods, storms, and droughts present the greatest challenge to Canadian agriculture. Give examples of how these threats would affect agricultural production and what impact that would have on Canadian consumers.

Agriculture and Climate Change

Climate change is expected to impact Canada's agriculture in both positive and negative ways. For example, warmer temperatures would make the growing season longer, but they could also increase crop damage due to heat stress and pest problems. Warmer temperatures may make it possible to grow crops farther north, but the soils will not be as rich. Impacts would vary by region and crop.

Agriculture is extremely sensitive to any changes in climate, particularly the levels of moisture available. Global warming will likely affect water supply for agriculture. For example, less **meltwater** from receding glaciers in the Rocky Mountains will mean less available water for Alberta and British Columbia agriculture during the dry summer months. The benefits of a longer growing season may then be offset by water shortages. Warmer winters may mean less protective snow cover and could also bring thaws that damage crops. As Figure 13–24 shows, the impact of climate change on agriculture will vary widely and have significant impacts on the Canadian economy.

Water and Climate Change

The uneven distribution of water resources and yearly variations in precipitation have led to droughts, floods, and water quality problems around the world. Many areas face dire prospects as increased pressure is put on this limited resource. For example, as the Himalayan glaciers (Asia's "water towers") melt due to global warming, the reduced water supply will have devastating effects on the human, agricultural, and industrial needs of South and Southeast Asia. Subsistence farmers living in the valleys of the Indus River in Pakistan, the Irrawaddy River in Myanmar, or the Mekong River in Cambodia, Laos, Thailand, and Vietnam may be further threatened by changing weather patterns.

Changes in ocean temperatures could have an effect on the temperatures of ocean currents. In turn, these ocean currents may affect the regularity and moisture content of winds, such as the monsoons of Asia. In 2009, an Indian newspaper reported that "Farmers from Uttar Pradesh and Bihar said the precipitation and the number of rainy days had come down significantly and disrupted the entire agricultural cycle in the region during the last five

©P

years." Changes in wind and precipitation patterns also bring damaging floods or droughts. The latter results in desertification as deserts expand into previously semi-arid areas. When rivers and lakes dry up in these areas, millions of people will be forced to leave their farms and livestock, becoming environmental refugees.

In Canada, changes in temperature and precipitation can affect **runoff**, evaporation, and the storage of water in lakes, soils, and glaciers. Arid regions, such as the Okanagan Valley and parts of the Prairies, will be particularly vulnerable due to present supply problems. Reduced flows from glaciers and less precipitation will decrease summer flows of rivers, which will in turn affect agriculture and salmon spawning. In winter, less ice cover, winter thaws, and snow-rain precipitation may increase the risk of flooding in many regions.

Despite its relative abundance of water on a per-capita basis, many regions of Canada have experienced water-related problems. Changes in water levels and warmer temperatures could increase bacteria and contamination in some areas. Elsewhere, increased flooding could flush urban and agricultural waste into rivers and municipal water systems. In coastal areas, rising sea levels may increase saltwater invasion into freshwater supplies. In the North, melting permafrost may make the ground unstable and affect the transmission of water supplies.

Melting glaciers and ice caps, and warming oceans, will result in rising sea levels. These changes will have a serious impact on Canada's coastline. Some effects might include cliff erosion, land destabilization, flooding of low-lying areas, and the disruption of infrastructure, such as roads and pipelines. Low-lying deltas, such as the Fraser River delta in British Columbia and the Mackenzie River delta in the Northwest Territories would be severely affected by a significant rise in sea levels.

KEY TERMS

meltwater melted snow or ice, including ice from glaciers

runoff water from rain and melting snow that cannot be held in the soil so makes its way into streams, rivers, lakes, and oceans

WEB LINK •

Visit the Pearson Web site to explore the possible effects of rising sea levels on Canadian cities.

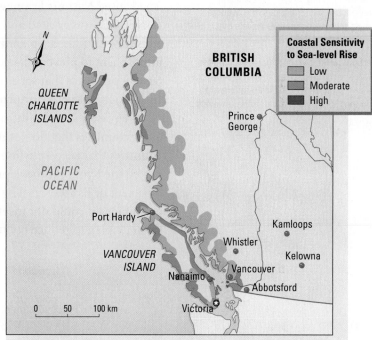

FIGURE 13–25 Coastlines of Canada likely to be affected by rising sea levels

PRACTICE QUESTIONS

1. Create a two-column chart with the headings "Ozone Depletion" and "Global Warming." Under each heading, list the causes, effects, and possible solutions to these issues.

2. How successful was the Montréal Protocol? Explain.

3. What areas of Canada might be most affected by changes in agriculture due to global warming? Give examples to support your answer.

4. Use a two-column organizer to show the advantages and disadvantages of global warming for Canadian agriculture. Do the advantages outweigh the disadvantages? Explain.

5. What effects will rising sea levels have on coastal communities?

6. **Patterns and Change** Describe how global warming will affect economic activity, settlement, and transportation in the future.

● How has the international community responded to climate change?

● What are the principal international agreements concerning the environment?

KEY TERMS

United Nations Framework Convention on Climate Change (UNFCCC) the UN's plan to keep greenhouse gas concentrations from increasing, created at the 1992 Earth Summit in Rio de Janeiro, Brazil

Kyoto Protocol an international agreement that sets binding targets for reducing greenhouse gas emissions; the average target is 5 percent of 1990 levels by 2008–2012

carbon credit if an organization produces more greenhouse gases than it is allowed, it can purchase a credit from an organization that is below its target emission levels

Taking Action on Greenhouse Gas Emissions

In 2006, noted economist Nicholas Stern released a report for the British government presenting a compelling case for decisive action against global warming. The Stern Review stated:

> *Our actions now and over the coming decades could create risks of major disruption to economic and social activity, on a scale similar to those associated with the great wars and the economic depression of the first half of the 20th century. And it will be difficult or impossible to reverse these changes.*
>
> *–Nicholas Stern*

Kyoto Protocol

The **United Nations Framework Convention on Climate Change (UNFCCC)** was created at the 1992 Earth Summit in Rio de Janeiro, Brazil. This treaty outlined a plan to stabilize greenhouse gas concentrations in the atmosphere to prevent dangerous interference with Earth's climate system. Several protocols that set emission limits came out of this convention, including the **Kyoto Protocol**. This document outlined target reductions for GHG emissions. It also introduced the system of **carbon credits**, which allow countries that do not meet their reduction targets to buy credits from countries that keep emissions below their allotted levels. In 1997, Canada signed the Kyoto Protocol, promising to reduce greenhouse gas emissions by 6 percent of its 1990 level by 2012. In 2007, the Canadian government announced it could not meet its Kyoto Protocol targets, and developed a separate plan to reduce pollution and GHG emissions (see Case Study).

Idea	Description
Carbon Tax	In 2008, British Columbia introduced a tax on fossil fuels to reduce use and meet the government's goal of reducing GHG emissions by 33 percent by 2020. The money raised is returned in reductions of other taxes.
Cap and Trade	A ceiling is put on emissions, and companies exceeding it must buy permits on the "carbon market" from companies under the allowable limit. If no permits are available, the rights to higher than targeted emissions could also be bought. These costs are meant to encourage companies to reduce emissions. The Western provinces and the U.S. favour this system.
Carbon Sequestration (locking away)	Carbon dioxide would be collected and shipped to a geologically suitable area below layers of impermeable rock. Storage areas might be depleted fossil fuel reservoirs. The technology is already in use with water and natural gas. Saskatchewan and Alberta are promoting this system.

FIGURE 13–26 Three approaches to limiting GHG emissions being discussed in Canada and the United States

Thinking Critically What might be the drawbacks of each of these approaches? How could governments be convinced to apply any of these approaches?

Bali Road Map

In 2007, delegates from 189 countries met in Bali, Indonesia, to prepare a new treaty to replace the Kyoto Protocol in 2012. Two groups emerged at the Bali conference. One group agreed with the European Union's support of the Kyoto model of absolute reduction in GHG emissions by 25 to 40 percent by 2020. The second group, which included Canada, Japan, Russia, and many Asia-Pacific Economic Cooperation members, supported the United States' call for flexible goals focused on reducing carbon intensity (the amount of carbon released per unit of energy produced). This idea was rejected by the EU group, who argued that it would not reduce overall emissions. The final agreement, called the Bali Road Map, encouraged countries to cooperate to fight climate change.

Moving to Sustainable Energy Sources

While political debates continue, Earth is still heating up. Most leaders agree that all nations need to move toward sustainable development and clean energy sources to slow down climate change. There are many sustainable sources of energy that could be used to lessen dependence on fossil fuels. These include wind turbines, solar power panels, tidal power, ground-source energy or geothermal power (which uses heat from underground sources where available), and biofuels derived from biomass (plant or animal material). The environmental group Greenpeace claims that by 2030 wind power could provide 15 percent of the world's electricity. Although all these alternative sources of energy have drawbacks, they are renewable without harmful emissions.

FIGURE 13–27 Wind turbines would be effective in windy locations such as along the coast of British Columbia or in the Alberta foothills.

Thinking Critically Why would some people oppose having wind turbines like these in their area?

Source	Advantages	Disadvantages
Hydroelectric power	Vast quantities of power. Dams and reservoirs control flooding and provide recreation.	Dams and reservoirs can cause environmental and social disruption. Transmission lines take land as right of way and emit waves.
Run-of-river hydropower	Emissions free. Minimum impact on river flow or fish.	Power plant, access roads, and transmission lines disrupt ecosystem. River levels may be affected.
Wind power	Emissions free. Easily installed for individual or large-scale use. Land can have other uses.	Need reliable, strong winds. Noisy and a visual pollutant. Threat to migrating birds.
Geothermal	No pollutants or emissions. Discharges are safe to recycle. No storage needed.	Expensive to build. Must be located in geologically active areas.
Tidal	Regular source. First turbines tested in Bay of Fundy in 2009.	Limited locations. Interferes with aquatic life and coastal transportation.
Biofuels	Biodegradable, readily available biomass; few pollutants when burned.	Not as efficient as fossil fuels. Some croplands used for ethanol, leading to higher food prices.

FIGURE 13–28 Advantages and disadvantages of various sustainable energy sources

Politics, Conferences, and Climate Change

FIGURE 13–29 Low-lying island nations like the Maldives are facing extinction if climate change cannot be controlled and sea levels continue to rise.

The author of the British government's 2006 Stern Review, a report on the economics of climate change, remarked: "The first thing that struck me... was the magnitude of the risks and the potentially devastating effects on the lives of people across the world. We were gambling the planet." Despite this warning, meaningful action at the international level has been elusive.

There are few today who deny that global warming is changing our relationship to the biosphere. The difficulty in finding an effective and realistic solution lies in getting the 192 member countries of the United Nations to agree on and implement a program to reduce greenhouse gas (GHG) emissions. Each nation wants to protect its right to develop and use its industries as it sees fit.

The politics of climate change were first evident at the 1992 Earth Summit in Rio de Janeiro, Brazil. The leaders could not agree on how to best deal with greenhouse gas concentrations in a way that worked for all nations. This debate essentially led to a postponement of any action until the next conference in Kyoto, Japan, held five years later.

Kyoto, 1997

The Kyoto Protocol established GHG emission targets for industrialized nations. Countries that ratified the protocol agreed to meet their given targets by 2012. The United States, which was the largest producer of greenhouse gases when the Kyoto Protocol was established, did not ratify the treaty.

As Figure 13–30 shows, compliance with Kyoto GHG targets has varied across different nations. Domestic politics have played a significant role in the failure of Kyoto in all but a few countries. In Canada, the Liberal government ratified the treaty and proposed steps to meet its targets, but emissions continued to rise. One reason for Canada's inability to meet its targets was that the federal government signed the agreement, but provincial governments regulate polluting industries. After the Conservative government under Prime Minister Stephen Harper came to power, it announced that Canada could not meet its limits in the Kyoto Protocol and developed its own plans to address air pollution and climate change in 2007. Due to the lack of social or economic changes that would reduce greenhouse gases, Canada continues to lead G8 nations in the growth of emissions.

©P

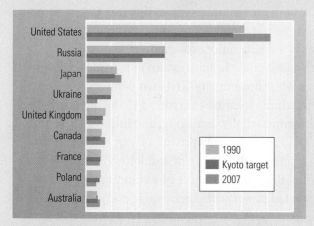

FIGURE 13–30 GHG emissions for selected countries who signed the Kyoto Protocol

Thinking Critically Why might some countries have signed but not ratified the protocol?

Bali, 2007

World leaders met again in Bali, Indonesia, to discuss climate change. The focus of this conference was on developing the next steps after the Kyoto Protocol and to come up with a timetable for meeting greenhouse gas emission targets. The final agreement, called the Bali Road Map, proposes long-term cooperation between nations to cut emissions and share technology that promotes clean, renewable energy. The road map was, by necessity, a compromise. It allows countries to determine how they can best address climate change by taking "nationally appropriate steps." While this clause is intended to make sure that developing countries are not handicapped by their targets, critics fear that industrialized nations may take advantage of this leeway.

Copenhagen, 2009

The UN held another meeting in Copenhagen, Denmark, to finalize the agreement outlined in the Bali Road Map. Once again, politics hampered efforts to come up with a plan that all nations could agree to. The dividing line fell between developed and developing nations. Both China and India, two of the world's greatest GHG emitters, take the position that global warming is caused by the accumulation of greenhouse gases from developed, industrialized countries and that poor, developing countries should not have their economic development restricted. The Prime Minister of India emphasized his country's position: "For us, the foremost priority is the removal of poverty, for which we need sustained rapid economic growth."

When President Obama entered office in 2009, the United States changed its position on climate change, which also influenced Canada. Prime Minister Harper noted that "The alignment of our climate change policies with those of the Obama Administration is a critical element of Canada's overall approach due to the close integration of our economies and our geographic proximity." This sentiment was reflected in Canada's support of the U.S. position at the Copenhagen Conference. When negotiations for a new treaty broke down, the U.S., China, India, Brazil, and South Africa worked together to draft a new Copenhagen Accord. This agreement did not include specific long-term targets for GHG emission cuts, but it did promise US$30 billion in aid over the next three years to help developing countries reduce their emissions. Canada supported the accord, but other countries felt that it was not a fair agreement because it was drafted by only a few powerful countries. The accord was not unanimously accepted, so it did not pass.

While developed and newly industrializing countries debate, nations facing the immediate consequences of global warming grow more frustrated. The president of the Maldives, an archipelago of 1200 islands that face steadily rising sea levels, expressed that frustration: "The Maldives has committed to becoming carbon neutral by 2020, using the wind and sun to power the entire nation. If that can happen in a relatively poor, developing country, it can happen anywhere. What we lack is not technology, but political will."

WEB LINK •
Visit the Pearson Web site to find out more about climate conferences and agreements.

Looking Further

1. Why is it so difficult for countries to reach an agreement to reduce GHG emissions?

2. Do you agree or disagree with Canada's position on the environment? Explain.

3. Do you support the position of India, China, and some developing countries? Why or why not?

4. **Perspectives** How are the perspectives of the Maldives and India, although opposed, both based on perceived needs for survival?

What might be the impact on
Canada's energy consumption
if the rest of Canada follows
the First Nations' example?

First Nations Lead the Way in Clean Energy

Many of Canada's First Nations communities are leading the way in adopting green energy solutions to meet their energy needs. Projects include small-scale hydro stations, wind generation, solar power, and new approaches to energy efficiency. These initiatives aim to provide reliable and sustainable energy sources while minimizing GHG emissions.

Many communities in remote locations are forced to use diesel generators that are expensive, environmentally damaging, and unreliable. Adopting alternative or green energy sources not only provides clean and sustainable energy supplies, but also economic development and jobs. The Taku River Tlingit First Nation in Atlin, B.C., is an example of a community that was able to replace diesel-generated power with a renewable energy project. A Tlingit-owned power company operates a run-of-river (meaning that it relies on the natural force of the river) two-megawatt power project. This will save 1.5 million litres of diesel and 4500 tonnes of greenhouse gases. The result is to reduce the community's carbon footprint by the same amount as removing 1600 cars from the road.

On Haida Gwaii (the Queen Charlotte Islands) the Haida Nation will partner with NaiKun Wind Energy to build a Hecate Strait wind-power project. The 110-turbine project will generate enough power to light 130 000 homes. This project will also create jobs and revenue for the Haida Nation.

At Sooke on Vancouver Island, the T'Sou-ke Nation has the largest system of solar panels operating in B.C. The band office has banks of solar panels that provide electricity and power batteries for emergencies or cloudy days. The fisheries building is powered entirely by solar power. With the solar panels and conservation initiatives, energy consumption on the reserve has dropped by 30 percent. Excess power is sold to B.C. Hydro. Another benefit has been training the band members as solar panel installers. The T'Sou-ke Nation has become an example for other remote communities.

There are many other First Nations communities adopting innovative green projects that set an example for the rest of Canada. As T'Sou-ke Chief Gordon Planes said: "We are going to change B.C. and we are going to change Canada."

FIGURE 13–31 The T'Sou-ke Nation is going solar powered as part of a community sustainability push. They have the largest solar-powered system in B.C. and will be selling power to B.C. Hydro. Here, T'Sou-ke Nation Elder Linda Bristol stands in front of some of the solar panels on the reserve. The residences in the background have small panels used for hot water heating only.

©P

Doing Our Part for the Environment

Since the 1992 Earth Summit, Canada has tried to make its economy more responsive to environmental concerns. In some areas, forest practices have improved significantly. Many communities have adopted waste recycling programs, and Canadian innovations have helped to turn sewage into fertilizer and develop more energy-efficient cars and buildings. Canadians have been less successful at reducing the use of pesticides and herbicides, or in cutting back paper and water consumption. Canada's boreal forests, groundwater supplies, and other resources are still being depleted at a concerning rate. Greenhouse gas emissions in Canada have increased, even after signing the Kyoto Protocol.

● How can we offset environmental threats at the local, national, and international levels?

Individuals Can Make a Difference

Canadians consume 15 times more energy than people in developing countries. Our small population can have as much impact on world energy and resources as a less developed country many times our size. But we can all do our part to help the environment by becoming active in the community and taking responsibility for our environmental footprint. Individuals can help fight climate change by recycling, composting, buying local, and using energy-efficient appliances, lights, and transportation. Each of us can conserve water by installing low-flush toilets and taking shorter showers. Drinking tap water rather than bottled water reduces water consumption and saves the energy needed to make and recycle plastic bottles. Reuseable shopping bags can help cut down on the billions of plastic bags used worldwide each year. These bags can make their way into oceans and rivers, where they can harm animals and their habitats.

As people like Simon Jackson demonstrate, individuals have the capacity to bring about change. Becoming aware of the state of the local environment is the first step. Find out about school-based groups or community organizations that are working to help protect the environment, and get involved. Our actions will help set the course for future generations, and as a report from the United Nations Environment Programme stated, our "present course is unsustainable and postponing action is no longer an option."

WEB LINK ●
Find out more about what individuals can do to help fight climate change by visiting the Pearson Web site.

FIGURE 13–32 Volunteers help to recycle donated computers in Vancouver. Many cities have special programs for recycling electronics.

PRACTICE QUESTIONS

1. What was the purpose of the Kyoto Protocol? What was Canada's involvement in this agreement?

2. What two viewpoints emerged from the Bali conference on greenhouse gas emissions in 2007?

3. Why have international efforts to reduce GHG emissions been ineffective? What might account for Canada's poor record in reducing emissions?

4. Which forms of sustainable energy would be practical in your area? Support your choices.

5. For what reasons have many First Nations communities turned to alternative energy sources? How might the example of these First Nations help other Canadians reduce their carbon footprint?

6. Provide specific steps individual Canadians can take to reduce their environmental footprint.

CHAPTER FOCUS QUESTION **How is global development causing environmental issues and what challenges do they pose for Canada?**

1. In this chapter you have read about the many ways that climate change is affecting Canada's environment. Use an organizer like the one below to categorize the challenges of climate change described in the chapter.

   a) In the first column, list the primary global causes of climate change.

   b) In the second column, list the secondary, or more localized, causes of climate change.

   c) In the third column, list the effects of climate change that are evident or visible in Canada.

   d) In the fourth column, list the long-term consequences for Canada and the world.

   e) In the last column, list some of the solutions proposed to help meet the challenges of climate change.

Primary Causes	Secondary Causes	Effects in Canada	Long-Term Consequences	Possible Solutions

2. Use the information you gathered above to develop an outline for an essay discussing Canada's role in contributing to climate change and the effects and consequences for the environment.

Vocabulary Focus

3. For each term below, write a sentence showing its relationship to environmental issues in Canada.

   a) ozone layer

   b) deforestation

   c) Montréal Protocol

   d) Kyoto Protocol

   e) groundwater

   f) greenhouse effect

   g) CO_2 emissions

Knowledge and Understanding

4. Explain how effective each of the following was in dealing with threats to the environment.

   a) The UN report *Our Common Future*

   b) United Nations creates the Intergovernmental Panel on Climate Change

   c) British Columbia government introduces a carbon tax on energy

   d) Agricultural Land Reserve established in British Columbia

©P

5. Describe the effects of global warming on each of the following:

   a) Arctic regions

   b) forests

   c) agriculture

6. List an advantage and a disadvantage for each of the following alternative energy sources:

   a) wind

   b) run-of-river hydro

   c) tidal

7. Note and give reasons for the Canadian government's record in reducing GHG emissions.

8. a) Why is global warming an environmental problem?

   b) Why is international cooperation needed to deal with this problem?

9. Make a list of the types of information you would need if you were sent to determine the amount of Canada's forests that should be preserved.

10. Make a list of some of the sources of water pollution in your community. Find out what action is being taken to deal with the worst examples of pollution.

11. How many of the causes of global warming can be found in Canada? Suggest actions that could be taken to deal with the emissions in your area.

Critical Thinking

12. How successful has the world been at living up to the goals of Agenda 21 in the past decades? Give specific examples from this chapter.

13. In a short paragraph, summarize the steps Canadians need to take to ensure that freshwater supplies are used in a sustainable way.

14. Explain which approach to limiting GHG emissions you would be in favour of and why.

15. Send an e-mail or a letter to the federal Minister of the Environment explaining why that department should give the highest priority to addressing the problems of Canada's forests.

16. Research a First Nations community in British Columbia and discover how they share their traditional lands and culture with tourists.

17. In a group, develop a proposal for a film on one of the issues in this chapter. Submit a story outline, cast, setting, soundtrack, and working title.

18. In a small group, write and perform a TV spot called "Water Minutes" (in the style of "Heritage Minutes"), promoting the benefits of water conservation.

19. Does it surprise you that Canada has not been at the forefront of reducing GHG emissions? Explain why or why not.

20. Suggest ways that the Canadian government can take more of an international leadership role in environmental sustainability.

Document Analysis

21. This statement was issued by British and U.S. scientists in 1997:

    It has often been assumed that population growth is the dominant problem we face. But what matters is not only the... number of people... but also how... much natural resource they utilize, and how much pollution and waste they generate. We must tackle [the problems of] population and consumption together.

    a) What is the problem of consumption? How would you tackle this problem on a personal level?

    b) Why is it difficult to solve the problem of consumption?

    c) Do you agree with the scientists' statement? Explain your answer.

    d) Could sustainable development successfully deal with the environmental problems caused by growing populations and consumption? Explain.

Use this Study Guide to bring together some of the key ideas relating to world population and resources, standards of living, environmental issues, and challenges facing Canada in the future. As you work through the following steps, keep in mind the Focus Questions in Chapters 11 to 13. Look for evidence in your understanding to answer these questions.

STEP 1 Unpacking Knowledge

Construct a chart similar to the one below. In groups of two or three, look through your notes and the textbook, and categorize and record information that you have learned regarding issues, causes, solutions, and challenges. Part of an example for the environment has been done for you.

	Issues	Causes	Solutions	Challenges
Population Trends				
Living Standards				
The Environment	rising sea levels	• sustained global warming • melting of polar ice caps	• global reduction in CO_2 emissions • relocation of settlements	• shifting ecosystems and habitats • loss of agriculture and sacred sites

STEP 2 Organizing Your Understanding

Create a Venn diagram based on the Chapter Focus Questions similar to the one below. Using your chart from Step 1, list the items that could be used as evidence in answering the Chapter Focus Questions. Remember that many issues, causes, solutions, and challenges are inter-related and will belong in the overlapping sections of the circles.

What is the significance of changes in global population for Canada and the world?

How do living standards in Canada compare with those of developing countries, and what is being done to close the poverty gap and improve human development around the world?

How is global development causing environmental issues and what challenges do these issues pose for Canada?

STEP 3 Making Connections

Choose one specific issue from your Venn diagram and use the steps below to consider how this global issue affects you and your community.

a. Brainstorm a list of all the ways in which the issue affects you and your community.

b. Use the Internet, the newspaper, and/or personal interviews to research ways in which your community is dealing with this issue.

c. Identify the challenges that your community faces to deal with the issue and put possible solutions into action.

d. Identify specific actions you can take on a personal level to begin dealing with the issue.

e. Present and discuss your findings with your classmates.

STEP 4 Applying Your Skills

Examine the data sources below and discuss the following questions:

a. What global issue is being represented?

b. What does the information in the source tell you about the issue?

c. How effectively and reliably does the source communicate information?

d. What questions do you have regarding the information in the sources or the issue itself?

e. What type of information is represented and where could you look to answer questions you may have regarding the issue?

Remember to use the skills you have gained through the chapters in designing graphs, evaluating web sites, and problem solving and decision making to assess the reliability of information, and to make global connections between your community, Canada, and the world.

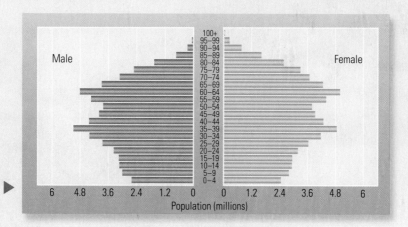

SOURCE 1: Population pyramid, Japan, 2010

SOURCE 2: Infant Mortality Rate, Life Expectancy, and Infant Deaths—Less Developed Countries (UN-based) Afghanistan

Year	IMR* Both Sexes	IMR Male	IMR Female	Life** Expectancy Both Sexes	Life Expectancy Male	Life Expectancy Female	Infant Deaths Both Sexes	Infant Deaths Male	Infant Deaths Female
2010	151.5	155.2	147.7	44.7	44.5	44.9	168 137	90 096	78 041

* Infant Mortality Rate (per 1000 births)
** Life Expectancy (in years)

SOURCE 3: Distribution of the world's poor

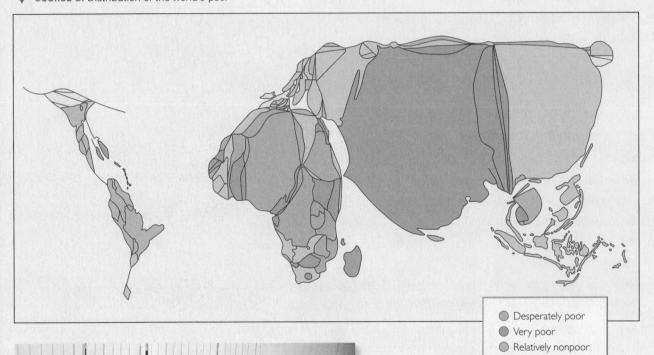

- ● Desperately poor
- ● Very poor
- ● Relatively nonpoor
- ○ Insufficient data
- ○ Industrial nations

SOURCE 4: Seniors practising yoga and meditation

SOURCE 5: Fish processing plant in China ▶

▲ **SOURCE 6:** Cartoon by a Swiss artist on the subject of climate change

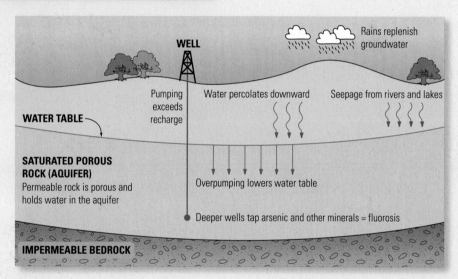

SOURCE 7: Diagram showing the process of groundwater depletion ▶

STEP 5 Thinking Critically

Assess the following quotations and choose an effective means to respond to the questions below.

> "We're in a giant car heading towards a brick wall and everyone's arguing over where they're going to sit."

> "Our personal consumer choices have ecological, social, and spiritual consequences. It is time to re-examine some of our deeply held notions that underlie our lifestyles."
>
> **–David Suzuki**

a) What is the brick wall—the consequences—to which Suzuki refers?

b) What roles do governments have in addressing these problems?

c) What roles can individuals have in diverting this "giant car"?

d) What are some challenges to these solutions?

CHECK the Pearson Web site for additional review activities and questions.

Exam Skills Handbook

CONTENTS

Regular review of information on individual chapter tests will help you study for a final exam that tests your knowledge of the entire course.

The "So What?" Test

A great strategy to use after each lesson or at the end of a chapter is to try the "So What?" Test. Think of the things you have learned and ask yourself, "So What?" to determine the importance of the event or topic. Your answer should help you put the information into a larger context so that you can remember it.

> **Topic:** Halibut Treaty 1923
>
> So What? Because it was the first treaty Canada signed without Great Britain, and it was important in signifying our independence as a nation.

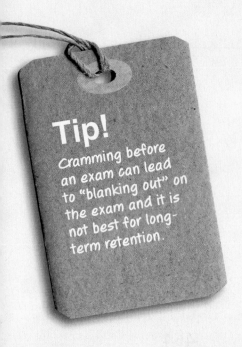

Tip!

Cramming before an exam can lead to "blanking out" on the exam and it is not best for long-term retention.

Know What to Study

Review your tests and look for patterns. What are your strengths? What are your weaknesses? Armed with this information, study those things that give you the most difficulty. By starting this way, you will spend most of your time reviewing the most challenging material. Topics you find easy will most likely be easy for you on the exam and should require less study time.

Make a list of the things that are most likely to give you difficulty on the exam. Once you have made your list, use it to study. Commit your list to memory. You might even take the first 10 minutes of the exam to write down key things that were on your list.

> **Topic:** National Identity
>
> - mobility
> - communications
> - movies
> - art
> - literature
> - sport

©P

Chunking

When you are looking at topics for review, ask yourself which topics go together and then study them one after the other to make the connections.

> <u>**Topics**</u>: Montréal Protocol, Kyoto Protocol, and Copenhagen Summit
>
> Even though these events took place in different decades, they are all linked because they are important international environmental agreements.

Another great strategy is "chunking your time." If you study for hours without a break, your brain will reach a point where it is overloaded and your retention of the material will drop significantly. Take a break after you have mastered a chunk of material. This will give your brain a rest before you move on to a new chunk of material.

Tip!
The brain naturally likes to chunk information into categories.

Know Your Learning Style

Different learning styles work for different people. Ask yourself these questions: "What am I good at?" "What things give me difficulty?" "What strategies have worked best for me in the past?" Here are some ideas to help you get started.

Visualizing
Draw diagrams and mind maps; create flow charts; use colour to organize your notes.

Hearing
Teach the concept to another student; explain the subject to someone unfamiliar with the material; create a song.

Doing
Create flashcards; build a model of a concept.

Learning Styles

USING THE TEXT TO STUDY

When teachers create final exams, they are faced with the difficult task of condensing a year's worth of work into a two-hour exam. Not everything can be tested. To avoid studying the wrong things, you can begin by determining the Big Ideas of the chapter, the units, and the course. The text has some great features to help you do this.

Finding the Big Ideas

The following image is a spread from Chapter 3 of this text. What text features do you notice that could help you determine the Big Ideas of the chapter?

> Can you answer these focus questions? These would be great long-answer or essay questions. Notice how they are also organized by theme. Think about how the events in the chapter match these themes.

> Here we have another great essay question.

> The key vocabulary is already listed. This would make a great study list.

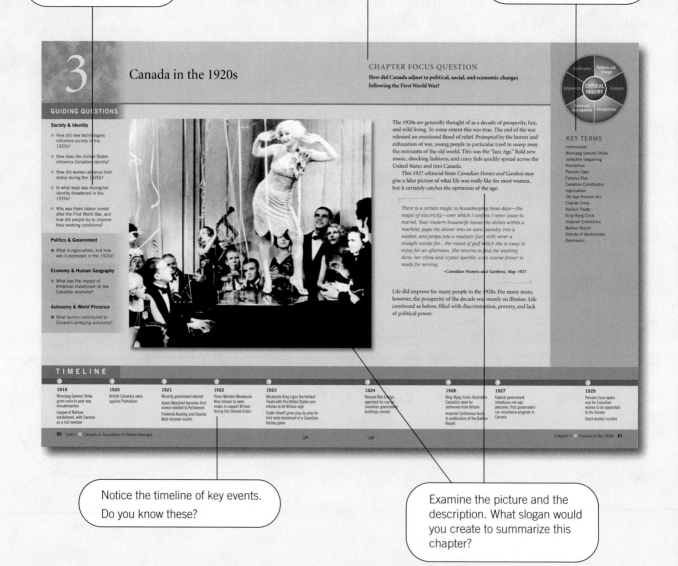

> Notice the timeline of key events. Do you know these?

> Examine the picture and the description. What slogan would you create to summarize this chapter?

©P

Finding the Details

Once you have determined the Big Ideas, the next step is ensuring you know the important details of the chapter. These will help you master the multiple-choice and short-answer questions.

The following text features can help you with

Practice Questions: Throughout every chapter, you will find Practice Questions that focus on important details. You may have already done them for your teacher. Study these and pay special attention to the ones you initially got wrong.

Chapter Review: A helpful Chapter Review appears at the end of every chapter. These were created around the important Big Ideas and details in the chapter. Use them the same way as you would use the Practice Questions.

Key Terms: Throughout the chapter, Key Terms are listed in the margin of the text. Scan the chapter and make sure you know the meaning of these Key Terms. You can also find their definitions in the Glossary at the end of the book.

Building Your Skills

Sometimes exam questions are created to see if you can apply your learning. Can you read a map? Can you interpret a cartoon? Can you present information in a graph? The text has some great features called Building Your Skills that focus on how to do these things. Making your own practice test lets you consider information from the viewpoint of teachers and examiners and lets you think of possible questions as well as their answers.

Reading a Map	Interpreting Cartoons	Designing Graphs
See Building Your Skills on page 145	See Building Your Skills on page 31	See Building Your Skills on page 360
General Tips Read the title of the map. What does it tell you?	**General Tips** If there is a title on the cartoon, what does it tell you?	**General Tips** Examine your data. What type of graph would work best?
What information is contained in the legend?	Look at the whole picture and the small details.	What information should appear on each axis?
How does your knowledge of the chapter help you understand the map?	How does your knowledge of the chapter help you understand the cartoon?	How does your graph make the data clearer?

©P

Note Taking

Summarize information for review later by taking notes. Writing down key points helps you to remember facts, dates, and events. Effective notes include the maximum amount of important information in the minimum amount of words. Here are two ways to record information as you read your text or listen in class. Choose the method that best suits your needs.

Tip!

- Keep notes short, neat, and organized
- Use key terms, events, dates, and personalities
- Underline or highlight important information
- Categorize notes under headings and subheadings
- Use your own words to aid your understanding

Two-Column Method

The following two-column method makes it easy to find information and is ideal for studying.

> Divide the paper into two columns, with the right side wider than the left.

Key Words

D.P. - Displaced Persons
Balts = people from Baltic countries
1952 Immigration Act

> If using abbreviations, give a definition under Key Words.

> Dates, key terms, events, and places. Be very brief for easy review.

Details

- 1946–1952 approximately 165 000 refugees and displaced persons came to Canada
- Balts (Estonian, Latvian, and Lithuanians) among first DPs to Canada after WWII
- Almost 20 000 Lithuanians, well-educated professionals & artists, came to Canada
- Immigration Act = blind to ethnic origin
- Economic boom = huge demand for labour, immigrants

> Use this column for the majority of your notes. Include important details, but be concise and organized.

> Use symbols like +, =, &, b/c (because), w/ (with), and w/o (without) to keep notes brief.

Outline Method

The outline method organizes information by topic, with details listed below the topic in descending order.

LIFE AFTER THE WAR
Canadian soldiers had difficulty adjusting to life back home after the war b/c
  Difficulties:
  - **Slow Passage Home:** Shipping soldiers home sometimes took years; kept them from family, loved ones
  - **Compensation:** Money insufficient
  - **Psychological Issues:** Shell shock, grief, depression affected returning soldiers = difficulty returning to "normal" life
  - **Political Scars:** Conscription had torn nation in two—French vs. English

©P

DESIGN YOUR OWN STUDY QUESTIONS

Creating and Using Flash Cards

Flash cards are two-sided study aids made on index cards, or squares of paper. You can use them by yourself, with a partner, or in a group in short, quick bursts or over extended periods of time. Try using them in game-show style or as straight rote memorization. Flash cards also lend themselves to alternate learning styles. Students who learn best kinesthetically (by movement) often get tremendous benefit by using flash cards while walking, pacing, speaking aloud, or by arranging them on bulletin boards or tabletops.

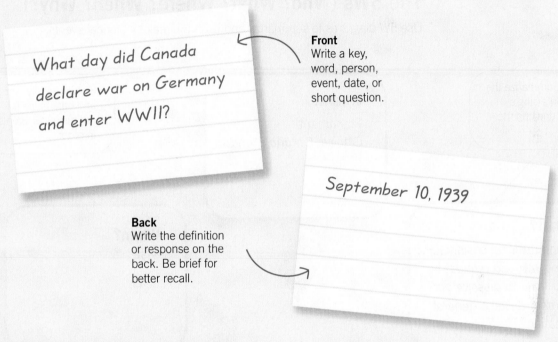

What day did Canada declare war on Germany and enter WWII?

Front
Write a key, word, person, event, date, or short question.

September 10, 1939

Back
Write the definition or response on the back. Be brief for better recall.

Creating Essay Questions

Practise using essay commands (see page 476) to write a sample essay question. Choose topics that are broad in scope, but fall within the major themes of Social Studies 11: Government and Politics; Autonomy and International Development; Human Geography; and Society and Identity.

- Ask yourself what impact the major historical events of the 20th century had on Canada.

- Consider ways in which Canada has grown as a nation as a result of the events of the past century, and try phrasing these as a question.

- Create an outline, complete with a thesis statement, in response to each sample essay question.

©P

When preparing for tests, quizzes, or the provincial exam, try using graphic organizers to simplify complex ideas, show connections, or highlight a series of events. To create an effective organizer, focus on the relationships among data and examine the impact of each of them. The best organizers are simple to read and understand, so you must also prioritize information and determine the most important material. Add colour coding, pictures, and/or symbols to your graphic organizer to further increase its utility, readability, and impact. Here are three different types of organizers:

The 5Ws (Who? What? Where? When? Why?)

Use 5W diagrams to summarize and examine major historical events.

Be brief. Summarize the key term in a single phrase or one concise sentence.

Where?
Parliament
Ottawa, Ontario, Canada

Knowing the year and date helps to put historical events in order.

What?
Constitutional crisis: GG Byng refused request by PM King to dissolve parliament & call a general election

When?
1925

King-Byng Crisis

Who?
Govenor General Lord Byng and Prime Minister W.L.M. King

Why?
Byng refused b/c he felt King should have resigned earlier. This was the first time a GG refused a PM

Use abbreviations for common words like b/c (because), w/ (with), and w/o (without).

©P

Cause and Effect Organizers

Cause and Effect organizers describe how events affect one another. Using this process helps you to see the growing impact of multiple causes leading to an event. The Cause and Effect diagram below lists the major causes of the First World War.

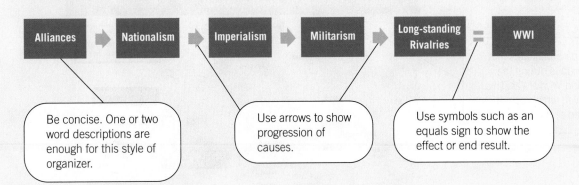

Be concise. One or two word descriptions are enough for this style of organizer.

Use arrows to show progression of causes.

Use symbols such as an equals sign to show the effect or end result.

Using Familiar Shapes as Organizers

Research suggests that it is easier to recall new information when it is presented in a familiar format. Below, a familiar shape is transformed into a graphic organizer.

Causes of The Great Depression

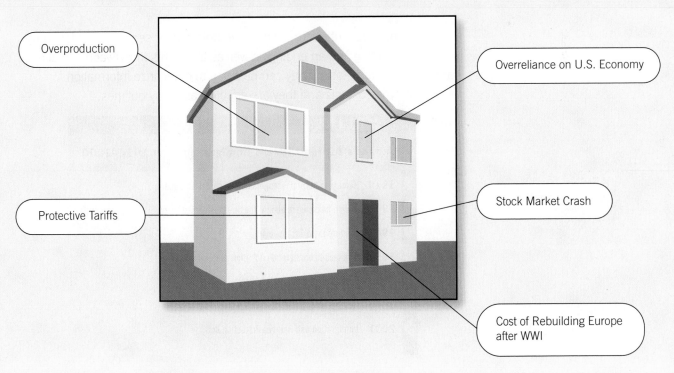

Maps and timelines are often used in tests and exams and make great study tools. When considering a map, be sure to look at the title, legend, and date, if given. Political boundaries changed considerably in the 20th century. Comparing with a more recent map will indicate where political boundaries have moved.

> This date indicates that the map is during the Second World War. This tells you which countries existed at the time.

Timelines present information in chronological or sequential order. They show a beginning and an ending as well as the points in between. Timelines are valuable study tools. They can help you to categorize information for nearly all types of tests and they are effective as essay outlines.

TIMELINE

Canada's Attitude Toward Immigration from 1914–2000

1914	Komagata Maru passengers denied entry into Canada
1939	Jewish passengers aboard the St. Louis denied entry
1947	Chinese Head Tax repealed
1952	Changes to Immigration Act allow preferred classes
1967	Introduction of the Points System
1976	Refugee and family provisions added
2001	Immigration and Refugee Protection Act

©P

HOW TO PREPARE FOR EXAMS

Do you know anyone who *likes* to write exams? Exams can be difficult. Some exams may leave you feeling nervous. Some may leave you feeling inadequate, and others may have content that leaves you in disbelief. The goal of this handbook is to minimize those feelings by giving you tips, advice, and strategies that will help you to succeed on your Social Studies exam.

Knowing What to Study

Often your teacher will provide a study outline, but if you are left with the task of creating your own, here are some great places to start.

Provincial Exams	School-based Exams
The B.C. Ministry of Education maintains a Web site that has helpful information for students regarding the provincial exams. It includes past exams and answer keys, information on the structure and time allotted to your exam, rules about what you can bring into your exam, and definitions for important terms. Visit the Pearson Web site to take a look.	Your teacher most likely gave you a course outline at the beginning of the year. The main ideas and topics for your course should be listed on the outline.
The B.C. Ministry of Education also publishes curriculum guides (IRPs) on their Web site. These documents outline the key concepts that should be taught in each course. See the IRP for your course on the Pearson Web site.	The IRP applies to all courses even if there is not a provincial exam.

Types of Questions

There are two generic types of questions—multiple choice and written answers.

Multiple Choice	Written Answers
*Traditional Multiple Choice	*Essays
Matching	Paragraphs
True/False	Fill in the blanks

These types of questions are on the Social Studies 11 Provincial Exam.

©P

Multiple-Choice Exams

Many multiple-choice exams are created so that the questions are in a special order. The two most common ways questions are ordered are in Chronological Order and Thematic Order. Knowing the organizational structure of the questions can be helpful.

Chronological Order

If the exam is in chronological order and you are debating whether the answer is the Battle of Passchendaele or the Battle of Sicily, look at the questions before and after. One of these battles is from the First World War and the other is from the Second World War. A chronologically ordered exam might give you the clue you need. The history section of the Social Studies 11 Provincial Exam is currently in chronological order.

Thematic Order

If the exam is in thematic order and you are debating between two answers, you might be able to determine the answer by understanding which theme cluster you are working on. If the theme cluster is women's achievements, you will know that the answer to the question will be one of the women's names listed.

Key Words

Three types of words—absolutes, negatives, and qualifiers—can give you clues.

Absolutes
- always
- never
- all
- none
- only

If these words are used, keep in mind that the correct answer would have to be absolutely true in all cases. These words are not often associated with correct answers.

Negatives
- none
- not
- never
- neither
- except

If the question uses one of these words, such as "Which of the following is *not* a cause of the war?" you are looking for the opposite of what you normally seek.

Qualifiers
- usually
- often
- generally
- may
- seldom

If these words are used, they are more than likely pointing you to a correct answer because it is rare to find something absolutely true in all circumstances.

©P

Relieving Stress and Avoiding Confusion

Multiple choice is a commonly used review and testing method. But for many students, multiple choice spells stress and confusion. There are a number of strategies for multiple-choice tests that apply to students across ability levels. You can overcome stress and avoid confusion by using these simple tips.

Answer the ones you know first. Answering the questions from top to bottom can often slow you down if you get stuck on the questions you do not know. Instead, quickly scan all the questions and start with the ones you feel confident about. Do not spend too much time on any one question. If a question seems to have no right answer, circle it and move on. Once all the questions have been read, go back and answer the ones you have circled.

Try to answer *before* looking at the choices. By predicting the answer before you look at the alternatives, you will feel more confident when you see the right answer and be less likely to be confused by incorrect ones.

Make sure you look at *all* the responses before choosing. This sounds simple enough, but students are often in such a hurry to finish that they do not take the time to thoroughly read all the options and therefore overlook the correct response.

Look for absolute terms such as *always, never, all,* and *none*. More often than not, absolute terms in a question indicate that the statement is false.

Look for answers with terms used by your teacher or your textbooks. If the language is familiar, it is likely that that answer is the correct one.

Use the process of elimination. When the answer is not immediately apparent, or if there seems to be multiple possible answers, try to eliminate two answers that seem the most blatantly wrong. Among the four different choices, two are usually noticeable distracters. Now, you have a 50–50 chance of choosing the correct answer.

Answer every question. Do not ever leave a multiple choice blank. You always have a 25 percent chance of getting the right answer; higher if you can eliminate one or more of the distracters. Return to your circled answers once you have answered all the questions you know. See if you can answer them now.

Do not change your answer. Often a question will seem to have two right answers. If you are unsure, use the strategies above and *then* make your final choice. Research shows that people who change their answers overwhelmingly change a correct one to a wrong one. Only change your answer if you are absolutely sure you made a mistake, for instance, if another question suggests the right answer, or it is revealed by another answer.

©P

TAKING NOTES FOR MULTIPLE-CHOICE EXAMS

The content of Social Studies 11 can be divided into four categories: Politics and Government, Autonomy and International Involvement, Society and Identity, and Human Geography. It is often useful for students to create study notes based on these topics. Remember that multiple-choice answers are often looking for "just the facts," so your notes should be concise. Below is an example of how to prepare study notes ideal for multiple choice.

Organize your information in a matrix chart. You may not have information for every column. To study, cover one or more columns and try to guess the correct response. Try to complete the unfinished columns below in your notebook.

Politics and Government

It is expected that students will be able to
- understand the political spectrum
- explain how Canadians can create change in the federal and provincial government
- explain how governments, provincial and federal, are formed in Canada
- describe major provisions of the Canadian Constitution, including the Charter of Rights and Freedoms
- assess the impact of the Charter on Canadian society

Politics and Government – Matrix

Key Word/Event	Date	Key Persons	Definition	Explanation or Effect
Political Spectrum		- citizens of a country - political parties	- refers to differences in ideology between the major political parties - Left = in favour of change, new ideas - Right = desire to keep traditions, little change	Left vs. Right Left parties: NDP, Green Party Centre party: Liberal Right parties: Conservatives; Bloc Québécois
Change in Government	Must be every 5 years, often every 4	- political party in power calls election - electorate votes	Election called, electorate votes in first-past-the-post system	First past the post = candidate with the most votes wins the riding; the party with the most ridings won is then in power
Formation of Government				
Provisions of Constitution				
Impact of Charter				

©P

The remaining three categories of Social Studies 11 curriculum as well as the learning objectives are shown below. You can create your own matrix charts for these categories to study for the exam.

Autonomy and International Involvement

It is expected that students will be able to
- describe Canada's political spectrum
- assess Canada's role in the First World War and the impact on the nation
- assess Canada's role in the Second World War and the impact on the nation
- describe Canada's participation in world events in regard to
    human rights
    United Nations
    Cold War
    modern conflicts

Human Geography

It is expected that students will be able to
- explain changes in world population in regard to
    population pyramids
    distribution and density
    demographic transition models
- compare Canada's standard of living with those of developing countries
- assess environmental challenges facing Canadians, including
    global warming
    ozone layer depletion
    fresh water quality and supply

Society and Identity

It is expected that students will be able to
- assess the development and impact of Canadian social policies and programs
- describe economic cycles including the Great Depression and the labour movement
- describe the social, political, and economic contribution of women in Canada
- assess the impact of Québec nationalism, conscription crises, bilingualism, and regionalism on Canadian unity and identity
- explain challenges faced by Aboriginal people in Canada during the 20th century and their responses, with reference to reserves, self-government, residential schools, and treaty negotiations

©P

INTERPRETING GRAPHIC INFORMATION, MAPS, AND TIMELINES

Sometimes multiple-choice questions present familiar information in unexpected ways. Examiners are giving you the opportunity to demonstrate your deep understanding of the content and making sure that you are able to analyze and discuss the information, as well as understand its application.

Graphic Information

Some multiple-choice questions will present information in a graphic organizer for you to analyze.

Use the following political spectrum to answer the question.

| Left | 1 | 2 | 3 | 4 | 5 | Right |

> All the data you need is in this spectrum. Another word for spectrum is scale.

Which number on the political spectrum reflects the position of the Green Party?

A. 1
B. 2
C. 4
D. 5

> You are asked to decide if the Green Party is Left or Right on the spectrum.

Use the following list to answer the question.

> What do you recall about these facts? What do they have in common? Do you recall the date or what world events were taking place?

- Establishment of relief camps
- On-to-Ottawa Trek
- Minimum wage and maximum hours of work a week

Which prime minister is associated with this list?
A. R.B. Bennett
B. W.L.M. King
C. A. Meighen
D. R. Borden

> Use the strategies on the previous pages to help you narrow down the choices.

©P

Maps

When presented with a map, be sure to read all of the information including the date, title, and labels, not just the images.

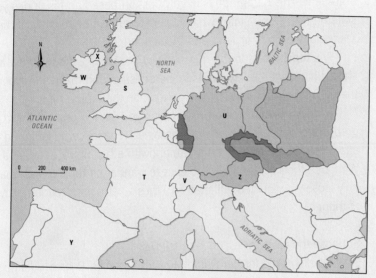

Which countries were neutral during the Second World War?

A. S, T, U

B. X, Y, Z

C. S, U, V

D. V, W, Y

Timelines

Examiners will often give you a list of events and ask you to put them in chronological order. Take your time and read through the options carefully.
If it helps, write the events down in the right order in the margin of your exam booklet.

Put the following Second World War battles into the correct chronological order.

1.	Hong Kong	1941 (first)
2.	D-Day	1944 – June (third)
3.	Antwerp	1944 – September (fourth)
4.	Sicily	1943 (second)

Write the correct order down on the paper beside the responses, then look for the answer that corresponds with the timeline you wrote.

A. 1, 2, 3, 4

B. 4, 3, 2, 1

C. 1, 4, 2, 3

D. 3, 2, 4, 1

©P

WRITING EXAM ESSAYS

By Grade 11, you are expected to be able to write a five paragraph essay by using the following construction.

Introduction

The introductory paragraph does not contain any factual evidence for your argument. This paragraph is largely opinion-based and includes your **thesis** statement. A thesis states what you are arguing and consists of three parts: the topic, the point of view, and the sequence.

The **topic** refers to the question you are being asked to write about. You should highlight the key words in the question and make sure you address them. The **point of view** is your position on the topic.

The **sequence** is the order in which you plan to present the content paragraphs that will follow. Keep your essay at a manageable length to demonstrate your ability to form an argument with a beginning, middle, and end. Without a thesis statement, it is easy to wander off topic or list ideas that are only loosely connected. Ultimately, a thesis helps your reader follow your train of thought.

Suppose the essay question is as follows:

To what extent did former Prime Minister Lester B. Pearson define the identity of modern Canada? Then your thesis might look like this, which includes your position on the topic:

Tip!

Follow these three steps to write a thesis.
1. Re-state the question or assignment.
2. Take a position on the issue.
3. Briefly state the themes of your content paragraphs in sequence.

Point of View

Lester Bowles Pearson, Canada's 14th prime minister, was largely responsible for defining modern Canada's national identity through social programs, political autonomy, and retooling our military for peacekeeping.

Sequence

©P

Content Paragraphs

The three content paragraphs must correspond to the sequence in the thesis statement. They must have a topic sentence and contain supporting details, facts, and information. In the case of the above thesis, your three paragraphs would describe social programs, political autonomy, and retooling the military for peacekeeping. Each content paragraph should have three facts and a concluding or transitional sentence. You might also include a relevant quotation to support your position.

Conclusion

The final paragraph summarizes what you have said. It need not be overly long, but you want to take this final opportunity to convince your reader. This is the place where you can express yourself with opinion and persuasive language to make an insightful conclusion.

Self Assessment of Your Essay

You can assess your work using the following essay checklist.

Tip!
If you are given a date range in the question, try to pick examples from the beginning, middle, and end of the date range.

Essay Checklist	
Introduction *Do you have...*	• an introduction? • a thesis statement(s) informing the reader of *all* three subjects you will discuss in your three body paragraphs? • a transitional or concluding sentence leading into the next paragraph?
Supporting Paragraphs *Do you have...*	• three body paragraphs, each with a topic sentence? • specific supporting detail (names, dates, events)? • a powerful quotation or statistic? • a concluding sentence or a transition sentence?
Conclusion *Do you have...*	• a concluding paragraph? • a topic sentence? • supporting sentences in which you summarize the topic and draw a conclusion? • a closing sentence?

©P

UNDERSTANDING COMMAND TERMS

When asked to write an essay response, read the question very carefully. Make sure you have a clear idea of what it is you are asked to do, and answer all aspects of the question. One reliable way to do this is to look at the **command terms**, which are a key to understanding not only what the question is asking, but also a guide to knowing how to answer. Here is a list of command terms and descriptions of what they are prompting you to do.

Command Term	Explanation	Sample Question and Expectations
Assess	Estimate the success, value, or the extent to which something has or has not been achieved. Give an informed judgement based on criteria. **Tip!** When assessing, you do not need to address weaknesses.	Assess the role of the Canadian International Development Agency in supporting developing nations. *You are expected to list the ways that CIDA has been effective in developing nations.*
Evaluate	Make judgements based on standards or criteria about the strengths and weaknesses of a particular situation.	Evaluate the role of the Canadian International Development Agency in supporting developing nations. When asked to evaluate, you are expected to list the successes and the failures and decide which was greater.
Compare	Describe how one event, issue, or personality is similar to another. This is often used in conjunction with contrast.	Compare the treatment of returning Canadian soldiers following WWI and WWII. *You are to describe the similarities between these two groups, despite the difference in eras.*
Contrast	Describe how one event, issue, or personality is different from another.	Contrast the treatment of returning Canadian soldiers following WWI and WWII. *Students are asked to describe the differences between these two groups.*

©P

Command Term	Explanation	Sample Question and Expectations
Describe	Give a detailed, factual account of an object, event, or concept. **Tip!** When *describing* a role, give a detailed account of *what* happened.	Describe the key events leading up to the First World War. *You are asked to list the key events leading up to the First World War in chronological order.*
Discuss	Discuss the various points of view and conflicting opinions on a particular topic, process, or concept, as well as the merit of these opinions.	Discuss the key events leading up to the First World War. *You are expected to list the key events leading up to the First World War and explain why and how they were important in creating that conflict.*
Explain	Give a fact-filled account of a topic, process, or concept. Provide evidence and reasons.	Explain the causes of the Depression in Canada. *You are expected to list the causes and explain why they led to the Depression.*
To What Extent	Describe the successes and failures of the given event, with emphasis on one or the other. Be sure to include the opposing point of view. **Tip!** When judging *to what extent*, examine the events and their impact in relation to what is being measured in the question.	To what extent could the Canadian government have minimized the hardships to Canadian citizens during the Depression? *You are expected to consider both sides of the statement (success and failure) and decide which side has the stronger argument.*

©P

THEMATIC ESSAY

There are several strategies for writing a successful essay. The thematic essay, sometimes called an analytical essay, is a useful technique to ensure you effectively answer the command term and include sufficiently detailed information.

Use the Mnemonic (memory trick) PERMS-G to categorize your information into themes. Each of these letters stands for a significant theme of social studies: **P**olitical, **E**conomic, **R**eligious, **M**ilitary, **S**ocial, and **G**eographical. Of course, not all of these themes will apply to the question. During the planning stage of your response, the most appropriate themes will become evident. Choose the three most relevant themes to form your body paragraphs.

Sample question: Discuss the issue of intolerance in Canada from 1900–2000.

In this sample essay question, the command term is discuss, which means you should spend time explaining why and how the events were important, as well as what happened. Use the Organization and Planning section on page 479 (opposite) to create a PERMS-G Chart to list all of your facts regarding the essay question. Once you have listed all of the facts pertaining to the essay topic, you are then able to construct your three supporting body paragraphs into themes. Use the details you have included to support your position in the essay, and be sure to mention your three themes in your thesis statement.

Sample Essay Outline

Thesis: Intolerance has been an ongoing issue in Canada during the 20th century, specifically in regard to the political climate and legislation, economic penalties for minorities, and social stratification.

Body 1 – Political details

Body 2 – Economic details

Body 3 – Social details

Conclusion

©P

Organization and Planning

> Sometimes a fact can belong to more than one category.

	Intolerance in Canada				
P (Political)	**E (Economic)**	**R (Religious)**	**M (Military)**	**S (Social)**	**G (Geography)**
• Continuous Passage Act detained passengers aboard the *Komagata Maru* in 1914 • prohibition of Japanese Canadians to live within 160 km of the coast as a war measure in WWII • Aboriginal children removed from their families as a result of the residential school system that stressed assimilation into "Canadian" culture • post-war reconciliation: Official Languages Act, Multicultural Policy, Multicultural Act, Immigration Act revisions, recognition of refugees	• Chinese head tax introduced in 1885 was increased from $50 to $100 in 1902 and again to $500 in 1903. • confiscation and selling of Japanese property during WWII	• strong anti-Semitism in the 1920s and 1930s • *St. Louis* incident, 1939	• minorities discouraged from participating in World Wars	• Vancouver race riots against Japanese and Chinese in 1907 • Aboriginal children forced to speak English and punished for using their own culture and language, causing a rift between them and their traditional values • resentment between traditional immigrants of British and French descent and new wave of immigrants	• establishment of the reserve system made Aboriginal peoples dependent on the Canadian government

> As you fill out the chart with all of your details, it will become clear which three themes contain the most, or most significant, information. Use these three themes as your body paragraphs.
>
> In this example, the Political, Social, and Economic themes have the most detailed information.

©P

TIMELINE ESSAY

An alternate to the thematic essay is the timeline essay. This type of essay considers the essay question from a chronological point of view and responds by grouping facts by decade or era. Generally speaking, one of the essay questions on the exam will suggest a timeframe—1914 to 2000—and one effective way to respond is to divide the 20th century into three major eras: the First World War and the Depression; the Second World War and the Cold War; and Post Cold War, which are naturally separated into three paragraphs.

Sample Question: Discuss the issue of intolerance in Canada from 1914–2000.

Use the Organization and Planning section on page 479 to create a PERMS-G chart to list all of your facts regarding the essay question. Once you have listed all of the facts pertaining to the essay topic, you are then able to construct your three supporting body paragraphs into eras (see opposite). Use the details you have included to support your position in the essay, and be sure to mention your three eras in your thesis statement.

Sample Essay Outline

Thesis: Intolerance has been an ongoing issue in Canada during the 20th century, with numerous instances of injustices during the First World War and the Depression as well as during the Second World War and the Cold War years, and finally moving toward reconciliation in the latter two decades of this century.

Body 1 – First World War/Depression—supporting details

Body 2 – Second World War/Cold War—supporting details

Body 3 – Post War—supporting details

Conclusion

©P

Organization and Planning

Intolerance in Canada	
First World War and the Depression, 1914–1939	- history of intolerance before 1914 like the Vancouver race riots against Japanese and Chinese in 1907 - 1914 *Komagata Maru* and Continuous Passage Act - Chinese head tax introduced in 1885 increased from $50 to $100 in 1902 and again to $500 in 1903. - 1923 Chinese Immigration Act - minorities discouraged from participating in World War - strong anti-Semitism in the 1920s and 1930s - 1939 *St. Louis* incident
Second World War and the Cold War, 1939–1988	- minorities discouraged from participating in World Wars - prohibition of Japanese Canadians to live within 160 km of the coast as a war measure - confiscating and selling of Japanese property - resentment between traditional immigrants of British and French descent and new wave of immigrants - Aboriginal children removed from their families as a result of the residential school system that stressed assimilation into "Canadian" culture - Aboriginal children forced to speak English and punished for using their own culture and language, causing a rift between them and their traditional values - point system introduced for refugees - 1969 Official Languages Act - 1971 Multicultural Policy - 1977 Immigration Act
Post Cold War, 1985–2000	- post-war reconciliation - 1988 Official Languages Act amended - 1985 Multicultural Act - 2000 Immigration and Refugee Protection Act - recognition of refugees - official apologies by prime ministers

RECOGNIZING FACT AND OPINION

Tip!

Certain words signal opinions. These include: always, best, most, many, a lot, usually, and anything ending with "est."

One area of essay writing that can be problematic for students is the distinction between facts and opinions. Facts are statements that can be proven or shown to be true. Facts are documented events. They include dates, events, people, and places. Numerical facts are amounts that are specific and can be counted (500, for example) or suggestive of an amount (many, few, some). Social studies essays are dependent on facts, and you, the writer, must include them to support your writing.

Opinions express how a person feels about something, a point of view, perspective, or bias. Opinions do not have to be based upon logical reasoning, but your essay will be more persuasive if your opinions are supported by facts. In fact, a good ratio to work toward is two to three facts to support every one opinion.

Consider the following passage:

Opinion: these are points of view and cannot be proven as fact.

Facts: These can be proven as accurate. Dates, numbers, places, and people's names are good indicators that the writing contains fact.

At first, most everything Canada contributed to the Second World War was in supplies. Mackenzie King, always a clever strategist, hoped that much of what Canada contributed could be in the areas of supply and training—and the issue of conscription could be avoided. The British Commonwealth Air Training Plan (BCATP) was absolutely tailor-made for this and was the best decision King ever made. In December 1939, Canada agreed to host and administer a training plan in which British instructors would train pilots and other flight personnel from all over the Commonwealth in Canada. There could not have been a better choice. Clear prairie skies and distance from enemy aircraft were clear advantages. Airfields were built on the Prairies and in other locations near small towns and villages and old aircraft were refitted and returned to service for training purposes. The program was a major Canadian contribution to the war effort. The BCATP trained more than 130 000 pilots, navigators, flight engineers, and ground staff. The total cost was over $2.2 billion, of which Canada paid more than 70 percent. Although a lot of money went into the program, it paid off in the end as Canada emerged as the strongest and bravest of all the former colonies in the commonwealth.

Use of the ending "est" is a good indicator of opinion.

©P

GLOSSARY

Words that appear in blue are your chapter Key Terms.

abdicate to give up a position of authority

Aboriginal Pipeline Group a group formed in 2000 to represent the interests of the Aboriginal peoples of the North in the proposed pipeline

Aboriginal title claims by Aboriginal peoples to lands that their ancestors inhabited

ace a fighter pilot who has shot down five enemy aircraft

acid precipitation any form of precipitation that is high in sulfuric and nitric acids as a result of pollution in the air

ad valorem tax a tax that is proportional to the value of goods

advance polls locations where people can vote in advance of election day

affirmitive action programs that are designed to help disadvantaged individuals or groups achieve equity

age cohort an age group in a population, for example, the number of people between the ages of 10 and 14

Agenda 21 a statement of environmental action, produced at the 1992 Earth Summit, that outlines actions that should be taken to protect the planet and achieve sustainable development

allegiance loyalty or faithfulness

alliance a union or agreement among groups working toward a common goal

Allies countries fighting against Germany during the Second World War, including Britain, France, Canada, Australia, New Zealand, and after 1941, the United States and the U.S.S.R.

amending formula a rule established in 1982 that states Canada's Constitution cannot be changed unless at least seven Canadian provinces, representing at least 50 percent of the population of Canada, approve

Anti-Ballistic Missile Treaty (ABMT) an agreement between the U.S. and the U.S.S.R. limiting strategic offensive weapons and defensive systems

anti-Semitism discrimination or hostility toward Jewish people

apartheid an official policy of racial segregation involving political, legal, and economic discrimination against non-whites

aquifer an underground layer of rock, gravel, etc., from which water can be drawn for wells and which is a source of springs

armistice an agreement by warring parties to end hostilities

arsenal of democracy a slogan coined by President Franklin D. Roosevelt in December 1940 promising to help the Allies fight the Germans by providing military supplies while staying out of the actual fighting

artillery large guns used to fire shells

assimilation adoption of the customs and language of another cultural group so that the original culture disappears

atomic bomb a bomb containing radioactive material, capable of destroying an entire city or region

authoritarian a form of government in which one individual or small group holds all the power and directs the lives of citizens

autonomy the power to govern oneself and make one's own decisions

Axis alliance between Germany, Italy, and Japan

baby boom the increase in the birth rate that occurred after the Second World War

backbenchers members of a legislature who are not Cabinet ministers, party leaders, or opposition critics

Balfour Report the conclusions of the 1926 Imperial Conference that acknowledged that Canada was an autonomous community within the British Empire

balloting voting

Battle of Britain an air campaign launched in 1940 by the Royal Air Force to stop the Germans from achieving air superiority

Battle of Hong Kong Japan's attack on the British colony of Hong Kong in which there were heavy Canadian losses

Battle of the Atlantic the struggle between the Allies and the Axis powers to control the Allies' shipping route across the Atlantic Ocean

bilateral aid assistance from one country to another

Bill 101 also called the "Charter of the French Language," Bill 101 strengthened the position of the French language in Québec

Bill 22 provincial legislation that made French the sole official language of Québec

biodiversity having a variety of life forms

biosphere regions of Earth occupied by living organisms, made up of all the ecozones

biplane an airplane with two sets of wings, one on top of the body, and one underneath

birth rate the number of births per 1000 people in a country in a given year

Black Christmas December 25, 1941, the date Hong Kong fell to the Japanese

Black Hand a terrorist group of Bosnian Serbs that was determined to free Bosnia from Austria-Hungary

Black Tuesday October 29, 1929, when the New York Stock Exchange collapsed

blitzkrieg German war tactic of surprise attacks by tanks and fighter planes

Bloc Québécois a federal party dedicated to Québec separation from Canada

Bloody Saturday June 21, 1919, when the Royal North-West Mounted Police charged a crowd of protesters during the Winnipeg General Strike

Bomarc missiles nuclear missiles that Canada agreed to accept from the U.S. during the Cold War; led to a rift in Canada/U.S. relations

Bomber Command the section of the RAF that directed the strategic bombing of Germany

bonded labour (or debt bondage) paying off a loan with labour rather than money; bonded labourers often work for very little pay and their labour is worth more than the original debt

boom and bust cycle a term used to describe a healthy (booming) economy and/or one that is failing (bust)

boom town a town that enjoys sudden prosperity or develops quickly

bourgeoisie the ruling or middle class

branch plants factories, offices, or other operations set up in Canada but owned or controlled by U.S. or other foreign companies

brand recognition awareness by the general public of characteristics associated with a particular product, business, or person (in the case of politics)

British Commonwealth an association of nations that were formerly colonies of the British Empire

British Commonwealth Air Training Plan (BCATP) a program to train pilots and aircrew during the Second World War; it produced half of all Commonwealth aircrew and is the largest air training program in history

bureaucracy officials and administrators who carry out the work of government

bureaucrats government officials and administrators

by-election an election held in a riding to fill a vacancy

Cabinet the group of ministers chosen by the prime minister who decide government policy; each Cabinet minister has a responsibility for a particular department

Cabinet solidarity the custom that Cabinet members must not show disagreement with government policies

Canada Council for the Arts the group that funds Canadian artists and supports the arts in Canada

Canadian Bill of Rights a federal document that set out the rights and freedoms of Canadians; it was enacted in 1960 under the leadership of Prime Minister John Diefenbaker

Canadian Charter of Rights and Freedoms the bill identifying human rights that are guaranteed to everyone in Canada; enacted in 1982 and embedded in the Constitution of Canada

Canadian Constitution the document that describes the powers and responsibilities of the government and its parts, and the rights of citizens

Canadian International Development Agency (CIDA) Canada's leading development agency for assistance to the developing world

Canadian Radio-television and Telecommunications Commission (CRTC) the agency that regulates the amount of foreign material broadcast over the airwaves in Canada and imposes rules requiring Canadian content

Canadiens French descendants of the original settlers of New France

capitalism an economic system in which the production and distribution of goods are owned privately or by shareholders in corporations who have invested their money in the hope of making a profit

capitalist one who believes in an economic system in which the production and distribution of goods are owned privately or by shareholders in corporations that have invested money in the hope of making a profit

carbon credit if an organization produces more greenhouse gases than it is allowed, it can purchase a credit from an organization that is below its target emission levels

carbon footprint the total amount of carbon dioxide (CO2) and other greenhouse gases emitted over the full life cycle of a product or service

carbon sink a reservoir that can absorb and store carbon dioxide from the atmosphere, including forests, peat, and oceans

carrying capacity the maximum number of people that can be sustained by an environment

casualties those injured, killed, captured, or missing in action

census the process of collecting, compiling, and publishing demographic, economic, and social data about all people living in a particular area

Central Powers the German Empire, the Austro-Hungarian Empire, the Ottoman Empire, and the Kingdom of Bulgaria

CFCs (chlorofluorocarbons) chemicals used in coolants, solvents, and aerosol cans that damage the ozone layer

Chanak Crisis the Canadian government's refusal in 1922, lead by King, to support British troops in defending the Turkish port of Chanak; the first time the Canadian government did not support the British military

Chief Electoral Officer an independent officer of Parliament responsible for federal elections

civil disobedience the act of intentionally breaking the law while protesting against laws one considers unjust

civil liberties basic individual rights protected by law, such as freedom of speech

civil servant someone who works for a government department

civil service the body of people who work in government administration

Clarity Act (Bill C-20) legislation passed by the Chrétien government requiring separatist referendums to pass with a "clear majority" rather than 50 percent plus 1, before Québec could negotiate separation

CO2 emissions Carbon dioxide emissions caused by burning of fossil fuels; largest contributor to global warming

coalition a formal alliance of political parties

coercion the use of force

Cold War a period lasting approximately from 1945 to 1989 when there was tension and hostility between the communist Soviet Union and its allies and the capitalist United States and its allies

collective bargaining negotiation of a contract between unions and management regarding such things as wages and working conditions

commodities goods or services that are bought or sold

communism a social and economic ideology that believes property, production, and distribution of goods and services should be owned by the public, and the labour force should be organized for the benefit of all members of society

communist one who believes that property and the production and distribution of goods and services should be owned by the public and that the labour force should be organized for the benefit of all; the application of the theory in the Soviet Union, China, Cuba, and other countries resulted in dictatorships by leaders of communist parties

comprehensive claims the assertion of the right of Aboriginal nations to large tracts of land because their ancestors were the original inhabitants

confidence in politics, it means support

conscientious objector a person who opposes war for religious or moral reasons

conscription forced enlistment in the armed forces of all fit men of certain ages

conservatism a political philosophy supporting traditional values and institutions and opposing sudden change

constituent a voter in a riding

contraception birth control

convoy a group of ships travelling together protected by an armed force

Co-operative Commonwealth Federation (CCF) Canada's first socialist party founded in the Prairies in 1932; advocated government control of the economy

cornucopians people who have optimistic views on population growth due to advances in science and technology

corporate tax a tax charged to businesses based on their total revenues

corvettes small, fast, warships built in Canada to help protect convoys in the Atlantic Ocean

counterculture a subculture, especially of young people, with values or lifestyles that are in opposition to those of the dominant, established culture

"cradle to grave" social security social assistance provided by the government, from birth to death

crimes against humanity widespread attacks against civilians, including murder, enslavement, deportation, and torture

Crown corporations businesses and industries owned by the Canadian government

cultural exceptionalism the belief that human values vary by culture and that human rights should be interpreted according to ethnic, cultural, or religious traditions

cut-off lands lands taken from reserves without consent of the Aboriginal peoples

D-Day June 6, 1944; the day Allied armies, including Canada, invaded France; the biggest Allied invasion of the Second World War

death rate the number of deaths per 1000 people in a country in a given year

deficit the amount of money a government owes when it takes in less money than it spends

deflation the opposite of inflation, deflation occurs when the price of goods and services falls

deforestation the process of destroying a forest and replacing it with something else

democracy a system of government in which people freely choose in elections who will govern them; principles and ideals of such a government, including free speech and the rule of law

democratic rights Charter rights to participate in a democratic society, including voting in elections, guaranteed by the Canadian Charter of Rights and Freedoms

demographic regulation the theory that population growth will level off as living standards improve

demographic transition model a model that shows changes in a population's birth and death rates and growth based on technological development

demography the study of population numbers, distribution, trends, and issues

dependency load the percentage of a population that is younger than 15 or older than 64 years of age

dependency ratio the proportion of the population (children and those over 65 years of age) that is being supported by the working age group

deport to send back to one's country of origin

deportation the act of sending someone back to his or her native land

depression a long period of severe economic and social hardship, massive unemployment, and suffering

Depression a severe economic downturn in the global economy in the 1930s

desertification the spread of desert-like conditions in an area, sometimes caused by human activity

developed countries the world's wealthiest countries; they have well-established infrastructures and their people are well-housed, healthy, and have good literacy skills

developing countries countries that have lower standards of living than developed countries; many have extensive poverty

dictator a ruler with unrestricted power, without any democratic restrictions

Dieppe Raid the 1942 trial raid by Canadian troops against Germany's occupation of Dieppe; Canada suffered heavy losses

direct democracy a system in which citizens vote directly on every issue

disenfranchised to be deprived of basic legal rights

displaced persons those who are forced to leave their native home because of war or for political reasons

dissolve Parliament to call an end to a sitting Parliament, at the request of the prime minister (or premier) to the Governor General (or Lieutenant-Governor in the provinces); followed by a general election

Distant Early Warning (DEW) radar stations in northern Canada set up between 1958 and 1960 to detect Soviet activity over the North Pole

distinct society a phrase that refers to the recognition of the unique nature of Québec within Canada; it often has the sense that Québec should have special powers and privileges to protect its language and culture

dogfight aerial duels between aircraft

doubling time the number of years it takes a country to double its population at its current growth rate

draft resisters citizens who refuse to join the army to fight in a war during conscription

Dunkirk port town in France from which a massive Allied evacuation took place in May 1940, when German forces conquered France

Earth Summit a meeting of world leaders, held in 1997 in Rio de Janeiro, Brazil, in 1992, to discuss environmental changes and sustainable development

ecological footprint the impact of humans on the environment

ecology the science concerned with the relationship between living things and their environment

ecotourism tourism to threatened areas that tries to be low-impact and small-scale

ecumene the populated area of the world

electoral district, riding, constituency a geographical area of a given size or population used as a unit in elections

electoral officers Elections Canada officials who count the votes

elite a group of people who hold power

embargo the prohibition by a government or organization that prevents certain goods from being shipped in or out of a country

emigration rate the number of people leaving a country in a given year per 1000 people

employment equity policies that ensure certain groups are given an advantage by employers, in particular women, people with disabilities, Aboriginal peoples, and visible minorities

enemy alien a national living in a country that is at war with his/her homeland

enfranchisement giving up one's status as an Indian

enumeration process of compiling a list of voters

equality rights Charter rights that guarantee people will not be discriminated against based on national or ethnic origin, religion, gender, age, or mental or physical disability

equalization payments a federal transfer of funds from richer to poorer provinces

equity groups certain groups of people who have traditionally been disadvantaged or discriminated against by employers

ethnic cleansing the elimination of one ethnic group from an area by another ethnic group

ethnocentric the belief that one's own culture is superior, and that other cultures should be judged by its values

excise tax an added tax on certain goods produced or sold in the country, for example, alcohol, gas, and tobacco

exponential rate a rapid rate of population growth as each generation doubles in size

extradition the surrender of a person accused of a crime from one country to another

family planning the concept of limiting the size of families

Famous Five five Alberta women who fought for the political status of women

fascism an authoritarian system of government that exercises complete power, suppresses opposition often through use of force, and encourages nationalism and racism

fascist a form of authoritarian government that is totalitarian and nationalistic

federalism a political system that divides power between federal and provincial legislatures

feminist a person who supports the idea that women are equal to men and deserve equal rights and opportunities

Final Solution the Nazis' plan to systematically kill all European Jews

first-past-the-post (FPTP) an electoral system in which the candidate who has more votes than any other candidate wins

fiscal pertaining to money issues

five-year plans Stalin's plans for economic development in the Soviet Union over five years

FLQ (*Front de libération du Québec*) a revolutionary movement founded to work for an independent, socialist Québec

foreign aid aid from rich, industrialized countries to poorer, developing countries

free trade trade between countries without tariffs, export subsidies, or other government intervention

Free Trade Agreement (FTA) the agreement that came into effect in 1989 between Canada and the United States to allow goods produced in each country to cross the border tariff-free

free vote members voting according to their own conscience

fundamental freedoms freedoms in the Charter that guarantee citizens are free to worship and believe what they wish, to express their opinions freely, to associate with whomever they wish, and to gather together peacefully with others

GDP per capita gross domestic product, or the total value of all goods and services produced in a country in one year, divided by the population

gender selection the choice of whether to keep a fetus based on its gender

genocide the systematic extermination of a religious or ethnic group

global warming the observed and projected increase in the earth's average temperature due to burning of fossil fuels and deforestation

globalization a process by which the regions and countries of the world are becoming economically and culturally interconnected

governor general the person who represents the British crown in Canada

greenhouse effect greenhouse gases trap heat in the atmosphere, causing Earth's temperature to rise

greenhouse gases (GHG) various gases in the atmosphere that absorb and emit radiation, including carbon dioxide, methane, nitrous oxide, and zone

groundwater water beneath Earth's surface in underground streams and other forms

Group of Seven group of Canadian landscape painters in the 1920s

habeas corpus the right of a detained person to be brought before a judge or other official to decide whether the detention is lawful

Halibut Treaty a 1923 treaty between Canada and the U.S. to protect halibut along the Pacific Coast; the first treaty negotiated and signed independently by the Canadian government

head tax the fee that Chinese immigrants were required to pay after 1885 in order to enter Canada

heavily indebted poor countries (HIPCs) countries at the low end of the UN Human Development Index that are in debt to developed nations

herbicides substances used to kill plants

Holocaust the Nazi imprisonment and murder of 6 million Jewish people and 5 million other peoples during the Second World War

homesteaders newcomers who claimed and settled land

honour rationing a civilian effort to consume less and conserve supplies on the home front

House of Commons the first legislative body of Parliament whose members are elected

Human Development Index the UN's index used to rank standards of living in its member countries

Hundred Days Campaign the final Allied offensive against the Central Powers on the Western Front, from August 8 to November 11, 1918

hydroelectric power electricity produced from the energy of falling water

ideology political and social principles or beliefs

immigration policy a nation's regulations surrounding immigration

immigration rate the number of new arrivals in a country in a given year per 1000 people

Imperial Conference a meeting of the leaders of the countries in the British Empire

imperialism the policy of one nation acquiring, controlling, or dominating another country or region

imperialists people who support imperialism, the policy of one nation acquiring, controlling, or dominating another

income tax a tax on personal income

Indian Act an Act created to regulate the lives of the First Nations of Canada

industrialization the overall change in a society from farm production and craftsmanship to mechanized manufacturing production

infanticide the act of killing an infant

inflation the rise in prices for goods and services that increases the cost of living and triggers demand for higher wages

infrastructure structures such as roads, railways, power grids, and communications links that are basic to the functioning of a modern economy, as well as buildings such as schools and hospitals

intercontinental ballistic missiles missiles equipped with nuclear warheads that have a range of 5500 kilometres

International Monetary Fund (IMF) an international organization designed to promote economic stability and development

internment camp a government-run camp where people who are considered a threat are detained

isolationism the policy of remaining apart from the affairs of other countries

Italian Campaign 1943 Allied battles to recapture Europe from the south, through Sicily and Italy

Juno Beach the nine-kilometre stretch of beach in France where Canadian troops landed on D-Day

Keynesian economics an economic theory named for John Maynard Keynes (1883–1946) who advocated government intervention in the economy, especially during economic downturns

khaki election the name given to the 1917 federal election because of Borden's efforts to win the military vote

King-Byng Crisis a situation that occurred in 1926 when Governor General Byng refused Prime Minister King's request to dissolve Parliament and call an election

Kristallnacht a coordinated attack against Jewish people and their property carried out by Nazis in Germany on November 9, 1938

Kyoto Protocol an international agreement that sets binding targets for reducing greenhouse gas emissions; the average target is 5 percent of 1990 levels by 2008–2012

labour movement groups organized to improve conditions for workers

laissez-faire an economic condition in which industry is free of government intervention

language rights Charter rights to receive government services in English or French and to be educated in either English or French

legal rights rights that guarantee people will be treated fairly by the legal system, including knowing why they were arrested, having access to a lawyer, and getting a fair and speedy trial

liberalism a political philosophy supporting individual freedoms and governmental protection of civil liberties

libertarianism a political ideology that supports maximum individual freedom and minimal government involvement in the lives of its citizens

Lieutenant-Governor the provincial representative of the Crown appointed by the Governor General

life expectancy the average number of years an individual is expected to live

literacy rate the percentage of a population that is able to read and write

lobby to try to influence the opinions and votes of public officials for or against a cause

lobbyist a person hired to represent the interests of a pressure group by influencing policy decision makers in the group's favour

Luftwaffe the German air force

majority government a government in which the ruling party has more than half of the total number of seats in the legislature

malaria a deadly infectious disease common in tropical climates, transmitted to humans by the mosquito

malnutrition poor, or lack of, nourishment

Manhattan Project the code name during the Second World War for the American plan to develop the first atomic bomb

marginalized to be pushed aside and made less important in terms of social standing and power

market economy an economic system in which individuals produce goods and prices are determined by supply and demand

Massey Commission a body set up by the federal government to study the state of Canadian culture

Medical Care Act an Act passed by Parliament in 1966 that provided free access to physician services for Canadians

Meech Lake Accord a package of constitutional amendments that would define Québec as a distinct society within Canada

megaproject a very large-scale, costly project to help develop infrastructure, such as building roads, dams, or irrigation systems

meltwater melted snow or ice, including ice from glaciers

merchant marine civilian ships and sailors that transported food, weapons, and munitions

middle power a nation that is not a superpower but has international influence

migrant a person who moves from one region to another

militarism a nation's policy of enlisting, training, equipping, and maintaining armed forces ready for war

Military Service Act a 1917 Act that made conscription compulsory for all Canadian men between the ages of 20 and 45, calling up the younger men first

Military Voters Act an Act that allowed men and women serving overseas to vote

Millennium Development Goals (MDGs) eight goals developed by the member states of the United Nations to close the gap in living standards between developed and developing countries

minority government a government in which the ruling party has more seats than any other party, but the other parties combined have more seats than the government

minority rights legal rights to ensure that specific groups which are vulnerable or disadvantaged are protected and able to achieve equality

mixed economy an economic system in which both individuals and the government produce and sell goods

mobility rights Charter rights that guarantee people the ability to move around or in and out of the country

Montréal Protocol an international agreement signed in 1987 to phase out the ozone-depleting chemicals CFCs

mortality death rate, calculated as number of deaths per 1000 people in a population

multiculturalism a policy of encouraging the expression of the cultures of many ethnic groups that make up a country's population

Multiculturalism Act or Bill C-93, was adopted in 1988 and provides a legal framework for multiculturalism in Canada

multilateral aid aid delivered through international organizations such as the UN and the World Bank

multinational corporations (MNCs) companies that do business in more than one country

national debt the amount of money owed by a federal government; most of Canada's national debt money is owed to Canadians who hold Government of Canada savings bonds, treasury bills, and so on

National Resources Mobilization Act an Act passed in 1940 enabling the government to do whatever was necessary for the war effort; it was amended in 1942 to allow conscription

nationalism devotion to and support of one's culture and nation, sometimes resulting in the promotion of independence

nationalists people who have a strong attachment to their culture or nation

nationalize move from private to government ownership

natural increase (NI) the rate at which a population increases (or decreases) in a year expressed as a percentage of the total population; calculated by subtracting the death rate from the birth rate

Nazis members of the National Socialist German Workers' Party; the Nazis were extreme nationalists who took power in 1933 and controlled every aspect of German life through a police state

neo-Malthusians people who share Malthus' pessimistic views regarding population growth

net migration the difference between the number of people immigrating to a country and the number of people emigrating

New Deal a series of programs, such as social assistance for the aged and unemployed, introduced by U.S. president Roosevelt in the 1930s to deal with the Depression

newly industrializing countries countries that are experiencing rapid economic and industrial growth; many are switching from agricultural to industrial economies

no man's land the area between the trenches of two opposing forces

nomination choosing a candidate to run for office

non-aggression pact an agreement between two countries not to attack each other

non-governmental organizations (NGOs) non-profit local, national, or international groups that work independently of government on issues such as health, the environment, or human rights

North American Aerospace Defence Command (NORAD) a defence agreement signed in 1958 between Canada and the United States (known as the North American Air Defence Agreement until 1981)

North American Free Trade Agreement (NAFTA) the agreement signed in 1992 and implemented in 1994 between the United States, Mexico, and Canada to create a free trade zone among the countries

North Atlantic Treaty Organization (NATO) the mutual defence organization set up to protect several Western European countries, Canada, and the U.S. from possible aggression from the U.S.S.R. after the Second World War

notwithstanding clause a clause in the Canadian Constitution (Section 33[1]) that enables Parliament or the legislature of a province to allow an Act to stand even though it contravenes the Charter of Rights and Freedoms

nutritional density a measure of how much nutrition in calories can be produced from a certain area; an area with fertile soil and adequate temperatures and precipitation will have a higher nutritional density than an area such as Canada's North

Office of the Prime Minister (PMO) the prime minister's political advisors and staff

official development assistance (ODA) aid given to developing countries through official government programs to promote economic development and the welfare of the people

Official Languages Act the Act that states that French and English are Canada's official languages, and that all federal institutions must provide services in English and French

Old Age Pension Act an Act passed in 1927 to provide social assistance to people over 70

On-to-Ottawa Trek a 1935 rail trip from Vancouver to Ottawa (stopped at Regina) by unemployed men to protest conditions at employment relief camps

one-child policy a policy adopted by China to control population growth

Operation Barbarossa Germany's unsuccessful invasion of the Soviet Union in 1941–1942, which broke the non-aggression pact and ultimately led to the Soviet Union joining the Allies

Order-in-Council an order signed by the Governor General (or the Lieutenant-Governor in the provinces) on the advice of the prime minister (or premier) and Cabinet; allows laws and regulations to be passed without a parliamentary vote

organic grown or produced without chemical fertilizers or pesticides

Organisation for Economic Co-operation and Development (OECD) originally created as the Organisation for European Economic Co-operation (OEEC) to administer the Marshall Plan to rebuild Europe after the Second World War; OECD's mission is to improve living standards in developing countries

overproduction more goods being produced than being sold; leads to a decrease in production, which leads to increased unemployment

ozone layer a thin layer of ozone in the atmosphere 15 to 30 kilometres above Earth; the ozone layer filters the sun's ultraviolet (UV) rays

paratroopers soldiers trained to parachute from airplanes onto combat areas

Paris Peace Conference a meeting in Paris in 1919 to discuss the terms of a peace agreement after the First World War

Parti Québécois (PQ) a Québec provincial party that advocates separation from Canada

partisan loyal to a party or cause

party discipline all party members voting the same way, as one voice

party platform a list of priorities and a plan for governing published by a political party

party whip a member of the legislature assigned the specific role of ensuring all members of their party are present in the legislature to support party interests

patriate to take control of power over a document from a former colonial government

patronage a favour, often a government position, given in return for political support

Pearl Harbor the Japanese bombing of the U.S. naval base in Hawaii

peatlands wetlands with soil formed mostly from decomposing plants

permafrost subsoil that remains frozen all year long

persecution to oppress or ill-treat because of race, religion, gender, sexual orientation, or beliefs

Persons Case a court case in which the Famous Five successfully fought to have women declared "persons" under Canadian law in 1929

pesticides substances used to kill pests such as unwanted plants and animals

plebiscite a direct vote by electors on an issue of public importance; the outcome of the vote may not be binding on the government

pogey relief payments by a government, sometimes in the form of vouchers for food and other essentials

polarize to go in opposite directions

policy of appeasement giving in to an aggressor's demands in the hopes that no more demands will be made

political spectrum a linear visual used to illustrate political ideologies, from left to right

polling stations locations where citizens in a riding vote

pollsters people who conduct public opinion polls

population density the number of people living in a given area; calculated by dividing the population by its area

population distribution the pattern of where people live in an area

population growth rate the rate at which a country's population increases or decreases; calculated by adding natural increase and net migration

population pyramid a bar graph that shows male and female populations back to back at age intervals of five years

populism a political movement that advocates the interests of ordinary people

populist someone who appeals to the concerns of ordinary citizens

precedent a legal decision that serves as a rule for future cases

pressure groups organized groups of individuals with common interests and concerns who attempt to pressure political decision makers; also known as interest groups

primary industry an industry that deals with the extraction or collection of raw materials, such as mining or forestry

private member's bill a bill introduced into the legislature by a member of the legislature who is not a member of the Cabinet

Privy Council Office (PCO) the office that organizes the work of the Cabinet

profiteering making a profit by raising prices on needed goods or producing poor quality materials

prohibition the banning of the sale and consumption of alcohol

proletariat the workers or lowest class

propaganda information, usually produced by governments, presented in such a way as to inspire and spread particular beliefs or opinions

prorogue Parliament to suspend Parliament for a period of time upon the prime minister's request to the Governor General

prorogue to postpone or suspend, as in Parliament

prosperity in the economic cycle, the period of economic growth and expansion

Protected Areas Strategy (PAS) a plan to preserve approximately 12 percent of B.C.'s provincial land for parks, recreation, and wilderness

protectionism a system of using tariffs to raise the price of imported goods in order to protect domestic producers

public service the government administration

Québec nationalism a movement advocating for the protection and development of Québécois culture and language

Québec sovereignty a movement advocating that Québec separate from the rest of Canada and become a country of its own

Quiet Revolution a period of rapid change and reform that modernized Québec society during the years 1960 to 1966 under the Liberal provincial government of Jean Lesage

ratified approved

recession less severe than a depression, a recession is a downturn in economic activity in which the value of goods and services declines

reconnaissance military search or exploration

recovery in the economic cycle, the period following a recession during which the value of goods and services rises

Red Paper Aboriginal response to the federal government's White Paper of 1969; the Red Paper caused the government to change its policies

Red Scare the fear that communism would spread to Canada

referendum a direct vote in which everyone is asked to either accept or reject a particular proposal

refugee a person displaced from his of her home and territory by war and other acts of aggression

Regina Manifesto platform of the Co-operative Commonwealth Federation party; it supported public ownership of industry and social programs to assist those in need

Regina Riot a riot that occurred when police attempted to clear On-to-Ottawa trekkers from a stadium in Regina

regional disparity differences in income, wages, and jobs in one area compared with another

regionalism a concern for the affairs of one's own region over those of one's country

reparations compensation from a defeated enemy for damages caused by war

representative democracy a system in which citizens elect a politician who then makes decisions for them

reserves land set aside by the government for the use of First Nations

residential schools government authorized schools, run by the churches, in which Aboriginal children lived apart from their families and were educated in Canadian culture

reverse discrimination discrimination against a majority group in order to give preference to a disadvantaged group

rhythm method a method of birth control in which a couple does not have intercourse during the time when a woman is likely to ovulate

Rowell-Sirois Report report of the Royal Commission on Dominion-Provincial Relations, a commission set up in 1937 to examine the Canadian economy and federal-provincial relations

royal assent the final stage a bill must complete before it is passed into law in which the Governor General (or Lieutenant-Governor in the provinces) signs or grants approval for the bill

Royal Commission on Bilingualism and Biculturalism a commission created by the federal government to recommend ways of enhancing and promoting the historically bilingual nature of Canada

rule of 70 the time it takes a country to double its population, approximately 70 divided by the country's growth rate

rule of law the principle that laws apply to all members of society equally; no one is above the law

runoff water from rain and melting snow that cannot be held in the soil so makes its way into streams, rivers, lakes, and oceans

Rwandan genocide the 1994 mass murder of nearly one million Tutsis in Rwanda

Schlieffen Plan Germany's plan to stage a two-front war with Russia in the east and France in the west

secondary industry an industry that deals with manufacturing or construction

self-determination the freedom for a group to form its own government

self-government the right of a colony or cultural group to define the structure, laws, and policies that will govern its affairs

Senate the second legislative body in Parliament consisting of appointed members whose role is to give sober second thought to the passage of bills

sharpshooter a person skilled in shooting

single transferable vote (STV) an electoral system in which parties gain seats by the proportion of votes won in large electoral districts

Slavic relating to peoples in eastern, southeastern, and central Europe, including Russians, Serbians, Croatians, Poles, Czechs, etc.

Social Credit Party political party founded in Western Canada; opposed to capitalism

socialism a political and economic system in which the means of production and distribution in a country are publicly owned and controlled for the benefit of all members of a society

socialist a believer in a political and economic system in which the means of production and distribution in a country are publicly owned and controlled for the benefit of all members of a society

sovereignty-association a proposal by Québec nationalists that Québec have political independence yet retain close economic ties or association with Canada

specific claims First Nations' claims to land based on the belief that the government did not fulfill its obligations under a treaty or other agreement related to money, land, or other assets

speculation buying shares "on margin" with the expectation that the value of the shares will increase enough to pay back the loan and make a profit

spin doctors people who publicize in a positive way the words and actions of politicians

standard of living a measure comparing how well people live in different countries based on three indicators: life expectancy, literacy rate, and gross domestic product (GDP) per capita

status quo the existing order of things

Statute of Westminster the law that changed the British Empire into the British Commonwealth; all commonwealth countries to be considered equal in status with Britain and able to make their own laws

sterilization a procedure by which a person's ability to reproduce is destroyed

stewardship careful management of resources to ensure that they are sustainable

structural adjustment programs (SAPs) programs designed by the World Bank and IMF to adjust the economies of developing countries as a condition of receiving loans

subsidies grants from the government, intended to help people

subsistence farming a form of farming in which the crops grown are used to feed the farmer and his or her family, with little or nothing left over to sell or trade

suffragist a person who advocates that women should have the right to vote

superpowers the term used to refer to the United States and Soviet Union in the post–Second World War period when both were engaged in building up powerful arsenals of weapons of mass destruction as deterrents against aggression

supply and demand the quantity of a product that is available and the market's desire for that product; the price of the product varies based on supply and demand

surface water water that is readily available on Earth's surface in streams, rivers, lakes, wetlands, and oceans

surplus the amount of money remaining when a government takes in more than it spends

sustainable development a way to maintain economic growth without damaging the environment

tabulating counting votes

tariffs taxes on imported goods

the Blitz the heavy, frequent bombing attacks on London and other British cities by Nazi Germany

tied aid aid given to a foreign country with conditions attached

total fertility rate the average number of children born over the lifetime of a typical woman in a particular country

total war the mobilization of the entire resources of a nation for war

totalitarian a form of government that uses intimidation, violence, and propaganda to rule all aspects of the social and political life of its citizens

totalitarian state a dictatorship in which the government uses intimidation, violence, and propaganda to rule all aspects of the social and political life of its citizens

trade and aid the process of stimulating the economies of developing countries with aid so that they can access global markets and trade with developed nations

trade union a group of workers who unite to achieve common goals in discussions with owners and management of businesses and industries

transient an unemployed person who moves from place to place in search of work

Treaty of Versailles one of the treaties that ended the First World War; it imposed strict sanctions on Germany

tribunal court of justice

Triple Alliance the alliance of Germany, Austria-Hungary, and Italy prior to the First World War

Triple Entente the alliance of France, Britain, and Russia prior to the First World War

troposphere the lowest level of Earth's atmosphere

ultraviolet radiation (UV) invisible rays from the sun that can cause skin cancer

undue hardship financial strain or excessive difficulty

Union Government the coalition government formed by Conservatives and some Liberals and independents that governed Canada from 1917 to 1920

Union nationale nationalist French-Canadian political party led by Maurice Duplessis

unionization the formation of labour unions

United Nations (UN) an organization established in 1945 to bring peace and security to the world.

United Nations Children's Fund (UNICEF) a UN organization that works to protect children's rights, to make sure the basic needs of children are met and to help children reach their full potential; originally called United Nations International Children's Emergency Fund

United Nations Educational, Scientific, and Cultural Organization (UNESCO) a UN organization that helps build peace, fight poverty, and promote sustainable development through education, the sciences, culture, communication, and information

United Nations Framework Convention on Climate Change (UNFCCC) the UN's plan to keep greenhouse gas concentrations from increasing, created at the 1992 Earth Summit in Rio de Janeiro, Brazil

Universal Declaration of Human Rights the United Nations outline of the rights to which all human beings are entitled

urbanization the move of people from farms to cities where jobs are available

vasectomy a form of male sterilization in which the tube carrying sperm from each testis is cut and tied

Victorian of or pertaining to the reign of Queen Victoria; also someone who shares the values of that period

Victory Bonds bonds issued by the Canadian government to support the war effort

voter apathy reluctance or lack of interest in voting

voters list a list of persons eligible to vote

war brides foreign women who married Canadian troops serving overseas and then immigrated to Canada after the war

war crimes the killing, torture, and hostage-taking of civilian populations, or the deliberate and extensive destruction of their property

War Guilt Clause an article in the Treaty of Versailles that made Germany responsible for starting the First World War

War Measures Act an Act that gives the federal government emergency powers during wartime, including the right to detain people without laying charges

war of attrition a military strategy based on exhausting the enemy's manpower and resources before yours are exhausted, usually involving great losses on both sides

Warsaw Pact a post–Second World War military alliance established in 1955 involving the Soviet Union and the Soviet block countries of Albania, Bulgaria, Czechoslovakia, East Germany, Hungary, Poland, and Romania

Wartime Elections Act an Act that gave the vote to Canadian women related to servicemen, but cancelled the vote for conscientious objectors and immigrants from enemy countries

Wartime Information Board board established in 1942 to coordinate wartime propaganda in Canada

wastewater water that has been used in homes or industries and, as a result, contains waste products

watermilfoil weed a plant that grows and spreads quickly, choking out native plants, affecting spawning areas for fish, and posing a safety problem if it grows around public beaches

watersheds river basins drained by a river and flowing into the same large body of water

Weimar Republic the democratic government in Germany after the First World War

welfare state a state in which the government actively looks after the well-being of its citizens

Western alienation the feeling on the part of Western Canada that federal policies favour Central Canada; it has led to the rise of several regional parties, including the Canadian Alliance Party

Western Front the area of fighting in western Europe during the First World War, characterized by trench warfare and inconclusive battles with heavy casualties on both sides

White Paper of 1969 the government report proposing dramatic changes to the lives of Aboriginal peoples, including the elimination of the Indian Act

Winnipeg General Strike massive strike by workers in Winnipeg in 1919

World Bank an international group of five financial institutions that provide financial and technical help to developing countries

World Health Organization (WHO) a UN agency that coordinates international health activities and helps governments improve health services

INDEX

CREDITS

bg/i: background/inset
t/c/b/l/r: top/centre/bottom/left/right

Photo Credits

x–xi (t l to r) iStock.com; iStock.com; Corbis–Dreamstime; photos.com; public domain; iStock.com; **x–xi (b l to r)** Shutterstock.com; Shutterstock.com; iStock.com; © Rob Melnychuk/Corbis; Shutterstock.com; © Hola Images/Alamy **Unit 1 2t** Canada Post Corporation; Veterans Affairs Canada. Reproduced with the permission of the Minister of Public Works and Government Services, 2007; © Lordprice Collection/Alamy; Glenbow Archives NA-2496-1; **3t** CP PICTURE ARCHIVE/National Archives of Canada/William Ivor Castle; Remember Hong Kong poster, #19700036-024, © Canadian War Museum; NAC; © CORBIS; **Chapter 1 4-5** City of Vancouver Archives CVA 371-917, W.J. Cairns; 6 Glenbow Archives NA-3509-8; **8** Library and Archives Canada; (c) Canada Post Corporation; **9** © The Slide Farm; **10** VPL #30625; **11** Image D-05577 courtesy of Royal BC Museum, BC Archives; **12** NAC/PA-48475; **13** City of Vancouver Archives CVA 99-2507, Stuart Thomson; **15** Woodruff/Library and Archives Canada/C-004745; **16bl** TRL T11245; **16br** Archives of Manitoba Foote 1491 (N2438); **17tl** © D. Hurst/Alamy; **17tr** © INTER

FOTO/Alamy; **17c** © Pictorial Press Ltd/Alamy; **17br** Glenbow Archives NA-2685-61; **17bl** © CP Images; **18** Archives of Ontario I0003361; **19b** CTA #SC244-136A; **19Ins** © David J. Green–Lifestyle/Alamy; **20** © Paul A. Souders/CORBIS; **21** THE CANADIAN PRESS/Larry MacDougal **Chapter 2 24** CP PICTURE ARCHIVE/National Archives of Canada/William Ivor Castle; **26** © Punch Ltd. London, UK; **27** © Mary Evans Picture Library/Alamy; **29** The Granger Collection, New York; **31** Source unknown; **32** Canada. Dept. of National Defence/NAC/PA-022759; **33bl** Library and Archives Canada, Acc. No. 1983-28-854; **33bc** NAC/95378; **36** NAC/PA-2468; **37** © Hulton-Deutsch Collection/CORBIS; **38** © NRT-Travel/Alamy; **39cr** Veterans Affairs Canada. Reproduced with the permission of the Minister of Public Works and Government Services, 2007; **39tr** William Rider-Rider/Canada. Dept. of National Defence/NAC/PA-002165; **40t** CWM 19920044-674, George Metcalf Archival Collection, Canadian War Museum; **40c** © Bettmann/CORBIS; **40b** Bettman/CORBIS; **41tl** Used with permission of Public Works and Government Services Canada; **41tr** The New York Times Company; **41c** Osprey Publishing Ltd.; **41b** Classic Image/Alamy; **42** Canada. Dept. of National Defence/NAC/PA-002826; **43** Library and Archives

Canada; © Canada Post Corporation; 44 Popperfoto/Getty Images; **45** NAC/C-57358; **46bl** Canada. Dept. of National Defence/NAC/PA-024435; **46tl** Archives of Ontario 7606-9024; **47** NAC/C-019944; **48tr** Veterans Affairs Canada. Reproduced with the permission of the Minister of Public Works and Government Services, 2007; **48tc** Reprinted with permission from Woodland Cultural Centre/Irma Coucill; **49** © Roberto Herrett/Alamy; **50** William Rider-Rider/Canada. Dept. of National Defence/NAC/PA-002279; **52** © Underwood & Underwood/CORBIS; **53** © Bettmann/CORBIS; **57** GA, Calgary NA3452.2 Chapter 3 **60** © Lordprice Collection/Alamy; **62** © Pictorial Press Ltd/Alamy; **63** CP/Jonathan Hayward; 64 Archives of Manitoba #N2762; **65** NAC/e000008187; **66** Glenbow Archives NA-3217-2; **67** Reprinted with permission from Denny May; **68tr** Glenbow Archives NA-4179-9; **68tl** Library and Archives Canada; © Canada Post Corporation; **68bl** © Bettmann/ CORBIS; **68br** Source unknown; **69cl** Whyte Museum of Canadian Rockies #NA 33-882; 69br Library and Archives Canada; © Canada Post Corporation; **70** NAC/PA-151007; **71** Image PDP00672 courtesy of Royal BC Museum, BC Archives; **72** The Granger Collection, New York; **73** © Andrew Balfour; **74** Image B-01060 courtesy of Royal BC Museum, BC Archives; **76** VPL #8956-D; **77** CP PHOTO/Winnipeg Free Press-Ken Gigliotti; **78** Glenbow Archives NA-3055-24; **79** Glenbow Archives NC-6-11899; **81** © Michael de Adder/Arizans.com; **87** © Michael Eddenden Chapter 4 **88** Glenbow Archives ND-3-6742; **90** © Hulton-Deutsch Collection/ CORBIS; **91** © Malcolm Mayes/Artizans.com; **94** Glenbow Archives NA-2496-1; **95** VPL #12749; **96** NAC/C-2997; **97** Special Collections, VPL #3035; **98cr** Yukon Archives #8533; **98Ins-c** NAC Acc. No. 1990-119-1; **101** NAC/C-087860; **103** CTA #SC244-1682; **104cr** Courtesy of CBC, cbc. ca; **104tl** Source unknown; **106** Glenbow Archives #NA-2377-1; **107 Vic** Davidson/Montréal Gazette/NAC/C-053641; **108** Glenbow Archives NA-3622-20; **109t** NAC/C-31058; **109b** AP Photo/Dario Lopez-Mills; **111bl** CP PHOTO/Stf/Files; **111t** © Lucien Aigner/CORBIS; **111br** Parks Canada; **112** Dale/Winnipeg Free Press/19 Jan 1931; **113** Dale/Winnipeg Free Press; **114** © Bettmann/CORBIS Chapter 5 **118** City of Vancouver Archives CVA LP **109**, Claude Dettloff; **120** © Paul Almasy/CORBIS; **121** Associated Press; **122b** © CORBIS; **122tl** © The Art Gallery Collection/Alamy; **123tr** © Bettmann/CORBIS; **123br** Associated Press; **127** NAC/PA-119013; **128** CP; **129** Courtesy of Ontario Jewish Archives. Reproduced with the permission of the Archives.nlc-10915; **130** Western Canadian Pictorial Index #A1279-38312; **131** TRL BDS 1939-45 Ind. Prod. #16; **132tl** NAC, Acc. No. 1987-72-105 The Hubert Rogers Collection, Gift of Mrs. Helen Priest Rogers; **132c** Maintenance Jobs in the Hangar by Paraskeva Clark, #14085, © Canadian War Museum; **134** © CORBIS; **137** Remember Hong Kong poster, #19700036-024, © Canadian War Museum; **138** NAC/PA-112993; **139** Associated Press; **140t** © INTERFOTO/Alamy; **140br** Library of Congress, cph 3c01012; **140bc** © Chris Howes/Wild Places Photography/Alamy; **140bl** Hulton Archive/Getty Images; **141tr** SSPL via Getty Images; **141tl** Ivan Cholakov Gostock-dot-net; **141b** NAC/a144981; **143** CP Photo; **144** NAC/PA-163938; **148b** Associated Press; **148tl** Alexander Mackenzie Stirton/ Canada. Dept. of National Defence/NAC/PA-134376; **149** Hulton Archive/ Getty Images; **150** Library of Congress, cph 3c13495; **151** Library of Congress, cph 3c13494; **152tl** © CORBIS; **152Ins-t** © Reuters/Bettman/CORBIS; **153** National Film Board of Canada. Photothèque/NAC; **154bl** National Film Board of Canada. Photothèque/NAC; **154br** The Advertising Archives; **155** TRL BDS 1939-45 Espionage #5; **156** McCord Museum M965.199.3242; **157** NAC; **159** CTA #1266-104988; **161** Associated Press Unit 1 Study Guide **163c** Library and Archives Canada; **163b** Canada. Dept. of National Defence/NAC/PA-024435; **164tr** National Film Board of Canada. Photothèque/NAC; **164c** NAC/C-2997; **164b** NAC/C-087860; **165b** NAC, Acc. No. 1987-72-105 The Hubert Rogers Collection, Gift of Mrs. Helen Priest Rogers Unit 2 Opener **166t** Michael Ochs Archives/Getty Images; NAC/PA-129625; © Bettmann/CORBIS; CP/AP/Thomas Kienzle; **167t** CP PICTURE ARCHIVE/ Fred Chartrand; CP PHOTO/str-Shaney Komulainen; CP Photo/ Chuck Stoody; Chapter 6 **168** AP Photo/RCA Victor; **170** Lambert/Getty Images ; **171Ins** © DeBrocke/ClassicStock/Corbis; **171b** © Allan Cash Picture Library/Alamy; **172** Michael Ochs Archives/Getty Images; **173** NBC Television/Courtesy of Getty Images; **174l** CP Images/Wisconsin Historical Society/Courtesy Everett Collection; **174r** Hulton Archives/Getty Images; **175** The Granger Collection, New York; **176** Photo courtesy National Ballet of Canada; **177** Public Archives of NS #G1066-2; **178** Glenbow Archives #NA-5719-4; **179** Gar Lunney/National Film Board of Canada. Photothèque/NAC/PA-191422; **180** NAC/C-123991; **181** NAC/PA-112693; **182** Craig Leonard Photograph Collection, Maritime History Archive, Memorial University, PF-328.30; **183cl** Nicolas Raymond/Shutterstock; **184** CWM 20010129-0543 © Canadian War Museum; **185br** AP Photo/Jeff McIntosh; **185tr** CP PHOTO 1999/NAC C-071095; **186cr** Dario Sabljak/Shutterstock; **186br** Maxx-Studio/ Shutterstock; 186bc Wire_man/Shutterstock; **186tr** Phant/ Shutterstock; 186cl SSPL/Getty Images; **186tl** AP Photo/ NASA; **187** © Radius Images/Alamy; **188** Hulton Archives/Getty Images; **190** NAC/PA-129625; **191** American Stock/Getty Images; **192** Getty Images; **195** NORAD; **196** Washington Post via Getty Images; **198** Spencer Platt/Getty Images; **200** CP/AP Images Chapter 7 **206** © Peter Arnold, Inc./Alamy; **207br** AP Photo/Dan Loh; **207tr** Michael Ochs Archives/Getty Images; **208** © Bettmann/CORBIS; **209** AP Photo/The Canadian Press, Jacques Boissinot; **210** Special Collections, VPL #85698; **211br** © Bettmann/CORBIS; **211cr** Courtesy of UNHCR; **212** CP PHOTO/Halifax Chronicle Herald; **213** CP PHOTO; **214** oksana perkins/Shutterstock; **215br** P.Uzunova/ Shutterstock; **215cr** Pearson Education Archives; **215tr** Pearson Education Archives; **216** CP Photo; **217** CP Photo/Peter Bregg; **218** CP/Montreal Star; **219** Roy Peterson; 220tl CP; **220bc** AP Photo; **221** CP; **223** © Joseph Heller/ CartoonStock; **225** © Fire-foxfoto/Alamy; **226bl** AP Photo/IBM, ho; **226br** AP-PHOTO/rw/bd; 226cr SSPL/Getty Images; **226tl** AP Photo/NASA; 226tr Popperfoto/Getty Images; **227br** © Greenpeace/ Robert Keziere; **228bl** Hulton Archive/Getty Images; **228tl** © TIME Inc.; **229** AP Photo; **230** AP Photo; **231** Dick Darrell/Toronto Star/GetStock; **232** Bernard Weil/GetStock.com; **232Ins** CP/Daniel Morel; **234** CP PICTURE ARCHIVE/Fred Chartrand; **235br** CIDA/ACDI; **235tr** CP PICTURE ARCHIVE/ Toronto Star/Frank Lennon; **239bc** CP PHOTO/Carl Bigras; **239br** © Bettmann/CORBIS Chapter 8 **240** CP PHOTO/str-Shaney Komulainen; **242t** David Cooper/ GetStock.com; **244bl** IBM; **244cl** SSPL/Getty Images; **244cr** michael ledray/Shutterstock; **244tr** Tatiana Popova/ Shutterstock; **244-5** © Stocktrek Images, Inc./Alamy; **245br** Press Association via AP Images; **245 br** inset Fedor Bobkov/Shutterstock; **245cl** Jeremy Swinborne/Shutterstock; **245tl** Vinicius Tupinamba/ Shutterstock; **245tr** Apple; **248** Dimo Safari; **249** Boris Spremo/GetStock.com; **250** THE CANADIAN PRESS/Fred Chartrand; **251** Courtesy of the AFN; **252** CP PHOTO/Tom Hanson; **253** CP PHOTO/Kevin Frayer; 25 Canadian Museum of Civilizaton; **255b** Canadian Museum of Civilizaton CMC #589-1736; **257** Roy Peterson/Vancouver Sun; **259** Canada Wide; **262** McCord Museum #M989_397_95; **263** CP PICTURE ARCHIVE/Winnipeg Free Press/Wayne Glowacki; **264** Reuters; **265** ©Toronto Star Syndicate[2003] all rights reserved; **266** McCord Museum #M986_286_111; **267** CP Photo/Chuck Stoody; **268** CP PHOTO/Tom Hanson; **270** TorStar Syndicate; **271** AP Photo/Richard Cross; **272** CP/AP/Thomas Kienzle; **273cr** © Colin Palmer Photography/Alamy; **273tr** AP Photo/Jeff Widener; **274** AP Photo/John Gaps III; **277** CP/ Tom Hanson; **278** AP Photo/Daniel Hulshizer Unit 2 Study Guide **283** CP Photo; **284** Cdn National Dept of Defence; **285** © Tim Dolighan Unit 3 Opener **286t** Hans Deryk/ GetStock.com; CP Photo/Aaron Harris; CP Photo/Ian Barrett; **287t** Toronto Star/GetStock.com; **339** CP Chapter 9 **290** CP Photo/Ian Barrett; **291** Katja Heinemann/Aurora Photos; **293** Press Association via AP Images; **294** © Tim Dolighan, dolighan.com; **295br** © Greenpeace; **295tr** Time Life Pictures/Mansell/Time Life Pictures/Getty Images; **296** CP Photo/Chuck Stoody; **297** © Superstock; **298** © Neil Beer/CORBIS; **300a** Conservative Party of Canada; 300b Liberal Party of Canada; **300c** Parti Bloc Quebecois; **300d** NDP Party of Canada; **300e** Green Party of Canada; **301** Right To Play; **302** CP Photo/Chuck Stoody; **303** CP; **306** THE CANADIAN PRESS/Hamilton Spectator-Ron Albertson; **307** CP; **309** Adrian Wyld/TCPI/The Canadian Press; **311** THE CANADIAN PRESS/Chris Young; **313** CP Photo/Aaron Harris; **315** Ins br Steve Russell/GetStock.com; **315br** Hans Deryk/GetStock.com; **317** © Off the Mark, offthemark.com; **318** Lisa Maree Williams/Getty Images; **320** © Tim Dolighan, dolighan.com Chapter 10 **322** CP/Boris Spremo; **324** Courtesy of Amnesty International; **325** © National Geographic; **326** CP/Amel Emric; **327** UN Photo; **328** Leon Neal/AFP/Getty Images; **332** CP/Fred Chartrand; **333** Toronto Star/GetStock.com; **338** Macleans; **339** CP; **342** CP; **343** CP/Fred Chartrand; **344** © Copyright Simon Fraser University; **349** AP Photo/Paolo Giovannini; **350** © Adam Woolfitt/CORBIS; **351** CP Unit 3 Study Guide **351** shutterstock.com; **353t** jochem wijnands/GetStock.com; **353b** CP Photo Unit 4 Opener **354t** Andrew Fox/GetStock.com; **354b** © Reuters/CORBIS; **355t** JanP/ Alamy, AEM5BT; © Bettmann/CORBIS; NASA; © Chetan Soni Chapter 11 **356** GS International/GetStock.com; **357** Andrew Fox/GetStock.com; **358bl** AP Photo/Altaf Qadri; **358br** © The Slide Farm; **359** © Reuters/CORBIS; **363** PRAKASH MATHEMA/AFP/Getty Images; **365** CDC/Photo Researchers, Inc.; 370 Source unknown; **373br** © Jan Butchofsky/CORBIS; **373bl** © James Marshall/CORBIS; **375** Special Collections, VPL #84175B; **379** © Riber/Svenska Dagbladet, Stockholm. Used in permission of Cartoonist & Writers Syndicate; **385cl** © Sheldan Collins/CORBIS; **385br** Wolf Kutnahorsky Chapter 12 **386** Ulet Ifansasti/ Getty Images; **392** BrazilPhotos/Alamy; **394** © ITAR-TASS [2008] all rights reserved; **396** © Reuters/CORBIS; 398 © Howard Davies/CORBIS; **399tr** © Yann Arthus-Bertrand/ CORBIS; 399br © Yann Arthus-Bertrand/CORBIS; 399Ins cr © Chinch Gryniewicz; Ecoscene/CORBIS; **401** Play Pump International; **403** © Paul Almasy/CORBIS; **405** Antonio Bolfo/Getty Images; **406** Archives du 7eme Art; **407** Sipa-Press/Mark Peters/Ponopress Int. Inc.; **408** Ulet Ifansasti/Getty Images; **409** © Barnabas Bosshart/CORBIS; 410 India Images/GetStock.com; **412** Courtesy of the Stephen Lewis Foundation; **413** CP PHOTO/Belleville Intelligencer–Jennifer Bell; **415** AP Photo/Alfred de Montesquiou; **416** J Marshall/GetStock.com; **417** Dr B Lynne Milgram; **419tl** AP Photo/ Christophe Ena; **419br** AP Photo/Manish Swarup Chapter 13 **424cl** NASA; **424bl** NASA; **425** AP Photo/Ajit Solanki; **427** Ontario Ministry of the Environment; **428** Fisheries Canada; **429** © Bill Beatty/Visuals Unlimited; **430** Ian McAllister/AllCanadaPhotos; **431** CP Photo/Lyle Stafford; **434** © Cameron Davidson/Alamy; **435** Darron R. Silva/Aurora Photos; **437** NASA; **440** CBC; **445** David Cooper/GetStock.com; **446** © Reinhard Dirscherl/Alamy; **448** Bruce Stotesbury, Times-Colonist; **449** CP/Darryl Dyck Unit 4 Study Guide **454cl** Angela Hampton/GetStock.com; **454b** Francis Li/GetStock.com; **455** Patrick Chappatte/Globe Cartoon

Literary and Source Credits

Chapter 1 **5** *The Globe*, October 15, 1904; **5** L.P. Hartley, *The Go-Between*, (London: Hamish Hamilton, 1953); **7** House of Commons Debates, October 23, 1903; **9** *The Canadian Annual Review of Public Affairs* Volume 7; **10** *cbc.ca*. June 11, 2008. http://www.cbc.ca/canada/story/2008/06/11/aboriginal-apology.html Last accessed Apr. 20, 2010; **10** Speech by Alan Li, Then President of the Chinese Canadian National Council, 1994; **11** Prime Minister of Canada: "Prime Minister Harper Offers Full Apology for the Chinese Head Tax" http://pm.gc.ca/eng/media.asp?id=1219, 22 June 2006. Reproduced with the permission of the Minister of Public Works and Government Services, 2009, and Courtesy of the Privy Council Office; **11** Harsha Walia, "Komagata Maru and the Politics of Apologies," Aug. 25, 2008. http://www.zmag.org/znet/viewArticle/18536 Last accessed Apr. 20, 2010, © Harsha Walia; **12** *Maclean's Canada's Century*, ed. Carl Mollins (Toronto: Key Porter Books, 1999), 233; **13** *The Daily Colonist*, May 8, 1907; **14** Pierre Berton, *The Promised Land: Settling the West 1896–1914*, (Toronto: Anchor Canada, 2002); **15** Quoted in Kenneth McNaught, *J. S. Woodsworth*, (Toronto: Fitzhenry & Whiteside, 1980), 15; **23** "Moving Experiences Video," *Living Histories Series*, www.distributionaccess.com Chapter 2 **25** Mark Moss, *Manliness and Militarism: Educating Young Boys in Ontario for War*, (Toronto: Oxford University Press, 2001), 144; **32** *The Mail and Empire*, August 5, 1914; **32** "Canada Enters the War," http://www.vac-acc.gc.ca/remembers/sub.cfm?source=history/firstwar/canada/Canada3, Department of Veterans Affairs, 2008. Reproduced with the permission of the Minister of Public Works and Government Services Canada, 2009; **33** *Canada and the Battle of Vimy Ridge* pp. 35 – vol. 1992. National Defence. Reproduced with the permission of the Minister of Public Works and Government Services, 2009; **34** *War Measures Act*, S.C. 1914, c. 2, s. 6; **36** *The Globe*, April 15, 1916; **37** *Canada and the Battle of Vimy Ridge* pp. 24 – vol. 1992. National Defence. Reproduced with the permission of the Minister of Public Works and Government Services, 2009; **38** Library and Archives Canada/ Francis Xavier Maheux fonds/MG30-E297, letter September 20, 1916; **43** Beatrice Hitchens Memorial Aviation Collection, University of Western Ontario; **43** William Avery Bishop, *Winged Warfare*, (Toronto: Totem, 1976); **43** Bishop File, Directorate of History, Department of National Defence. Reproduced with the permission of the Minister of Public Works and Government Services Canada, 2009; **46** Excerpt from ***Tapestry of War***. Copyright © 1992 by R. & A. Gwyn Associates. Published by HarperCollins Publishers Ltd. All rights reserved; **48** Department of Indian Affairs, *Annual Report 1913-1914*, (Ottawa), xxvii; **48** Diamond Jenness, *The Ojibwa Indians of Parry Island: Their Social and Religious Life*, (Ottawa: J.O. Patenaude I.S.O., 1935), 53; **50** House of Commons Debates, 1917, 2184 & seq.; **54** Quoted in Erika Storey, *A Childhood in Bohemia*, (Bury St. Edmunds, England: Arena Books, 2009), 187; **55** George Woodcock, *A Social History of Canada*, (Toronto: Penguin, 1988), 297. By permission of the Writers' Trust of Canada; **55** Jonathan Vance, *Death So Noble*, (Vancouver: UBC Press, 1997); **57** "What About the Pandemic Risk?" In "Avian Influenza Frequently Asked Questions," *World Health Organization*. http://www.who.int/csr/disease/avian_influenza/avian_faqs/en/#areall Last accessed Apr. 20, 2010; **59** © Government of Canada. Reproduced with the permission of the Minister of Public Works and Government Services Canada (2010). **Source:** Library and Archives Canada/Sir Robert Borden fonds/MG26-H, vol. 69, file OC 318 (2), pages 35868-35869, Reel C-4314. http://www.collectionscanada.gc.ca/ firstworldwar/025005-2600.019-e.html Chapter 3 **61** "Next Month with *Canadian Homes and Gardens*," *Canadian Homes and Gardens* (May 1927): 13; **66** *Winnipeg Citizen*, May 17, 1919; **66** W.R. Plewman, *Toronto Star*, May 23, 1919; **71** Quoted in J. Russell Harper, *Three Centuries of Canadian Painting*, (Toronto: Oxford University Press, 1973), 29; **73** Lord Sankey, Privy Council Judgement, October 18, 1929; **73** Quoted in Linda Rasmussen et al., *A Harvest to Reap: A History of Prairie Women*, (Toronto: Women's Press, 1976), 214; **75** Quoted in *Basic Call to Consciousness*, ed. Akwesasne Notes (Summertown, Tennessee: Book Publishing Company, 2005), 53; **79** Excerpt from ***Right Honourable Men***. Copyright © 1994 by Michael Bliss. A Phyllis Bruce Book. Published by HarperCollins Publishers Ltd. All rights reserved; **83** Lord Balfour, *Summary of Proceedings at the Imperial Conference*, (London: 1926); **84** Ralph Allen, *Ordeal By Fire: Canada, 1910–1945*, (Toronto: Doubleday Canada, 1961), 221–2; **84** P.E. Corbett, "The New Canadianism," *Contemporary Review* (October 1931): 479–83; **84** Speech by Warren Harding, U.S. President, Vancouver, 1923; **85** Robert McKee, Then Chair of the Vancouver Board of Trade, 1929 Chapter 4 **89** James Gray, *The Winter Years*, (Toronto: Macmillan, 1966, 1976), 108–11; **92** Library and Archives Canada/Canada. Royal Commission on Dominion-Provincial Relations. Report of the Royal Commission on Dominion-Provincial Relations 1867-1939 (1940)/AMICUS 5435504/Vol. 1. P. 150; **95** *Ten Lost Years, 1929-1939* by Barry Broadfoot. Copyright © 1973, 1997 by Barry Broadfoot. Published by McClelland & Stewart Ltd. In Trade Paperback in 1997. Used with permission of the publishers; **96** Sydney Hutcheson, *Depression Stories*, (Vancouver: New Star Books, 1976), 64–5; **97** From *The Concubine's Children* by Denise Chong. Copyright © Denise Chong, 1994. Reprinted by permission of Penguin Group (Canada), a Division of Pearson Canada Inc. From *The Concubine's Children* by Denise Chong (Penguin, 1994). Copyright © 1994 Denise Chong. With permission of the author; **97** Quoted at http://www.abcbookworld.com/view_author.php?id=4531 Last accessed Apr. 20, 2010; **98** Quote by Terry Reksten, *The Illustrated History of British Columbia*, published 2004 by Douglas & McIntyre: an imprint of D&M Publishers Inc.; **98** *Ten Lost Years, 1929-1939* by Barry Broadfoot. Copyright © 1973, 1997 by Barry Broadfoot. Published by McClelland & Stewart

Ltd. In Trade Paperback in 1997. Used with permission of the publishers; **98** *Ten Lost Years, 1929-1939* by Barry Broadfoot. Copyright © 1973, 1997 by Barry Broadfoot. Published by McClelland & Stewart Ltd. In Trade Paperback in 1997. Used with permission of the publishers; **99** Nellie McClung, *The Stream Runs Fast,* (Markham, ON: Thomas Allen Publishers, 2007); **99** *The Wretched of Canada: Letters to R.B. Bennett, 1930–1935,* ed. Linda M. Grayson and Michael Bliss (Toronto: University of Toronto Press, 1971). © University of Toronto Press 1971. Reprinted with permission of the publisher; **100** Mederic Martin, "Go Home Young Woman," *Chatelaine* (Sept. 1933): 10; **100** Quote by Terry Reksten, *The Illustrated History of British Columbia,* published 2004 by Douglas & McIntyre: an imprint of D&M Publishers Inc.; **101** R.B. Bennett, quoted in Robert Bothwell, Ian Drummond, and John English, *Canada 1900–1945,* (Toronto: University of Toronto Press, 1987), 260; **105** "Republican Party Platform, 1936." *Proceedings 21st Republic National Convention.* Quoted in John T. Woolley and Gerhard Peters, *The American Presidency Project* [online]. Santa Barbara, CA. http://www.presidency.ucsb.edu/ws/?pid=29639 Last accessed Apr. 20, 2010; **105** Quoted in R.C. Brown and M.E. Prang, *Confederation to 1949,* Vol. 3, (Toronto: Prentice Hall, 1966), 244–5; **105** Quoted in R.C. Brown and M.E. Prang, *Confederation to 1949,* Vol. 3, (Toronto: Prentice Hall, 1966), 249; **112** Michael Bliss, *Right Honourable Men,* (Toronto: HarperCollins, 1994), 123; **112** © Government of Canada. Reproduced with the permission of the Minister of Public Works and Government Services Canada (2010). **Source:** Library and Archives Canada/ William Lyon Mackenzie King fonds/Diaries/MG26-J13, August 26, page 3; **113** © Government of Canada. Reproduced with the permission of the Minister of Public Works and Government Services Canada (2010). **Source:** Library and Archives Canada/William Lyon Mackenzie King fonds/ Diaries/MG26-J13, Sunday, February 13, 1898. http://www.collections canada.gc.ca/databases/ king/index-e.html **Chapter 5** **119** "Broadcast, outbreak of war with Germany, 3 September 1939," *Historical Royal Speeches and Writings: George VI (1936–1952).* http://www.royal.gov.uk/pdf/ georgevi.pdf Last accessed Apr. 20, 2010; **127** © Government of Canada. Reproduced with the permission of the Minister of Public Works and Government Services Canada (2010). **Source:** Library and Archives Canada/William Lyon Mackenzie King fonds/Diaries/MG26-J13, Tuesday, March 29, 1938 (Page 2); **127** © Government of Canada. Reproduced with the permission of the Minister of Public Works and Government Services Canada (2010). Library and Archives Canada/William Lyon Mackenzie King fonds/Diaries/MG26-J13), Tuesday, June 29, 1937 (Pages 10-11). http://www. collectionscanada.gc.ca/databases/king/ index-e.html; **129** *Winnipeg Free Press,* July 19, 1939; **129** Equality Rights, Canadian Charter of Rights and Freedoms. In Part I of the Constitution Act, 1982. Assented to March 29th, 1982. http://laws.justice.gc.ca/en/charter/1.html#anchorbo-ga:l_I-gb:s_3; **130** House of Commons, Proceedings of the 6th Session of the 18th Parliament; **130** *House of Commons Debates, Official Report,* (Ottawa: King's Printer, 1917–39). 1939; **138** Winston Churchill, *The Second World War Vol. 2,* (London: Cassell, 1948–1954). Reproduced with permission of Curtis Brown Ltd, London, on behalf of The Estate of Winston Churchill. Copyright © Winston S. Churchill; **142** Thomas Hunter, Royal Regiment of Canada veteran, quoted in extract from *Our War* by Christopher Somerville, published by Orion. Weidenfeld & Nicolson is an imprint of The Orion Publishing Group, London. © 1998 Christopher Somerville. Reproduced by permission of Sheil Land Associates Ltd.; **143** Ross Munro, "Sees Canadian Army Fight Hun," *Windsor Daily Star,* Aug. 20, 1942; **144** Strome Galloway, *A Regiment at War: The Story of the Royal Canadian Regiment, 1939–1945* (Privately printed, 1979), 109; **148** Quoted in Blake Heathcote, *A Soldier's View: The Personal Photographs of Canadians at War 1939–1945,* (Toronto: Doubleday Canada, 2005), 267. Testaments of Honour; **150** Robert Oppenheimer, quoted in "The Decision to Drop the Bomb," television documentary produced by Fred Freed, *NBC White Paper,* 1965. © 2010 NBC Universal, Inc., All Rights Reserved; **150** William Leahy, *I Was There,* (New York: Whittlesey House, 1950), 441; **151** "Statement Offered by Brigadier General Paul W. Tibbets (USAF, retired) at the Airmen Memorial Museum on June 8, 1994 upon the Acceptance of the Air Force Sergeants Association's Freedom Award." News Release by Airmen Memorial Museum. June 9, 1994. Copyright Airmen Memorial Museum; **151** Karl von Clausewitz, 1819, quoted in Gwynne Dyer, *War,* (New York: Crown Publishers, 1985), 75; **152** King Whyte, *Letters Home 1944–1946,* (Woodstock, ON: Seraphim Editions, 2007), 105; **156** © Government of Canada. Reproduced with the permission of the Minister of Public Works and Government Services Canada (2010). **Source:** Library and Archives Canada/William Lyon Mackenzie King fonds/Diaries/MG26-J13, Tuesday, June 9, 1942 (Page 1). http://www.collectionscanada.gc.ca/databases/king/index-e.html; **159** Barry Broadfoot, *Six War Years, 1939-1945: Memories of Canadians at Home and Abroad,* (Toronto: Doubleday, 1974), 10. Used with permission of Dolores Broadfoot; **161** Harry S. Truman, "Radio Report to the American People on the Potsdam Conference, August 9, 1945," *The American Presidency Project.* http://www.presidency.ucsb.edu/ws/index.php?pid=12165&st=&st1= Last accessed Apr. 20, 2010 **Study Guide 1** **163** Mr. MacInnis quoted in House of Commons Debates, June 26, 1935. **Chapter 6** **169** John Kirkwood, *Vancouver Sun,* Sept. 3, 1957; **188** Mackenzie King, House of Commons Debates, Spring 1941; **192** © Government of Canada. Reproduced with the permission of the Minister of Public Works and Government Services Canada (2010). Source: Library and Archives Canada/Clifford W. Harvison fonds/MG31-E119, Vol. 1, File 1-6, "What Communists Have Achieved," Page 6; **192** "Anti-Communist Ballot Cuts Out All but Two," *The Globe and Mail,* January 2, 1948; **192** "The Red Scare: Canada Searches for Communists During the Height of Cold War Tensions." 2001. http://www.cbc.ca/history/EPISCONTENTSE1EP15CH1PA2LE.html Last accessed Apr. 20, 2010; **192** House of Commons, Oct. 16, 1970 **Chapter 7** **205** FLQ, "Revolution by the People for the People," March 1963; **209** CBC television clip, first broadcast on Dec. 21, 1967. http://archives.cbc.ca/politics/rights_freedoms/topics/538/ Last accessed Apr. 20, 2010; **211** House of Commons Debates, 3rd Session, 28th Parliament, Vol. 8, Oct. 8, 1971; **213** Statement of Government of Canada on Indian Policy, 1969 (The White Paper); presented to the first session of the twenty-eighth Parliament by the Honourable Jean Chretien, Minister of Indian Affairs and Northern Development. Ottawa: Indian and Northern Affairs Canada, 1969. http://www.ainc-inac. gc.ca/ai/arp/ls/pubs/cp1969/cp1969-eng.asp Reproduced with the permission of the Minister of Public Works and Government Services Canada, 2010; **213** Harold Cardinal, *The Unjust Society: The Tragedy of Canada's Indians,* (Mel Hurtig Publishers, 1969); **220** CBC television clip, first broadcast on Oct. 13, 1970. http://archives.cbc.ca/war_conflict/civil_unrest/clips/610/ Last accessed Apr. 20, 2010; **221** "The Charter of the French Language," Gouvernement du Québec. http://www.olf.gouv.qc.ca/english/charter/#t1status Last accessed Apr. 20, 2010; **222** Pierre Trudeau, *Memoirs,* (Toronto: McClelland & Stewart, 1993), 136; **222** René Lévesque, *Memoirs,* (Toronto: McClelland & Stewart, 1986), 247; **222** J.L. Finlay and D.N. Sprague, *The Structure of Canadian History,* (Toronto: Prentice Hall, 1984), 444; **222** Robert Bothwell, Ian Drummond, and John English, "Quebec and the Constitution: Phase One," *Canada Since 1945: Power, Politics, and Provincialism,* (Toronto: University of Toronto Press, 1989), 373. © University of Toronto Press 1981, 1989. Reprinted with permission of the publisher; **224** Peter Lougheed, Federal-Provincial Conference on Energy, Ottawa, January 22, 1974; **224** "Catalogue F1-21/1982E," Department of Finance. Reproduced with the permission of the Minister of Public Works and Government Services, 2010; **233** Michael Byers, "Afghanistan: Wrong Mission for Canada," *The Tyee,* Oct. 6, 2006. http://thetyee.ca/Views/2006/10/06/Afghanistan/ Last accessed Apr. 20, 2010; **233** Andrew Coyne and Paul Wells, "Afghanistan: Noble fight or Lost Cause?" *Macleans,* Nov. 1, 2009. http://www2. macleans.ca/2009/11/01/afghanistan-noble-fight-or-lost-cause/3/ Last accessed Apr. 20, 2010; **234** © Government of Canada. Reproduced with the permission of the Minister of Public Works and Government Services Canada (2010). Source: Library and Archives Canada/Pierre Elliott Trudeau fonds/Series 011, Vol. 63, file 13; **237** Paul Kaludjak, "Sovereignty and Inuit in the Canadian Arctic," *Arctic Peoples,* Nov. 18, 2006. http://www.arcticpeoples.org/news/item/83-sovereignty-and-inuit-in-the-canadian-arctic Last accessed Apr. 20, 2010 **Chapter 8** **247** Gary Engler, "Dr. Fry defends her job and policies." *Vancouver Sun,* November 19, 1997, A13. Material reprinted with the express permission of: "Pacific Newspaper Group Inc.", a CanWest Partnership; **247** House of Commons Debates, 1st Session, 35th Parliament, Hansard No. 108, Oct. 18, 1994; **250** Prime Minister Harper Offers Full Apology on Behalf of Canadians for the Indian Residential Schools System, June 11, 2008. http://www.ainc-inac.gc.ca./ai/rqpi/apo/ndex-eng.asp. Reproduced with the permission of the Minister of Public Works and Government Services, 2010, and Courtesy of the Privy Council Office; **251** "Residential Schools Timeline," Catherine Rolfsen/ *Vancouver Sun,* June 9, 2008. http://www.canada.com/topics/news/national/story.html?id=171cc0a7-3790-4b30-ab29-d70e69bf0be5 Last accessed Apr. 20, 2010; **252** *The Royal Proclamation of 1763.* Found at http:// www.bloorstreet.com/200block/rp1763.htm Last accessed Apr. 20, 2010; **253** Quoted in federal government press release, April 13, 2000; **254** From *Three Day Road* by Joseph Boyden. Copyright © Joseph Boyden, 2005. Reprinted by permission of Penguin Group (Canada), a Division of Pearson Canada Inc.; **255** From *Written in the Stone: An Architectural Tour of the Canadian Museum of Civilization,* by Douglas Cardinal, www.civilization.ca/cmc/exhibitions/cmc/architecture/tour10e. shtml © Canadian Museum of Civilization, 2010; **256** Canada Mortgage and Housing Corporation (CMHC). Census-based housing indicators and data, 2004. http://www.cbc.ca/news/background/ aboriginals/status-report2006.html All rights reserved. Reproduced with the consent of CMHC. All other uses and reproductions of this material are expressly prohibited; **256** "Royal Commission on Aboriginal People at 10 Years: A Report Card," *Assembly of First Nations.* http://www.afn.ca/ cmslib/general/ afn_rcap.pdf Last accessed Apr. 20, 2010; **260** Claire Lehan, "Separatism Is an Issue for All of Canada, Not Just Québec," *TheRecord.com,* Jan. 25, 2006. http://www. therecord.com/ fed_election2006/fed_election2006_ 0601258115.html Last accessed Apr. 20, 2010; **261** Intellectuals for the Sovereignty of Quebec (IPSO), "Québec Sovereignty: A Legitimate Goal." http://www. rocler.qc.ca/turp/eng/Intellectuals/ Intel.htm Last accessed Apr. 20, 2010; **261** "Remarks of Grand Chief Matthew Coon Come, Canada Seminar: October 28, 1996, Harvard Center for International Affairs and Kennedy School of Government," *NativeWeb.org.* http://www.nativeweb.org/pages/ legal/coon_come.html Last accessed Apr. 20, 2010; **262** *CBC Sunday Morning,* broadcast on March 4, 1990. Michel Cormier, reporter. http://archives.cbc.ca/programs/682-5323/page/2/ Last accessed Apr. 20, 2010; **268** "Why We Do It," *Campaign Against Child Poverty.* http://www.childpoverty. com/eng/why.html Last accessed Apr. 20, 2010. Courtesy of Campaign 2000, a cross-Canada network of partners working to end child/family poverty: www.campaign 2000.ca; **270** "Kyoto Protocol," *David Suzuki Foundation.* http://www.davidsuzuki.org/climate_ Change/Kyoto/ Last accessed Apr. 20, 2010; **271** "Initiatives for peace and security." Remarks in the House of Commons, Ottawa, Feb. 9, 1984. Ottawa: Department of External Affairs, Statements and Speeches No. 84/2; **279** www.international.gc.ca. Reproduced with the permission of Her Majesty in Right of Canada, represented by the Minister of Foreign Affairs, 2010; **281** Prof. Donald Fleming, University of British Columbia, "Kosovo and Canada's participation in NATO's war." Letter to Bill Graham, Chair, Standing Committee on Foreign Affairs and International Trade, April 21, 2000. Found at http:// www.balkanpeace.org/index.php?index=/content/background_studies/lan/ lan01.incl Last accessed Apr. 20, 2010 **Study Guide 2** **283** Romeo Dallaire, quoted in "'Peacekeeping has failed in this era,' says Dallaire," CBC News, Sept. 28, 2006. http://www.cbc.ca/canada/story/2006/09/28/ dallaire-peacekeepers.html Last accessed Apr. 20, 2010; **284** Broadcast on Oct. 13, 1970. http:// archives.cbc.ca/war_conflict/civil_unrest/clips/610/ Last accessed Apr. 20, 2010; **284** FLQ communiqué from the Liberation cell, released on December 8, 1970; **285** "Jean Chretien: True Grit," *CTV.ca.* http://www.ctv.ca/generic/WebSpecials/jean_chretien/ Last accessed Apr. 20, 2010. CTV Television Inc.; **285** "Jean Chretien: True Grit," *CTV.ca.* http://www.ctv.ca/generic/WebSpecials/ jean_chretien/Last accessed Apr. 20, 2010. CTV Television Inc.; **285** Jean Chrétien quoted in House of Commons Debates, 2nd Session, 37th Parliament, Hansard No. 071, Mar. 17, 2003; **285** David Eaves, *From Middle to Model Power: Recharging Canada's Role in the World,* (Toronto: Canada25, 2004), 79 **Unit Opener 4** **355–6** *2007 World Population Data Sheet,* Population Reference Bureau, 7–10. http://www.prb.org/pdf07/07WPDS_Eng. pdf Last accessed April 20, 2010 **Chapter 9** **295** Nelson Mandela Foundation Centre of Memory & Dialogue. "Nelson Mandela Sentenced to Life Imprisonment 44 Years Ago." http://www.nelson mandela.org/index.php/news/article/nelson_ mandela_sentenced_to_life_44_years_ago/ Last accessed Apr. 20, 2010; **300** "Canada General Election 2008," *The Political Compass.* http://www. politicalcompass. org/images/canada2008.png Last accessed Apr. 20, 2010; **303** "Interview: General Romeo Dallaire." *Frontline. PBS.* Fall 2003. http://www.pbs.org/wgbh/pages/frontline/shows/ ghosts/interviews/ dallaire.html Last accessed Apr. 20, 2010. Courtesy WGBH-TV Boston. Copyright © 1995–2010 WGBH Educational Foundation; **304** "Canada's System of Government," http://www2.parl.gc.ca/Sites/LOP/AboutParliament/ Forsey/institutions_01-e.asp, 2010; **309** "Peter Stoffer's Kingdom for a National Tartan Day," *Globe and Mail,* Jan. 15, 2010. http://www.theglobeandmail.com/ news/politics/peter-stoffers-kingom-for-a-national-tartan-day/article1433105/ Last accessed Apr. 20, 2010; **316** Elections Canada. Jon H. Pammett and Lawrence LeDuc, "Table 57: Importance of Reasons for Not Voting in the 2000 Election, by Age Cohorts (percentages)," in *Explaining the Turnout Decline in Canadian Federal Elections: A New Survey of Non-voters,* p. 66. http://www. elections.ca/loi/tur/tud/TurnoutDecline.pdf Last accessed Apr. 20, 2010; **319** "Voter Turnout at Federal Elections and Referendums, 1867–2008," *Elections Canada.* http://www.elections.ca/content.asp? section=pas&document= turnout&lang=e&textonly =false Last accessed Apr. 20, 2010; **319** http://www.idea.int/vt/ countryview.cfm?id=15 Last accessed Apr. 20, 2010. Reproduced by permission of International IDEA from "IDEA: Voter Turnout: Country View: Australia." © International Institute for Democracy and Electoral Assistance 2009 **Chapter 10** **323** Nobel Lecture, December 11, 1989. © The Nobel Foundation 1989; **325** "The Universal Declaration of Human Rights," *United Nations.* http://www.un.org/en/ documents/udhr/ Last accessed Apr. 20, 2010; **328** From *The Concubine's Children* by Denise Chong. Copyright © Denise Chong, 1994. Reprinted by permission of Penguin Group (Canada), a Division of Pearson Canada Inc. From *The Concubine's Children* by Denise Chong (Penguin, 1994). Copyright © 1994 Denise Chong. With permission of the author; **332** Multani v. Commission scolaire Marguerite-Bourgeoys, 2006 SCC 6, [2006] 1 S.C.R. 256; **334** R. v. A.M., 2008 SCC 19, [2008] 1 S.C.R. 569; **335** "Annual Report 2008–2009," *BC Human Rights Tribunal,* p. 43. http://www. bchrt.bc.ca/annual_reports/Annual_ Report_2008-2009.pdf Last accessed Apr. 20, 2010; **336** "Annual Report 2008–2009," *BC Human Rights Tribunal,* p. 6. http:// www.bchrt.bc.ca/annual_reports/Annual_Report_2008-2009.pdf Last accessed Apr. 20, 2010; **337** Oscar Wilde, *Oscar Wilde's Wit and Wisdom: A Book of Quotations,* (Mineola, NY: Dover Publications, 1998); **338** Fundamental Freedoms, Canadian Charter of Rights and Freedoms. In Part I of the Constitution Act, 1982. Assented to March 29th, 1982. http://laws. justice.gc.ca/en/charter/ 1.html#anchorbo-ga:l_I-gb:s_2; **338** Mark Steyn, "Why the Future Belongs to Islam," http://www. macleans.ca/article.jsp? content=20061023_134898_134898 Last accessed Apr. 20, 2010; **338** Section 13, Canadian Human Rights Act (R.S., 1985, c. H-6). Part I. Proscribed Discrimination. http:// laws.justice.gc.ca/eng/H-6/page-2.html; **338** "Tribunal Weighs Rights Complaint Against Maclean's," Canwest News Service, June 7, 2008; **338** Joseph Brean, "Dismissal of Maclean's Case Wrong: Elmasry," *National Post,* Sept. 20, 2008; **338** "PEN Canada's Position on Federal and Provincial Human Rights Commission Legislation," PEN Canada, June 13, 2008. http://www. pen-canada.ca/media/June132008-statement.pdf Last accessed Apr. 20, 2010; **339** Shelley Wright, "Canada Joins Australia in Condemnation by Indigenous Groups Before the UN," *Peace Writes Newsletter,* University of Sydney's Centre for Peace and Conflict Studies, No. 2000/2 (October 2000): p. 3; **342** http://www.scc-csc.gc.ca/court-cour/ju/spe-dis/bm03-03-07-eng.asp Reproduced with the permission of the Supreme Court of Canada, 2010; **342** Public Service Alliance Canada Pay Equity Bulletin #42, June 28, 2000; **342** Janet Steffenhagen, "Universities Hiring, but White Males Need not Apply," *Vancouver Sun,* Sept. 17, 1999, A1. Material reprinted with the express permission of: "Pacific Newspaper Group Inc.", a CanWest Partnership; 343 British Columbia (Public Service Employee Relations Commission) v. BCGSEU, [1999] 3 S.C.R. 3; 343 "Lowering the Bar," *The National Post*, Sept. 11, 1999. http://www.nationalpost.com/commentary.asp?f= 990911/765098&s2=editorials Last accessed Dec. 15, 2009; 345 Rich Daly, "Fewer Young Criminals May Face Life-Without-Parole Sentences," *Psychiatric News* 44, no. 22 (Oct. 16, 2009): 16. Reprinted with permission from Psychiatric News, (Copyright 2009). American Psychiatric Association; 346 "Convention on the Rights of the Child," *United Nations*. http://www2.ohchr.org/ english/law/ crc.htm Last accessed Apr. 20, 2010; 346 "Child Rights in Action: Path to the Convention on the Rights of the Child," United Nations Special Session on Children, 8–10 May 2002." http://www. unicef.org/specialsession/rights/path. htm Last accessed Apr. 20, 2010; 346 "Ministry of Children and Family Development: Ministry Overview," *Government of British Columbia.* http://www.mcf. gov.bc.ca/about_us/overview.htm Last accessed Apr. 20, 2010; 347 House of Commons, unanimous all-party resolution, November 24, 1989; 347 "2009 Report Card on Child and Family Poverty in Canada: 1989–2009." http://www. campaign2000.ca/reportCards/ national/2009English C2000NationalReportCard.pdf Last accessed Apr. 20, 2010. Courtesy of Campaign 2000, a cross-Canada network of partners working to end child/family poverty: www. campaign2000.ca **Chapter 11** Statistics Canada information is used with the permission of Statistics Canada. Users are forbidden to copy this material and/or redisseminate the data, in an original or modified form, for commercial purposes, without the expressed permission of Statistics Canada. Information on the availability of the wide range of data from Statistics Canada can be obtained from Statistics Canada's Regional Offices, its World Wide Web site at http://www. statcan.gc.ca, and its toll-free access number 1-800-263-1136. 358 United Nations, "The World at Six Billion," p. 3. http://www. un.org/esa/population/publications/ sixbillion/sixbilpart1.pdf Last accessed Apr. 20, 2010. © United Nations. Reproduced with permission. The United Nations is the author of the original material; 361 "World Population Prospects: The 2008 Revision Population Database," *United Nations.* http://esa.un.org/unpp Last accessed Apr. 20, 2010. © United Nations, 2009. Reproduced with permission. The United Nations is the author of the original material; 361 Adapted from: Statistics Canada, http://www.statcan.gc.ca/ pub/11-516-x/pdf/5500092-eng.pdf Last accessed Apr. 20, 2010; 362 "World Population Prospects: The 2008 Revision Population Database," *United Nations.* http://esa.un.org/unpp Last accessed Apr. 20, 2010. © United Nations, 2009. Reproduced with permission. The United Nations is the author of the original material; 363 Adapted from: Statistics Canada, "Immigrants in Canada: A Portrait of the Foreign-born Population, 2006 Census: Immigration: Driver of Population Growth," *2006 Census: Analysis Series,* Catalogue no. 97-557-X1E2006001; 367 "World Population Prospects: The 2008 Revision Population Database," *United Nations.* http://esa.un.org/unpp Last accessed Apr. 20, 2010. © United Nations, 2009. Reproduced with permission. The United Nations is the author of the original material; 370 "World Population Prospects: The 2008 Revision Population Database," *United Nations.* http://esa.un.org/unpp Last accessed Apr. 20, 2010. © United Nations, 2009. Reproduced with permission. The United Nations is the author of the original material; 373 Tania Branigan, "China's Gender Imbalance 'Likely to Get Worse,'" *The Guardian,* May 19, 2009. http://www. guardian.co. uk/world/2009/may/19/china-gender-ratio-women-men Last accessed Apr. 20, 2010. Copyright Guardian News and Media Ltd 2009; 376 "Immigration Admission Levels 1995–2005," http://www. cic.gc.ca/EnGLIsh/department/media/backgrounders/2006/2006-10-31.asp Citizenship and Immigration Canada, 2006.Adapted and reproduced with the permission of the Minister of Public Works and Government Services Canada, 2010; 377 Adapted from: Statistics Canada, *Aboriginal Peoples in Canada in 2006: Inuit, Métis and First Nations, 2006 Census.* Catalogue no. 97-558-XIE. http://www12.statcan.ca/english/ census06/analysis/aboriginal/pdf/97-558-XIE2006001.pdf Last accessed Apr. 20, 2010; 378 William R. Catton, *Overshoot: The Ecological Basis of Revolutionary Change,* (Champaign, IL: University of Illinois Press, 1982); 378 Mathis Wackernagel and William E. Rees, *Our Ecological Footprint: Reducing Human Impact on the Earth,* (Gabriola Island, BC: New Society Pub, 1996) **Chapter 12** 387 Ban Ki-moon, "Foreward," *The Millennium Development Goals Report 2008,* (New York: United Nations, 2008), 3; 388 United Nations Development Programme (UNDP), *Human Development Report 2009,* published 2009, Palgrave Macmillan. Reproduced with permission of Palgrave Macmillan; 390 "Millennium Development Goals," *United Nations.* http://www.un.org/ millenniumgoals/Last accessed Apr. 20, 2010. © United Nations. Reproduced with permission. The United Nations is the author of the original material; 393 *The Challenge of Slums: Global Report on Human Settlements 2003.* © United Nations, 2003. Reproduced with permission. The United Nations is the author of the original material; 393 "New UN-HABITAT Report Says Urban Dwellers Badly Off." June 19, 2006. http://www.unhabitat.org/content.asp?cid= 3177&catid =5&typeid=6&subMenuId=0 Last accessed Apr. 20, 2010. © United Nations, 2006. Reproduced with permission. The United Nations is the author of the original material; 394 "Poverty Profile 2007: Fast Facts for 2007 (2007)," http://www.ncwcnbes.net/en/research/ povertyprofile2007/ bulletin1.html *National Council of Welfare,* 2009. Reproduced with the permission of the Minister of Public Works and Government Services Canada, 2010; 395 United Nations Development Programme, *Human Development Report 2007/08,* published 2007, Palgrave Macmillan. Reproduced with permission of Palgrave Macmillan; 398 United Nations Development Programme (UNDP), *Human Development Report 2009,* published 2009, Palgrave Macmillan. Reproduced with permission of Palgrave Macmillan; 401 Lorenzo Cotula et al., *Land Grab or Development Opportunity?* (Rome: Food and Agriculture Organization of the United Nations, 2009); 401 Food and Agriculture Organization of the United Nations, "From Land Grab to Win-Win," *Economic and Social Perspectives,* Policy Brief 4 (June 2009): p. 1. ftp://ftp.fao.org/ docrep/fao/011/ak357e/ak357e00.pdf Last accessed Apr. 20, 2010; 401 Kristi Heim, "Is Offshore Farming a Good Thing for Africa?" *Seattle Times,* June 1, 2009. http:// seattletimes.nwsource.com/ html/thebusinessofgiving/2009286536_is_offshore_farming_a_good_thi.html Last accessed Apr. 20, 2010. Copyright 2009, Seattle Times Company. Used with permission; 403 United Nations Development Programme (UNDP), *Human Development Report 2009,* published 2009, Palgrave Macmillan. Reproduced with permission of Palgrave Macmillan; 404 UNICEF, *The Progress of Nations 1999,* (New York: UNICEF, 1999), 4–5. http://www.unicef.org/ pon99/ Last accessed Apr. 20, 2010; 405 UNICEF, *The State Of The World's Children 2008,* (New York: UNICEF, 2007). http://www. unicef.org/sowc08/docs/sowc08. pdf Last accessed Apr. 20, 2010; 405 Chris Niles, "Worldwide Deaths of Children Under Five Decline, Continuing Positive Trend," *UNICEF: Young Survival and Development,* Sept. 10, 2009. http://www. unicef.org/childsurvival/ index_51095.html Last accessed Apr. 20, 2010; 405 "U5 Mortality—Background," *UNICEF Australia,* Sept. 10, 2009. http://www.unicef.com.au/More/ MediaCentre/ Mediareleases/Background Underfivemortality/tabid/387/ Default.aspx Last accessed Apr. 20, 2010; 406 "Introduction," *Child Soldiers: The Shadow of Their Existence,* (War Child: 2007). http://www. reliefweb.int/rw/lib.nsf/db900sid/ EMAE-779QSP/$file/ war%20child-child%20 soldiers-2007. pdf?openelement Last accessed Apr. 20, 2010; 407 David Smith, "Malawi's child tobacco pickers 'being poisoned by nicotine,'" *The Guardian,* Aug. 24, 2009. http://www.guardian.co.uk/world/ 2009/aug/24/malawi-child-tobacco-pickers-poisoned Last accessed Apr. 20, 2010. Copyright Guardian News and Media Ltd 2009; 408 Craig Kielburger, Founder, Free the Children. "Say It Right." *Canadian Coalition for the Rights of Children.* http://rightsofchildren.ca/youth/sir_kiel Last accessed Apr. 20, 2010; 408 Quoted in Edelweiss F. Silan, "Child Labor in Asia: A Review." http://www.hurights.or.jp/asia-pacific/no_25/ 02childlabor.htm Last accessed Apr. 20, 2010; 409 United Nations Development Programme, *Human Development Report 2006,* published 2006, Palgrave Macmillan. Reproduced with permission of Palgrave Macmillan; 409 A. Prüss-Üstün et al., *Safer Water, Better Health: Costs, Benefits and Sustainability of Interventions to Protect and Promote Health,* (Geneva: World Health Organization, 2008), p. 10. http://whqlibdoc.who.int/publications/ 2008/9789241596435_eng.pdf Last

accessed Apr. 20, 2010; 409 "Burden of Disease and Cost-Effectiveness Estimates," *World Health Organization.* http://www.who.int/water_sanitation_health/ diseases/burden/en/index.html Last accessed Apr. 20, 2010; 411 UNAIDS and World Health Organization, *09 Aids Epidemic Update,* (Geneva: UNAIDS, 2009), 11. http://data.unaids.org/pub/ Report/2009/JC1700_Epi_Update_2009 _en.pdf Last accessed Apr. 20, 2010. Courtesy UNAIDS; 414 Based on Table 1 from OECD (2009), Development aid at its highest level ever in 2008, www.oecd. org/dac; 414 Stockholm International Peace Research Institute (SIPRI), *SIPRI Yearbook 2009: Armaments, Disarmament and International Security* (Oxford University Press: Oxford, 2009), 179; 416 "Countries of Focus." http://www.acdi-cida.gc.ca/acdi-cida/ACDI-CIDA.nsf/eng/ home *Canadian International Development Agency,* 2009. Reproduced with the permission of the Minister of Public Works and Government Services Canada, 2010; 419 "Human Rights, Global Markets: Some Issues and Challenges for Canadian Foreign Policy." http://dsp-psd.tpsgc.gc.ca/ Collection-R/ LoPBdP/BP/bp416-e.htm Reproduced with the permission of the Minister of Public Works and Government Services Canada, 2010; **419 Canada and China: A Good and Frank Relationship to Build on 2009.** http://www.pm.gc.ca/ fra/media.asp?id=3010 Reproduced with the permission of the Minister of Public Works and Government Services, 2010, and Courtesy of the Privy Council Office; **421** United Nations Development Programme (UNDP), *Human Development Report 2009,* published 2009, Palgrave Macmillan. Reproduced with permission of Palgrave Macmillan **Chapter 13** 424 "World Scientists' Warning to Humanity," Nov. 18, 1992. http://www.worldtrans. org/whole/warning.html Last accessed Apr. 20, 2010; 424 "Earth's Ecosystems," *Climate Change Science Compendium 2009,* p. 34. http://www.unep.org/pdf/ccScience Compendium2009/cc_ ScienceCompendium2009_ch4 _en.pdf Last accessed Apr. 20, 2010; 429 "United Nations General Assembly Declares 2011 as International Year of Forests," http://www.un.org/ News/Press/docs/ 2006/ga10565.doc.htm Last accessed Apr. 20, 2010. © United Nations, December 21, 2006 (GA/10565 ENV/DEV/907). Reproduced with permission. The United Nations is the author of the original material; 431 Kelly McManus, "30 U 30: Simon Jackson, 27," *North Shore Outlook,* October 14, 2009; 432 AQUASTAT database. *Food and Agriculture Organization of the United Nations.* www.fao.org/nr/water/ aquastat/main/index.stm Last accessed Apr. 20, 2010; 432 *New Report Highlights Crucial Role of Water in Development,* Press Release No 2009-21, UNESCOPRESS, March 12, 2009 © UNESCO 2009 http://www.unesco.org/new/en/media-services/single-view/news/new_report_highlights_crucial_role_of_water_in_development/browse/8/back/18276/ Used by permission of UNESCO; 432 *Water in a Changing World: The United Nations World Water Development Report 3* © UNESCO 2009. Used by permission of UNESCO; 434 Quoted in Erin Aylward, "Topic: Canada's Role in North America," Policy eDiscussions, #382 of 407, http://www. dfait-maeci.gc.ca/ cip-pic/ discussions/NA-AN/ediscussion/381.aspx? lang=eng Foreign Affairs and International Trade Canada, 2007. Reproduced with the permission of the Minister of Public Works and Government Services Canada, 2010; 435 Center for Strategic and International Studies and Sandia Laboratories, *Global Water Futures: Addressing Our Global Water Future,* September 2005; 435 IPCC 2008: Climate Change and Water. Technical Paper of the Intergovernmental Panel on Climate Change, p. 102. IPCC Secretariat, Geneva; 436 Peter Gleick, *The World's Water 1998–1999: The Biennial Report on Freshwater Resources,* (Washington, DC: Island Press, 1998; 436 United Nations Development Programme, *Human Development Report 2006,* published 2006, Palgrave Macmillan. Reproduced with permission of Palgrave Macmillan; 437 UNEP, Production and Consumption of Ozone Depleting Substances, 1986–1998, October 1999. via ciesin.org. Quoted at http://www. nationmaster.com/graph/env_cfc_con-environment-cfc-consumption%20emissions Last accessed Apr. 20, 2010; 438 "Information on Greenhouse Gas Sources and Sinks: Canada's 2007 Greenhouse Gas Inventory—A Summary of Trends," 1, Environment Canada. Reproduced with the permission of the Minister of Public Works and Government Services Canada, 2010; 438 Based on Climate Change 2007: Mitigation of Climate Change. Working Group III Contribution to the Fourth Assessment Report of the Intergovernmental Panel on Climate Change, Figure TS.1b. Cambridge University Press; 438 2009 World Population Data Sheet, Population Reference Bureau, 2. http://www.prb.org/pdf09/09wpds_eng.pdf Last accessed Apr. 20, 2010; 438 "Greenhouse Gas Emissions," Canada's Oil Sands, 2009. http://www. canadasoilsands.ca/ en/issues/greenhouse_gas_ emissions.aspx Last accessed Apr. 20, 2010. Courtesy of CAPP (Canadian Association for Petroleum Producers); 438 "Tar Sands," Sierra Club Prairie. http://www. sierra club .ca/prairie/ tarnation.htm Last accessed Apr. 20, 2010; 439 Climate Change 2007: Synthesis Report. Contribution of Working Groups I, II and III to the Fourth Assessment Report of the Intergovernmental Panel on Climate Change, Summary for Policymakers (SPM). IPCC, Geneva, Switzerland; 440 United Nations Environment Programme, "Earth Systems," *Climate Change Science Compendium 2009,* 9. http://www.unep.org/pdf/ ccScienceCompendium2009/cc_ Science Compendium2009_ch1_en. pdf Last accessed Apr. 20, 2010; 442 "Figure 3: Potential Impacts of Climate Change on Agricultural Crops in Canada," http://www.adaptation.rncan.gc.ca/ perspective/summary_5_e.php *Natural Resources Canada,* 2007. Reproduced with the permission of the Minister of Public Works and Government Services Canada, 2010; 442 "Climate Change and Impacts and Adaptation: A Canadian Perspective," http://www.adaptation.rncan.gc.ca/ perspective/summary_5_e.php *Natural Resources Canada,* 2007. Reproduced with the permission of the Minister of Public Works and Government Services Canada, 2010; 442–3 "Farmers Voice Their Concern Over Impact of Climate Change," *The Hindu,* Nov. 5, 2009. http://www.thehindu.com/ 2009/11/05/stories/ 2009110557740700.htm Last accessed Apr. 20, 2010; 443 "Coastal Sensitivity to Sea-Level Rise," http://atlas.nrcan.gc.ca/site/english/ maps/climatechange/potentialimpacts/ coastalsensitivity-sealevelrise *Natural Resources Canada,* 2007. Reproduced with the permission of the Minister of Public Works and Government Services Canada, 2010; 444 Nicholas Stern, "Summary of Conclusions," *Stern Review: The Economics of Climate Change,* p. vi. http://www.hm-treasury.gov.uk/d/ CLOSED_SHORT_executive_summary.pdf Last accessed Apr. 20, 2010. Reproduced under the terms of Click-Use Licence; 446 Nicholas Stern, *The Economics of Climate Change,* (Cambridge, NY: Cambridge University Press, 2007), p. vi. Reproduced under the terms of Click-Use Licence; 447 "Who's Meeting Their Kyoto Targets," *David Suzuki Foundation.* http://www. david-suzuki.org/files/climate/cop/Meeting_Kyoto_Targets.pdf Last accessed Mar. 15, 2010. David Suzuki Foundation (www.davidsuzuki.org). "National Greenhouse Gas Inventory Data for the Period 1990–2007," in *United Nations Framework Convention on Climate Change.* http://unfccc.int/ resource/docs/2009/sbi/eng/12.pdf Last accessed Apr. 20, 2010. © United Nations, October 21, 2009 (FCCC/SBI/2009/12). Reproduced with permission. The United Nations is the author of the original material; 447 "Backgrounder: Canada's Action on Climate Change 2009." Reproduced with the permission of the Minister of Public Works and Government Services, 2010, and Courtesy of the Privy Council Office; 447 Mohamed Nasheed, "Climate Change Requires a Real Movement," *The Huffington Post,* Sept. 20, 2009. http://www.huffingtonpost.com/mohamed-nasheed/ climate-change-requires-a_b_292747.html Last accessed Apr. 20, 2010; 448 Quoted in Judith Lavoie, "Small T'Sou-ke Reserve One of Most Solar-Power-Intensive in Country," *Victoria Times Colonist,* July 18, 2009; 449 United Nations Environment Programme, *Global Environmental Outlook 2000,* (London: Earthscan, 1999). http://www.unep.org/geo2000/english/0016.htm Last accessed Apr. 20, 2010; 451 "Joint Statement by the National Academy of Sciences and the Royal Society of London," Nov. 4, 1997. http://www.nasonline.org/site/PageServer?pagename=NEWS_ statement_NAS_11041997_ RoyalSoc_sustainable_consumption Last accessed Apr. 20, 2010 **Study Guide 4** 454 "International Data Base (IDB)," *U.S. Census Bureau.* http://www.census.gov/ ipc/www/idb/ informationGateway.php Last accessed Apr. 20, 2010; 455 "David Suzuki," *Heroes for a Better World.* http://www.betterworldheroes.com/pages-s/suzuki-quotes.htm Last accessed Apr. 20, 2010; "Consumer Culture No Accident," *David SuzukiFoundation.* http://www.davidsuzuki.org/ about_us/Dr_David_Suzuki/Article_Archives/weekly 03070301.asp Last accessed Apr. 20, 2010